THE PRACTICE OF CONSUMER LAW

Seeking Economic Justice

Second Edition

Robert J. Hobbs
Stephen Gardner

Contributing Author: Carolyn L. Carter

National Consumer Law Center
77 Summer Street, 10th Floor Boston, MA 02110
www.consumerlaw.org

National Association of Consumer Advocates
1730 Rhode Island Ave. NW, Ste. 710 Washington, DC 20036
www.naca.net

About NCLC

The National Consumer Law Center, a nonprofit corporation founded in 1969, assists consumers, advocates, and public policy makers nationwide who use the powerful and complex tools of consumer law to ensure justice and fair treatment for all, particularly those whose poverty renders them powerless to demand accountability from the economic marketplace. For more information, go to www.consumerlaw.org.

Ordering NCLC Publications

Order securely online at www.consumerlaw.org, or contact Publications Department, National Consumer Law Center, 77 Summer Street, Boston, MA 02110, (617) 542-9595, FAX: (617) 542-8028, e-mail: publications@nclc.org.

Training and Conferences

NCLC participates in numerous national, regional, and local consumer law trainings. Its annual fall conference is a forum for consumer rights attorneys from legal services programs, private practice, government, and nonprofit organizations to share insights into common problems and explore novel and tested approaches that promote consumer justice in the marketplace. Contact NCLC for more information or see our web site.

Case Consulting

Case analysis, consulting and co-counseling for lawyers representing vulnerable consumers are among NCLC's important activities. Administration on Aging funds allow us to provide free consulting to legal services advocates representing elderly consumers on many types of cases. Massachusetts Legal Assistance Corporation funds permit case assistance to advocates representing low-income Massachusetts consumers. Other funding may allow NCLC to provide very brief consultations to other advocates without charge. More comprehensive case analysis and research is available for a reasonable fee. See our web site for more information at www.consumerlaw.org.

Charitable Donations and Cy Pres *Awards*

NCLC's work depends in part on the support of private donors. Tax-deductible donations should be made payable to National Consumer Law Center, Inc. For more information, contact Suzanne Cutler of NCLC's Development Office at (617) 542-8010 or scutler@nclc.org. NCLC has also received generous court-approved *cy pres* awards arising from consumer class actions to advance the interests of class members. For more information, contact Robert Hobbs (rhobbs@nclc.org) or Rich Dubois (rdubois@nclc.org) at (617) 542-8010.

Comments and Corrections

Write to the above address to the attention of the Editorial Department or e-mail consumerlaw@nclc.org.

About This Volume

This is the Second Edition of *The Practice of Consumer Law* with a 2006 companion CD-Rom. Continuing developments can be found in periodic revisions to this volume and in NCLC REPORTS.

Cite This Volume As

National Consumer Law Center, The Practice of Consumer Law (2d ed. 2006)

Attention

This publication is designed to provide authoritative information concerning the subject matter covered. Always use the most current edition and supplement, and use other sources for more recent developments or for special rules for individual jurisdictions. This publication cannot substitute for the independent judgment and skills of an attorney or other professional. Non-attorneys are cautioned against using these materials to conduct a lawsuit without advice from an attorney and are cautioned against engaging in the unauthorized practice of law.

Copyright

© 2006 by National Consumer Law Center, Inc.
All Rights Reserved

ISBN 1-931697-86-8

Library of Congress Control Number 2005910045

About the Authors

Robert J. Hobbs is an NCLC staff attorney and Deputy Director. He has been writing and consulting since 1972 on debt collection and other consumer credit issues. Prior to that, he was a staff attorney with New Orleans Legal Assistance. He worked on the enactment of the Fair Debt Collection Practices Act, 1980 Truth in Lending Act amendments, and the FTC Holder and Credit Practices rules. He is also the author of *Debt Collection Harassment* (1982) and *Fair Debt Collection* (1987, 1991, 1996, 2000, 2004) and edits *Consumer Law Pleadings on CD-Rom* (2005 with Index Guide). He advises attorneys on their clients' fair debt collection claims, was counsel to amicus curiae in *Heintz v. Jenkins*, 514 U.S. 291 (1995), has served on the FRB's Consumer Advisory Council, and is a founder and a former board member and treasurer of the National Association of Consumer Advocates. He helps coordinate NCLC's fall Consumer Rights Litigation Conference and the spring Fair Debt Collection Practices Act Conference.

Stephen Gardner is Director of Litigation for the Washington, D.C.-based advocacy group Center for Science in the Public Interest. He also consults with attorneys on their consumer cases in an of-counsel relationship with NCLC. He was formerly the co-chair of the National Association of Consumer Advocates, on the Board of Directors of Consumers Union, on the FRB Consumer Advisory Council, and an NCLC Consumer Law Fellow. He has also served as the Assistant Dean of Clinical Education and visiting assistant professor of law at Southern Methodist University, and was an assistant attorney general in Texas and New York. In 1991, he coordinated efforts of numerous attorneys general and the FTC to investigate and bring law enforcement actions against the major consumer reporting agencies.

His publications include "How Green Were My Values: Regulation of Environmental Marketing Claims," *Toledo Law Review* (1991); *See Dick and Jane Sue: A Primer on State Consumer Protection Laws* (American Law Institute 1992); and *Caveat Vendor* (editor)(State Bar of Texas 1980–1982). The Center for Science in the Public Interest inducted Mr. Gardner into their Nutrition Action Hall of Fame in 1991; he was named to *Adweek Magazine*'s Top Ten Enemies of Advertising in 1991; and he received the National Association of Attorneys General's Marvan Award in 1988.

Carolyn L. Carter is NCLC's Deputy Director for Advocacy, and was formerly co-director of Legal Services, Inc., in Gettysburg, Pennsylvania and director of the Law Reform Office of the Cleveland Legal Aid Society. She is the editor of *Pennsylvania Consumer Law* and the First Edition of *Ohio Consumer Law*, author of *Repossessions* (6th ed. 2005), co-author of *Unfair and Deceptive Acts and Practices* (1997, 2001, 2004), *Consumer Warranty Law* (1997, 2001), and *Automobile Fraud* (2d ed. 2003), and contributing author to *Truth in Lending* (5th ed. 2003), *Fair Debt Collection* (5th ed. 2004), *The Cost of Credit* (2000, 2005), *Foreclosures* (2005), and *The Practice of Consumer Law* (2d ed. 2006). She was the 1992 recipient of the Vern Countryman Consumer Law Award.

Acknowledgements: A number of other attorneys authored or co-authored individual chapters, and are acknowledged at the beginning of their chapters. This book is truly a community effort. Thanks to Dick Feferman, John Roddy, Mary Fons, Chris LeFavre, Ron Burdge, Hyung Choi, Len Bennett, and the many others who have shared their experiences and insights about starting and developing a consumer law practice at the annual National Consumer Rights Litigation Conferences. Thanks to Kathleen Keest, Kevin Brown, and Elizabeth Renuart for their work on the historical development of usury laws; Dick Rubin for his assistance on the Rule 68 discussion; Mary Kingsley for research on SLAPP issues; Robert Bigelow for his research and analysis of ethical issues; and Stuart Rossman and Dan Edelman for their analysis of class actions. Special thanks to Adrienne Calhoun who assembled a number of the materials. We are also grateful for the assistance of many other members of the NACA/NCLC community, too numerous to name here.

Finally we especially thank Dorothy Tan for editorial supervision; Nathan Day for editorial assistance; Shirlron Williams for assistance with cite checking; Mary McLean for indexing; Xylutions for typesetting services; and Neil Fogarty of Law Disks for preparing the CD-Rom.

About the National Association of Consumer Advocates

The National Association of Consumer Advocates is a nationwide organization of more than 1000 attorneys who represent hundreds of thousands of consumers victimized by fraudulent, abusive and predatory business practices. As an organization fully committed to promoting justice for consumers, NACA's members and their clients are actively engaged in promoting a fair and open marketplace that forcefully protects the rights of consumers, particularly those of modest means.

Today, unfortunately, the fundamental consumer protections that we have all come to depend upon are under attack. This can be seen in the watering down of federal regulations and the preemption of strong state consumer protection laws. It can be seen in the systematic attack on a consumer's right to access our nation's justice system, either cynically through "tort reform" or surreptitiously through the use of binding mandatory arbitration clauses in every conceivable consumer contract. Finally, it can be seen in the ever-growing presence of unscrupulous and deceptive business practices that our members and their clients bear witness to each and every day.

In the years ahead, NACA will be focused on promoting an agenda that lays the groundwork for rebuilding a consumer justice system that will be based on our nation's fundamental sense of fairness, equity and honesty.

The Benefits of Joining NACA

Besides becoming part of a dynamic organization committed to seeking economic justice (naca.net), membership in NACA includes the following benefits:

- **Litigation support** and consultation services to members by NACA's Executive Director and General Counsel, Ira Rheingold, who has extensive experience in predatory mortgage lending and other deceptive business practices litigation.
- **An annual NACA directory**, organized by members' areas of interest, which is a valuable resource for members to obtain assistance and advice from each other or to refer business.
- **NACA's newsletter**, published four times annually, provides substantive articles on key issues such as predatory lending, automobile fraud, RESPA, fair debt collection, and fair credit reporting. It includes thoughtful reviews of current topics as well as practice pointers.
- **Complimentary copy of *The Practice of Consumer Law: Seeking Economic Justice*,** with companion CD-Rom.
- **Consideration** for membership in substantive and legal practice listserv groups.
- **Access to the NACA website, www.naca.net**, including a "Members Only" section. The site contains NACA publications, articles, briefs, links to consumer sites, a library for NACA members and other useful material.
- **Discounts on the purchase** of consumer law manuals published by the National Consumer Law Center.
- **Several conferences** each year bring together the best and brightest consumer law experts to provide training on novel and tested legal theories and strategies for obtaining economic justice for consumers.
- **NACA's Issues Committee** is available to assist in high-impact cases with amicus curiae briefs, drafted by NACA staff or volunteers.
- **Legislative assistance in both drafting and mobilizing** advocates in support of local, state, and federal consumer protection initiatives.
- **Annual Lobby Day,** which provides an opportunity for our members to meet with their congressmen on issues of concern to consumers and their advocates.

What Your Library Should Contain

The Consumer Credit and Sales Legal Practice Series contains 17 titles, updated annually, arranged into four libraries, and designed to be an attorney's primary practice guide and legal resource in all 50 states. Each manual includes a CD-Rom allowing pinpoint searches and the pasting of text into a word processor.

Debtor Rights Library

2004 Seventh Edition, Special Guide to the 2005 Act, and 2005 CD-Rom, Including Law Disks' 2005 Bankruptcy Forms

Consumer Bankruptcy Law and Practice: the definitive personal bankruptcy manual, from the initial interview to final discharge, including consumer rights as creditors when a company files for bankruptcy. The Special Guide to the 2005 Act includes a redlined Code, Interim Rules, a date calculator, new forms, pleadings, and software, means test data, and a new questionnaire and client handout.

2004 Fifth Edition, 2005 Supplement, and 2005 CD-Rom

Fair Debt Collection: the basic reference, covering the Fair Debt Collection Practices Act and common law, state statutory and other federal debt collection protections. Appendices and companion CD-Rom contain sample pleadings and discovery, the FTC Commentary, *all* FTC staff opinion letters, and summaries of reported and unreported cases.

2005 First Edition with CD-Rom

Foreclosures: a new volume covering VA, FHA and other types of home foreclosures, workout agreements, servicer obligations, and tax liens. The CD-Rom reprints key federal statutes, regulations, interpretations, and handbooks, and contains numerous pleadings.

2005 Sixth Edition with CD-Rom

Repossessions: a unique guide to motor vehicle and mobile home repossessions, threatened seizures of household goods, statutory liens, and automobile lease and rent-to-own default remedies. The CD-Rom reprints relevant UCC provisions, summarizes many other state statutes, and includes many pleadings covering a wide variety of cases.

2002 Second Edition, 2005 Supplement, and 2005 CD-Rom

Student Loan Law: student loan debt collection; closed school, false certification, disability, and other discharges; tax intercepts, wage garnishment, and offset of social security benefits; repayment plans, consolidation loans, deferments, and non-payment of loan based on school fraud. CD-Rom and appendices contain numerous forms, pleadings, letters and regulations.

2004 Third Edition with CD-Rom

Access to Utility Service: the only examination of consumer rights when dealing with regulated, de-regulated, and unregulated utilities, including telecommunications, terminations, billing errors, low-income payment plans, utility allowances in subsidized housing, LIHEAP, and weatherization. Includes summaries of state utility regulations.

Credit and Banking Library

2003 Fifth Edition, 2005 Supplement, and 2005 CD-Rom

Truth in Lending: detailed analysis of *all* aspects of TILA, the Consumer Leasing Act, and the Home Ownership and Equity Protection Act (HOEPA). Appendices and the CD-Rom contain the Acts, Reg. Z, Reg. M, and their Official Staff Commentaries, numerous sample pleadings, rescission notices, and two programs to compute APRs.

2002 Fifth Edition, 2005 Supplement, and 2005 CD-Rom

Fair Credit Reporting: the key resource for handling any type of credit reporting issue, from cleaning up blemished credit records to suing reporting agencies and creditors for inaccurate reports. Covers credit scoring, privacy issues, identity theft, the FCRA, the new FACT Act, the Credit Repair Organizations Act, state credit reporting and repair statutes, and common law claims.

2005 Third Edition with CD-Rom

Consumer Banking and Payments Law: unique analysis of consumer law (and NACHA rules) as to checks, money orders, credit, debit, and stored value cards, and banker's right of setoff. Also extensive treatment of electronic records and signatures, electronic transfer of food stamps, and direct deposits of federal payments. The CD-Rom and appendices reprint relevant agency interpretations and pleadings.

2005 Third Edition with CD-Rom

The Cost of Credit: Regulation and Legal Challenges: a one-of-a-kind resource detailing state and federal regulation of consumer credit in all fifty states, federal usury preemption, explaining credit math, and how to challenge excessive credit charges and credit insurance. The CD-Rom includes a credit math program and hard-to-find agency interpretations.

2005 Fourth Edition with CD-Rom

Credit Discrimination: analysis of the Equal Credit Opportunity Act, Fair Housing Act, Civil Rights Acts, and state credit discrimination statutes, including reprints of all relevant federal interpretations, government enforcement actions, and numerous sample pleadings.

Consumer Litigation Library

2004 Fourth Edition, 2005 Supplement, and 2005 CD-Rom

Consumer Arbitration Agreements: numerous successful approaches to challenge the enforceability of a binding arbitration agreement, the interrelation of the Federal Arbitration Act and state law, class actions in arbitration, collections via arbitration, the right to discovery, and other topics. Appendices and CD-Rom include sample discovery, numerous briefs, arbitration service provider rules and affidavits as to arbitrator costs and bias.

2002 Fifth Edition, 2005 Supplement, and 2005 CD-Rom

Consumer Class Actions: A Practical Litigation Guide: makes class action litigation manageable even for small offices, including numerous sample pleadings, class certification memoranda, discovery, class notices, settlement materials, and much more. Includes a detailed analysis of the Class Action Fairness Act of 2005, recent changes to Rule 23, and other contributions from seven of the most experienced consumer class action litigators around the country.

2005 CD-Rom with Index Guide: ALL pleadings from ALL NCLC Manuals, including Consumer Law Pleadings Numbers One through Eleven

Consumer Law Pleadings on CD-Rom: Over 1000 notable recent pleadings from all types of consumer cases, including predatory lending, foreclosures, automobile fraud, lemon laws, debt collection, fair credit reporting, home improvement fraud, rent to own, student loans, and lender liability. Finding aids pinpoint the desired pleading in seconds, ready to paste into a word processing program.

Deception and Warranties Library

2004 Sixth Edition, 2005 Supplement, and 2005 CD-Rom

Unfair and Deceptive Acts and Practices: the only practice manual covering all aspects of a deceptive practices case in every state. Special sections on automobile sales, the federal racketeering (RICO) statute, unfair insurance practices, and the FTC Holder Rule.

2003 Second Edition, 2005 Supplement, and 2005 CD-Rom

Automobile Fraud: examination of title law, odometer tampering, lemon laundering, sale of salvage and wrecked cars, undisclosed prior use, prior damage to new cars, numerous sample pleadings, and title search techniques.

2001 Second Edition, 2005 Supplement, and 2005 CD-Rom

Consumer Warranty Law: comprehensive treatment of new and used car lemon laws, the Magnuson-Moss Warranty Act, UCC Articles 2 and 2A, mobile home, new home, and assistive device warranty laws, FTC Used Car Rule, tort theories, car repair and home improvement statutes, service contract and lease laws, with numerous sample pleadings.

National Consumer Law Center ▪ 77 Summer Street ▪ 10th Floor ▪ Boston MA ▪ 02110
(617) 542-9595 ▪ FAX (617) 542-8028 ▪ publications@nclc.org
Order securely online at www.consumerlaw.org

NCLC's CD-Roms

Every NCLC manual comes with a companion CD-Rom featuring pop-up menus, PDF-format, Internet-style navigation of appendices, indices, and bonus pleadings, hard-to-find agency interpretations and other practice aids. Documents can be copied into a word processing program. Of special note is *Consumer Law in a Box*:

December 2005 CD-Rom

Consumer Law in a Box: a double CD-Rom combining *all* documents and software from 17 other NCLC CD-Roms. Quickly pinpoint a document from thousands found on the CD through keyword searches and Internet-style navigation, links, bookmarks, and other finding aids.

Other NCLC Publications for Lawyers

issued 24 times a year

NCLC REPORTS covers the latest developments and ideas in the practice of consumer law.

2006 Second Edition with CD-Rom

The Practice of Consumer Law: Seeking Economic Justice: contains an essential overview to consumer law and explains how to get started in a private or legal services consumer practice. Packed with invaluable sample pleadings and practice pointers for even experienced consumer attorneys.

First Edition with CD-Rom

STOP Predatory Lending: A Guide for Legal Advocates: provides a roadmap and practical legal strategy for litigating predatory lending abuses, from small loans to mortgage loans. The CD-Rom contains a credit math program, pleadings, legislative and administrative materials, and underwriting guidelines.

National Consumer Law Center Guide Series are books designed for consumers, counselors, and attorneys new to consumer law:

2005 Edition

NCLC Guide to Surviving Debt: a great overview of consumer law. Everything a paralegal, new attorney, or client needs to know about debt collectors, managing credit card debt, whether to refinance, credit card problems, home foreclosures, evictions, repossessions, credit reporting, utility terminations, student loans, budgeting, and bankruptcy.

First Edition

NCLC Guide to Mobile Homes: what consumers and their advocates need to know about mobile home dealer sales practices and an in-depth look at mobile home quality and defects, with 35 photographs and construction details.

First Edition

NCLC Guide to Consumer Rights for Immigrants: an introduction to many of the most critical consumer issues faced by immigrants, including international wires, check cashing and banking, *notario* and immigration consultant fraud, affidavits of support, telephones, utilities, credit history discrimination, high-cost credit, used car fraud, student loans and more.

First Edition

Return to Sender: Getting a Refund or Replacement for Your Lemon Car: Find how lemon laws work, what consumers and their lawyers should know to evaluate each other, investigative techniques and discovery tips, how to handle both informal dispute resolution and trials, and more.

Visit **www.consumerlaw.org** to order securely online or for more information on all NCLC manuals and CD-Roms, including the full tables of contents, indices, listings of CD-Rom contents, and **web-based searches of the manuals' full text**.

National Consumer Law Center ▪ 77 Summer Street ▪ 10th Floor ▪ Boston MA ▪ 02110
(617) 542-9595 ▪ FAX (617) 542-8028 ▪ publications@nclc.org
Order securely online at www.consumerlaw.org

Finding Aids and Search Tips

The Consumer Credit and Sales Legal Practice Series presently contains seventeen volumes, nine supplements, and seventeen companion CD-Roms—all constantly being updated. The Series includes over 10,000 pages, 100 chapters, 100 appendices, and over 1000 pleadings, as well as hundreds of documents found on the CD-Roms, but not found in the books. Here are a number of ways to pinpoint in seconds what you need from this array of materials.

Internet-Based Searches

www.consumerlaw.org

Electronically search every chapter and appendix of all seventeen manuals and their supplements: go to www.consumerlaw.org/keyword and enter a case name, regulation cite, or other search term. You are instantly given the book names and page numbers of any of the NCLC manuals containing that term, with those hits shown in context.

www.consumerlaw.org

Current indexes, tables of contents, and CD-Rom contents for all seventeen volumes are found at www.consumerlaw.org. Just click on *The Consumer Credit and Sales Legal Practice Series* and scroll down to the book you want. Then click on that volume's index, contents, or CD-Rom contents.

Finding Material on NCLC's CD-Roms

Consumer Law in a Box CD-Rom

Electronically search all seventeen NCLC CD-Roms, including thousands of agency interpretations, all NCLC appendices and almost 1000 pleadings: use Acrobat's search button* in NCLC's *Consumer Law in a Box CD-Rom* (this CD-Rom is free to set subscribers) to find every instance that a keyword appears on any of our seventeen CD-Roms. Then, with one click, go to that location to see the full text of the document.

CD-Rom accompanying this volume

Electronically search the CD-Rom accompanying this volume, including pleadings, agency interpretations, and regulations. Use Acrobat's search button* to find every instance that a keyword appears on the CD-Rom, and then, with one click, go to that location on the CD-Rom. Or just click on subject buttons until you navigate to the document you need.

Finding Pleadings

Consumer Law Pleadings on CD-Rom and Index Guide

Search five different ways for the right pleading from over 1000 choices: use the *Index Guide* accompanying *Consumer Law Pleadings on CD-Rom* to search for pleadings by type, subject, publication title, name of contributor, or contributor's jurisdiction. The guide also provides a summary of the pleading once the right pleading is located. *Consumer Law Pleadings on CD-Rom* and the *Consumer Law in a Box CD-Rom* also let you search for all pleadings electronically by subject, type of pleading, and by publication title, giving you instant access to the full pleading in Word and/or PDF format once you find the pleading you need.

Using This Volume to Find Material in All Seventeen Volumes

This volume

The Quick Reference at the back of this volume lets you pinpoint manual sections or appendices where over 1000 different subject areas are covered.

---

* Users of NCLC CD-Roms should become familiar with "search," a powerful Acrobat tool, distinguished from "find,"another Acrobat feature that is less powerful than "search." The Acrobat 5 "search" icon is a pair of binoculars with paper in the background, while the "find" icon is a pair of binoculars without the paper. Acrobat 6 and 7 use one icon, a pair of binoculars labeled "Search," that opens a dialog box with search options.

Summary Contents

Contents

Chapter 3 Starting a Private Consumer Law Practice

Chapter 4 Making Money on Small Consumer Claims

Chapter 5 The Importance of Legal Services Consumer Law Specialization

Chapter 6 Consumer Advocacy in Government and Academics

Chapter 7 Ethical Issues in the Practice of Consumer Law

Chapter 11 Keeping America's Economy Strong: Enforcing Consumer Protection Laws as Congress Intended

Chapter 12 A Guide to Price Traps in Mortgage Loans

Chapter 13 Saving a Client's Home Through Bankruptcy

Chapter 14 Is That Arbitration Clause Unconscionable? PROVE IT!

Chapter 15 Car Cases 101: Creating the Interview Form

Chapter 16 Formal and Informal Discovery

Chapter 17 Expert Witnesses

Chapter 20 Consumer Litigation's Tax Consequences for Prevailing Clients

Chapter 21 Trial of Consumer Cases

Chapter 22 Consumer Law Remedies in Individual Suits

Chapter 23 Common Defenses and Defense Tactics

Chapter 24 Consumer Class Actions

Chapter 25

Chapter 26 Historical Development of Consumer Law: Usury Laws

CD-Rom Contents

Practice of Consumer Law

Key Internet Links (Appendix B)

Pleadings by Type

Notice Letters

Rejection or Revocation of Acceptance (*Consumer Warranty Law*, Appendix J.1)
TIL Rescission (*Truth in Lending*, Appendix E)

Complaints, Answers

Defective Used Car (*Consumer Warranty Law*, Appendix K.3)
Used Car's Undisclosed Wreck History (*Automobile Fraud*, Appendix E.2)
Answer and Counterclaim to Automobile Deficiency Claim (*Repossessions and Foreclosures*, Appendix D.1)
Defective Mobile Home (*Consumer Warranty Law*, Appendix K.6)
Breach of Implied Warranty of Merchantability (*Consumer Warranty Law*, Appendix K.2.2)
Debt Collection (Appendix C)
Hospital Collection
Wrongful Setoff of Social Security Funds
TILA (*Truth in Lending*, Appendix D)
HOEPA (*Truth in Lending*, 2002 Supplement, Appendix F.2)
Mortgage Servicer Practices
Discrimination in Offering of Home Mortgage and Appraisal Practices (*Credit Discrimination*, Appendix F.1)
Fair Credit Reporting (*Fair Credit Reporting*, Appendix I.1.3)
Payday Loan (*The Cost of Credit*, Appendix F.1)
Small Loan Usury (*The Cost of Credit*, Appendix E.3)
Trade School Fraud (*Student Loan Law*, Appendix E.5.1)
Long-distance Telephone Overcharges
Foreclosure Rescue Scam (NY)
Foreclosure Rescue Scam (IL)

Combined Interrogatories and Document Requests

Debt Collection (*Fair Debt Collection*, Appendix E.1)
Hospital Collection
TIL (*Truth in Lending*, Appendix G)
Mortgage Servicer Practices
Trade School Fraud (*Student Loan Law*, Appendix F.2)
Foreclosure Rescue Scam (IL)

Document Requests

Warranty Litigation (*Consumer Warranty Law*, Appendix L.3)
Used Car's Undisclosed Wreck History Directed to Dealer (*Automobile Fraud*, Appendix F.2.2)
Used Car's Undisclosed Wreck History Directed to Lender (*Automobile Fraud*, Appendix F.2.3)
Mobile Home Case (*Consumer Warranty Law*, Appendix L.7)
Mortgage Discrimination Case (*Credit Discrimination*, Appendix G.4)
Fair Credit Reporting Case (*Fair Credit Reporting*, Appendix I.3.1)
Foreclosure Rescue Scam (NY)

Interrogatories

Warranty Litigation (*Consumer Warranty Law*, Appendix L.2)
Defective Used Car Sale (*Consumer Warranty Law*, Appendix L.6)
Zip Code Redlining (*Credit Discrimination*, Appendix G.3)
Fair Credit Reporting (*Fair Credit Reporting*, Appendix I.2.1)
Foreclosure Rescue Scam (NY)

Requests for Admissions

Small Loan Usury (*The Cost of Credit*, Appendix E.3)

Practice of Consumer Law

Pleadings by Subject

The Practice of Consumer Law Appendices on CD-Rom

Word Pleadings and Practice Aids on CD-Rom

Chapter 1 Overview: The Practice of Consumer Law

By Robert Hobbs[1]

1.1 Overview

1.1.1 The Basics

The number of private lawyers practicing consumer law has grown tremendously in the last decade. While there are no hard numbers, a dozen years ago NCLC could identify only about eighty private lawyers specializing in representing consumers. Today, the National Association of Consumer Advocates boasts over 1000 members, the majority of whom are in private practice, with many from government and legal aid. The National Association of Consumer Bankruptcy Attorneys has over 2000 members. While not every consumer law practice is able to maintain itself over the long run, the majority are thriving nowadays, and some consumer law firms are growing steadily.

The success of consumer law is not evinced simply by the number of lawyers but by the ever increasing success of the cases brought by those lawyers on behalf of consumers. Shifts in the law and in public attitudes underlie these changes. More and more Americans expect products to work as advertised. They demand to be treated honestly and fairly in the marketplace. Judges and juries are reflecting these public values in their judgments, which increasingly promote economic justice and punish deceptive merchants and devious lawyers.

The success of the practice of consumer law is also expressed in the career satisfaction that is apparent among consumer law lawyers as compared with other lawyers. Surveys of lawyers working for traditional law firms over the years have indicated that there is a large group of lawyers who are unhappy with their work of representing large, wealthy corporations. On the other hand, many, many consumer lawyers will tell you of their great satisfaction in successfully representing ordinary people against large corporations. While some consumers are not enjoyable clients and not all consumer cases are successful, most consumer lawyers are finding a meaningful purpose in their career accomplishing what they do for their consumer clients.

The practice of consumer law does not require a private practice. Consumer law is also practiced by legal services lawyers, government lawyers, academics, and public interest lawyers. This book addresses the practice of consumer law in this broad sense.

The goals of this book are to provide information that will help lawyers decide whether to try a consumer law case, show them how to get started, and assist them in preparing their cases. This book begins with the basics, and the content becomes progressively more advanced. Do not neglect the companion CD-Rom to this volume which, in addition to the appendices, contains scores of pleadings, discovery materials, motions and memoranda of law, sample retainers, and trial materials.

1.1.2 Consumer Law Encompasses Many Areas of Law and Means Different Things to Different People

There is a tremendous breadth to consumer law. For example, there are dozens of different laws in each state addressing consumer credit, sales of automobiles, and general deceptive sales practices. With this breadth may come the need to specialize. Many in private practice specialize in one type of consumer case, at least initially. Because of this

1 In his thirty years at NCLC, Robert Hobbs has specialized in consumer credit issues, with particular attention to fair debt collection practices. He was the designated consumer representative in the Federal Trade Commission rulemakings on creditor remedies and preservation of consumers' claims and defenses. He has testified on and proposed amendments adopted as part of the Fair Debt Collection Practices Act and the Truth in Lending Act and has participated in drafting NCLC's Model Consumer Credit Code (1974). He writes NCLC's popular treatise, *Fair Debt Collection*; the bimonthly newsletter on fair debt collection and repossession, *NCLC REPORTS* Debt Collection and Repossessions Ed.; and *The Practice of Consumer Law*. He also edits NCLC's annual *Consumer Law Pleadings (Cumulative CD-Rom and Index Guide)*. He is Deputy Director of NCLC, a former member of the Consumer Advisory Council to the Federal Reserve Board, a former Director and Treasurer of the National Association of Consumer Advocates, Inc., and a graduate of Vanderbilt University and the Vanderbilt School of Law.

need for specialization, one person's practice is unlikely to be like another's. If one area of consumer law turns out to be unappealing to you, keep looking! There are many others.[2] Chapter 5 discusses consumer law practice in legal aid, and Chapter 6 talks about the practice in government and academics.

1.1.3 Consumer Law Practices May Change from Year to Year

Chapter 3 discusses how to start a private consumer law practice. Chapter 9 discusses some of the different areas in which consumer law specialists work. While one of the themes of those chapters is to find a niche in which you can achieve mastery of an industry's practices and the law applying to that industry, some lawyers develop several niches over a period of time while others are content to keep their practice more narrowly focused. Some "niche" law practices develop as the industry develops so that the laws used and types of cases taken may change over time.[3]

1.2 The National Consumer Law Center's Legal Practice Series Gets You Started

National Consumer Law Center's (NCLC) specialized manuals on consumer law are one key to a successful consumer law practice. The manuals save you not only hours of research but are a compendium of the best advice amassed over several decades from the top consumer law lawyers. They are authoritative and kept up to date with *NCLC REPORTS*, our newsletter, and annual supplements. For many types of consumer cases the specialized NCLC manuals are essential.[4] To find which volume to refer to, check the Quick Reference in the back of this volume or go to www.ConsumerLaw.org and press the button labeled "Keyword Search NCLC Manuals."

1.3 NCLC Provides Case Consulting and Expert Witnesses for Many Consumer Cases

NCLC regularly provides case consulting services with the aim of providing the surest footing for each consumer case. For most cases, NCLC charges a fee based on the time required to provide the case analysis. In other instances, outside funding allows NCLC to provide case advice without a fee. This funding has permitted NCLC to waive fees for advocates for low-income consumers in Massachusetts and for legal services lawyers representing elderly clients with consumer problems. NCLC's website or the Boston office can provide you with more information on this case advice and analysis. In other cases, particularly those involving mortgage and consumer credit analysis, NCLC can sometimes provide expert witness analysis. Other expert witnesses are listed in Appendix D and on the companion searchable CD-Rom to this volume.

1.4 The Annual Consumer Rights Litigation Conference Boosts Your Consumer Practice

Each fall about 600 consumer lawyers from around the country meet to share ideas and enhance the practice of representing consumers. The conference is a great opportunity to get advice and inspiration. Fax (617-542-8028) or write NCLC to be added to the conference mailing list. A small number of scholarships to the conference are awarded each year based on financial need. Details about the next conference are posted on www.ConsumerLaw.org in July.

1.5 Joining the National Association of Consumer Advocates (NACA) Puts You in the Center of the Network of Consumer Lawyers

NACA is a non-profit group of attorneys and advocates committed to promoting consumer justice and curbing abusive business practices that bias the marketplace to the detriment of consumers. Its membership is comprised of over 1000 law professors, public sector lawyers, private lawyers, legal services lawyers, and other consumer advocates across the country. In the decade since NACA's creation, NACA has established itself as one of the most effective advocates for the interests of consumers in this country.

Member benefits of the National Association of Consumer Advocates include the following:

- Litigation support and consultation services to members by NACA's Executive Director and General Counsel, Ira Rheingold, who has extensive experience in class action and unlawful business practices litigation
- An annual NACA Directory, organized by members' areas of interest, which is a valuable resource for members to obtain assistance and advice from each other or to refer business
- NACA's Newsletter, published four times annually, provides substantive articles on key issues such as

2 See Ch. 9 and Appx. D, *infra*, for ideas on specialty areas.

3 *See* Appx. D, *infra*.

4 Call NCLC at (617) 542-9595 or go to www.ConsumerLaw.org for publications information and online ordering.

automobile fraud, RESPA, fair debt and fair credit, with practice pointers
- Access to the NACA website, found at www.naca.net, which contains NACA publications, a directory of members, articles, briefs, links to consumer sites, a library for NACA members, and other useful material
- Discounts on the purchase of consumer law manuals published by the National Consumer Law Center
- Several conferences each year, bringing together the best and brightest consumer law experts to provide training on novel and tested legal theories and strategies for obtaining economic justice for consumers
- The availability of NACA's Issues Committee to assist in high-impact cases with *amicus curiae* briefs, drafted by NACA staff or volunteers
- A number of targeted e-mail groups—on class actions, FDCPA, mortgage fraud and other topics—hosted by NACA
- A mentor program by NACA that matches newer attorneys with skilled and experienced lawyers

For more information call NACA, (202) 452-1989, or visit its website at www.naca.net.

1.6 Your Feedback to the Authors Is Welcomed

This is a work in progress. We believe that this book has tremendous value for someone considering or starting a consumer law practice as well as for the more experienced consumer lawyer faced with a novel challenge. We believe that the book's future potential is even greater. Your feedback to make this book more comprehensive will be appreciated. Write or e-mail the authors with your comments or additions.[5]

5 Bob Hobbs may be reached at RHobbs@NCLC.org, Carolyn Carter at ccarter@cvn.net, and Steve Gardner at atsteve@consumerhelper.com.

Chapter 2 The Consumer Movement

By Stephen Brobeck and Robert J. Hobbs

2.1 History and Dynamics of the Consumer Movement in the United States[1]

2.1.1 Overview

The consumer movement consists of the organized efforts of individual citizens and private not-for-profit organizations to enhance the rights and collective welfare of consumers. The primary goal of the movement is to advance efficiency and equity in the marketplace. Although the consumer movement is a global phenomenon, this entry focuses primarily on the consumer movement in the United States. The U.S. consumer movement is itself highly diverse, with activity at the local, state, and national levels. This entry focuses mainly on the movement at the national level. (Movement developments at the grassroots level are summarized in the entry on "State and Local Consumer Organizations"[2] and treated in greater detail in entries on specific state and local groups.)

Within the United States, individuals such as Ralph Nader and Esther Peterson and organizations such as Consumers Union and the Consumer Federation of America exemplify the consumer movement. The consumerist philosophy of these activist individuals and organizations is often shared by parties outside the movement itself—consumer-oriented legislators and regulators, journalists, scientists, educators, and consumer affairs personnel working in businesses. While these parties have supported the movement and contributed to its achievements, their primary allegiance is typically to an entity or set of values separate from the consumer movement.

The U.S. consumer movement is diverse in the goals, levels of commitment, and social background of its participants. The movement contains people who are motivated by economic issues and seek benefits for themselves as well as those who are guided by moral concerns and who pursue benefits for others. The movement is entrepreneurial in the sense that it relies heavily on the activity of full-time professionals who generate support and mobilize resources aimed at particular issues, but it is also characterized by spontaneous, short-term, grassroots action. Whereas the consumer movement has largely attracted white, middle-class participants, it has also afforded leadership opportunities to women and racial minorities.

Diversity within the consumer movement is particularly pronounced with respect to preferred tactics and strategies. The movement is largely reformist in terms of its basic acceptance of existing economic and political institutions and its attempt to solve consumer problems, often in collaboration with business interests. Nevertheless, the movement also contains more radical elements who believe that existing institutions require fundamental change and who distance themselves from business interests.

Members of the movement also differ in other respects. One segment seeks policies that expand consumer alternatives and encourage informed choices among them, while another segment takes the more paternalistic view that choices that might prove harmful to consumers should be restricted (for example, by limiting the availability of alcohol and tobacco or by punishing those who do not use seatbelts or motorcycle helmets). Finally, some consumer organizations (for example, the American Council on Science and Health) define their role as advocacy against government interventions on behalf of consumers, even when these interventions are supported by the majority of consumer organizations.

In sum, the U.S. consumer movement consists of a broad and loosely coordinated set of individuals and private not-for-profit organizations that consciously seek to advance the welfare of consumers. These movement participants share

1 Section 2.1 is reprinted with the permission of Stephen Brobeck, Executive Director of the Consumer Federation of America, for which permission we are very grateful. This section is largely from Robert O. Herrmann & Robert N. Mayer, Encyclopedia of the Consumer Movement, U.S. Consumer Movement: History and Dynamics (1997). The editors of this book have updated this material where needed.

2 *See also* Erma Angevine, Consumer Activists: They Made a Difference (Mt. Vernon, NY: Consumers Union Found., Inc., 1982); Robert O. Herrmann, *Participation and Leadership in Consumer Movement Organizations*, 47 Journal of Social Issues (1), 119–134 (1991); Robert N. Mayer, The Consumer Movement: Guardians of the Marketplace (Boston: Twayne 1991).

an equally broad and loosely constructed set of values and beliefs about the situation of consumers. This flexibility in the structure and goals of the consumer movement allows for diversity in the commitment, motives, preferred strategies, and geographical location of movement participants.

2.1.2 The First Era: The Early 1900s

In the early days of the nation, consumers' welfare depended in large part on their own skills and on the honesty and competence of local storekeepers. Both consumers and storekeepers were forced to depend on past experience in judging goods, since they had little in the way of technical information, trademarks, or grades to guide them. The laws governing trade focused on ensuring orderly commerce rather than on protecting consumers specifically. Fraud and adulteration were frequent and difficult to control since many items were in bulk form and moved through many hands on their way to the consumer.

The economic life of the country and the situation of consumers changed rapidly in the last four decades of the nineteenth century. Industrial output and employment increased fivefold. The population doubled and became increasingly urbanized. Nationwide markets developed as manufacturers of consumer goods began to trademark their wares, advertise them in the new mass-circulation magazines, and ship them via the growing rail system to remote areas.

In about 1900, a new group of political reformers concerned with the problems of a more urban and industrialized society emerged in the urban middle and professional classes. These reformers of the Progressive movement were joined by the veterans of the Populist movement of the previous decade and sought to use the power of government to bring about the social and economic reforms they believed were needed.

A variety of reform organizations concerned with local social problems and political corruption appeared between 1890 and 1900. One such group, a voluntary organization of middle- and upper-class "do-gooders," sought to improve working conditions by education, research, and selective retail patronage. The first Consumers' League, formed in New York City in 1891, began its work by preparing an approved "white list" of shops that paid fair wages, had reasonable hours, and maintained sanitary conditions. They asked consumers to concentrate their patronage on these shops. In 1898, the local groups joined in a national federation, the National Consumers League (NCL), the first national consumers' organization. By 1903, the national organization had branches in twenty states. While the League's early investigations focused on working conditions, more recently NCL has worked mainly on consumer issues.

For three decades after the Civil War, workers' real incomes grew steadily. But, beginning in 1897, these gains turned to losses as a long chain of increases in consumers' costs of living began. Between 1900 and 1914, with the help of unions, private-sector workers were able again to increase their real annual incomes. But the pressure of price increases was felt keenly by government employees and others on fixed incomes. Trusts, corporate schemes to eliminate competition and control prices, became a focus of blame for the new rise in prices. The muckraking journalistic exposés of the period both reflected and fed the suspicions of the public about the trusts.

McClure's magazine became a muckraking publication by accident when it commissioned a study of Standard Oil, the largest American trust, as a follow-up to a series it had run on great American business achievements. Beginning in 1902, the series by Ida Tarbell showed that Standard Oil had grown through bribery, graft, fraud, violence, and the destruction of competition. It created a sensation, encouraging several other new mass-circulation magazines to use exposés of corruption in business and government as a device to build circulation. Life insurance companies, railroads, trusts, and politicians were all scrutinized, and the demand for reform grew.

The nationwide rail network and the development of refrigerated rail cars opened a national market to food processors and meat packers. The packers' and canners' understanding of the principles of food safety and preservation was rudimentary, and preservatives were used liberally. Official attention to the problem in the Division of Chemistry of the U.S. Department of Agriculture began with the arrival of Dr. Harvey W. Wiley in 1883. In the course of their investigations, Wiley and his staff cataloged 1400 pages of documented cases of adulteration, but they were unable to arouse much interest among the public or Congress. To dramatize the problem, Wiley created a "poison squad," a volunteer group of healthy young men whom he fed a diet of typical food adulterants in order to determine their effects. Although the tests proved little, they made excellent copy for the media.

Beginning in 1892, a series of unsuccessful attempts were made to obtain federal pure food legislation. Opposition to the bills came from three groups: business and regional interests affected by the proposed legislation, southern Democrats reluctant to grant increased powers to the federal government, and those who believed that other legislative matters were more pressing. Another attempt was made in 1902. This bill made little headway, but support for new legislation was gathering and included the General Federation of Women's Clubs, the National Consumers League, and state food and dairy chemists. The muckraker press aided with exposés on the dangers of adulterated food and the hazards of unlabeled patent medicines laced with opiates and alcohol. Despite this support, the efforts for new legislation failed.

In 1904, after Theodore Roosevelt was elected president in his own right, he was urged by consumer advocates to support pure food legislation. In his annual message to Congress the following year, Roosevelt urged the enactment of a pure food and drug law. After Senate passage, the proposed law stalled in the House. Then, in 1906, Upton Sinclair's *The Jungle* was published. This fictional exposé of the working conditions in the Chicago meat packing houses nauseated the public with its graphic descriptions of adulteration techniques and unsanitary conditions. The president's reaction was similar to the public's. He was, moreover, concerned about the deficiencies in federal inspection detailed in the book. When two independent investigations bore out Sinclair's charges, Roosevelt put his support behind the passage of meat inspection legislation.

After Senate passage of the bill, the groups opposing meat inspection legislation hoped to water it down in the House, but Roosevelt urged the House to action. To his message he appended the first portion of the report made by the federal officials who had checked conditions at his request. The report touched off a new wave of indignation. Sales of meat and meat products had dropped by half, and the loss of European markets was threatened. The packers then began to realize that a strengthened system of federal inspection was the only way to save their reputations. A bill, the Meat Inspection Act, quickly passed Congress and was signed by the president. The momentum created by the meat inspection issue also carried the Pure Food Bill to the floor of the House, where it also was passed quickly. The fight for the pure food law finally had been won, but only after two decades of effort, the help of a full-scale scandal, and strong presidential support.

The Progressives' battle with the corporate trusts, the fight for pure food, rising prices, and the growing volume of advertising all helped to make the public aware of their interests as consumers as distinguished from their interests as workers or property owners. This appearance of a consumer consciousness is perhaps the most important result of the first era of the consumer movement. In 1914, Walter Lippmann pointed out the growing political power of consumers as an interest group and noted that "we hear a great deal about the class-consciousness of labor; my own observation is that in America today consumers' consciousness is growing very much faster."

There was little activity in the consumer movement during the next decade. The accelerated rise in prices between 1914 and mid-1920 created hardships for many. For others, especially businessmen and farmers, wartime income increases outran price increases. Patriotic fervor, wartime scarcities, and postwar readjustment diverted attention from consumer problems.

2.1.3 The Second Era: The 1930s

In the 1920s, consumer incomes rose gradually while prices remained relatively stable. Times were good for all but the farmers. Consumers were inundated with advertising from billboards, electric signs, newspapers, magazines, and the new medium of radio. Not surprisingly, then, sales of autos, refrigerators, vacuum cleaners, radios, and phonographs were brisk.

Although the public was little concerned about consumer issues, educators began to recognize the need for more and better consumer education. Consumer problems had been a major concern of home economists from the formative years of their association at the turn of the century. In the mid-1920s, they became concerned about the "scanty amount of economics in our home economics" and began new research into consumer problems. About the same time, Henry Harap proposed a comprehensive curriculum for consumer education based on a comparison of actual consumption patterns and scientifically based standards in his book, *The Education of the Consumer.*

As the decade passed, vague discontent grew among consumers who were purchasing new and unfamiliar consumer durables, food items, and personal hygiene products with little solid information to guide them. This discontent found expression in 1927 in *Your Money's Worth*, a book by Stuart Chase and F. J. Schlink. The book, subtitled *A Study in the Waste of the Consumer's Dollar*, attacked advertising and high-pressure salesmanship and called for scientific testing and product standards to provide consumers with the technical information they needed to make purchase decisions. The book, which gave expression to widely felt concerns, became a best-seller and a Book-of-the-Month Club selection.

At the close of their book, Chase and Schlink proposed the formation of a consumer-sponsored organization to do product testing and described the testing activities of a local "Consumers' Club" in White Plains, New York. Inquiries from readers convinced Schlink that the local group should be expanded. In 1929, Consumers' Research was formed to perform this testing work on a larger scale. The new organization was only one of a number of new product testing laboratories that appeared in the late 1920s. The potential of scientific testing of consumer goods was accepted widely; several major department stores and trade associations also began testing laboratories about this time.

The Great Depression made the problems of consumers far more immediate and compelling than they had been in the 1920s. Reduced incomes and unemployment forced most consumers to consider how to spend more wisely. The problems of consumers were aggravated by a flood of shoddy merchandise at bargain prices. In the first years of the depression, real bargains in distress sale merchandise were offered and sold well. As these stocks were exhausted, they were replaced with inferior merchandise that played on consumers' belief that real bargains were still available. These false bargains created a widespread belief that the quality of clothing, shoes, and sheets had deteriorated. This feeling created further support for quality testing and grade labeling of consumer products, which continued to be major themes of the consumer movement throughout the 1930s.

Business and its excesses in the 1920s were blamed for the debacle of the 1930s, and much of the blame was focused on advertising. There were increasing concerns among consumers that advertising encouraged wasteful proliferation of brands, led to unwise spending, and added to the cost of consumer goods while providing little useful information. These concerns were given new voice in a new book by Arthur Kallet and F. J. Schlink of Consumers' Research, *200,000,000 Guinea Pigs*, which appeared in 1933. This book was followed by several other "guinea pig" books—*Skin Deep*; *Counterfeit*; *Partners in Plunder*; *Eat, Drink and Be Wary*; and *Guinea Pigs No More*—all devoted to debunking (a favorite word of the time) nationally advertised products.

The development of the National Recovery Administration (NRA) program of codes regulating industrial competition led to the first formal representation of the consumer interest in the federal government. The National Industrial Recovery Act, passed in June 1933, provided for industrial, labor, and consumer advisory boards to participate in the code-making process. The Consumer Advisory Board experienced persistent difficulty in influencing the work of the NRA because, unlike the Industrial and Labor Advisory Boards, it lacked the backing of any organized pressure group. NRA administrators saw no need for special consumer representation. They were not persuaded by the argument that consumers, workers, and sellers each have separate interests and that the public interest is the resolution of conflicts among divergent groups for the good of all. They preferred equating the consumer interest with the public interest and firmly believed they represented the public interest. During the early 1930s, Consumers' Research (CR) developed under the close control of Schlink, who insisted that CR concentrate on product testing and stay clear of broader social and economic issues. In 1935, Consumers' Research was divided by a bitter strike over unionization of its employees. An association of CR subscribers originally formed to help settle the strike became the nucleus of a new organization, Consumers Union (CU).

From the beginning, CU tested products and disseminated the results in its magazine as well as concerned itself with a broad range of consumer and social problems. Consumers Union grew rapidly and, within three years, its membership passed that of Consumers' Research. In 1939 and 1940, CU and the consumer movement came under a cloud when alleged Communist influences in Consumers Union and thirteen other consumer organizations were investigated by the House Un-American Activities Committee. Although the Dies Committee was able to prove little beyond the fact that CU's director, Arthur Kallet, was highly critical of the capitalist system, CU's reputation was temporarily tarnished.

By the 1930s, the Pure Food and Drug Act of 1906 was badly in need of revision. Early in the 1930s, the New Deal administration did offer a new bill that would have extended the powers of the Food and Drug Administration (FDA) to include cosmetics as well as food and drugs and to cover both labeling and advertising. The FDA dramatized the need for new legislation with an exhibit of useless and dangerous patent medicines, unsafe cosmetics, and adulterated foods. The press dubbed the exhibit "The Chamber of Horrors." When hearings began on the bill in 1933, the American Home Economics Association and the National Congress of Parents and Teachers were the only groups actively supporting it. The opposition characterized the bill as an interference with consumer choice and "the right of self-medication." The newspapers, cowed by fear of lost advertising revenue or for other reasons, gave little attention to the bill.

In 1935, President Franklin D. Roosevelt sent a message to Congress urging passage of new legislation to strengthen the FDA but never gave the measure full support. Historian Charles O. Jackson suggests that the legislation was considered to be a reform proposal rather than part of the crucial New Deal recovery program. Without either strong administration or public support, the measure failed. In 1936, Ruth Lamb's *American Chamber of Horrors* documented the FDA's case in print and carried it to a wider audience. Other concerned groups joined in the fight.

A shocking tragedy finally provided the impetus for congressional action. In 1937, a liquid form of a sulfa drug for infections was placed on the market. Although the drug was safe in capsule form, the liquid form (elixir sulfanilamide) relied on a toxic solvent. It proved lethal, and over 100 people died, including several children. A new section was added to the proposed bill requiring that manufacturers prove the safety of new drugs to the satisfaction of the FDA before placing them on the market. In June 1938, a much modified version of the bill finally was passed.

By the late 1930s, some businesses that had become concerned about the impact of the consumer movement commissioned a survey to assess its effects on public attitudes. In 1940, public opinion researcher George Gallup reported that about one-quarter of those questioned in his study had read one of the "guinea pig" books, and about half of this group said they had changed their buying habits as a result of what they had read. About one-fifth said they had read research reports of one of the product rating services. Gallup found that the movement had developed its greatest strength among teachers, well-educated groups, the wealthy, and the young. He concluded that the movement had made considerable headway and was likely to continue to grow because of its strength among influential groups.

2.1.4 The Third Era: The 1960s and 1970s

The tempo of activity in the consumer movement and its impact had increased throughout the 1930s. Consumerism undoubtedly would have gained even greater influence in the next few years if the coming of World War II had not diverted attention to the problem of national survival. As its contribution to the war effort, consumer education turned its attention to resource conservation, adjustment to scarcities and rationing, and the consumer's role in fighting inflation. Consumers Union membership fell by a third as a result of the Dies Committee investigation and declining interest in buying information in a period of wartime shortages.

With the end of the war, Consumers Union's circulation began a remarkable upward climb as consumers sought product information to guide them in spending their wartime savings. Circulation grew from 50,000 in 1944 to almost 500,000 in 1950. There was, however, little activity among grassroots consumer organizations.

Although prices rose rapidly in the early years of the Korean War, so did wages, and memories of World War II shortages seem to have stilled consumer protests. A resurgence of interest in consumer education came in the early and middle 1950s as families struggled with the problems of meeting installment payments, financing new homes, choosing life insurance, and selecting television sets and other new durables. In the late 1950s, however, consumer education and other life adjustment courses in the secondary schools suffered setbacks when increased emphasis was given to basic disciplines after the USSR's launch of the first Sputnik satellite in late 1957.

In 1953, the Council on Consumer Information was formed by a group of consumer educators to encourage fact-finding on consumer problems and the dissemination of consumer information. The group instituted a newsletter, a pamphlet series with analyses of policy issues and self-help information aimed at the general public, and a program of annual conferences. The group, whose membership consisted chiefly of college and secondary school teachers and extension workers, grew steadily.

Despite the relative quiet of the 1950s, flare-ups of consumer concern did occur. One such incident came after the publication of Vance Packard's *The Hidden Persuaders* in 1957. Packard, accepting at face value the ad agencies' and market researchers' claims about their powers in influencing consumers, argued that the public was being manipulated without realizing it. The resulting round of charges and countercharges received extensive press coverage and showed that, given the right issues, there still was public interest in consumer problems.

The beginning of the third era of the consumer movement often is dated from John F. Kennedy's Consumer Message to the Congress in the spring of 1962. In fact, Kennedy's influence may have begun even earlier. Historian Arthur Schlesinger, Jr., has pointed out that, in Kennedy's 1960 campaign, he "communicated, first of all, a deeply critical attitude toward the ideas and institutions which American society had come in the fifties to regard with such enormous self-satisfaction." Schlesinger argues that the widespread acceptance of these views released the nation's capacity for self-criticism, which had been checked by complacency and McCarthyism in the 1950s. This self-critical perspective was reflected in a succession of examinations of the nation's social and economic problems, many of which deeply involved consumers: Michael Harrington's *The Other America* (1962) on the problems of the poor; Rachel Carson's *The Silent Spring* (1962) on the hazardous effects of pesticides; Jessica Mitford's *The American Way of Death* (1963), an exposé of funeral industry practices; and David Caplovitz's *The Poor Pay More* (1963) on the problems of low-income consumers.

In the preamble to his Consumer Message to Congress in March 1962, President Kennedy enunciated the now famous Consumer Bill of Rights: the right to safety; the right to be informed; the right to choose; and the right to be heard in government decision-making. The main body of the message outlined the need to improve existing programs and to implement new ones. The regulation of food and drugs was one of the areas singled out by Kennedy for special attention.

The weaknesses of the existing laws in ensuring that drugs on the market were both effective and safe had become clear in Senator Kefauver's hearings on the regulation of the drug industry. New drug legislation came only after a new tragedy forced action upon the Congress. Word of the thalidomide case reached the public in June 1962. The drug, a sedative and morning sickness drug for pregnant women, had resulted in severe birth defects in Europe. Fortunately, the drug had been kept off the market in the United States by deliberate delays within the FDA. By August, legislation expanding the powers of the FDA had been passed and signed into law.

To implement the fourth right of his Consumer Message, the right to be heard in government proceedings affecting consumers, Kennedy asked the Council of Economic Advisers to appoint a Consumer Advisory Council. Although the functions of the council were strictly advisory, the consumer interest never before had been represented at so high a level. The council undertook comprehensive studies of consumer needs but had limited impact on Congress and public consciousness.

About this same time, a new surge of interest in consumer education occurred. Educators and the public both came to recognize that consumer education was an important and useful subject for all students, college-bound and vocational, and boys and girls alike. New curricula continued to stress both buymanship techniques and money management and gave new emphasis to the problems and uses of installment credit. Agricultural extension and adult education activity in consumer education also increased greatly during the 1960s. These efforts were supported by an active consumer publication program by the federal government.

As a result of its rapid growth during the 1950s, Consumers Union was publishing nearly one million copies of

Consumer Reports at the time of its twenty-fifth anniversary in 1961. CU increasingly came to view itself as an organization to educate consumers rather than just as a disseminator of product test results. It concerned itself with educating consumers about all phases of their relationship with the market: interest rates, guarantees and warranties, life insurance, product safety, and doctor selection. In addition, Consumers Union provided leadership and funding for the development of other consumer organizations, including an organization of consumer educators (formerly the Council on Consumer Information, now the American Council on Consumer Interests) and an international federation of consumer product testing agencies (formerly the International Organization of Consumers Unions, now Consumers International).

State attorneys general took a prominent place in the consumer movement. Led by Louis Lefkowitz of New York beginning in the late 1950s, and Walter Mondale of Minnesota and Ed Brooke of Massachusetts soon after, the states' attorneys general began developing consumer protection offices which brought suit against unfair and deceptive business practices. The state AGs also sought legislation to deal with consumer problems, often setting the course for federal consumer protection laws. Some offices established mediation programs that encouraged settlement of consumer disputes through informal means. With fewer resources in Washington, D.C., to protect consumers from abuse, the state AGs began in more recent years to act in multi-state working groups in dealing with interstate frauds.

Early in his administration, President Lyndon Johnson recognized that public and congressional interest in consumer problems was growing and that consumer legislation could allow him to build a domestic legislative record with minimal budgetary outlays. In February 1964, he sent a consumer message to Congress urging passage of twelve new laws, including measures on truth in lending, meat inspection, drug inspection, and pesticide control.

In January 1964, Johnson created the new White House post of special assistant for consumer affairs and appointed Esther Peterson to fill it. She played several key roles—as a spokesperson for consumers before Congress, as a publicist for the administration's program of consumer legislation, and as a promoter of local consumer organizations.

By early 1969, there were state consumer organizations in twenty-nine states and nine major city- or county-supported organizations. These organizations provided support to the consumer representatives in state and local governments and became increasingly skilled at putting together temporary coalitions to advance the cause of consumers in the state legislatures.

After the liberal landslide in the election of 1964, the possibilities for new consumer legislation improved. In the spring and summer of 1965, hearings were held on tire and auto safety. The hearings revealed the lack of any deep concern over safety problems in either industry and ended inconclusively after the auto manufacturers argued that principal responsibility for auto safety lay with the driver.

The view that manufacturers bore little responsibility for automobile safety was challenged a few months later by Ralph Nader. His book, *Unsafe at Any Speed*, presented evidence that auto accidents and injuries were typically the result of faulty engineering, construction, and design. Public concern mounted and, in his State of the Union message in January 1966, President Johnson promised new legislation. During the hearings on the proposed legislation, the news broke of General Motors investigation of Nader's background and activities. Congressional opinion was alienated by this interference with a key witness. The safety legislation that passed later that year was significantly stronger than the bill originally proposed by the White House and, two years later, the National Highway Traffic Safety Administration was established. In 1966, after five years of congressional inaction, Senator Phillip Hart's (D-MI) "Truth in Packaging" bill was passed and signed into law.

During the first years of the 1960s, consumer prices rose gradually. This made a sudden jump in food prices in 1966 a major cause for consumer concern. Suddenly, large groups of consumers were faced with a noticeable decline in purchasing power. Consumer discontent found open expression in October in a wave of consumer boycotts of food stores. Store contests and games, which had been used widely in the previous year, were the focus of blame, although the real problem was short supplies of meat and produce.

After Ralph Nader's successful efforts in promoting auto safety legislation, he developed a pattern of action. For each issue, he built a well-documented case with information that he and his "Raiders" had searched out or obtained from concerned insiders in industry and government. Then, he enlisted congressional interest and support. At the same time, he publicized his findings in the press and in his lectures. He institutionalized this exposê approach by founding the Center for Study of Responsive Law.

Government regulatory agencies were a major target of early "Raider" efforts. These agencies included the Federal Trade Commission, the Food and Drug Administration, and the Interstate Commerce Commission. The resulting reports argued that the agencies had not been aggressive enough or had become captives of the special interests they were supposed to regulate. As a result of his contacts in Congress, Nader had far more impact than the muckrakers of the early 1900s or the "guinea pig" authors of the 1930s.

One of Nader's early exposês was of the unsanitary conditions in meat packing plants that sold only intrastate and thus were not subject to federal regulation. This problem was remedied with the passage of the Wholesome Meat Act of 1967, which was signed in a White House ceremony that included Upton Sinclair, then nearly 90 years old.

In 1966, Esther Peterson proposed the creation of a federation of consumer organizations. In 1967, such an organization, the Consumer Federation of America, was organized by Consumers Union, state and local consumer organizations, consumer cooperative groups, and labor unions. Its principal purpose was the representation of the consumer interest before Congress and federal regulatory agencies. Its conference, Consumer Assembly, continues to be one of the largest annual gatherings of consumer advocates from around the nation.

In 1968, the legislative pace quickened. In his State of the Union Message and his Consumer Affairs Message in February, President Johnson called for passage of a long list of consumer bills. During the course of the year, a truth in lending bill finally was passed, eight years after the original bill was introduced by Senator Paul Douglas (D-IL). Other new legislation on poultry inspection, pipeline safety, fraudulent land sales, and hazardous appliance radiation also was approved.

Richard Nixon continued the tradition of delivering a consumer message to Congress. In his 1969 message, he offered a Buyer's Bill of Rights that made significant additions to the Consumer Bill of Rights enunciated by John Kennedy. Most importantly, Nixon added the right to register dissatisfaction and to have complaints heard and weighed. He also proposed to give the Office of Consumer Affairs more permanent status by seeking congressional authorization to replace the executive order by which it had been established.

In 1972, Congress created the Consumer Product Safety Commission (CPSC). The new agency combined some existing regulatory activities—such as regulation of flammable fabrics—with new ones, including regulation of toys, recreation equipment, and household cleaners and chemicals. In 1975, Congress passed another major piece of legislation, the Magnuson-Moss Warranty Act, which strengthened the consumer's right to redress.

During the 1970s, a variety of national consumer organizations with specialized interests sprang up. In contrast to the broader agendas of earlier organizations, these groups focused more narrowly on such issues as auto safety (Center for Auto Safety), food safety and nutrition (Center for Science in the Public Interest, Community Nutrition Institute), medical issues (Public Citizen's Health Research Group), and local marketplace information (Center for the Study of Services). Highly entrepreneurial, these organizations established themselves as visible, influential advocates for the consumer interest. Over time, they found innovative ways to finance their activities with a combination of grants, supporter contributions, and publication sales.

In his 1976 campaign, Jimmy Carter campaigned as an outsider, calling for better fiscal management by government and reductions in the bureaucracy. Carter's legislative efforts were hampered by the fragmentation of the Democratic majority and the need for fiscal restraint. The increasing public disillusionment with government, which Carter had played upon as a candidate, also proved a handicap when he proposed governmental solutions to social and economic problems.

A watershed in the third era of activity was the defeat, in 1978, of legislation to create an agency for consumer advocacy. The idea of a Department of Consumers to parallel the Departments of Commerce and Labor had been discussed for some time. In the 1970s, under the leadership of Ralph Nader, attention shifted to creating a consumer advocacy agency that would have no regulatory powers of its own but could monitor the activities of other government agencies and intervene in their regulatory decision-making. This structure was urged by Nader, who believed that regulatory responsibility is incompatible with advocacy activity.

The defeat of the consumer advocacy agency proposal came after nine years of effort by one of the largest and most active consumer coalitions in history—The Consumer Federation of America—many of whose member organizations, Consumers Union, the Nader network, and about 100 corporations and trade groups were faced by a new, broad coalition of business interests. These business opponents of the proposal foresaw an agency with extensive powers and the ability to intervene in all aspects of government. They argued that the proposed agency would create a new bureaucracy, increase the complexity of regulatory hearings, and force the disclosure of trade secrets.

The bill's defeat appears to have had several causes. Because it focused on process rather than the control of specific risks or abuses, the bill did not arouse the level of public support that more specific protection proposals often do. Another problem was that, for the first time, business had built a broad and powerful coalition to oppose a consumer proposal. In the face of this strong opposition, the consumerist camp became deeply divided on the questions of whether, when, and how to compromise.

After the congressional defeat of proposals for a consumer advocacy agency, the Carter administration tried another approach to representing the consumer interest in government. Using an executive order, Carter called for the creation of consumer affairs programs in major federal agencies. The plan, which created consumer advocates in each agency, drew praise from many consumer leaders but was criticized by Ralph Nader. He concluded that the advocates would have little real clout since they lacked subpoena power and the power of judicial review and were unlikely to criticize their bosses. After the Carter administration, these consumer offices remained but functioned as information disseminators to those outside government rather than as advocates.

Despite the defeat of the consumer advocacy agency bill, the Carter administration did succeed in moving the consumer interest forward on some fronts. Several leading consumer advocates were appointed to key regulatory posts, where they succeeded in reinvigorating their agencies. In addition, several deregulatory proposals designed to increase competition were put into effect, including the 1978 deregulation of the airline industry. Aggressive antitrust action against AT&T by the Justice Department eventually led to the 1984 breakup agreement that separated long-distance operations from local telephone operating companies. There were setbacks, however. No-fault auto insurance was defeated and, in 1979, Congress imposed restrictions on a number of major FTC investigations.

2.1.5 Recent Decades

The Ronald Reagan administration promoted both economic and social (especially health and safety) deregulation. To implement its program of deregulation, the Reagan administration reduced enforcement activities by cutting agency appropriations and appointing agency heads with a narrower view of their agency's mission. These changes were particularly visible at the FTC, where there were cutbacks in both antitrust and advertising regulatory activities, and at the Consumer Product Safety Commission. While the public supported many of the economic deregulation proposals, proposals for health, safety, and environmental deregulation met with resistance. The pressures of the Reagan cutbacks and the experience of lobbying together for the agency for consumer advocacy proposals brought the organizations of the consumer movement more closely together. In his early years, Ralph Nader had been dubbed "the Lone Ranger of the consumer movement" because of his unwillingness to collaborate with other segments of the movement. Beginning in the late 1970s, the Nader network, Consumers Union, and the Consumer Federation of America increasingly worked together in *ad hoc* issue coalitions.

During the 1980s, a top priority of the Nader network was to establish citizen groups at both the national and state levels funded by small contributions from many consumers. This funding approach had been successful in creating Public Interest Research Groups, or PIRGs, on college campuses. The principal result of these efforts was the formation of a few citizen utility boards (CUBs). These CUBs lost much of their ability to organize when they were denied access to utility mailings in a 1986 Supreme Court decision.

The activities of the consumer movement in the late 1970s and early 1980s were hampered by serious financial problems. During this period, "stagflation" and recession cut revenues from contributions and subscriptions. Movement revenues also suffered a major reduction when the Reagan administration eliminated most grants and contracts to consumer groups. Consumers Union, the Consumer Federation of America, and the Nader flagship organization, Public Citizen, all experienced financial problems. As economic conditions improved during the 1980s, and as consumer leaders devoted more attention to building stable funding bases, the movement recovered financially. The revenues of Consumers Union doubled during the 1980s. It used some of its substantial surpluses to fund state and local consumer groups and to increase aid for consumer organizations in the Third World.

The consumer movement lost much of its visibility during the 1980s. After some media coverage of the movement's protests of the Reagan administration's budget cuts and regulatory rollbacks, media attention shifted elsewhere. Despite this lack of coverage, the movement continued to push its agenda and was able to promote some narrowly focused but significant reforms. Mandatory seat-belt-use laws were passed in virtually every state, and a federal passive restraint standard was finally implemented after a decade-long battle. Important victories were also won in the area of financial services, with consumers gaining new rights with respect to cashing checks and taking out home equity loans.

The George H. W. Bush administration proved somewhat more receptive to consumer protection concerns than had the previous one. In particular, the first President Bush made several strong appointments to regulatory agencies. Important changes in nutritional labeling were instituted by the FDA at congressional request despite strong objections from livestock interests. The new labels added information on such problem constituents as sodium, saturated fat, and cholesterol and also added information on fiber content.

During the first Bush presidency, consumers also won the right to standardized disclosure of interest on savings accounts, and the FTC (spurred by aggressive actions from state attorneys general) issued guidelines for environmental marketing claims (for example, "ozone friendly," "recyclable," "photodegradable"). The rapid proliferation of computers during the late 1980s and early 1990s led to increased concern about consumer privacy, especially with respect to credit and medical records. No new federal legislation was passed to safeguard consumer privacy, but several firms and industry groups addressed this concern through self-regulatory policies.

As a Democrat, President Bill Clinton might have been expected to be sympathetic to consumer issues. Consumer groups were able to persuade Congress to pass the Home Ownership and Equity Protection Act in 1994, which provides some protection against predatory mortgage lending, and the Consumer Credit Reporting Reform Act of 1996, which targets the high level of inaccuracy of the information in consumer credit reports. While Clinton's efforts to reform health care were applauded by the consumer movement, he never developed a concrete set of priorities regarding consumer issues before losing his Democratic majority in the Congress in the 1994 elections. Nevertheless, consumer protection efforts continued during Clinton's administration, mostly in the form of regulatory decisions. The FTC issued rules to discourage abusive practices involving 900-telephone numbers (1993) and fraudulent telemarketing efforts

(1995). The CPSC also regained some of its vigor, especially in the area of protecting children. Thus, even in the absence of major new legislation and without a president explicitly committed to traditional consumer issues, the consumer movement enjoyed successes both before and after the 1994 elections.

As a Republican, President George W. Bush was assumed not to be a supporter of consumer protection initiatives. However, Bush appointments to the FTC have continued effective enforcement of many consumer protection laws and have pushed for a national do-not-call directory for consumers to escape from telemarketers. Banking regulators appointed by the administration have increasingly engaged in backdoor deregulation of credit by preempting traditional state regulation of consumer credit without providing effective federal safeguards against predatory lending. Republican majorities in Congress have recognized the importance of fighting consumer frauds and have not yet rolled back important consumer protections, with the significant exception of diminishing consumers' bankruptcy protections.

2.1.6 Overarching Patterns

2.1.6.1 General

Since the U.S. consumer movement's origins in the last decade of the nineteenth century, the movement has experienced several periods of especially intense activity, corresponding roughly to the Progressive era of the early twentieth century, the New Deal period of the 1930s, and the Great Society of the 1960s and early 1970s. While consumerist activity continued in between these three peaks, a striking feature of the American consumer movement remains its periodic (and, some might argue, cyclical) character. One important feature of all three periods has been diminished public confidence in business and heightened confidence in government and, by implication, new regulatory controls. In addition to the movement's periodic character, five other general patterns can be seen in the movement's century-long history: institutionalization, specialization, professionalization, changing strategies, and internationalization.

2.1.6.2 Institutionalization

Social movements, by their very nature, challenge a society's existing arrangements and ways of thinking. When these movements first arise, they must struggle to be taken seriously by both the general public and policy makers. At the same time that an emerging social movement seeks support and legitimacy, opponents of the movement attempt to discredit and de-legitimize it. Social movement leaders may be described by their opponents as naive do-gooders, self-appointed elitists seeking to impose their values on others, or enemies of capitalism and democracy. This entry has already reviewed the allegations of Communist influence aimed at Consumers Union during the late 1930s. In the 1960s, consumer leader Ralph Nader was variously criticized as arrogant, uncompromising, authoritarian, paranoid, puritanical, and devoid of economic common sense. Another consumer leader, FTC Chairman Michael Pertschuk, was accused of turning the commission into a "national nanny."

Despite criticism leveled at the leaders, organizations, and basic ideology of the consumer movement, it has gradually grown in its public legitimacy. At the same time, the movement has become more institutionalized and permanent. The movement has established a set of ongoing organizations with a relatively reliable financial base and a pool of leaders who rely more on professional and organizational skills than on charisma to achieve movement goals. The institutionalization of the consumer movement has also brought forth institutionalized responses on the part of government and business. Consumer affairs departments have been created within government agencies and large corporations, and professional associations have been established for consumer agency administrators (National Association of Consumer Agency Administrators), state utility consumer advocates (National Association of State Utility Consumer Advocates), and consumer affairs professionals in business (Society of Consumer Affairs Professionals in Business).

A final aspect of the consumer movement's institutionalization is its growing self-reflexiveness and awareness of its history. Consumers Union has published several books and produced a film (*America at Risk: A History of Consumer Protest*) on the history of the consumer movement. Under the guidance of Professor Richard L. D. Morse, an archive of consumer movement documents was established at Kansas State University in the late 1980s. During the early 1990s, consumer leader Helen Nelson produced a film (*Change Makers: The Struggle for Consumer Rights*) and established an archive based on videotaped interviews with thirty-five prominent consumer activists. Stephen Brobeck, executive director of the Consumer Federation of America, published an annotated bibliography of resource materials on the consumer movement. That encyclopedia marks a further step in the institutionalization of the consumer movement.

2.1.6.3 Specialization

The number of national, state, and local consumer organizations has increased dramatically since the early days of the consumer movement. A 1992 study by the Consumer Federation of America counted more than 400 such organizations. More striking than the increase in the sheer number of consumer organizations has been the emergence of groups specializing in a particular domain or on a particular set of issues. Whereas organizations such as the National Consumers League, Consumers Union, Public Citizen, and the Consumer Federation of America remain "generalists" in the consumer field, a number of other organizations have established themselves as experts in particular areas such as food safety and nutrition, health care, automobile safety, credit cards, insurance, privacy, consumer law, and telecommunications fraud.

The division of consumer organizations into generalist and specialist organizations has occurred largely on an unplanned basis. To the extent that there is coordination among these diverse organizations, it is sometimes accomplished through the Consumer Federation of America, the continuing personal influence of Ralph Nader, or the formation of temporary coalitions devoted to a particular action or issue.

Given the number and diversity of consumer organizations, it should not be surprising that competition and conflict sometimes exist. Differences in tactics are, however, more prevalent than differences in goals. Some organizations are comfortable working collaboratively with business organizations, while other organizations view contacts with business as compromising their integrity. Honest differences of opinion can also exist regarding when and how much to compromise in seeking legislative solutions to consumer problems. Still, overt conflict among consumer organizations is rare; and, given the need to stretch resources across a large number of issues, most organizations are only too pleased to let another group take the lead on a particular issue.

2.1.6.4 Professionalization

Consumer advocates have become increasingly professionalized over time. Many of the movement's first leaders were either volunteers (usually homemakers) or people who had careers in other domains (as chemists, economists, lawyers, or engineers). They had little formal training in consumer affairs and could not claim to be experts in more than one consumer area, if that. Today, consumer leaders are full-time professionals who can build a career in consumer affairs or public interest advocacy. To deal effectively with technical issues such as telecommunications policy, public utilities, pharmaceutical safety, and financial services, it is no longer possible for consumer leaders to rely on righteous indignation. They have become increasingly knowledgeable in specialized areas and able to prepare and critique technical documents. Moreover, consumer leaders have gained considerable expertise in the methods of political action—from conducting direct-mail solicitations and lobbying legislators to organizing ballot initiatives and taking cases to the U.S. Supreme Court. In sum, work in the area of consumer affairs has been transformed from a part-time, uncompensated, and transient task conducted primarily by homemakers to a full-time, compensated, career-oriented occupation capable of attracting talented men and women.

2.1.6.5 Changing Strategies

From its earliest days, the consumer movement has relied on a mix of political strategies, including seeking change directly from businesses and using governmental laws and regulations to alter business conduct. For example, consumerists at the turn of the twentieth century urged consumers to buy from a "white list" of companies whose labor practices stood above the suspect standards of the day while, at the same time, pressing for federal legislation to ensure the safety of foods and pharmaceutical products.

A similar mix of political strategies can be seen today, only the mix is much broader. Along with boycotts are "buycotts," efforts to direct consumer spending and investing toward firms whose social performance is particularly laudatory. Efforts to educate consumers have expanded from classrooms and meetings organized by agricultural extension agents to the airwaves and the Internet. Consumer advocates have also gained skill in using the state initiative and referendum process to make consumer policy or give strong direction to state legislators. Similarly, consumerists have honed their skills in the judicial arena, learning how to use the courts to block undesirable actions and sustain past successes.

Still, the primary tactic of the consumer movement is lobbying governments for legislative and regulatory action. Some of the lobbying attempts to limit seller behavior by setting minimal standards for safety or performance or by outlawing certain goods and services. Automobile safety standards and the drug approval process fall in this category. Other efforts are directed at expanding consumer choice (for example, airline, telecommunication, and banking deregulation) or making choices more informed (for example, requiring disclosure data on product performance or price).

Overall, the general thrust of the U.S. consumer movement has been less an effort to influence consumer product choices and more an attempt to alter seller behavior directly through legislative and regulatory means. That is why the movement's strategies are somewhat centralized and focused on Washington, D.C., and capitals of the most populous states.

2.1.6.6 Internationalization

In its early years, the consumer movement in the United States developed in relative isolation from the consumer-oriented activities in other countries (for example, consumer cooperatives and housewives' organizations). Since around 1960, the consumer movements of the world have become increasingly interlinked. In many instances, the U.S. consumer movement has set the pace for other nations but, in other cases, the U.S. has "imported" consumerist ideas from abroad.

The single most important event in the internationalization of the U.S. consumer movement was the formation in 1960 of the International Organization of Consumers Unions (IOCU). IOCU, whose name was changed to Consumers International in 1994, was initially intended to spread the practice of comparative product testing, pioneered in the United States by Consumers' Research and Consumers Union, to other industrialized nations. Over time, IOCU has become a vehicle for spreading consumer advocacy protection and education to both more and less developed nations.

By virtue of its size and influence, the U.S. consumer movement has been responsible for the diffusion of specific elements of consumer policy. These policies span the areas of safety (for example, passive restraints in automobiles; smoking bans on airplanes; systematic national collection of product-related injury data), information (for example, permitting comparative advertising; requiring disclosure of energy efficiency data and nutritional information), competition (for example, airline and telecommunications deregulation), and redress (for example, lemon laws; cooling-off periods; and class action lawsuits). On the other hand, the United States has adopted consumer policies pioneered in other nations. These policies include mandatory seat belt use laws (Australia), rotating cigarette warnings (Sweden), environmental seals of approval (Germany), accelerated drug approval (United Kingdom), and consumer ombuds (the Nordic countries).

During the 1990s, the U.S. consumer movement has found itself increasingly drawn into a set of issues that are international by their very nature: free trade and environmental protection. Consumer groups in the United States, which once ignored issues related to trade liberalization and protectionism, confronted consumer issues raised by the North American Free Trade Agreement (NAFTA) and the latest round of the General Agreement on Tariffs and Trade (GATT). In contrast to consumer groups in Europe, which were cautiously supportive of free-trade agreements like the GATT, most U.S. consumer groups tended to take the position that the lower prices brought about by free trade were not worth the threat to strict consumer and environmental standards posed by free-trade agreements. A notable exception was Consumers Union, which supported the trade agreement.

Environmental issues also are pushing the U.S. consumer movement to think more globally. In the United States, the consumer and environmental movements have developed largely in parallel, with relatively little interaction except over issues such as pesticides, energy conservation, and recycling. In the rest of the world, the relationship between the consumer and environmental movements is more intimate. The Dutch product testing magazine, for instance, considers a product's environmental impact as an integral part of its overall product rating, whereas Consumers Union in the United States does not. As consumer organizations in the United States increasingly come into contact with those of other nations, especially those of formerly socialist nations and the less developed world, environmental issues may occupy a more important position in the priorities of the U.S. movement.

2.1.6.7 Persisting Tensions Within the Movement

If a social movement is to endure, it must solve, or at least manage, a number of problems. Some of these problems involve the movement's identity and internal relationships, including the problem of preserving a tough, combative spirit. Other problems involve the movement's relationship to its external environment, especially the problems of obtaining adequate financial and human resources and maintaining its legitimacy among the public and policy makers.

A set of persisting problems concerns the consumer movement's proper goals and scope. Should the movement focus on a narrow set of issues that arise from individual purchases of goods and services in the private market, or should it focus on a broader set of economic issues that includes the availability and quality of public services and the fairness of tax policy? Organizations within the U.S. consumer movement differ in how broadly they define consumer issues but, relative to the consumer movements of less developed countries—with their heavy emphasis on providing basic necessities and obtaining redress from unresponsive, government-owned enterprises—the U.S. movement operates with a relatively narrow definition of consumer issues.

Closely related to the issue of scope is the problem of balancing the interests of middle-class and poor consumers. With a few notable exceptions, the U.S. consumer movement has primarily recruited its participants from the middle class and pursued issues relevant to middle-class consumers. Consumer advocates show little regard for the argument that mandating a consumer safety and performance feature will increase a product's price and therefore make it less affordable for low-income consumers. Nevertheless, there are several notable areas in which consumer advocates have devoted special attention to problems of low-income consumers: price increases that threaten access to electricity, natural gas, telecommunications, and banking services; discrimination in credit and insurance markets; and excessive price differences between inner-city and suburban stores. Still, most of the U.S. movement's activities are based on the assumption that consumers have more difficulty spending money wisely than earning it.

Consumer organizations are not only sensitive to the charge that they have a middle-class bias but also to the charge that they are self-appointed and out of touch with the real desires of consumers. Critics of the U.S. consumer movement contend that it was consumer advocates, not consumers, who wanted the ineffective interlock seatbelt system on cars, mandatory motorcycle helmet laws, a ban on saccharin, and conservative rules for approving new drugs. Thus, a continuing challenge for the movement is to be accountable to the consuming public and to their financial contributors while still being able to pursue consumer problems that may be only dimly perceived or imperfectly understood by these constituencies.

A further internal problem involves coordination of movement activities. As would be expected of organizations that were established at different times, in different locales, and for different purposes, the organizations of the consumer movement guard their autonomy. Efforts at coordination are further complicated by differences in preferred tactics, especially the question of whether consumer groups should work with, and even accept funds from, business groups. Consumers Union and the organizations founded by Ralph Nader are very cautious about contact with business interests, while groups like the National Consumers League and the Consumer Federation of America are more accommodating toward business interests.

The most basic external problem of any social movement is to "mobilize resources," that is, to obtain the financial and human resources necessary to support the movement's activities. Despite favorable tax treatment, the organizations of the consumer movement constantly face the problems of financial insecurity and personnel turnover. Even those organizations that have established a relatively firm financial base usually can not match resources with business-financed opponents.

An additional external problem of the consumer movement is being able to operate credibly in dealing with increasingly complex issues. Issues may require knowledge of biology, chemistry, and physics (for example, food irradiation and genetically engineered food); geology and transportation systems (for example, natural gas and electricity regulation); economics (for example, trade liberalization and telecommunications deregulation); and medicine (for example, health care reform and pharmaceutical regulation). It is difficult for consumer organizations to develop the expertise and confidence to address such complex issues and then obtain the necessary expertise to lobby effectively.

The task of dealing with increasingly technical issues is often complicated by the uneasiness of many consumer advocates with scientists, even ones sympathetic to the consumerist perspective. The culture of the scientist and the activist are quite different. Whereas the activist sees issues in relatively black-and-white terms, the scientist tends to consider all sides of an argument. The activist needs research that directly addresses a particular policy proposal; the scientist is concerned with policy implications but also with more basic and enduring scientific questions. The activist needs the research results almost immediately; the scientist will be ready when he or she is satisfied that the work meets certain professional standards of quality. The activist wants research results that are clear-cut and dramatic, while the scientist wants to hedge and qualify findings. Unfortunately consumer advocates have failed to form productive relationships with consumer-oriented academics in the natural and social sciences, although the blame for this appears to fall on both camps.

A final persisting tension in the consumer movement is the management of its relationships with other social movements, especially organized labor and the environmental movement. Historically, the ties between the consumer movement and organized labor have been very close, and labor unions continue to participate actively in the National Consumers League and the Consumer Federation of America. Labor unions have provided financial support, manpower, and their militant tradition of standing up to injustice to the U.S. consumer movement. At the same time, the consumer movement sometimes finds itself at odds with the position of organized labor, especially on issues relating to trade protection, through which consumer benefits in terms of lower prices and greater choice may come at the expense of domestic jobs.

The consumer movement also must negotiate its relationship with the environmental movement. While the consumer and environmental movements have similar reformist ideologies, recruit resources from similar segments of society, and face similar problems as public interest movements, they also have areas of potential conflict. The efforts of environmentalists to protect the natural environment may require consumers to pay higher prices for goods (for example, auto air conditioning coolants), face restricted choices (for example, reduced access to ecologically sensitive areas), or endure inconveniences (for example, product recycling). Conversely, environmentalists sometimes view consumerists as contributing to, rather than challenging, the materialism and "consumerism" of modern industrialized societies. *Consumer Reports*, they might argue, should not even compare the relative merits of large, luxury cars; instead, the magazine should tell consumers to avoid all such gas-guzzlers. These tensions between the consumer and environmental movements are often overcome or submerged, but neither movement can take the other's support for granted.

2.1.7 Contributions

Despite the problems facing social movements in general and the consumer movement in particular, the U.S. consumer movement has a century-long history and a substantial record of achievement. The actions of the consumer movement have resulted in a long list of laws, regulations, and judicial decisions that have improved consumer welfare. The consumer movement's greatest accomplishments, however, may have relatively little to do with these specific, concrete accomplishments. The movement's most enduring effects may be sensitizing the mass media, businesses, and consumers themselves to consumer interests.

Individuals now recognize that they have distinct interests as consumers and that these interests must be continually guarded. Individuals are aware that they have certain rights as consumers regarding safety, information, competition, representation, redress, education, and privacy. Consumers who complain about shoddy products or poor service are no longer regarded as cranks and whiners but rather as people who are taking the time to stand up for themselves and others. When citizens consider alternative candidates for public office, they not only want to know where a candidate stands on national defense, the economy, civil rights, and abortion, but also on consumer protection issues.

The mass media, too, have been strongly influenced by the consumer movement. While they were at first resistant to the idea of covering consumer issues for fear of alienating advertisers, the mass media have become an important force for educating consumers. While programs and articles are rare that explicitly and regularly cover consumer topics, many of the health, safety, and financial exposés carried by the mass media involve consumer topics. Similarly, media coverage of the legislative, administrative, and judicial actions of government contains a large share of consumer-relevant news. Furthermore, the media themselves have instituted "reader advocates" or other mechanisms to be responsive to their own customers.

Finally, the consumer movement has had an enduring effect on the business community. Progressive marketers no longer view themselves as trying to "sell" something to consumers but rather as trying to meet consumer needs and build ongoing relationships with consumers. Many companies have special consumer affairs representatives, consumer advisory panels, or complaint-handling offices. Treating customers properly and listening to consumer leaders has been embraced as both a moral obligation (part of corporate social responsibility) and a necessary part of maximizing long-term profitability.

The U.S. consumer movement has experienced three periods of intense activity in this century. One might ask whether there will be another such period. Certainly, the pace of legislative and regulatory action on behalf of consumers has slackened compared to its peak in the 1960s and the first half of the 1970s. Moreover, the issues that galvanized the movement in the past were relatively straightforward ones, involving dramatic problems of safety and fairness. Most of the consumer problems that remain, or are likely to arise, are more complex. They are less likely to lend themselves to dramatic exposés by "issue entrepreneurs" and spectacular media coverage.

Is a fourth era of consumer activism unlikely, then? Perhaps a more appropriate question might be: will a fourth era be necessary? The consumer movement is so thoroughly institutionalized, and the values of the movement are so fully embedded in society, that it may be accurate to say that the third era has never really ended. Even under Republican administrations, consumer organizations and their allies in government and corporation settings have remained remarkably focused on consumer welfare and effective in carrying out their missions. Future achievements will be more difficult, requiring careful study and preparation, skillful coalition building, and persistent political pressure. But the influence of the U.S. consumer movement is becoming permanent because its role has become indispensable.[3]

2.2 Legal Services and the Consumer Movement

2.2.1 General

The terms Legal Aid and Legal Services generally refer to local community programs that provide civil legal representation to low-income individuals without charge. These free services are provided by lawyers and other legal workers who are usually full- or part-time employees of a legal aid program, although sometimes a panel of private lawyers is used.

Civil representation refers to cases and legal matters outside of the criminal justice system. In the criminal justice system, a person charged by the government with a criminal violation of the law will be entitled to the services of a public defender if the person is unable to afford a lawyer. If the legal matter is not criminal in nature, a person unable to afford a lawyer may sometimes be able to secure legal representation from a legal aid or legal services program. The civil matters most commonly handled by legal aid attorneys are divorce and other family matters, public benefits disputes, housing matters including evictions, and consumer cases, but the range of available services may be considerably broader. The number of legal aid offices and attorneys is far too inadequate to ensure that representation is available to all qualified individuals who need it.

Legal services have at times played an important role in consumer law. From 1970 to 1995, a substantial portion of consumer law cases contested in the courts involved clients represented by legal aid attorneys. Legal services programs probably closed more than a quarter million consumer cases in 1994. Typical consumer cases involve car purchases and leases, debt collection harassment, home improvement contracts, credit and loan contracts and mortgages, various forms of credit insurance and related products, credit discrimination, and a wide variety of unfair and deceptive acts and practices, although the complete list is nearly endless. Most of the private attorneys specializing in consumer protection law today once practiced with a legal services program.

3 *See* www.lsc.gov.

Until the last decade, many of the most important consumer cases were litigated by legal services programs. These are cases that affect a great number of consumers or help define how a consumer protection law will be interpreted and applied. Some of the Supreme Court cases establishing a consumer's constitutional right to notice of court proceedings initiated by a creditor and the right to be heard in court were argued and won by legal services attorneys.

2.2.2 *Types of Legal Aid Programs*

A community may host different kinds of legal aid offices. Every community is served by a legal services office funded in part by the federal government through the Legal Services Corporation. This Corporation is a private, non-profit organization, but it is funded by Congress and governed by a board appointed by the President. The Corporation in turn funds local programs governed by a local board of directors that sets the local program's priorities. As a result, programs in many parts of the country may handle consumer cases, for example, while programs in other places do not. Every county in the country falls within the service area of a legal services program funded by the Legal Services Corporation. Nationwide, there are about 140 such programs.[4] Because of increasing restrictions on their services by the Legal Services Corporation, some localities have set up separately funded programs that can provide a fuller range of services to their low-income clients. These programs are most often funded by state funds, client fees, foundation grants, or court attorney fee awards.

Many communities, especially cities, host other legal aid programs as well. Most are small, single-office programs, serving a small community or a special group of clients or specializing in a particular subject. For example, a neighborhood might have a church- or foundation-sponsored legal clinic serving the area; other legal aid offices might be established to assist elderly clients, disabled clients, or prisoners; or a legal services program might handle only housing cases or civil rights matters. Some law schools have clinical programs for the students that offer free or low-cost legal services.

Nearly all legal aid offices are intended to serve individuals who otherwise would not have access to professional legal assistance. Most serve only low-income individuals. Offices receiving funds from the federal Legal Services Corporation have income eligibility guidelines tied to the poverty level. A few, such as those serving older Americans, have no income guidelines.

2.2.3 *History of Legal Aid*

The first legal aid program was established in 1876 in New York City as a private charitable effort to assist recent German immigrants. Thereafter, the American Bar Association and Reginald Heber Smith promoted legal aid societies to serve the "deserving poor." Beginning in Boston in 1900, legal aid societies were formed in most major cities, usually with the support of lawyers, United Way Organizations, and other local public and private funders. For the most part, these organizations eschewed all but routine individual legal matters.

Legal services as we know it today was profoundly shaped in the 1960s. At the beginning of the decade, legal aid societies employed only about 200 full-time attorneys nationwide. National foundations began to experiment with full-service legal services programs focusing on chronic problems of poverty as part of a growing anti-poverty movement in the country.

Under President Johnson, and extending until 1974, the federal Office of Economic Opportunity established neighborhood legal services offices in many parts of the country as part of its War on Poverty. These offices were established under local community control and outside the control of state and local governments. In addition, a few national organizations, such as the National Consumer Law Center, were funded to shape and support the local delivery of legal services. The first in a series of important poverty law cases began reaching the Supreme Court.[5]

The legal rights of poor people as newly voiced with legal services program assistance raised political controversy at the local level and in Congress. In an effort to insulate federal financial support for legal aid from political controversy, responsibility for the legal services program was removed from the federal bureaucracy and transferred to a newly created private non-profit Legal Services Corporation. In 1974, the Corporation was proposed by President Nixon and created by Congress with strong support from the American Bar Association. Funding is appropriated annually by the Congress.

Under the Legal Services Corporation, funding for legal services increased to the point where there was one legal services attorney funded by the Legal Services Corporation for every 5000 poor persons, and every county in the country was served. However, the political controversy surrounding legal services work never ceased, and federal funding has been debated and varied ever since. Today it is significantly lower than in 1980 but significantly higher than in the 1960s. At the same time, local funding has increased

4 *E.g.*, Fuentes v. Shevin, 407 U.S. 67 (1972) (replevin of consumer goods without notice and opportunity for a hearing violated due process); Goldberg v. Kelly, 397 U.S. 254 (1970) (termination of public welfare benefits without notice and hearing violated due process); Thorpe v. Hous. Auth., 386 U.S. 670 (1967) (housing authority's decision to evict a tenant and terminate their public housing benefits without a prior hearing and notice violated due process).

5 *See* www.ConsumerLaw.org.

significantly in many states. Even so, overall funding is still low. Less than fifteen percent of the civil legal needs of the poor are being met.

2.3 The National Consumer Law Center, Inc.

The National Consumer Law Center (NCLC) is the leading national expert on legal and policy issues concerning low-income consumers. It is known to many as the "Nation's Consumer Law Experts." The Center is best known for its informed and well-researched advocacy on behalf of low-income consumers, its research of public policy matters affecting the legal needs and rights of low-income consumers, and its publications[6] and treatises on consumer, energy, and public utility law.

The Center, or NCLC, is a non-profit organization located in Boston, Massachusetts, with an office in Washington, D.C. Its work, however, is national in scope, and it is commonplace for Center staff to be engaged in projects with public agencies, community groups, and lawyers across the country. The board and staff of the Center itself are drawn from around the country.

Consumer law is a broad jurisdiction for the Center's work. Topics of focus have ranged from insurance and warranties to housing and access to markets. The primary emphasis over the years, however, has been consumer credit, debt and finance problems, and the affordability of necessities of life such as home heat, utility services, home repairs, and home mortgages.

As experts in consumer law and policy, National Consumer Law Center staff serve as a resource to: lawyers representing low-income clients; public agencies designing and administering laws and programs serving the poor; legislatures and policy-makers; and private non-profit and for-profit organizations and companies with special concerns for low-income consumers. The Center is not a place for individual consumers to call and write for assistance, although some Center publications may be of interest to the general public and may be purchased from the Center; Center staff are more likely to be found assisting those agencies and advocates who provide direct service to low-income consumers.

The National Consumer Law Center was founded in 1968–69 at the Boston College School of Law. Professor William Willier, a well-known commercial law professor and consumer advocate, was the moving force in getting the Center started with the active support of the law school's dean, Father Robert Drinan. Following Professor Willier, the Center's Executive Director was Richard Hesse, formerly a legal services attorney in Pennsylvania. During his tenure, the Center established itself as a national representative of the interests of low-income consumers. The next director, beginning in 1975, was Mark Budnitz. Mr. Budnitz left the clinical program at Boston University School of Law to join the Center, where he had previously served as the litigation director. During his tenure, the Center expanded its advocacy into areas of energy law and policy. Following Mr. Budnitz, Robert Sable became director in 1979. Mr. Sable was former Civil Director of the Cleveland Legal Aid Society and Deputy Director of the Center. The current director, Willard P. Ogburn, began in 1987. Mr. Ogburn is a former Massachusetts Deputy Commissioner of Banking and former Deputy Director of the Center as well. During Mr. Sable's and Mr. Ogburn's tenures, the Center greatly expanded its publications and greatly diversified its funding base. Throughout its history, the strength of the Center has been its staff of highly expert legal and technical specialists drawn to the Center from across the country.

Initial funding was provided by the federal Office of Economic Opportunity (OEO) as part of the nation's War on Poverty. OEO was then funding new legal services neighborhood organizations to ensure that low-income Americans had access to lawyers and the ability to protect and assert their rights in court and in public affairs. To support and complement the work of local legal services offices, OEO funded a small number of national backup centers, beginning with the Center on Social Welfare Policy and Law at Columbia University School of Law followed shortly by other centers, including the National Housing Law Project (at Boalt Hall, Berkeley), the Center for Law and Education (at Harvard Law School), and the National Consumer Law Center (at Boston College School of Law). Ever since, NCLC has worked closely with legal services programs, which now serve every part of the country.

In 1973, the Center separated from Boston College for financial reasons, incorporated as a non-profit, tax-exempt organization, and moved into space in downtown Boston. Until 1995, the single largest source of financial support was OEO funding and funding from one of its successors, the federal Legal Services Corporation. Today, its funding includes: a changing variety of public and private grants, including foundation support and contracts from public and private national and local organizations; donations; *cy pres* awards; and income from publications, conferences, and services; as well as a variety of other sources. In recent years, the budget of the National Consumer Law Center has risen to five million dollars a year.

Following its founding, the Center's impact was felt almost immediately on state consumer credit laws. The National Conference on Uniform State Laws, using funds provided by the retail credit and financial services industry, drafted and proposed a Uniform Consumer Credit Code for adoption by each state. The Code contained many provisions detrimental to consumers in many states. In response, the National Consumer Law Center drafted a National Consumer Act, and later a Model Consumer Credit Act, and joined with local advocates to oppose adoption of the Code

6 15 U.S.C. § 1692.

unless it was amended to be more favorable to consumers. Thereafter the Code was withdrawn and revised to reflect many improvements proposed by the Center. At the same time, the National Consumer Act and the Model Consumer Credit Act have served as models for state law provisions in both so-called Code states and non-Code states and for the Fair Debt Collection Practices Act.[7]

Language and policies drafted by the Center have been adopted or have influenced consumer protection laws at both the state and federal levels. In addition, to state credit codes, Center work is reflected in laws and regulations on debt collection, pre-paid service contracts, interest rate ceilings, credit insurance, warranties, and other matters. National consumer protection laws similarly reflect Center expertise. Many parts of the federal Consumer Protection Act reflect the testimony and draftsmanship of Center staff, including especially the Truth in Lending Act, the Fair Debt Collection Practices Act, and the Home Ownership Equity Protection Act. In addition, federal programs to help ensure affordability of utility services, especially home heating, have been shaped by NCLC expertise.

Sometimes the rights of low-income consumers are the subject of agency adjudication or rule-making. Center staff have frequently testified before public utility commissions and worked with utility advocates to ensure fair treatment for low-income households. The Center is especially well known for having created, fostered, and helped to implement "percentage of income plans" or PIPs, which seek to match the need for essential life-saving utility services with the ability of low-income households to pay, programs which can benefit all ratepayers. At the federal level, the Center served as appointed public advocates for the Holder in Due Course and the Credit Practices Rules adopted by the Federal Trade Commission to require basic fairness in the consumer credit marketplace.

The Center will also undertake litigation when important principles are at stake. Center attorneys have appeared and participated in ground-breaking cases before federal and state courts at all levels, including the United States Supreme Court. The cases have established constitutional due process rights of consumers, especially debtors; expanded standards of deception and unfairness; secured appropriate interpretations of consumer protection laws; caused hundreds of million of dollars of illegal overcharges by oil companies to be set aside for the benefit of low-income households; and attacked hidden illicit automobile finance fees discriminating against African-American and Hispanic consumers. Generally such litigation is handled in conjunction with local advocates.

In addition to advocacy, the Center undertakes research and public policy analyses addressing the circumstances of low-income households in the area of consumer and energy law. For example, the Center has released a series of reports (for example, "Out in the Cold" and "Cold, Not By Choice") analyzing the devastating impact of energy and utility costs on low-income households. Another report was the first to detail the impending crisis (and possible solutions) for low-income households caused by water and sewer bills rising as a result of clean water initiatives. Yet another study on growing home equity lending practices led to federal reform legislation. Private entities also commission NCLC studies on particular industry practices or emerging consumer problems or alternative public policy responses. Many of NCLC's reports are on its website, www.ConsumerLaw.org, and available for purchase by phone.

The Center's seventeen-volume *Consumer Credit and Sales Legal Practice Series* is an encyclopedic collection of practice manuals and treatises widely respected and used by the legal profession. Each volume addresses a topic of consumer law—such as debt collection, credit reporting, unfair and deceptive acts and practices, utility customer service, bankruptcy, or sales of goods and services—and is a guide to all major related state and federal statutes and judicial interpretations, providing extensive analysis and practice resources. The books are standard reference materials. Two regular newsletters are published by the Center: *NCLC REPORTS* highlights new developments and consumer law trends, and *Energy and Utility Update* reports on low-income energy policy developments. In addition, numerous monographs, books, and reports are available.

NCLC publications are primarily addressed to lawyers, advocates, and specialists, although many studies are of broader interest. A few consumer education pieces are developed and distributed from time to time. The *NCLC Guide to Surviving Debt* (2005) provides practical advice for consumers who find themselves overcome with debt, while being particularly appropriate for counselors, social workers, clergy, and organizers who work with financially distressed households.

The Center is also the sponsor of an annual conference on consumer law, and its staff participate regularly as presenters at conferences, training seminars, and continuing legal education sessions. Its first Consumer Law Specialist Training Conference was held in Kansas City in 1976. Today, its popular Consumer Rights Litigation Conference and Consumer Class Action Symposium are held each fall, in a different city each year, with nearly 600 advocates attending the four days of training and meetings. Its first Annual Low Income Energy Conference was held in 1987 and, after a hiatus of several years, NCLC co-sponsored a conference on energy restructuring in September 2002.

The Vern Countryman Consumer Law Award is presented once a year by the Center to one of the nation's top consumer law attorneys. The Award recognizes at least ten years of exceptional consumer law practice or an achievement which

---

7 National Association of Consumer Advocates, 1730 Rhode Island Avenue, N.W., Suite 805, Washington, D.C. 20036, (202) 452-1989, fax (202) 452-0099, www.naca.net.

profoundly affects the rights of a large number of low-income consumers. The Award was funded by friends of Professor Countryman, a founding trustee of the National Consumer Law Center, upon his retirement from Harvard Law School.

2.4 National Association of Consumer Advocates, Inc. (NACA)

The National Association of Consumer Advocates is a non-profit association of attorneys and consumer advocates committed to representing customers' interests. Its members are private and public sector attorneys, legal services attorneys, law professors, and law students whose primary focus is the protection and representation of consumers. NACA also has a charitable and educational fund incorporated under section 501(c)(3). Since its founding in 1993, it has grown to include over 1000 members. It is headquartered in Washington, D.C.

NACA's mission is to promote justice for all consumers by maintaining a forum for communication, networking, and information-sharing among consumer advocates across the country and by serving as a voice for its members and consumers in the ongoing struggle to curb unfair and abusive business practices that adversely affect consumers. From its inception, NACA has focused on issues that involve predatory, fraudulent, or deceptive business practices affecting consumers.[8] It website, www.NACA.net, provides a directory of its members and other useful information.

NACA provides to its members a newsletter on consumer law and practice topics, networking, mentoring and list-servs, a membership directory, ethical standards, support for legislative initiatives, training conferences, and malpractice insurance.

8 *Id.*

Chapter 3 Starting a Private Consumer Law Practice

3.1 The Discussion

A lawyer may come to the decision to start a consumer law practice for a number of different reasons. You may be a recent law graduate. You may be an experienced lawyer who decides to change specialties. Or you may be a consumer lawyer in the public or non-profit, but *salaried*, sector who has decided to go out on your own as a private consumer lawyer. Similar considerations apply in each instance. However, there is no single right or wrong way to do it, so this chapter is presented as a discussion among several experienced and successful consumer lawyers. These lawyers are John Roddy of Boston, Joanne Faulkner of New Haven, Steve Gardner of Dallas, and Bob Hobbs with the National Consumer Law Center in Boston.

John Roddy is a partner in the Boston law firm of Roddy, Klein & Ryan and a graduate of Boston College Law School. He formerly served as an assistant attorney general in the Consumer Protection Division of the Massachusetts Attorney General's Office and as Legislative Counsel to former Attorney General Frank Bellotti. John's practice is restricted to the representation of consumers victimized by predatory business practices. John frequently writes and lectures on consumer law and class action litigation for diverse organizations, including the Practicing Law Institute, the National Consumer Law Center, the Review of Banking and Financial Services, Massachusetts Continuing Legal Education (MCLE), and the Florida Bar Association. He is a board member of the Massachusetts Appleseed Foundation and a sponsor member of the National Association of Consumer Advocates.

Joanne S. Faulkner is in solo practice in New Haven, Connecticut, that is restricted to consumer matters, preferably for persons who can not afford to pay a lawyer. She is a past chair of the Consumer Law section of the Connecticut Bar Association and past editor of its newsletter. Joanne was a member of the Federal Reserve Board's Consumer Advisory Council and has served on advisory committees to the Connecticut Law Revision Commission. She was on the Board of Directors of the National Consumer Law Center and is presently a trustee of NCLC. Joanne frequently lectures on consumer laws and has assisted NCLC in updating various manuals, including *Fair Debt Collection* and *Fair Credit Reporting*, and their respective supplements. Her successes include *Connecticut v. Doehr*, 111 S. Ct. 2105 (1991) (due process, pre-judgment attachments), and *Clomon v. Jackson*, 988 F.2d 1314 (2d Cir. 1993) (FDCPA violated by attorney who allows collection agency to use his name). Joanne is a graduate of Cornell Law School (L.L.B. 1963) and was admitted to practice in New York in 1963 and in Connecticut in 1967.

Steve Gardner is, in addition to being the co-author of this book, the Director of Litigation for the Center for Science in the Public Interest, a health and nutrition advocacy group based in Washington, D.C. While in private practice, Steve represented such organizations as the Center for Auto Safety and Public Citizen. He was Assistant Dean of Clinical Education and visiting assistant professor of law at Southern Methodist University and an assistant attorney general in Texas and New York. Steve has served as a member of the Board of Directors of Consumers Union, an officer in the National Association of Consumer Advocates and, like Joanne, was a member of the Consumer Advisory Council of the Federal Reserve Board. He has written numerous articles on a variety of consumer protection topics. He is a graduate of the University of Texas at Austin and the University of Texas School of Law.

In his thirty-plus years at NCLC, Robert Hobbs has specialized in consumer credit issues, with particular attention to fair debt collection practices, usury, rent-to-own plans, Truth in Lending, and home defense. Bob's extensive consumer law experience includes having briefed and argued *Mitchell v. W.T. Grant Co.* before the United States Supreme Court. He was the designated consumer representative in the Federal Trade Commission rulemakings on creditor remedies and preservation of consumers' claims and defenses. Bob has testified on and proposed amendments adopted as part of the Fair Debt Collection Practices Act and the Truth in Lending Act and has participated in drafting NCLC's Model Consumer Credit Code (1974). Bob writes NCLC's popular and respected treatise *Fair Debt Collection* and compiles and edits *Consumer Law Pleadings* as well as the edition of *NCLC REPORTS* on debt collection and repossession. He is Deputy Director of NCLC, a former member of the Consumer Advisory Council to the Federal Reserve Board, a former Director of the National Association of Consumer Advocates, and a graduate of Vanderbilt University and the Vanderbilt School of Law.

3.2 Considerations Before Starting a Practice

Roddy: The demands of a small practice are never-ending. In addition to being a lawyer, you have to engage in marketing, accounting, tax work, personnel matters, and a host of other administrative duties. These ancillary activities are not enthralling but they have to be done. The point of having your own consumer practice is to make your practice conform to your ideals and interests. To accomplish this goal, you must do what you are compelled to do, what you have an affinity for, what excites you, what generates enthusiasm. You can then use the energy that your enthusiasm for the work generates to provide the impetus for doing the things which are necessary to running the practice but are not enjoyable. So, if the actual lawyering part of your practice isn't satisfying, then what is the point of the exercise?

Gardner: Absolutely. Be sure that you want to do consumer protection work as a private lawyer. The rewards are wonderful but largely of a non-material nature. That is, you are unlikely to get rich, but you will both make money and otherwise be well rewarded with the appreciation of the consumers for whom you advocate. If you see consumer law as the road to riches, take a u-turn and try another path. This is especially important at the outset of your practice, when the financial movement will be almost completely out your door and not into your bank account.

Faulkner: It will take about six months, longer for some types of cases, for your cash flow to get going satisfactorily. You may be able to get along without staff for a few months, or, if computer-proficient, for years. Start with the basic equipment: two phone lines (one for the fax), voice-mail or an answering machine, a computer with a high-speed modem, printer, copier, and fax. Then see how it goes before committing to support staff.

Gardner: Any lawyer who wants to start his or her own practice absolutely must know how to use a computer, e-mail, and the Internet. After I left the attorney general's office, I practiced first out of my garage apartment and then in a shared-space office but did not hire a secretary for about a year. That way, I only had to worry about paying myself. I could not have done this if I had not been skilled at using a computer.

Faulkner: Start your practice where you want to. Consumer law does not require that you impress clients with elegant office space or even that you have office space at all. More and more lawyers are practicing out of space in their homes. Screening potential clients over the phone, and asking them to send the documents, takes up much less time than a meeting in an office, for both of you. Meet the client in a public place (coffee shop, courthouse waiting room, etc.) on the rare occasion when a meeting seems desirable. Take depositions at the court reporter's offices.

Gardner: I don't totally agree. Unless it is financially essential, try to have a physical office outside your own home. Although you certainly don't have to impress your clients, you should try to reassure them that their lawyer has some stability. Practicing out of a back bedroom just doesn't give that assurance. You will also get treated more seriously by opposing counsel if you have an appearance of permanence. However, this does not mean that you have to opt for the top floor of the biggest bank building in town. Most office buildings offer fairly cheap space for just one office, including "virtual" offices that provide an address, phone, and conference room without a private space.

Hobbs: It can be important to meet your clients face to face. Some of us find it more satisfying when we are advocating for someone we have actually met. Meeting with clients is energizing for some lawyers. Meeting with your client helps gauge credibility, and clues from body language may uncover facts that would strengthen their case—for example, the amount of stress they are under or their confusion about a deceptive practice. Meeting with clients does require an appropriate but not luxurious space. More than that, it requires control: self-control to let them tell their story themselves and control to get the rest of the needed story and to end the meeting without wasting time.[1]

Faulkner: Consider business suites, which give you an address, answering service, and place to meet even if you mostly work at home. Often lawyers start out in a small law office with space- and staff-sharing arrangements.

Gardner: I have a small office, with space- and staff-sharing arrangements. When I was in private practice, I found that the best way for me to manage my time and to choose only the cases I really want was to keep my overhead as low as possible.

3.3 Get Clear Fee Agreements and Keep Time Carefully

Gardner: At the outset, be sure to enter into a fee agreement with each client. The agreement does not have to be formal (I use a two-page letter), but it must set forth the complete understanding between you and your client.[2] One of the most important components of this agreement is the money—how you will be compensated and who pays expenses. Most consumer lawyers agree that it is best that the client share somehow in the risk of the lawsuit, even if this is merely by paying a small retainer, a small share of the fees as they accrue, or the costs. A client who pays a buck a minute to talk to the lawyer will quickly get to the point. In a closely related point, the only way you will make money is to keep excellent track of your time. Almost every

1 *See also* Ch. 15, Car Cases 101: Creating the Interview Form, *infra*.

2 See § 7.6, *infra*, and the companion CD-Rom for sample retainer forms.

consumer case will be fee-shifting—you'll get your money from the defendant based on time—rather than a percentage of the client's recovery. If you don't have good, contemporaneous time records, you are likely to see your fees cut by the judge or the jury. In any event, keeping records lets you see how you are allocating your efforts, to try to eliminate wasteful efforts.

Hobbs: Fee agreements raise difficult and complex issues that are addressed in § 7.6, below. Some practitioners believe that their contingent fee in their retainer agreement is essential to a viable practice and use a contingent fee even in cases where there is a fee-shifting claim. This may not agree with professional rules of conduct in other states.

3.4 Choose a Specialty

Roddy: Start with a niche which you can make your own, establish your practice in this area, then gradually expand. In the consumer law area, there are a number of potential domains: credit reporting and identity theft, home mortgage fraud, Truth in Lending, RESPA, debt collection, odometer fraud, equal credit, car leasing—the list is extensive. In each of these areas you should be able to find more than enough work, for two reasons: First, there aren't a lot of people competing with you. Chances are, you are the only person or firm doing this kind of work within one hundred square miles. Second, there are so many scams and unscrupulous businesses in each practice territory that your principal case management task should be to decide which case is the most egregious, not how to find one.

Faulkner: Consumer law itself is a niche. With the help of the NCLC manuals, take cases in several areas. Narrow your field down only when your time becomes limited or your interests become clearer. When you are starting out, make sure that you have some short-term fee-shifting cases, where the financial result seems clear at the outset so you can get your cash flow off to a good start. Ex-legal-service people should not be afraid to ask the opponent for fees and should not undervalue their services. Check around for the local hourly rate and charge your opponents accordingly.

3.5 Use Truth and Justice As Your Ally

Roddy: Let your attitude infuse your work. Allow your particular values, style, and manner of writing and speaking to identify your briefs, letters, and arguments. Most legal matters are presented in a dispassionate and artificially objectified style, which has come to be accepted as the norm and the preferred mode of behavior. But this method of "argument" was created in part to make arguing an inequitable position more psychologically palatable. Of course, the presumption here is that you will be arguing positions which are founded on a desire to provide equity, not deny it. Assuming this to be the case, recognize that this stance, which you have consciously adopted by your decision to represent only consumers, is a tremendous asset. In his recent book,[3] Gerry Spence advances one simple theme—speak from the heart and don't equivocate. Lawyers are disliked and mistrusted by people because they are (many times accurately) perceived as engaging in double-speak. This hair-splitting bothers anyone who cares about fairness.

Lawyers are bound to make such arguments on behalf of their clients if they are legally tenable. But I wonder if the lawyers who make such arguments feel that there was any essential justice or fairness to the legal proposition they are advancing. The closer arguments like this get to the edge of legal viability, the harder it is for anyone to make them with true conviction.

The converse is also true. If you believe in what you are saying, your argument has more force. And, if you are trying to achieve a fair result for someone who has been treated unfairly, you have in most cases the unspoken allegiance of the judge as well. Arguing from this position provides an emotional and psychological advantage that offsets the usual economic advantage of the other side. This conviction in your approach and goals makes the practice inherently satisfying. It makes arguments more enjoyable to write and speak. Most importantly, it also makes you feel good about yourself. The adversary system is probably unavoidable. But if you don't feel good about what you do, why keep doing it? What is the point of making clever intellectual or technical legal arguments, particularly winning ones, if the result is that you achieve a favorable outcome for your client but an unfair result for some person who is equitably in the right but on the losing side in court?

Gardner: Some years back, when the tactics of defense counsel in several cases were making my legal life miserable, I slumped in my office and muttered, "I hate being a lawyer." Then, with a start, I realized that actually I hated other lawyers. If he had practiced, Sartre would have said "Hell is other lawyers." Once I had this realization, I was able to prevent the tactics from bothering me, choosing instead to deal with these lawyers as the overgrown but under-matured children they were.

3.6 Link Up with Others

Gardner: It is essential to establish links to other lawyers doing similar or related work, especially if you are a solo practitioner. You need to have a sympathetic ear to bend and someone to bounce ideas off. The annual Consumer Rights Litigation Conference, sponsored each fall by NCLC and the National Association of Consumer Advocates (NACA), is the single best way to meet others who have committed themselves to consumer law. In addition to offering a great

3 G. Spence, How to Argue and Win Every Time (1996).

series of lectures and discussions on the widest possible variety of consumer topics, the Conference presents an unparalleled opportunity to meet, buttonhole, or just plain hang out with other lawyers in this area. When I went into private practice, after about fifteen years in the public sector, one of the first things I did was attend the Conference with the explicit goal of meeting private lawyers who shared my interests. To my delight, I found that there were many, and they were all trapped where they couldn't run away from me.

Roddy: NACA has established a network of lawyers who are trying to change things for the better or at least repair some of the harm done by people who confuse business with predation. We can all give this network a large boost by simply communicating. Often you learn something more valuable than the item of information you were seeking. This type of communication also helps to psychologically bolster both the person seeking help and the one giving it. The flip side is, of course, when someone in this community asks for your help, don't think about what's in it for you, just help out.

Gardner: To become a member of NACA, call NACA's Washington office at (202) 452-1989 or visit its website, www.naca.net. It's the best way to get into the network. Also get on NCLC's mailing lists. Between them, NCLC and NACA maintain several e-mail groups for specialized topics, such as auto fraud, debt collection, and class actions. And both NCLC and NACA offer specialized conferences on specific topics such as credit reports, debt collection abuses, bankruptcy, auto fraud, and others.

Roddy: Ask mentors for help. Don't be shy or embarrassed, as if you're too experienced to ask or learn. Call the people you meet at the Consumer Rights Litigation Conference—those you hear speaking—or in the media who make comments on listservs or whom you have read about. Ask for insights, even pleadings. As long as you are not competing for the same clients or cases in the same geographic area, most people are more than willing to share their experiences with you.

Gardner: Even if you *are* in the same area and the same specialization, most consumer lawyers will be happy to talk with you. However, keep in mind that all lawyers have nothing to sell but our time, so don't abuse the free advice you seek. When I get a call from someone I don't know from Adam, I am always pleased when the call starts off with a sincere offer to pay me for the discussion. I invariably refuse this offer, but it tells me the caller values my time, and I appreciate it.

Faulkner: Networking is the best way to get case referrals. Network in your local bar association. Send a newsletter to bar members letting them know what kind of cases you are interested in. When lawyers know you "specialize," they will not fear losing a client by referring someone to you. Bankruptcy, family, and personal injury lawyers see lots of consumer problems and don't know what to do about them. Let them know you are around and what they can do to identify cases you are interested in.

Gardner: Let me add to that last point. Consumer bankruptcy lawyers see many people with consumer problems and are sympathetic to those problems but do not wish to get involved in the litigation of those problems. People seeking bankruptcy advice are particularly likely to have financing problems, repossessions, debt harassment, and other credit-related issues. It may be that resolving those problems can avoid the need for a bankruptcy, or it may be that the problem is worth litigating in connection with a bankruptcy. In many instances, the bankruptcy trustee will agree to the consumer litigating the case outside of the bankruptcy court. Get to know bankruptcy lawyers and establish a formal or informal referral system, always taking your local ethical rules into account. Very importantly, reciprocate—send clients to them who would benefit from their expertise.

Roddy: There is strength in a common purpose and shared values. It's hard to keep going if you're depressed, overwhelmed by the amount of work, the scorched-earth tactics or incivility of the other side, your negative cash flow, or the legal business itself. In addition, the best substitute for personal experience is the ability to draw on the experience of others. For these reasons, if you can rely on a network of experienced people who have already been through the situation you are first encountering, you have established a tremendous resource. It also helps to have someone who's in the same boat reinforce your view of things and approach to a particular problem.

3.7 Make Technology Work for You

Gardner: As I said earlier, you must be computer literate. You should also be computer functional. That is, you must have e-mail that you check many times a day, and you must be able to use the computer as a word processor. Spend the money necessary to get the hardware you need and you will find it pays for itself quite quickly. For example, a scanner with text conversion software can save someone quite a bit of re-typing, which is especially important if that someone is you. A scanner can also double as a fax machine at your desk, eliminating the steps necessary to fax from a dedicated fax machine. Although you need a separate fax machine for incoming faxes, using the scanner saves time and effort. Although my office has a good stand-alone fax machine, and although I have a great assistant, I find that it is quicker and easier to scan and fax rather than seeking out my assistant to get her to go stand at the dedicated machine. And don't try to save money by ignoring Westlaw or Lexis—changes to consumer law happen every day and it is a false economy to try to save money by not subscribing. Get good software—everyone has Word or WordPerfect, but it is also essential to have good financial software like Quicken, a full copy of Adobe Acrobat (not just Acrobat Reader), and a simple time-keeping system.

Roddy: Computer networks provide a sort of community. Using e-mail is often a better way to communicate with your peers, who may not be able to take the time to talk on the phone but who can more easily share their knowledge by responding to an e-mail message at the end of the day. In addition, when people are sharing pleadings or other written work, sending the digitized form of the document saves the work of re-inputting a fax into your computer and enables some extremely fast brief-writing when deadlines are approaching.

Gardner: I do most of my work with co-counsel, usually out of state. I now make it a requirement that co-counsel be fully computer literate and functional. I want to be able to communicate by e-mail and to exchange drafts over the Internet. Otherwise, it is just too much work on my end to coordinate with faxes and mailed copies, especially from across the country.

A low-tech way to simplify your practice, especially if you don't have a support staff, is to use client questionnaires. You can mail or e-mail a questionnaire to prospective clients at the time of the initial contact and decide whether to interview them based on the information they provide. Some prospective clients may balk at filling out a questionnaire but, frankly, if someone doesn't want to spend thirty minutes of his own time and would rather spend an hour of mine, I don't want him for a client. Sample questionnaires are included in Appendix B, but you should modify them to meet your own needs and specialization.

3.8 Market Yourself and Your Practice

Roddy: Marketing is an area that can not be overemphasized. If you're enthusiastic about what you do, you naturally talk about it with everyone, not just people or entities you have targeted for marketing efforts. This enthusiasm comes out in your voice and demeanor, so, without consciously trying to persuade someone, your presentation is made that much more compelling by the honest conviction it carries. People are infected by enthusiasm and drawn to projects that appeal to their sense of what's right. In addition, those people who may not directly help or hire you often refer others and tell others about what it is you are doing.

Gardner: The very idea of "marketing" oneself as a lawyer may make your lip curl with the non-professionalism of it all. Get over it. Every lawyer is engaged in marketing of one kind or another, whether it is through public speaking, media appearances, websites, or traditional advertising. Every time you leave your office, you are marketing yourself. Do it with disdain if you must, but do it and do it well.

Roddy: Each person has a particular approach, but every lawyer can at least take a few hours at night to write a piece for the local newspaper on an interesting consumer rip-off. Unless you are the editor's child or are well-known, it is unlikely that you can get such pieces into the big metro paper. However, bigger is not necessarily better. Many people assume that a lawyer who is published in the *Washington Post* is too big, too expensive, or too busy for their small-debt-collection problem, for example, but will call the lawyer who wrote the same piece in the neighborhood journal.

Gardner: I agree absolutely with the idea of writing articles for smaller newspapers, but I have to disagree with the idea that you are not likely to get a piece in a major paper. Newspapers are always interested in topical pieces, perhaps as an op-ed or maybe [a column by] a guest columnist. Contact the editorial department to learn how best to submit a piece, and read pieces already published to see the style and substance that your paper will publish.

Roddy: If you write about even the most basic protections and the extraordinary remedies of the FDCPA,[4] leasing act,[5] TILA,[6] UDAP laws[7]—whatever you are doing that is current—you can expect a substantial response. People will come out of the woodwork in response because no one ever told them what their rights were before, and, even if they had some knowledge, they didn't know any lawyers who would help them enforce those rights. Even small articles in small papers reach large numbers of potential clients.

Gardner: In addition to submitting pieces for print media, find a way to let radio and television stations know that you are available to shoot your mouth off on consumer topics. You can do this in any number of ways. The easiest way is to practice in the area, preferably on cases that gather press attention. But you can achieve similar results more proactively, without shilling. Your local bar association may conduct call-in programs with local radio or television stations; participate and the producer will remember you the next time a story comes in on that topic. The idea of a guest editorial also applies to electronic media, although it may be tougher to break through the clutter. The best place to start may be a talk radio station, by letting the on-air person or the producer know that you would like to come on for an hour to talk about a specific topic or to take calls. To know what you can ethically say, review § 7.3, *infra*. Also consider the Internet. You can have your own website for very little investment, with your name and address, an online questionnaire, and some simple information and links to other sites.[8] Even cheaper is blogging. It's very popular now but, doubtless, it will fade and be replaced by something else, possibly podcasting, which gives you the opportunity to reach those who don't feel like reading.

Roddy: My less-is-more philosophy can be applied in any number of other ways, at no cost. Local clubs, the Lions

---

4 Fair Debt Collection Practices Act, 15 U.S.C. § 1692.

5 15 U.S.C. § 1667.

6 15 U.S.C. § 1630.

7 *See* National Consumer Law Center, Unfair and Deceptive Acts and Practices (6th ed. 2004).

8 See § 7.2, *infra*, about lawyer advertising.

Club, the Rotary, the Knights of Columbus, church groups, elder assistance programs, etc., all welcome lawyers who are trying to help their members and who have something interesting to say. Virtually none of these people will have any idea of the nature of the rip-offs you address or of the remedies which they can achieve with your legal assistance. Once again, even if no one from the Lions Club meeting calls you in the next month, it is more than likely that they will refer someone else or tell someone else about what you do.

Faulkner: Contribute to bar association newsletters. Become active in bar association sections and the bar's referral service. Most referrals come from other lawyers.

Roddy: The key is getting the word out. Educating people not only about their rights but about the accessibility of legal help (that is, you) to vindicate those rights is critical. Which avenues you take are up to you but, without marketing, unless you are very fortunate, it is difficult to get a large volume of the right kind of cases.

Hobbs: Another source of cases is your local legal service program and the referral programs they use. Sign up with them for the type of cases that you specialize in. Co-counseling with legal service lawyers can also be rewarding for private lawyers.

3.9 Practice Law But Have a Life

Gardner: Anyone choosing to be a consumer lawyer must be driven by a desire to serve consumers rather than just to make money. However, although you like your work, you must not let it control your life. I have come up with a list of the *Top Ten Ways to Have a Life and Then (and Only Then) a Law Practice*. They are:

1. *Get help!* Many of us try to do too much of our work ourselves. As soon as your practice is up and running, get good secretaries, legal assistants, etc. Limit your work to the work that requires a law license to do—like going to court. Most of the rest is the boring stuff, anyway. Also, try to work with co-counsel. At best, you'll have someone with whom to share ideas, strategies, and work. At worse, you'll have someone to blame.

2. *Don't take bad cases.* Most of us got into representing plaintiffs because we want to help them out. This should still be the driving force, but don't try to help those whom you really can't help. This is compulsive and won't work—both you and your client will end up sorry for it.

3. *Don't retain bad cases.* The retentive corollary to Rule 2. If you get into a case that you discover is no good—whether on the facts, the law, the client, or whatever—don't keep at it.

4. *Remember—Testosterone should be a controlled substance.* Don't try to out-macho the defense lawyer. They have lots of minions, and we don't. More work for us is just more billables for them.

5. *Lie about your job.* Don't talk about being a lawyer away from work. No one else really cares, unless they want free advice. Others will treat you as though you had just said you were a drug dealer. I tell people I'm a shoe salesman.

6. *Ignore the man behind the curtain.* In other words, don't do what others tell you to do (except judges). Follow your own instincts, or you'll get work dumped on you.

7. *Don't marry your kin.* Two lawyers in one household attain critical mass. And they are often primarily critical of each other.

8. *Have kids.* Unless you marry your kin. Having children gives a good perspective on life and the law and the relative importance of each on the Great Mandala. Plus, it's easier to accept childishness from opposing counsel when you can see that she just missed an important developmental step at age 5. If you can't or won't have kids, consider a pet, especially the high-maintenance kind like a Shih-Tzu that only eats scrambled eggs and spits up hairballs daily. Much the same experience as a kid, except you can't train a pet to mow your yard.

9. *Have a hobby or other consuming passion.* This augments the kid/pet rule. As long as you care more about it than the law. You need something you'd truly rather be doing.

10. *Get out of Dodge before sundown.* Don't regularly work late hours or weekends. Doing so creates a vacuum that will fill itself with more work.

Hobbs: I would add one more: take Steve's Rules with a grain of salt and a touch of humor.

Gardner: Killjoy.

3.10 Conclusions

Roddy: These ideas simply lay out a few guideposts which may be helpful to people who are establishing a small-firm consumer law practice. Much of the practice of law is necessarily a trial-and-error process. Take what is useful, try what looks interesting, and develop your own rules of practice that conform to the goals which you hold for yourself. Don't be afraid to ask others for help, but don't be afraid to try your own ideas, even when they conflict with the conventional wisdom.

Gardner: If you're reading this chapter, it's a very good sign that you want to think about what you plan to do before you do it. As long as you think it through, go with it. As a fine lawyer whom I know says, "I may be in error, but I'm never in doubt."

Chapter 4

Making Money on Small Consumer Claims

By Manuel H. Newburger[1]

4.1 Introduction

Consumer law has evolved in many respects over the last thirty years. Many consumer attorneys have drifted away from the more traditional aspects of consumer law into those "glamorous" areas such as class actions, representation of the "business consumer," high-dollar deceptive insurance practice litigation, large-scale construction defect litigation, and business opportunities suits. This article, however, is intended to assist attorneys interested in finding a profitable way to return to the more traditional types of consumer litigation, that is, claims involving personal, family, or household goods or services, collection practices, landlord-tenant disputes, etc.

4.2 Screening the Claim

4.2.1 The Expert's Report

In taking on the small consumer case, it is critical to make a speedy decision as to the viability of the consumer's claim. Speed, however, is not a function of haste in evaluating the case but rather of eliminating as much as possible the attorney's investment of time in the pre-evaluation process. At least one way to accomplish this goal is to not even let the consumer into your office until he or she has already assembled a case file. For example, some lawyers do not ordinarily meet with a consumer until he or she has a written expert's report which, in the case of complaints regarding services, details the defects in the services and, in the case of goods, details exactly what is wrong with the goods and either the cost of repair or, alternatively, the diminution in value as a result of the consumer's complaints.

Frequently, the consumer will report in the initial phone conversation that "my mechanic says he will come to court and testify about all of the horrible stuff that this dealership did." All too often, however, such experts either refuse to testify at trial or "wimp out" in depositions. Although there is no absolute protection from this problem, at least one solution is to refuse to consider the case unless a competent expert has already been willing to commit, in writing, to the position asserted by the consumer.

For many attorneys, one of the crucial factors in making the small consumer case pay is the requirement that the *client* pay all expenses as they are incurred. The consumer who will not spend a few hundred dollars to get an expert evaluation of his or her case is often one who is less than sincere about an injustice and more interested in using an attorney to bully their way to a quick settlement. The requirement of the expert's report therefore serves a valuable secondary screening function.

4.2.2 The Chronology/Client File

It is, of course, critical to have a complete file and history on the case. It is therefore advisable when scheduling the initial appointment to require that the potential client bring copies of *every single document* pertaining to the case, together with a complete chronology of events. A typical statement to prospective clients should be to the effect that "you can never be too detailed, too specific, or too comprehensive in your chronology of events."

At least one fairly effective way to obtain an accurate chronology from the client is to ask that it be written over a period of not less than a week. The initial draft can be written in one or two sittings and should then be put aside for at least two or three days. If, during that time, the client thinks of additional matters that he or she thinks were not included, those should be written down on a separate piece of paper. After the passage of two or three days, when the chronology is not so fresh in the client's mind as to make effective proofreading impractical, he or she should go back, review the chronology for any missing facts, compare it to any additional notes made in the interim, and discuss it with

1 Great appreciation is due for the contribution of this chapter to Manuel H. Newburger, Barron & Newburger, P.C. (1212 Guadalupe, Suite 104, Austin, Texas 78704, 512-476-9103, fax 512-476-9253, mnewburger@bnpclaw.com). Mr. Newburger represents both businesses and consumers in his practice and has been an expert witness for consumers in fair debt collection cases.

any friend, spouse, or fact witness whose insights would be helpful in filling in any blanks.[2]

Many clients have computers, and it is helpful to have the client furnish the chronology in electronic form. This will save time later when preparing pleadings, discovery responses, and summary judgment affidavits. Scanning copies of critical documents and photographs at the start of the case will provide similar benefits, and the relatively low cost of an all-in-one color printer/scanner/fax/copier makes such scanning easy and inexpensive.

4.3 The Initial Client Interview[3]

4.3.1 Importance of Client Bringing Key Documents

Assuming that the client comes to the initial interview with everything that you have requested, the initial interview should run speedily. If he or she has not brought the items that you have requested you may wish to (i) reschedule the meeting until all of the requested documentation can be made available or (ii) proceed with the meeting but, recognizing that you already have a client cooperation problem, make a mental note to increase your retainer accordingly.

4.3.2 Minimum Liability Facts—the "MLF"

In analyzing the consumer's claim, examine the documents and chronology for what may be described as Minimum Liability Facts (MLF). The MLF may be defined as those independent facts apparent from either (1) the face of the documents or (2) the incontrovertible portion of the consumer's story as would give rise to liability under either a consumer protection statute or a common law theory of liability, regardless of the credibility of the client's remaining claims. For example, if a consumer's contract provides that interest will not run for the first thirty days after a bill is mailed, and he or she has received a letter or bill demanding interest during the interest-free period, you have the MLF necessary to establish a cause of action for usury. Regardless of any other creative or tenuous theories of liability or damages that you may assert as to any other aspects of the case, you will enter the case knowing that, at a minimum, your client has the ability to recover certain statutory penalties plus attorney fees.

As a second example, in reviewing a potential case against a lender, you discover that the lender's attorneys have sent a demand letter that is not in conformity with the requirements of the federal Fair Debt Collection Practices Act. Again, you have located your MLF. The violation appears on the face of the documents and, even if the consumer has no demonstrable actual damages, federal case law holds that attorney fees and statutory damages are recoverable upon mere proof of a violation, regardless of whether any actual damages exist.[4]

Because of the number of consumer statutes that provide for penalties, attorney fees, or both, an MLF can ensure a minimum recovery for the attorney who takes the small case. Identifying an MLF can therefore give an attorney a comfort zone ensuring that, regardless of the value of a case, attorney fees for the handling of the case should be recoverable at trial.

Of perhaps equal importance, putting together the MLF at the outset of the case will enable a plaintiff to respond to a defendant's motion for summary judgment with a cross-motion for such relief.

4.3.3 Identify All Liability and Damage Issues

Once a meritorious case has been identified, try to identify all potential legal theories of recovery and to calculate all arguably recoverable elements of damages. When the fee agreement is prepared, client authorization should be obtained to demand or sue for those damages.

4.4 The Fee Agreement

4.4.1 General Considerations

4.4.1.1 Mandatory Agreements

Having decided to take a case, a good fee contract is needed in order to protect your fees. In the context of contingent-fee agreements, a written contract is essential. In fact, under many state ethical rules, it is *mandatory*.[5] In the case of hourly-fee agreements, a written contract is strongly recommended and, at a minimum, the basis of the fee should be communicated to a client before or within a reasonable time after commencing the representation. Again, some state ethics rules may make it mandatory.

2 Appendix B, *infra*, contains checklists, questionnaires, and chronology forms that may be helpful in this initial stage.

3 *See also* Chapter 15, *infra* ("Car Cases 101: Creating the Interview Form"); Appx. B, *infra* ("Checklists and Questionnaires").

4 *See, e.g.*, Emmanuel v. Am. Credit Exch., 870 F.2d 805 (2d Cir. 1989).

5 *See, e.g.*, Tex. Discip. R. Pro. Cond. 1.04(d); Tex. Gov. Code Ann. § 82.065; § 7.6.4, *infra*.

4.4.1.2 The Fee Agreement Should Be Established at Once

Establish the fee agreement prior to or as part of the creation of the attorney-client relationship. Contracts between attorney and client negotiated subsequent to establishment of the relationship are viewed with suspicion and are closely scrutinized for unfairness and overreaching.[6] Furthermore, there is a taint of fraud that attaches by presumption to agreements made in the course of the attorney-client relationship, but this taint does not attach to a contract made at the inception of employment.[7] A fee arrangement entered into prior to the inception of representation is still reviewable to determine whether the attorney breached his fiduciary duty to the client by charging the specified fee and whether the specified fee was clearly excessive under the applicable state bar disciplinary rules.[8]

4.4.1.3 Amending the Fee Agreement

Despite the best of intentions, circumstances can arise which were not envisioned at the time a fee agreement was made. An adversary (or client) can file bankruptcy, new causes of action can accrue, or counterclaims can be filed that were not reasonably able to be anticipated based on the information originally furnished by the client. It is proper to modify a fee agreement after the inception of litigation when the opposing party brought in new issues and parties not contemplated by the original fee agreement.[9] Nevertheless, many lawyers prefer to try to anticipate in the original contract as many such circumstances as can reasonably be imagined. On the other hand, other experienced lawyers do not try to bind the client to every conceivable contingency, instead focusing only on the most likely prospects and providing generally for modification when there are changed circumstances.

4.4.1.4 Inequality of Bargaining Power

In preparing a fee contract, one should keep in mind that an attorney fee agreement is essentially an adhesion contract. The client has virtually no bargaining power if he or she wants the lawyer's services, and the client is not going to seek the advice of another attorney on the meaning and consequences of the fee agreement. Instead, the client counts on the lawyer to explain the meaning of contractual provisions, most of which are included for the benefit of the attorney, not the client.

The relationship between attorney and client has been held to be highly fiduciary in nature, and the courts have therefore created a presumption of unfairness or invalidity attaching to a contract between them. The burden of showing the fairness and reasonableness is on the attorney.[10] The fiduciary duty extends even to preliminary consultations concerning employment, and one can not create a fee agreement in breach of the duty on the theory that representation does not commence until there is a contract.[11]

A fee agreement may be attacked for fraud, negligence, misrepresentation, or overreaching and, when any such attack is made, consideration will be given to the relative knowledge of the parties.[12] Attorney fee agreements are of special interest and concern to courts and will not be enforced on the same basis as ordinary commercial contracts.[13] Thus, be meticulous and mindful of the inequality of bargaining power when drafting and negotiating fee agreements.

4.5 Contingent-Fee Contracts

4.5.1 Setting Forth All the Terms

For the reasons set forth above, the contingent-fee agreement should specifically set forth all of the terms and conditions of the attorney-client relationship. Some provisions should be included in the contract to define the relationship clearly.

4.5.2 Percentage of Recovery[14]

> Attorney is assigned 1/3 of the total benefit or recovery to Client (whether monetary or non-

6 Sec. & Exch. Comm'n v. W.L. Moody & Co., 363 F. Supp. 481, 484 (S.D. Tex. 1973).

7 Cole v. McCanlies, 620 S.W.2d 713, 715 (Tex. Civ. App.—Dallas 1981, writ ref'd n.r.e.).

8 Nolan v. Foreman, 665 F.2d 738 (5th Cir. 1982, reh'g denied, 671 F.2d 1380). *See* § 7.6.1, *infra*.

9 Gill v. Randolph, 269 S.W.2d 529, 532 (Tex. Civ. App.—Galveston 1954, writ ref'd n.r.e.). *See also* Sec. & Exch. Comm'n v. W.L. Moody & Co., 363 F. Supp. 481, 484 (S.D. Tex. 1973).

10 Archer v. Griffith, 390 S.W.2d 735 (Tex. 1965); Ames v. Putz, 495 S.W.2d 581, 583 (Tex. Civ. App.—Eastland 1973, writ refused). Cf. Plummer v. Bradford, 395 S.W.2d 856, 860 (Tex. Civ. App.—Houston 1965, no writ) (holding that there is no presumption of unfairness or inequitable conduct by the attorney unless there has been a pleading or claim raising such issues).

11 Nolan v. Foreman, 665 F.2d 739 (5th Cir. 1982, *reh'g denied*, 671 F.2d 1380).

12 Johnson v. Cofer, 113 S.W.2d 963, 965 (Tex. Civ. App.—Austin 1938, no writ).

13 Magana v. Platzer Shipyard, Inc., 74 F.R.D. 61 (S.D. Tex. 1977).

14 There may be almost as many ways to ethically structure a contingent fee as there are consumers lawyers. Ethical standards for fees provide constraints that vary state by state and must be carefully followed. Within ethical standards it is important to set fees that are sufficient to sustain a legal practice in the long run without charging an excessive fee. Court-awarded fees alone have proven insufficient for many practices and sufficient for others.

monetary), unless the portion of any settlement or court award that is designated as attorney fees exceeds one-third of the total benefit or recovery, in which case Attorney is assigned the attorney fees portion of the settlement or award. In the event that Client receives real or personal property in payment of Client's claims, Attorney is assigned ____________.

The critical issue is the full disclosure of the contingent arrangement. If fees are to be determined on a sliding scale, from demand through appeal, those terms must be stated. It is difficult to argue that appeal is an eventuality that could not be considered at the start of representation, and any requirement of additional fees for appeal should be included in the original contract.

4.5.3 The Hourly Recovery

The suggested language above leaves open the possibility that a jury might award more in attorney fees than the contingent percentage agreed to by the client. This is a critical part of the fee agreement, as one of the problems with the small consumer claim is that 30% to 40% of the consumer's damages does not even approach the cost of generating a demand letter and complaint. If, however, you seek fees based on the actual time put into the case, the small amount of damages need not limit the fee recovery. Even when they greatly exceed the actual damages awarded to the consumer, attorney fees have been held to be reasonable and necessary.[15]

For example, the Texas Supreme Court's opinion in *Arthur Andersen & Co. v. Perry Equip. Corp.*[16] makes it clear that a plaintiff's attorney must produce evidence to prove that the amount of fees was both reasonably incurred and necessary to the prosecution of the case. The court's opinion makes it clear that the finder of fact is to consider the factors set forth in the Texas Disciplinary Rules of Professional Conduct in making its determination of fees and that the fees must be stated as a specific dollar amount rather than as a percentage of the judgment. The court's opinion allows the fact finder to consider the contingent-fee agreement, but the disciplinary rule also requires consideration of the time required on the case. It is crucial to track the hours expended on every case in order to be able to recover those fees at trial.

Consumer statutes such as the Texas Deceptive Trade Practices Act or the Fair Debt Collection Practices Act have mandatory fee-shifting provisions that make it possible for consumers who otherwise could not afford attorneys to secure legal representation. Even in a mandatory fee-shifting case, however, a prevailing plaintiff must be able to prove the reasonableness and necessity of the fees sought.

4.5.4 Sanctions

Attorney is also assigned all attorney fees that may be awarded as sanctions by any Court.

Since sanctions are normally awarded to the party and not the attorney, the failure to include such a clause might entitle the attorney to only the contingent percentage of any sanctions.[17]

4.5.5 Equitable Relief

In the event of a settlement or judgment for rescission, Client agrees to pay Attorney for all time incurred on Client's behalf at the rate of $ _____ per hour.

It may well be overreaching to try to charge a percentage of the restitution award, as this would completely undermine the effort to restore the parties to their original positions. Unfortunately, this is an unfair result for the attorney, who is only being paid an hourly rate on a contingent basis, and many lawyers are reluctant to take on rescission and restitution (or revocation-of-acceptance) cases except on an hourly basis.

4.5.6 Early Termination by the Client

If Client withdraws the claim or suit from Attorney prior to the conclusion of the case, Client agrees to pay Attorney's usual hourly rate for all time expended on same and to reimburse all of Attorney's expenses in connection with Client's case. Attorney's present hourly rate is $_____ per hour. Attorney may give Client thirty days'

15 *See* Owens v. Howe, 365 F. Supp. 2d 942 (N.D. Ind. 2005) ($12,037.50 in fees on $1,000 in statutory damages); IFG Leasing Co. v. Ellis, 748 S.W.2d 564 (Tex. App.—Houston [14th Dist.] 1988, no writ) (award of attorney fees upheld even though the consumer was only awarded a certificate of title and no monetary damages); Seabury Homes, Inc. v. Burleson, 688 S.W.2d 712 (Tex. App.—Fort Worth 1985, no writ), ($15,000 in attorney fees approved on a recovery of $2000 in actual damages); Jack Roach Ford v. De Urdanavia, 659 S.W.2d 725 (Tex. App.—Houston [14th Dist.] 1983, no writ) ($20,000 in attorney fees approved on a recovery of $500 in actual damages); Tate v. Wiggins, 583 S.W.2d 640 (Tex. Civ. App.—Waco 1979, no writ) ($14,500 in attorney fees approved on a recovery of $1000 in actual damages to one of the plaintiffs and $1400 to the other); Gradisher v. Check Enforcement Unit, 2003 U.S. Dist. LEXIS 753 (W.D. Mich. 2003) ($69,872 in fees on $1,000 in statutory damages). *See also* National Consumer Law Center, Fair Debt Collection § 6.8.1 (5th ed. 2004 and Supp.).

16 945 S.W.2d 812 (Tex. 1997).

17 *See* Shula v. Lawent, 359 F.3d 489 (7th Cir. 2004) (noting that fee award is the property of the client); Satellite Earth Stations E., Inc. v. Davis, 756 S.W.2d 385, 387 (Tex. App.—Eastland 1988, writ denied).

written notice of increases in Attorney's usual hourly rate as it applies to this paragraph.

As a general matter, if the former client in a contingent-fee case pleads and proves good cause for discharge, the attorney is not entitled to recover under the contract of employment. The attorney may, however, recover under *quantum meruit* for services rendered up to the time of discharge.[18]

Unfortunately, however, if the client contests the fee, the reasonable value of the attorney's services is a fact issue to be determined by the trier of fact.[19] This means that a jury may well have to determine the "value" of your services. It may therefore be beneficial to have the client agree in advance on the value of those services.

4.5.7 *Payment of Expenses by the Client*

> Client's expenses shall be borne by Client. It is specifically understood that copies, postage, fax transmissions, delivery charges, court costs, expenses of litigation, expenses for expert witnesses, and deposition costs and fees, are expenses of the Client and not Attorney and (when possible) shall be paid by Client to Attorney in escrow prior to the time such costs are incurred or paid.

As noted above, one crucial factor in making the small consumer case profitable is the refusal to advance expenses for the client. At the billing rate of the average attorney, the time investment in getting a case to trial is such that the client receives a bargain just by getting a contingent arrangement in any case that involves less than $50,000 in actual damages. It is not cost-effective to advance expenses in a small case and doing so can destroy the profit margin.

The only exception to this rule is the indigent client. The client who can not afford to pay expenses may be able to file suit with an affidavit of inability to pay costs.

4.5.8 *Disclaimer of Warranties or Solicitation*

> Client now specifically certifies that Client voluntarily came to the office of Attorney seeking employment of Attorney and that Client's business was not solicited in any manner whatsoever. Client has received no promises of remuneration or loans of any kind from Attorney. Client acknowledges that Attorney has made no warranties or promises as to the outcome of Client's case.

In these days of bad public image and well-publicized cases of alleged solicitation and barratry, it is wise to address such matters in the fee agreement.

4.6 Addressing the Client's Damages

4.6.1 *Communicating with Client*

Given the potential for sanctions under Fed. R. Civ. P. 11 and its state law equivalents, it is advisable to require the client to specify the nature and type of damages claimed. (Those damages should also be documented as part of the case history.) Since some statutes limit recovery in the event of an excessive demand, this may be insurance against future complaints by the client. The danger in doing this is the possibility that the client will later assert that you somehow warranted the recoverability of those damages. The following form is suggested, as a starting point, but may require editing depending on state law.

> **AUTHORIZATION FOR DAMAGES DEMAND**
>
> The undersigned Client hereby authorizes Attorney to demand the following damages in connection with Client's case against ______________________.
>
> ______________________.
>
> *Client understands and agrees that attorney does not warrant the recoverability of such damages.*
>
> EXECUTED this _____ day of _______, 200 __.
>
> ______________________

4.6.2 *The Demand Letter*

Some statutes require a written demand as a condition precedent to the filing of suit or, alternatively, to the recovery of certain types of damages.[20] Because one of the keys to profitability on small consumer cases is an efficient use of time, it is advisable to prepare the demand letter in anticipation of the lawsuit. Thanks to word processors, a properly worded demand letter can be turned into a complaint with little effort.

The demand letter is also the opportunity for the consumer's attorney to make as many persuasive and/or self-serving

18 Rocha v. Ahmad, 676 S.W.2d 149, 156 (Tex. App.—San Antonio 1984, writ dismissed). *See also* Universal Acupuncture Pain Servs., P.C. v. Quadrino & Schwartz, P.C., 370 F.3d 259 (2d Cir. 2004) (lawyer fired without good cause in a contingent-fee matter is entitled to compensation for reasonable value of his services even if client has not recovered).

19 Rocha v. Ahmad, 676 S.W.2d 157 (Tex. App.—San Antonio 1984, writ dismissed); Gulf Paving Co. v. Lofstedt, 188 S.W.2d 155, 160, 144 Tex. 17, 27, 28 (1945).

20 *See, e.g.*, Tex. Bus. & Com. Code Ann. § 17.505; Tex. Ins. Code Ann. art. 21.21, § 16(e); Tex. Civ. Prac. & Rem. Code Ann. § 38.002; Mass. Gen. L. ch. 93A, § 9(3). On the other hand, some lawyers never send demand letters that are not legally required because it is a way to diminish the strategic advantage of a defendant's filing a SLAPP suit before the consumer can file a complaint. *See* § 23.8, *infra*.

statements and descriptions of the consumer's claim as are useful to convince the potential defendant that the case should be settled before suit is ever filed. It is a good idea to use the demand letter to anticipate and rebut in advance defenses that can be reasonably anticipated, such as "as-is" sales or other waivers of warranties. An adequate description of how a transaction was unconscionable can undermine such defenses.

4.6.3 The Complaint

4.6.3.1 Getting It Right the First Time

Once the decision has been made to file suit, one should keep in mind the need for efficient use of time in drafting the complaint. While there is always time to do it right the second time, profitability in a small case depends on spending as little time as possible generating unnecessary pleadings.[21]

4.6.3.2 Pleading the Facts

If the client has furnished a complete chronology, pleading the facts in the lawsuit should be a relatively simple matter. Furthermore, if the demand letter is sufficiently detailed, it can be inserted into your form complaint with minimal changes.

Notwithstanding the usual rule against pleading one's evidence, many experienced consumer attorneys recommend that, whenever possible, any documents that establish liability on their face be made exhibits to the complaint. This approach serves two fundamental purposes: First, at any hearing in which the court takes time to read the pleadings in the case before proceeding, the judge will get to see those damning documents and may form an opinion about the defendant before any argument begins. Second, pleading the evidence may well push the case to a speedy settlement, especially in cases with "smoking gun" exhibits such as demands for usurious interest or egregious debt collection act violations.

4.6.3.3 Pleading the Theories of Liability

Again, in the interest of efficiency, all potential legal theories of liability should be pleaded in the original complaint.[22] Because elements of proof differ under different theories of recovery, many attorneys plead all claims arising under overlapping or mutually exclusive theories. For example, most UDAP cases will overlap with claims for breach of warranty, breach of contract, fraud, negligent misrepresentation, or negligence. One need not be particularly crafty or artful to find those overlaps and be certain that they are pleaded in the alternative to the UDAP cause of action.

Beyond overlapping legal theories, there are also those that may be described as mutually exclusive, that is, theories that are similar but negate each other. For example, one may plead that fraud took place but, alternatively, it is advisable to plead that, if the defendant's misrepresentations were not made intentionally and knowingly, then they were made negligently and without the exercise of ordinary care and prudence. This will leave open the possibility of a winning verdict even if the jury finds that there was no intent to deceive.

In addition to pleading theories of recovery, it is advisable to plead any statutory standards that may be applicable. The same may be said of disciplinary rule violations by attorneys and insurance regulation violations by an insurance agency or carrier.

4.6.3.4 Pleading Damages

In many small consumer cases, it is quite possible there may be items that are not truly "damages." Among the non-damage items that may be available are: usury penalties and forfeitures; Truth in Lending Act penalties; Consumer Credit Code penalties; Article 9 penalties; and Odometer Act penalties.

Non-monetary remedies may include: rescission and restitution; injunctive relief; receivership; and even forfeiture of a defendant's ability to do business in the state.

4.6.3.5 Checklist of Statutory Causes of Action

The following checklist (while hardly all-inclusive) may be useful in streamlining the process of identifying potential theories of liability with MLFs. These types of statutes often provide for attorney fees and/or penalties in addition to damages, thereby allowing a case to be profitable even in the face of small damages.

Common Types of State Statutory Causes of Action

- Business Opportunity Act
- Career Counseling Services Act
- Consumer Credit Code
- Contest and Gift Giveaway Act
- Credit Services Organizations Act
- Debt Collection Act
- Deceptive Trade Practices Act (UDAP)
- Declaratory Judgments Act
- Disclosure by Uninsured Financial Institutions
- Disclosure to Purchaser of Property

---

21 The companion CD-Rom this volume contains sample pleadings that may be helpful. See also NCLC's annual publication *Consumer Law Pleadings on CR-Rom.*

22 But see § 8.2, *infra*, for the opposite approach.

- Fraud in a Real Estate or Stock Transaction
- Health Spa Act
- Home Improvement Contract
- Home Solicitation Transactions Act
- Insurance, Unfair Competition and Unfair Practices
- Invention Development Services Act
- Labeling, Advertising, and Sale of Kosher Foods
- Manufactured Housing Standards Act
- Membership Camping Resort Act
- Motor Vehicle Commission Code
- Notary Public (Representation as Attorney)
- Optometry Act
- Personnel Employment Services
- Removal of Unauthorized Vehicles from Parking Facilities or Public Highways
- Rental-Purchase Agreements
- Residential Service Company Act
- Self-Service Storage Facility Liens
- Sham Sales of Homesteads
- Speech Pathologists and Audiologists
- Talent Agencies
- Telephone Solicitation
- Timeshare Act
- Usury

Common Federal Statutory Causes of Action

- Bank Tying Act
- Consumer Leases
- Consumer Product Warranties
- Credit Repair Organizations Act
- Electronic Fund Transfer Act
- Equal Credit Opportunity Act
- Fair Credit Reporting Act
- Fair Debt Collection Practices Act
- Interstate Land Sales Act
- Odometer Act
- RICO
- Truth in Lending Act
- Usury

4.6.3.6 Serving Discovery with the Pleadings

One of the most useful tools in the plaintiff's arsenal is the ability to serve discovery with the complaint in those jurisdictions where such service is permitted. Even if you choose not to use this approach, you may wish to prepare all discovery at the same time as you prepare the complaint. It is not particularly difficult to work up a basic set of boilerplate discovery that can then be custom-adjusted to track the factual and legal issues of each case.[23]

For example, in a suit against a lender you will want the consumer's entire loan file and the minutes of all directors and loan committee meetings that addressed such loan(s). In a suit against an attorney or collection agent for Fair Debt Collection Practices Act violations, you will want copies of collection letters sent over a several-year period preceding the date of suit. The histories of attorneys' collection practices have been found relevant to fundamental issues in several cases.[24]

In a case involving Truth in Lending Act violations, you will want copies of all forms, procedures, and procedure manuals used by the seller or lender in its consumer transactions in order to establish whether there could be a bona fide error defense. In a suit involving a defective vehicle, you will want all service and sales records dealing with the vehicle.

4.6.3.7 First Strike

One of the problems in handling small consumer cases is the delay built into the system. For a UDAP case in states such as Massachusetts and Texas, a demand letter will ordinarily have to be sent before a suit for damages can be filed. As most defendants fail to take advantage of their opportunity to settle, this is likely to simply be a wasted period of time.[25]

Because so many cases involve multiple grounds of recovery, it may be possible to file the suit on all non-UDAP causes of action and serve the defendant, within the span of a few days, with a demand letter, complaint, and first round of discovery. This prevents the defendant from finding an attorney who will accept a minimal retainer to file a general denial or to simply write a response to a letter. Instead, within the first sixty to seventy-five days, the defendant is assured of having to incur substantial legal fees if an immediate settlement can not be reached.

While this strategy should be used judiciously and in compliance with the applicable ethical standards for attorneys, the fact remains that, on a meritorious consumer case, the first strike approach can persuade a defendant to settle quickly.

The other advantages to the first strike approach are that (1) the defendant and its attorney are much more likely to take you seriously, given the fact that you have done more than merely send a letter and (2) jumping into discovery at such an early stage may well provide the necessary information to make a partial summary judgment feasible or make more effective the taking of the case to alternative dispute resolution.

---

23 The companion CD-Rom to this volume contains sample discovery. See also NCLC's annual publication *Consumer Law Pleadings on CD-Rom*.

24 *See, e.g.*, Crossley v. Lieberman, 868 F.2d 566 (3d Cir. 1989); Mertes v. Devitt, 734 F. Supp. 872 (W.D. Wis. 1990).

25 *See generally* R. Alderman, 15 Caveat Vendor 25 (1990).

4.7 The Early Summary Judgment Motion

One of the least-utilized tools available to plaintiffs' attorneys is the motion for partial summary judgment. A court may grant summary judgment to a plaintiff on the issue of liability alone, even though there may be a genuine issue as to the amount of damages. The plaintiff's burden of proof for such a motion is met if he or she presents summary judgment evidence that would be sufficient to support an instructed verdict at trial.[26] The affidavit of an interested party witness will support a summary judgment "if the evidence is clear, positive and direct, otherwise credible and free from contradictions and inconsistencies, and could have been readily controverted."[27]

Many issues in a typical small consumer case may be ripe for an early summary determination. A summary judgment motion that addresses only minor issues may seem to be a waste of time, but in most cases every victory, however small, serves an overall beneficial effect for the plaintiff.[28] Beyond the strategic demoralizing benefit of partial summary judgments, there are obvious benefits to narrowing the issues, simplifying the case, and identifying those matters that are really in dispute.

As indicated above, the ideal small consumer case is one in which the issue is damages and not liability. A motion for partial summary judgment therefore affords a clear opportunity to lock in liability. Many statutory causes of action—such as those pursuant to the usury statute, consumer credit code, and state and federal debt collection practices acts—will appear on the face of documents that can be made exhibits to a motion for partial summary judgment. The trial court may therefore have the opportunity to give the plaintiff all of the findings necessary to support liability for such damages as are found by the trier of fact and, in many instances, judgment for statutory damages such as those arising pursuant to 15 U.S.C. §§ 1640 and 1692k, Article 9, or usury statutes. In addition to all other considerations, a partial summary judgment for statutory penalties can be useful in setting the lower boundary of settlement negotiations.

An early motion for summary judgment may also provide benefits similar to those derived from a deposition, that is, locking in a witness's testimony as well as discovering what that testimony will be. Nothing in the summary judgment rule prohibits a plaintiff from filing a motion for partial summary judgment on all of the ultimate issues of liability, even if it is anticipated that many of those issues might be disputed. Obviously, in order to defeat such a motion, the defense will find it necessary to file affidavits in response that address each of the matters set forth in the plaintiff's affidavits. This enables the plaintiff to obtain disclosure of sworn testimony of those fact witnesses, many times providing for wonderful impeachment when depositions are actually taken.

While it is true that the plaintiff will be giving away much of his or her testimony, the fact remains that most of that information would be discoverable in a competently recorded deposition anyway. The risk to the plaintiff in what is given away is therefore substantially less than the burden to the defendant who must, almost immediately after answering, lay its cards on the table.

Finally, in the area of special remedies, the partial summary judgment can provide an additional incentive for the defendant to want to settle. For example, if the statutes under which liability is proven provide for injunctive relief to restrain or prevent violations, the granting of a permanent injunction on partial summary judgment can have an extremely demoralizing effect. Such a ruling almost guarantees a strong push by the defendant to settle. A judicious plaintiffs' attorney will therefore provide defense counsel with a reasonable opportunity to reach a settlement before the permanent injunction order is signed.

4.8 Requests for Admissions

Another extremely useful tool for plaintiffs' attorneys is requests for admissions.[29] Particularly in "general denial" states, the use of requests for admissions to narrow the issues is extremely attractive. Consider using a separate request for admission on each and every issue that may be raised in a consumer suit, subject to local rules limiting the number of such requests. Unfortunately for the average defense attorney, this can sometimes mean having to answer well over a hundred requests. Moreover, a defendant must be careful in answering those requests since a bad-faith denial could support an award of expenses and attorney fees to compensate for the effort of proving the truth of the matter on which the request was made. Again, in the never-ending search for statutory attorney fees, requests for admissions can provide another way to get attorney fees in a suit in which such fees might not otherwise be recoverable, such as a claim for fraud.

4.9 Choice of Court

The appropriate choice of court in which to file a small consumer suit is a more critical strategic decision than

26 Braden v. New Ulm State Bank, 618 S.W.2d 780, 782 (Tex. Civ. App.—Houston [1st Dist.] 1981, writ ref'd n.r.e.).

27 Republic Nat'l Leasing Corp. v. Schindler, 717 S.W.2d 606, 607 (Tex. 1986); Danzy v. Rockwood Ins. Co., 741 S.W.2d 613, 615 (Tex. App.—Beaumont 1987, no writ).

28 *See generally* M. Musashi, A Book of Five Rings, The Fire Book, to Injure the Corners 78 (Overlook Press 1974).

29 The companion CD-Rom to this volume contains a sample request for admissions.

would appear at first glance. In some jurisdictions, getting hearings or trials in a limited-jurisdiction court will be significantly faster and easier than getting them in a court of general jurisdiction. The downside, however, is the limit on the potential recovery as well as the fact that there may be only six jurors instead of twelve.

What is perhaps less obvious to most attorneys is the potential desirability of filing suit in a justice of the peace court or small claims court. In addition to the limited jurisdiction, there are normally two other reasons why attorneys often object to filing suit in such courts. The first is that the justice of the peace may not be an attorney. In almost all cases, however, that is of little consequence if the plaintiff is willing to provide an adequate set of briefing and explanation of the law for the court.

The second reason normally cited for not filing in justice of the peace court is the right of trial de novo on appeal. This is not a valid reason. For example, in order to appeal a judgment from a Texas justice of the peace court to the county court at law, a defendant must post a bond on appeal, normally in the amount of twice the amount of the judgment.[30] This means that the plaintiff whose judgment is appealed from justice court should, in fact, be in far better shape than a plaintiff who starts out in county court at law, since the appeal from justice court will require the posting of a bond to secure payment of the judgment.

There is often yet another objection when neither the rules of evidence nor the rules of procedure are applicable in small claims court. Attorneys often view such a court as a free-for-all forum. While this may be extremely undesirable for a defendant, the plaintiff's attorney with really egregious circumstances may find that it is extremely beneficial to be able to put before the court or jury evidence that would normally not be admissible. Furthermore, the limited discovery available in small claims court prevents an aggressive defense attorney from excessively running up your time investment in the case and from engaging in abusive discovery tactics.

Even if the case is appealed and a trial *de novo* becomes necessary, the original trial should have provided the sort of discovery normally available only through a deposition. While it is true that there is no record of the justice court trial, any question asked at the trial can be asked in a subsequent deposition.

The primary negative to being in justice court or small claims is that certain remedies may not be available. For example, Texas Civil Practice and Remedies Code § 65.021 provides that injunctions may be granted by a district or county court, but a justice court can not issue an injunction.

On the opposite end of the spectrum, it may well be desirable to file suit in the court of general jurisdiction if there is any possibility of seeking class action relief. As the risk of possible class certification can be a monstrous sword hanging over the head of a defendant, serious thought should be given to this issue before deciding not to file in district or circuit court. Of course, a class action is no longer a "small consumer claim." Class Action is covered in Chapter 23 of this book.

4.10 Conclusion

The small consumer case, if efficiently handled, can be both profitable and emotionally satisfying. It is possible to do justice for those who otherwise could not afford access to the legal system, turning such work from pro bono into a profit center. Granted, one must be selective as to what cases will be taken, but careful choices can yield significant rewards.

30 Tex. R. Civ. P. 571.

Chapter 5 The Importance of Legal Services Consumer Law Specialization

By Will Ogburn[1]

5.1 The Importance of Consumer Protections to Low-Income Households

There are three reasons why consumer law is important to a legal services practice. First, consumer law addresses common needs of legal services clients. Financial crises, fraud, harassment, and economic victimization of the low-income population are all too common. Over 14% of the caseload of the nation's legal services programs is classified as consumer cases. The number is even higher if you consider the fact that a lot of consumer law issues are classified under other rubrics. But in either case, this is one of the largest case-load areas for legal services. Moreover, legal-needs surveys consistently show that legal services are meeting only the tip of the iceberg of client needs—a much smaller portion than for many other areas of practice. In short, client demand for consumer law assistance is high.

Second, consumer law is more than what immediately springs to mind. In the practice of poverty law, consumer law can not be understood as it is defined in law school. It does indeed involve the mastery and application of a large body of consumer protection statutes. But limiting the scope of consumer law practice so narrowly to that kind of "consumer case" ignores the wider range of legal redress available to address our clients' economic plight. Such a narrow practice is also irrelevant to the client entering the office door whose family or healthcare crisis means inevitable financial crisis as well; whose complaint of being unable to pay the bills may stem from unemployment as well as over-extended finances; or whose effort to provide for a child means a second mortgage and the threatened loss of a home. It is important not to categorize a problem too narrowly as a "consumer law" issue or not a "consumer law" issue, thereby losing sight of the real needs of the client. Precisely because our clients are poor, their economic fortunes are often at stake whatever the nominal reason for seeking legal service. As a result, consumer law in its broadest sense must be an integral part of any effort to address the needs of our client community.

The third principal reason consumer law is important for legal services stems from the nature of poverty in America. Competition is the essence of our free market system. It is the engine of enterprise upon which so much of our national economy rests, and it is the bread and butter of our clients' economic world—some would say jungle—in which they must obtain the necessities of life. One characteristic of competition is that it spawns pressure among competitors to test the limits of the rules of the game in order to get ahead. The temptation is especially great when consumer needs border on the desperate or when consumers live on the fringe outside the mainstream of the economy. Too often our clients deal with the shysters and two-bit players or with large institutions adept at skimming essential resources from those in need—or indeed with anyone willing to test the limits or traverse the line of fraud, fairness, and decent behavior—in order to make a buck.

The limits on this competitive behavior are the limits imposed by consumer law. Whenever we bring a case on behalf of a particular client, we are reinforcing the rules that apply to everyone. Enforcing these laws on behalf of our clients not only brings them a measure of redress but also helps define the practice of the marketplace in which all our clients and all Americans must operate.

Consumer law in a very real sense is the law of the marketplace, the means by which daily transactions are regulated and the marketplace is policed. It lies at the core of our economic system, establishing the rules of fair dealing, transfer of ownership, and rights of use. As such it affects, in thousands of ways, the daily lives of all our clients and all Americans. It addresses shoddy merchandise, personal finances, insurance coverages, access to basic commercial services (for example, credit, check cashing, depositing social security checks), constitutional rights (for example, due process, garnishment protection, shut-offs, and the right to bankruptcy), fraud and deception, purchases,

1 Will Ogburn is the Executive Director of the National Consumer Law Center. He wishes to thank Kathleen Keest and NCLC staff who contributed to the development of the ideas in this chapter.

rentals, and a broad range of other commercial transactions in which a consumer may participate.

Consumer law is both statutory law and common law. It is the law of deception and good faith, fraud and "meeting of the minds," and the myriad standards of right and wrong developed and passed on through case law and notions of fair play. And of course, it is the law of statutes designed to control how household items can be taken away, checks processed, products warranted, personal and credit files restricted, disclosures made, and on and on through a thousand details of daily commerce. The subject of consumer law may be the entire breadth of those rules that regulate the economy at the transactional level at which our clients participate. In this sense, consumer law is the warp and woof of our economic system, all the rules that balance the responsibilities and obligations of all parties to any potential consumer transaction.

Consumer law is an important facet of poverty law. It is a body of special protections in economic transactions. For a clientele strapped for money, these protections can make the difference between getting by and total failure and can be an essential ingredient for escaping poverty. Consumer law is also an important aspect of other poverty law specialization. The problems of health costs, home ownership and access to rental housing, job security, and family stability often can not be adequately addressed without considering the nexus between financial well being and the other areas of need.

5.2 The Special Role of Legal Services

Legal services' practice of consumer law is especially important and effective. Until the Office of Economic Opportunity (OEO) expanded the scope and nature of legal aid practice, little consumer law litigation existed. Over the years, the strength and vitality of consumer law has been derived in large part from the effective practice of consumer law by neighborhood legal services attorneys across the country. Today, as we respond to the daily needs of clients walking into our offices, we are the key actors in defining and developing the issues and determining the routine applications of consumer law. Moreover, by enforcing the laws and regulations on behalf of our own clients, legal services has done much to enforce and define the rules of the marketplace for poor people and for all Americans.

Even so, the unmet consumer law needs of our clients are very substantial. Every legal-needs survey of low-income populations has shown consumer law problems to be among the most frequently cited areas in which additional resources are needed. And even though the practice of most consumer law by legal services programs is reported under housing, health, and other categories, caseload reports still place consumer cases among the top four areas of legal services practice.

Client groups served by legal services have a specific need for effective consumer law advocacy. Neighborhood groups challenging the pattern of exploitation of certain local merchants (or outside organizations doing business in the community) require the assistance of lawyers. Legal advice is necessary to identify predatory and other illegal patterns of unfair practices and to pursue individual and classwide remedies.

Similarly, when market rates and rules are set by a regulatory body, low-income clients and client groups require the tools of legal advocacy to ensure that their interests and rights are recognized. Improperly inverted electric rates, unfair fuel adjustment clauses, proposals for local measured telephone services, and the like, all raise issues that can not be adequately addressed by our clients without legal and expert technical assistance. When these issues are not addressed by legal services, the interests of the low-income population are usually not addressed.

With proper backup support, consumer law does not have to be practiced by specialists. Indeed, since consumer law is often one essential aspect of a problem that may involve welfare, housing, health, employment, education or other issues, its practice is appropriately integrated into other priority areas. However, given the critical role consumer law can play in attacking many chronic problems of poverty and preventing others, it is also suitable to a high degree of specialization. The range and complexity of consumer law has, like welfare law, been compared to the tax code.[2] For this reason, it is appropriate for any program, even if it does not specialize in consumer law, to have at least some consumer law specialists to provide support and assistance in identifying and pursuing useful consumer law remedies.

5.3 Consumer Law and the Poor

No matter what kind of legal problem a low-income client has, consumer law solutions must be considered. For example:

- Consumer law protects *income levels and public benefits*. Much legal services work tends to focus on the

2 Consider, for example, a typical home improvement case, one perhaps trying to prevent a foreclosure. It can involve more than a dozen state and federal laws: the state's usury statute, Retail Installment Sales Act, mechanics lien laws, the Uniform Commercial Code (re: security interests), Home Solicitation Sales Act, debt collection and foreclosure laws, licensing laws, the Unfair and Deceptive Acts and Practices (UDAP) statute, and tort laws of fraud and negligence, as well federal laws on preempting state usury ceilings, Truth in Lending, the FTC rules on holder in due course, credit practices, and door-to-door sales, and perhaps the Fair Credit Reporting and Equal Credit Opportunity Acts. In all likelihood, the typical case would also involve federal and state laws on debt collection, property exempt from execution, and perhaps bankruptcy, and might involve—depending on the facts—a plethora of other laws as well.

income side of a family's personal ledger. Consumer law often addresses the other side of the ledger. Every time a family is cheated on a purchase, every time they pay out a higher and higher percentage of their income on exorbitant interest, they decrease the essential income available to support their family just as effectively as a cut in wages or benefits.

- Consumer law prevents *financial crises, foreclosures or evictions, and loss of jobs.* A client whose wages are garnished, whose savings account of SSI benefits is attached, whose fear of harassment forces him to pay a disputed debt, may be fired, may fail to pay the rent or mortgage, or may sacrifice other necessities of life. Consumer law addresses problems before they inevitably lead to catastrophe.
- Bankruptcy can protect a *public housing tenant from eviction.* Consumer law can force the housing authority to keep the tenant even when there are no state law remedies available. Filing for bankruptcy automatically stops an eviction. The tenant may wipe out the back-rent debt or be entitled to a reasonable payment plan, allowing the tenant to stay in her home.

The range of consumer law is epic. It extends from home foreclosures, second mortgage scams, flipping, home improvements and exemptions laws; from repossessions, lemon laws, repairmen liens; and from utility rates and terminations, usury ceilings, and debt collection harassment; to access to credit and reasonable check-cashing facilities, the application of unfair and deceptive acts and practices statutes to landlord tenant law, student loans and vocational school fraud, predatory practices, and insurance law.

The key is that consumer law is not just a specialty of poverty law. It is a range of legal applications that present exceptional tools to deal with the fundamental problems of poverty and legal services clients. It can be an important aspect of nearly any personal crisis that brings a low-income client to a legal services office. In this way, consumer law is a critical part of any poverty law practice.

5.4 Consumer Law As Income Protection

The single act of removing federal interest rate ceilings and preempting state usury laws cost poor people a greater loss in disposable personal income than even the most draconian proposal to cut welfare in the last decade.

Income is both the most universal and essential resource for low-income households, required to secure everything from foods and medical care to housing and health. It can be protected through benefit programs or jobs, on the one hand, and through consumer protections on the expenditure side. The loss of income to a welfare cut or to an insurance scam each diminish the ability to obtain and protect the necessities of life.

In fact, consumer law protects both the income coming in and the income going out. Jobs and employment income are protected by laws limiting employer contacts by debt collectors and by restricting the amounts and frequency of garnishment of paychecks. Public benefits are protected by laws exempting them from garnishment, attachments, and encumbrances and by principles of tracing, say, social security benefits into and out of a savings account claimed by a creditor.

But most of consumer law addresses the expenditures that dissipate our clients' income. For example, laws dealing with product warranties, with the over-extension of credit and costs of credit (usury), with fraud and deception and unfairness, all protect consumers from costly waste and abuse. Consumer protection laws help prevent unnecessary squandering of income by preventing debt collection harassment, ensuring one's right to due process of law before income and property is taken, and making it possible for low-income clients to know the important terms of the transaction beforehand. Similarly, utility rate case work prevents the low-income community from paying more than their fair share for basic needs, while public subsidies of low-income home weatherization and conservation efforts (and private subsidies ordered by utility commissions) lessen strains on family budgets. These and a wide range of additional laws and consumer law practices help ensure that essential income can be wisely husbanded and available for other needs.

5.5 Consumer Law As Asset Protection

The two most important and expensive assets low-income clients have are houses and cars. For a surprising number of our clients, their single largest asset and their greatest security for old age and financial emergency is their ownership of a home. More than one third of households with income of below $10,000 dollars occupy their own home. Seventy percent of retired persons own their home.

Today there is an onslaught by ever more brazen creditors threatening the pattern of homeownership among low-income people. Whenever there is home "equity," there is now an aggressive campaign to convert that equity into money with loans and lines of credit that assign homeownership rights to creditors. Only strong consumer law advocacy can attack these abuses through individual and class action litigation, law making, and publicity. Otherwise, millions of poor people will be deprived of their family homes and primary economic asset.

The second most important asset for many low-income households is an automobile. In all but a few densely populated urban areas, car ownership is an essential of life and a necessity for employment. Yet nothing has produced the consistently high volume of complaints and the plethora of legislation that car problems have. The scope of consumer protections extend from rights to cure defaults to used car lemon laws, from regulated credit rates to licensing laws, from warranties to special concerns with odometer tampering and selling poorly rebuilt wrecks.

Even aside from homes and cars, consumer assets are often at risk. The standard consumer credit transaction is frequently secured by furniture, televisions—indeed everything our clients may own. Recently we have even begun to see liens taken out by municipal hospitals for emergency health services. A good consumer law practice can protect consumers from these liens and other threats to the limited assets that our clients own.

5.6 Consumer Law Guarantees a Fresh Start

For our clients, the constitutional right to declare bankruptcy is different than for other Americans. Instead of something that occurs when a person faces financial disaster, bankruptcy for our clients can provide a way to get out of poverty. At the point when our clients have a chance to get a job, for example, bankruptcy gives them what the Supreme Court has called "a fresh start." By getting rid of the old debt load they may have acquired (often directly related to illness and staggering hospital bills or an extended layoff, when they needed to keep their family afloat), they can take on the job, get their family and themselves out of poverty, and have that "fresh start." Bankruptcy work is important as a means of seeing clients escape the shackles of poverty.

In other important but less dramatic ways, consumer law provides an opportunity to get out of a jam, rethink a commitment and change direction, and in the end avoid a train of events that can lead to the failure to pay enough rent to avoid eviction, to garnishment and the loss of a job, or to other serious personal crises. With careful legal advocacy, transactions secured by real estate often may be rescinded for up to three years. Door-to-door sales, often so hard to turn down, may be cancelled. The purchase of used cars and other products that do not work may be rejected or revoked. With timely and aggressive legal services representation, clients can turn a mistake that has the potential of bringing down the financial house of cards into a new opportunity.

5.7 Consumer Law As Access to Necessities of Life

Few needs are as basic as home heat. By dint of hard work and good advocacy, an essential federal grants program has been established and supplemented widely at the state level to help ensure that low-income households can afford to get through the winter without freezing. But it is far from enough. Moreover, the varieties of supplemental programs are in a state of flux and will demand careful attention throughout the decade. The problems of continuing access to utility services (not just heat, but electricity, telephones, and water as well) are not going away and are in fact being heightened by federal cuts.

Entire low-income communities are strangled by lack of access to credit and essential finances. Individual welfare recipients may pay 1% to 2% of their total income just for the privilege of cashing their checks. "Easy credit" is all too often available, but reasonable credit is not available when it is truly needed. The Community Reinvestment Act has served to focus attention on such community needs, and it has at times provided an important vehicle for extracting appropriate investments from reluctant financial institutions. However, until the long-term needs of poor neighborhoods are addressed effectively by national policy, creative solutions and advocacy will be necessary.

New obstacles are arising for tenants seeking new apartments or who need critical insurance coverage. Tenant blacklists and the new landlord-tenant reporting services ensure that, in tight markets, a single complaint or a landlord's misspoken word effectively bars a person from securing adequate shelter. Mandatory automobile insurance can be priced out of the affordable range for poor persons who need a car just to get to work or to have access to medical care. The availability of long-term-care insurance on reasonable and fair terms may well mean the difference between a respectable life situation and a life of despair. Effective advocacy is necessary to ensure effective access to most essential services.

5.8 Consumer Law As Crisis Mitigation

For the poor, a vicious cycle often exists between individual and family crisis and financial difficulties. The loss of a job, the onset of illness, divorce, or unexpected death of a family member: each can mean dire, drastic financial repercussions. In many cases these events pull people into poverty. In other cases, they render intolerable already unacceptable circumstances. In addition to addressing the immediate cause of distress, it is also necessary to address the financial stress these problems cause. Debts must be put off or avoided, homes and other assets must be protected and, if the opportunity for improvement arises, the opportunity must not be overshadowed by the continuing effects of the financial crisis.

Just as family crises bring on financial crises, financial distress is a primary cause of family stress. A repossessed car may lead to the loss of a job. A hospital bill may lead to the loss of a home. Studies show that the burden of debts is a frequent cause of family tensions, marital breakdowns, and illness. Often good and adequate legal responses to many of these pressures are available, which, if timely, can prevent one problem from cascading into even more serious ones.

5.9 Cycles of Consumer Law

5.9.1 Overview

Shortly after the birth of the national legal services program, there was an explosion of legislation, litigation, and new consumer case law. At the time, however, there was little developed consumer law as it is understood today. The most prominent consumer law reform on the scene was a national effort paid for by the credit industry to reform state credit and consumer protection laws. The Uniform Consumer Credit Code (UCCC, or the "U-triple-C") was said to do for consumer law what the Uniform Commercial Code had recently done for commercial law—except that in fact it enshrined a number of principles vigorously opposed by consumers. With hindsight, one can now say that this industry effort heralded the beginning of a period of rapid and sweeping changes bringing radical improvements to consumers generally and low-income consumers specifically.

First, the national movement to enact the early version of the Uniform Consumer Credit Code was halted. The National Consumer Law Center (NCLC) and legal-services-represented clients were at the center of the debate. That version of the UCCC was defeated, to be replaced by a lengthy series of consumer-oriented model statutes ranging from the Model Consumer Credit Code to specific proposals for specific industries that have since found their way into federal and state laws across the country.

At the same time, fundamental violations of notions of judicial and governmental fairness spawned constitutional challenges nationwide. Constitutional procedural rights were established. A series of Supreme Court (*Sniadach*, *Fuentes*, *Memphis Light*, etc.) and other cases established constitutional rights of due process in the area of consumer law that are still expanding today. A consumer is entitled to notice and a hearing before a court before judgment is rendered, before property is executed upon, before wages may be garnished, before municipal services may be discontinued, and before a creditor may use the auspices of the state to collect a debt. These principles sound so basic and uncontroversial today, but they were hard fought when legal services helped establish the breakthroughs years ago. Echoes of the fights are still heard in current battles to ensure that consumers get notice of which property is exempt from seizure before the fact.

Substantive rights soon followed: the right to rescind second mortgage transactions up to three days, and sometimes three years, from the date of the transaction; the right to cancel home solicitation sales; the right to privacy about one's credit (and personal) history; the right to credit on equal terms with white males; the right to raise one's defenses against the purchaser of one's debt paper; the right not to be harassed for money claimed to be owing; and, that most elemental of rights, the right to know the terms of the transaction. None of these rights are yet perfected, but all are firmly established.

In relatively few years, consumers gained the federal Truth in Lending Act, limits on garnishments, the Equal Credit Opportunity Act, the Fair Credit Reporting Act, restrictions on unsolicited credit cards and the Fair Credit Billing Act, a Fair Debt Collection Practices Act, the Electronic Fund Transfer Act, a federal Odometer Act, Interstate Land Sales Fraud laws, the Community Reinvestment Act, and a major reform of the bankruptcy laws (the principle elements of which have survived successive industry onslaughts).

Disclosure laws bear special mention. While grounded in earlier state laws, the federal Truth in Lending law has left an indelible mark on consumer law. Not only did it send a message to consumers and attorneys alike that it is now viable to seek private remedies through the courts for violations of consumer laws—changing the nature of consumer law practice forever—it established three abiding principles of import. First, it is good public policy to provide for minimum statutory damages for violations of consumer protection laws, especially those difficult or expensive to prove. Second, in order to encourage the private enforcement of consumer laws, it is proper to require attorney fee awards for prevailing consumers. Third, the basic terms of a transaction should be made known to the consumer so that informed judgment is possible.

States have done much the same and more, adding to the list lemon laws, "plain English" rights, future services laws, strengthened state unfair and deceptive acts and practices (UDAP) laws, somewhat tighter insurance practices laws, exemption rights, limited deficiency judgments, door-to-door sales laws, and a slew of other innovative and locally designed consumer protections.

Legislation begat regulation. The era of rulemaking followed the lead of the legislatures and often had an equally profound impact upon the lives of poor persons. Many of the federal laws called for rulemaking, and that rulemaking expanded the reach of the law considerably (for example, Truth in Lending and the four-installment rule; Equal Credit and the effects test). In addition, the Federal Trade Commission went further. It promulgated the Holder-in-Due-Course rule that required retailers to include in their credit forms a clause providing that assignees could not cut off the consumer defenses. The Credit Practices Rule forbid *inter alia* confessions of judgments, dragnet security interest clauses, pyramiding late fees, and several other than common unfair and widespread practices. A vocational school rule took the first steps to protect students. The funeral rule sought to introduce basic protections in that realm. At the same time, state rulemaking expanded and many state attorneys general began aggressive and creative enforcement of consumer protection laws. Legal services clients played a prominent role in nearly every one of these advancements.

If the 1970s brought new consumer protections, the 1980s meant protecting established consumer rights. Legal services consumer litigation continued unabated, but the era of deregulation overcame Washington. While some old rights continued to expand, clients had to fight hard to protect earlier gains. The client victories of the 1980s were no less consuming or important than those of the 1970s. Efforts to keep overburdened debtors from having a fresh start under the bankruptcy laws, or to freely permit coerced reaffirmations of discharged debts, were beaten back in a clear David and Goliath confrontation. Efforts to repeal rescission rights, to permit hidden charges, and to keep consumer cases out of federal court, all part of the effort to gut federal consumer protection law, were largely defeated. Yet victories such as these, unlike those of the previous decade, were not accompanied by a sense of progress and improvement.

The 1980s had other hallmarks as well. The government became the single biggest collector of debts claimed to be owed by those in economic need. And, just as income and programmatic support for those in poverty were severely cut back, deregulation brought new hardships to the poor. Whatever the overall merits of economic deregulation, it has undeniably unleashed the greedy instincts of unscrupulous operators: annual percentage rates exceeding 100%; home loans designed to cause default and foreclosure; the inability to get quick and easy access to the proceeds of government checks, and on and on through an endless list of economic abuses and scams. In the 1980s, the low-income consumer has often had to fight harder just to stay even.

5.9.2 Consumer Law in the Last Decade

Nothing has happened to diminish the importance of consumer law in the future. Indeed, the contentiousness of the 1980s has already defined areas of importance for the years ahead: the effects of deregulation, the need to save homes, and developing responses to the government as debt collector, as examples. Each is discussed below. But more general themes are also apparent: consumer law will be striving to reintroduce and expand basic notions of fairness and responsibility into judicial and legislative deliberations of consumer rights. Emerging areas are already identifiable. Still, it is of course impossible to know when the course of time will actually lead. Many signs already indicate a new era of regulation and legislative responsiveness to low-income consumer needs. It seems clear that we are approaching an era of considerable client activism with many opportunities for change.

5.9.3 Deregulation: The Poor Paying More

A pattern has emerged in those deregulated industries that affect poor people most directly. The result is that poor people pay more for basic services and necessities of life. The fear is that as poor people pay more for less, the dangers of creating an underclass of poor are increased.

In industry after industry, deregulated companies have moved swiftly to compete with their new competitors. To compete, they need to invest heavily in new technology and in new markets. The most attractive markets are upscale consumers and industry.

To raise money necessary for this expansion and "advancement," they increase their charges in whatever captive market they have. More often than not, poor people are part of the captive market and are charged more by companies seeking to make new and better services available to the upper segments of the market.

The essential regulated services most needed by low-income consumers are heat and electricity, telephones, and basic banking. Basic telephone charges are up, electric rates reflect costs of industrial conservation programs, and check fees have skyrocketed. Billions upon billions of dollars are at stake. The trend toward even greater charges for basic services is clear. Legal services clients can respond and protect themselves only with direct legal assistance. In order to adequately represent client interests, there must be resources of expertise and technical assistance capable of addressing complex regulatory and economic issues in specialized forums.

5.9.4 Equity Lending—Saving Homes

No form of credit has grown faster than home-equity lending. It takes the form of second mortgages, wrap-around mortgages, home-secured credit cards, home-equity lines of credit, mechanics liens, seductive home improvement contracts, and on and on. Official government policy is no longer "borrow only as necessary" but instead fosters a consumer's right to "enjoy" the equity in one's home. Millions of low-income Americans own homes and, for many, it is the only financial security they bring on their own into old age. The result is that the poor are taking on debts at exorbitant rates with huge numbers of points and other hidden charges and impossible terms. Defaults and foreclosures are legion and when an economic turndown spreads across the nation, tragedy will hit.

The key to saving the homes of low-income households lies not in foreclosure expertise but in the ability to address the underlying credit transactions and patterns of deceptive behavior that entrap consumers in unfair mortgage transactions. A concerted community-wide effort will be necessary to stem the sudden loss of family homes among the poor.

5.9.5 Government As Debt Collector

Two happenings involving government debts may characterize the 1990s. First, the federal government increasingly used the summary powers of the IRS to enforce unproven claims of consumer debt by withholding tax refunds or earned income tax payments. Second, the government farmed out growing numbers of student and veteran loans and benefit overpayment claims to private nationwide debt collection firms for collection. In both instances the constitutional and consumer protection rights of consumers must be defined, enforced, and monitored.

This is novel territory. The governmental processes being established are designed to collect money swiftly and efficiently, and often cut off traditional rights and opportunities to contest the legitimacy of the claims or the fairness of the results. Litigation and administrative advocacy will set the course for years to come and affect astronomical amounts of our clients' disposable income.

5.9.6 Emerging Standards of Fairness

In addition to challenging the specific legacies of the last decades, a broader front is necessary to challenge the widespread growth and inventiveness of practices and institutions that increasingly rob low-income consumers of their vital resources. The emerging standard of fairness is one profound development that promises a pervasive impact on consumer rights.

For years, the course of consumer protection has been marked by detailed, specific legislation setting forth clear terms of behavior. Recently, however, as deregulation has taken hold and new scams and outrages occur, consumers are faced with new injustices. Statutory law has been unable to keep up. Consequently, courts are faced with an unusual volume of cases presenting clear wrongs and no obvious solutions. The first signs of a newly revitalized common law emphasizing "good faith" actions, fiduciary responsibilities, and unconscionability are now visible. The return to basic, general standards of fairness offers some promise of fertile, active case development at the state level. What is at stake is a new common law for consumer transactions that would alter the balance between low-income consumer and merchant.

5.9.7 Ultimate Control—Ultimate Liability

Another broad attack on abuse is to hold liable the party with ultimate control over the marketplace. Behind every neighborhood creditor is a financer. Unscrupulous creditors can not survive without the financial backing of a larger institution. If the financers are liable for the abusive acts of the creditor, one can be sure that the credit market will be better policed.

Few credit transactions occur without the powerful backing of an established financial institution. For example, the door-to-door salesman hawking home improvements can only survive if a bank or finance company is willing to extend credit or buy the consumer paper. Or, an overreaching second-mortgage company must be able to package its mortgages and sell them on the securities market or to out-of-state banks. Such institutional investors, however, shield themselves from liability for these abuses by artful contract drafting, recourse agreements, failing to make rudimentary inquiries, and turning their back to telltale signs of mischief. The challenge is to use the Racketeer Influenced and Corrupt Organizations (RICO) Act, standards of negligence, principles of notice (defining holder-in-due-course status), rights of rescission and cancellation, and joint enterprise claims to hold liable those financers who persist in funding unethical practices and thereby to force the unscrupulous creditors out of business.

5.9.8 Deep Pockets and Personal Liability

Consumer law practice by legal services attorneys traditionally seeks client redress from corporate or business defendants. However, true justice and restitution is often thwarted by legal fictions and because the real profits pass quickly through the business structure to owners or third parties. Those with the money, the deep pockets, hide behind the corporate veil, principles of independent contractors, and a maze of obscure relationships and covers.

Yet the law is not necessarily as rigid as many believe. Several attorneys general have made a practice of suing principals as well as corporate defendants. Common law and statutory law provide ways of reaching the real culprits. Recent legal literature is addressing these issues directly. With careful research and guidance, legal services practice will come to routinely incorporate more effective claims and proofs of expanded liability, benefiting current clients and, again, policing the market as well.

5.9.9 Finding the Bad Apple

In addition to pursuing new claims with broad applications to the growing range of consumer abuses, new tactics are necessary too. The market in which low-income consumers find themselves has been inundated with new institutions, new actors, and old actors in new roles. At the same time, the ways in which low-income consumers are disadvantaged have increased many fold as limits on commercial behavior fade. It has become increasingly important to focus on those specific actors and those specific patterns of practice that do the most harm in low-income communities.

It was not so very long ago that banks entered the consumer credit market. Recently, savings and loans and securities firms have entered the market. Now we are seeing an explosion in the sources of credit for consumers in general and low-income consumers in particular, and especially in the accompanying variety and ingenuity of fraudulent and abusive schemes. The full brunt of this growth will be felt in the coming years. Today, in addition to finance companies and neighborhood sources of credit, banks, and credit unions, credit is being hawked by loan brokers, first- and second-mortgage companies, "cheap credit" advertisements in the newspapers, door-to-door salesmen, get-rich-quick schemers reading legal notices of foreclosures, "credit clinics," and too many others. All have enjoyed success; the amount of consumer credit extended has ballooned and grown beyond historical mile posts. The rates of foreclosure reach 50% in some communities. The poor carry more than their own heavy share. It is certain that legal services offices will see an astronomical growth in the number of over-extended clients facing financial disaster. This growth alone will require innovative, efficient, and thoughtful programmatic responses.

One response, consistent with the increased computerization of case load tracking systems, is to focus particularly on marketplace actors who are found to repeatedly disadvantage our clientele. By matching claims and defendants for all consumer law suits brought within a program's service area, patterns of misbehavior can be identified. The worst actors can be targeted for considered, economical, coordinated legal offensives. By marshalling evidence cutting across many cases, patterns of abuse and fraud can be more easily established. The strength of an individual case can be buttressed by similar claims in tens of hundreds of other complaints by other consumers. And when appropriate the consumer claims can be joined in a massive assault on the wrongdoer. By focusing early on the worst actors, the limited resources available to our clients can be brought to bear on the biggest and most important community problems.

5.9.10 Dealing with Retailers' Inappropriate Use of Compulsory Arbitration

Increasingly in the last two decades, shoddy finance companies and retailers have sought to insulate themselves from judicial accountability by inserting arbitration clauses in their retail contracts. By doing so they have sought to select a forum that may be biased in their favor, is not bound by the law, and may not entertain class action relief or punitive damages. The effect if upheld would be to insulate fraud and other overreaching. Attacks on the bias and expense of arbitration have met with mixed success. Some arbiters have awarded punitive damages and provided class relief although others have not. Much needs to be done to thwart this strategy of irresponsibility.

5.9.11 Challenges Lay Ahead

Consumer law has come a long distance already but still has miles to go. By virtue of the voice given low-income consumers by legal services programs, the face of consumer law has changed radically. The next decade is certain to alter the balance of consumer rights again. The cycle of change has come full circle. The coming decade of consumer law practice offers another opportunity to affect vital interests of poor Americans for decades to follow.

5.10 Seven Lessons of Consumer Law Practice in Legal Services

1. *Most poverty law deals with family income—benefits, employment,* etc. Consumer law deals with family expenses. To the client, saving $1000 in recurring debt expenses is as important as $1000 in increased benefits or salaries, yet many legal services programs focus on benefits and ignore consumer law. Legislative changes are similar. Increased interest rates or insurance rates may be more costly for our clients than a welfare cut.

2. *Many consumer issues are critical to well being, for example, saving houses from foreclosure, saving cars necessary for jobs, enhancing dignity and a sense of fairness in dealing with debt collectors.*

3. *Consumer law has powerful solutions.* TIL rescission can eliminate the mortgage on a home; bankruptcy can eliminate or reduce the debt on an overpriced car; class actions can change the practices of creditors preying on the whole low-income community; RICO can bring treble damages.

4. *Consumer law has critical legal tools for all aspects of legal services.* For example, bankruptcy can be used to prevent evictions in public and private housing; deceptive practice statutes can be used to counter nursing-home, migrant-farmworker-camp, mobile-home, and landlord abuses; and many consumer protection tools can be used to protect the elderly from home improvement scams. Much of legal services practice of consumer law arises out of other specialty areas.

5. *Consumer law is the law of markets and private contracts.* Much of legal services work is concerned with the law of public entities, but this is basically a free enterprise country and most of the law in general reflects that fact.

6. *The changing marketplace intensifies the need for representation and advocacy.* Deregulation combined with increased capital investment means that, while businesses seek upscale customers, expenses are being loaded onto the most inelastic customers, that is, our clients who struggle to obtain the necessities of life. With regard to telephones, credit and banking services, electricity, insurance, and in other areas, an increasing proportion of our clients' income goes toward maintaining just the basic services. Not a few

clients drop out and become part of a permanent underclass with no phone and no access to financial institutions or other necessities.

7. *Clients can address systemic consumer problems as well as individual problems and can also attack local marketplace abuses.* Neighborhoods can use consumer law to attack local abusive practices of merchants and utility companies and obtain relief and a sense of empowerment.

5.11 Tips for Starting a Consumer Law Specialty in Legal Services[3]

- The first step is for the program to become committed to the importance of consumer law as a powerful tool for helping the low-income community. If you don't have that commitment, don't give up: the support often follows the work rather than precedes it. If you don't have support, then focus on an area where you can generate good client stories, do those cases, and then the program support will follow. If you build it . . . .
- Set up your office so that you really are specialized. Consider an office policy that turns away clients whose problems are not covered by a specialist or assigns them to a program that has generalists who take all the cases falling outside of the specialty areas. Work with your program's intake staff regularly to identify the appropriate cases to refer to you. Review the intakes handled by the intake workers in your target area—this gives you a better sense of the problem and also alerts you to cases you want that they've missed.
- Pick a particular community problem to focus on. It could be predatory mortgage lending, used-car scams, fraudulent vocational schools, or hospitals overcharging uninsured patients or balance-billing Medicare patients. Each of these problems has multiple legal approaches and requires the advocate to learn the jargon and practices of very different industries. Get your feet on the ground addressing one community problem before expanding your practice to another problem.
- Find out what resources and support you have available and develop what you need that is not available. Check out state and national support centers and find out where they can help you. For example, NCLC has some funds to help legal services programs with the consumer law problems of the elderly but not other types of problems. Are there state or topical "listservs" and task forces on the community problem you are addressing? Are there helpful materials in the program or state pleadings bank? Train the intake people in your program to screen for the cases that you are looking for. Send the intake staff revised intake forms or questions to identify the appropriate clients or clients who have had experiences with particular rogues.
- Build alliances and coalitions with your state attorney general, local consumer complaint office, law school professors and clinical instructors, consumer journalists, the better business bureau, consumer credit and housing counselors, the local police, and academic and community experts on the community problem you are focusing on. Schedule trainings on the topic and have individuals from these organizations speak about and get accustomed to providing educational support to your project. These allies can be your experts in helping develop strong cases.
- If you are in a legal-services-funded program that can not pursue class actions or attorney fee awards, focus on the types of cases that are not being pursued by private consumer attorneys and other legal services programs. Cases involving vocational school fraud and used-car dealers would be likely candidates.
- If you are a legal services program funded substantially through attorney fee-shifting, choose an area that has good fee potential and is not being explored by private consumer attorneys and other legal services programs. Used-car fraud and the areas of predatory mortgage lending may be likely candidates, but take great care to separate the strong claims from the weaker ones.[4]
- Explore legislative and administrative law approaches to the community problem that you have focused on. Talk to other staff and those in the community who pursue legislative and administrative solutions for advice on how and where to get started. People in restricted programs can, should, and must do legislative and administrative advocacy. Alan Houseman at CLASP wrote a memo addressing what restricted programs can do after lobbying restrictions were put into effect, and people need to know what they can. You can collaborate with groups, participate in coalitions, and provide information about pending legislation. Importantly, restricted programs can do comments on all public rulemaking for their clients—and there are very few consumer friendly comment and even fewer consumer-friendly comments with a poverty focus. Perhaps the main point is that people in restricted programs need to stay informed and engaged with other groups.
- Get the NCLC treatises on your area of focus and come to NCLC and NACA trainings on the problems that face your client community.
- The media can be an important tool. Using the media is a great way to find good cases and to educate consumers about new scams and which traps to avoid. Also,

3 Thanks to Carolyn Carter, Dianne Thompson, and Michelle Weinberg for their contributions to this section.

4 *Cf.* Frye v. Tenderloin Housing Clinic, Inc., 16 Cal. Rptr. 3d 583 (Cal. App. 2004) (non-profit housing clinic may be required to disgorge its 35% contingent fee to the tenants it represented because it was not registered as a non-profit legal assistance organization and non-profit legal assistance organizations are not permitted to charge attorney fee).

media exposure, if it's positive, unequivocally builds program support for doing consumer work. People need to cultivate relationships with the press and both answer questions from the press and seek the press out when they have good cases.

- Community consumer education is an important tool to stymie consumer fraud before it spreads. Publicizing consumer work is a great way to get clients and community support. Funders love it, the community really does gain something from it, and you get cases/clients and referrals too.

Another point to add would be that even LSC-restricted programs may offer plenty of advocacy. For example, they can offer legislative advocacy if a legislator requests. Martha Bergmark, Diane Thompson, or other advocates could add more detail.

Another suggestion is to publicize the consumer work as a way of contacting clients and getting community support. A final suggestion is to contact social services agencies to increase referrals.

Chapter 6 Consumer Advocacy in Government and Academics

By Stephen Gardner

6.1 Overview

Consumer advocacy in government and in academia are worth exploring, both for a lawyer who is looking for help with a specific consumer's problem or on a particular abusive practice and for a lawyer who seeks an alternative to private or legal services practice.

This chapter covers the following:

- State government consumer protection
- Federal government consumer protection
- Consumer protection in academia
- Opportunities for working as a consumer lawyer in government and academia

6.2 State Government Consumer Protection

6.2.1 General

Consumer protection lawyers in state government generally work for three separate and distinct entities: state attorneys general, regulatory boards, and state or local consumer protection agencies. Of these, the state attorneys general (AGs) are generally most active and most effective in protecting the rights of consumers.

6.2.2 State Regulation of Consumer Practices Developed Many Years Ago

The earliest large-scale attempt by states to regulate deceptive advertising came as the result of a 1911 model statute proposed by Printer's Ink, an advertising industry trade journal. Approximately forty-four states adopted one version or another of the proposed statute. For example, California Business and Professions Code § 17500, which is the California version of this model law, first appeared in amended form in the California Penal Code in 1915 and, in 1941, was transferred to the Business and Professions Code. Similar to most of these statutes, it provides in pertinent part:

> It is unlawful for any person, firm, corporation . . . with intent directly or indirectly to dispose of real or personal property or to perform services, . . . or to induce the public to enter into any obligation relating thereto, to make or disseminate or cause to be made or disseminated before the public in this state, . . . in any newspaper or other publication, or any advertising device, . . . any statement, concerning such real or personal property or services, . . . or concerning any circumstance or matter of fact connected with the proposed performance or disposition thereof, which is untrue or misleading, and which is known, or which by the exercise of reasonable care should be known, to be untrue or misleading . . . .

The model statute did not contain an element of scienter, but eleven states that adopted this statute added a scienter element.

Led by Louis Lefkowitz of New York beginning in the late 1950s, Democrat Walter Mondale of Minnesota and Republican Ed Brooke of Massachusetts soon after, the state AGs began developing consumer protection offices that brought suit against unfair and deceptive business practices. The state AGs also sought legislation to deal with consumer problems, often setting the course for federal consumer protection laws. The consumer movement and state law enforcement involvement with it, as we know it today, really traces its origins to the 1960s.

On March 15, 1962, President Kennedy delivered his landmark message, *On Protecting the Consumer Interest*.[1] In it, he set forth four basic rights of consumers:

1. The right to safety, including the right to be protected against the marketing of goods that are hazardous to health or life

2. The right to be informed, including the right to be

1 1962 Cong. Q. 890–893 (1962).

protected against fraudulent, deceitful or misleading information, advertising, labeling and other such practices, and the right to be given the facts necessary to make informed choices

3. The right to choose among a variety of products and services at competitive prices

4. The right to be heard, including the right of consumer interests to receive full and sympathetic consideration in the formulation of government policy

In concluding his message, President Kennedy said that, for there to be a fuller realization of these consumer rights, there was a need, in certain areas, for new legislation and a need for existing government programs to be strengthened and improved. He also established a Consumer Advisory Committee, that issued a report dealing with each of the consumer rights he had set forth.[2] Since President Kennedy's message, state legislatures have added a fifth consumer "right"—the right of a consumer to recover damages and attorney fees from a seller who violated the consumer's rights.

"Consumer Protection has generated more interest among attorneys general in recent years than any other single area of activity."[3] Starting in the 1960s, state legislators and politicians realized that an increasingly complex marketplace was causing more and more problems for the average consumer. No longer did most consumers go down to a Mom and Pop store to buy what they needed (if in fact they ever did). Sales transactions became more and more impersonal, products were perceived as being less reliable than in "the good old days," and service was no longer what was being sold.

A number of generic "model" laws were proposed as ways of equalizing the consumer's "reduced" position in the sales transaction. The Uniform Deceptive Trade Practice Act (UDTPA),[4] originally drafted by the Legislative Research Center of the University of Michigan in 1964 and revised in 1966, was approved by the National Conference of Commissioners on Uniform State Laws and the American Bar Association. Section 2 of the uniform version lists eleven specifically defined deceptive trade practices, including: trademark and trade name infringement, passing off goods as those of another, bait and switch, disparagement, misrepresentations of standards, origins or quality of goods, misleading price comparisons, and a catch-all provision that covers "conduct which similarly creates a likelihood of confusion or of misunderstanding." Thirteen states adopted the UDTPA in some form.[5]

The Uniform Consumer Sales Practices Act (UCSPA)[6] was approved by the National Conference of Commissioners on Uniform State Laws and the American Bar Association in 1971. The UCSPA prohibits unconscionable and deceptive sales practices. In section 3(b), examples of eleven types of deceptive conduct are set forth, but these are not meant to be an exclusive listing of deceptive practices. There is some overlap with the eleven listed deceptive practices of the UDTPA. Three states adopted the UCSPA in some form.[7]

The Unfair Trade Practices and Consumer Protection Act (UTP-CPA) was developed by the FTC and Council of State Governments. Starting in the mid-1960s, the FTC began cooperating with state and local law enforcement officials in antitrust and consumer protection matters to a far larger degree than ever before. In 1971, the FTC issued a tentative draft Model Law for State Government, which came in the wake of its proposal that states adopt "Mini-FTC Acts." The Model, in section 2, combines the basic language of section 5(a)(1) of the Federal Trade Commission Act[8] with the eleven specifically delineated deceptive practices of the UDTPA and some of the prohibited practices of the UCSPA for a total of nineteen "unfair methods of competition and unfair or deceptive acts or practices in the conduct of any trade or commerce" that are declared to be "unlawful." Nine states adopted the UTP-CPA in some form.[9]

6.2.3 *State Attorney General Consumer Protection Authority*

Regardless of the model law from which they were developed, state UDAP laws usually provide for enforcement of their requirements in two ways—by public law enforcement agencies and by private individual and class-action litigants. The encouragement of private actions is primarily to achieve the goal of turning citizens into what are usually called "private attorneys general" who vindicate frauds against the public by private actions.

Generally, the various acts allow the state attorney general to seek injunctive relief and civil penalties in various situations, to accept assurances of voluntary compliance, and to obtain restitution for consumers. They usually give the attorney general broad administrative powers, including the right to conduct hearings, issue subpoenas, and promulgate regulations.

---

2 The First Report of the Consumer Advisory Committee (Washington GPO 1963).

3 National Association of Attorneys General Committee on the Office of the Attorney General, Report on the Office of Attorney General (1971).

4 In its uniform version it can be found at 7A U.L.A. 265 (West, Master Edition, 1985).

5 *See* National Consumer Law Center, Unfair and Deceptive Acts and Practices § 3.4.2.4 (6th ed. 2004).

6 In its uniform version it is found at 7A U.L.A. 231 (West, Master Edition 1985).

7 *See* National Consumer Law Center, Unfair and Deceptive Acts and Practices § 3.4.2.3 (6th ed. 2004).

8 "Unfair methods of competition in commerce, and unfair or deceptive acts or practices in or affecting commerce, are declared unlawful." 15 U.S.C. § 45.

9 *See* National Consumer Law Center, Unfair and Deceptive Acts and Practices § 3.4.2.2 (6th ed. 2004).

In addition to the state attorney general, local prosecuting attorneys often have the ability to enforce the state's consumer protection statutes to the same degree as does the state attorney general. This ability, however, is exercised differently in different states. For example, several California district attorneys are vigorous enforcers of California's consumer protection laws. In contrast, the district and county attorneys in Texas rarely independently enforce Texas consumer protection laws.

Even in those cases in which the attorney general or local prosecuting agency has not been involved, the principles enunciated in the cases brought by the public agencies have been the cornerstone of many major private consumer protection actions.

Approximately thirty state attorneys general have the added ability to interpret their consumer protection statutes by way of rule making. Generally the requirements for rule making follow the dictates of each state's administrative procedures act. Certain consumer statutes provide that the attorney general's regulations have the force of law,[10] while others merely say that a violation of a regulation is prima facie evidence of a violation of the consumer protection act.[11]

Interestingly, while California and New York enjoy two of the most active attorneys general in enforcing their consumer protection laws, they are also among those states in which the attorney general has no rule-making authority. However, even in states where the attorney general lacks rule making authority, companies are often apprised of the attorney general's interpretation and enforcement policy on the consumer protection laws by virtue of business advisories and other less formal expressions of opinion and policy.

6.2.4 State Regulatory Board Consumer Protection

Many states also enforce consumer protection statutes through various administrative licensing boards, bureaus and departments that usually are under the control of the state's executive branch. They regulate a variety of industries, from insurance to utilities to auto repair. Although they are industry-specific, many of these agencies have laws and regulations similar in language.to the state's general statutes that prohibit untrue or misleading advertising or the use of unfair or deceptive trade practices. Most of these agencies have broad rule making authority that can supplement or expand on the general consumer protection laws. Courts interpreting these agencies' laws and regulations, because of the similarity in language to the state's general statutes, often rely on the interpretations that have been given to the general statutes.[12]

A third, but less common, type of state consumer protection comes in the form of a consumer protection agency, which has broad regulatory authority over companies that abuse consumers. Usually, a state consumer protection agency supplements, but does not supplant, the activities of the state attorney general.

6.2.5 Cooperating with a State Consumer Protection Agency

Consumer lawyers may well find it an advantage to enlist the aid of a state consumer protection official, whether the attorney general or another agency. The public assistance can either supplement the private representation or replace it completely.

One valuable form of assistance is the mediation function offered by virtually every state attorney general and consumer protection office. A lawyer may get a call from a consumer whose rights appear to have been abused but whose case may result in such a small amount of actual damages that it is not economically efficient to offer to represent the consumer on a contingent basis—and plainly abusive to suggest that the consumer pay a fee of $250 to resolve a $100 dispute. Referring this consumer to a state mediation office can provide the consumer the very realistic opportunity of some relief, at no cost. Referrals also make sense in the case of larger claims that involve an impecunious defendant.

In a similar vein, it may be a good idea to seek cooperation from a state official even if the private lawyer is planning to sue.[13] State laws often grant the state official advantages and powers that a private person, and his or her lawyer, do not have. Examples include the following:

1. The ability to sue for any false, misleading, or deceptive act or practice, not limited to the laundry list of specific types of illegality that many state UDAP laws contain. Thus, any act that the state official can convince a jury or judge is false, misleading, or deceptive is illegal and subject to sanctions.

2. A panoply of discovery devices that are available without filing suit, including the right to take depositions and to subpoena documents. For example, these laws often empower the attorney general to take depositions and to issue subpoenas *duces tecum*—all before filing suit. There is no requirement that the attorney general may have concluded that any particular company is violating the law—this provision usually allows discovery without a lawsuit as long as the attorney general has reason to believe that it is

10 *See* National Consumer Law Center, Unfair and Deceptive Acts and Practices § 3.4.4 (6th ed.2004 and Supp).

11 *Id.*

12 *See, e.g.*, Ford Dealers Ass'n v. Dept. of Motor Vehicles, 32 Cal. 3d 347 (1982); Jack Criswell Lincoln-Mercury Inc. v. Haith, 590 S.W.2d 616 (Tex. Civ. App. 1979).

13 *Consumer Action Handbook* lists the address and contact information for these various offices. It is published annually by the Consumer Information Center, U.S. General Services Administration, and available online at http://consumeraction.gov/caw_state_resources.shtml.

in the public interest to determine *whether or not* there is a UDAP violation. The purpose of this type of provision is to allow an attorney general, without taking the extremely public step of filing suit, to investigate and determine whether a company's acts are actually deceptive and/or whether it is in the public interest to file suit.

3. Available remedies that are often more effective than private damages. For example, an attorney general may be able to bring an action in the name of the state against a person to restrain any violation of the UDAP law without prior notice and without needing to identify any individual consumer who is harmed by the practice. The attorney general usually has the right to seek penalties and broad injunctive relief, in addition to restitution and damages for individual consumers.

Of course, as state officials are usually quick to emphasize, their role is to protect the public interest in general. Some, but not necessarily all, of the information obtained through these discovery processes may be statutorily confidential. And the state official may develop a different litigation strategy than the private lawyer, possibly to the exclusion of the private lawyer. Nonetheless, in many instances, cooperating with the state official may be the right thing to do.

Another method is to work with the state attorneys general on a consumer problem as a special attorney general for the particular case or group of cases. Many state attorneys general conducted tobacco litigation in this manner, with the special attorneys general compensated on a contingency-fee basis out of the common funds generated by the cases. The advantage for the consumer lawyer of becoming a special attorney general is that hr or she obtains the attorney general's investigatory and remedial powers.[14] The advantage to the attorney general is that the attorney general may undertake an enforcement action that he or she otherwise does not have the resources for. With the increasing use of arbitration clauses by retail merchants to avoid litigation and the rule of law, the special attorney general may proceed without regard to the arbitration clause as he or she is not a party to that contractual provision.[15]

6.3 Federal Government Consumer Protection

6.3.1 General

The prime force in federal consumer protection is the Federal Trade Commission (FTC), which has the mandate to protect American consumers from "unfair or deceptive acts or practices in or affecting commerce."[16] The FTC also has the duty to prohibit false advertising of food, drugs, devices, and cosmetics.[17]

The FTC has authority to bring an administrative proceeding or to seek judicially ordered injunctive relief. It can also seek penalties and restitution.

The FTC exercises its mandate through rule-making. It sometimes issues Trade Regulation Rules, which have the force and effect of law. The Rules regulate a variety of areas, including credit practices,[18] used car sales,[19] and the funeral industry.[20]

The FTC also issues policy statements, which are not themselves binding law but which reflect the FTC's interpretation of its authority. Policy statements also cover a variety of practices, including environmental marketing claims,[21] price advertising,[22] and the use of celebrity testimonials.[23]

Trade Regulation Rules, policy announcements, and other broad-based steps are reserved for industry-wide issues. The FTC also takes enforcement action against individual companies engaged in unfair or deceptive practices. These actions are as wide and varied as the imaginations of those who set out to cheat consumers.

Other federal agencies, such as the Federal Reserve Board with respect to Truth in Lending, regulate specific aspects of consumer protection at the federal level. However, for one-stop shopping for consumer protection, the FTC is the best bet.

6.3.2 Cooperating with the FTC

The FTC is a deliberate and usually slow-moving beast. It does not act willy-nilly or, in most instances, quickly. Unlike state consumer protection agencies, the FTC does not offer a formalized mediation process, although it does accept consumer complaints in writing or through its website, www.ftc.gov. Since the volume of complaints is one factor in the FTC's decision to pursue an investigation, it is often a good idea to send a copy of private complaints to the Consumer Protection Division of the FTC.

Unlike many state attorneys general and other state officials, the FTC conducts its investigations internally and in secret, making any flow of information a one-way street. The FTC will accept and consider anything a private lawyer or a consumer may offer but will not publicly or privately

14 *See* National Consumer Law Center, Unfair and Deceptive Acts and Practices Ch. 10 (6th ed. 2004 and Supp).

15 *See* National Consumer Law Center, Consumer Arbitration Agreements § 6.4.3 (4th ed. 2004).

16 15 U.S.C. § 45(a)(1).

17 15 U.S.C. § 53(a). The Food and Drug Act has similar authority over deceptive labels for food and drugs. *E.g.*, 21 U.S.C. § 341 *et seq.*

18 16 C.F.R. § 444.

19 16 C.F.R. § 455.

20 16 C.F.R. § 453. *See* National Consumer Law Center, Unfair and Deceptive Acts and Practices Ch. 5 (6th ed. 2004).

21 16 C.F.R. § 260.

22 16 C.F.R. § 233.

23 16 C.F.R. § 255.

comment on an investigation, discuss its activities, or even confirm whether or not a company is under investigation until it is ready to file a formal complaint or to announce that it has reached a settlement.

The FTC staff may be a great source of information once a complaint is filed. FTC staff may share information and insights about the defendant or the industry. When private and FTC litigation is proceeding against the same defendant, it is often in every party's interest to coordinate settlements in a way that provide the most consumer protection without conflicting or duplicative remedies.

6.4 Consumer Protection in Academia

Many, if not most, law schools operate clinical programs that provide legal representation, either through legal services or similar programs or through in-house legal clinics. Many of these clinical programs include consumer representation. The degree of representation differs at each law school. Some offer only advice. Some provide only administrative representation. Some provide full litigation representation for their clients.

For details about which schools have clinics, a good place to start is the Clinical Legal Education Association, which has its website at www.cleaweb.org.

Because the eligibility for representation is usually based on income, and because the number of clients in any program is relatively small, clinical programs will rarely offer an alternative to private lawyer representation, but they can provide additional resources and cooperative work on a common consumer problem.

Academic consumer protection can be passive as well as active, in the form of consumer law courses that teach law students about state and federal consumer protections and encourage the development of consumer protection specialization. Many law professors have taken leading positions in strengthening protections for consumers by providing the analytical framework for change,[24] the factual case for change,[25] or the legislative advocacy necessary to effect the change.

24 *E.g.*, D. Skeel, Jr., *Vern Countryman and the Path Of Progressive (and Populist)*, 113 Harvard L. Rev. 1075 (Mar. 2000); C. Mansfield, *The Road to Subprime "Hel" Was Paved with Good Congressional Intentions: Usury Deregulation and the Subprime Home Equity Loan Market*, 51 SCLR 473 (Spring 2000).

25 *E.g.*, Ian Ayres, *Fair Driving: Gender and Race Discrimination in Retail Car Negotiations*, 104 Harv. L. Rev. 817 (Feb. 1991); H. Sterling and P. Shragg, *Default Judgments Against Consumers: Has the System Failed?*, 67 Denver L. Rev. 357 (1990).

6.5 Working in Government and Academia

For the recent law graduate who is interested in developing a consumer protection specialization or the more experienced consumer lawyer who is looking for a change of pace, positions in government or academic consumer protection are worth serious consideration.

State attorneys general often have offices in the major metropolitan areas of the state, providing a choice of places to live and work. Other state consumer protection and regulatory agencies are usually based in the state capital. There may also be local consumer protection offices to consider.

Unfortunately, one of the by-products of a federalist society is that there is no central place to apply for positions or even to learn of their availability. The National Association of Attorneys General (750 First Street, NE, Suite 1100, Washington, DC 20002, 202-326-6000) often has information about assistant attorney general positions available in the various states. The office has a staff person assigned to consumer protection. Checking with the particular office may be the best course.

Similarly, the National Association of Consumer Agency Administrators (1010 Vermont Avenue, NW, Suite 514, Washington, DC 20005, 202-347-7395) may have information about jobs available at its member agencies.

The FTC does not have a great deal of turnover—and, thus, positions—but it does offer the opportunity to work at the primary consumer law enforcement agency. Although based in Washington, the FTC also has regional offices around the country in major cities, including New York, Chicago, Dallas, Atlanta, and San Francisco. The application process is very formalized. Jobs are usually posted with the Office of Personnel Management, and applications must use the Federal Standard Form 171.

Nothing, however, can substitute for actively beating the bushes by contacting each and every office and asking if positions are available or about to become available. Here is where networking can be invaluable, enabling one to learn of positions that may not even be publicly posted.

Looking for a position at a law school is in one way quite simple but in most ways somewhat particularized. Once a year, in the fall, all law schools conduct the "Faculty Recruitment Conference"—charmingly called "the Meat Market" by those attending. The Association of American Law Schools (AALS) (1201 Connecticut Avenue, NW, Suite 800, Washington, DC 20036, 202-296-8851) conducts the Faculty Recruitment Conference. Its website is www.aals.org.

A prerequisite to the Faculty Recruitment Conference is getting oneself listed in the online Faculty Appointments Register, which provides a brief resume of each person interested in law faculty jobs. The deadline for inclusion in the Register is in the late summer preceding the Faculty Recruitment Conference, and there is a fee of approximately $245.

Before the Faculty Recruitment Conference, a lawyer can read through the AALS Placement Bulletin—which contains positions for which each law school wishes to interview—and then contact each law school seeking an interview at the Faculty Recruitment Conference. The law school may respond by proposing an interview.

Anyone interested in applying for a position as law professor or clinician should take part in this process. A good article describing the process appears on the AALS website at www.aals.org/frs/index.html. It begins with the point that the teaching applicant should be able to intelligently express his or her commitment to teaching law before the first interview.

Aside from this process, there is also the more particularized method of contacting each school to learn of other positions it may have available. Some clinics hire staff attorneys, full- or part-time, to assist the clinical faculty in supervising the students, and they may well not interview for these positions at the Faculty Recruitment Conference.

Some law schools also employ practitioners as adjunct faculty to teach specialized courses, such as consumer law, that are not within the expertise or teaching desires of their regular faculty. An adjunct professor is not full-time, not tenure-tracked, and not usually well-paid. However, if one has the time or the inclination to teach for reasons other than remuneration, an adjunct position can be very fulfilling professionally. Virtually the only way to learn of the availability of these adjunct positions is through direct contact with the law school, usually through the law school's academic associate dean.

6.6 Conclusion

Consumer lawyers should not hesitate to use the resources of governmental consumer protection offices and law school clinics. Many clients whose cases are too small to warrant a contingent fee, or who can not afford even a small retainer, can often get all the help needed through these free or low-cost programs.

As a corollary, lawyers who want to do consumer protection work but do not want to go into private practice should consider both governmental and academic positions in addition to legal services jobs. Each offers unique and uniquely satisfying opportunities for consumer advocacy.

Chapter 7 Ethical Issues in the Practice of Consumer Law

By Robert Hobbs and Stephen Gardner

7.1 Introduction

This chapter is designed to alert the lawyer to ethical problems that can arise in a consumer law practice. It examines ways to reach out to potential clients, arrange fees with clients, and share office space resources with others. It also looks at the ethics of tape recording a witness's statement. This chapter focuses on the American Bar Association's model standards that are often the basis for state ethical rules. However, ethical rules for lawyers are determined at the state level, requiring careful research of local rules and rulings by the reader. Additional ethical issues involving class actions are discussed in § 24.4, *infra*, and issues involving undercover investigations in Chapter 27, *infra*.

7.2 Providing the Public Information About Your Consumer Law Practice

7.2.1 The ABA Ethical Rules on Lawyer Advertising and Outreach: Introduction

Before the twentieth century there were few limitations on how lawyers could advertise their availability to serve clients. "Lawyer advertising and solicitation were common and generally lawful in the Nineteenth Century. . . . The most renowned lawyer who advertised was . . . Abraham Lincoln. In addition to newspaper advertising, Lincoln wrote letters soliciting business from the railroads, which were among the wealthiest clients in central Illinois in the mid-1800s."[1]

But even then, except in the larger cities, a lawyer's reputation among colleagues at the bar, and among the townspeople, was usually the best way to become known as a competent attorney. And in cities the neighborhoods were in effect small towns, so the same ways of publicizing one's ability worked. Ethical rules relevant to all lawyers were not widely applied.

With the establishment of the American Bar Association (ABA) as a nationwide organization, the spread of lawyers from coast to coast, and the need for multi-state advice on legal problems, many ABA members felt that a written code of conduct would be appropriate. On August 27, 1908, the Association adopted its original canons (Canons of Professional Ethics). In 1969 the ABA revised the canons and replaced them with a model code (Model Code of Professional Responsibility), which was "adopted by the vast majority of state and federal jurisdictions." Both of these provided limitations on advertising by lawyers.

In 1977 the Supreme Court issued its opinion in *Bates v. State Bar of Arizona*,[2] holding that state bans on lawyer advertising were unconstitutional under the First Amendment but allowing the states to regulate lawyer advertising to the extent needed to protect consumers.

The ABA revised its rules within six weeks to address the unconstitutional aspects of its "Model Code of Professional Responsibility" and then reexamined the rules in depth between 1977 and 1982. The resulting revised "Model Rules of Professional Conduct"[3] was issued in 1983. A number of amendments to these rules have been adopted since. In 1998 the ABA's Commission on Advertising reexamined Rules 7.1, 7.2, and 7.3 in light of emerging technologies and published its findings in a White Paper.[4] In 2002, the ABA amended its rules on advertising and issued "Guidelines for Responsible Lawyer Advertising."

Some states have adopted the Model Rules; others tailored some of the rules to the state's needs. In 1990, Florida

1 ABA Commission on Advertising, A Re-Examination of the ABA Model Rules of Professional Conduct Pertaining to Client Development in Light of Emerging Technologies—A White Paper Presented for the Purpose of Discussion, 3 (July 1998) (citing David H. Donald, Lincoln (1996)), *available at* www.abanet.org/legalservices/clientdevelopment/ethicswhitepaper.html.

2 433 U.S. 350 (1977).

3 The model rules are published by the ABA. The model rule with some of the 2002 amendments were available at www.abanet.org/cpr/e2k-report_home.html.

4 The report is available at www.abanet.org/legalservices/clientdevelopment/ethicswhitepaper.html.

adopted a complete set of its own advertising rules, with greater controls on both advertising and solicitation.[5] The ABA website currently maintains a directory of states' rules on lawyer advertising.[6] While any lawyer should know the ABA position on ethical matters, it is essential to know the rules of the state or states where you practice.

7.2.2 ABA Rule 7: "Information About Legal Services"

7.2.2.1 Overview

Rule 7 has five parts that consider

1. the kinds of statements a lawyer may use to contact potential clients;
2. the communication techniques that may be used and the records that must be kept;
3. personal solicitation of potential clients;
4. fields of practice and certification; and
5. the firm's name and letterhead.

Each of these is discussed below. Check regularly for changes in your local court rules and integrated bar associations and also check for new court and bar association ethics opinions.

7.2.2.2 Rule 7.1: Communications Concerning a Lawyer's Services

Rule 7.1 covers all communications that a lawyer makes about his or her services, whether oral or written. The rule prohibits the lawyer from making "a false or misleading communication about the lawyer or the lawyer's services." The rule also states that a "communication is false or misleading if it contains a material misrepresentation of fact or law or omits a fact necessary to make the statement considered as a whole not materially misleading."

The ABA's Commentary to Rule 7.1 says advertisements about the results the lawyer has obtained for a client (such as damages, or the number of favorable verdicts, or client endorsements) would ordinarily violate the Rule by creating unjustified expectations unless the specific factual and legal circumstances of the successful case are detailed. The Commentary goes on to indicate that comparisons of results or fees with those of other lawyers may be deceptive if the comparison would lead to unjustified expectations or the comparison had not been substantiated. A disclaimer could avoid the possibility of deception.

7.2.2.3 Rule 7.2: Advertising

Rule 7.2(a) specifies that lawyers may generally advertise their services. The Commentary states that lawyers should be able to make their services known "through organized information campaigns . . ." to assist "the public's need to know about legal services." It recognizes this need as particularly acute in the case of persons of moderate means who have not made extensive use of legal services. The Commentary also notes that television is a powerful media to get information to the public, "particularly persons of low and moderate means." ABA amendments in 2002 made clear that advertising on the Internet and using e-mail are permissible.

ABA Rule 7.2(c) specifies that the advertisement include the name and office address of at least one lawyer or law firm. The commentary indicates that an advertisement may include "the lawyer's name or firm name, address and telephone number; the kinds of services the lawyer will undertake; the basis on which the lawyer's fees are determined, including prices for specific services and payment and credit arrangements; a lawyer's foreign language ability; names of references and, with their consent, names of clients regularly represented; and other information that might invite the attention of those seeking legal assistance."

ABA Rule 7.2(b) prohibits the lawyer from giving anything of value to anyone for recommending the lawyer's service, except that the lawyer can pay for advertisements, pay the regular membership fees of a qualified lawyer referral service, and buy a law practice under Rule 1.17. Although this Commentary does not discuss referral fee arrangements, this comment authorizes one lawyer to recommend another when the referring lawyer does not share in the fee.

7.2.2.4 Rule 7.3: Personal Contact with Prospective Clients

This rule about initiating personal contact with prospective clients with whom the lawyer has not had a prior relationship is **very strict**. ABA Rule 7.3(a) states that a lawyer may not, either in person, by telephone, or real-time electronic communication contact a possible client when the purpose is to get professional employment and "a significant motive for the lawyer's doing so is the lawyer's pecuniary gain." ABA Rule 7.3(b) prohibits contacts if the prospective client has let the lawyer know that she or he does not want to be solicited or if the solicitation "involves coercion, duress or harassment."

ABA Rule 7.3(c) adds the requirement that the words "Advertising Material" must appear on the outside of the envelope in the case of letters. For recorded and electronic messages, these words must be included as part of both the beginning and the end of the message. This disclosure is

5 Florida Rules of Professional Conduct, Chapter 4 (2002). *See also* The Florida Bar: Petition to Amend the Rules Regulating the Florida Bar—Advertising Issues, 571 So. 2d 451 (Fla. 1991).

6 The directory is available at www.abanet.org/legalservices/clientdevelopment/adrules.html.

required when dealing with individuals whom the lawyer knows need legal assistance but with whom the lawyer has had no prior family or professional relationship. The Commentary also says that Part (c) "does not apply to communications sent in response to requests of potential clients or their spokespersons or sponsors" or to general announcements such as "changes in personnel or office location."

ABA Rule 7.3(d), like the Commentary to Rule 7.2(c), provides an exception from Rule 7.3 for prepaid or group legal services not owned or controlled by the lawyer. And the Commentary states that none of Rule 7.3 is "intended to prohibit a lawyer from contacting the representatives of organizations or groups that may be interested in establishing a group or prepaid legal plan." The Commentary continues, however, with detailed limits on how the lawyer and such organization may interact.

7.2.2.5 Rule 7.4: Communication of Fields of Practice

ABA Rule 7.4(a) states that a lawyer "may communicate the fact that the lawyer does or does not practice in particular fields of law." For those who practice consumer law, observance of this Rule is particularly important. The Commentary states that subject to Rule 7.1's prohibition of "false and misleading" statements, a lawyer who practices in one or more fields may say that she or he is a specialist or specializes in a particular area of law. Because the label of specialist suggests a level of expertise, a lawyer starting to concentrate on consumer cases or a type of consumer case would be better off describing his or her field of practice as limited to or focused on those types of cases but should not indicate that he or she is a specialist until some experience has been in obtained in those cases.

ABA Rule 7.4(d) provides that a lawyer shall not state or imply that a lawyer is certified as a specialist in a particular field of law unless certified by the state bar or ABA.[7]

7.2.2.6 Rule 7.5: Firm Names and Letterheads

The guiding principle of ABA Rule 7.5 is: Thou shalt not make false or misleading statements. A lawyer in private practice may use a trade name (for example, ABC Legal Clinic), so long as that name complies with Rule 7.1 and does not imply any connection with a government agency or public or charitable legal service organization. To help multi-state firms, ABA Rule 7.5(b) permits the use of the same firm name in different states, but the letterhead and other sources (such as Martindale-Hubbell) must indicate which lawyers are **not** admitted to practice in the state where the office is located. ABA Rule 7.5(c) prohibits a firm from using, as part of its name, the name of a lawyer "holding public office . . . during any substantial period" when the lawyer is not "actively and regularly practicing with the firm." ABA Rule 7.5(d) states: "Lawyers may state or imply that they practice in a partnership or other organization only when that is the fact." The Commentary says that lawyers who share office facilities, but not the responsibility for each other as partners, can not call themselves "Smith and Jones."[8]

7.3 Consumer Education Through Public Speaking, the Press, and the Radio

Lawyers are encouraged to provide information to the public about their individual legal rights and responsibilities.[9] This should not be done in a way that gives individual legal advice, solicits clients face to face, overstates the speaker's legal qualifications, or is otherwise deceptive.[10] Within those constraints, a lawyer may offer his speaking services to organizations, talk appropriately about her qualifications, and offer that someone who asks about their own legal problem may benefit from the advice of counsel.

One bar suggests the following to its members who engage in public speaking:

- To avoid giving individual advice, it would be prudent for the lawyer to advise the attendees that the lawyer's discussion in regard to questions will be general and not intended as individual advice for specific problems. In addition, it may be helpful for the attorney to remind the attendees not to divulge confidential information.
- To avoid improper solicitation, a lawyer conducting or speaking at a legal seminar must refrain from making statements or suggestions that the seminar attendees should seek the attorney's counsel. However, the attorney may make a general statement to the attendees regarding his or her availability, including his or her telephone number, address, and whether the lawyer provides free initial consultation.[11]

A lawyer participating in a radio talk show about legal issues should be extremely careful not to impart individual advice.[12]

---

7 The American Bar Association has not certified any organizations in the field of consumer law. Some state bars, such as Texas, have done so.

8 See § 7.4.4, *infra*, for additional discussion of this topic.

9 *See* Utah State Bar Ethics Advisory Op. Comm. Op. No. 98-15 (Jan. 29, 1999).

10 *See* Ohio Formal and Informal Op. 94-13 (Dec. 2, 1994).

11 *Id.*

12 S.C. Bar Advisory Op. 94-27 (Jan. 1995).

7.4 Office Organization

7.4.1 General

The organization and operation of the lawyer's office raises certain liability and ethical issues that should be kept in mind by those who practice consumer law. The lawyer may become responsible for the actions of employees and associates as the office grows unless specific steps are taken to limit responsibility for each other. If a relationship is established with another lawyer, care must be used to ensure that the ethical and legal responsibilities arising from the relationship are those intended. ABA Rule 5, "Law Firms and Associations," requires lawyers in various relationships to take steps to ensure each other's compliance with the Rules of Professional Conduct. Associated attorneys also must be concerned about whether the rules of conflicts and confidentiality apply as if they were a partnership.

7.4.2 The Sole Practitioner

While the first two parts of ABA Rule 5 apply to a lawyer who practices in a law firm, Rule 5.3 applies to office staff and requires them to be supervised to ensure compliance with the lawyer's ethical obligations. The lawyer is responsible for the ethical violations of his employee that he knows about or ratifies. Once the lawyer has other lawyers who work for her—either as subordinates or in the same office facilities when cases are referred within the office or if the lawyer refers a case to another lawyer—Rule 5.1 requiring each lawyer to be responsible for the ethics of the other may become applicable.

7.4.3 Partnerships

ABA Rule 5.1 requires a partner or other supervising lawyer to ensure that other lawyers in the organization abide by the Rules of Professional Conduct. Conversely, Rule 5.2 requires the subordinate to comply with the Rules except in certain cases in which the supervisor determines that the action does not violate the Rules. Rule 7.5 specifically regulates the use of a firm name, like "Smith & Jones," that indicates a partnership.

7.4.4 Office Sharing or the "Professional Association"

Many law offices are not partnerships but share facilities, personnel, or both. Each lawyer may have his or her own office, but two lawyers may share the services of a secretary or legal assistant, and everyone uses a common library. In some cases, a common telephone number is used. These affiliations are also subject to Rule 7.5 on firm names. Local ethical rulings may start with the premise that the public may be misled if associated lawyers who are not partners do not take steps to disclose that they are not responsible for each other as if they are partners. In all office-sharing arrangements, insurance against malpractice and other kinds of liability (for example, if a client slips during a visit) should be a major consideration. One article[13] suggests that, to avoid partnership by estoppel, attorneys in an association should implement the following measures:

- each lawyer in an office-sharing arrangement should use his own stationary, business cards, and telephone number;
- each lawyer in the association should write a letter to every other lawyer in the association stating that she does not consent to any attorney in the association holding herself out as a partner and that she should not do so;
- if an attorney is being assisted in the matter by another attorney, he should seek client consent, stating the capacity in which the other attorney is assisting and that the other attorney is not a partner;
- place a sign in the reception area stating the attorneys share space, but are not partners;
- the lawyers in the office should not refer to each other as partners;
- the lawyers should not have common bank accounts and liability insurance;
- the lawyers should minimize the extent to which they work together on cases and cover cases for each other;
- bills should indicate they come from the individual attorneys and not refer to or mention other attorneys in the association or the association itself; and
- to the extent more than one attorney works on a matter, each should send out separate bills.

Use of the term "professional association" alone may not avoid partnership by estoppel. The Massachusetts [ethics] Committee has declined to opine on whether that term is deceptive when used to describe lawyers who are not partners. However, it has stated that the term is ambiguous and may imply a partnership.[14] The Massachusetts Appeals Court seized upon this opinion to state "that the use of the term 'professional association' may well suggest a partnership to the public which is unlikely to distinguish among partnerships, professional corporations, and professional associations."[15]

13 George C. Rockas, *Lawyers for Hire and Associations of Lawyers: Arrangements That Are Changing the Way Law Is Practiced*, 40 Boston Bar J. 8 (Nov./Dec. 1996).

14 MBA Op. 85-2 (1985).

15 Atlas Tack Corp. v. Dimasi, 37 Mass. App. Ct. 66, 637 N.E.2d 230 (1994).

7.5 Referrals

Frequently, a firm will refer a matter to a lawyer who specializes in a particular field of law. Those who practice consumer law are often the recipients of such referrals (for example, when a consumer who is represented by a bankruptcy attorney is referred to a consumer law attorney). Again, the Rules imposing responsibility on one lawyer for the ethical behavior of the other may apply, even though the lawyers may be miles apart. One particular problem that could arise is when the referral is from a lawyer in a different state that has different rules of conduct. The lawyers in such a situation may be responsible for complying with the rules of both states.[16]

ABA Rule 1.5(e) applies to division of fees when the lawyers are not in the same firm. It has these requirements:

- The fee is divided proportionately to the services provided by each lawyer, unless each lawyer assumes joint responsibility for the representation.
- The client agrees to the arrangement in writing, including the share of each lawyer.
- The total fee is reasonable.

This rule liberalized the many states' former prohibitions on referral fees, although a handful of states have retained their prohibitions on referral fees.[17] A sample co-counseling agreement based on the liberalized rule is included in Appendix A.3, *infra*, and on the companion CD-Rom to this volume.

7.6 Fee Agreements and Disclosures

7.6.1 Fees Must Be Reasonable

The fundamental rule for fee agreements is provided by ABA Rule 1.5(a), which states that a lawyer's fee and expenses may not be unreasonable.[18] The prior requirement that fees be reasonable may still be the rule in many states.[19] Rule 1.5(a) contains eight parts covering the factors that determine whether a fee is reasonable; Rule 1.5(b) deals with the need to advise the client about how fees are determined; Rules 1.5(c) and (d) address contingent fees; and Rule 1.5(d), which is discussed in § 4.5, *supra*, covers dividing fees with a lawyer not in the same firm.

16 *See* ABA Rule 5.5(b).

17 *See* Murray H. Gibson, Jr., *Attorney-Brokering: An Ethical Analysis of the Model Rules of Professional Conduct and Individual State Rules Which Allow This Practice*, 19 J. Legal Prof. 323 (1995) (the article cites Colorado, Hawaii, and Wyoming among the states banning referral fees).

18 "A lawyer shall not make an agreement for, charge, or collect an unreasonable fee or an unreasonable amount for expenses." ABA Rule 1.5: (a).

19 *See* www.law.cornell.edu/ethics/comparative.

7.6.2 Factors in Determining a "Reasonable Fee"

ABA Rule 1.5(a) lists the factors that should be considered in deciding whether a fee is reasonable. Most of these factors, in one form or another, have been included in most codes of conduct over the years:

- Time and labor required
- Novelty and difficulty of the questions involved
- The skills needed to perform this legal service properly
- Whether accepting this specific matter will preclude the lawyer from accepting other employment and this factor is apparent to the client
- Fees usually charged for similar services in the community
- The amount involved
- The results obtained
- Time limitations imposed by the client
- Time limitations imposed by circumstances of the matter
- Nature and length of the professional relationship with the client
- The lawyer's experience
- The lawyer's reputation
- The lawyer's ability
- Whether the fee is fixed or contingent

7.6.3 Agreement on Fees

The lawyer and the client should agree on how the lawyer's fee will be determined, whether the client is to pay anything in advance as a retainer or toward costs, when payments are due during the representation, and any credit arrangements. The Commentary to Rule 1.5 prohibits any agreement that might "induce" the lawyer to curtail his or her services to the client or to perform services in a way that is contrary to the client's interests. It also cautions against using wasteful procedures in an hourly-rate fee agreement. Clearly the lawyer can not do things that are against the Rules, even when the client wants them done.[20]

The Commentary to Rule 1.5 also states that the agreement should not limit the service a lawyer provides unless the limitation is clearly explained to the client. The lawyer should not agree to provide partial services for an hourly fee if the partial services do not meet the client's needs. But the Commentary does approve, as proper, the definition of the "extent of services in light of the client's ability to pay."

20 *See* ABA Rule 1.2(e).

7.6.4 Need for Written Agreement

If there is a contingent-fee agreement, the fee agreement must be in writing and signed by the client.[21] While the Rule does not demand that there be a written fee agreement in other cases, ABA Rule 1.5(b) requires the lawyer who has not represented a client regularly to communicate the fee basis to the client before or shortly after beginning legal services and preferably in writing. As a practical matter, a written fee agreement with **all** clients, agreed to before the representation begins, is a wise move; it avoids misunderstandings at a later date, especially if the client does not win. It is required in some jurisdictions. If the client may be subject to paying the alternative minimum tax on the recovery of attorney fees and/or damages in the case, notice to seek expert tax advice regarding this potential tax liability, discussed in Chapter 20, *infra*, should be written.

7.6.5 Contingent Fees Must Be Reasonable

Most consumer lawyers depend upon contingent-fee agreements with their clients. The general rule of ethics is that there may be a contingent-fee agreement that depends on the outcome of the matter except in certain domestic and criminal types of representation. The Commentary notes that, if the lawyer has any doubt about the contingent fee being in the client's best interest, he or she should offer alternative ways of setting and paying the fee and should explain the implications of each method.

The contingent-fee agreement must

- state how the fee is to be determined;
- spell out the percentage(s) that the lawyer earns if:
  —the matter is settled, or
  —there is a trial, and
  —there is an appeal;
- state what litigation and other expenses are deducted from the recovery; and
- state whether deductible expenses are deducted **before** or **after** the contingent fee is calculated.

ABA Rule 1.5(c) requires that, when the contingent-fee matter is concluded, the lawyer shall provide the client with a written statement that

- states how the matter turned out and,
- if there is a recovery,
  —the amount remitted to the client and
  —how this amount was determined.

Contingent-fee agreements are often critical to providing consumers access to representation in the legal system. This is often because the cost of representation will likely exceed the amount of fees paid by the defendant pursuant to a court award or settlement. In most situations, contingent fees are necessary because the consumer can not afford to pay legal fees out of their income. Most private consumer attorneys obtain most of their fees on a contingent basis. Some may charge an hourly fee for initial consultations because of the drain on resources that consultations may become; others do not, particularly at the beginning of their practice, or may charge a reduced rate for consultation.

On the other hand, some consumer lawyers are able to require payment of their hourly fees as they accrue and maintain a practice they find satisfying. Clients who are able to pay fees as they accrue are likely to have higher incomes, limiting the type of case that the attorney pursues. Some of the largest punitive damage and class action claims have involved lower-income clients with a claim against a retailer that was targeting lower-income consumers.

The amount of the contingent fee must be reasonable in light of the factors enumerated in Rule 1.5. If the client's claim does not involve any novelty or other risk, some state ethical rulings in other contexts have indicated that a contingent-fee agreement would not be appropriate. However, if a contingent fee is necessary because the client can not afford to pay a fee until there is a recovery, the better approach in a very low-risk case may be to provide in the retainer agreement that the amount of fees will be determined by the actual time reasonably spent on the case at a reasonable hourly rate. Because of potential fact disputes, collectability problems, and unpredictable bona-fide-error and other defenses available in consumer litigation, very few consumer cases are likely to be truly low risk.

While fee-shifting statutes provide increased access to lawyers for consumers, the attorney fee awards are often insufficient in themselves in providing for sufficient remuneration to ensure a continuing law practice. Fee-shifting claims must be addressed in contingent-fee agreements so that it is assured that the attorney will not violate ethical rules prohibiting the splitting of an attorney fee.[22] Stressing the freedom of clients to contract with the attorneys, the Supreme Court held that a $406,000 contingent fee (40% of the total recovery) that exceeded the $117,000 lodestar fee determined by the court was permissible and not inconsistent with the federal civil rights statute's fee-shifting policies.[23] While the Supreme Court did not rule on ethical

21 ABA Rule 1.5(b). Sample retainer forms may be found in Appendix A, *infra*, and on the companion CD-Rom to this volume.

22 *Cf.* Stair v. Turtzo, Spry, Sbrocchi, Faul & Labarre, 564 Pa. 305, 768 A.2d 299 (2001) (client's claim to two-thirds of attorney fee award in a employment discrimination action should not have been dismissed when the retainer agreement ambiguously provided that the attorney fee was 33% of the recovery and the only recovery was the attorney fee; fee-splitting was not addressed).

23 Venegas v. Mitchell, 495 U.S. 82 (1990). *See also* Gobert v. Williams, 323 F.3d 1099 (5th Cir. 2003) (in an employment

issues, other courts have allowed contingent fees in claims involving a fee-shifting statute.[24] Some courts have approved of the fee agreement providing the greater of the loadstar award or a percentage contingent fee but have disallowed fee agreements for both a contingency and the loadstar award.[25]

Law review articles examining the reasonableness of contingent-fee agreements point out that the review of those agreements by the courts is infrequent; the courts often analyze the reasonableness of the fee, not based on the time of retainer but from the time of settlement or judgment, exercising hindsight to reduce the fee but not to increase it; courts often give little deference to the agreement represented in the retainer agreement.[26] This suggests that the consumer attorney may need to consider the reasonableness of the fee at both junctures. However, for an attorney to be successful in a practice requires substantial fees to cover not only the expenses in that case but also the expenses in cases in which recovery is not possible because the merits turn out to be not strong enough or the defendant's bank accounts are empty.

When the consumer action involves a class action with recovery of attorney fees from a common fund, the normal percentage used is 20% to 30%,[27] with 40% to 50% being the upper limit.[28] Smaller percentages are on occasion used in cases involving very large funds.[29]

---

discrimination case, 35% of the recovery plus the court-awarded attorney fees was not unreasonable under the employment act, following *Venegas*).

24 *See, e.g.*, Cambridge Trust Co. v. Hanify & King, P.C., 721 N.E.2d 1 (Mass. 1999) (in a fee disagreement between a commercial client with a UDAP claim and its lawyer, the court upheld the lawyer's claim that it was ethically and contractually entitled to a fee of about 30% of the combined compensatory damages ($2,032,301) and the lodestar fee award ($409,200) less some expenses and credits; client argued this was excessive); Luna v. Gillingham, 57 Wash. App. 574, 789 P.2d 801 (1990) (when retainer ambiguously provided that the attorney fee was to be calculated on the "gross recovery," clients entitled to the fee-shifting award being treated as a credit to their contingent fee rather than as a part of the gross recovery).

25 *See, e.g.*, Laster v. Cole, 2000 U.S. Dist. LEXIS 8672, 2000 WL 863463 (E.D.N.Y. June 23, 2000) ($200 per hour was a reasonable rate and $5490 a reasonable fee for the case, but the retainer agreement that the client would pay 50% of the recovery to the attorney provided double payment and the attorney fee was reduced by the $100 the consumer was to pay out of the recovery); State *ex rel.* Okla. Bar Ass'n v. Weeks, 969 P.2d 347 (Okla.), *cert. denied*, 525 U.S. 1042 (1998) (fee agreement in a civil rights employment discrimination case provided for fees of 50% of the recovery plus any lodestar fees; held to be unreasonable, providing for recovery of "dual" fees; attorneys claimed that, because of the likelihood of low damages in an employment discrimination case and the failure of the courts to award adequate loadstars, the fee of $20,000 for the contingency plus $23,417 lodestar negotiated with the defendant was necessary to sustain civil rights representation; court responded that the greater of the two should be sufficient or the attorneys would have to pursue a change in policy by the federal courts or Congress).

26 *See* J. Perillo, *The Law of Lawyers' Contacts Is Different*, 67 Fordham L. Rev. 443 (1998); T. Schneyer, *Legal Process Constraints on the Regulation of Lawyers' Contingent Fee Contracts*, 47 DePaul L. Rev. 371 (1998). *See also* Gisbrecht v. Barnhart 535 U.S. 789 (2002) (court should start with the fee provided by the retainer and can measure its presumptive reasonableness against the value of the services provided); Bandura v. Orkin Exterminating Co., 865 F.2d 816 (7th Cir. 1988) (30% contingent fee reasonable in a UDAP case, but 50% contingent fee if case appealed was admitted to be excessive given the total damages of $625,000).

27 In *Paul, Johnson, Alston & Hunt v. Graulty*, 886 F.2d 268, 272 (9th Cir. 1989), the Ninth Circuit held that a trial court could use the "percentage" method as well as the "lodestar," noting "with approval that one court has concluded that the 'bench mark' percentage for the fee award should be 25 percent." In *Bebchick v. Washington Metropolitan Area Transit Commission*, 805 F.2d 396, 406–07 (D.C. Cir. 1986), the District of Columbia Circuit Court of Appeals held that, "[w]here the fees, as here, will come out of a 'common fund,' 'a reasonable fee is based on a percentage of the fund bestowed on the class.' " (citation omitted) The court held that 25% was "a reasonable percentage for otherwise uncompensated attorneys."

On remand in *Harman v. Lyphomed*, 945 F.2d 969 (7th Cir. 1991), a federal district court in Chicago awarded 20% of the $9.9 million settlement fund to counsel. 787 F. Supp. 772 (N.D. Ill. 1992). In *Camden I Condominium Association, Inc. v. Dunkle*, 946 F.2d 768, 774–75 (11th Cir. 1991), the court stated that "[t]he majority of common fund fee awards fall between 20% to 30% of the fund" and that "district courts are beginning to view the median of this 20% to 30% range, i.e., 25%, as a 'bench mark.' " *See also In re* Workers' Compensation Ins. Antitrust Litig., 771 F. Supp. 284 (D. Minn. 1991) (awarding 22.5% of the more than $50,000,000 recovery); *In re* Businessland Secs. Litig., 1991 U.S. Dist. LEXIS 8962, [1991] Fed. Sec. L. Rptr. (CCH) ¶ 96,059 (N.D. Cal. June 18, 1991) (awarding a 30% fee); Sanders v. Robinson Humphrey/Am. Express, Inc., 1990 U.S. Dist. LEXIS 11492, [1990 Transfer Binder] Fed. Sec. L. Rep. (CCH) ¶ 95,315 (N.D. Ga. May 23, 1990) (awarding 30% of $16.84 million settlement fund); Lubliner v. Maxtor Corp., 1990 U.S. Dist. LEXIS 3930 (N.D. Cal. 1990) (30% fee award); *In re* Activision Secs. Litig., 723 F. Supp. 1373, 1378 (N.D. Cal. 1989) ("in class action common fund cases the better practice is to set a percentage fee and that, absent extraordinary circumstances . . . the rate should be set at 30%"); Mashburn v. Nat'l Healthcare, Inc., 684 F. Supp. 679, 692 (M.D. Ala. 1988) ("The majority of common fund fee awards fall between 20% to 30% of the fund"); *In re* Warner Communications Secs. Litig., 618 F. Supp. 735, 749–50 (S.D.N.Y. 1985) ("[t]raditionally, courts in this Circuit and elsewhere have awarded fees in the 20%–50% range in class actions").

28 Both "lodestar" and "percentage" cases have awarded fees in the higher range. *See, e.g., In re* Ampicillin Antitrust Litig., 526 F. Supp. 494 (D.D.C. 1981) (45%); Clark v. Cameron-Brown Co., 1981 U.S. Dist. LEXIS 12824, [1981] Fed. Sec. L. Rptr. (CCH) ¶ 98.014 (M.D.N.C. Apr. 6, 1981) (30% of $3 million settlement fund) (lodestar).

29 In *Brown v. Phillips Petroleum Co.*, 838 F.2d 451, 454, 456 (10th Cir.), *cert. denied*, 488 U.S. 822 (1988), the Tenth Circuit approved a trial court's award of a flat 16.5% of a $75 million "common fund" class action recovery, giving weight to "the amount involved and the results obtained."

The majority of federal courts today endorse awarding a percentage of the benefit to the class, with some adjustment for the amount of effort spent. The Eleventh Circuit and the District of Columbia Circuit have held that use of the percentage method is mandatory in common fund cases.[30] The Ninth[31] and Tenth[32] Circuits have indicated a preference for use of the percentage method. The Seventh Circuit has endorsed the percentage approach,[33] but some decisions can be read as leaving the selection between the percentage and lodestar method up to the discretion of the district judge, reviewable only for abuse.[34] The First,[35] Sixth,[36] and Eighth[37] Circuits have stated that use of the percentage method is now permitted. The Fifth Circuit continues to use the "lodestar."[38] The Third[39] and Second Circuits[40] purport to authorize a percentage award but "encourage" the district court to "cross-check" it against a lodestar, a hybrid methodology which preserves the worst features of the lodestar calculation.

30 Swedish Hosp. Corp. v. Shalala, 1 F.3d 1261, 1265–71 (D.C. Cir. 1993); Camden I Condo. Ass'n v. Dunkle, 946 F.2d 768–74 (11th Cir. 1991).

31 Hanlon v. Chrysler Corp., 150 F.3d 1011 (9th Cir. 1998) (district court's choice of methodology is reviewed for abuse of discretion); Six Mexican Workers v. Ariz. Citrus Growers, 904 F.2d 1301 (9th Cir. 1990); Paul, Johnson, Alston & Hunt v. Graulty, 886 F.2d 268 (9th Cir. 1989).

32 Gottlieb v. Barry, 43 F.3d 474 (10th Cir. 1994) (percentage of the fund method preferred in common fund cases, but either method permissible); Brown v. Phillips Petroleum Co., 838 F.2d 451, 454 (10th Cir. 1988).

33 *In re* Cont'l Ill. Secs. Litig., 962 F.2d 566 (7th Cir. 1992).

34 Cook v. Niedert, 142 F.3d 1004, 1011–12 (7th Cir. 1998); Florin v. Nationsbank of Ga., 34 F.3d 560 (7th Cir. 1994) (the decision whether to use a percentage method or a lodestar method remains in the discretion of the district court).

35 *In re* Thirteen Appeals Arising Out of the San Juan DuPont Plaza Hotel Fire Litig., 56 F.3d 295, 307 (1st Cir. 1995).

36 Rawlings v. Prudential-Bache Properties, Inc., 9 F.3d 513, 516 (6th Cir. 1993).

37 Johnston v. Comerica Mortgage Corp., 83 F.3d 241 (8th Cir. 1996) (it is within the discretion of the district court to choose which method to apply).

38 Longden v. Sunderman, 979 F.2d 1095, 1099 (5th Cir. 1992) ("This circuit utilizes the 'lodestar method' to calculate attorneys' fees"); Strong v. BellSouth Telecommunications Inc., 137 F.3d 844, 850 (5th Cir. 1998) (same).

39 *In re* Rite Aid Corp. Sec. Litig., 396 F.3d 294 (3rd Cir. 2005); *In re* Prudential Ins. Co. Am. Sales Litig., 148 F.3d 283 (3d Cir. 1998) (percentage of recovery method favored in cases involving a common fund, while lodestar method used when nature of recovery does not allow determination of the settlement's monetary value; second method should be used to cross-check initial fee calculation).

40 Wal-Mart Stores, Inc. v. VISA U.S.A., Inc., 396 F.3d 96 (2d Cir. 2005); Goldberger v. Integrated Resources, Inc., 209 F.3d 43 (2d Cir. 2000) (noting wasteful and inefficient aspects of lodestar approach, but concluding that district courts may use either approach).

7.6.6 Fee Dispute Resolution

ABA Rule 1.5 does not have any provisions on resolving fee disputes. However, the Rule's Commentary says that, when an alternative dispute resolution procedure has been established by the bar, the lawyer(s) should consider submitting the dispute to such procedure when it is voluntary.

In some states, an attorney who is terminated in a contingent fee case without good cause may be entitled to recover the value of her services from the former client.[41] When a prior counsel has been discharged, the new attorney should clearly provide in his retainer who is to pay the prior attorney, the client or the new attorney, with the new attorney responsible in the absence of another clear agreement.[42] A client may sue the lawyer for taking a fee in excess of the reasonable value of the legal services provided.[43] A lawyer may not ethically report the non-payment of a fee to a credit reporting agency in some states.[44]

7.7 The Client's Authorization to Sue as a Class Representative

After identifying a case as a potential class action, discuss with the client the possibility of bringing the suit on behalf of a class.[45] Spend sufficient time explaining the class device and the duties of the class representative so that the client understands the implications of bringing a class action instead of an individual one. Even an unsophisticated client can usually understand that a class action may be appropriate when a business has injured a group of people in the same general manner. The client should be advised whether or not counsel would be willing to undertake the case on an individual basis and, if so, on what terms.[46]

41 *E.g.*, Universal Acupuncture Pain Servs., P.C. v. Quadrino & Schwartz, P.C., 370 F.3d 259 (2d Cir. 2004) (applying N.Y. law) (entitled to fee even before client's claim recovered).

42 *E.g.*, Malonis v. Harrington, 442 Mass. 692, 816 N.E.2d 115 (2004).

43 *E.g.*, Monday v. Robert J. Anderson, P.C., 77 P.3d 855 (Colo. App. 2003) (former client failed to prove that the reasonable value of her former attorney's services settling a car accident claim was less than the $33,000 contingent fee charged based on 33% of the award).

44 *E.g.*, Op. 04-20 Md. State Bar Ass'n. Comm. on Ethics, 20 ABA/BNA Law. Manual on Prof'l Conduct 361 (June 14, 2004) (credit report would violate lawyer's confidentiality requirement.).

45 *See also* Chapter 24, *infra* (Consumer Class Actions).

46 A private attorney would not take a case in which the named plaintiff's personal claim is only a few hundred dollars except on a class basis. There is nothing wrong with informing a client that counsel will undertake the case only on a class basis, if this is in fact the case. Even for larger individual claims, a private attorney might have to charge a percentage contingency or retainer so large in relation to the size of the claim that non-class litigation would not be feasible.

It is also necessary to explain any negative aspects of filing the client's case as a class. If it is likely that a particular class action might take longer than an individual action[47] or that the plaintiff might have to be present in court at trial, the possibilities should be explained to the client. The need for appearances for depositions and for court approval of any settlement should be explained. The plaintiff should be made aware that, once a class action is filed, the plaintiff can not ordinarily settle individually. On the other hand, if the case is successful, it may be possible for the class representative to obtain compensation for the time and effort incurred in acting as the representative.[48]

This conversation should take place on the client's first office visit or as soon thereafter as possible. Good communication with the client at the initial stage of representation will effect the development of an appropriate attorney-client relationship and later allow the client, at deposition, to recall authorizing the case to be filed as a class action. This latter point is important to impress on the client because defendants will often attack the clients' adequacy of representation with deposition questions regarding their authorization of the case as a class action.

The client should be given a full explanation of the class representative's duties and obligations. Clients who have suffered monetary damages or who have had substantial problems with a company are often eager to take up the class "banner" to help others who were harmed because of the same practice. However, the client must understand the role and obligations of the class representative.

When a client agrees to file the case as a class action, it is very important that the client sign an authorization form that includes the following disclosures:

(1) The client is authorizing the attorney to file a class action if the attorney's investigation discloses that a class action is appropriate.
(2) Costs (court filing and service costs, deposition costs, and the costs of sending the class notice) will be advanced. If applicable, clients should be told that they are ultimately liable for all or for a pro rata share of these costs, in the event that the defendant wins the case.[49] The ABA Model Rules of Professional Conduct authorize attorneys to advance litigation costs, the repayment by clients of which may be contingent on the outcome of the matter.[50] The Model Rules also allow a lawyer representing an indigent client to pay court costs and expenses of litigation on behalf of the client.[51] While these American Bar Association Model Rules are adopted widely, practitioners should be careful to ascertain whether rules of ethics in their state still require the named plaintiff to be ultimately responsible for costs.
(3) The attorney will seek an award of fees to be paid by the defendant or from the class recovery if the suit is successful in obtaining either a judgment or settlement. The right to fees should be the attorney's, and the client should assign them to the attorney as consideration for being represented.[52] It may be desirable to provide that the client agrees not to waive these fees as a condition for settlement. This subject is discussed in more detail in National Consumer Law Center, *Consumer Class Actions: A Practical Litigation Guide* Ch. 15 (5th ed. 2002 and Supp.).
(4) The client agrees to cooperate by appearing at deposition and trial, providing documents upon request, and remaining in touch with counsel. In addition, the client should agree to notify the attorney if he or she considers seeking relief under the bankruptcy laws, which may divest the client of the claim.
(5) If the client is contributing toward fees or expenses, this should be spelled out. If the client's contribution is to be paid in the future, the consequences of non-payment should be stated.

A sample authorization form is contained in Appendix A, *infra*, and on the companion CD-Rom to this volume.

7.8 Trial Publicity

ABA Rule 3.6 limits the statements that a lawyer[53] may make about pending case. The rule seeks to strike a balance

47 Frequently this is *not* the case because a defendant has a much greater incentive to resolve in a timely manner a class action rather than an individual one.

48 *See* National Consumer Law Center, Consumer Class Actions: A Practical Litigation Guide § 11.8 (5th ed. 2002).

49 When the named plaintiff can not afford to repay costs, most states now allow that costs may be advanced by counsel and that the attorneys may even assume ultimate responsibility for the costs if there is no recovery in the litigation. Brame v. Ray Bills Fin. Corp., 85 F.R.D. 568 (N.D.N.Y. 1979); Am. Bar Ass'n, Model Code of Prof'l Responsibility and Code of Judicial Conduct, Disciplinary Rule 5-103(b) (1980); Am. Bar Ass'n, Model Rules of Prof'l Conduct and Code of Judicial Conduct, Rule 1.8(e) (1983); Am. Bar Ass'n, Comm. on Ethics and Prof'l Responsibility, Informal Op. 1361 (1976). A number of federal courts have held that Rule 23 permits class counsel to advance fees and costs irrespective of state law to the contrary. *See* National Consumer Law Center, Consumer Class Actions: A Practical Litigation Guide § 9.4.3 (5th ed. 2002).

50 Am. Bar Ass'n, Model Rules of Prof'l Conduct and Code of Judicial Conduct § 1.8(e).

51 *Id. See also* Brame v. Ray Bills Fin. Corp., 85 F.R.D. 568 (N.D.N.Y. 1979) (attorneys for non-profit organization have no financial stake in case's outcome, so no ethical violation in advancing costs, repayment contingent on a successful outcome); Am. Bar Ass'n, Comm. on Prof'l Ethics, Informal Op. 1361 (1976).

52 If the defendant is notified of such an assignment, any attempt by the client to waive the attorney's right to fees without the consent of the attorney is ineffective. Zeisler v. Neese, 24 F.3d 1000 (7th Cir. 1994).

53 A lawyer may not need to be associated with the case to be subject to this stricture. *See* Conn. Bar Ass'n, Comm. on Prof'l Ethics Informal Op. 99-3 (Jan. 11, 1999).

between the right to free speech and the right to a free trial.[54]

The Commentary to the Rule states:

> It is difficult to strike a balance between protecting the right to a fair trial and safeguarding the right of free expression. Preserving the right to a fair trial necessarily entails some curtailment of the information that may be disseminated about a party prior to trial, particularly where trial by jury is involved. If there were no such limits, the result would be the practical nullification of the protective effect of the rules of forensic decorum and the exclusionary rules of evidence. On the other hand, there are vital social interests served by the free dissemination of information about events having legal consequences and about legal proceedings themselves. . . . It also has a legitimate interest in the conduct of judicial proceedings, particularly in matters of general public concern. Furthermore, the subject matter of legal proceedings is often of direct significance in debate and deliberation over questions of public policy.[55]

The primary standard in the ABA Rule 3.6a provides:

> A lawyer . . . shall not make an extrajudicial statement that the lawyer knows or reasonably should know will be disseminated by means of public communication if the lawyer knows or reasonably should know that it will have a substantial likelihood of materially prejudicing an adjudicative proceeding.

The Commentary to ABA Rule 3.6 gives examples of statements that would fall within this stricture. They include statements about the credibility of witnesses, the nature of the evidence, evidence that would be inadmissible, and criminal charges against a defendant without a statement that the charges are only accusations and the defendant is presumed innocent until found guilty. These examples do not necessarily apply to civil cases in which there may not be a jury involved.

ABA Rule 3.6(b) gives examples of statements a lawyer may make about a case or investigation:

> Notwithstanding paragraphs (a) and (b) (1–5), a lawyer involved in the investigation or litigation of a matter may state without elaboration:
> (1) the general nature of the claim or defense;
> (2) the information contained in a public record;
> (3) that an investigation of the matter is in progress, including the general scope of the investigation, the offense or claim or defense involved and, except when prohibited by law, the identity of the persons involved;
> (4) the scheduling or result of any step in litigation;
> (5) a request for assistance in obtaining evidence and information necessary thereto;
> (6) a warning of danger concerning the behavior of a person involved, when there is reason to believe that there exists the likelihood of substantial harm to an individual or to the public interest . . . .[56]

There is broad press interest in consumer cases. In any given week, there is usually at least one consumer story included in television news magazines like *20/20* and *60 Minutes*. Publicity of consumer cases serves the important goal of educating the public about consumer frauds so that others can be wary of similar schemes. Publicity can also inform public policy debate over consumer protection laws and remedies. For example, there is public criticism—sometimes justified and sometimes not—of high punitive damage and attorney fee awards. However, the availability of any legal representation for complex consumer cases usually depends on the availability of attractive punitive damages or attorney fees. The model rules and state ethical standards require counsel to be careful when discussing a pending case or investigation with the press.[57]

7.9 Agreements Not to Represent Future Clients Against a Business Are Unethical

Some defense counsel may attempt to condition a settlement on the consumer lawyer's agreement not to sue the defendant again on behalf of another client. This offer must be strongly rejected because it is clearly unethical.

ABA Model Rules of Professional Conduct, Rule 5.6(b), prohibits an "agreement in which a restriction on the lawyer's right to practice is part of the settlement of a controversy between private parties." The commentary to ABA Rule 5.6(b) explains:

> The rationale of the Model Rule 5.6 is clear. First, permitting such agreements restricts the access of the public to lawyers who, by virtue of their background and experience, might be the very

---

54 *See* Gentile v. State Bar of Nev., 501 U.S. 1030 (1991) (Nevada equivalent of Rule 3.6 valid on its face, but unconstitutionally applied to discipline a lawyer's statements critical of the police department and the prosecutor).

55 Commentary to Rule 3.6, ABA Model Rules of Prof'l Conduct (2002).

56 Rule 3.6(c), ABA Model Rules of Prof'l Conduct (2002).

57 A related issue arises from protective orders and confidentiality agreements sought by defendants in consumer cases. *See* Chapter 18, *infra* (" 'Come Out With Your Hands Up!'—Trade Secrets, Protective Orders and the Smoking Gun"). Another good source of information on protective orders and confidentiality agreements is the Trial Lawyers for Public Justice in Washington, D.C. *See* www.tlpj.org.

> best available talent to represent these individuals. . . . Second, the use of such agreements may provide clients with rewards that bear less relationship to the merits of their claims than they do to the desire of the defendant to "buy off" plaintiff's counsel. Third, the offering of such restrictive agreements places the plaintiff's lawyer in a situation where there is conflict between the interests of present clients and those of future clients.

This rule has been adopted widely by the states.[58] It is probably a violation of the ethics rules for the defense counsel to make this offer, since it constitutes a request that the consumer lawyer act unethically. The best approach is to advise defense counsel that what they ask is unethical and allow them to withdraw the offer.

7.10 Communicating with a Defendant's Employees

If a defendant is a large company, it is often desirable to contact the employees of that defendant—either before a lawsuit or after filing—to learn what the defendant is up to. This usually arises from one of two motivations: (1) a wish to obtain testimony that can be used to impeach the defendant's official position or even to improve your own case or (2) a plan to use a tester or investigator to obtain independent proof of the defendant's practices.

The initial ethical consideration is the same in either context. However, because the use of testers or investigators involves additional considerations, it will be covered separately in § 7.12, *infra*. The guidepost is the ABA Rules of Professional Conduct Rule 4.2:

> Rule 4.2. Communication with Person Represented by Counsel
>
> In representing a client, a lawyer shall not communicate about the subject of the representation with a party the lawyer knows to be represented by another lawyer in the matter, unless the lawyer has the consent of the other lawyer or is authorized to do so by law or a court order.

Thus, if you want to contact an employee of a company before suit is filed and with no knowledge that the company has counsel, then you are essentially free to do so.

Note also that the rule provides that you can not contact someone whom you know is represented by a lawyer "regarding that subject" about which you are contacting them. This means that you are not precluded from contacting a company just because you recall that the company was represented in another matter at a time in the past. However, if the company has a general counsel, you should assume that the company is "represented by another lawyer regarding that subject," as long as the subject involves the company's activity.

But all is not lost. Comment 7 to ABA Rule 4.2 also defines what it is to communicate with the company:

> [7] In the case of a represented organization, this Rule prohibits communications with a constituent of the organization who supervises, directs or regularly consults with the organization's lawyer concerning the matter or has authority to obligate the organization with respect to the matter or whose act or omission in connection with the matter may be imputed to the organization for purposes of civil or criminal liability. Consent of the organization's lawyer is not required for communication with a former constituent. If a constituent of the organization is represented in the matter by his or her own counsel, the consent by that counsel to a communication will be sufficient for purposes of this Rule. *Compare* Rule 3.4(f). In communicating with a current or former constituent of an organization, a lawyer must not use methods of obtaining evidence that violate the legal rights of the organization.[59]

First, do not call management. This is an easy one. The commentary to the rule prohibits "communications with a constituent of the organization who supervises, directs or regularly consults with the organization's lawyer concerning the matter or has authority to obligate the organization with respect to the matter."[60]

But in some states you can usually contact a non-management employee, with the exception noted below.[61] The Rule does not prohibit "interviewing a potential witness,

58 *E.g.*, Ala. Rules of Prof'l Conduct Rule 5.6(b); Alaska Rules of Prof'l Conduct Rule 5.6(b); Ariz. Rules of Prof'l Conduct Rule 5.6(b); Ark. Rules of Prof'l Conduct Rule 5.6(b).

59 *Cf.* Tex. Disciplinary Rule of Prof'l Conduct R. 4.02(c):

> For the purpose of this rule, "organization or entity of government" includes: (1) those persons presently having a ***managerial responsibility*** with an organization or entity of government that relates to the subject of the representation, or (2) those persons presently employed by such organization or entity and ***whose act or omission in connection with the subject of representation may make the organization or entity of government vicariously liable*** for such act or omission . . .

(emphases added)

60 *See, e.g.*, Midwest Motor Sports v. Arctic Sales, Inc., 347 F.3d 693 (8th Cir. 2003) (tape recordings of managerial employee excluded as unethically obtained); Tex. Ethics Op. 474 (June 1991). All Texas ethics opinions may be reviewed at the Internet site maintained by the University of Houston, www.law.uh.edu/ethics/Opinions/ethicssubjectindexb.html.

61 See Ch. 27, *infra*, discussing the wide variation in state and federal court interpretations and the choice-of-law issues on this point, with some courts allowing almost no employee contacts and others allowing contacts with any employee not involved in

other than a party to the suit, even though such witness may be an employee of a party to the suit, where such attorney makes a full disclosure of his connection with litigation and explains the purpose the interview."[62]

The one sticky area is if you want to contact the employee who is in fact the cause of the problem to your client. Comment 7 to Rule 4.2 prohibits contact with an employee "whose act or omission in connection with the matter may be imputed to the organization for purposes of civil or criminal liability" One court has applied this to prohibit contact with an employee to obtain admissions against the interest of the employer, although the court noted a division of authority on this point.[63] This would almost certainly prohibit seeking to create vicarious liability of the corporation by contacting an employee. But one ethics opinion seems to take it further, prohibiting contact if the conduct by the employee is "the subject of the controversy."[64] The best practice here is to avoid that type of contact.

7.11 Taping Telephone Calls

If the client wants to sue but additional evidence regarding liability is needed, the lawyer and client should explore various means of obtaining it. In states where it is not considered criminal eavesdropping, evidence of the deceptive or illegal practice and of the client's credibility might be obtained by tape recording a call between your client and the prospective defendant.

The FCC ruled some years ago that a consumer's tape recording, without the beep tones ordinarily required by telephone company tariffs, was not a violation of telephone tariffs; the tape was admissible evidence before the FCC and should have been considered by the telephone company. The company had denied being abusive in the telephone conversation and had sought to suppress the recording.[65] The tape recording revealed abusive language.

However, state criminal eavesdropping statutes may also prohibit tape recording of a telephone conversation without the consent of all parties.[66]

A law review article found that it was legal in thirty-six states for one party to a phone conversation to secretly tape the conversation.[67] Even in states where recording without consent or warning "beeps" is illegal, the consumer might call to explain his or her inability to pay, to announce retention of counsel, or to respond to a dunning letter and take notes of that conversation. The client should keep paper and pen by the telephone and take notes of future collection calls. As an alternative to secret recording, the client may set up tape recording equipment and inform the debt collector that he or she is taping the call.

In states where such tape recording is illegal, it is unethical for a lawyer to make or use secret recordings.[68] If you live in a state where secret recording is legal, is it ethical for you to ask your client to tape future calls?

The answer depends on the state you are in.

There is a long line of opinions holding that it is unethical for a lawyer to record telephone conversations without telling the other party simply because it looks sleazy or, in the words of ethics mavens, fails to avoid the appearance of impropriety or is deceptive because it is not expected.

The granddaddy of these opinions was ABA Opinion 337 (1974)[69] which held that recording without consent was

management or in the actions creating the company's alleged liability.

62 Tex. Ethics Op. 17 (Dec. 1948).

63 Midwest Motor Sports v. Arctic Sales, Inc., 347 F.3d 693 (8th Cir. 2003).

64 Tex. Ethics Op. 461.

65 Maller v. New England Tel. & Tel. Co., 44 F.C.C.2d 614 (1973). *See also* United States v. Lihman, 421 F.2d 981 (2d Cir.), *cert. denied*, 400 U.S. 991 (1970) (tape recording of a telephone conversation by the victim of a swindler found admissible in a criminal fraud prosecution).

66 *E.g.*, Mass. Gen. L. Ann. ch. 272, § 99 (1968). *See* Commonwealth v. Hyde, 434 Mass. 594, 750 N.E.2d 963 (2001) (no exception to criminal eavesdropping when one party to the conversation consents to taping); C. Bast, *What's Bugging You? Inconsistencies and Irrationalities of the Law of Eavesdropping*, 47 DePaul L. Rev. 837, 868–881 (1998) (listing state laws allowing one-party consent to taping); www.rcfp.org/taping (summarizing each state's law on taping conversations). *See also* Bartnicki v. Vopper, 532 U.S. 514 (2001) (criminal prosecution of journalist for publishing illegally recorded private, but newsworthy, conversation violated First Amendment free speech protections when an unknown third party intercepted the call and anonymously gave it to the journalist; the interceptor would be criminally responsible).

67 C. Bast, *What's Bugging You? Inconsistencies and Irrationalities of the Law of Eavesdropping*, 47 DePaul L. Rev. 837, 868–881 (1998) (listing Alabama, Alaska, Arkansas, Arizona, Colorado, District of Columbia, Georgia, Hawaii, Idaho, Indiana, Iowa, Kansas, Kentucky, Louisiana, Maine, Minnesota, Mississippi, Missouri, Nebraska, Nevada, New Jersey, New Mexico, New York, North Carolina, North Dakota, Ohio, Oklahoma, Rhode Island, South Carolina, Tennessee, Texas, Utah, Virginia, West Virginia, Wisconsin, and Wyoming as allowing one-party taping). *See also* Or. Rev. Stat. § 165.540 (may permit person at home to record telephone calls).

68 *See* N.C. State Bar Ass'n Op. 192 (Jan. 13, 1995) (lawyer may not listen to a client's illegal tape recording); Ct. Bar Ass'n Informal Op. 94-30 (Oct. 19, 1994); State *ex. rel.* Neb. State Bar Ass'n v. Schleich, No. 5-97-1214 (Neb. 1998) (repentant lawyer suspended for six months for illegally taping wife's phone conversation prior to instituting divorce). *But cf.* Bar Counsel v. Curry (Ma. Board of Bar Overseers May 11, 2005) (Special Hearing Officer's Report) (not unethical for Massachusetts counsel to set up a meeting to secretly record a conversation with another Massachusetts lawyer in New York, a one-party consent state; Massachusetts is a two-party consent state; Massachusetts counsel's use of the ruse that they were interviewing the former judge's clerk for a job was unethical when counsel was actually trying to uncover improprieties by the judge for whom the lawyer had clerked), *available at* www.mass.gov/obcbbo/ccd.pdf.

69 ABA Formal Op. 337 (1985). *See also* Nissan Motor Co., Ltd. v. Nissan Computer Corp., 180 F. Supp. 2d 1089 (C.D. Cal.

conduct involving fraud, dishonesty, or misrepresentation that is prohibited by Rule 8.04(a):

> A lawyer shall not: . . . (3) engage in conduct involving dishonesty, fraud, deceit or misrepresentation . . . .

However, in 2001, the ABA reversed itself and held, in Opinion 01-422, that "the mere act of secretly but lawfully recording a conversation inherently is not deceitful." The 2001 opinion takes the position that the non-consensual tape recording of a conversation to which the recording attorney is a party is not unethical if it is lawful in that state and the recording attorney does not falsely deny that the conversation is being recorded. An increasing number of states' ethics opinions had already held it ethical to tape record without the other party's consent in states where it is legal, including Hawaii,[70] Maine,[71] Mississippi,[72] New York,[73] Oklahoma,[74] and Oregon.[75] The 2001 opinion was influenced by those decisions.

The ABA noted that many states disagree with this new position of the ABA, but the opinion is likely to result in more states adopting the new ABA position.[76]

The next question is: Can a lawyer get around any prohibition by having the client do the taping? The answer to this is easy: NO, NO, NO. A lawyer can never have the client do something that it would be unethical for the lawyer to do. As noted in Texas Ethics Opinion 514:

> An attorney, however, may not circumvent his or her ethical obligations by requesting that clients secretly record conversations to which the attorney is a party. Under these circumstances, the attorney would be ethically required to advise the other parties of the electronic recording, in advance. An attorney may not solicit the aid of his or her clients to undertake an action that the attorney is ethically prohibited from undertaking. (*See* DR 8.04 (a)(1) (discussing violations of the disciplinary rules through the acts of others).)

But that same ethics opinion also provides:

> This brings the committee to the issue of whether an attorney can ethically advise a client to electronically record a telephone conversation to which the client is a party, without first informing all other parties involved. Both Texas and federal law permit a party to a conversation to tape record that conversation without first informing the other parties that the conversation is being recorded. (*See* 18 U.S.C. § 2511 (2)(d); Tex. Penal Code Ann. (Vernon 1986).) An attorney is required to provide his or her client with both an accurate statement of the law, and an honest opinion of the consequences likely to result from a particular course of conduct. (*See* Comment 7 to DR 1.02.) Hence, ***an attorney may advise his or her client that both Texas and federal law permit the client to electronically record conversations without first informing the other parties involved, where the equities of the situation merit such advice.***

Tex. Ethics Op. 514 (emphasis added). The Bar giveth and the Bar taketh away. After saying you can not get a client to do something you are ethically prohibited from doing, the Opinion seems to say you can tell the client what she or he could do and let them move forward with a nudge and a wink.

If you are going to tape record, you should bear in mind how courts react. Some courts have allowed at least the limited evidentiary use of a secretly obtained tape recording[77] while others have refused to allow its use even if their refusal may have helped perpetuate a fraud.[78] Two cases illustrate this antipathy:

2002) (taping of opposing counsel without consent would be criminal and unethical and enjoined).

70 Haw. Op. 30 (July 27, 1995) (not per se unethical when legal, but must be made and used in an ethical way).

71 Me. Prof'l Ethics Comm. Op. 168, 14 Me. Bar J. 132 (Mar. 9, 1999).

72 Attorney M v. Miss. Bar, 621 So. 2d 220 (Miss. 1992) (attorney's call to treating physician was explicitly involving a malpractice claim putting the doctor on notice that his statement was for potential re-publication, therefore no deceit was involved in the tape recording of the conversation, and action for unethical conduct was dismissed). *See Propriety of Attorney's Surreptitious Sound Recording of Statements By Others Who Are Or May Become Involved in Litigation*, 32 A.L.R.5th 715.

73 N.Y. County Ethics Op. 696 (1993) (invalidated prior contrary opinion).

74 Okla. Bar Ass'n Op. 307 (Mar. 5, 1994) (lawyer must disclose recording if asked to avoid deceit).

75 Or. State Bar Op. 1991-74 (may record phone conversation if it is legal to do so; may not secretly tape record an in-person conversation).

76 *See Minn. Lawyers Professional Responsibility Board Repeals Its Opinion #18 That Prohibited Secret Tape Recording*, *at* www.courts.state.mn.us/lprb/fc060302.html (Apr. 18, 2002).

77 *See also* 20th Century Wear, Inc. v. Sanmark-Stardust Inc., 747 F.2d 81 (2d Cir. 1984) (unethically obtained secret tape recording admissible to refresh witnesses recollection to promote the truth-finding process); Koller by and Through Koller v. Richardson-Merrell, 737 F.2d 1038 (D.C. Cir. 1984), *vacated on other grounds*, 472 U.S. 424 (1985) (unethical secret tape recording of witness was not misconduct that would disqualify *pro hac vice* counsel, as taping was motivated by desire to get at the truth), *rev'd on other grounds*, 472 U.S. 424 (1984).

78 *See* Iowa S. Ct. Bd. of Prof'l Ethics and Conduct v. Plumb, No. 91/95-1852 (Iowa 1996) (taping private conversation with magistrate was unethical even if done to record threats of false accusation of drug dealing). *See also* Parrot v. Wilson, 707 F.2d 1262 (11th Cir. 1983) (any work product privilege that may have applied to a taped conversation was lost because of the unethical secret tape recording), *cert. denied*, 464 U.S. 936 (1983); Meacham v. Outdoor World Corp., 12 ABA/BNA Lawyers Manual on Prof'l Conduct 443 (N.Y. Sup. Ct. Nov. 27, 1996)

> ***Secretly taped interviews with witnesses are considered unethical***, see *Chapman & Cole*, 865 F.2d at 686, ***and do damage to that system, regardless of whether the attorney or the client operates the tape recorder***. See *Otto*, 177 F.R.D. at 701. Combining this disruption of the system with the inherent unfairness of allowing one party to use the tapes to further their case while preventing the other party from doing the same requires the Court's conclusion. See *Pfeifer*, 1997 WL 276085, at *3. Work product protection, therefore, is not available for the secretly recorded tapes in this case.

Smith v. WNA Carthage, L.L.C., 200 F.R.D. 576, 579 (E.D. Tex. 2001) (emphasis added).

> We also observe that an Ethics Opinion concerning an attorney's obligation to inform all parties before tape recording a conversation was published during the same month as this recording occurred. *See* 59 Texas Bar Journal 181 (Ethics Opinion 514) (Feb. 1996). ***We emphasize that Ethics Opinion 514 is a legally binding part of Rule 8.04(a)(3), supra, and is applicable to all attorneys licensed in this state.***

McWhorter v. Sheller, 993 S.W.2d 781 (Tex. App.—Houston [14 Dist.] 1999) (emphasis added).

For another court's opinion, *see Mena v. Key Food Stores Co-Op.*, 195 Misc. 2d 402, 758 N.Y.S.2d 246 (Sup. Ct. Kings Co. 2003). In *Mena*, the court stated that "[c]ontemporary ethical opinions hold that *a lawyer may secretly record telephone conversations* with third parties without violating ethical strictures *so long as the law of the jurisdiction permits such conduct*." *Id.* at 406, 758 N.Y.S.2d at 248 (citing American Bar Association Formal Ethics Opinion 01-422 (2001), and New York County Lawyers' Association on Professional Ethics, Opinion No. 696 (1993) [emphases added]). The *Mena* court further explained that "the attorney's conduct, even had it involved more hands on participation than it actually did, should not be subject to condemnation under the disciplinary rules and does not warrant the *extreme sanction* of *suppression* [of the tape] or [the attorney's] *disqualification*." *Id.* at 407, 758 N.Y.S.2d at 250 (emphases added).

All of this suggests that a victim's tape recording of an abusive telephone call may either be admissible evidence or may reveal the victim's violation of a state criminal eavesdropping statute, depending on the state law. However, an attorney may be engaging in unethical conduct if he or she tape records an abusive phone call without consent of all the parties, regardless of the state criminal laws.

Because of the criminal and ethical constraints on surreptitious tape recordings of telephone conversations, lawyers should proceed very cautiously, carefully researching local ethical and criminal standards. A lawyer may not advise a client to engage in criminal conduct. A lawyer who does so may incur criminal responsibility for the crime. If surreptitious tape recording is unethical for the lawyer but legal for others, a lawyer advising a client on the subject must avoid even an appearance of impropriety.

Some abusive companies may be so hardened to their own tactics as to give consent to their phone conversation being taped by the consumer. Moreover, some companies will admit to routinely tape recording their own calls without using a beep tone, and their own recording may be available evidence of an abusive telephone call. Also, some companies leave messages on the consumer's telephone answering machine. On such occasions the client should be instructed to bring to the attorney the tape containing the company's message in order that it may be preserved as evidence.

There are numerous other possibilities for corroborating abusive phone calls, although leg work is often required. Corroborating evidence may be obtained in the following ways:

- Have a reliable third person call the company to get the company's explanation of the calls may confirm the client's version of their content.
- Other victims of the company's telephone practices may be located through their complaints to a Better Business Bureau, an attorney general's office, or other consumer complaint office.
- A former employee of the company may be able to confirm the company's telephone practices.[79]
- Companies routinely maintain logs of their contacts, although most are not so callous or foolish to enter evidence of their abuse, for example, noting a late-night phone call or a call to a neighbor.[80]

7.12 Using Undercover Testers or Investigators

Sometimes it may be necessary to send an investigator or tester to a prospective defendant in order to obtain documentation of what the defendant is up to. When this author was with the Texas Attorney General, he used undercover investigators extensively because, in his experience, if the investigators showed up at Defendant's door and said, "Hello, we're investigators with the Texas Attorney General. Would you mind telling me whether you are engaged in the widespread screwing of your customers?," they were not likely to get a true picture of things. Similarly, a private

(disqualified class counsel for secretly taping adverse party's phone call).

79 Turnover is often high among debt collection employees.

80 *See* National Consumer Law Center, Fair Debt Collection § 2.4.5 (5th ed. 2004 and Supp.).

attorney may want to test a prospective client's story or simply obtain additional information on the prospective defendant.

Step One, of course, is whether it is ethical to contact the defendant by talking to its employees, as discussed above. If it is ethical, go to Step Two. Step Two is whether it is lawful to have the tester tape the conversation. As discussed above, it is probably just fine. Step Three is the actual visit. While it is true that an accurately recorded undercover visit with an unsuspecting weasel can be very probative, it is also true that the act itself may look somewhat sleazy. This is the primary consideration before using a tester—or at least using a tester for anything other than a work product that will not be disclosed.

For considerations regarding the use of undercover testers and investigators, see Chapter 27, *infra* ("The Use of Testers and Investigators in Civil Litigation," by Professor David Hricik of the Mercer University School of Law).[81]

7.13 Conclusion

This chapter has just scratched the surface of the interplay between ethical and practical considerations that is part of being a consumer lawyer. However, the issues covered here are (1) the ones most likely to arise and (2) good examples of how one can be an effective and ethical advocate for consumers.

81 Consumer & Personal Rights Litigation Newsletter, Vol. VIII, No. 3 (ABA Section of Litig., Summer 2003). Professor Hricik also maintains an Internet site on ethical issues that is an excellent source, www.hricik.com/business.html.

Chapter 8

Fifty Ways to Lose a Winner, or, "Kids! Don't Try This at Home!"*

By Bernard Brown, Cary Flitter, Stephen Gardner, Bryan Kemnitzer, Laura McDowall, and Janet Varnell

8.1 Introduction

We have organized into four areas the following fifty stupid things at least one of us has done:

Triage: Mistakes to avoid when considering a lawsuit

Trial: Mistakes to avoid during a lawsuit

Practical: Mistakes to avoid just about any time

Personal: Mistakes to avoid all the time

We hope our stupidity contributes to your wisdom.

8.2 Triage: Mistakes to Avoid When Considering a Lawsuit

But I like a big, fat complaint. Do you really need twelve causes of action? What is your case really about? There may be a myriad of different causes of action you can dream up, but which will win the case? Which ones might be thrown out on demurrer or motion for summary judgment, or which might you decide you need to get rid of at trial? Which of those causes of action are going to go to the jury or the trier of fact? For each one that is taken out during litigation, the defendants are going to claim victory. Sometimes the KISS principle is the best strategy: Keep It Simple, Stupid.

Talking directly to a prospective defendant—BAD MOVE. Don't do it! I actually had two cases in my early years of practice in which defendants in depositions swore the very same lie: that I had promised them we wouldn't sue them. (Neither ended up having the nerve to try repeating those lies when it came time for trial, fortunately.) Look, we're going after people who committed outright fraud in many instances. It can be no surprise if they fabricate lies about our conversations. And it can put you in a terrible position—it can make you and your conduct merely the red herring issue that they want for a distraction in the case, obviously without respect to the merits. It can make you close to being a witness in the case. So the best way to handle this threat is prevention—don't talk with them. In some cases you may want to have a legal assistant talk with them, but even that must be done very carefully, for the above reasons as well as ethical ones.[1]

When going on a journey, it always is a good idea to check your map. A business plan is like a map. The biggest and most frequent mistake I make is failing to look at and follow my business plan everyday. I am amazed at the lawyers who operate without any written business plan at all. I have had one in place for eight years and it has undergone very little revision. I have a summary of my plan on a dry erase board that hangs on my office wall, and I try to look at it every day so I can focus on what makes my business work in making day-to-day decisions about what cases to take and how to prioritize my daily efforts and those of my employees. I owe any success I have enjoyed to our ability to work in accordance with our business plan. Nearly every significant problem I have had in my law practice can be traced to my failure to act in accordance with the business plan.

Don't be a hog. As plaintiff lawyers, we are taught to take the "kitchen sink" approach to litigation, meaning that we tend to throw everything but the kitchen sink into our complaint. Yet, compromising simplicity in favor of breadth often can unnecessarily complicate the case you are trying to prove. I have a multitude of examples in which I caused myself undue headache by trying to prove claims that did not suit my facts, but I can count on one hand the times that I wished I had included additional claims. Similarly, do you really need to handle everything that the company ever did

* Not copyrighted, since the authors do not assert that anything herein constitutes intellectual property. Some of the points are discussed in the first person singular, but we do not identify the person who first identified each point because (1) we don't want to single out anyone for abuse and (2) we can't really remember the source.

1 See §§ 7.10, *supra*, and 27.3, *infra*, regarding the ethics of interviewing employees.

wrong to anyone at any time in this one case? I now try to remind myself that an elephant is best eaten one bite at a time.

Speaking of hogs, don't go back to the trough right after you have been fed. I learned the hard way that we can not ignore the basic psychological reluctance that a defendant or its counsel will develop to "feeding" (that is, paying) the same plaintiff lawyers and their clients twice when there is little time between feedings. We learn so much about a company, its practices, and the legal claims in any given case that the natural result is for us to turn right around and sue it again. It seems like a good idea at the time, but I discovered that you set yourself up for an unfair fight for yourself and your client simply because the defense feels targeted and that you, personally, are the terrorist. Why not translate what you learn in a given case and then look around for the last defendant's competitor who may be engaged in a similar practice? You will find that you can use the information gained in a positive way and the former defendant will respect you for leveling the playing field enough that its resistance will be lessened the next time you do sue it.

Want to hear about my great new theory? How many new, innovative cases are you able to take at one time? We like to think we are on the cutting edge of consumer litigation and bring various cases that are innovative in protecting consumers. But if they're innovative for us, they're very innovative for the defense attorneys and the judges. There may not be any law on the issues, and new law will have to be decided and is expensive. This is not to say that you should not raise innovative legal arguments. We encourage that but not in every case. Make sure you have a number of tried and true cases that will help pay for the practice and keep you in practice.

Don't put all your eggs in one basket. I have sued financial advisors for failing to diversify a client's portfolio when the obvious risk associated with having too much of one good thing cost them their life savings. From time to time, I forget that I need to have both bread and butter and some gravy too. Legislation or developing case law can wipe your plate clean in one fell swoop if you fail to put enough irons in the fire.

Have you ever done hard time?, or, Fool me twice, shame on me. I learned at my extremely nice client's deposition that he had been confined to prison for approximately half his life. You don't need a jailhouse lawyer for a client if you can help it. I had to settle extremely cheaply mid-stream, when the client called to warn me that I might be reading about him in the newspaper and that he was headed back to the Big House.

It's a great case! Really! *Really. Really*? In my earlier years of practice I lapsed—as many attorneys do—into talking myself into how good a case was. I would talk to people I was working with on the case, and we would all agree with each other how right we were. This was, I now think, exactly the wrong thing to do. You miss the problems because you're not really looking for them. I work extra hard now at finding every possible fault in a case, both before taking the case and as it proceeds. I love to talk with people of a conservative bent who know nothing of the case, describe to them the facts in as plain and non-plaintiff-oriented a way as possible, and hear all their thoughts. I love to hear from the defense attorneys everything they think is wrong with the case. I love to listen to their side during mediations. The last thing you want is to have the jury or judge tell you about the problems in the case that you just didn't catch through ideological preoccupation, lack of diligence, or simple lack of perspective.

How many lawyers does it take to screw in a light bulb? In the beginning of my career, I was often lured into what some call copycat litigation. In filing the case, I either knew there were already similar cases on file or that, given the nature of the case, other cases surely would follow. With the constantly evolving creativity of the corporateers in our capitalist economy, there will always be plenty of wrongdoing to go around. It was and continues to be a mistake to get into those situations because you always end up wasting time, talent, and money in a nasty cannibalistic effort to protect your own cornbread and beans. It makes us all look bad and, while you are busy fighting with your own kind, sneaky, thieving corporations are running amok! I conclude that it is much better to make your own pie and eat it rather than spending your time arguing about how big a slice of the communal pie you deserve.

I'll show that stupid defense lawyer! It's all about principle. Do not take and fight cases simply because you do not like the defense attorney and want to prove something. And, likewise, be careful of the company that wants to teach you a lesson. A multi-state car dealer decided it was paying too much money to us on cases, so it hired an attorney to fight us on every case, on every issue, and make it extremely expensive for us to proceed with litigation. If this is going to happen, you better make sure you have a good case. You better make sure that you have the right forum. And you better make sure that you can afford to fully litigate the case.

Inflate client expectations too much and the bubble WILL burst. Salespeople understand this. Happiness for any particular client often has very little to do with how high a recovery is compared with recoveries in similar cases. I've started with clients who called our office wondering if they could just get at least a price break on the rebuilt wreck they bought and ended up thinking that, if they didn't get $200,000, they were going to be upset. By contrast, I normally have clients who start out with similarly low expectations and, at the end of the case, are very pleasantly surprised by the results we get for them (even with relatively modest results). Do you want happy clients? (Let me answer that for you—you really want happy clients.) Then work right away from the beginning—before you take the case or sign the contract—to make sure their expectations are low enough that you will be able to make them happy. If they have expectations that are too high, don't take the case. And keep their expectations in the right place throughout the case.

Oh, boy! I get to challenge an arbitration provision! We have all faced arbitration provisions, though initially we put our heads in the sand and thought it would never happen to us. We currently have three cases involving arbitration, two of which we have won at the trial level and one that is pending.[2] Our fees for those three cases are close to $1,000,000 and we haven't done much discovery, if any. Unless you are TLPJ or some non-profit that obtains money from other sources, you can not stay in business simply fighting arbitration clauses.

It's okay, my client's a jerk, but he's got a great case. We have made more mistakes by taking cases for clients who are difficult, if not impossible. The fact that such a potential client might have a good—or even a very good—case does not justify taking the case. The difficult client who turns out to be a nightmare for you probably was a nightmare for the defendant, and the defendant may have a number of stories about your client's behavior that will reduce the value of your case. If your client is not nice, the fact that the law, technically, may be on your side might become irrelevant.

But I like being up in the mountains! Where do you want this case to be tried and heard? Keep in mind that most cases settle. Who is going to be your judge hearing law and motions? Who is the judge hearing the discovery issues? You definitely don't want to do what we did with a case involving theft etching devices, when we argued the devices were actually insurance. We filed in a Sierra Foothill county where the judge was not interested in our esoteric arguments regarding insurance and dealers not licensed to sell insurance.

So what if the defendant doesn't have any money? Your client may be great and very sympathetic. You may be in the right forum and the legal issues may be tried and true issues, but, if your defendant is a deadbeat used-car dealer that disappears the moment the case is going to cost the dealership money, you really haven't done your client or yourself a service. There is a major limitation on how many pro bono cases you can take and stay in business, in particular, those cases that you didn't think were going to be pro bono.

8.3 Trial: Mistakes to Avoid During a Lawsuit

Your client needs to hear those defense questions from you first. "Mr. Smith, what is your basis for saying in your petition that my client acted 'maliciously'?" "Ms. Jones, you already had decided to buy this vehicle before the salesman told you it never was wrecked, isn't that right? So you didn't rely on what he said when you decided to buy it, isn't that right?" There are a number of defense stock-in-trade questions for consumer plaintiffs in depositions, and I'm certainly one who learned the hard way to make sure I cover those with the clients in preparing for their depositions.

Client, what client? Don't settle a case for a terrific settlement amount on a presumption of authority to do so, since you may have to deal with the aftermath when the client does not accept the news and recommendation.

Ass, meet You and Me. I didn't line up a witness to authenticate a document at trial, assuming that, because the defendant produced the key document in discovery, authenticity would not be questioned.

Try not to expose yourself. I explained my entire case to opposing counsel, including my "favorite fact" about what one of the two defendants did (she was representing both defendants) in the hope of jump-starting settlement talks. Instead, the lawyer took the "favorite fact" to the other defendant, withdrew from representing the "favorite fact" defendant, and the case was delayed another year and a half while new counsel got up to speed.

Telling a judge you don't want to talk settlement . . . hmmm. I've learned the hard way that, with most judges these days, you just can't appear to oppose settlement talks, no matter what has transpired so far and how extreme the defendants' positions are. Even if you know settlement efforts are farcical, it is important to at least pay lip service to the value of continued settlement talks. Any other posture tends to make you appear as part of the problem to the judge, no matter that the actual problem may be a "Stalingrad" defense and low-ball offers.

Judges can be camels carrying too many straws, too. I've made the mistake of overworking judges. You have all kinds of perfectly valid motions (especially discovery motions), you work long and hard to put all this good stuff together, and you end up—surprise!—running into judicial hostility. No, it's not fair, but it's perfectly understandable. Judges are bureaucrats and people and, just like other people, they generally will respond badly if asked to do too much work. The moral to the story: Make your first appearances with the judge count, make them very good, and watch closely (and draw back if necessary) if you have to ask the judge to work a lot.

All courts are basically the same, yeah? If you are in a new court and you don't get, read, understand, and follow the local rules, you may find yourself getting "hometowned" with a vengeance.

Don't be an alien in your legal community. It definitely is swimming upstream to try to work through the legal system as a complete outsider. I've pretty much done that, because I've never been really comfortable with the "mainstream bar." But, in dealing with judges and defense counsel

2 *See* Consumer Arbitration Agreements (4th ed. 2004 and Supp.).

who are always part of the mainstream bar, I have had to get better at being comfortable with them. The judges certainly aren't the enemy after all (we'll leave aside those relatively few judges who really do have inappropriate motives). And defense counsel, while often behaving badly, are better regarded as simply an obstacle than as the problem we're addressing. At any rate, I've had to get better at getting along with all of these "mainstream bar" people, and I wish I had climbed this particular hill a long time ago. Rather than a bad thing, it contributes in a good way to emotional maturing, to getting better at genuinely understanding and working with people with whom you often may disagree.

Sure, go ahead, talk to my client without me. Never let the other lawyer talk with your client. Opposing counsel threatened my client then filed a motion with the court claiming (falsely) that, during the conversation, he learned that my client was hot for the defendant's settlement offer but that his greedy lawyer (me) was interfering with the settlement.

I assume judges know most of the law—don't they? Of course judges know very little consumer law—just look at your bookshelf full of NCLC manuals and consider how very little consumer law is taught in law schools, and it is obvious that judges generally will know little about this stuff. They generally know a lot of law in certain subject areas—or about things they handle often (like procedure, jurisdiction, evidence, local rules)—but not about consumer law and not the deeper areas of theory on most points. With this understanding, it behooves us to fully expect to educate judges (which one only does oh so deferentially!) and to expect that most judges will only learn a certain amount in any given case. This also points us towards trying hard to use theories the judges already understand and accept and only to go deeply into consumer law or theory when it is really necessary—and then only with judges who will travel that road with us.

If you start defendants thinking low, they're harder to get high. Salespeople know that people are satisfied with things that meet their expectations. Defendants and their insurance carriers will pay what they expect to pay, but they will fight and delay paying more than they expect to pay. If their frame of reference in a case starts in the range of $30,000, say, it will be very hard to get them to pay $100,000. Making initial low offers can give them that low frame of reference. I've done that and run into surprised responses and emotional resistance from the other side when we later hiked our demands to a much higher level. By the same token, making high demands early can get them started toward the right frame of reference, the right expectations. (Of course other considerations—such as looking bad to a judge or looking unsuccessful when fee-application time comes—should make one careful about demanding too much too soon.) The whole tone with which the case is discussed in the initial communications is critical in getting a defendant's expectations moving in the right direction. Giving a case the "big case aura" is important.

Do the math. This prompted a sarcastic rebuke from the judge at the final hearing (to my shock) that she'd never heard of charging the class for a "*Daubert* hearing celebration luncheon." The earlier *Daubert* hearing went well, although the court held the ruling in abeyance pending defense experts; in the meantime, the case settled. Although we did go out for lunch, I was mortified that my co-counsel recorded the $350 lunch cost as an expense, much less described it that way. The judge concluded, "And I was going to strike much of his testimony, anyway!"

What was I saying, again? Trying a brilliant case but, for a variety of reasons, missing the point.

So you think a judge thinks like a schoolteacher? When I started practice, I thought of judges a lot like I thought of teachers—they would sit there and make academic decisions based on analysis of the law. Whoo! Was that a limited and misleading view! Judges are almost all quite political or they wouldn't have gotten to their positions. They generally come from the "inside," from the mainstream establishment, which of course is dominated by business. Their friends are usually successful insiders, often "country club" types. Judges who want to move up—for example, to a court of appeals or some such—are extremely political animals, even more sensitized to political winds than other judges. And almost all judges are highly sensitive to political winds and to the problem of making waves. Suffice it to say that judges ordinarily should be thought of as highly political creatures, very tuned in to political forces at work in their jurisdictions. In my experience, it turns out almost to be ironic (but thankfully true) that most judges can be reached with fairness arguments of the kind that would move most juries.

Are you sure you want to say anything? When you are in court, it is very important that you listen to the judge and opposing counsel. You may have a brilliant argument prepared, but it may be more important not to say anything. Are you winning? Are you sure you want to say anything else? If you are winning, it is much better to not say anything for fear that, if you do, you may lose. If tentative rulings in motion practice are in your favor, do not repeat everything in your papers. Do not upset the court.

You mean the jury has to answer that question? You must prepare the jury submission form long before closing argument. I recently had a judge question why plaintiff's attorneys do not prepare the jury submission form prior to filing a complaint. Too often, we think the case is great and file a complaint with a number of causes of action, only to do the research in response to a demurrer, motion for judgment on the pleadings, motion for summary judgment or, in a worst-case scenario, motion for non-suit after putting on our case.

8.4 Practical: Mistakes to Avoid Just About Any Time

Just the facts. Always tell a reporter what you know and what you believe, not what you think the reporter wants to hear. And don't try to spin your case—you are not a PR professional.[3]

Dress for success. Assume you will be going to court on a moment's notice any day. I once had to show up for an emergency bankruptcy hearing in jeans and a polo shirt, which I had worn because we were having a snowstorm.

Sure, I can do that. It doesn't sound like it will take much time. Don't accept the role of Local Counsel without any real responsibility or veto power. Otherwise, for the privilege of billing 0.3 hours, you get a large package in the overnight mail at noon which you are to sign without so much as reading (much less agreeing with) and hand-file at the courthouse by the close of business.

Rise to defense counsel's bait and you'll get hooked. Don't do it! Just don't do it. For all these reasons—it doesn't accomplish anything, wastes time and energy, adds to your own discomfort, alienates judges (doesn't matter if you're right or wrong) and, perhaps worst of all, simply distracts you from what you should be thinking about. Keep yourself squarely focused, always, on getting where you're going. Live in your own positive internal world, think positively about where you're going, and let these storms of sound and fury to blow all around you signifying nothing. This doesn't mean you never respond if opposing counsel, say, accuses you in a brief of misconduct. Even then, it is often better not to respond directly to such accusations but, instead, to simply vigorously pursue your strong arguments.

Penny-wise really is pound-foolish. Don't try to do things on the cheap. Pleadings shouldn't have typos and be printed or bound poorly. If you need a scanner, get one. If you need to have it there the next day, don't mail it and hope for the best.

History repeats itself. Because the issues in a case were identical to those in another case, I used an old brief. Just to be consistent, apparently, I left in the old plaintiff's name.

Department of Redundancy Department, I missed a hearing because I didn't calendar it (only once in twenty-five-plus years, but still . . .). Keep a calendar and have your secretary or assistant keep one as well. Enter dates the very moment you get a notice. In my case, the opposing counsel passed the case—he was one of those you can trust.

"Just one look" just ain't enough. I've filed a pleading with extra pages (in one case, a notice of my daughter's overdraft). I've filed a brief in which the copies were missing a page. Sure, you are sick of the thing by that point, but what does it take to do one final review?

Insist on final cut. My secretary typed a remark I'd jotted on a Post-It Note and my then-associate approved inclusion of a footnote that I thought was a patent joke. I had said, "like the colorful Joe Pesci character from *My Cousin Vinnie,* one could summarize defendant's position thusly: '*Everything they just said is bulls.'* " And so it appeared—verbatim—in the brief, to my mortification.

Win a case—prepare those sound bites! Right after a jury verdict you can expect press contacts. You're tired, things are swimming all around you, and you're not geared to do more work. But—my hard experiences have taught me—that you need to write up your sound bites *right now*. Be really well prepared to take this highly valuable moment to get the *right* message across. Make sure you have the affirmative message you want to get across well prepared. Talk about *solutions*. Talk *constructively*. Talk about other affirmatives that help the cause—like the lack of law enforcement that is at the root of so many of these problems. In my early years of practice, I underestimated how badly the negative image of mainstream personal-injury lawyers rubs off onto us "white hat" consumer attorneys. Even when we're doing what we know is the "good guy" work that almost every citizen who understands wants us to do, we will generally be thought of—at least initially—as though we were attorneys for the plaintiffs in the McDonald's coffee case (yes, I know perfectly well that, if one knows the true story of that case, the attorneys would look very good, but, in fact, that is not the public perception, which is my point). The public is extremely ready to think of us as being just greedy and out to get as much money as possible—so, in preparing remarks for the media (*always* prepare them!), look your remarks over with a cynic's eye and make sure you do nothing that helps play into that (mis)perception.

Skip the Notary! Unsworn statements under penalty of perjury may be substituted in many instances for a notarized statement required by federal law.[4]

Pull up, Sparky! Sometimes, though, it's okay to hold back when you are talking to a reporter, at least in the level of vitriol. That is, call the defendant "greedy" and not a "greedy scum-sucking Capitalist-tool pig."

8.5 Personal: Mistakes to Avoid All the Time

Don't leave well enough alone. As we used to say of the Soviets, "Trust with verification." Unless you know for sure that your co-counsel will act as promised, follow up and make sure. This makes for a little more work but a lot less heartache and headache.

Can I call you? Don't date clients. Be cautious of befriending them.

Call me anytime. Don't give a client your home or cell phone number if you value time off.

---

3 *See* §§ 7.3, 7.8, *supra*.

4 *See* 28 U.S.C. § 1746.

You mean I have to run a business? Don't make the mistake of running your law practice like a charity organization. If you keep employees who are not productive, are not team players, take advantage of you, do not do the work assigned to them, and refuse to learn and be productive, you must replace them with people who are willing to be productive and compatible.

Do unto others. Many years ago, I capitalized on an error made by my opposing counsel to gain a relatively small benefit for my client. The position I took made my opposing counsel look really bad to his client and to the large law firm where he worked, and he later lost his job. Now, every time I see this lawyer, who was and is a basically decent guy, I feel like a complete heel.

Walk softly and carry a big stick. What is it about lawyers and their egos that draw them, like moths to the light, to talk to anyone who will listen about their great case—or, worse yet, themselves? I have gained a far greater advantage by flying under the radar and doing a good job than I ever got by announcing my exploits to the world. Whenever I talk to the media (or anyone else, including the plaintiffs' class action bar) about my cases, I generally end up with a few too many cooks in the kitchen. I quickly realized that this was a grave error and have long since enjoyed a previously unanticipated advantage: The defendants and their counsel consistently underestimate us. I now understand it is standard procedure for defense counsel to look through all publicly available information. Some among our bar would argue that it is better to have an impressive reputation so the defendants will somehow respect and fear us so much that they will—I don't know—maybe surrender without a fight. I have yet to meet an adversary from the defense class action bar who did not believe they were smarter and better resourced than any plaintiff's lawyer.

Keep the home fires burning. I have allowed myself to be distracted by the "real problems" in my practice as my third grader was describing the awful behavior of her best friend on the school playground; when I bought only bakery cupcakes for my fifth grader to share with his classmates in honor of his birthday; when I realized that the most "quality time" I spend with my two teenaged sons is only when they join me in campaigning for candidates; when I have fallen asleep while my husband was talking to me; when, in general, I have failed to consistently put my family first before this grueling job.

Chapter 9 Troublesome Businesses and Common Legal Approaches

By Carolyn Carter[1]

9.1 Familiarity with Trade Practices Key to Successful Representation

One key to providing effective representation is developing an understanding of the best and worst practices of the business that your client is complaining about. Because of this, successful consumer lawyers tend to begin their practices by limiting their focus to one, perhaps two, industries and types of cases. This chapter surveys some of the industries and types of cases around which lawyers have developed consumer law practices. The attorney biographies in Appendix D give further information and insight on specialization in individual law practices.

9.2 Automobile Fraud

9.2.1 Introduction

An astonishing percentage of car sales involve fraud, deception, or unfair conduct. There are a number of reasons that automobile fraud is so prevalent. The sheer volume of American car expenditures is enormous—hundreds of billions of dollars a year. In addition, both by necessity and by dealer ingenuity, car purchases are complex. A sale involves compliance with state titling and registration laws and often involves trade-ins, financing, leasing, physical damage and liability insurance, credit insurance, service contracts, options, and other fees. This complexity provides ample opportunities for confusion and deception.

Dealer profits on sales of new cars are small. Instead, dealers make their profits from financing, insurance, service contracts, added charges and options, repairs, and the sale of used cars. There is enormous financial pressure to make profits on these items to offset the dealer's inability to make profits on the sale of the car itself.

A used-car sale offers all the same potential for abuse as a new-car sale, plus the fact that the buyer does not really know what he or she is buying. The used car's history is easily misrepresented or kept hidden, and consumers often do not know a used car's real value. Abuses in the sale of used cars are aggravated because buyers tend to have lower educational levels, less marketplace experience, and marginal credit ratings, thus giving dealers even more leverage to take advantage of buyers.

Perhaps the most important factor involved in automobile fraud is a culture at many car dealerships, wholesalers, and other segments of the industry in which cheating consumers is an acceptable, or the only, way to do business. The single rule of the game is "buyer beware." The fact that Unfair and Deceptive Acts and Practices (UDAP) statutes and other laws have abandoned "buyer beware" as a legal framework has not made an impact on the actual practices of these merchants. Commission structures, quotas, training, and supervision place relentless pressure on sales personnel and their supervisors to deceive and take advantage of consumers, and they do so in a very sophisticated and routinized manner.

9.2.2 Misrepresentation or Non-Disclosure of Vehicle's Adverse History

The number of consumers defrauded each year by concealment or misrepresentation of a car's adverse history is in the millions. This includes

- odometer tampering, mis-disclosure of the accuracy of

---

1 Carolyn Carter is Deputy Director of Advocacy at NCLC. She was formerly co-director of Legal Services, Inc., in Gettysburg, Pennsylvania, and director of the Law Reform Office of the Cleveland Legal Aid Society. She is the editor of *Pennsylvania Consumer Law* and the first edition of *Ohio Consumer Law*; co-author of *Automobile Fraud* (2003), *Consumer Warranty Law* (2d ed. 2001), *Unfair and Deceptive Acts and Practices* (6th ed. 2004), *Repossessions and Foreclosures* (5th ed. 2002 and Supp.); and contributing author to *Fair Debt Collection* (5th ed. 2004 and Supp.), *Truth in Lending* (5th ed. 2003 and Supp.), and *The Cost of Credit: Regulation, Preemption, and Industry Abuses* (3d ed. 2005). She is the 1992 recipient of the Vern Countryman Consumer Award and is currently a member of the Federal Reserve Board's Consumer Advisory Council.

an odometer, and misrepresentation about a vehicle's mileage;
- sale of flooded or wrecked cars, including sale of salvage vehicles, without disclosure of that adverse history;
- sale of stolen cars and cars with similar title problems without disclosure;
- sale of cars that have been returned to the manufacturer as lemons or that have some other history of mechanical problems, without disclosure of that history;
- misrepresentation of the number of prior owners or the prior use of a vehicle as a rental or leased car, taxicab, or police car;
- misrepresentation that a demonstrator, program car, previously titled car, or other used car is new;
- concealment that a car is a gray market vehicle (that is, it was manufactured for a foreign market); and
- non-disclosure that a new car was damaged and repaired before it was sold to the consumer.

All of these frauds are analyzed in detail in National Consumer Law Center's (NCLC) manual *Automobile Fraud*. These and related frauds "hang together" in one volume because investigational techniques are quite similar, the same legal claims may be available, and the same litigation issues arise. In addition, a single vehicle may have more than one problem in its past, for example, both a rolled-back odometer and concealed wreck damage.

These cases often present excellent facts for a common law fraud claim. Punitive damages can be significant, especially since the dealer is often a repeat offender and may have placed the unknowing buyer in an unsafe car. A parallel claim under a state Unfair and Deceptive Acts and Practices (UDAP) statute may offer treble damages and attorney fees and will usually have a lower standard of proof. Other potential claims can be based on

- state and federal odometer statutes, most of which offer multiple damages and attorney fees;
- state lemon laundering, salvage vehicle, damage disclosure, and other motor vehicle laws;
- the warranty provisions of the Uniform Commercial Code;
- state and federal racketeering laws; and
- the common law doctrine of mistake, which can unwind the deal for the consumer even if the seller is entirely innocent.

Practitioners handling these types of automobile fraud cases usually investigate and select cases carefully and focus on just a few cases at a time. Often there are many potential defendants in addition to the selling dealer, such as prior dealers and owners in the chain of title, the manufacturer in the case of a laundered lemon, auto auctions, floor plan financers, repair shops, insurance companies that paid for and then concealed wreck damage, and the entity that financed the sale for the consumer.[2]

NCLC's manual *Automobile Fraud* gives advice on how to investigate, plead, litigate, and settle these claims, providing adequate relief for the consumer and appropriate compensation for the attorney. The book includes numerous sample pleadings, *voir dire* questions, opening and closing arguments, and jury instructions. One perspective offered in the book is that it is relatively easy to investigate and prove automobile fraud. In a number of cases, class actions may also be effective. NCLC's annual Fall conference usually devotes a full track of courses to automobile fraud litigation.

9.2.3 Automobile Warranties and Repairs

Consumer complaints about defective new and used vehicles are widespread and form the backbone of many consumer law practices. The Uniform Commercial Code (UCC) provides the basic law of warranty in all states except Louisiana. The UCC has a number of shortcomings for consumers, however. State lemon laws fill some of these gaps by making it easier for a vehicle buyer to obtain a refund or replacement. Every state has a new car lemon law, and a number of states have a similar statute or some other special protection for buyers of used cars.[3] In many states, the lemon law requires the manufacturer to pay attorney fees to a prevailing consumer. Some lemon laws also offer multiple damages or penalties.

The federal Magnuson-Moss Warranty Act[4] also offers attorney fees and can often be pleaded as a parallel claim to a UCC warranty claim. Many states also treat a breach of warranty, or a violation of the state lemon law, as a UDAP violation, making multiple damages and attorney fees available.[5]

Practitioners handling automobile warranty issues often develop fairly high-volume practices. They develop expertise in car defects and have ongoing relationships with mechanics who can diagnose and testify about car defects.

Automobile warranty issues, including new and used car lemon laws, are examined in detail in National Consumer Law Center, *Consumer Warranty Law* (2d ed. 2001 and Supp.). The manual also includes a full chapter on all aspects of the Magnuson-Moss Warranty Act, eight chapters analyzing UCC warranty law, and a companion CD-Rom with pleadings, interview forms, and sample jury papers and arguments. Automobile repair practices when a warranty is

2 *See* National Consumer Law Center, Automobile Fraud Chs. 2, 9 (2d ed. 2003 and Supp.).

3 *See* National Consumer Law Center, Consumer Warranty Law Chs. 13, 14, Appx. F (2d ed. 2001 and Supp.).

4 15 U.S.C. §§ 2301–2312. The Act is analyzed in detail in National Consumer Law Center, Consumer Warranty Law Ch. 2 (2d ed. 2001 and Supp.).

5 *See* National Consumer Law Center, Consumer Warranty Law § 11.1 (2d ed. 2001 and Supp.).

not in effect are treated in chapter 16 of that manual and in *Unfair and Deceptive Acts and Practices* § 5.4.1 (6th ed. 2004).

A lemon law practice often leads to odometer fraud, lemon laundering, and salvage fraud cases. For example, investigation of a vehicle defect may show that it is not a standard warranty problem but resulted from concealed wreck damage. Chapter 15, "Car Cases 101: Creating the Interview Form," *infra*, discusses how to conduct the client intake interview in such cases. A lemon law practice can also lead to cases involving deceptive pricing and sales techniques, discussed in the next section. Thus, many lemon law practitioners find themselves branching out into other areas of automobile fraud.

9.2.4 Deceptive Pricing, Financing, and Sales Techniques

9.2.4.1 General

Even without concealment of a car's adverse history or warranty violations, deception abounds in vehicle sales. Deceptive sales and financing techniques often underlie a consumer's other problems with a vehicle. The possible claims are varied. Some, such as UDAP claims, allow multiple damages and attorney fees in many states. If the dealer failed to disclose the financing or lease terms properly, the federal Truth in Lending Act or Consumer Leasing Act provides actual damages, statutory damages, attorney fees, and federal jurisdiction. Violations of the notice requirements of the Fair Credit Reporting Act and the Equal Credit Opportunity Act are also common in vehicle sales.

9.2.4.2 Dealer Add-Ons and Other Financing Deception

An area of substantial dealer abuse involves financing and trade-ins. Financing frauds are quite varied but generally involve the consumer paying more in finance charges than the dealer initially promised or than the consumer was led to expect. One of the most notorious games played by car dealers is to add extra charges, fees, and options that inflate the agreed-upon price and provide almost pure dealer profit with little or no benefit to the consumer. Kickbacks to dealers from lenders are also common.

The biggest profit centers for car dealerships are credit insurance, GAP insurance, and service contracts, also known as extended warranties or mechanical breakdown insurance. These items are dramatically overpriced. Dealers do not adequately disclose that they get to keep a large cut of the item's price as a commission, and they may not provide promised benefits. The worst practice, though, is selling these items to consumers who do not realize they have a choice in their purchase or even understand that they are paying for them.

State UDAP statutes provide a broad and flexible remedy for all types of dealer misrepresentation, non-disclosure, and overreaching. National Consumer Law Center, *Unfair and Deceptive Acts and Practices* (6th ed. 2004), examines these statutes in detail and analyzes

- how to find dealer documents to substantiate abuses (§ 5.4.2);
- packing of extras, such as rust-proofing, insurance, service contracts, document charges, and dealer kickbacks on financing into the contract (§ 5.4.3);
- unfair dealer negotiation practices (§ 5.4.4);
- automobile pricing misrepresentations (§ 5.4.7);
- misrepresentation of the condition, features, or prior use of the vehicle (§ 5.4.6);
- excessive prices for used cars (§ 5.4.6.12); and
- deception as to how much the trade-in is really reducing the purchase price (§§ 5.4.4.4, 5.4.4.6).

Attempts by a consumer to enforce a service contract are covered in National Consumer Law Center, *Consumer Warranty Law* Ch. 18 (2d ed. 2001 and Supp.) and unfair denials of credit, gap, or other types of insurance claim are discussed in § 5.3 of another NCLC manual *Unfair and Deceptive Acts and Practices*. For state law regulating the rate and nature of automobile credit, see National Consumer Law Center, *The Cost of Credit: Regulation, Preemption, and Industry Abuses* (3d ed. 2005).

When consumers do not obtain physical damage insurance on their cars, their lender may purchase forced-placed insurance, which is insurance to cover the risk of loss to the car that is selected by the lender but is paid for by the consumer. The lender may purchase the insurance from the company that promises the most money or other benefits for the lender even if the consumer is forced to pay an outrageous amount for the product, which is of little benefit for the consumer. This issue is examined in *Unfair and Deceptive Acts and Practices* § 5.3.11 (6th ed. 2004).

9.2.4.3 Yo-Yo Sales

Yo-yo sales are another prevalent practice. In a yo-yo sale, the consumer signs a contract for a vehicle and is allowed to drive it away on the promise that the dealer will arrange financing. Later the consumer may be told that the deal fell through and that a higher price, more options, a different car, or less advantageous financing are necessary. If the consumer wants to unwind the deal, the dealer may claim that the consumer's trade-in has already been sold or may refuse to return the down payment. Yo-yo sales are also sometimes called "spot delivery" because the consumer buys and takes possession of the car on the spot.

The best source for analysis of these various abuses is in *Unfair and Deceptive Acts and Practices* § 5.4.5 (6th ed. 2004). Yo-yo sales often involve violations of the Truth in

Lending Act and the notice requirements of the Equal Credit Opportunity Act and the Fair Credit Reporting Act as well as misrepresentations and violations of state motor vehicle laws.[6]

9.2.4.4 Vehicle Leasing

Leasing is an important profit center for dealers and a frequent area of automobile fraud. The Federal Consumer Leasing Act, Regulation M, and state leasing statutes set out disclosure requirements and standards about early termination and default penalties. These are examined in detail in National Consumer Law Center, *Truth in Lending* Ch. 10 (5th ed. 2003 and Supp.). Early termination and default also raise issues very similar to a car repossession. These issues are examined in National Consumer Law Center, *Repossessions* Ch. 15 (6th ed. 2005).

Leasing also involves numerous abuses as to the terms of the lease, for example, stealing trade-ins, down payments, and rebates, higher capitalized costs or lease charges than represented, manipulation of residual values, misrepresentation about other lease terms, or even deception about whether a transaction is or is not a lease. Effective challenges to these practices can often be based on state UDAP statutes.[7]

9.2.4.5 Automobile Subleases and Brokerage

A common scam is for a "broker" to prey on consumers who want to get out of automobile leases or credit agreements. The broker offers to sub-lease the car to another consumer who will make the payments. Such brokers charge large fees for a practice that is illegal if done (as it invariably is) without the creditor's permission. Payments may never be forwarded to the lender, and insurance coverage may not be kept up. More on sublease scams is set out in National Consumer Law Center, *Unfair and Deceptive Acts and Practices* § 5.4.10 (6th ed. 2004).

9.2.4.6 Credit Reports

To help size up the consumer and negotiate a purchase price, car dealers often pull a consumer's credit report almost as soon as the consumer enters the dealership. This use is illegal under federal law.[8] Unauthorized access to the consumer's credit report is usually easy to detect because it is recorded in the consumer's credit record, which the consumer can obtain from the credit reporting agency. Another issue concerning credit reports arises when consumers stop credit or lease payments for legitimate reasons but the lender reports the consumer to a credit reporting agency as being in default. In addition, the Fair Credit Reporting Act and the Equal Credit Opportunity act require notice to a consumer whose application for credit is rejected or acted upon adversely. All of these issues are covered in National Consumer Law Center, *Fair Credit Reporting* (5th ed. 2002 and Supp.) and *Credit Discrimination* (4th ed. 2005).

9.2.4.7 Discrimination

Studies have found that women and minorities pay more at car dealerships.[9] There are also indications that they are discriminated against with regard to the amount they pay for automobile loans and leases. The Equal Credit Opportunity Act and similar state laws provide powerful remedies for discrimination. While discrimination claims typically require intensive factual development, a strong case can lead to substantial damages and attorney fees. For more on discrimination claims, see National Consumer Law Center, *Credit Discrimination* (4th ed. 2005).

9.2.5 Repossessions and Collection Activity

Automobile repossessions, repossession sales, and deficiency claims are important areas of automobile fraud. Their significance to a consumer lawyer is accentuated because consumers often will not go to a lawyer after they have been defrauded at the time of a car's purchase—or even after their car is repossessed—but *will* go to a lawyer after the creditor sells the car and brings a deficiency claim.

In addition to claims arising from the repossession and sale itself, the buyer can usually raise any claims regarding the sale of the vehicle in response to a deficiency action. In most cases this is true even if the creditor bringing the deficiency action is not the original seller of the vehicle but is an assignee or a lender who financed the sale. The FTC's Holder Rule[10] and many similar state laws[11] make assignees of retail installment contracts liable for the claims and defenses that the consumer could assert against the dealer, with affirmative liability capped at the amount the consumer

6 *See generally* National Consumer Law Center, Truth in Lending (5th ed. 2003 and Supp.).

7 *See* National Consumer Law Center, Unfair and Deceptive Acts and Practices § 5.4.8 (6th ed. 2004).

8 *See* National Consumer Law Center, Fair Credit Reporting §§ 9.2.2.3, 9.2.4.1 (5th ed. 2002 and Supp.).

9 *See* National Consumer Law Center, Credit Discrimination § 8.5 (4th ed. 2005); Ian Ayres, *Fair Driving: Gender and Race Discrimination in Retail Car Negotiations*, 104 Harv. L. Rev. 817 (1991). *See also* A. Munnell, G. Tootell, L. Browne & J. McEneaney, *Mortgage Lending in Boston: Interpreting HMDA Data, reprinted in* the Am. Econ. Rev. 25–53 (Mar. 1996).

10 16 C.F.R. § 433. The FTC's Holder Rule is analyzed in detail in National Consumer Law Center, Unfair and Deceptive Acts and Practices § 6.6 (6th ed. 2004).

11 *See* National Consumer Law Center, Unfair and Deceptive Acts and Practices § 6.6.5.3 (6th ed. 2004).

has paid. Lenders have the same liability if the seller refers consumers to, is affiliated with, or has a business arrangement with that lender.

A number of affirmative claims are available for repossession abuses. The Uniform Commercial Code offers actual or statutory damages for violations of its repossession and sale standards. Many state retail installment sales acts or other statutes mandate additional protections for consumers. Tort claims such as trespass and conversion are also available for wrongful repossession and offer the possibility of punitive damages. Often a UDAP claim can also be fashioned, affording the possibility of multiple damages and attorney fees. In addition, the Fair Debt Collection Practices Act, which offers actual damages, statutory damages, and attorney fees, applies to some repossession practices and to third parties' attempts to collect deficiencies on behalf of creditors.[12] The rights and responsibilities of secured parties under all of these laws are examined in detail in *Repossessions* (6th ed. 2005).

9.3 Sale and Rental of Housing; Home Improvements

9.3.1 Home Sales

A family's home is its largest single investment. When the seller or real estate agent has concealed serious defects in the home, the buyer faces not only potential loss of shelter but also a major financial setback.

Attorneys representing defrauded home buyers should consider UDAP and common law fraud theories. UDAP statutes, which are applicable to real estate sales in most states, provide more flexible standards than fraud for determining deception and often offer statutory damages and attorney fees. State real estate laws may set additional standards. Many states have a real estate recovery fund to compensate victims of fraud by licensed real estate agents and brokers.

For problems with the condition of a home, most states hold that the sale of a new home by a builder carries with it some common law warranty of its quality. In addition, about twelve states have statutes mandating a warranty regarding at least some features of a new home, and about fifteen states require that a warranty accompany the sale of a new condominium. The seller or builder may also have given an express warranty. Federal law requires that homes built pursuant to a loan guaranteed by the Veteran's Administration or financed by the FHA pursuant to the National Housing Act carry a warranty that the dwelling is in substantial conformity with the plans and specifications.[13] All of these laws are analyzed in detail in *Consumer Warranty Law* Ch. 16 (2d ed. 2001 and Supp.).

9.3.2 Property Flipping Schemes

In property flipping schemes, a speculator buys dilapidated residential properties at low prices and resells them to unsophisticated first-time home buyers at huge markups. Often the speculator makes cosmetic repairs to the property or promises the buyer that repairs will be made after closing. Typically the speculator works with loan officers, closing agents, attorneys, building inspectors, and appraisers who aid in securing financing and keeping the buyer in the dark.

The primary claims in property flipping cases are fraud, UDAP violations, and civil conspiracy claims.[14] Discrimination claims may also be appropriate if the speculator targets a minority group or another protected class.[15] Claims under the federal or state credit repair laws[16] or a federal or state RICO statute[17] are also possible and may offer enhanced remedies and procedural advantages. Adding all the players as parties to a lawsuit is important because the speculator may be long gone or without assets by the time the consumer becomes aware of the fraud.

9.3.3 Manufactured Homes and Mobile Home Parks

Mobile home sales are subject to many of the same incentives and schemes for cheating consumers that exist for automobiles. Financing for mobile homes tends to be expensive and the expected life of a mobile home relatively short, undermining the purchaser's pursuit of inexpensive housing. Moreover, mobile homes are easily damaged in transit and in the setup process. All of this leads to a variety of ways that lawyers can help mobile home consumers. *Consumer Warranty Law* Ch. 15 (2d ed. 2001 Supp.) and *Unfair and Deceptive Acts and Practices* § 5.4.12 (6th ed. 2004) are most targeted to this area of representation. Key claims are UCC warranty and Magnuson-Moss warranty claims and claims under state UDAP and mobile home laws.

Some mobile home owners own the land on which the home sits, but many rent a lot from a mobile home park.

12 *See* National Consumer Law Center, *Fair Debt Collection* (5th ed. 2004 and Supp.).

13 38 U.S.C. § 3705; 12 U.S.C. § 1701j-1.

14 *See* National Consumer Law Center, Unfair and Deceptive Acts and Practices § 5.5.5.4 (6th ed. 2004).

15 *See* Honorable v. Easy Life Real Estate Sys., Inc., 100 F. Supp. 2d 885 (N.D. Ill. 2000) (denying defendants' motion for summary judgment on § 1981 and Fair Housing Act claims). *See* National Consumer Law Center, Credit Discrimination (4th ed. 2005).

16 *See* National Consumer Law Center, Fair Credit Reporting Ch. 15 (5th ed. 2002 and Supp.).

17 *See* National Consumer Law Center, Unfair and Deceptive Acts and Practices § 9.2, 9.3 (6th ed. 2004).

Mobile home parks often have onerous rules for their tenants. Eviction can occur quickly after even a minor default. UDAP statutes and state mobile home park statutes, in addition to general state landlord-tenant law, are the primary legal resources to help mobile home park tenants as to their relationship with the park.[18]

9.3.4 Rental Housing

Fraud, deception, and unfair practices abound in the rental housing market. While state landlord-tenant laws are the primary source of law in this area, attorneys who represent tenants must also be familiar with consumer protection laws, which offer significant remedies for landlord abuses. In particular, UDAP statutes have often been used to challenge unfair rental agreements, sub-standard housing conditions, failure to make repairs, rent overcharges, unjustified withholding of security deposits, deceptive notices to quit, and illegal self-help eviction.[19] The federal Fair Debt Collection Practices Act and state debt collection laws may also provide tenants a remedy for deceptive or abusive rent collection methods.[20]

9.3.5 Home "Improvement" Scams

The typical home "improvement" scam involves selling a product—water filtration, driveway paving, siding, roof repairs, or replacement windows—at an inflated price. The seller then fails to deliver all of the goods promised or performs shoddy or incomplete work. The house actually may be worse off for the "improvement." There are all sorts of variations on this basic theme of fraud and deception.[21]

The complaint is often brought against the financer of the sale under the FTC Holder Rule[22] because the seller has disappeared or is inadequately capitalized. Remedies are often under UDAP statutes and state home improvement statutes.[23] Unconscionability and fraud claims may also be available.

Some fraudulent home improvement companies work hand-in-glove with predatory lenders, so an analysis of the financing of the transaction is particularly important. The three-day right to cancel certain home-secured credit transactions that the Truth in Lending Act affords can be extended for up to three years if certain key financial disclosures were not made correctly.[24] If the finance charges are so high that the transaction is covered by the Home Ownership and Equity Protection Act (HOEPA), special protections apply.[25]

9.4 Sale of Other Goods and Services

9.4.1 Introduction

Many of the issues described in the preceding sections that arise in the sale of vehicles, real property, and home improvements also arise in the sale of other goods and services. The discussion that follows highlights a few industries that have particularly troubled histories or that present particular problems for consumers.

9.4.2 Telemarketing Fraud

Telemarketing fraud is a huge international industry. Prize promotions, in which the victim is required to make some payment to acquire the prize; bogus business and investment opportunities; advance fee credit card offers; and sale of credit card protection services are common telemarketing frauds.

The FTC's Telemarketing Sales Rule[26] prohibits the worst of these telemarketing abuses. The statute under which the rule was adopted offers a private cause of action, but only when each plaintiff's damages exceed $50,000.[27] A second federal statute, the Telephone Consumer Protection Act,[28] along with a rule adopted under it by the Federal Communications Commission, forbids a few telemarketing techniques, for example, early morning and late-night calls. While the substantive prohibitions of the FCC's statute and rule are narrower than the FTC's, the FCC's statute offers a private cause of action with fewer limitations. Both the FTC's and the FCC's rules also prohibit calls to consumers who have registered on the nationwide do-not call list. Claims under state UDAP statutes and state telemarketing statutes are also possible. *Unfair and Deceptive Acts and Practices* § 5.9 (6th ed. 2004) discusses all of these remedies in detail.

Since fraudulent telemarketers often conceal their assets or disappear and may even operate from foreign countries,

18 *See* National Consumer Law Center, Unfair and Deceptive Acts and Practices § 5.5.1 (6th ed. 2004).

19 *See id.* § 5.5.2.

20 *See* National Consumer Law Center, Fair Debt Collection (5th ed. 2004 and Supp.).

21 *See* National Consumer Law Center, Unfair and Deceptive Acts and Practices § 5.6 (6th ed. 2004).

22 16 C.F.R. § 433. *See* National Consumer Law Center, Unfair and Deceptive Acts and Practices 9.2.9 (6th ed. 2004).

23 *See id.*; National Consumer Law Center, Consumer Warranty Law § 17.7, Appx. I.3, K.4 (2d ed. 2001 and Supp.); National Consumer Law Center, Consumer Law Pleadings No. 2, §§ 4.2, 4.3, No. 3, § 1.1, No. 4, Ch. 1 (2002 Cumulative CD-Rom and Index Guide).

24 *See* National Consumer Law Center, Truth in Lending Ch. 6 (5th ed. 2003 and Supp.).

25 *See* § 10.5.2, *infra*; National Consumer Law Center, Truth in Lending Ch. 9 (5th ed. 2003 and Supp.).

26 16 C.F.R. § 39.

27 15 U.S.C. § 6104(a).

28 47 U.S.C. § 227; 47 C.F.R. § 64.1200.

collection of a judgment is often difficult. In many situations, the FTC, state consumer protection authorities, and federal and state criminal prosecutors are better equipped to obtain redress for consumers. Defrauded consumers should complain to all of these public authorities and should protect themselves from further fraud by registering with the nationwide do-not-call list enforced by the FTC and the FCC.[29]

9.4.3 Vocational Schools and Student Loans

Fraudulent vocational schools flourished in the 1970s and 1980s when the federal student loan program was a heavy, indirect funder of those fly-by-night enterprises. Their legacy remains in attempts to collect student loans from the 1970s and 1980s as well as in new schools spawned in their image. More recently, private student loan programs have funded fraudulent vocational schools.

The typical fraudulent vocational school recruited inner-city youths and, in some cases, homeless people to start classes that were typically overcrowded, without skilled instructors, and without the necessary teaching equipment. Attendance by teachers and students was typically poor, attrition high, and motivation and morale low. Schools often closed in the middle of a course of study. Typically the principals would flee before a civil judgment could be obtained against them. As a result, private lawyers usually have been unsuccessful in obtaining a fee by representing consumers against vocational schools. Most of the law enforcement has been relegated to the criminal justice system, legal services lawyers, and pro bono efforts.

Even if a suit against the fraudulent school is not feasible, there are ways to help student loan debtors. Many student loans, whether fraudulent or not, are collected by private collection agencies. Students may have claims under the Fair Debt Collection Practices Act[30] if the collection agency uses deceptive or abusive tactics. Student loans can be discharged in bankruptcy if the student proves substantial hardship.

Another avenue of relief is to seek discharge of the debt under one of several Department of Education programs. Discharge is available if (1) the school closed while the student attended or within ninety days after the student withdrew; (2) the school falsely certified that the student had the ability to benefit from a course of study; or (3) the student withdrew but the school failed to refund the portion of the tuition that was required by the contract. The Department of Education will consider requests to discharge whole groups of students who were affected by the same practice. Discharge is also available if the student is now permanently and totally disabled. The Department of Education also offers a variety of repayment and loan consolidation alternatives that can ease the student's financial burden.

National Consumer Law Center, *Student Loan Law* (2d ed. 2002 and Supp.), is a comprehensive analysis of vocational school fraud and student loan issues.

9.4.4 Immigration Consultants or Assistants

The number of scam artists preying upon immigrants seeking assistance in obtaining legal residence, work authorization, or citizenship has risen dramatically in recent years. While honest and responsible immigration consultants exist, unscrupulous consultants claim that they are attorneys or that they have close connections to the Immigration and Naturalization Service (INS). Some use titles such as notary public or *notario* to deceive people into believing that they are lawyers. In many Spanish-speaking countries, a *notario* is an attorney, often possessing more credentials than other lawyers.

Unscrupulous immigration consultants take advantage, in many different ways, of immigrants' lack of sophistication and the changing nature and complexity of immigration law. Typical scams include:

- Charging exorbitant fees for immigration services and then failing to file any documents
- Filing false asylum claims on behalf of victims who do not speak or read English and have no idea what the application contains
- Charging fees to prepare applications for non-existent immigration programs or for legitimate programs for which the client does not qualify, such as asylum or labor certification

Victims of these scams not only lose large sums of money but also are likely to suffer serious harm to their immigration status.

Several states have enacted statutes that regulate non-attorneys who assist consumers on immigration matters.[31] Most of these statutes exempt accredited representatives[32] and non-attorneys who work for non-profit agencies or law school legal clinics.[33] Challenges to fraudulent immigration consultants can also be based on the state UDAP statute,

29 Consumers can register on the do-not-call list by calling 1-888-382-1222 (TTY 1-866-290-4236) or visiting www.ftc.gov/donotcall.

30 15 U.S.C. § 1692. *See* § 10.7, *infra*.

31 *See* National Consumer Law Center, Unfair and Deceptive Acts and Practices § 5.12.2 (6th ed. 2004).

32 An accredited representative is a non-attorney working for an organization accredited by the board of Immigration Appeals. 8 C.F.R. § 292.1(a)(4), 8 C.F.R. § 292.2.

33 *See, e.g.*, Ariz. Rev. Stat. § 12-2702; Cal. Bus. & Prof. Code § 22440; 815 Ill. Comp. Stat. Ann. 505/2AA(a-5); Mich. Comp. L. Ann. § 338.3455; Minn. Stat. § 325E.031(5); N.M. Stat. Ann. § 36-3-4; Wash. Rev. Code § 19.154.030.

common law fraud, or statutes forbidding unauthorized practice of law.

9.4.5 *Telephone Service*

The provision of long-distance telephone service has become deregulated, increasing the opportunities for deceptive and unfair practices by telephone service providers. "Slamming," the illegal practice of switching a customer's telephone service provider without that customer's knowledge or consent, is prohibited by an FCC rule[34] and similar statutes in some states. "Cramming" is the illegal practice of placing unauthorized, misleading, or deceptive charges on a phone bill. The FCC's Truth in Billing rule is intended to deter cramming by making phone bills easier to decipher.[35] UDAP challenges to these practices are also possible.[36] National Consumer Law Center, *Access to Utility Service* Ch. 2 (3d ed. 2004) discusses these and other practices. The provision of local phone service by large, incumbent carriers is regulated by the state's utility commission. In addition to regulating rates, many of the protections regarding matters such as denial of service, deposits, and disconnection rules are also regulated by the state utility commission.

Telephone rates have historically been insulated from challenge by the "filed rate doctrine," which bars suits against regulated entities for unreasonable rates whenever the rates have been approved by regulatory authorities. Since the FCC has discontinued regulating interstate telephone rates, this shield may no longer be available to long-distance telephone service providers.[37]

9.4.6 *Timeshares, Resort Memberships, Health Spas*

Timeshare and resort firms entice consumers to visit their facilities, ranging from luxury condominiums to campsites, with the lure of free prizes and the possibility of winning a big ticket item. They then engage in high-pressure sales tactics that are described in detail in *Unfair and Deceptive Acts and Practices* §§ 5.5.5.10, 5.9.5 (6th ed. 2004). Some companies continue the scam by misrepresenting the services that they provide in reselling timeshares. UDAP statutes and telemarketing statutes offer claims against these companies. Some states have consumer protection laws that are targeted specifically at abuses in the sale of timeshares and resort memberships.

Some health spas use similar high-pressure techniques to sell memberships. Many states now have laws restricting the length of health spa contracts—affording a right to cancel—and providing other protections.[38]

9.4.7 *Nursing Homes, Assisted-Living Facilities*

Nursing homes and assisted-living facilities may run afoul of consumer protection laws and laws targeted directly at these industries when they provide sub-standard care, abuse residents, deny access to relatives, double-bill for the same service, or mistreat Medicaid patients. *Unfair and Deceptive Acts and Practices* § 5.11.3 (6th ed. 2004), discusses some of the law protecting residents of these facilities. While the federal Nursing Home Reform Law[39] does not give residents a private cause of action, violations of that law may be actionable under a state UDAP statute. Assisted-living facilities are less regulated than nursing homes, so there are fewer specific standards, but the broad and flexible prohibitions of state UDAP statutes can usually still reach deception or unfair practices by these facilities.

9.5 Debtors' Rights and Credit Reporting

9.5.1 *Debt Collection Harassment*

Harassment by debt collectors creates enormous distress for financially strapped consumers and their families. The boundaries of fair debt collection practices are set by federal law for debt collection agencies and collection attorneys and by state law for creditors.

Lawyers in private practice have established a variety of types of practices around representing consumers who have been subject to debt collection activities that cross those boundaries. Some of these lawyers specialize in a high volume of small-damages cases while others specialize in class actions against debt collectors. Many consumer lawyers do a combination of small cases and class actions, joining co-counsel to pool resources and experience in the larger cases. Still other consumer lawyers focus on cases

---

34 47 C.F.R. § 64.1100 *et seq.*

35 47 C.F.R. § 64.2400 *et seq.*

36 Note that the FCC has recently extended the Truth in Billing rules to apply to wireless carriers, 70 Fed. Reg. 29979 *et seq.* (May 25, 2005) (to be codified at 47 C.F.R. § 64.2400) but at the same time has opened a proceeding to examine whether state laws regarding billing practices are preempted. 70 Fed. Reg. 30044 *et seq.* (May 25, 2005).

37 *See* National Consumer Law Center, Access to Utility Service § 2.8 (3d ed. 2004).

38 National Consumer Law Center, Unfair and Deceptive Acts and Practices § 5.9.3.1 (6th ed. 2004).

39 42 U.S.C. §§ 1395i-3, 1395r.

with gross misconduct and high individual damages. Debt collection abuse cases may involve large awards, including million-dollar awards.[40]

The federal Fair Debt Collection Practices Act[41] is the primary vehicle for debt collection harassment claims. Since it offers statutory damages and attorney fees, it is a powerful vehicle to enforce consumer rights. One weakness in the law, however, is that as a general rule it only applies to independent debt collectors, not creditors collecting their own debts. State debt collection practices statutes and UDAP statutes are more likely to apply to creditors. In addition to these statutory claims, debtors are sometimes able to assert tort claims such as invasion of privacy, intentional infliction of emotional distress, and defamation, which have the advantage of offering punitive damages in most states. All of these legal theories are analyzed in detail in National Consumer Law Center, *Fair Debt Collection* (5th ed. 2004 and Supp.). The book also includes a wealth of practice tools such as interview forms and sample pleadings. NCLC also sponsors an annual training in the winter on fair debt collection litigation for new and experienced lawyers.

9.5.2 Consumer Credit Counseling

Many consumer debtors enroll in a consumer credit counseling program in hopes of gradually working their way out of debt. The traditional credit counseling agency offers education, credit counseling, and debt management plans under which the consumer pays a monthly sum to the agency to distribute to the consumer's creditors.

While many of these agencies are legitimate, the industry has expanded and changed rapidly in recent years. Some charge high fees that reduce the debtor's ability to pay creditors. Some have engaged in aggressive telemarketing that the FTC has alleged violated the nationwide do-not-call list rule.[42] Some credit counseling agencies are no more than non-profit intake operations for profit-making businesses, and the IRS has denied several credit counseling organizations' applications for tax-exempt status. Even the traditional credit counseling agencies have been charged with failing to disclose that the majority of their funding comes from creditors,[43] failing to inform consumers of their bankruptcy rights, failing to remit payments promptly to the consumer's creditors, and failing to disclose fees.[44]

There are a number of possible remedies for problems with credit counseling. The broad definition of "credit repair organization" in the federal Credit Repair Organizations Act (CROA) might apply to credit counseling organizations, but there is an exception for non-profit organizations.[45] However, some of the prohibitions in the CROA apply to any individual, not just to credit repair organizations. Also, it may be possible to persuade a court to look behind the IRS determination of non-profit status when an organization is clearly abusing it.[46]

Another possible claim is violation of a state debt pooling law or credit counseling law.[47] Many state laws specifically prohibit the business of debt pooling (also known as debt management plans, debt consolidation, budget planning, or debt prorating). While most of these laws have no specific provision for private enforcement, violations should be UDAP violations.[48] However, many of these laws explicitly exempt most non-profits from at least some requirements.

9.5.3 Debt Settlement, Debt Elimination

A number of businesses prey on overburdened consumer debtors. Debt-settlement or debt-negotiation companies purport to settle consumers' debts at deep discounts. Typically, the company advises consumers to stop paying their creditors. Instead, the consumer pays the debt-settlement company. Once the consumer has accumulated enough money, the company contacts the consumer's creditors and proposes to settle the consumer's debt for a fraction of the claim. One problem with this approach is that the non-payment ruins the consumer's credit rating, likely costing the consumer more over the long run than the consumer saved through the settlement of the debt. These companies also may charge high fees and make excessive claims about what they can do

40 *See* Household Credit Servs. v. Driscol, 989 S.W.2d 72 (Tex. App. 1998). *See also* National Consumer Law Center, Fair Debt Collection § 9.2 (5th ed. 2004 and Supp.).

41 15 U.S.C. § 1692 *et seq.*

42 *See* www.ftc.gov/opa/2004/07/dmfs.htm (FTC complaints).

43 As a result of a settlement with the FTC in 1999, NFCC now includes in its best practices standards that member agencies must disclose this possible conflict. *See* Stephen Gardner, *Consumer Credit Counseling Services: The Need for Reform and Some Proposals for Change*, 13 Advancing the Consumer Interest (Fall 2001/Winter 2002).

44 *See, e.g.*, FTC v. Credit-Care, Inc., 5 Trade Reg. Rep. (CCH) 23,296 (N.D. Ill. 1992) (consent decree) (alleging that Credi-Care kept a significant portion of consumer payments, assessed unfair fees, processed payments so slowly that most accounts became delinquent, and stopped payments on drafts sent to creditors when consumers tried to cancel the agreement).

45 15 U.S.C. §§ 1679–1679j. *See* National Consumer Law Center, Fair Credit Reporting Ch. 15 (5th ed. 2002 and Supp.). Many states also have credit repair laws.

46 *See* Zimmerman v. Cambridge Credit Counseling Corp., 2005 WL 1273956 (1st Cir. May 31, 2005) (IRS determination of tax-exempt status not dispositive on the issue of whether providers were exempt from the CROA).

47 *See* National Consumer Law Center, Unfair and Deceptive Acts and Practices § 5.1.2.3.2 (6th ed. 2004) (citing each state's credit counseling law).

48 *See, e.g., In re* Fricker, 115 B.R. 809 (Bankr. E.D. Pa. 1990). *See generally* National Consumer Law Center, Unfair and Deceptive Acts and Practices § 3.2.7 (6th ed. 2004).

for the consumer. The number of consumers who are able to pay the company's fees and enough money to settle their debts may be very small.

The federal Credit Repair Organizations Act and state analogs apply to debt-settlement companies that pitch their services as improving the consumer's credit rating or credit record.[49] Debt settlement companies are generally for-profit so do not fall within the federal statute's exemption for non-profit organizations. State UDAP laws clearly apply, and recent FTC actions against debt-settlement companies are persuasive precedent as to the unfair and deceptive nature of some of their practices.[50] Some states have enacted new legislation to cover debt-settlement agencies, or these states' credit counseling law may be broad enough to cover them.

Another type of fraud aimed at desperate debtors is debt elimination. Some debt-elimination companies prepare, for a fee, a spurious instrument with a title such as "bond for discharge of debt" or "redemption certificate." By presenting the instrument, the debtor supposedly forces the creditor to relinquish the debt. The Office of the Comptroller of the Currency (OCC), which regulates national banks, has warned banks against these schemes and asserted that creating or presenting such instruments may be a federal crime.[51]

Another scheme sets up an arbitration that is programmed to produce a ruling that the debt is invalid. This technique is likely to be unsuccessful, and a debtor who pays for this service certainly has a UDAP claim and possibly also a fraud claim for the misrepresentation of the technique's features, legality, and likelihood of success. The federal Credit Repair Organizations Act or a state analog may give the consumer additional claims, as these schemes are often marketed as methods for consumers to improve their credit records.[52] The activities of some of these companies may also amount to the unauthorized practice of law.

9.5.4 Credit Reporting

A person's credit standing is a significant and vital financial asset. Information contained in a consumer's credit reporting file affects not only access to, but also the cost and terms of, home mortgages, car loans, other forms of consumer credit, residential tenancies, employment, and even insurance.

A consumer's credit reporting file includes data reported by companies that have done business with the consumer, plus public record information—deaths, marriages, divorces, bankruptcies, court judgments, lawsuits. Credit reporting agencies play an integral and expansive role in the United States economy as they facilitate, or in many cases frustrate, consumers' access to credit. The industry sells more than 550 million credit reports a year. Credit scores, which are increasingly replacing the credit report as a means of evaluating creditworthiness, are used by more than 75% of mortgage lenders and over 90% of credit card issues.[53]

The federal Fair Credit Reporting Act (FCRA)[54] is the primary resource for resolving consumers' credit report problems. It offers a private cause of action, including attorney fees and in some circumstances statutory or punitive damages, for violation of many of its provisions.

Most FCRA claims fall into one of three general categories. The first is the unauthorized access to the consumer's credit report by a salesperson, an employer, or an adversary in litigation, for example, a spouse in a divorce proceeding.[55] A second common violation is the credit reporting agency's failure to maintain reasonable procedures to ensure the maximum possible accuracy in the credit report on the consumer.[56] Often it will be advantageous to frame this claim as a failure of the credit reporting agency to follow the procedures mandated by the FCRA when the consumer disputed the information in the report.[57]

A third common type of FCRA claim focuses on the entity that furnished the incorrect information to the credit reporting agency. While the FCRA sets accuracy standards for furnishers of information, there is no private cause of action to enforce those standards. However, the consumer does have a private cause of action against a furnisher who fails to reinvestigate a report after the consumer has disputed the information with the credit reporting agency.[58]

Credit reporting issues often arise in connection with identity theft, through which an imposter uses key elements of the consumer's financial identity to obtain credit and goods in the consumer's name. This is one of the fastest growing types of financial crimes, with billions of dollars of losses each year.[59] The general requirements of the FCRA can help identity theft victims remove negative information

49 15 U.S.C. §§ 1679–1679j. *See* National Consumer Law Center, Fair Credit Reporting Ch. 15 (5th ed. 2002 and Supp.).

50 FTC v. Innovative Sys. Tech., Inc., d.b.a. Briggs & Baker, CVO 4-0728 (C.D. Cal. complaint filed Feb. 4, 2004); FTC v. Nat'l Consumer Council *et seq.*, Case No. SACV-04-0474 CJC (C.D. Ca., complaint filed April 23, 2004), *available at* www.ftc.gov/os/2004/05/040423ncccomplaint.pdf. *See also* § 10.4.5 (telemarketing and "Do Not Call" laws).

51 *See* OCC Alert 2003-12 (Oct. 1, 2003), *available at* www.occ.treas.gove/ftp/alert/2003-12.doc.

52 The federal Act is found at 15 U.S.C. §§ 1679-1679j. The federal Act is reprinted, and all state credit repair laws cited and summarized, in National Consumer Law Center, Fair Credit Reporting Appxs. A, B (5th ed. 2002 and Supp.).

53 *See* National Consumer Law Center, Fair Credit Reporting § 14.3 (5th ed. 2002 and Supp.).

54 15 U.S.C. §§ 1681-1681v.

55 *See* National Consumer Law Center, Fair Credit Reporting §§ 9.2.2.3, 9.2.4.1 (5th ed. 2002 and Supp.).

56 *See* National Consumer Law Center, Fair Credit Reporting §§ 9.2.2.1, 9.2.2.2 (5th ed. 2002 and Supp.).

57 *Id.* §§ 7.6, 7.7, 9.2.2.9.

58 *Id.* § 3.14, 9.2.3.3.

59 *See* National Consumer Law Center, Fair Credit Reporting § 13.5.5 (5th ed. 2002 and Supp.).

from their credit reports. In addition, amendments to the FCRA adopted in 2003 provide a few special protections for victims of identity theft. For example, consumers can request fraud alerts and block theft-related debt from their credit reporting files.[60]

Because of the complexity of the FCRA and the need to master arcane facts about the credit reporting industry, practitioners who handle FCRA cases often find themselves specializing in that area, sometimes along with one or two other areas of consumer law, like debt collection. Since credit reporting issues also arise in the context of vehicle sales and mortgage financing, non-specialists should also be familiar with the FCRA. NCLC's manual *Fair Credit Reporting* is a key resource for attorneys handling FCRA cases. National Association of Consumer Advocates (NACA) holds annual trainings on FCRA litigation in the Spring, and several sessions of NCLC's annual Fall conference cover FCRA litigation issues.

9.5.6 Credit Repair Organizations

Credit repair organizations tell consumers that, for a fee, they can remove negative items from a credit history. Sometimes, they encourage consumers to establish a new credit identity by using an Employer Identification Number instead of their social security number, a seemingly fraudulent and possibly criminal solution to a bad situation. Another technique is to flood credit reporting agencies with spurious disputes of items in the consumer's credit record. A 2004 FTC Study estimated that, over a one-year period, almost 2.5 million people in the United States fell victim to credit repair scams.[61]

Generally, these agencies do nothing legitimate that consumers can not do for themselves free of charge.[62] Indeed, consumers may be better positioned to deal with their credit histories by themselves, as many credit bureaus refuse to deal with credit repair agencies and ignore the dispute letters they generate. A consumer will have far greater success by drafting individualized letters, which are not as likely to be considered frivolous as a repair agency form, and save paying the repair organization's fee.

Credit repair agency abuses are amenable to a UDAP approach. The federal Credit Repair Organizations Act and similar state laws offer additional remedies, including statutory damages and attorney fees. Federal and state RICO claims are also possible.[63] In addition, the FTC Telemarketing Rule prohibits many specific practices when credit repair services are sold through telephone calls.[64]

9.5.7 Consumer Bankruptcy

Rather than focusing on a particular industry, a bankruptcy practice focuses on the intricacies of the Bankruptcy Code. Most practitioners maintain a low-fee, high-volume practice. This is the largest area of consumer law practice, with the National Association of Consumer Bankruptcy Attorneys (NACBA) claiming 3000 members.

While most bankruptcy cases are handled by attorneys concentrating in that area, non-bankruptcy attorneys who handle consumer cases should also have a working knowledge of bankruptcy law and be prepared to associate with a bankruptcy attorney to litigate some clients' cases. For example, bankruptcy court has distinct advantages as a forum for some predatory mortgage lending cases.[65]

Many consumer attorneys start out with a practice that focuses on bankruptcy and then expand into other areas. Bankruptcy clients often have experienced violations of federal and state debt collection laws or are driven to consider bankruptcy because of a fraudulent transaction. In the alternative, many bankruptcy practitioners develop referral relationships with attorneys who handle these types of consumer cases.

National Consumer Law Center, *Consumer Bankruptcy Law and Practice* (7th ed. 2004), is an essential practice tool in this area. It analyzes in detail all issues affecting consumer bankruptcies, including the changes made by the 2005 amendments to the Bankruptcy Code. It also includes over a hundred forms, pleadings, notices, and sample letters on a companion CD-Rom.

9.6 Predatory Mortgage Lending and Home Defense

9.6.1 Predatory Mortgage Lending

Many Americans in the middle and upper economic classes are used to getting competitive interest rates and paying few fees to buy homes, refinance their mortgages, purchase cars and other consumer goods, take vacations, repair their homes, and send their children to college. The "prime" or "conventional" lending market serves these homeowners.

For those whose credit is blemished to any degree and others who are steered to unconventional lenders, the "subprime" mortgage market can be a very different experience. At its worst, the interest rates on loans are priced for

60 *See* National Consumer Law Center, Fair Credit Reporting §§ 16.1.1a.2; 16.6.1a.4.1 (5th ed. 2002 and Supp.).

61 *Consumer Fraud in the United States: An FTC Survey*, (Fed. Trade Comm'n, 2004), at 32.

62 *See* National Consumer Law Center, Fair Credit Reporting Ch. 13 (5th ed. 2002 and Supp.).

63 *See* National Consumer Law Center, Unfair and Deceptive Acts and Practices §§ 9.2, 9.3 (6th ed. 2004).

64 *See id.* § 5.9.2.3.6, *infra*.

65 See Ch. 13, *infra*.

profit, not risk. Abusive mortgage lenders may charge points[66] and fees in excess of 10% (and more) of the principal.

Repeated refinancing or "flipping" of the loan is another abuse. Each refinancing triggers a new round of points and fees that are charged up front and added to the principal. Interest is earned on these points and fees over the life of the loan as well as on the points and fees carried over from the old loan. The borrower may also have to pay a prepayment penalty upon refinancing. The result is an ever-increasing principal and a severe reduction in the equity in the home.

A segment of the subprime market engages in "asset-based lending," looking only to the value of the home rather than the borrower's ability to pay from liquid assets. When the borrower is unable to pay, the lender forecloses on the home.

Causes of mortgage lending abuses include

- federal preemption of state interest rate ceilings and other protections in the 1980s, and similar actions on the state level;
- the rise in real estate values, giving homeowners equity in their homes that attracts predatory lenders;
- reverse redlining—the abandonment of low-income neighborhoods by mainstream banks, creating a vacuum that high-rate lenders have rushed to fill;
- securitization of mortgage loans and the rise in the secondary mortgage market, which have enabled mortgage companies specializing in home equity lending to operate more profitably and with little capital; and
- amendments to the Internal Revenue Code that retained deductibility of interest only for home-secured loans.

Many predatory mortgage loans are originated by mortgage brokers, home improvement contractors, or mobile home dealers.

Litigating predatory mortgage loan cases is a rewarding practice that provides enormous benefits to victimized consumers. These cases tend to require a fair amount of individual factual development, discovery, and legal analysis. Attorney fees are available for a number of the most common statutory claims.

The Truth in Lending Act, and the Home Ownership and Equity Protection Act (HOEPA) amendments to that law, are the primary resources for helping homeowners victimized by predatory lending. The Truth in Lending Act requires the lender to disclose the key terms of the transaction to the consumer in standardized, clear language.[67] For certain non-purchase money home mortgage transactions, the consumer has the right to rescind the transaction for up to three years if the lender did not make certain material disclosures properly.[68] Consumers can also seek actual and statutory damages and attorney fees.[69]

HOEPA singles out a class of high-rate mortgage transactions and subjects them to special regulation.[70] If the transaction carries such a high interest rate, or has such high points and fees, that it qualifies as a HOEPA loan, then certain terms and practices are prohibited and the lender is required to give special advance disclosures.[71] Predatory lenders often attempt to conceal the fact that a loan qualifies as a HOEPA loan because they want to avoid these requirements, so determining whether HOEPA covers a transaction is a key first step in analyzing it. Remedies for violations can include rescission, actual and statutory damages, a special enhanced damages award, and attorney fees. National Consumer Law Center, Truth in Lending (5th ed. 2003 and Supp.), is an essential resource for litigating under either TILA or HOEPA.

The Fair Housing Act[72] and Equal Credit Opportunity Act[73] are also useful in predatory mortgage lending cases. The former prohibits discrimination in residential real-estate-related transactions, and the latter prohibits discrimination in granting credit or the terms of credit. Both allow actual damages, punitive damages, equitable relief, and attorney fees. Furthermore, while discrimination cases require extensive discovery and factual development, the ECOA also requires creditors to follow certain procedures when they grant or deny credit. Predatory lenders often shortcut these procedures and the complementary procedural requirements of the Fair Credit Reporting Act, giving the consumer more easily proven claims under these statutes.

The Real Estate Settlement Procedures Act (RESPA)[74] is another useful statute. It requires disclosure of settlement costs in real estate transactions. While RESPA does not create a private cause of action for violation of these disclosure requirements, these violations may be actionable as a violation of a state UDAP statute. RESPA also prohibits kickbacks from companies providing settlement services; prohibits steering of borrowers to title insurance companies; requires various notices to consumers; and requires mortgage loan servicers (entities that bill the consumer, receive payments, pass payments on to the owner of the loan, etc.) to audit escrow accounts, pay out escrowed money properly, and respond to requests from consumers about their accounts. For many of these requirements, the statute does create a private cause of action, in many instances including

66 One point equals 1% of the principal.

67 *See* National Consumer Law Center, Truth in Lending (5th ed. 2003 and Supp.).

68 15 U.S.C. § 1635.

69 15 U.S.C. § 1640.

70 *See* 15 U.S.C. § 1602(aa) (definition of HOEPA-covered transactions); National Consumer Law Center, Truth in Lending Ch. 9 (5th ed. 2003 and Supp.).

71 15 U.S.C. § 1639.

72 42 U.S.C. § 3605.

73 15 U.S.C. § 1691.

74 12 U.S.C. §§ 2601–2617.

statutory damages and attorney fees.

Claims against predatory mortgage lenders can also be based on the following:

- State and federal Racketeer Influenced and Corrupt Organization (RICO) laws. Treble damages and attorney fees are available under the federal statute and many state counterparts. RICO cases are extremely complex, however, so should not be undertaken lightly.
- State Unfair and Deceptive Acts and Practices (UDAP) statutes. These statutes prohibit deceptive practices, usually in broad, flexible terms. Many also prohibit unfair practices or offer statutory, multiple, or punitive damages and attorney fees. Before relying on a state UDAP statute, however, the attorney should make sure that it does not exempt credit transactions, real estate transactions, or the financial institution in question.
- Common law fraud. Neither credit nor real estate transactions will be exempt from common law fraud. Attorney fees are not generally available, but punitive damages are available in most jurisdictions, and a common law fraud claim can often be combined with a statutory claim that offers attorney fees.
- Unconscionability. Article 2 of the Uniform Commercial Code, which applies to transactions in goods, allows a court to find that a contract or term is unconscionable.[75] For non-goods transactions, the common law or another statute may establish a similar standard. The UCC also imposes a duty of good faith and fair dealing.[76]
- Broker laws. Loan brokers, typically compensated by commission, are the driving force for much predatory lending. A number of states have laws regulating mortgage loan brokers. In some states, a Credit Services Organization law may regulate both credit repair organizations and loan brokers.[77] A statute or the common law may also impose a fiduciary duty upon the broker.
- Home improvement contract laws. Many predatory mortgages arise out of fraudulent home improvement contracts. States may have special laws regulating these contractors. Common law warranties may arise regarding the quality of the work. Because of the FTC's Holder Rule,[78] these claims can be asserted against the lender in most circumstances.

National Consumer Law Center, *STOP Predatory Lending: A Guide for Legal Advocates* (2002), is an introduction to predatory lending and the ways to challenge it. For the litigator, National Consumer Law Center manuals *Truth in Lending* and *The Cost of Credit: Regulation, Preemption, and Industry Abuses* are essential resources.

9.6.2 Foreclosure Defense

Many homeowners who seek help regarding a foreclosure will have fallen victim to a predatory lender. Others, however, fall behind on their mortgage payments simply because of financial problems caused by divorce, illness, loss of a job, or some other reversal.

Every state has a statute governing the foreclosure of real estate, and some states have statutes dealing specifically with home mortgage foreclosures. Some states require foreclosure to be by judicial process and, in these states, court rules and procedures are also an important source of law. In other states, creditors can foreclose on a home without judicial involvement through a power of sale. In these states, a homeowner who wants judicial scrutiny of the foreclosing creditor's action must initiate suit.

The homeowner may be able to stop a foreclosure by challenging the underlying debt on grounds such as fraud, usury, or violation of the Truth in Lending Act, HOEPA, or a state UDAP statute. Many states also require the lender to offer the homeowner a right to cure the default by paying the past due amount plus certain specified costs and fees by a certain deadline. Even if the mortgage holder has followed all the proper procedures and there are no substantive grounds to challenge the right to foreclose, an attorney or a housing counselor may be able to negotiate a workout agreement.

All of these issues are discussed in detail in National Consumer Law Center, *Foreclosures* (2005). Attorneys who help consumers avoid foreclosure should also be familiar with bankruptcy law,[79] as bankruptcy can be an effective means of saving a home.

9.6.3 Home Rescuer Foreclosure Rescue Scams

Some companies use public records to identify those whose homes are being foreclosed and offer, for a fee, to help save the home. The company may imply it will offer re-financing or other effective techniques to stave off foreclosure. Instead, the company just files a bankruptcy petition for the homeowner or refers the consumer to a bankruptcy attorney. Since these businesses typically misrepresent their services, UDAP claims are often successful against them.[80]

75 U.C.C. § 2-302.

76 U.C.C. § 1-203.

77 *See* National Consumer Law Center, Fair Credit Reporting Ch. 15 (5th ed. 2002 and Supp.).

78 16 C.F.R. Part 433.

79 *See* National Consumer Law Center, Consumer Bankruptcy Law and Practice (7th ed. 2004).

80 *See* National Consumer Law Center, Unfair and Deceptive Acts and Practices § 5.1.2.1 (6th ed. 2004); National Consumer Law Center, The Cost of Credit: Regulation, Preemption, and Industry Abuses Ch. 11 (3d ed. 2005).

In addition, the Bankruptcy Code has special requirements and remedies if the company helps the consumer file a bankruptcy petition.[81]

An even more insidious type of "home rescue" induces the consumer to convey the home to the home rescuer, who then leases it back to the consumer. Often the home rescuer misleads the consumer about the import of the papers. If the sale and leaseback is disclosed at all, the home rescuer usually makes a vague and false promise that the consumer can repurchase the home at a future date.

Even though it is disguised as a sale and leaseback, the transaction may be considered a consumer credit transaction under the Truth in Lending Act, giving the consumer potential statutory damage and rescission claims.[82] In addition, a few states have statutes specifically directed at home rescuers.[83] The homeowner will also likely have claims under the state UDAP statute, common law fraud, the state home solicitation sales law, state credit laws, a state or federal telemarketing statute, a state real estate licensing or transfer laws, or a state or federal credit repair organization statute, depending on how the transaction was solicited and consummated.[84] Since home rescuers typically re-sell or mortgage the home as soon as they get title, it is important to act quickly and to name as defendants all parties who may have interests in the property or who may have been involved in the fraud. Failure to comply with the state's formal requirements for deeds should be investigated early. Home rescuers often cut corners on these formal requirements, but there is usually only a very short period of time to challenge a deed on these grounds.

9.7 Non-Mortgage Credit and Fringe Lenders

9.7.1 Banks, Thrifts, Credit Unions, Finance Companies, and Retail Installment Sellers

Banks, savings and loan associations (also known as thrift institutions), and credit unions are the traditional mainstream providers of non-mortgage (as well as mortgage) credit. These institutions may be chartered under either federal or state law. Since they not only extend credit but also accept deposits, they are known as depository institutions.[85]

Lenders such as consumer finance companies traditionally served the subprime market. These lenders operate under state laws that authorize a higher rate of interest and typically require licensing and supervision by a state agency. In recent years, however, consumer finance companies are being edged out by extremely high-rate fringe lenders such as payday lenders and auto pawn lenders.

Retail sellers can also extend credit by allowing payment for their merchandise over time. Typically a state retail installment sales act authorizes and regulates the extension of credit by sellers. Instead of waiting for the buyer to make installment payments, the seller may assign the installment sales contract to an acceptance company for a lump sum. Then the consumer makes the installment payments to the acceptance company.

When litigating against one of these entities, common claims are

- violation of the law under which the creditor operates, for example, a state or federal banking law or retail installment sales act;
- contract law claims;
- violation of the requirements under the Uniform Commercial Code and other state law for repossession and sale of collateral;
- violation of state debt collection practices laws (the federal Fair Debt Collection Practices Act generally applies only to independent debt collectors, not creditors collecting their own debts, but many state laws apply to creditors);
- claims under state Unfair and Deceptive Acts and Practices statutes, unless the statute exempts financial institutions; and
- Claims that could be asserted against the seller of goods or services for which the credit was extended to purchase. The FTC's Holder Rule[86] allows these claims to be asserted against the entity that financed the sale if it had a relationship with the seller as defined by the Rule.

9.7.2 Credit Cards

Charge cards were introduced in about 1914 by department stores, hotels, oil companies, and Western Union.[87]

---

81 11 U.S.C. § 19. *See also* National Consumer Law Center, Consumer Bankruptcy Law and Practice § 15.6 (7th ed. 2004).

82 *See, e.g.*, James v. Ragin, 432 F. Supp. 887 (W.D.N.C. 1977). *See generally* National Consumer Law Center, Truth in Lending § 2.5.3, Ch. 6 (5th ed. 2003 and Supp.).

83 *See* Cal. Civ. Code §§ 1695.1–1695.17 (home equity purchasers), 2945.1–1945.11 (foreclosure consultants).

84 *See* National Consumer Law Center, Unfair and Deceptive Acts and Practices §§ 5.1.2.5, 5.1.17, 5.8, 5.9 (6th ed. 2004).

85 See National Consumer Law Center, The Cost of Credit: Regulation, Preemption, and Industry Abuses Ch. 2 (3d ed. 2005) for a fuller exposition of the nature, history, and role of these lenders.

86 16 C.F.R. Part 433.

87 This summary of the development of the credit card industry is based on Diane Ellis, *Bank Trends—The Effect of Consumer Interest Rate Deregulation on Credit Card Volumes, Charge-Offs, and the Personal Bankruptcy Rate* (1999), *available at*

These cards could only be used to purchase the issuer's goods and services, and the balance had to be paid in full each month. In the 1950s, Diners' Club and American Express began issuing general purpose cards that could be used at a variety of vendors. Several years later, banks entered the market and introduced credit cards, which allowed balances to be carried over from one month to the next. In the 1960s, groups of banks created national credit card transaction processing systems under the names VISA and MasterCard. The great explosion in credit card lending, however, began in 1978 when the Supreme Court ruled that national banks could export interest rates from their home states by issuing credit cards to residents of other states.[88]

The intense marketing of credit cards is characterized by teaser rates, bait-and-switch offers, and false promises of fixed rates and other favorable terms.[89] Some credit card lenders increase their income through high late fees, manipulation of due dates and posting dates, over-limit fees, transaction fees, inactivity fees, penalty interest rates that are imposed if a payment is late, and low minimum payments that allow finance charges to build up over a longer period of time.[90]

Advocates representing consumers on credit card issues generally rely on contract law and the credit card law of the state that governs the issuing creditor. The Truth in Lending Act[91] requires disclosure of certain information when the consumer first obtains the credit card and thereafter in monthly bills. These claims are often suitable for class action treatment. In addition, the Fair Credit Billing Act[92] gives the consumer a procedure to challenge improper crediting of payments, charges for merchandise that was not received, and other billing errors.

9.7.3 Payday Loans

Payday loans go by a variety of names, including "deferred presentment," "cash advance," "deferred deposit," or "check loan," but they all work similarly. The consumer writes a check to the lender or authorizes the lender to debit his or her bank account for the amount borrowed plus a fee. For example, to receive $300 in cash, the consumer might have to write a check for $360. The typical annual percentage rate (APR) is at least 390% and can exceed 1000%.[93] The lender then holds the check (or debit agreement) for up to a month, until the customer's next payday or receipt of a government check. When payday arrives, a consumer who still does not have enough money to pay the check can pay another fee to extend the loan. If, on the other hand, the lender deposits the check and it is returned for insufficient funds, the consumer will incur bounced check charges. In addition, the lender may threaten to involve the criminal justice system, a tactic that is possible only because a check, rather than a mere promissory note, is involved.

These loans are marketed as a quick and easy way to get cash until the next payday. To qualify, consumers need only be employed for a period of time with the current employer or receive government benefits, maintain a personal checking account, and show a pay stub and bank statement. Credit reports are not routinely reviewed.

Abuses in making and collecting payday loans occur in a variety of ways. Cash-strapped consumers are rarely able to repay the entire loan when payday arrives, because they need the new paycheck for current living expenses. Lenders encourage these consumers to roll over or refinance one payday loan with another, payday after payday. Many borrowers are unable to climb off this debt treadmill.

Payday lenders have obtained laws legalizing their charges and practices in a number of states. In states that prohibit or restrict the practice, payday lenders may claim that they are not making loans at all. For example, some lenders use "cash back ad sales" as a subterfuge. The consumer "buys" an advertisement of one line for every $100 borrowed and pays an "ad fee" of $33 per $100—for an annual percentage rate of 860%—and gives the lender a signed check for $133, payable in two weeks. In another subterfuge, payday loans are offered by a local "front" for an out-of-state bank that is chartered in a state that does not have a usury ceiling. The payday lender then claims that it is able to export the out-of-state bank's permissible interest rate and ignore usury laws in the borrower's home state.

There are a number of potential claims against payday lenders. First is the often-complex question of whether the lender is violating a state usury law. These issues are analyzed in National Consumer Law Center, *The Cost of Credit: Regulation, Preemption, and Industry Abuses* (3d ed. 2005). Threats or use by a lender of criminal bad check laws to collect the debt may violate the state unfair or deceptive trade practices act. Such conduct also violates state fair debt collection practices acts that apply to creditors as collectors (and the federal act when the collector is a third party).

Payday loans are credit as defined by Truth in Lending, and these lenders' Truth In Lending disclosures are often inaccurate.[94] In addition, some state enforcement agencies have uncovered numerous violations of state payday loan laws during annual audits.

---

www.fdic.gov/bank/analytical/bank/bt_9805.html.

88 Marquette Nat'l Bank v. First Omaha Serv. Corp., 439 U.S. 299 (1978).

89 MassPIRG Education Fund, A Road Map to Avoiding Credit Card Hazards (Mar. 2001).

90 *Id.*

91 15 U.S.C. § 1601 *et seq.*

92 15 U.S.C. §§ 1666–1666j. *See* National Consumer Law Center, Truth in Lending § 5.8 (5th ed. 2003 and Supp.).

93 *See* National Consumer Law Center, The Cost of Credit: Regulation, Preemption, and Industry Abuses § 7.5.5 (3d ed. 2005).

94 *See* National Consumer Law Center, Truth in Lending § 2.5.5 (5th ed. 2003 and Supp.).

9.7.4 Pawnbrokers and Title Pawn Lenders

Pawnbrokering is not a new phenomenon. Traditional pawns are structured as pledges or conditional sales of the borrower's personal property to the pawnbroker, subject to the borrower's right to redeem. The pawnbroker takes physical possession of the property, paying the customer up to 50% of the value of the item. The consumer may redeem the property by paying a higher amount, usually a month later. If the consumer does not redeem the collateral, the pawnbroker keeps it and sells it.

Every state has enacted pawn statutes that regulate this type of lending to one extent or another. They may allow such high interest and fees that the permissible annual percentage rate exceeds 200%. Pawn transactions are subject to the disclosure requirements of the federal Truth in Lending Act.

Auto title loans are becoming prevalent, especially in the South. They were designed to take advantage of the special treatment afforded pawn transactions, but they are actually just secured loans, as the debtor turns over only the title, not the car itself. Such lenders usually limit the loan amount to 30% of the book value of the car, making the loans a risk-free investment. The typical title loan is a one-month single-payment loan with an annual percentage rate ranging from 200% to 300%.

Abuses abound in this industry. Borrowers who can not make the payment when it comes due often pay another fee to extend the loan. This cycle can create a debt treadmill. In addition, the tile lender holds title and may be entitled to repossess the car. Usually, the lender sells the car and keeps the entire sale price if it is not required to return the equity to the consumer. Some lenders obtain used car dealer licenses, sell the repossessed car to themselves, and then re-sell to other consumers on the retail market. The profit can be enormous.

Under the guise of regulating these transactions, a few states have passed statutes that permit auto title pawn lending.[95] In the other states, title lenders may claim they are operating legally under state pawnbroker laws. However, state pawnbroker laws typically do not allow loans while the lender holds just the title to the car rather than the car itself. If the lender can not take shelter under the state pawnbroker law, it will almost surely be in violation of state restrictions on interest rates and loan terms. In addition, title pawn lenders are subject to the Truth in Lending Act.[96] Title pawn lenders often do not provide Truth In Lending disclosures at all or, if they do, the disclosures may be inaccurate. A wrongful repossession claim may be raised when the pawnbroker or lender did not obtain a valid security interest in the car or title.[97] The borrower may also have claims of fraud, misrepresentation, and unfair or deceptive practices.

9.7.5 Refund Anticipation Loans

Tax refund anticipation loans ("RALs") are another type of high-cost credit. Tax preparers advertising "instant refunds" lend the taxpayer the amount of the refund, minus fees. By accepting the loan, taxpayer gets money about ten days before the tax refund would normally arrive.

Regardless of how these transactions are treated under state usury law, they are credit transactions for purposes of the TILA. The TILA's broad definition of credit—"the right granted by a creditor to a debtor to defer payment of debt or to incur debt and defer its payment"[98]—clearly encompasses such a transaction. Most tax refund lenders acknowledge that the transaction is a loan and that TIL disclosures must be made, but a few fringe operators attempt to cast the transaction in a form that will enable them to avoid complying with TILA and other credit legislation.

9.7.6 Rent to Own (RTO)

Rent-to-own (RTO) businesses are essentially appliance and furniture retailers, except that they arrange lease agreements instead of installment sales contracts for consumers who can not pay cash. An RTO lease agreement contains several special features. First, the lease is short term, so "rental" payments are due weekly or monthly. Second, the lease is structured as a series of one-or two-week loans, renewable at the consumer's option. Theoretically, the lease need not be renewed at the end of each weekly or monthly payment period. Third, the lease includes a purchase option that enables the customer to obtain title to the goods by making a final payment in a specified amount after making weekly or biweekly rental payments for a specified number of weeks.

The RTO industry originally crafted these transactions as leases in order to mask their installment sales nature. In this way, the industry attempted to avoid state interest rate caps in state retail installment loan laws. The short renewable term also avoids the disclosures that the federal Truth in Lending or Consumer Leasing Act would otherwise require.

In the 1980s, litigation in many states successfully challenged the industry's claim not to fall under state Retail Installment Sales Acts. In response, however, the industry successfully lobbied for protective legislation. Industry-drafted legislation has been adopted in all but a few states.[99]

RTO transactions carry astronomic undisclosed interest rates. For example, a nineteen-inch new color television

95 National Consumer Law Center, The Cost of Credit: Regulation, Preemption, and Industry Abuses § 7.5.2.3 (3d ed. 2005).

96 National Consumer Law Center, Truth in Lending § 2.5.2 (5th ed. 2003 and Supp.).

97 *See* National Consumer Law Center, Repossessions § 3.5.5 (6th ed. 2005).

98 15 U.S.C. § 1602(e).

99 National Consumer Law Center, The Cost of Credit: Regulation, Preemption, and Industry Abuses § 7.5.3.5 (3d ed. 2005).

may sell for $300. At the RTO store, the customer will pay about $16 per week for 52 weeks ($832). The difference between the retail price of $300 and the cost to purchase through a lease is $532. The annual percentage rate for this transaction is 254%.

Legal challenges are still possible. Causes of action can include unconscionability in the pricing, fraud and unfair and deceptive practices, wrongful repossession, breach of warranty, debt collection harassment, violation of restrictions on home solicitation sales, breach of the peace and, occasionally, even violation of a state RTO law.[100]

---

100 *Id.* § 7.5.3.6.

Chapter 10 Analysis of Consumer Transactions

By Carolyn Carter[1] and Kathleen Keest[2]

10.1 Consumer Law: Wide and Deep

There are so many consumer protection laws that most consumer law practitioners are forced to specialize, focusing on a few practices of a particular industry.[3] The typical sale of a car using a retail installment sales contract may involve the federal Truth in Lending Act, the Equal Credit Opportunity Act, Magnuson-Moss Warranty Act, federal and state odometer laws, and the Federal Trade Commission's Rules on Preservation of Claims and Defenses, Used Cars, and Creditor Practices. In addition, the transaction may involve the state usury law, retail installment sales act, Uniform Commercial Code articles 2, 3, and 9, insurance laws, unfair and deceptive acts and practices (UDAP) statute, lemon law, and vehicle title laws.

To make this law more accessible, the National Consumer Law Center (NCLC) publishes a multi-volume series of manuals on consumer law.[4] NCLC also hosts an annual conference in the fall on consumer law and takes part in local consumer law training events throughout the year.

1 Carolyn Carter is Deputy Director of Advocacy at NCLC. She was formerly co-director of Legal Services, Inc., in Gettysburg, Pennsylvania, and director of the Law Reform Office of the Cleveland Legal Aid Society. She is the editor of *Pennsylvania Consumer Law* and the first edition of *Ohio Consumer Law*; co-author of *Automobile Fraud* (2003), *Consumer Warranty Law* (2d ed. 2001), *Unfair and Deceptive Acts and Practices* (6th ed. 2004), *Repossessions and Foreclosures* (5th ed. 2002 and Supp.); and contributing author to *Fair Debt Collection* (5th ed. 2004 and Supp.), *Truth in Lending* (5th ed. 2003 and Supp.), and *The Cost of Credit: Regulation, Preemption, and Industry Abuses* (3d ed. 2005). She is the 1992 recipient of the Vern Countryman Consumer Award and is currently a member of the Federal Reserve Board's Consumer Advisory Council.

2 Kathleen Keest is Senior Policy Counsel at the Center for Responsible Lending in Durham, N.C. Prior to that, Kathleen was with the Office of the Attorney General of Iowa in its Consumer Protection Division, serving as Deputy Administrator of the Iowa Consumer Credit Code. From 1985 to 1996, she was a staff attorney with the National Consumer Law Center, specializing in federal and state credit litigation.

3 *See* Ch. 3, *supra*; Appx. E, *infra*.

4 *See* What Your Library Should Contain, *supra*; visit www.ConsumerLaw.org or call NCLC, 617-542-9595 for information.

10.2 A Map of Consumer Protection Legislation

One way of taking a systematic look at a consumer transaction is to track its history and examine each stage from access to credit, to advertising and inducement, to disclosure of credit terms, to performance, and finally to collection in light of applicable federal and state laws. Even if a client presents a problem dealing with just one stage of a transaction, it is helpful to look forward and backward to analyze the causes and side effects of the problem.

The following is a kind of travel guide to the major statutes applicable to each of these stages. From there, refer to the NCLC manuals for a more detailed look at the issues to be examined.

Although this outline focuses on statutes, practitioners should remember that common-law contract and tort claims and defenses also serve as critical tools. NCLC's manuals discuss the most useful common law principles as well as statutory claims.[5]

10.3 Access to Credit

10.3.1 General

Was there a problem obtaining access to credit or obtaining the desired terms of credit? Predatory lenders often target a particular class of victims, such as elderly or minority homeowners, to market their highly disadvantageous credit terms. Federal and state laws prohibiting credit discrimination go to the heart of these abuses. Even when discrimination can not be shown, the Equal Credit Opportunity Act and the Fair Credit Reporting Act have procedural requirements that are designed to alert consumers

5 For example, *Fair Debt Collection* discusses defamation, invasion of privacy, and other tort claims for debt collection abuses; *Automobile Fraud* discusses common law fraud; Consumer Warranty Law discusses negligence; and *Cost of Credit: Regulation, Preemption, and Industry Abuses* discusses common-law lender liability claims such as breach of fiduciary duty and unconscionability.

when the creditor is switching them to abusive credit terms. Many creditors ignore these inconvenient requirements, giving the victimized consumer powerful claims.

10.3.2 Equal Credit Opportunity Act

The Equal Credit Opportunity Act (ECOA)[6] proscribes discrimination in any aspect of the credit transaction on the basis of

- race, color, religion, national origin, sex or marital status, or age (assuming age of capacity);
- the applicant's income being entirely or partly from a public assistance program, including but not limited to TANF, HUD subsidies, food stamps, social security disability, SSI, unemployment compensation, and veterans' benefits; and
- the applicant's good-faith exercise of a right under the Consumer Credit Protection Act.[7]

The ECOA also requires that an applicant be given notice of adverse actions and an opportunity to obtain an explanation for adverse actions. It limits the types of questions a creditor may ask a potential borrower and requires that information furnished by a creditor to a credit-reporting agency reflect that both spouses participate in a credit account.

The ECOA authorizes actual and punitive damages and attorney fees. The practitioner should pay particular attention to Regulation B[8] rather than in the ECOA itself because most of the detailed requirements are found in Regulation B. Many states have their own credit discrimination laws, usually found in the state credit or civil rights act.[9]

10.3.3 Fair Credit Reporting Act

The Fair Credit Reporting Act[10] (FCRA) applies to credit reporting agencies, users of credit reports, and creditors and others who furnish information to credit reporting agencies. In 2003, the FCRA was amended by the Fair and Accurate Credit Transactions Act[11] (FACTA), which provides consumers with important additional rights relating to credit reports, identity theft, and credit scores.

The FCRA establishes standards for access to and use of credit reports. It also sets standards of accuracy for credit reports, prohibits the reporting of obsolete information, and requires various notices to consumers. Consumers have the right to disclosure of the contents of their files, including, in certain cases, the source of the information and the identity of those to whom a report has been given within a specified time. The FCRA also provides a mechanism for obtaining a reinvestigation of disputed information and the deletion of incorrect information as well as the right to include the consumer's explanation of the dispute if the disputed information is not to be deleted.

A credit report user who takes adverse action on the basis of the report must disclose certain information concerning the report to the consumer, either automatically or upon request.

The FCRA makes credit reporting agencies liable for damages and attorney fees, plus punitive damages, for willful violations. If a creditor or other entity that originally reported negative information fails to cooperate when the credit reporting agency requests a reinvestigation, it too faces liability under the federal statute.[12] Many states also have legislation governing credit reporting.[13]

Because of the FACTA amendments to the FCRA, consumers now have the right to one free report each year from each of the three national credit reporting agencies.[14] A good early step in evaluating a credit transaction is to have the consumer obtain a free report from at least one of the national credit reporting agencies.[15] The credit report may contain negative items that will explain why the consumer could not get credit. If the consumer is fighting a fraudulent merchant, the credit report will show whether the merchant has made a negative report on the consumer. It will also show who has accessed the consumer's credit report recently and when they did so. All of this information can help the advocate develop a picture of the players, their actions, and more potential claims.

---

6 15 U.S.C. §§ 1691–1691f. *See generally* National Consumer Law Center, Credit Discrimination (4th ed. 2005).

7 The Consumer Credit Protection Act, 15 U.S.C. §§ 1601–1693r, includes the Truth in Lending Act, the Fair Credit Billing Act, the Consumer Leasing Act, the federal restrictions on wage garnishment, the Fair Credit Reporting Act, the Fair Debt Collection Practices Act, the Electronic Fund Transfer Act, and the Equal Credit Opportunity Act itself.

8 12 C.F.R. §§ 202.1–202.14.

9 National Consumer Law Center, Credit Discrimination Appx. E (4th ed. 2005).

10 15 U.S.C. §§ 1681–1681t.

11 Pub. L. No. 108-159 (Dec. 4, 2003).

12 15 U.S.C. §§ 1681s-2(b), 1681o, 1681n.

13 *See* National Consumer Law Center, Fair Credit Reporting Appx. B (5th ed. 2002 and Supp.).

14 15 U.S.C. § 1681j(a), *amended by* Pub. L. No. 108-159, § 211 (Dec. 4, 2003). *See* National Consumer Law Center, Fair Credit Reporting § 4.4.2.1 (5th ed. 2002 and Supp.).

15 The free credit reports may be obtained from a centralized source by calling 1-877-322-8228 or visiting www.annualcreditreport.com.

10.4 Advertising and Inducement

10.4.1 FTC and Truth in Lending Requirements

Was there improper disclosure, deception, misrepresentation, or omission of information in (1) advertising the credit terms, (2) inducement to the contract, or (3) explanation of the contract terms?

The Federal Trade Commission Act generally prohibits unfair or deceptive acts or practices in or affecting commerce.[16] The Federal Trade Commission (FTC) has issued many trade regulation rules defining unfair or deceptive acts in specific kinds of transactions, including the Credit Practices Rule,[17] the Holder Rule,[18] the Used Car Rule,[19] and the rule establishing a cooling-off period for door-to-door sales.[20] These rules include many restrictions on deceptive tactics that induce consumers to enter into transactions.

Unfortunately, the FTC Act does not provide a private cause of action for consumers to enforce these rules. The federal Truth in Lending Act also regulates advertisements regarding credit costs and terms[21] but also lacks an explicit private right of action for violation of these requirements. Nonetheless, a violation of one of these federal statutes will usually constitute a violation of the state unfair and deceptive acts and practices statute, described next.

10.4.2 State Unfair and Deceptive Acts and Practices (UDAP) Statutes

All fifty states and the District of Columbia have statutes that prohibit deceptive business practices.[22] Most also prohibit unfair or unconscionable practices. All jurisdictions except Iowa authorize a private right of action for damages, and most provide enhanced remedies such as treble damages, punitive damages, minimum statutory damages, and attorney fees to the prevailing consumer.

State UDAP statutes are the workhorses of consumer law. Most accommodate a broad, flexible definition of deception and unfairness and are thus well-suited to attack emerging forms of consumer fraud. Although there are issues in a few states regarding coverage of certain defendants such as lenders, real estate sellers, and regulated industries, the typical UDAP statute is broadly applicable to all or almost all businesses that deal with low-income consumers.

Since state UDAP statutes usually prohibit deception and unfairness in general terms, courts often look to other sources of law for guidance. Many consumers have successfully used the state UDAP statute as a vehicle for enforcing FTC rules or requirements under other statutes and regulations designed to protect consumers.[23]

10.4.3 Common Law Fraud

State UDAP statutes were enacted to liberalize the rules of common law fraud and, in many instances, a UDAP claim is preferable to a fraud claim. Nonetheless, when there is evidence that the defendant's deceptive inducement was intentional, or when the consumer can develop proof of repeated instances of the same type of deception, a common law fraud claim should be considered.[24] A significant advantage of a common law fraud claim is the possibility of punitive damages in most jurisdictions. While the proof requirements are stricter, restrictions on a UDAP statute's scope will not apply to a common law fraud claim. In addition, in some states a jury trial is not available for UDAP claims but is available for common law fraud claims.

10.4.4 Racketeer Influenced and Corrupt Organizations Act

The Racketeer Influenced and Corrupt Organizations Act (RICO)[25] has been used to attack various forms of fraud, including consumer fraud. Civil penalties include treble damages and attorney fees.[26] RICO claims must be based on a pattern of racketeering activity or collection of an illegal debt, terms that are defined in the statute and judicial decisions. In addition, there are complicated requirements involving the relationship between the defendant and an enterprise. Case law interpreting RICO is complex and in a constant state of flux, and there is some judicial hostility to it. Thus, if this approach is considered, care should be taken to follow the latest developments. Many states have RICO laws of their own, most of which provide for a simpler private cause of action based on a wider range of predicate offenses. NCLC's *Unfair and Deceptive Acts and Practices* contains a detailed discussion of the application of both federal and state RICO statutes to consumer fraud.[27]

16 15 U.S.C. § 45(a)(1). *See* National Consumer Law Center, Unfair and Deceptive Acts and Practices (6th ed. 2004).
17 16 C.F.R. Part 444.
18 16 C.F.R. Part 433.
19 16 C.F.R. Part 455.
20 16 C.F.R. Part 429.
21 15 U.S.C. §§ 1661–1665a; 12 C.F.R. §§ 226.16, 226.24.
22 *See* National Consumer Law Center, Unfair and Deceptive Acts and Practices (6th ed. 2004).
23 *See* National Consumer Law Center, Unfair and Deceptive Acts and Practices § 3.2.7 (6th ed. 2004).
24 Common law fraud is discussed in detail in National Consumer Law Center, Automobile Fraud Ch. 7 (2d ed. 2003 and Supp.).
25 18 U.S.C. §§ 1961–1968.
26 18 U.S.C. § 1964.
27 *See* National Consumer Law Center, Unfair and Deceptive Acts and Practices §§ 9.2, 9.3 (6th ed. 2004).

10.4.5 Telemarketing Laws

If the transaction was conducted over the telephone, a state or federal telemarketing law may apply. The FTC's Telemarketing Sales Rule[28] prohibits telemarketers from calling people who register on the nationwide do-not-call list and also prohibits a litany of deceptive and abusive practices. Most states have similar laws.

10.4.6 Cancellation Rights

The advocate should always determine whether the consumer has the right to cancel the transaction under a statute or rule. An FTC Rule creates a three-day right to cancel a door-to-door or off-premises sale of goods or services.[29] Most states have similar rules or statutes. Federal law also creates a three-day right to cancel any contract with a credit repair organization[30] and any non-purchase money consumer credit transaction in which the creditor takes a security interest in the borrower's primary dwelling.[31] Many states also have statutes giving consumers the right to cancel certain types of transactions, such as health spa contracts or timeshare purchases. If the seller or creditor failed to make proper disclosure of the right to cancel under these statutes or rules, typically the consumer has a continuing right to cancel that can be exercised long after the three-day period has expired.

10.5 Are the Contract Terms Properly Disclosed and Do They Comply with Applicable Statutes and Regulations?

10.5.1 Disclosure Requirements of the Federal Truth in Lending Act

The Truth in Lending Act,[32] passed in 1968, was Congress's first foray into consumer protection since it had broadened the FTC Act in 1938 to cover consumer fraud. The main thrust of the Truth in Lending Act is not to regulate credit terms but to require accurate, uniform disclosure of those terms.

Actual damages, statutory damages, and attorney fees are available for violations. For certain non-purchase money residential mortgage credit, the borrower may rescind the transaction for up to three years in some circumstances.

10.5.2 Home Ownership and Equity Protection Act (HOEPA)

The Home Ownership and Equity Protection Act of 1994 (HOEPA)[33] was Congress's primary response to the predatory lending crisis. HOEPA singles out certain high-rate mortgage loans and subjects them to special disclosure requirements and restrictions on terms. A high-rate loan is defined as one in which (1) the annual percentage rate exceeds the interest rate for U.S. Treasury bonds by a certain number of percentage points, or (2) the total dollar amount of points and fees paid by the borrower at or before closing exceeds a certain percentage of the total loan amount.[34] Purchase-money loans, reverse mortgages, and open-end credit are not covered.

If a creditor enters into a credit transaction covered by HOEPA and does not comply with the special disclosure requirements, includes a prohibited term, or engages in a prohibited practice, the consumer has the remedies provided by the Truth in Lending Act: actual damages, statutory damages, attorney fees, and, in some cases, the right to rescind the transaction.[35] In addition, HOEPA allows the consumer to recover an enhanced statutory damage award consisting of all finance charges and fees paid by the consumer.[36] HOEPA also makes assignees of the obligation liable for all claims and defenses that could be asserted against the original creditor, up to a certain cap.[37]

10.5.3 State Credit Laws

Businesses that prey on low-income consumers often impose unconscionable finance charges. The first step in analyzing such a transaction is to determine whether a state credit law applies to the transaction: a retail installment sales

28 16 C.F.R. Part 310. *See* National Consumer Law Center, Unfair and Deceptive Acts and Practices § 5.9 (6th ed. 2004).

29 16 C.F.R. Part 429. *See* National Consumer Law Center, Unfair and Deceptive Acts and Practices § 5.8.2 (6th ed. 2004).

30 15 U.S.C. § 1679d. *See* National Consumer Law Center, Fair Credit Reporting Ch. 15 (5th ed. 2002 and Supp.).

31 15 U.S.C. § 1635. *See* National Consumer Law Center, Truth in Lending Ch. 6 (5th ed. 2003 and Supp.).

32 15 U.S.C. §§ 1601–1667e. The Federal Reserve Board has promulgated Regulation Z, 12 C.F.R. Part 226, and Regulation M, 12 C.F.R. Part 213 (consumer leasing), and issued an Official Staff Commentary to provide greater specificity as to disclosure requirements. The Act, the appropriate regulation, and the Commentary should all be consulted when analyzing a transaction. All are included in the appendices to National Consumer Law Center, Truth in Lending (5th ed. 2003 and Supp.).

33 15 U.S.C. §§ 1602(aa), 1639; Regulation Z, 12 C.F.R. §§ 226.31–226.34. HOEPA is analyzed in detail in National Consumer Law Center, Truth in Lending Ch. 9 (5th ed. 2003 and Supp.).

34 The calculations for determining whether a loan meets either of these two triggers are discussed in detail in National Consumer Law Center, STOP Predatory Lending: A Guide for Legal Advocates (2002) and National Consumer Law Center, Truth in Lending Ch. 9 (5th ed. 2003 and Supp.).

35 15 U.S.C. §§ 1640(a), 1639(j), 1635.

36 15 U.S.C. § 1640(a)(4).

37 15 U.S.C. § 1641(d).

act, motor vehicle installment sales act, installment loan law, rent-to-own statute, payday loan law, small loan act,[38] secondary mortgage act, or comprehensive consumer credit law such as the Uniform Consumer Credit Code. Determining whether a particular state statute applies to a transaction is sometimes surprisingly difficult, as the creditor may attempt to disguise one type of transaction as another in order to avoid regulation.

When a state credit law applies, it will govern the cost of credit, including the finance charge, authorized additional charges, and delinquency and deferral charges. These statutes often place limitations on other credit terms, such as security interests, prepayment rights, and creditors' enforcement rights. Specific remedies available to the consumer are often prescribed.

After determining that a state credit statute applies to the transaction, the advocate has another hurdle to overcome. Several federal statutes, including the Depository Institutions Deregulation and Monetary Control Act of 1980,[39] the Alternative Mortgage Transactions Parity Act,[40] and the National Bank Act[41] preempt state usury laws as to interest rates, charges, or certain types of loan terms, at least with respect to certain types of lenders or certain types of transactions.[42] Under some of the preemption statutes, states have the right to opt out of the effects of the federal preemption. Practitioners should always determine whether federal preemption applies to the transaction under analysis. The consumer's advocate should make sure that any creditor who invokes federal preemption has complied with all the federal statute's preconditions.

10.5.4 Credit Practices Rule

The FTC's Credit Practices Rule[43] places limitations on certain credit contract terms. Among other things, the rule prohibits non-purchase-money security interests in household goods, pyramiding late charges, confessions of judgment, wage assignments, and waivers of exemption.[44] It also requires specific disclosures to co-signers of the risks they are undertaking.[45] As is true for other FTC rules, there is no private cause of action to enforce this rule, but most courts have held that terms that violate the rule are unenforceable and that inclusion of such terms is a UDAP violation.[46]

10.5.5 Special State Laws Applicable to Particular Types of Transactions

Many states have special laws applicable to transactions with particular types of providers such as health spas, loan brokers, credit repair organizations, telemarketers, membership campgrounds, and buyers clubs.[47] These laws generally provide some substantive requirements as to the terms of the transaction and the seller's obligations. Many provide a private cause of action or explicitly state that a violation is a UDAP violation.

10.6 Performance

10.6.1 Warranties

If the transaction was a sale, did the seller perform its obligations? Article 2 of the Uniform Commercial Code (UCC) establishes numerous types of warranties related to the sales of goods and services.[48] Article 2 is in effect in every state except Louisiana.

The Magnuson-Moss Warranty Act[49] sets minimum standards for warranties and disclosure requirements of warranty terms. The Act also prescribes standards for informal dispute-settlement procedures. Damages and attorney fees are authorized. In some cases, this Act provides more protections to consumers than state law.

Every state also has a lemon law that expands the rights of the buyers when a new car can not be conformed to the warranty within a reasonable number of repair attempts. A number of states also have used car lemon laws or other special protections for buyers of used cars. Many states also have laws that mandate or regulate warranties on mobile homes, assistive devices such as wheelchairs and hearing aids, newly built homes, and condominiums. Common law warranties apply to services such as automobile repair in most jurisdictions.

All of these sources of warranty law are analyzed in National Consumer Law Center, *Consumer Warranty Law* (2d ed. 2001 and Supp.).[50] A number of treatises on UCC warranty law are also available.

38 The state small loan act may be known as a regulated loan act, consumer loan act, or industrial loan act.

39 12 U.S.C. §§ 1737f-7 note, 183 1(d), 1730g note, 1735f-7 note.

40 12 U.S.C. §§ 3801–3805.

41 12 U.S.C. § 85.

42 *See* National Consumer Law Center, Cost of Credit: Regulation, Preemption, and Industry Abuses Ch. 3 (3d ed. 2005).

43 16 C.F.R. Part 444.

44 *Id. See* National Consumer Law Center, Unfair and Deceptive Acts and Practices § 5.1.3.1.9 (6th ed. 2004).

45 16 C.F.R. Part 444.

46 *See* National Consumer Law Center, Unfair and Deceptive Acts and Practices § 5.1.1.2.10 (6th ed. 2004).

47 See National Consumer Law Center, Unfair and Deceptive Acts and Practices Ch. 5 (6th ed. 2004) for a survey of UDAP statutes and other state laws applicable to particular types of transactions.

48 UCC §§ 2-313 to 2-315.

49 15 U.S.C. §§ 2301–2312; 16 C.F.R. Parts 700–703. *See* National Consumer Law Center, Consumer Warranty Law Ch. 2 (2d ed. 2001 and Supp.).

50 *See, e.g.*, James J. White & Robert S. Summers, Uniform Commercial Code (4th ed. 1995).

10.6.2 Odometer Law

Federal law prohibits tampering with odometers and establishes disclosure standards.[51] Treble damages or $1500, whichever is greater, plus attorney fees are authorized. Many states have also enacted legislation dealing with odometer tampering.[52]

10.6.3 FTC Used Car Rule

The FTC Used Car Trade Practices Rule requires used-vehicle dealers to disclose whether the car carries a warranty.[53] The rule also prohibits any misrepresentation about the vehicle's mechanical condition or the terms or existence of a warranty. As is true for other FTC rules, there is no implied private right of action. Still, the Rule is useful as a basis for state UDAP or Magnuson-Moss claims.

10.7 Collection

10.7.1 Fair Debt Collection Practices Statutes

Is the debtor being harassed for payment? Are the borrower's assets being threatened?

The federal Fair Debt Collection Practices Act (FDCPA) regulates collection practices of third-party collectors.[54] With a few exceptions, it does not cover creditors collecting their own debts. The Act regulates communications to third parties and prohibits harassment, abuse, false or misleading representations, and unfair practices. It also requires collectors to notify debtors that they may challenge the validity of the debt and require the collector to verify it. Damages, statutory penalties, and attorney fees are authorized.

In many states, there are state laws that go beyond the FDCPA and regulate collection practices of both third-party collectors and creditors. These statutes may be found in state consumer codes, UDAP statutes, or collection agency licensing laws.[55]

National Consumer Law Center, *Fair Debt Collection* (5th ed. 2004 and Supp.), is a comprehensive analysis of federal and state debt-collection practices statutes and the numerous decisions interpreting them. It also analyzes common law tort claims that can often be asserted in conjunction with or in lieu of a statutory claim.

10.7.2 Repossession

Article 9 of the UCC[56] specifies creditors' duties and consumers' rights with respect to the repossession and disposition of collateral. A creditor who fails to comply with Article 9 requirements in a consumer transaction is liable for actual damages or, for some violations, a statutory damage award of the finance charge plus 10% of the principal.[57] Under the uniform version of Article 9, a smaller statutory damage award ($500) is also available for violation of certain requirements regarding such matters as notice to the consumer of the amount of the deficiency, responses to requests for information, and termination of the security interest when an obligation has been paid.[58] A creditor's failure to comply with Article 9 may also bar it from recovering a deficiency judgment. Article 9 was revised extensively in 1999, and all fifty states plus the District of Columbia have adopted the revised version.

Many states also have non-UCC statutes that restrict repossession of collateral or the creditor's right to collect a deficiency. Typically these laws apply only to certain types of transactions, such as retail installment contracts. Wrongful repossession may also give the consumer remedies under tort law and, in some circumstances, under the federal Fair Debt Collection Practices Act.[59]

10.7.3 Foreclosure of Residential Property

10.7.3.1 State Foreclosure Laws

Every state has a law governing foreclosure. Some states require the creditor to file a judicial action to foreclose on real estate. Others authorize a non-judicial foreclosure procedure in which the creditor has the right to sell the property, usually after giving the homeowner notice. Many states require the creditor to afford the homeowner an opportunity to cure the default and avoid the sale or to redeem the property after the sale by paying the total outstanding balance and costs. All of these—as well as the creditor's compliance with the procedures required by the foreclosure

51 49 U.S.C. §§ 30501–30505; 49 C.F.R. §§ 580.1–580.17. *See* National Consumer Law Center, Automobile Fraud Chs. 3, 4 (2d ed. 2003 and Supp.).

52 *See* National Consumer Law Center, Automobile Fraud Ch. 5 (2d ed. 2003 and Supp.).

53 16 C.F.R. Part 455. *See* National Consumer Law Center, Consumer Warranty Law Ch. 14 (2d ed. 2001 and Supp.).

54 15 U.S.C. §§ 1692–1692o. *See* National Consumer Law Center, Fair Debt Collection Chs. 3–7 (5th ed. 2004 and Supp.).

55 *See* National Consumer Law Center, Fair Debt Collection Ch. 11 (5th ed. 2004 and Supp.).

56 National Consumer Law Center, Repossessions and Foreclosures (5th ed. 2002 and Supp.); James J. White & Robert S. Summers, Uniform Commercial Code (4th ed. 1995).

57 U.C.C. § 9-625. California and Louisiana did not adopt this statutory damage provision, however, and in Oregon the amount is $1000 plus attorney fees.

58 U.C.C. § 9-625(e), (f).

59 *See* National Consumer Law Center, Repossessions and Foreclosures Ch. 13 (5th ed. 2002 and Supp.).

law—options should be explored. In addition, it may be possible to negotiate a workout agreement before the foreclosure sale.[60]

10.7.3.2 Truth in Lending Rescission

Rescinding the contract (and voiding the security interest that threatens foreclosure) is sometimes an available remedy.

If the credit is (1) secured by a security interest or lien arising by operation of law in (2) the consumer's principal dwelling and (3) the credit is for consumer purposes (but not for the acquisition of the property or dwelling), the Truth in Lending Act may give the consumer up to three years to rescind the transaction. Rescission voids the security interest and cancels any obligation to pay finance charges (even if accrued) or closing costs.[61] The consumer has an unconditional right to cancel for three business days after consummation of the transaction, but this right can be extended up to three years if the creditor has failed to make certain key Truth in Lending disclosures properly.[62] If the mortgage transaction qualifies as a HOEPA loan, as described above, there are additional grounds on which the right to rescind can be extended. Statutory and actual damages under the Truth in Lending Act and HOEPA can also help make a workout of the mortgage affordable by offsetting part of the balance.

10.7.3.3 State Credit Regulation Laws

State credit regulation laws, such as licensing laws or other usury laws, provide relatively stiff penalties for certain violations.[63] Unless they are preempted by federal law,[64] these provisions can be used to stop a foreclosure by voiding the transaction.

10.7.3.4 Cooling-Off Period

Many home improvement contracts arise from home solicitation sales. The FTC rule concerning a cooling-off period for door-to-door sales provides a three-day right to cancel covered transactions.[65] Many states have enacted similar statutes.[66] Most courts hold that the right to cancel extends until the seller gives proper notice of the right to cancel. As a result, a non-complying contract can often be cancelled years later.

60 *See id.* Chs. 16, 17.
61 15 U.S.C. § 1635.
62 *Id.*
63 *See* National Consumer Law Center, Cost of Credit: Regulation, Preemption, and Industry Abuses Ch. 10 (3d ed. 2005).
64 *See id.* Ch. 13.
65 16 C.F.R. Part 429.
66 *See* National Consumer Law Center, Unfair and Deceptive Acts and Practices § 5.8 (6th ed. 2004).

10.7.4 Garnishment and Attachment

Federal law limits the amount of earnings that can be garnished by most judgment creditors.[67] It also prohibits employers from firing employees because their wages have been garnished for any one indebtedness.[68] Most courts have held that there is not an implied federal cause of action to enforce the prohibition against discharge, but usually the worker will be able to assert a state law claim of wrongful discharge.[69]

All states have statutes setting forth prescribed procedures for garnishment and limitations on the amounts and types of assets that can be garnished. In some states, the restrictions on wage garnishment go beyond those provided by federal law.[70]

Federal statutes also protect certain types of income from garnishment, such as Social Security and SSI benefits.[71] All states also have statutes that specify property that is exempt from execution to satisfy a judgment.[72]

10.7.5 Bankruptcy

It is common knowledge that bankruptcy can give a debtor a fresh start. Deciding whether a chapter 7 or a chapter 13 proceeding is more appropriate, or what to do about secured debts, may be less obvious. NCLC's bankruptcy manual[73] is a practical reference for consumer advocates. It discusses bankruptcy and public housing evictions, utility shutoffs, and other situations that cross boundaries of legal services specializations. Designed both for the generalist and the specialist, the manual includes hundreds of sample forms and pleadings, as well as software for preparing bankruptcy forms and schedules.

10.8 Conclusion

This guide to analyzing consumer transactions does not encompass the whole world of consumer law, which can cover insurance, rate setting, fraud, and other torts. It is, however, a starting point for getting the basics of a consumer law practice. It is presented as a road map, and it is a map that can lead to approaches to countless problems faced by consumers.

67 15 U.S.C. §§ 1671–1677.
68 15 U.S.C. § 1674(a).
69 *See* National Consumer Law Center, Fair Debt Collection § 12.4.1.6 (5th ed. 2004 and Supp.).
70 *See* National Consumer Law Center, Fair Debt Collection § 12.4.3 (5th ed. 2004 and Supp.).
71 42 U.S.C. § 407 (Social Security benefits); 42 U.S.C. § 1383(d)(1) (SSI).
72 *See* National Consumer Law Center, Fair Debt Collection Ch. 12 (5th ed. 2004 and Supp.).
73 National Consumer Law Center, Consumer Bankruptcy Law and Practice (7th ed. 2004).

Chapter 11

Keeping America's Economy Strong: Enforcing Consumer Protection Laws as Congress Intended

By Tom Domonoske[1]

11.1 Introduction

Beginning in 1969, Congress began passing important statutes designed to allow our free-market economy to function properly. These statutes are collected in the Consumer Credit Protection Act (CCPA), 15 U.S.C. §§ 1601–1693r. For instance, the Truth in Lending Act, Title I of the CCPA, was passed by Congress on May 29, 1968, P.L. 90-321, "to assure meaningful disclosure of credit terms so that the consumer will be able to compare more readily the various credit terms available to him." 15 U.S.C. 1601. *See* Beach v. Ocwen, 523 U.S. 410, 413 (1998). The Act is designed to promote "the efficient functioning of a free economic system" by providing consumers with information that allows them to shop for the best possible credit terms. Mourning v. Family Publications Service, Inc., 411 U.S. 356, 363–64 (1973). When consumer lawyers enforce the CCPA, the lawyers are implementing the will of Congress to strengthen the economy by ensuring that accurate information is used in market decisions. In this way, effective enforcement of all parts of the CCPA, the Truth in Lending Act, the Fair Credit Reporting Act, the Equal Credit Opportunity Act, and the Fair Debt Collection Practices Act, is necessary to keep the American economy strong. As consumer lawyers, we are never merely advocating for our individual client's rights, we are in fact protecting the American way from the danger posed by inefficient markets.

[1] Tom Domonoske is consumer law specialist and acclaimed lecturer practicing in Virginia. He first practiced law in California and then as a legal aid lawyer in rural Virginia. From July 1996 through August 2000, he was a Senior Lecturing Fellow at Duke Law School. While at Duke, he maintained a small consumer law practice in Virginia through an Of Counsel relationship with the Law Office of Dale W. Pittman, another ex-legal-aid lawyer. In August 2000, he returned to the practice of law in Virginia with that office.

11.2 The Basic Problem: A Completely Unregulated Market Does Not Work

The basic premise of the market economy is that a knowledgeable seller and a knowledgeable buyer will come together and make a decision in their own interests. Under the market theory, the combined effect of the many millions of such decisions on all levels of the economy is an ever-increasing efficiency in the distribution of goods and services. The ever-increasing efficiency is to occur because, through innovation and creativity, sellers will be continually and necessarily motivated to "build a better mouse-trap." Although this system creates the possibility and the reality of large disparities in income and wealth, the inequalities of that disparity are accepted as a necessary by-product of the efficiencies and benefits of the market system.

In actual practice, certain controls and protocols are necessary to make a market perform properly.

> The truth is that market fundamentalism is itself naive and illogical. Even if we put aside the bigger moral and ethical questions and concentrate solely on the economic arena, the ideology of market fundamentalism is profoundly and irredeemably flawed. To put the matter simply, market forces, if they are given complete authority even in the purely economic and financial arenas, produce chaos and could ultimately lead to the downfall of the global capitalist system.

George Soros (1998). Consequently, even those people like George Soros who believe strongly in the power of the market understand that the market forces must be directed to ensure the viability of the market system.

One of the important factors is honest information. If a seller of any type of goods or services misrepresents the value of the goods or services, buyers will purchase from that seller rather than from a different seller who is actually providing better goods or services. In the same way that millions of separate transactions between a knowledgeable buyer and seller can produce a functioning economy, millions of separate transactions based on misinformation will pervert and fundamentally harm an economy.

11.3 The Engines That Work Together to Create an Inefficient Market

11.3.1 Shameful Greed

Despite an attitude that gained acceptability in the 1980s, greed is not good. Unfortunately, because the market system allows for the financial rewards of transactions to be distributed based on individual decisions, huge disparities of wealth are a reality of our system.

> As wages fell for the typical worker, executive pay soared. From 1989 to 2000, the wage of the typical (i.e., median) chief executive officer grew 79.0%, and average compensation grew 342%. In 1965, CEOs made 26 times more than a typical worker; this ratio had risen to 72-to-1 by 1989 and to 310-to-1 by 2000. U.S. CEOs make about three times as much as their counterparts abroad.

The State of Working America, Economic Policy Institute.

The potential to live like royalty in the midst of others who struggle daily is a lure too strong for many. The Enron debacle is a prime example of a whole system of managers and executives who found no problem in using misrepresentations to funnel millions of dollars into their own pockets. Whether the misrepresentation is made by a used-car dealer about a car's accident history or by a corporate executive about the debts and profits of the company, the fundamental fraud is the same: a misrepresentation of value to illegally acquire dollars. Once the dollars are in a bank account, whether they were obtained honestly or dishonestly does not alter the ability to spend those dollars freely.

As society is increasingly fragmented, corporations and the people that identify with corporations lose touch with average citizens. Unfortunately, a class of people has developed, called corporatists, who live, think, and act differently than ordinary citizens. This process can best be seen by the generational change since World II in military service. In World War II, powerful wealthy families commonly sent their sons into harm's way. Future presidents like John Kennedy were on the front lines, living and mixing and risking death with other Americans from all walks of life. Currently, the idea of a Kennedy or Bush or Lay son or daughter going to serve in combat in a place like Iraq not only seems unlikely but also seems somehow wrong. "Why would they do that?" is the implicit question when such an idea is entertained. Well, the cultural change created by the corporatists, by gated communities where part of America lives without ever developing the ties that bind them to the rest of America, is what enables the validity of that question.

Although this simplistic example is not meant as an explanative model for societal change, the effect of executive pay jumping from twenty-six times the average worker's pay to 310 times the average worker' pay is one measurement of the distance that has been created between the executive class and the working class. The gap has increased over ten-fold and although dollars readily jump the divide in one direction, community ties no longer cross it. The wide gulf that has opened up between the corporatists and the vast majority of the rest of the population is expressed by those corporations that exist merely to prey upon people and extract value from them.

11.3.2 Generally Accepted Procedures Instead of Honest Procedures

The gulf between the corporatists and the average citizen has led to a complete breakdown of accountability, measured not by community standards other than the generic "generally accepted procedures." As long as the corporation follows "generally accepted procedures," its managers, lawyers, accountants, and other corporatists have convinced themselves that nothing else is required. Under "generally accepted procedures," many corporatists have allowed greed to dictate their actions. Viewed properly, their actions are often just simply fraud.

Many generally accepted procedures and rooted in initially proper concepts that are then twisted to circumvent the truth. For instance, the October 23, 2002, Washington Post's Business section ran an article titled *Pension Reports Return to Haunt U.S. Companies*. Under generally accepted procedures, large corporations report profit on pension plans as income to the corporation. Because the actual returns on the investments in the pension plans vary each year, large swings in profits on the pension plans may give a misleading idea of a corporation's real profits. To decrease the volatility of such swings, the generally accepted procedure is for these corporations to use an estimated percentage return each year on the plans. The problem is that, in the past few years, many pension plans have not only been performing far below historic estimates but have also been losing money.

Consequently, some companies have been reporting an overall profit by using an estimated return of 8% or 9% on a pension plan, even though the pension plan actually lost money and the corporation overall actually lost money. Of the fifty largest U.S. companies in 2001, $54 billion of pension income was reported in this way even though the plans lost $38 billion. This one "generally accepted procedure" thus accounted for a misrepresentation of $90 billion to all investors in these fifty companies.

This $90-billion misrepresentation was made to investors who use the information to decide which companies to invest in and how much to invest. The best way to test any generally accepted procedure is to imagine an ordinary American utilizing the procedure. When a consumer applies for a loan, the consumer must disclose financial information in the same way corporations disclose financial information to investors. Imagine the consumer who fills out the credit application that asks net worth information. The consumer could use "generally accepted procedure" to estimate the value of her IRA account as if she received an 8% return last year when in fact she lost 35% over the last two years; she could put down that her IRA was worth over $116,000 rather than $65,000. The creditor who extended credit on such misinformation would scream fraud and perhaps seek criminal charges.

By using such "generally accepted procedures," the corporatists truly believe that they and their corporations are no longer held to the standards of behavior applied to normal citizens. These procedures have poisoned the behavior of the corporations and, at all levels of the economy, introduced false information into market transactions.

11.3.3 Debt Is the American Way

Household debt grew much more rapidly than household income in the last decade. By 2001, total household debt exceeded total household disposable income by nearly 10%. Households in the middle of the wealth-distribution spectrum absorbed the largest share of this run-up in debt. While low nominal interest rates have made it easier for households to carry the greatly expanded debt, many households appear to be straining. Recent government data show that 14% of middle-income households have debt-service obligations that exceed 40% of their income; 9% have at least one bill that is more than sixty days past due.

Comparing household debt of 2002 to household debt of the previous decades reveals a shocking development in the American economy. As of February 2002, household credit stood at approximately $1.75 trillion dollars—a dramatic increase from $6 billion when the Truth in Lending Act was passed. Consumer spending is recognized as the engine that keeps our economy going, and consumer credit is the fuel for that engine. If this fuel is impure, the engine can sputter or stall. Bankruptcies, both corporate and personal, rise as credit obligations exceed ability or desire to pay. Because credit that is granted on imperfect or faulty information is imperfect or faulty fuel, misinformation in credit transactions stall our economy.

11.3.4 Advertising Works

The huge advertising budgets and all the work by advertising firms are not wasted. Advertising, done properly, works and motivates people to want more than they have. A common idea is that almost everyone, regardless of income, believes that, if they had $10,000 per year, they could afford all they wanted. Level of income is merely the yardstick by which each person is judged suitable for targeting by advertisements for goods that are just beyond their current reach.

As a recent Saab advertisement stated, you are simply a boring person if you can not put $3500 down and spend $399 per month on a car. Despite the rational knowledge that all non-Saab owners are not really boring, it is human nature to tend to measure others through their public display of material possessions. Advertising feeds on such tendencies, and people can spend an enormous of time trapped into living by such yardsticks.

The combination of effective advertising and easy availability of credit results in many impracticable credit purchases. When purchasers willingly enter into transactions that are not in their best interest, the market can never function properly.

11.3.5 The Result of These Factors

The result of the unmitigated greed, the loss of community values, the acceptance of debt, and the effectiveness of advertising has created some disturbing statistics. The wealthiest 1% of all households control about 38% of national wealth, while the bottom 80% of households hold only 17%. This disparity in wealth then directly translates into disparity of political power.

In 2002, default rates on home loans were at historic highs when interest rates were at historic lows. That is a telling sign of an ailing economy. Across the country, retirement funds have been threatened by massive declines in the stock market, and large corporate bankruptcy filings dominate the news. The United State's foreign trade deficit continues to set new records. This article does not attempt to explain the connection between all these events, but such events show the need to develop the controls that are necessary to allow our market economy to perform properly.

11.4 The Controls Selected by Congress to Increase the Efficiency of the Market

Congress has already acted: the Truth in Lending Act (TILA), the Equal Credit Opportunity Act (ECOA), the Fair Credit Reporting Act (FCRA), the Fair Debt Collection Practices Act (FDCPA) all regulate the credit economy. They make possible an environment for credit transactions constitute the only permissible structure within which individual credit decisions are to be made. Regarding the TILA, the Supreme Court has recognized that Congress created this "barrier between the seller and the prospective purchaser in the form of hard facts." Mourning v. Family Publications Service, Inc., 411 U.S. 356, 377 (1973). Most important, it also stated that Congress changed "the philosophy of 'Let the buyer beware' to one of 'Let the seller disclose.' " *Id.*

A few simple principles are incorporated into these federal statutes:

- TILA—tell them what the deal will be before they sign
- ECOA—tell them what action was taken and why
- FCRA—tell them what information was used and where it came from
- FDCPA—do not lie to collect an unpaid debt

Under the TILA, each creditor is required to place accurate TILA disclosures in each consumer's possession before the consumer signs to accept the credit. Under the ECOA, within thirty days after receiving an application from a consumer, each creditor must accurately inform the consumer of the action taken on the application. Under the FCRA, a creditor must inform the consumer about the information that was used to evaluate the credit. Under the FDCPA, debt collectors must not lie to consumers to coerce them to pay an alleged debt.

These principles ensure that the market functions properly and that people have the information to make knowledgeable credit decisions. At their core, these principles merely mandate honesty. The required disclosures are not invasive notices that mandate disclosure of trade secrets. The required disclosures are simply information that is necessary to have the market perform properly according to the underlying theory of the market. Because a seller will want the buyer to have as little information as possible and thereby increase how much the buyer will pay, these statutes are necessary to ensure the existence of informed consumers.

These principles are fundamentally designed to protect the business that "builds the better mouse trap." In theory, the consumers will choose to give their business to those businesses that are delivering better value or lower prices. The honesty mandated by these statutes gives a more efficient credit business the means to effectively compete with a less efficient credit business. Corporations that violate these statutes are stealing business from those that comply. To effectively enforce these statutes, every consumer lawyer should recognize and argue that he or she is working on behalf of the honest creditors to curb anti-competitive behavior by those businesses that act in unlawful and criminal ways.

Because these statutes were designed to strengthen the American economy, willful violations as a matter of practice are efforts to weaken our economy. Consumer lawyers are truly acting in the national interest by enforcing these statutes. The phrase "private attorney general" expresses the relevance of these statutes. Judges will be motivated to enforce the statutes if the very important policies behind them are explained.

11.5 Countering the Argument That a Consumer with Debts Is a Bad Person

The basic defense offered in most consumer cases is that the consumer is at fault for not paying all his or her bills. Let Congress explain the true situation:

> One of the most frequent fallacies concerning debt collection legislation is the contention that the primary beneficiaries are "deadbeats." In fact, however, there is universal agreement among scholars, law enforcement officials, and even debt collectors that the number of persons who willfully refuse to pay just debts is miniscule. Prof. David Caplovitz, the foremost authority on debtors in default, testified that after years of research he has found that only 4 percent of all defaulting debtors fit the description of "deadbeat." This conclusion is supported by the National Commission on Consumer Finance which found that creditors list the willful refusal to pay as an extremely infrequent reason for default.

Senate Report No. 95-382 on the FDCPA. That report also states that "[t]he Commission's findings are echoed in all major studies: the vast majority of consumers who obtain credit fully intend to repay their debts. When default occurs, it is nearly always due to an unforeseen event such as unemployment, overextension, serious illness, or marital difficulties or divorce."

The statutes in the CCPA were necessary to protect the economy because of the bad actions of certain industries. "The committee believes that the serious and widespread abuses in this area and the inadequacy of existing State and Federal laws make this legislation necessary and appropriate." *Id.* These are not merely legislative history comments but can also be found in the express words of Congress regarding all these statutes.

In 15 U.S.C. § 1692, under the Congressional findings and declaration of purpose:

> (a) There is abundant evidence of the use of abusive, deceptive, and unfair debt collection practices by many debt collectors. Abusive debt collection practices contribute to the number of personal bankruptcies, to marital instability, to the loss of jobs, and to invasions of individual privacy.
>
> (b) Existing laws and procedures for redressing these injuries are inadequate to protect consumers.
>
> (c) Means other than misrepresentation or other abusive debt collection practices are available for the effective collection of debts.

> (d) Abusive debt collection practices are carried on to a substantial extent in interstate commerce and through means and instrumentalities of such commerce. Even where abusive debt collection practices are purely intrastate in character, they nevertheless directly affect interstate commerce.
>
> (e) It is the purpose of this subchapter to eliminate abusive debt collection practices by debt collectors, to insure that those debt collectors who refrain from using abusive debt collection practices are not competitively disadvantaged, and to promote consistent State action to protect consumers against debt collection abuses.

Similarly, the Congressional Findings and Statement of Purpose of the ECOA make the same point:

> The Congress finds that there is a need to insure that the various financial institutions and other firms engaged in the extensions of credit exercise their responsibility to make credit available with fairness, impartiality, and without discrimination on the basis of sex or marital status. Economic stabilization would be enhanced and competition among the various financial institutions and other firms engaged in the extension of credit would be strengthened by an absence of discrimination on the basis of sex or marital status, as well as by the informed use of credit that Congress has heretofore sought to promote. It is the purpose of this Act to require that financial institutions and other firms engaged in the extension of credit make that credit equally available to all creditworthy customers without regard to sex or marital status.

Under 15 USC § 1601, the "Congressional findings and declaration of purpose" for TILA is equally clear:

> (a) Informed use of credit
>
> The Congress finds that economic stabilization would be enhanced and the competition among the various financial institutions and other firms engaged in the extension of consumer credit would be strengthened by the informed use of credit. The informed use of credit results from an awareness of the cost thereof by consumers. It is the purpose of this subchapter to assure a meaningful disclosure of credit terms so that the consumer will be able to compare more readily the various credit terms available to him and avoid the uninformed use of credit, and to protect the consumer against inaccurate and unfair credit billing and credit card practices.

Under 15 U.S.C. § 1681, the FCRA "Congressional findings and statement of purpose" explains how inaccurate credit information harms our economy:

> (a) Accuracy and fairness of credit reporting
>
> The Congress makes the following findings:
>
> (1) The banking system is dependent upon fair and accurate credit reporting. Inaccurate credit reports directly impair the efficiency of the banking system, and unfair credit reporting methods undermine the public confidence which is essential to the continued functioning of the banking system.
>
> (2) An elaborate mechanism has been developed for investigating and evaluating the creditworthiness, credit standing, credit capacity, character, and general reputation of consumers.
>
> (3) Consumer reporting agencies have assumed a vital role in assembling and evaluating consumer credit and other information on consumers.
>
> (4) There is a need to insure that consumer reporting agencies exercise their grave responsibilities with fairness, impartiality, and a respect for the consumer's right to privacy.
>
> (b) Reasonable procedures
>
> It is the purpose of this subchapter to require that consumer reporting agencies adopt reasonable procedures for meeting the needs of commerce for consumer credit, personnel, insurance, and other information in a manner which is fair and equitable to the consumer, with regard to the confidentiality, accuracy, relevancy, and proper utilization of such information in accordance with the requirements of this subchapter.

All of these statutory provisions make the same point. Congress has determined that, to make the market perform properly, these statutes must be followed. To enforce these statutes, the court and the defendant must fully understand the importance of compliance with the statutes. Because of the importance of these statutes, a consumer advocate must cite these provisions and connect the harm that violations pose to our national interest. Consequently, a consumer advocate is really working on behalf of the law-abiding businesses that are losing customers because of the anticompetitive action of the businesses that violate the statutes; the consumer advocate is also working on behalf of the country as a whole to sustain and support the life-blood of our economy.

The Congressional Record can also be used to provide a citation to all of these important truths. Regarding the FCRA and the importance of accurate credit information, "[i]f these reports are not accurate, or if they are distributed without a legitimate purpose, then our whole society suffers. Consumers may be unfairly deprived of credit, employment, and their privacy. And businesses may lose out on the opportunity to gain new customers." 140 Cong. Rec. H9809, September 27, 1994 (statement of Representative Kennedy).

11.6 Real Individual Harm Results from Violations of These Statutes

After ensuring that a judge understands the policies and purposes of these statutes, the consumer advocate must explain the real individual harm that results from these violations. In passing each of these statutes, Congress documented those harms. The FCRA states: "[t]he credit reports they compile determine whether a consumer will obtain a mortgage, a car or business loan, a job, and even an apartment." *Id.*

A common problem in the credit reporting industry involved inaccurate information resulting from identity theft. Anyone who has been subject to such a problem will know the frustration that results.

> And it was clearly insulting having a collection agency calling you constantly at home, leaving messages, when you get a live person on the phone, threatening you if you didn't pay your bill that you'd be listed as a deadbeat. It was mind-numbing. . . . The collection agency, even after I reached Target, consistently tried to call and disrupt me at all hours of the day.
>
> I can only imagine the senior citizen who has had their card stolen having fear of these type of tactics on the phone, threatening that they would lose their home, that they'd lose their credit, that they'd be taken seriously. And some may even pay the bill that they did not owe simply to get rid of harassers.

Hearing Before the Subcommittee on Social Security Of the Committee on Ways and Means, House of Representatives, 106th Cong., 2d Sess. (July 17, 2000), Delray Beach, Florida, Serial No 106-43 (statement of Rep. Mark Foley).

This testimony from Representative Foley is not unique in content but is rather unique as a first-person account from an elected member of Congress. If more members of Congress were similarly abused by corporate practices, then we could see even better statutory protections for both the economy and for individual consumers. For instance, if Representative Foley had been a victim of a consumer fraud and then forced into arbitration as a result of small print clause on the back of the fourth page of a form contact, then perhaps the Federal Arbitration Act would be amended to protect consumers.

Information is power and, to the extent that a consumer is denied information, the consumer loses power. Although the loss of that power is hard to value, it is always a loss. Especially when the federal government has given the consumer an automatic right to that information, no defendant can credibly claim that the information is not important. Late delivery of the TILA disclosures is the main problem under the TILA in the context of retail sales. A barrier to full compliance of the TILA is that consumers do not know about the creditor's obligation to deliver the TILA disclosure prior to signing. An analogy would be if few citizens know that police officers are required to give a Miranda warning when arresting a suspect and few officers were actually giving the required warning. Those citizens would then not be aware of that they were not receiving the mandated disclosure. Similarly, because consumers do not know they are entitled to TILA disclosures and that the disclosures are to be used to shop for credit, most consumers are not even aware of the vital information being withheld from them.

A final important fact about the statutes outlined above is that they were developed in close consultation with the regulated industry. Each statute is fine-tuned for ease of compliance and lack of barriers to legitimate business practices. Consumer advocates also need to show how the statutes work together and that the statutes are simple to comply with. If a judge believes a statute is a barrier to business rather than a benefit to the market, the judge will probably be more reticent to enforce it.

As consumer lawyers become better at explaining and enforcing these statutes, the industry will respond. This response may be compliance—it may be an effort to allow non-compliance to continue. Mandatory pre-dispute binding arbitration clauses have become increasingly prevalent as the means by which some corporations avoid changing practices that violate the law.

11.7 Conclusion

The basic principles of the federal consumer statutes are easy to state and make sense. Mandated honesty and required disclosures create an informed consumer public and protect honest businesses.

The statutes of the CCPA are designed to keep our economy strong, and strong enforcement of them is in the national interest. Without honest and accurate information in the market, the market misfires. The Enron and Worldcom debacles are examples of the tremendous harm that results when market decisions are manipulated through use of false information. Truth in individual decisions is important because of the cumulative effect of those decisions.

The real question for all lawyers is what to do with the tremendous opportunity afforded to them by a law license. Individually, we can work to enforce these statutes and help victims and thereby help our economy, or we can sell our services to the highest bidder trying to achieve the opposite.

By linking the violation of each statute to the purposes of the statute, we can clarify the issues and enforce the statutes as intended. The reason to do so is simple. "No one has the right to take for granted his own advantages over others in health, in talents, in ability, in success, in a happy childhood or congenial home conditions. One must pay a price for all these boons. What one owes in return is a special responsibility for other lives." Albert Schweitzer, *Reverence for Life*.

Chapter 12 A Guide to Price Traps in Mortgage Loans[1]

By Kathleen Keest[2]

12.1 Introduction

Escalator items in and out of the price tag, in and out of the instant loan, are like burglar tools of equity skimmers. This article discusses how consumer advocates can recognize and challenge these practices. With just such tools as these, for example, an equity skimmer can hold a note with a $46,000 principal from which the consumer has received real consideration of only about $25,000 over the life of their relationship.[3]

12.2 Interest Rate (the "Note Rate")

Note rates on subprime home equity loans are above market rate, often considerably so, though some may offer teaser rates (See Variable Rates, below.) Before the Home Ownership and Equity Protection Act (HOEPA),[4] regional subprime mortgage companies would write note rates at 20% to 24%. Such rates would trigger HOEPA coverage. The incidence of note rates this high may have declined since HOEPA, which, if true, is certainly a good thing.[5] The major nationwide subprime mortgage lenders often charge in the range of 11% to 17% but frequently have many of charges folded into the principal.

Practice Tip: Compare the note rate on the promissory note with the APR on the Truth in Lending (TIL) disclosure statement. In almost all mortgages, the APR will be higher, because TIL's definition of "finance charge" items is broader than most state laws. Of most relevance, TIL includes all points, and now all brokers' fees (in all loans closed since September 30, 1996[6]) in the finance charge. When the points are within the market norm (1–3 points), the difference between the APR and note rate will not be great. When there is a big difference between the APR and note rate, it is a clue that there are many "prepaid finance charges," like points that have been charged. (One notorious pre-HOEPA subprime lender had note rates of 15–18%, and APRs of 28–29%; it charged 25–40 points, which reminds us why HOEPA exists.) If theres an itemization of the amount financed, there will be a line item disclosing the prepaid finance charge. If there is no itemization of the amount financed, do the following calculation:

note principal
– "amount financed" on TIL disclosure statement
= the amount of charges the lender considered to be prepaid finance charges

(That does not mean the lender is right—but it tells you what his or her thinking was.)

Policy Note: Subprime lenders justify their rates by saying they are dealing with "risky" borrowers. However, it is not that easy. First, most of the loans are fully secured by the

1 Reprinted from National Association of Consumer Advocates' *The Consumer Advocate* (July–Aug. 2002).

2 Kathleen Keest is Senior Policy Counsel at the Center for Responsible Lending in Durham, N.C. Prior to that, Kathleen was with the Office of the Attorney General of Iowa in its Consumer Protection Division, serving as Deputy Administrator of the Iowa Consumer Credit Code. From 1985 to 1996, she was a staff attorney with the National Consumer Law Center, specializing in federal and state credit litigation.

3 *See, e.g.*, National Consumer Law Center, Consumer Law Pleadings Ch. 2 (Cumulative CD-Rom and Index Guide).

4 Home Ownership and Equity Protection Act, 15 U.S.C. § 1639. *See* National Consumer Law Center, Truth in Lending Ch. 9 (5th ed. 2003 and Supp.).

5 However, one of the interesting developments in the last five years may have been a "rate creep" back upward. Reviewing data from securitized sales (because that is the only place rates are reported), Professor Mansfield found that while the median rate did not much vary between 1995 and 1999 (between 11–12%), the distribution around the median changed dramatically, with many more loans being made in the 13–18% range. Furthermore, in 1995, the chart flattens out at a top rate of 17–17.99%, while in 1999, the chart flattens out at the 19–19.99% rate. *See* Cathy Lesser Mansfield, *The Road to Subprime "HEL" Was Paved with Good Congressional Intentions*, 51 So. Car. L. Rev. 473, Graph 2 p. 578, and Graph 6 p. 586 (Spring 2000).

6 On loans closed prior to that date, whether broker fees had to be considered a finance charge depended upon the facts of any given transaction. While it was fact-specific then, virtually all lenders put broker fees in the amount financed anyway, so it was a big loophole. The loophole was closed by the change that went into effect in 1996.

collateral—the home. Second, by a recent Freddie Mac estimate, as many as 30% of borrowers in the subprime market could qualify for the prime market. Some borrowers are likely to be in the subprime market as a result of target marketing decisions made by lenders and/or a result of "sucker pricing" rather than risk pricing. Generally, market forces do not work as well in the subprime market, so it frequently may cross the line from "risk-based pricing" to "opportunistic" or "sucker-pricing." Third, the pricing in many subprime loans is such that it creates risk rather than compensates for risk. In other words, the borrower's income stream might well support a reasonably priced loan but, with all the pricing bells and whistles, it becomes unaffordable. *See generally* National Consumer Law Center, Cost of Credit: Regulation and Legal Challenges § 11.3 (3d ed. 2005). Special Note on Precomputed Contracts and the Rule of 78s: This is not likely to come up except in home improvement contracts or mobile home contracts with terms of 60 months or less. A precomputed contract is one in which the legal obligation is cast in terms of the total obligation—the sum of the principal plus the anticipated interest to be earned over the scheduled life of the loan. In such transactions, if the consumer pays off the loan early, then to hold the consumer to that would be to make them pay interest for a time when they no longer are using the money, unjustly enriching the lender. Consequently, most states require a rebate of unearned interest. The Rule of 78s is a pre-computer short-hand formula that lets one estimate the earned interest without doing the labor-intensive amortization calculation. However, the Rule favors the lenders, letting them have more than actuarially precise accounting would allow. On a long-term debt, it really distorts the earnings by a significant amount, hence in 1992 it was outlawed on consumer transactions with terms of 61 months or longer. 15 USC § 1615. *See generally* National Consumer Law Center, Cost of Credit: Regulation, Preemption, and Industry Abuses §§ 5.2.2 (3d ed. 2005).

12.3 Variable Rates

Variable rate loans can be constructed to make a loan become very expensive, but in ways that are difficult for consumers to ascertain. The fact that it is a variable rate loan at all may be obscured. There may be a teaser rate, or the terms may otherwise be constructed so that the cost will inevitably rise—after the consumer is hooked. Some of the predatory lending variable rates are designed to only go up—and to significantly increase payments when they do. The initial rate may be a "teaser rate," which is relatively low in the first year or two, and then the regular rate, with a high margin over the index rate, will kick in, usually with rising payments. Some call these "exploding rate" loans.

12.4 Points ("Origination" Fees, "Discount" Fee, etc.)

There are several advantages to a lender to load a loan with points. These include the following:

- They enable the lender/broker to low-ball the rate in marketing & sales pitches when financed. They disappear into the note principal and therefore out of the interest rate. Though TIL's advertising rules and UDAP laws should limit the lender's use of the lower "rate" when they talk about the note rate, most do focus on the note rate. ("This APR is just something the government makes us tell you.")
- When financed, they increase the yield from the note rate because of compounding.
- Since points are a percentage-based fee, loading up the principal with points is self-feeding, as is loading up the principal with all the other kinds of fees. (See credit insurance, below, on "self-reinforcing feedback loops." This is another example of a self-feeding cost in credit pricing.)
- Since points are generally considered "earned" at consummation, they increase the lender's effective yield upon prepayment.[7] This protects its yield against early payoff or refinancing by other lenders. But it's especially true when the lender refinances its own loans, as that extra yield becomes embedded in the principal (and amount financed) of the new loan. So embedded, the points now disappear even from the TIL price tag in the new loan and serve to increase the cost of the new loan.

Resources: National Consumer Law Center, Cost of Credit: Regulation, Preemption, and Industry Abuses §§ 5.6, 7.2.2, (3d ed. 2005); National Consumer Law Center, Truth in Lending § 3.7.5 (5th ed. 2003 and Supp.).

Some states limit the number of points, but many do not. And even in states where there are point limits on the books, federal law may preempt those limits.

12.5 Other Closing Costs/Junk Fees

There is a whole laundry list of closing costs. Some are considered finance charges under TIL always (for example, mortgage guaranty insurance premiums); others may be excluded if certain preconditions are met. Regulation Z,

7 Example: A note principal of $6169, of which $1169 represents points and $5000 the real proceeds to consumer; five-year term at 15% note rate. If prepaid after two years, the non-rebate points give the lender an effective yield of 29 1/2%, almost double the note rate. *See* National Consumer Law Center, Cost of Credit: Regulation, Preemption, and Industry Abuses § 5.5.2.2.1 (3d ed. 2005).

§ 226.4(c)(7); National Consumer Law Center, Truth in Lending §§ 3.9 (5th ed. 2003 and Supp.). For substantive law purposes, see National Consumer Law Center, Cost of Credit: Regulation, Preemption, and Industry Abuses §§ 7.2, 7.3 (3d ed. 2005)). These lenders often charge a lot more for the standard categories of closing costs than other lenders do, impose duplicative charges,[8] or charge for every conceivable thing (underwriting fees, warehousing fees, mailing fees, wire fees, processing fees, signing fees, turning-on-the-light fees—the "junk fees"). Not all of these fees will necessarily go into the lenders' pockets: some will go to third parties. Some fees will stay with the lender (who may keep the excess portion of the fees, for example), or some theoretical third parties may actually be the same people as the lender. Whether the fees stay with the lender or not, it still benefits from the compounding effect of inflated principals. The percentage-based fees (for example, points) will have a higher dollar value, and the yield from the note rate will have a higher dollar value because of the inflated basis upon which they are calculated.

12.6 Brokers' Fees

Brokers play a huge role in the subprime mortgage market. One of the distorting impacts of their role is the "reverse competition." A broker may steer a borrower to a particular lender, not because that lender will offer the best deal for the consumer, but because the lender offers the best broker compensation package. The broker's compensation may be out in the open; there may even be a broker's compensation agreement, included among the other papers, by which the consumer agrees to pay some amount. But the broker may also have a compensation arrangement with the lender that will increase the cost of the loan to the borrower. He or she may get some of the points or take a slice of the note rate. (These are called yield-spread premiums or overages. They may also be called "kickbacks."[9]) As with points, broker fees are also often percentage-based—and so here, too, it is a self-inflating cost. Broker fees have the same positive impact on the lender (and negative cost on the borrower) as do other fees that are financed. For this reason, some lenders may set up a structure wherein they get to wear two hats—as lender and broker. It never hurts to check to see who the principals are at the broker and lender companies to see if there is overlap.

In any case, the broker permits the lender to "outsource" many of its costs at origination to someone else, passing those costs on to borrowers.[10] It also permits lenders to market more cost-effectively. The lender can target its marketing to brokers, offering them incentives to deliver customers who, in turn, ultimately fund the cost.

Resources: See National Consumer Law Center, Unfair and Deceptive Acts and Practices § 5.1.3 (6th Ed. 2004); Cost of Credit §§ 7.3.2, 11.5.4 (3d ed. 2005).

12.7 Credit Insurance

Credit insurance insures the debt in the event something happens to the borrower. Credit life insurance will pay off the outstanding balance (maybe) if the borrower dies. Credit disability insurance will make monthly payments (maybe) if the borrower's employment income is interrupted. Less frequently written into home equity lending is involuntary unemployment credit insurance (IUI), through which some payments are made (for a limited time horizon) if the borrower involuntarily loses his or her job. In theory, this is a good concept. In reality, it is less so, particularly in the subprime market. Credit insurance is very expensive in relation to the benefits offered, and lenders profit in a number of ways. As with the broker arrangements, the marketplace is distorted by the reverse competition: the lenders shop for the best deal for themselves, not their customers. Many major lenders have decided it's such a good deal that they have set up their own insurance affiliates.

Front-end commission/compensation: There is a great deal of commission or "producer compensation" built into the premium. Commissions exceed 35% overall and are higher for some kinds of lenders.[11]

Back-end compensation: The creditors may get back-end compensation, for example, in the form of "experience rebates." (This may help explain why some creditors may be less than helpful about assisting borrowers to collect on their credit insurance when death or disability strikes.)

Reinsurance: Even if the insurance sold looks like it is produced by a non-related company, there may be some arrangements whereby the money ultimately ends back up in an affiliated insurance company's hands. Reinsurance is insurance that insurers purchase, so the "independent" product may then be transferred back to the affiliated insurer.

Its price is self-inflating: Though not calculated on a percentage basis, credit insurance is also priced by a self-feeding mechanism.

Single upfront premiums are typically priced based on the total obligation. This includes the interest (which is calculated on a principal that includes the premiums) and the insurance premiums themselves. This is called "gross cov-

8 *E.g.*, Therrien v. Resource Fin. Group, 704 F. Supp. 322 (D.N.H. 1989).

9 *See generally* National Consumer Law Center, The Cost of Credit: Regulation, Preemption, and Industry Abuses § 7.3.2 (3d ed. 2005).

10 Lenders argue that brokers permit lenders to offer rates at lower costs, saving money on brick and mortar buildings, and increasing the geographic boundaries of their market area. However true that may be in the prime market, the negative effect of reverse competition is the more apparent result to many of those representing borrowers in this market.

11 Consumers Union & Center for Economic Justice, *Credit Insurance: The $2 Billion A Year Rip-Off: Ineffective Regulation Fails to Protect Consumers* 17 (Mar. 1999).

erage."[12] Some states have mandated "net coverage," at least for life premiums. Pricing is also time-sensitive, both directly and indirectly. (Directly, premiums cost more to insure more years; indirectly, they are based on a total of payments, including interest, which itself is time-sensitive. How the principle plays out is illustrated in *Besta v. Beneficial Loan Co. of Iowa*, 855 F.2d 532 (8th Cir. 1988)). *See also* National Consumer Law Center, Cost of Credit: Regulation, Preemption, and Industry Abuses § 8.5.4.2 (3d ed. 2005) (especially note 584).

Credit insurance is so expensive that, on more expensive mortgage loans, creditors may only insure part of the debt. The creditors fear that at some point they will encounter market resistance. Also, credit insurance regulations may prohibit insuring more than ten years of a loan. With partial insurance, for example, credit life may only insure $10,000 of a $40,000 debt or ten years of a fifteen-year mortgage; credit disability may only insure two of ten years of the debt. Partial insurance may create issues about whether the borrowers understood that the debt wasn't being totally insured.

Interest is calculated on it: The premium cost is on the principal/amount financed side of the ledger. Interest is calculated on a higher principal, increasing the interest yield. It is also off the price tag. (In theory, it is a "dual benefit" charge, benefiting both borrower and lender. The borrower is protected against default in the event of income disruption; it is added security for the lender. Therefore, TIL and most state law permit "voluntary" insurance to be excluded from interest and the finance charge/APR price tags.)

Rebates are usually calculated by the Rule of 78s: In the event of early payoff, including by refinancing, the rebate is calculated in most states by the creditor-friendly accounting method, the Rule of 78s. (There are also concerns that rebates may, in too many cases, not be made at all. See above.) Those are the structural ways in which credit insurance is a price trap. Other issues can arise, such as selling insurance to someone unable to benefit (for example, selling insurance to people past the age of eligibility; selling disability insurance, which typically has an "actively at work" precondition, to a retired or already disabled person; selling life insurance to someone with a medical history that would have made them ineligible). *See generally* National Consumer Law Center, Cost of Credit: Regulation, Preemption, and Industry Abuses § 8.5.5 (3d ed. 2005).

While the selling of credit insurance has proliferated in the subprime market, events of the last year may substantially reduce its presence (at least in its current form). In response to enormous public criticism, litigation, state legislative pressure, and a Senate Banking Committee hearing on predatory lending,[13] the two largest sellers of credit insurance—Citigroup and Household Finance—publicly announced that they no longer will offer the product. Even more significantly, in 2001, the Federal Reserve Board issued a final rule amending HOEPA to require credit insurance premiums to be counted toward the HOEPA "8% fees and points" trigger. (The regulation, 12 CFR § 226.32(b)(1)(iv), will take effect on October 1, 2002.) Because credit insurance is always costly, almost any home mortgage loan that contains it will be subject to HOEPA coverage. As many lenders now avoid making HOEPA loans, in large part because of the increased difficulty in selling these loans to the secondary market, we can expect to see much less "typical" credit insurance being sold. However, because this insurance has been such a significant profit center for industry, expect to see similar products being offered that will cynically attempt to avoid HOEPA coverage (that is, debt cancellation agreements).

Resources: Consumers Union and Center for Economic Justice, *Credit Insurance: The $2 Billion A Year Rip-Off: Ineffective Regulation Fails to Protect Consumers* (March 1999); National Consumer Law Center, Cost of Credit: Regulation, Preemption, and Industry Abuses Ch. 8 (3d ed. 2005).

12.8 Non-Credit Insurance and Other Ancillary Contracts

Mortgage loans, especially those to the elderly, may also have non-credit insurance added in. Non-credit insurance means that it does not insure the debt itself. It may be a term life insurance policy or "accidental death and dismemberment." Non-credit insurance has all the traits of credit insurance: expensive in relation to benefits; producer compensation; reinsurance; the compounding effect because interest is charged on it; and off the credit price tag. It is also easy to confuse the consumer into thinking it is credit insurance. But there are some advantages to the lender even greater than with credit insurance, particularly for flipping purposes: these insurance policies don't have to be rebated when a loan is prepaid. They get to keep all the revenues, since the policies stay in force. And this kind of insurance may have higher age cut-offs, permitting the insurance to be sold to older borrowers who are age-ineligible for credit insurance. However, it is doubtful that many claims are ever submitted on these products, particularly when they are written during a series of flippings. I have not seen loss-ratios but, given the character of the product and the way these products are sold, it may well be that they are quite

12 This is how single-premium upfront credit insurance is priced. Credit insurance can also be priced on a monthly-premium basis, which is the type typically offered in prime-market mortgages.

13 *See Hearing on Predatory Mortgage Lending: The Problem, Impact and Responses*, (July 26–27, 2001), *at* www.senate.gov/~banking/01_07hrg/072601/

low.[14] Many consumers are not even aware they bought it at all or what exactly it is; without this basic understanding, the consumer is not likely to file a claim.

Resources: National Consumer Law Center, Cost of Credit: Regulation, Preemption, and Industry Abuses § 8.5.4.3 (3d ed. 2005). *See also id* § 8.5.5 (3d ed. 2005.)

12.9 Balloon Loans

Balloon loans serve lenders in a couple of important ways. First, many of these lenders like to base their sales pitch on monthly payments—keep the prospect's eye away from the credit price tag and onto the monthly payments. They can low-ball the monthly payment but still get the benefit of the high costs and high rate.

Example (a real one):

Note principal: $17,500
Note rate: 15.25%
15 years: 179 monthly payments of $224.78, plus $16,000 balloon

After 14 years and 11 months, this borrower would have paid $40,236 on this $17,500 loan and still owe a final balloon payment of $16,000. When that $16,000 balloon is due, the borrower will be 80 years old. Had the monthly payments been just $23/month more, it would have amortized the loan to $0 in that same amount of time and saved the borrower nearly $12,000 overall. The second benefit for lenders is that it encourages refinancing. Some predatory lenders used to write one- or two-year balloons, but HOEPA prohibited balloons on HOEPA loans of under five years. So most balloons will show up only on loans that are for sixty-month terms or more. However, there's a flipping practice that uses balloon notes to generate quick refinances. Lawyers representing consumers report lenders writing fifteen-year balloons, like the one above, and then three months or so later, calling to say, "You've got a balloon loan—wouldn't you like to refinance that into a non-balloon." They then get to book a new loan with new costs—all the advantages of refinancing a balloon but without having to wait out its maturity.

12.10 Accounting

Daily basis accounting: Daily basis accounting calculates interest on an actual "as paid" basis. It is not inherently wrong or unfair. It is, in fact, the true actuarial method. If your payment gets there twenty-two days after the last one, twenty-two days of earned interest is calculated and applied to interest, the remainder to principal. If payments are made early, the loan will pay down more quickly, saving you interest overall. On the other hand, if your payment gets there forty days after your last payment, forty days of interest will have been earned, so less will go to reduce principal. Frequent gaps will mean the balance is paid down more slowly, and you pay more interest overall.

Most mortgages are written as interest-bearing rather than precomputed transactions,[15] but many mortgage companies, for ease of accounting, treat the monthly payments as if they were precomputed. That is, they just apply them according to the amortization schedule, charging extra only if the late payment trigger date has passed. That will hurt the people who always pay ahead but help the people who pay behind. Presumably, the companies feel that it will all balance out over the entire portfolio, but this is not necessarily true.

As noted, daily basis accounting is a neutral practice. But it is possible that more subprime lenders do it than mainstream lenders. With higher rates, it will cost more to "slow paying" consumers. And many borrowers (in both prime and subprime markets) may believe that there is a grace period and think they are being savvy to wait to pay during that "grace period." (Look at your payment coupon: it probably says "due on the 1st, if not paid by the 15th, pay a late charge of $______). Not so. If you put your payment in the mail on the 7th, you may avoid the late charge, but you still will be paying a penalty. If the borrower does this chronically, it can add several thousand dollars to the overall cost of the loan and lead to a big surprise come pay-off time.

Delayed crediting of payments on daily basis account loans: While daily basis accounting is a neutral accounting method, there is suspicion that some lenders (mortgage and credit card[16]) are either very inefficient in posting, or purposefully delay, the payments they receive so that even borrowers who send in timely payments end up getting stuck paying extra interest. If the delay is long enough, it might even result in late fees.

12.11 Prepayment Penalties

The contract may build in a penalty, for example, two to six months' interest if the loan prepays. (Sometimes it will call for prepayment penalties only within the first three to five years.) This locks consumers in, keeping them from refinancing with a lower-rate lender when they figure out just how bad a deal this is. Some of the lenders go so far as to impose the penalty even when they refinance the loan themselves. (Not all do, however.) State laws limiting or

14 The loss-ratio is the ratio of premiums earned to benefits paid. The higher the loss-ratio, the more of each premium dollar goes back to insureds in benefits paid, meaning it is a better value for consumers.

15 *See* National Consumer Law Center, The Cost of Credit: Regulation, Preemption, and Industry Abuses § 4.5 (3d ed. 2005).

16 For open-end credit, there is a provision of TIL that requires payments to be credited as of the date of receipt. 15 U.S.C. § 1666c, Reg. Z § 226.10. Some state laws may have prompt posting requirements for mortgage loans as well.

prohibiting prepayment penalties may be preempted by federal law, especially the Alternate Mortgage Transactions Parity Act. *See* 12 U.S.C., § 3800, 12 C.F.R. § 560.220.

12.12 Refinancing and "Flipping"

In the business of selling debt, there are only a few ways to grow: get more people in debt, get them deeper in debt, keep them there longer, get other lender's customers, or a combination of those ways. Keeping existing customers in debt has long been a mainstay of finance companies. Historically, more than two-thirds of finance-company loans have been written to existing customers. The above laundry list shows how each item individually can add to the price of any given loan. But the resulting whole is greater than the sum of its parts. Refinancing compounds the financial impact on the consumer: the presence of these kinds of charges in the prior loan inflates the payoff amount on the prior loan that is folded into the principal/amount financed of the new loan, upon which a new round of fees, charges and add-ons are added. . . . And so it goes, as Kurt Vonnegut might say.

Resources: National Consumer Law Center, Cost of Credit: Regulation, Preemption, and Industry Abuses Ch. 6 (3d ed. 2005); National Consumer Law Center, Consumer Law Pleadings (Cumulative CD-Rom and Index Guide).

12.13 General Resource for Fair Lending Issues

There are fair lending implications to these kinds of practices. All of the practices have an impact on the price of credit, though not all do so in a way that shows up overtly on credit price tags. The frequency and degree to which borrowers in protected classes pay more for credit because of the impact of such practices raise the specter of what has come to be called "reverse redlining." It's not that members of protected classes are denied credit; it's that they pay more for it for reasons that have nothing to do with legitimate indicia of creditworthiness.

Lenders often say that subprime credit costs more because the borrowers are more risky. The extent to which that is true about the price tags for credit—interest rate, points, broker fees (the argument is that brokers have to work harder to get a loan for a riskier borrower)—is not yet established empirically. However, when members of protected classes are more frequently the victims of such machinations as packing and flipping and padding, there is no legitimate basis for even pretending that "credit risk" is at issue. Those practices are about making risk, not compensating for it; those practices are about "sucker pricing," or "opportunistic pricing," not "risk-pricing."

The experience from advocates working in this field for many long years suggests that elderly and minority borrowers are impacted most heavily by such practices. Certainly, the less educated the borrowers, the more likely they are to be on the short end of the stick. While this cumulative experience, too, has not been empirically established except in isolated cases,[17] it is an issue that cries out for stringent scrutiny.

The issue of price discrimination is now coming to the fore. Two federal district courts in 2000 ruled that price discrimination stated a cause of action under fair lending laws. *See Honorable v. Easy Life Real Estate System*, 100 F. Supp. 2d 885 (N.D. Ill. 2000); *Hargraves v. Capital Cities Mortgage Co.*, __ (D.D.C. 2000). Litigation is also challenging auto lenders for discriminatory pricing. *See* Diana B. Henriques, *Extra Costs on Car Loans Draw New Legal Attacks*, N.Y. Times (Oct. 27, 2000), at 1.

Resources: National Consumer Law Center, Credit Discrimination (4th ed. 2005).

It is not sufficient to say that these lenders offer credit to underserved consumers. There's a difference between "productive credit" and "destructive debt," and it is important that we know who is offered which kind.

---

17 In some "reverse redlining" cases against specific lenders, discriminatory pricing has been statistically established sufficient for regulators to obtain consent judgments.

Chapter 13 Saving a Client's Home Through Bankruptcy

By John Rao[1]

13.1 Overview

Consumers facing a home mortgage foreclosure, property tax sale, or forced sale on a judicial lien may find that bankruptcy is the only effective option for saving their home. Chapter 13 is the most commonly used form of bankruptcy in consumer home defense, as it provides a powerful right generally unavailable under state law, namely, the right to de-accelerate a mortgage default and cure the default by paying the arrearage in installments over a period generally not exceeding three to five years.[2] The bankruptcy filing also invokes an "automatic stay" that stops virtually all collection proceedings, including home foreclosures and sheriff sales. In addition, bankruptcy can be used in some situations to modify home secured obligations. The bankruptcy court also can be a favorable forum for challenging a predatory mortgage.

13.2 Curing Defaults Outside Bankruptcy

Before proceeding with bankruptcy, counsel should explore the possibility of resolving the mortgage default outside bankruptcy. You may attempt to negotiate for your client a workout agreement providing for a repayment plan similar to that available under chapter 13. The advantage of a workout is that it will avoid payment of trustee fees and obligations to other creditors. Though such agreements may be difficult to negotiate when the client is in serious default, mortgage lenders and servicers may consider such proposals under their loss mitigation procedures. In some instances, lenders may agree to a loan modification, possibly providing even greater benefits to the client than would be available under chapter 13. The client also might consider refinancing, but care should be exercised to avoid high-cost loans that may only provide temporary relief for the client and may result in a loss of home equity. And, a loan workout should not be considered on a predatory loan when more effective remedies are available through litigation.[3]

13.3 Pre-Filing Issues—Gathering the Necessary Information

Your clients must provide you with the information necessary to accurately prepare the bankruptcy schedules.[4] You will need to obtain a complete list of creditors and a current address, account numbers, and balances owed for each debt. It is more important in chapter 13 than in chapter 7 to know the precise amount owed on each debt as this may affect the feasibility of the plan. Particularly in cases in which your clients are proposing to pay less than 100% to unsecured

1 John Rao is a staff attorney at the National Consumer Law Center focusing on consumer credit and bankruptcy issues and providing technical assistance and litigation support to attorneys in a wide range of consumer law cases. He also participates in the Center's litigation efforts. He has served as a panelist and instructor at numerous bankruptcy and consumer law trainings and conferences and has served as a trainer for housing counselors and attorneys on predatory mortgage lending issues. John is editor of NCLC's manual *Consumer Bankruptcy Law and Practice* manual, co-author of NCLC's manual *Repossessions and Foreclosures*, and contributing author to NCLC's manuals *Student Loan Law* and *Stop Predatory Lending*, and *NCLC REPORTS* Bankruptcy and Foreclosures Ed. He is also a contributing author to *Collier on Bankruptcy* (Matthew-Bender) and the *Collier Bankruptcy Practice Guide*. John is a member of the board of directors for the National Association of Consumer Bankruptcy Attorneys and the American Bankruptcy Institute. Prior to coming to the Center, John served as head of the consumer law unit at Rhode Island Legal Services.

2 To be eligible to file a chapter 13 case, a consumer debtor's total debt may not exceed the monetary limits set forth in 11 U.S.C. § 109, which currently are $307,675 for unsecured debt and $922,975 for secured.

3 For an overview of predatory lending, *see* National Consumer Law Center, *Stop Predatory Lending: A Guide for Legal Advocates* (2002 Edition).

4 A sample bankruptcy questionnaire is provided in Appendix H to National Consumer Law Center, *Consumer Bankruptcy Law and Practice* (7th ed. 2004). An updated version of the questionnaire reflecting the 2005 Act changes is found in Appendix H to National Consumer Law Center, *Consumer Bankruptcy Law and Practice, Special Guide to the 2005 Act* (2005).

creditors or to avoid a judicial lien, you also should try to obtain a copy of a recent appraisal of your clients' home. The trustee or secured creditor simply may not rely upon the tax assessment value.

It also is very important that your clients provide you with a realistic budget of income and expenses (following the form of bankruptcy Schedules "I" and "J") so that you can determine the amount of "disposable income" to be dedicated for monthly plan payments. For clients with income above the state median income, amendments made to the Code by the 2005 Bankruptcy Act ("the 2005 Act")[5] require that their expenses be calculated using a "means test" formula found in § 707(b)(2)(A) and (B) and that additional forms be prepared and filed with the bankruptcy court.[6]

Clients who are desperate to save their home often underestimate their expenses so as to convince you and the court they can afford the chapter 13 plan payments. Thus, you must spend some time reviewing these schedules with your clients to ensure that they can live within the proposed budget.

13.4 Preparing the Chapter 13 Plan

As part of the initial bankruptcy filing, your clients will need to file a plan that describes how they propose to deal with their creditors. In a chapter 13 case filed to stop a mortgage foreclosure, the primary objective of the plan is to cure the mortgage default. Under 11 U.S.C. § 1322(b)(5) of the Bankruptcy Code, a mortgage arrearage, including reasonable pre-petition foreclosure expenses, can be cured within a "reasonable time." Depending upon the mortgage contract language and applicable non-bankruptcy law, the plan may need to provide for interest on the arrearage.[7]

The plan may provide that your clients will make the ongoing, post-petition mortgage payments, often referred to as payments made "outside" the plan, directly to the mortgage lender. In some districts, the bankruptcy court may require that these ongoing mortgage payments be paid through the plan and disbursed by the trustee's office. As in so many areas of bankruptcy practice, counsel should carefully review any specific chapter 13 requirements contained in local bankruptcy rules.

5 Pub L. No. 109-8 (2005).

6 11 U.S.C. § 1325(b)(3). *See also* National Consumer Law Center, Consumer Bankruptcy Law and Practice, Special Guide to the 2005 Act § 6.2.3 (2005).

7 U.S.C. § 1322(e). *See also* National Consumer Law Center, Consumer Bankruptcy Law and Practice § 11.6.2.7.2 (7th ed. 2004).

13.5 Plans Involving "Strip Down" or "Strip Off"

Under general bankruptcy principles as set forth in § 506 of the Code, an undersecured claim may be bifurcated into its secured and unsecured portions. The creditor's secured claim is therefore limited to the value of the collateral.[8] To the extent that the claim exceeds the value of the collateral, it is unsecured and may be treated less favorably. Section 1322(b)(2) of the Code permits this modification of secured claims in chapter 13. However, an exception to the general modification rule applies to claims secured "only" by a security interest in real property that is the debtor's principal residence.[9]

Significantly, the protection against modification afforded to home mortgage lenders is not unlimited. In each of the following situations, a home-secured loan may be modified:

- If senior liens on the property exceed the value of the home, then a junior lien creditor whose lien effectively is "underwater" can be treated as a wholly unsecured claim in chapter 13. The creditor's security interest is rendered void and "stripped off." The circuit courts have unanimously held that this form of lien modification is not barred by the Supreme Court decision in *Nobleman*,[10] and no attempt was made by the 2005 Act to overrule these cases.
- If the claim is not secured "only" by the debtor's home, such as when additional security is provided, the mortgage may be modified or "stripped down." The 2005 Act attempts to limit modification on these grounds by adding a definition of "debtor's principal residence" in § 101 of the Code, that is defined as "a residential structure, including incidental property . . . ."[11] A definition of "incidental property" is also added by the 2005 Act that refers to property rights going beyond the ownership of the structure and includes rights to "prop-

8 To satisfy the "present value" requirement of § 1325(a)(5)(B)(ii), interest generally must be paid on the secured portion of the bifurcated claim. This may present an opportunity to significantly reduce the interest paid on a high-cost loan. The Supreme Court in *Till v. SCS Credit Corp.*, 124 S. Ct. 1951 (2004), held that a formula method is to be used for calculating the interest required, with the prime rate of interest as the starting point, adjusted by a factor for risk. *See* National Consumer Law Center, Consumer Bankruptcy Law and Practice § 11.6.1.3.3.5 (7th ed. 2004).

9 11 U.S.C. § 1322(b)(2). *See* Nobleman v. Am. Savings Bank, 508 U.S. 324 (1993).

10 See *In re* Zimmer, 313 F.3d 1220 (9th Cir. 2002); *In re* Lane, 280 F.3d 663 (6th Cir. 2002); *In re* Tanner, 217 F.3d 1357 (11th Cir. 2000); *In re* Bartee, 212 F.3d 277 (5th Cir. 2000); *In re* McDonald, 205 F.3d 606 (3d Cir. 2000). *See also In re* Mann, 249 B.R. 831 (B.A.P. 1st Cir. 2000); *In re* Lam, 211 B.R. 36 (B.A.P. 9th Cir. 1997).

11 11 U.S.C. § 101(13A)(A).

erty commonly conveyed with a principal residence in the area where the property is located, easements, rights, appurtenances, fixtures, rents, royalties, mineral rights, oil or gas rights, profits, water rights, escrow funds, or insurance proceeds," as well as all replacements or additions.[12] Courts had differed prior to the 2005 Act regarding whether some of the rights enumerated in the new definition of "incidental property" were additional collateral that removed a secured claim from the protection against modification in § 1322(b)(2).[13] The specificity in the new definition of "incidental property" clarifies that security interests in types of property not enumerated, such as appliances, furniture, bank accounts, motor vehicles, or property of entities other than the debtor, will permit the mortgage loan to be modified.[14] Indeed, an additional security interest in any type of property not commonly conveyed with a principal residence in the area where the property is located should permit modification. The 2005 Act also does not overrule decisions that had permitted modification if the security interest includes other real estate or rental units, such as multi-family homes.[15] However, the new definition of incidental property will overrule decisions permitting modification based on additional security in rents and profits from the property[16] and mortgage escrow accounts.[17]

- If the claim is not secured by a security interest in "real property" that is the debtor's principal residence, then the secured loan may be modified. Before the 2005 Act, it was clear that a lien secured by real estate upon which a mobile home was situated was not secured solely by real property that was the debtor's principal residence if the mobile home did not constitute real property under applicable non-bankruptcy law.[18] The new definitions added by the 2005 Act may have been intended to protect mobile home lenders by defining "debtor's principal residence" to mean a residential structure, without regard to whether it is attached to real property.[19] However, the new definition does not appear to alter the treatment of mobile homes, because no change was made to § 1322(b)(2). While a mobile home may be the debtor's principal residence under the definition, it would still be personal property under applicable non-bankruptcy law and therefore the debt would not be secured "only by a security interest in real property" that is the debtor's principal residence.[20] Only if a mobile home or cooperative is real property under applicable non-bankruptcy law would the limitations on modification apply, even though the mobile home or cooperative is considered the debtor's principal residence.
- If a mortgage has a final payment that comes due during the pendency of a chapter 13 plan, it may be modified.[21] This can be helpful in dealing with short-term, high-cost mortgages, particularly those having balloon payment obligations.

13.6 Lien Avoidance

Under § 522(f)(1), a debtor may avoid a judicial lien to the extent it impairs an exemption to which the debtor is entitled in the property, such as a judgment lien on the homestead.[22] In 1994, Congress amended § 522(f) to specifically adopt a mathematical formula for determining whether a lien can be avoided. Application of this formula can result in the total[23] or partial avoidance[24] of a judicial

12 11 U.S.C. § 101(27B). The purpose of this amendment appears to be to further define "debtor's principal residence," which is used in § 1322(b)(2).

13 *See* National Consumer Law Center, Consumer Bankruptcy Law and Practice § 11.6.1.2.2 (7th ed. 2004).

14 *E.g.*, Sapos v. Provident Inst. of Savs., 967 F.2d 918 (3d Cir. 1992) (wall-to-wall carpeting additional security); *In re* Libby, 200 B.R. 562 (Bankr. D.N.J. 1996) (mortgage included additional security in debtor's account at the creditor bank); *In re* Escue, 184 B.R. 287 (Bankr. M.D. Tenn.1995) ("refrigerator, space heater, and similar items" additional security even though described as "fixtures" in mortgage documents); *In re* Bouvier, 160 B.R. 24 (Bankr. D.R.I. 1993) (claim secured not only by mortgage but also by personal property of debtors' corporation).

15 Lomas Mortgage, Inc., v. Louis, 82 F.3d 1 (1st. Cir. 1996) (holder of mortgage on three-unit building that included debtor's residence not protected from modification); *In re* McGregor, 172 B.R. 718 (Bankr. D. Mass. 1994) (bifurcation permitted on four-unit building where debtor uses one unit as residence); *In re* McVay, 150 B.R. 254 (Bankr. D. Or. 1993) (security interest in property used as "bed and breakfast" not secured solely by debtor's residence).

16 *In re* DeCosta, 204 B.R. 1 (Bankr. D. Mass. 1996); *In re* Heckman, 165 B.R. 16 (Bankr. E.D. Pa. 1994) ("rents of the premises" are additional collateral).

17 *In re* Donadio, 269 B.R. 336 (Bankr. M.D. Pa. 2001) (security interest also covered escrow account for taxes and insurance); *In re* Stewart, 263 B.R. 728 (Bankr. W.D. Pa. 2001).

18 *E.g.*, *In re* Thompson, 217 B.R. 375 (B.A.P. 2d Cir. 1998) (mobile home is personalty under New York law). *See also* National Consumer Law Center, Consumer Bankruptcy Law and Practice § 11.6.1.2.4 (7th ed. 2004).

19 11 U.S.C. § 101(13A). It includes an individual condominium or cooperative unit as well as a mobile or manufactured home or a trailer.

20 11 U.S.C. § 1322(b)(2).

21 11 U.S.C. § 1322(c)(2). *See also* Am. Gen. Fin. v. Paschen (*In re* Paschen), 296 F.3d 1203 (11th Cir. 2002).

22 State law limitations on the homestead exemption generally do not apply in the bankruptcy context. *See In re* Weinstein, 164 F.3d 677 (1st Cir.), *cert. denied*, 527 U.S. 1036 (1999) (limitation in state homestead statute for debts existing before debtor claimed exemption not applicable in bankruptcy). The 2005 Act amends § 522 of the Code by imposing certain limitations on state homestead exemptions when claimed in a bankruptcy case. *See* National Consumer Law Center, Consumer Bankruptcy Law and Practice, Special Guide to the 2005 Act Ch. 8 (2005).

23 *See, e.g., In re* Jakubowski, 198 B.R. 262 (Bankr. N.D. Ohio 1996).

24 In *In re Silveira*, 141 F.3d 34 (1st Cir. 1998), the debtor sought

lien. The lien avoidance procedure is initiated by the filing of a motion.[25] Lien avoidance under § 522(f) applies equally in chapter 7 and chapter 13 proceedings. If the judicial lien is avoided in a chapter 13, the claim can be treated as an unsecured claim under the debtor's plan.

13.7 Requirements for Plan Confirmation

- Best Interest of Creditors Test. The plan must provide that unsecured creditors will be paid no less than what they would receive if the debtor's property were liquidated under chapter 7.[26] To the extent that the debtor's property is fully exempt under the federal or state exemption scheme (depending on whether the debtor's state has opted out of the federal bankruptcy exemption scheme),[27] the plan may be confirmed even if it provides nothing or only a small amount to unsecured creditors.
- Disposable Income Test. If an objection to plan confirmation is filed, the bankruptcy court must determine whether the debtor is proposing to commit to the plan all of his or her "projected disposable income" for at least three to five years.[28] The focus of this test generally is on the debtor's projected expenses and whether they are reasonably required for the support of the debtor and the debtor's dependents.[29]
- Good Faith Test. Another important requirement is that the plan be proposed in "good faith and not by any means forbidden by law."[30] While plans providing 0% or very small dividends to unsecured creditors are not per se proposed in bad faith, such plans generally will receive close scrutiny, even in the absence of any formal objection. The test of good faith in low- or no-dividend cases often is very fact-specific. Thus, the court will carefully review the debtor's schedules, particularly the income and expense schedules, to determine whether additional payments could be made to unsecured creditors.

13.8 Automatic Stay Limitations Based on Repeat Filings

The 2005 Act imposes a number of new restrictions on repeat bankruptcy filings. These new provisions must be considered in determining whether the debtor's bankruptcy filing will invoke the automatic stay and stop a pending foreclosure sale.

If the consumer has had a prior bankruptcy case dismissed within the year before the petition is filed, the automatic stay will terminate thirty days after the case is filed.[31] However, the debtor may request that the court extend the stay as to all or some creditors.[32] The debtor must demonstrate that the case has been filed in good faith, often by showing that circumstances have changed.

If a debtor has had two or more cases dismissed within the year before the petition, the automatic stay does not go into effect upon the filing of the case.[33] On a motion filed by the debtor within thirty days after filing of the later case, the court may order the stay to take effect as to all or some creditors upon a showing by the debtor that the case has been filed in good faith.[34]

The automatic stay is not applicable as to the enforcement of a security interest in real property if the debtor files a case during a period when the debtor is ineligible to be a debtor under § 109(g), relating to certain previous filers, or in violation of a prior court order prohibiting the debtor from being a debtor in another case.[35] In addition, the automatic stay may not apply to specific property for a period of two years after an *in rem* order has been entered in a prior case relating to the property, though the debtor may move in a subsequent case for relief from the *in rem* order based upon changed circumstances or for good cause shown.[36]

---

to avoid a judicial lien in the amount of $209,500 on homestead property valued at $157,000 that was encumbered by a $117,680 mortgage. Since the sum of all liens on the property plus the debtor's $15,000 exemption was $342,180, the amount of impairment that could be avoided was $185,180, resulting in the creditor retaining a lien in the amount of $24,320. The First Circuit found that partial lien avoidance in this manner was consistent with Congress' inclusion of the phrase "to the extent that" in both § 522(f)(1) and § 522(f)(2)(A). *See also In re* Falvo, 227 B.R. 662 (B.A.P. 6th Cir. 1998).

25 *See* Fed. R. Bankr. P. 4003(d) and 9014.

26 *See* 11 U.S.C. § 1325(a)(4).

27 11 U.S.C. § 522(b)(1).

28 11 U.S.C. § 1325(b)(1).

29 For clients with income above the state median income, the 2005 Act requires that expenses be calculated using a "means test" formula found in § 707(b)(2)(A) and (B). *See* 11 U.S.C. § 1325(b)(3); National Consumer Law Center, Consumer Bankruptcy Law and Practice, Special Guide to the 2005 Act § 6.2.3 (2005).

30 11 U.S.C. § 1325(a)(3).

31 11 U.S.C. § 362(c)(3); National Consumer Law Center, Consumer Bankruptcy Law and Practice, Special Guide to the 2005 Act § 7.3.2.1 (2005).

32 11 U.S.C. § 362(c)(3)(B).

33 11 U.S.C. § 362(c)(4); National Consumer Law Center, Consumer Bankruptcy Law and Practice, Special Guide to the 2005 Act § 7.3.2.2 (2005).

34 The 2005 Act did not amend any of the provisions of § 1301, and no mention of the co-debtor stay is made in § 362(c)(3) or (c)(4). Thus, the stay limitations under these subsections do not prevent the application of the stay provided under § 1301 as to any actions taken against a co-debtor on a consumer debt of the debtor.

35 11 U.S.C. § 362(b)(21); National Consumer Law Center, Consumer Bankruptcy Law and Practice, Special Guide to the 2005 Act § 7.3.2.5 (2005).

36 11 U.S.C. § 362(b)(20) and § 362(d)(4); National Consumer Law Center, Consumer Bankruptcy Law and Practice, Special Guide to the 2005 Act § 7.3.2.6 (2005).

13.9 Post-Confirmation Defaults and Relief from Automatic Stay

In chapter 13 cases in which the debtor is attempting to cure a mortgage default, the mortgage holder may attempt to obtain relief from the automatic stay to foreclose on the property. Under 11 U.S.C. § 362(d), a secured creditor may seek relief based on two different theories.

The first ground for relief is based on the catch-all provision found at § 362(d)(1), which provides that the stay may be lifted "for cause." This most often involves the argument by the secured creditor that it has not been provided with adequate protection or that there has been a default on plan payments. This argument may be countered by establishing that there is a sufficient "equity cushion" in the property and that the debtor is proposing a reasonable plan modification providing for cure of any post-petition arrearage.

The second ground for relief requires proof of two specific elements: (1) that the debtor does not have an equity interest in the property and (2) that such property is not necessary for an effective reorganization.

Section 362(g) generally has been interpreted to require that the creditor seeking relief has the burden to establish the validity and perfection of its security interest, the amount of the debt and other allowable costs included in its claim, and the amount of the debtor's equity in the property. While the debtor has the burden of proof with regard to the remaining issues, the question of adequate protection often is determined by the equity in the property, which the creditor usually is required to prove is lacking.

13.10 Proper Crediting of Plan Payments

Under a new provision in the 2005 Act, a creditor's willful failure to credit payments received under a confirmed plan in accordance with the plan constitutes a violation of the injunction of § 524(a).[37] Although § 524(a) previously was limited to violations of the discharge order, § 524(*i*) is not limited to acts occurring after discharge. The section does not apply, however, if confirmation of the plan has been revoked, the plan is in default, or the creditor has not received the plan payments as required by the plan.

Presumably, this provision is a response to decisions in which courts questioned whether they had the ability to remedy a creditor's failure to credit payments properly. For example, it provides a remedy that the Eleventh Circuit found missing in *Telfair v. First Union Mortgage Corp.*,[38] when a chapter 13 debtor challenged a creditor's application of plan payments to charges not provided for under the plan.

37 11 U.S.C. § 524(i).

38 216 F.3d 1333 (11th Cir. 2000).

It also makes clear that a failure to properly credit plan payments that results in a creditor asserting that the debtor is in default post-discharge is not simply a matter for state courts to resolve, but rather a critical issue that must be resolved by the bankruptcy court to ensure that the provisions and purposes of a plan are effectuated.

The willfulness requirement of § 524(i) should not be a significant obstacle for debtors. As in § 362(k)(1), willfulness should be interpreted to mean simply that the creditor intended to commit the act, that is, credit the payment in the manner it did; the debtor should not need to prove that the creditor intended to violate the Code or the plan provisions.[39] Absent a creditor's proof that the improper crediting was a mistake in conflict with the creditor's normal procedures, the creditor should be presumed to have intended its acts.

Section 524(i) also provides that the failure to credit payments must cause material injury to the debtor, a requirement that should be met in virtually every case involving a secured creditor. The failure to properly credit payments will almost always result in a higher payoff balance for the debtor and therefore a larger lien on the debtor's property than if the payments were credited properly. A creditor that has collected the payments made by the debtor under the plan and credited them in a manner leading to a higher balance remaining on a debt has caused a material injury to the debtor. Similarly, a creditor who has reported negative information on the debtor's credit report about non-payment or collection efforts with respect to fees resulting from the improper crediting of payments has caused a material injury to the debtor.

A common example of such injury is the assessment of post-petition charges to the debtor that are not in accordance with the terms of the confirmed plan. If a creditor could subvert the terms of a plan simply by adding such charges, the cure of a default under the plan would be meaningless. As with other aspects of the injunction under § 524(a), a court can hold a creditor in contempt for violating § 524(i).[40]

13.11 Liquidating Chapter 13 Plans

For some clients, a chapter 13 plan may not be feasible because their income is insufficient to fund a plan or they have excessive unsecured debt that must be paid due to application of the "best interest of creditors" test. Even in this situation, a client may elect to file bankruptcy so as to gain the protection of the automatic stay while attempting to liquidate the property. The client may be able to exempt and recover potential equity in property that would result from a voluntary sale during the bankruptcy and that probably would have been lost at a foreclosure or other forced sale.

39 *See* National Consumer Law Center, Consumer Bankruptcy Law and Practice § 9.6 (7th ed. 2004).

40 *See* National Consumer Law Center, Consumer Bankruptcy Law and Practice § 14.5.1.4 (7th ed. 2004).

13.12 Asserting Non-Bankruptcy Claims and Defenses

As part of the bankruptcy claim determination process, consumer claims and defenses may be asserted in response to a creditor's proof of claim.[41] Since the bankruptcy court generally is more familiar with federal consumer protection and state lending laws than are state courts, it may be a favorable forum for litigating consumer defenses to creditor's claims, providing a much quicker resolution than in state court.[42] In non-judicial foreclosure states, bankruptcy also may permit consumer defenses to be adjudicated without having to obtain injunctive relief in state court, eliminating the need to satisfy procedural requirements such as the posting of bonds.

For example, a consumer may object to the secured claim of a predatory mortgage holder because the mortgage was rescinded based on violations of the TILA or HOEPA. To the extent the TIL rescission is enforced in the bankruptcy proceeding, some courts have held that the consumer's tender obligation may be treated as an unsecured claim.[43]

Bankruptcy court also can be a favorable forum for defeating arbitration clauses so that consumer claims may be litigated in court. Because of the conflict between the Bankruptcy Code and the Federal Arbitration Act,[44] courts generally have held that bankruptcy judges have discretion to deny enforcement of an arbitration clause, particularly as to "core proceedings" such as lien avoidance or modification actions.[45]

13.13 Conclusion

Bankruptcy may present the best opportunity for consumers to save their home from foreclosure and get a fair result in a consumer action against the lender. Though local experience will vary considerably, bankruptcy judges tend to be less dismissive of consumers who are in default on a debt, as they are accustomed to dealing with consumers in financial trouble. They are likely to have had more exposure to unscrupulous creditor practices and may be less deferential to large financial institutions. In some cases, bankruptcy judges may be far more knowledgeable about commercial and consumer law than their state or district court counterparts. For the many reasons discussed in this article, clients facing the loss of their home should be advised of the options available under bankruptcy law.

Counsel without Bankruptcy Court experience may want to consider referring cases to an experienced consumer bankruptcy practitioner.[46] Bankruptcy Court is a unique forum with its own vocabulary and rules. Counsel filing his or her first case should seek assistance from a local bankruptcy attorney or bankruptcy trustee or attend a local CLE on consumer bankruptcy.

---

41 *E.g.*, *In re* Maxwell, 281 B.R. 101 (Bankr. D. Mass. 2002) (debtor allowed to assert by way of recoupment time-barred claim under the Fair Debt Collection Practices Act against mortgage servicer).

42 Such claims and defenses normally fall within the bankruptcy court's jurisdiction under 28 U.S.C. § 1334(b) or may be treated as a "core proceeding" under 28 U.S.C. § 157(b).

43 *See In re* Williams, 291 B.R. 636 (Bankr. E.D. Pa. 2003) (court treated consumer's tender obligation as unsecured and did not make rescission conditional upon tender but required debtor to classify tender claim separately and pay it in full over life of chapter 13 plan); *In re* Rodrigues, 278 B.R. 683 (Bankr. D.R.I. 2002); *In re* Fidler, 226 B.R. 734 (Bankr. D. Mass. 1998); *In re* Myers, 175 B.R. 122 (Bankr. D. Mass. 1994) (chapter 13 debtor not required to tender sums advanced by lender as condition precedent to rescission of mortgage). *See also* Ray v. Citifinancial Inc., 228 F. Supp. 2d 664 (D. Md. 2002) (bankruptcy court may condition TIL rescission upon tender but also has discretion to reduce or eliminate creditor's lien without requiring tender based on equitable considerations).

44 The presumption under the Federal Arbitration Act that valid arbitration agreements should be enforced is often in direct conflict with the goal of bankruptcy jurisdiction to have one centralized forum for the prompt resolution of disputes affecting the bankruptcy estate. *See Zimmerman v. Continental Airlines, Inc.*, 712 F.2d. 55 (3d Cir. 1983); *In re* Hemphill Bus Sales, Inc., 259 B.R. 865 (Bankr. E.D. Tex. 2001); *In re* Knepp, 229 B.R. 821 (Bankr. N.D. Ala. 1999) (court finds "inherent conflict" between FAA and Bankruptcy Code).

45 *See In re* Mintze, 288 B.R. 95 (Bankr. E.D. Pa. 2003), *aff'd*, 2003 WL 22701020 (E.D. Pa. 2003) (court refused to enforce arbitration clause because of potential impact on other creditors and questions about arbitrator's neutrality); *In re* Larocque, 283 B.R. 640 (Bankr. D.R.I. 2002) (denying enforcement of arbitration clause to decide Truth in Lending rescission issues); *In re* Hicks, 285 B.R. 317 (Bankr. W.D. Okla. 2002) (potential costs of arbitration would adversely affect debtor and creditors); *In re* Cavanaugh, 271 B.R. 414 (Bankr. D. Mass. 2001).

46 A directory of consumer bankruptcy attorneys may be found at www.nacba.org.

Chapter 14 Is That Arbitration Clause Unconscionable? PROVE IT![1]

By F. Paul Bland Jr.[2]

14.1 Factual Record Key to Fighting Unfair Arbitration Clauses

Fighting a mandatory arbitration clause is not for the lazy, the meek, or those exclusively inclined to broad abstractions. The key to success for a consumer advocate who wishes to avoid having his or her client forced into a particularly unfair arbitration system is both simple and difficult: one should put a powerful factual record before the court. The case law is riddled with pro-arbitration decisions in cases in which the plaintiffs did not offer a single piece of evidence to support their arguments that a given arbitration clause was particularly unfair.

Beginning with the premise that having an empty factual record is a poor approach, this article will suggest several ways that enterprising counsel can prove that a given arbitration clause is unconscionable.[3] In most states, a person attempting to prove that a contract provision such as an arbitration clause is unconscionable must establish two factors: (a) that it was adopted in a manner that is procedurally unconscionable and (b) that it includes provisions that are so one-sided or unfair as to be substantively unconscionable. In many cases, both factors can only be established with admissible evidence of facts.

14.2 Proving Procedural Unconscionability

In most states, it is much easier to prove procedural unconscionability than it is to prove substantive unconscionability, and courts regularly enforce procedurally unconscionable contracts. Nonetheless, it is important that counsel for consumers do not forget to prove that this required element is present in a given case.

While the nomenclature and sometimes the doctrine varies from state to state, most states look at two factors in determining if a contract is procedurally unconscionable: oppression and surprise. It is not always necessary to prove both factors, however, as many states require only that one of the two be present.

"Oppression" is sometimes defined as the absence of meaningful choice. This is often interpreted as merely requiring a showing that a provision fits into the category of a "contract of adhesion." All that this phrase means in most states is that a contract was promulgated on a take-it-or-leave-it basis (such as a standard form contract in which the consumer may not change or negotiate any of the printed terms) and that the contract was drafted by the more powerful party. In some states, it is enough to show that a contract is a contract of adhesion to establish that it is also procedurally unconscionable.

Some courts have held that consumer lawyers must prove—and not merely allege—this point. Some courts will not assume that a standard form contract is a contract of adhesion, and some plaintiffs have been compelled into arbitration solely because their counsel did not realize that it was necessary in that court to prove this point with admissible evidence. Many defendants will simply stipulate that a given contract was not negotiable—this is, in fact, generally true in consumer contracts, and many companies do not want to go through discovery to prove something that they can not seriously deny. If a defendant will not stipulate to this fact, however, a consumer attorney must establish through a Request for Admission, through an Interrogatory,

1 Reprinted from the National Association of Consumer Advocates, *The Consumer Advocate* (July–Aug. 2002).

2 F. Paul Bland, Jr., co-president of the NACA Board of Directors, is a staff attorney with Trial Lawyers for Public Justice and co-author of National Consumer Law Center, Consumer Arbitration Agreements (4th ed. 2004). He would like to thank Mike Quirk, Kate Gordon, and Khalid Elhassan, all of whom have done a great deal of research and thinking that contributed immeasurably to the ideas set forth in this article.

3 It is important to note that these facts will simply not be present in many cases. While the points discussed in this article do not begin to exhaust the arguments that are available to resist the enforcement of an arbitration clause, it is important to understand that not all arbitration clauses are unconscionable.

or by deposition that the company does not allow, and has never allowed, a consumer to refuse or re-write the arbitration clause.[4]

Some courts also look to a second factor in considering oppression or "meaningful choice": whether a consumer could have gotten the same service or product from another company in the area. Consumer lawyers should spend time and effort to prove this fact when possible. In *American General Finance v. Branch*, 793 So. 2d 738 (Ala. 2000), *cert. denied*, 122 S. Ct. 342 (2001), NACA members Barry Ragsdale and Garve Ivey built up a substantial factual record to establish that all but two sub-prime lenders in the consumer's home city required borrowers to agree to arbitration clauses and, thus, "the market was virtually closed to consumers seeking comparable financing without agreeing to arbitration provisions." This showing helped the plaintiffs win the first ruling ever from the Alabama Supreme Court that an arbitration clause was unconscionable.[5]

In *Ting v. AT&T*, 182 F. Supp. 2d 902 (N.D. Cal. 2002), Jim Sturdevant and I proved that Spring, MCI, Quest, and Working Assets Long Distance all had arbitration provisions similar to AT&T's clause. We also discovered that AT&T customer service would write to customers who questioned the arbitration clause that "[a]ll of the other major long distance carriers have included an arbitration provision in their service agreements." The court looked closely at the "meaningful choice" factor in finding that AT&T's arbitration clause was procedurally unconscionable: "Finding a carrier who did not contain such a provision was not easy." 182 F. Supp. 2d at 929.

As I mentioned above, many courts evaluating procedural unconscionability also look at whether consumers are likely to be "surprised" by a contract provision. Some consumer lawyers who have not put on any evidence on this issue have lost motions to compel arbitration from courts whose opinions stress that no one is excused from a contract merely because he or she did not bother to read it. When possible, consumer attorneys should attempt to prove that an arbitration clause was presented to their clients in a way that made it unlikely they would read it and in a way that made it reasonable and predictable that they would not see it. It is important to recognize, however, that proving this fact by itself generally does not demonstrate that a given arbitration clause is unconscionable, it only helps to show that one element of procedural unconscionability is present.

How can surprise be proven? Here are several illustrations of ways I have seen consumer lawyers establish that a particular arbitration clause was a surprise to consumers. NACA members Dan Hedges and Bren Pomponio demonstrated in one case that a closing agent held the pages of an agreement curled up so that their clients could not see anything but the signature lines. In another case, NACA members Tom Domonoske and Dale Pittman got a car salesman to admit that his normal practice is to tell buyers that the arbitration clause is just an option they have, proving that the consumers would be surprised to later be told that it was mandatory. In yet another case, NACA member Suzanne Keys used a readability expert to demonstrate that an arbitration clause was written in a manner that made it likely that most people with a college education could not understand the clause.

In the *Ting* case, we proved that (a) AT&T's own documents showed that it did not want its customers to become concerned about the details of the arbitration clause;[6] (b) AT&T's own internal marketing studies showed that it knew that few of its customers would read the clause; (c) a well-respected marketing expert, Todd Hilsee of Hilsoft Notifications, Inc., opined that the mailing that enclosed the arbitration clauses was ineffective from a communications standpoint and that the arbitration clause itself was not likely to be noticed; and (d) one of the most renowned pollsters in the country, Celinda Lake of Lake Snell & Perry, conducted a survey that established that only a small percentage of AT&T's customers had noticed the arbitration clause, and fewer still believed that they had agreed to it. The court's opinion reflects that this evidence was helpful in varying degrees to prove that the clause was procedurally unconscionable. 182 F. Supp. 2d at 930.

14.3 Substantive Unconscionability

14.3.1 Introduction

Mike Quirk of TLPJ, Jon Sheldon of the National Consumer Law Center, and I have written a manual entitled *Consumer Arbitration Agreements: Enforceability and Other Options*. As that manual demonstrates in great detail, there are quite a few factors that may be involved in establishing that a given arbitration clause is substantively

4 Some companies have begun to address this issue by including arbitration clauses in fine print underneath a statement to the effect that the consumer may refuse the arbitration clause and still receive the product or service addressed in the remainder of the contract. To the extent that marketing experts or other data, combined with the testimony of the consumers in a case, can demonstrate that such "choices" are not meaningful because the "option" is presented in a manner designed to ensure that consumers are not aware of it, many courts may not give much weight to such language.

5 I should disclose that I was involved in that case. Barry and Garve gave the author and TLPJ an opportunity to join them as co-counsel in resisting the bank's petition to the U.S. Supreme Court for certiorari, and the Supreme Court ultimately denied that petition.

6 The Court stated: "AT&T characterized the de-tariffing process as a non-event, thereby imposing on its customers the artificial notion that they would be unaffected by the changes resulting from the de-tariffing." 182 F. Supp. 2d at 930.

unconscionable in a given jurisdiction.[7] Because there is not room in this article to address each of these factors, I will focus on just two of them: arbitration clauses that impose prohibitively expensive costs upon consumers and arbitration clauses that bar consumers in certain types of cases from effectively vindicating their rights by prohibiting consumers from bringing their claims on a class-wide basis.

14.3.2 Five Points to Consider in Proving That an Arbitration Clause Imposes Excessive Fees

More courts have refused to enforce arbitration clauses on the grounds that they imposed prohibitive costs upon individuals than on any other grounds.[8] Nonetheless, there are all too many cases in which courts enforced arbitration clauses that would in fact impose prohibitive costs upon consumers because the consumer attorneys failed to build an adequate factual record. This article will offer several suggestions on how to avoid this problem.

First, it is important to recognize that the vast majority of arbitration systems imposes two types of fees: filing fees that are paid to the arbitration service provider (for example, the American Arbitration Association, JAMS, or the National Arbitration Forum) for their administrative services, and the fees that are paid to the actual arbitrator(s) for handling and deciding the case. The second category of fees—the arbitrators' fees—are generally much greater than the filing fees, but a number of judicial opinions reflect a mistaken impression that the only fees that a court needs to consider are the filing fees.

Second, consumer attorneys should realize that, while filing fees can often be ascertained from the official rules of the arbitration service provider, the arbitrators' fees generally can not be determined without discovery. Even with discovery, it is usually impossible to ascertain the precise fees likely to be charged in a case because different arbitrators charge different amounts. Nonetheless, consumers can usually obtain data from arbitration service providers as to the range of fees charged by arbitrators in a given area and the average fees charged by those arbitrators. Generally speaking, it takes the service of a subpoena or at least the threat of formal discovery processes to get the arbitration service providers to cough up this kind of information. For example, I have received in discovery documents from the AAA which demonstrate for Chicago the fee range for AAA arbitrators is $750 to $5000 for a day of hearings; the average (mean) is $1800; and the median is $1698. Similar statistics appear in affidavits from AAA officials for a half a dozen other cities. This kind of information is likely to prove extremely important in demonstrating that a given arbitration clause will impose significant costs upon a consumer.

Third, consumer lawyers should recognize that the amount of arbitration fees is likely to depend upon the amount of time required to arbitrate a case. All too often no evidence or argument is made on this point, and courts have several times assumed in opinions that relatively complex matters would be arbitrated in a single day. If a given consumer's case poses factual or legal complexities that will cause it to take several days or more to arbitrate, counsel needs to find a way to establish this fact to the court. I have seen courts base their findings as to the cost of arbitration upon the assumption that the arbitration can be completed in a single hour, in settings in which that assumption almost certainly seemed to be untrue but in which counsel had not made any kind of showing on the point to the court.

Fourth, some (but not all) courts look to the personal wealth of the consumer to determine whether arbitration fees will be prohibitive in a given case. Accordingly, when a consumer has relatively modest means and can not easily afford to pay significant arbitration fees, these facts should be established through an affidavit. The Third Circuit has even suggested that the affidavit should be supported by documents such as tax returns and records of expenses, assets, etc. *See* Blair v. Scott Specialty Gases, 283 F.3d 595 (3rd Cir. 2002).

Fifth, counsel should pay close attention to address the current version of the rules of arbitration service providers. The AAA, for example, has recently amended its rules for some consumer disputes in a manner that it claims will greatly reduce the fees that are paid by consumers and will shift those fees to businesses. It is not yet clear whether these changes are as significant as AAA claims, but they establish that practitioners need to focus upon the correct set of rules.

---

7 It is often pointed out to me that companies can write their arbitration clauses in ways that evade each of these problems, such as by paying all the fees and expenses of arbitration. My answer is simple: that has to be true. When one studies the U.S. Supreme Court's many opinions expansively interpreting the Federal Arbitration Act, it becomes clear that no argument can be made under the current law that all arbitration clauses are unconscionable. The only argument that can be made is that some clauses that are drafted to be particularly one-sided and unfair are unconscionable.

8 For a sample of recent cases in which courts refused to enforce arbitration clauses, at least in part because of high arbitration costs, see *Circuit City Stores, Inc. v. Adams*, 279 F.3d 889 (9th Cir. Feb. 4, 2002); *Ting v. AT&T*, 182 F. Supp. 2d 902 (N.D. Cal. 2002); *Popovich v. McDonald's Corp.*, No. 01C6622, 2002 WL 47965 (N.D. Ill. Jan. 14, 2002); *Bailey v. Ameriquest Mort. Co.*, No. CIV. 01-545, 2002 WL 100391 (D. Minn. Jan. 23, 2002); *Camacho v. Holiday Homes, Inc.*, 167 F. Supp. 2d 892 (W.D. Va. 2001); *Ball v. SFX Broad., Inc.*, 165 F. Supp. 2d 230 (N.D.N.Y. 2001); *Lelouis v. W. Directory Co.*, 2001 U.S. Dist. LEXIS 12517(D. Or. Aug. 10, 2001); *Gourley v. Yellow Transp., L.L.C.*, 178 F. Supp. 2d 1196 (D. Colo. 2001); *Phillips v. Assocs. Home Equity Servs.*, 179 F. Supp. 2d 840 (N.D. Ill. 2001); *Giordano v. Pep Boys—Manny, Moe & Jack, Inc.*, No. CIV. A. 99-1281, 2001 WL 484360 (E.D. Pa. Mar. 29, 2001); and *Mercuro v. Super. Court*, 96 Cal. App. 4th 167, 116 Cal. Rptr. 2d 671 (Cal. Ct. App. Feb. 13, 2002).

14.3.3 Challenging Arbitration Clauses That Prohibit Class Actions

A number of consumers have argued that arbitration clauses may not be enforced when they prohibit class actions (either explicitly or effectively). Unfortunately, the majority of these challenges have failed. The two most prominent of these failed challenges are *Johnson v. West Suburban Bank*, 225 F.3d 366 (3d Cir. 2000), *cert. denied*, 121 S. Ct. 1081 (2001) and *Randolph v. Green Tree Fin. Corp.*, 244 F.3d 814 (11th Cir. 2001), but there are quite a few others. One common thread through most of these cases is that the plaintiffs treated the cases principally as posing legal rather than factual issues. Typically, the plaintiffs in these cases argued that Congress intended that class actions be available under a given statute (such as the Truth in Lending Act) and argued that, in principle, prohibiting class actions would undermine the effectiveness of these statutes. While I am extremely sympathetic to these arguments, they have failed far more often than they have succeeded.[9]

There is another way of pursuing this issue, however, and that is to weave an argument from generally applicable principles of state contract law and a rich factual record and to stay away from broad generalities of federal law. In *Ting v. AT&T*, Jim Sturdevant and I argued that, based on the facts of that particular case, requiring plaintiffs to proceed on an individual basis will prevent them from effectively vindicating their legal rights. This argument is consistent with the Federal Arbitration Act—the Supreme Court has stated that the reason that arbitration clauses are generally to be enforced is that they generally permit parties to effectively vindicate their legal rights. In addition, most states do not permit exculpatory clauses that would deny individuals any meaningful remedy for wrongs done to them, and contracts that would have such an effect are regularly found to be unconscionable. Accordingly, if the facts in a particular case show that the plaintiffs can not pursue their statutory claims unless they are permitted to proceed on a class action basis, then a contract provision barring class actions will be found unconscionable in that case.

How does one prove that barring class actions will deny consumers any meaningful remedy? In *Ting v. AT&T*, Jim Sturdevant and I took discovery against AT&T relating to other class actions that had previously been filed against the company. We also gathered information about successful class actions that had been prosecuted against some other major long-distance carriers. We then contacted the attorneys who had represented the plaintiffs in those cases and learned that virtually all of them would be willing to testify that they would not have been able to pursue the claims at issue in those cases—even if the claims were valid—if they were unable to proceed on a class action basis. In one of those cases, for example, NACA member Seth Lessor had obtained a class-wide settlement worth 100 cents on the dollar against AT&T and, in another case, NACA members Robert Green and Eric Gibbs had obtained a settlement of more than $80 million from MCI. None of these witnesses ultimately had to testify at the trial, as AT&T stipulated to what they would have said rather than face this litany of damaging testimony. We also produced expert testimony from a number of experienced consumer attorneys familiar with the kinds of cases that are and are not brought and who had reviewed a number of the complaints in other class actions that had been brought against AT&T. These experts each testified that all or nearly all consumers with such claims would not have been able to find competent counsel to handle their claims on an individual basis, in or out of arbitration, even if their claims were entirely valid.

The approach ultimately succeeded, and the court held that "the prohibition on class actions will prevent class members from effectively vindicating their rights in certain categories of claims, especially those involving practices applicable to all members of the class but as to which any consumer has so little at stake that she can not be expected to pursue her claim." 182 F. Supp. 2d at 931. The key here is to develop a very strong factual record and not to rely upon common sense (which tragically has not been the governing force in the development of arbitration jurisprudence) or upon generalities of federal law.

14.4 Conclusion

When the U.S. Supreme Court decided to enforce the arbitration clause in *Green Tree Financial Corp. v. Randolph*, 531 U.S. 79 (2000), many consumer advocates lamented the decision as a disaster for the civil justice system. Surprisingly, the opposite has happened, as several dozen courts have refused to enforce arbitration clauses in particular cases for a variety of reasons. As one illustration of how the Court's emphasis on the plaintiff's burden of proof in the *Randolph* case has proven to be a stimulating dose of discipline for consumer attorneys, it has driven counsel to prove to court after court the reality that forced arbitration is very often far more expensive to consumers and employees than litigating claims in court. If more consumer lawyers follow this trend, the results are likely to be much brighter for their clients.

9 One notable exception is a significant win achieved by NACA member Phil Rogers in *Lozada v. Dale Baker Oldsmobile, Inc.*, 91 F. Supp. 2d 1087 (W.D. Mich. 2000).

Chapter 15 Car Cases 101: Creating the Interview Form[1]

By Ronald L. Burdge[2]

15.1 Introduction

"In the old days . . . ," as we sometimes say, a new client conference started out with our scribbling notes on a yellow pad. That was all we had, so that was all we used. It was certainly better than nothing, if only slightly. The seasoned attorney knew what to ask and why to ask it. But the newcomer attorney not only found himself not being sure why something should be asked but often having no idea what should be asked about. Moreover, even the seasoned attorney could easily forget to cover everything. That is the whole reason for using a standard New Client Conference Form.

A New Client Conference Form should cover all of the basics, in a systematic and organized fashion that is easy to follow, makes sense to the attorney, and is easily followed by the client. The fundamental objective is to get as much information as necessary, as quickly as you can, and then to impart as much information as necessary as quickly as you can. Ideally, the New Client Conference Form should facilitate the process of the conference by guiding and directing it (that is, "keeping it on track") and facilitating the discussion of every key aspect involved in such a conference—all in less than an hour of your time. With that in mind, you can create your own New Client Conference Form.[3]

15.2 Areas to Be Covered

First, think about the areas covered in the usual new client conference: the basic information about the client, the basic information about the vehicle, the possible claims, and the attorney fee arrangement. In one way or another, everything else is only another part of one of these topics.

The structure of the New Client Conference Form should make sense to the client as well as to you. Obviously, you have to "get" information before you can "give" an analysis back to the client. Thus, the first part of the form should be information-gathering and the last part of the form should be answer-giving.

15.3 Basic Information on Client

At the beginning you want identification of your client, including such obvious things as name, address, and telephone number. However, you should also ask for identification of the referral source (that is, "how did you hear about me?"). This enables you to send a personal "thank you" to the referring source and to gauge where to invest your marketing efforts for future business development. Also, ask for e-mail address information. Many people are "net savvy" and the instantaneous communication of e-mail is often greatly appreciated by the client.

Finally, consider getting work telephone numbers and times. It is useful to have a relative's or friend's contact information in case the matter lasts for an extended period of time. One way to get all of this information, and more, without the attorney ever asking a single question is having an "intake sheet" filled out by the client before the conference starts. The format can be similar to what doctors and dentists use for a new client.

1 Reprinted from the National Association of Consumer Advocate, The Consumer Advocate (Sept./Oct. 2001).

2 Ronald L. Burdge is in the private practice of law in Dayton, Ohio, and is known throughout Ohio as a leading consumer law attorney who has represented literally thousands of consumers in "lemon" car lawsuits over the last twenty years and who actively co-counsels and coaches other consumer law attorneys. He has authored articles and lectured on the Ohio Lemon Law, Assistive Device Lemon Laws, and Recreation Vehicle Lemon Laws. Although the majority of his court cases have involved defective motor vehicle litigation, he has also represented consumers in UDAP, product defect, odometer tampering, contract breach, fraud, and commercial litigation in both state and federal courts throughout Ohio, in Indiana and Kentucky. With extensive trial and appellate experience related to motor vehicles and dealership business practices, he has also successfully argued cases in various courts of appeals and the Ohio Supreme Court. He is a member of numerous bar associations, has obtained several multi-million dollar verdicts, and has handled numerous ground-breaking consumer law and lemon law cases.

3 See also Appendix B, *infra*, and the companion CD-Rom for sample questionnaires.

15.4 Basic Information on Vehicle

The conference should then shift to the basic information about the vehicle. In a typical car case, the basic information about the vehicle includes the obvious and the not so obvious: not only the make, model, year, odometer reading at sale and now, and identification of the dealer, but also the identity of the financier and whether or not it was financed by dealer.

Obviously the new client will bring many documents with him or her to this conference and much of the information can be readily obtained from the documents. You can either photocopy the documents or you can simply make notes from them or from answers given by the new client.

However, photocopying documents takes time and necessarily means either you leave the room or a distraction will occur in the form of someone entering the room and to get the documents and make copies and then returning. This distraction will cause a loss of focus by both the new client and the attorney and should be avoided. All of the focus during this conference should be on the new client.

You also will want to know if the client received repair documents every time they picked the vehicle up from the repair shop. That will enable you to look through the documents to independently verify and identify the complaints and defects—and what the dealer did about those during repair attempts. A simple question with a "yes" or "no" response for you to circle when going through the form is sufficient (that is, "Did you get a repair order every time you got the vehicle back from the shop?").

Also make a note of the warranty length and who the warranty is from (that is, in the case of a used car, is there a warranty from the dealer?). Likewise, make a note on the existence and length of any service contract (along with who the provider is—the dealer or some third party).

Many times a car dealer will argue that a consumer is complaining only because of "buyer's remorse" or because the vehicle has been damaged in an accident and the consumer wants a newer one. Anticipating this defensive argument, during the conference you can also ask the questions: "has the vehicle ever been wrecked or damaged by you or while you had it?" and "can you afford the loan payments?" Having these answers in advance gives you the ability to quickly retort if and when the defense argument is raised later.

At this point you have gathered the basic information about the client and the vehicle, and you are ready to find out what is wrong with the vehicle. In a new-car scenario you should probably start off with the Lemon Law definition questions for your jurisdiction to get a quick overview (that is, days out of service, number of times in the shop, three or four times in for the same problem, etc.).

After the overview questions are out of the way, begin to make a list of the defects (item by item) and note whether or not each one has been fixed yet. Also make a note on the number of times each defect was worked on by a dealer.

Sometimes the new client wants to talk more about the issues involved with a complaint or two (that is, "it happened on the interstate while I was between two trucks and the kids were in the back seat screaming and I was afraid I was going to have an accident when it stalled"). You can be certain that the new client will always have more to say than merely what you are asking. For that reason, near the list of defects you should place four or five blank lines across the page so that you can make any additional notes that you deem necessary. Here you want to make note of those "silver bullet" remarks you can use later.

Some of these defects will be of a "deadly" nature, and it is easy to put an asterisk by each of those as you go through the interview for later emphasis. Sometimes you can recognize a complaint as being about a deadly defect, and sometimes you must ask a client what they thought about it (that is, "was this problem serious enough that it could have caused an accident or someone could have been hurt?").

By this time you now know everything about the client and the car problems, right? Wrong.

Now it is time to ask the more fundamental question, which will help determine your "target" defendants. You might ask, "Looking back on what was said to you at the time you were first buying the car, do you think that there was anything the car dealer lied to you about, or do you think we are really just simply talking about a bad car?"

More times than not, this question will allows you learn everything you need to know about the relationship between the dealer and the new client. You can explain the definition of fraud, but that can be confusing and misleading. A direct question can give you a heads up on the issue without getting into too much unnecessary detail. Often a client will not realize what is happening to them during the sales process, but "20-20 hindsight" always helps later and a souring repair experience often causes the new client to reconsider the sales process more carefully.

With these considerations out of the way, the only thing left for you to find out from the new client is what it is the client wants. Typically, a new client is going to want one or more of several different things: a replacement vehicle, their money back (that is, a "buyback"), repairs, or other monetary recovery.

15.5 Now It Is Your Turn to Talk

If you are on schedule, you should now be about twenty minutes into the interview. Now, it is time to "turn the tables" and begin telling the client what you think, what they can and can not do, how long it would take, what it would cost, and what they can expect out of it. As you do that, you should be making notes on what you say on the rest of the form in a systematic manner. That way, at any time in the future, you can look at the notes you made and tell what it was you said and what you were thinking as you were talking about the client's case with them.

The rest of the conference will primarily be concerned with explaining the new client's alternatives, what legal claims may exist, and the attorney fee arrangement. Some additional important points to be discussed with clients are developed in Chapter 19, *infra*, regarding realistic client expectations for the case and Chapter 20, *infra*, on potential client income tax liability for attorney fees and damages.

15.6 The Possible Claims

At the outset of your explanation of the new client's rights, you need to explain what alternatives he or she is facing. Typically, the new client with a "bad car" only has a few choices to make. He or she can go back to the dealer or call up the manufacturer and continue to complain. A second choice is to file for arbitration, if the manufacturer has an arbitration process. A third choice is to file a law suit.

After explaining the alternatives available, you need to cover the legal claims that can exist in the case. Remember, you are not trying to get the client to become a lawyer—only to get him or her to understand the basics of the legal claims involved. At this part of the New Client Conference Form, you should have a list of all the most frequently used claims that are brought in a car case being filed in court, by name only. That way you can simply circle those that are applicable. You should also make a note of who the "target" defendant is in each claim, along with the applicable statute of limitations.

One of those claims will likely be for fraud. Fraud is "fact intensive," so it would be a good idea to draw one or two blank lines below on which to note what the essential fact was that you had in mind for fraud.

15.7 The Attorney Fee Agreement

By this point in the process, you have obtained information and given answers sufficient for the client to know his or her legal rights. The only thing left to cover is the attorney fee arrangement you will use.[4]

Obviously, if the New Client Conference Form is to be kept short and simple, the attorney fee agreement is not likely to be contained within it. But you should consider placing an outline of the attorney fee agreement on the New Client Conference Form. A separate written fee agreement should exist, but having an outline on the form will enable you to always know what the terms were for that particular case and remind yourself to cover them during the conference. As you are reviewing this with the new client during the conference, you can simply check off each area as you discuss it.

Ideally, the New Client Conference Form should be no more than two pages long. Remember, the more pieces of paper you must "shuffle" as you go through the conference, the more distracting it will be for the client and yourself.

The New Client Conference Form should be structured in a way that works best for the particular attorney. Your style may call for one section of the form to be moved to a different place than the sequence suggested here. You may routinely discuss something not even mentioned in this article, perhaps because of the peculiarities of the law in your jurisdiction.

The basic idea is to create a standard New Client Conference Form that you can use for every intake conference. Such a form will naturally and easily guide you through the conference, help you stay focused, obtain all information necessary for you to be able to advise the client, guide you through the answer-giving phase of the conference, and memorialize in a written fashion all important things that are said during the conference. Such a form will be simple and easy to use, enhancing a methodical and systematic approach to the new client conference. With that, you can become more confident in yourself—and the new client will see that and be encouraged to retain you.

---

4 See Appendix A, *infra*, for sample retainer forms.

Chapter 16 Formal and Informal Discovery

By Carolyn Carter[1]

16.1 Informal Pre-Suit Discovery

16.1.1 Client Documents, Witnesses, Public Records

Thorough pre-suit investigation enables the consumer to start a case in a strong position, in command of key evidence. Before filing suit, the attorney should obtain and review all the client's documents and all documents the client can obtain from others. For example, a client can document payments by requesting bank records. The client can also obtain credit reports to determine whether a dealer or financer has made a negative report to a credit reporting agency. In automobile fraud cases, the vehicle's title history should be obtained and the vehicle should be inspected. Experts can be retained and products inspected prior to suit.

The attorney can also begin tracking down and interviewing witnesses before suit. If state ethical rules permit,[2] the attorney should try to locate and interview former employees of defendant corporations. It is best to get a signed or even sworn statement from any witnesses who may change their testimony.

Public records are also available before suit: records from licensing agencies, title records, corporate records, SEC filings, mortgages, deeds, and records of lawsuits. Information about the structure and policies of manufacturers, sellers, and creditors is available on the Internet, as are guidelines and ethical standards published by trade organizations. Information about post office box holders and a new address can be obtained from the local postmaster if needed to serve legal process.[3]

Regardless of what formal discovery produces,[4] the consumer's attorney should conduct an independent investigation to uncover pattern evidence. Court dockets, records of complaints to government and consumer protection agencies, complaint websites, and motor vehicle or real estate transfer records are among the ways to locate other victims of a fraud.

16.1.2 The Consumer's Statutory Right to Obtain Information from Opposing Parties

16.1.2.1 Introduction

A number of statutes require creditors or other parties to respond to consumer requests for information. Invoking these statutes is an excellent part of pre-suit investigation. In addition, some of these statutes provide for statutory damages if the party fails to respond properly to the request for information, potentially giving the consumer an additional claim. The most significant of these useful statutes are outlined below. Many of them give the consumer the right to dispute debts as well as the right to obtain information, but only the latter provisions are described in this section.

16.1.2.2 Qualified Written Requests Under RESPA

The Real Estate Settlement Procedures Act (RESPA) requires a mortgage servicer (the entity that bills the consumer and accepts payments) to respond to a consumer's "qualified written request" for information on the loan.[5] A qualified written request should be considered as a first step on behalf of any client who has a problem relating to the

---

1 Carolyn Carter is Deputy Director of Advocacy at NCLC. She was formerly co-director of Legal Services, Inc., in Gettysburg, Pennsylvania, and director of the Law Reform Office of the Cleveland Legal Aid Society. She is the editor of *Pennsylvania Consumer Law* and the first edition of *Ohio Consumer Law*; co-author of *Automobile Fraud* (2003), *Consumer Warranty Law* (2d ed. 2001), *Unfair and Deceptive Acts and Practices* (6th ed. 2004), *Repossessions and Foreclosures* (5th ed. 2002 and Supp.); and contributing author to *Fair Debt Collection* (5th ed. 2004 and Supp.), *Truth in Lending* (5th ed. 2003 and Supp.), and *The Cost of Credit: Regulation, Preemption, and Industry Abuses* (3d ed. 2005). She is the 1992 recipient of the Vern Countryman Consumer Award and is currently a member of the Federal Reserve Board's Consumer Advisory Council.

2 *See* § 7.10, *supra*.

3 *See* 39 CFR § 265.6(d)(4)(ii); request form in Appx. B.2.9.

4 *See* § 16.1.2, *infra*.

5 12 U.S.C. § 2605(e).

balance due on a mortgage, including problems with crediting of payments, calculation of interest, and addition of other charges.

The duty to respond to a qualified written request applies to servicers of "federally related" mortgages. Almost all mortgages are federally related, as the term includes HUD mortgages, mortgages originated by federally insured lenders, mortgages originated by creditors who make or invest in $1 million or more in residential real estate loans per year, and mortgages bought by Fannie Mae, Freddie Mac, or other major secondary market lenders.[6] The mortgage must be on residential real property of one to four units.[7] HUD states that this duty does not apply to home equity lines of credit, but this is contrary to the statute and may not be enforceable.[8] RESPA does not preempt stronger state servicing laws, and a number of states have similar statutes that apply to a broader spectrum of loans or give greater consumer rights.[9]

A "qualified written request" is simply one that identifies the borrower and the account and explains an error or provides sufficient detail about the information sought by the borrower.[10] The request can not be made on a payment coupon or similar document used to pay the mortgage, however.[11]

Within twenty business days, the servicer must acknowledge receipt of the request, and, within sixty business days, either

- correct the account and notify the consumer;
- conduct an investigation and state the reasons why the account is correct, with the name and phone number of a servicer employee who can provide further information; or
- provide the information requested or explain why it is not available and also provide the name and phone number of a servicer employee who can provide further information.[12]

6 12 U.S.C. § 2602(1).

7 *Id.*

8 *See* National Consumer Law Center, Repossessions and Foreclosures § 19.2.1 (5th ed. 2002 and Supp.). Even if this RESPA right does not apply to home equity lines of credit, the FCBA rights set out in § 16.1.2.8, *infra*, do apply and provide different and probably stronger consumer protections, although they must be asserted within a shorter time limit.

9 *See* National Consumer Law Center, Repossessions and Foreclosures Appx. M (5th ed. 200 and Supp.). For example, Alaska, Kansas, Maryland, Minnesota, Utah, and Washington statutes give the servicer only fifteen days to respond. *See* National Consumer Law Center, Repossessions and Foreclosures Appx. M (5th ed. 2002 and Supp.).

10 12 U.S.C. § 2605(e)(1)(B). A sample qualified written request is found in National Consumer Law Center, Repossessions and Foreclosures Appx. O.5.1 (2004 Supp.).

11 *Id.*

12 12 U.S.C. § 2605(e)(1)(A), (2).

The servicer need not respond if the request is sent more than a year after "the date of transfer of service" or the amount was paid in full.[13] This clearly is meant to apply when an old servicer is no longer handling the loan or the loan is paid in full. Some servicers interpret this, however, as requiring the consumer to make the request within the first year that the servicer takes on a loan *and* within a year of the act or omission.

If the servicer fails to comply with a qualified written request, RESPA provides a private cause of action for actual damages, attorney fees, and costs, plus $1000 additional statutory damages if there is a pattern or practice of noncompliance.[14]

16.1.2.3 Finding Out What Entity Holds the Consumer's Obligation

In this age of securitization, it is often difficult to determine what entity actually owns the consumer's obligation. The entity that is billing the consumer may be merely a servicer, billing the consumer on behalf of a trust or other entity that owns the obligation.

A consumer who wants to file suit about an obligation needs to know who holds it, as that entity may be a necessary party. Finding out what entity actually owns the obligation is particularly important for consumers who are considering rescinding a transaction under the Truth in Lending Act,[15] as they will want to send a rescission notice not only to the original creditor but also to the current holder of the obligation.[16]

The Truth in Lending Act (TILA) gives consumers the right to make a written request of the servicer, which must then provide the name, address, and telephone number of the owner of the obligation.[17] This duty applies to any consumer credit transaction as defined by the Truth in Lending Act. The Truth in Lending Act does not provide any explicit private remedies for violation of this duty, however.[18] For transactions covered by RESPA,[19] a RESPA private cause of action will be available if the request for the identity of the holder is part of a RESPA-qualified written request.

16.1.2.4 Obtaining Information About Debts in Collection

A debt collector as defined by the Fair Debt Collection Practices Act (FDCPA) must give the debtor a validation

13 24 C.F.R. § 3500.21(e)(2)(ii).

14 12 U.S.C. § 2605(f).

15 15 U.S.C. § 1635.

16 *See* National Consumer Law Center, Truth in Lending § 6.6.4.2 (5th ed. 2003 and Supp.).

17 15 U.S.C. § 1641(f)(2).

18 15 U.S.C. § 1640 provides remedies for creditors but does not mention servicers.

19 *See* § 16.1.2.2, *supra*.

notice, setting forth the debtor's right to dispute the debt or any portion of it, and to require the creditor to identify the original creditor.[20] The consumer has thirty days after receiving this notice to dispute the debt or ask for the identity of the original creditor. Upon receiving a request, the collector can take no collection action until it provides the requested information to the consumer.[21] If the consumer disputes the debt, the creditor must mail verification of it to the consumer.[22] If a collector violates these requirements, FDCPA remedies include statutory damages up to $1000, actual damages, and attorney fees.[23]

16.1.2.5 Explanation of Amount Creditor Seeks as Deficiency After Selling Collateral

When a creditor seeks a deficiency after it sells a motor vehicle, mobile home, or other personalty, the Uniform Commercial Code requires the creditor to provide the consumer with an explanation of the amount of the deficiency it is seeking. The consumer also has the right, at no charge, to obtain this explanation once every six months.[24] This is helpful if the consumer did not receive or retain the notice provided by the creditor and also because the deficiency amount being sought may increase over time.

The creditor must send the explanation within fourteen days of the consumer's request. The explanation contains much useful information, including how the deficiency was calculated, any rebates of unearned interest, the sale proceeds, and the types of expenses and total amount of expenses charged to the consumer.[25]

Remedies for non-compliance are actual damages, plus $500 if the creditor has a pattern or practice of non-compliance.[26]

16.1.2.6 Identifying the Collateral for an Obligation

In some small loans and credit union debts, it may be unclear what collateral the creditor is presently claiming because of the operation of future advance clauses, cross-collateral, and allocation of payment issues. Section 9-210 of the Uniform Commercial Code allows the consumer to send a request reasonably identifying the consumer and the account number, and asking the creditor to approve or correct a list of collateral provided by the consumer. The creditor has fourteen days to send a statement of the collateral. The consumer is entitled to one free statement a year, and the price of additional statements is capped at $25. If the creditor fails to comply with § 9-210 without reasonable cause, the consumer has an action for actual damages plus $500.[27]

16.1.2.7 Determining the Balance on a Secured Obligation

Often a consumer's legal problem will involve a question or dispute about the amount owing to a creditor. For car loans and other secured transactions, UCC § 9-210 provides consumers with the right to get information on the amount due.

The consumer can proceed in either of two ways. The first alternative is to send the secured party a request for an accounting of the unpaid obligation. The request must be signed (electronically or manually) and must reasonably identify the transaction.[28] Then the secured party has fourteen days to send the consumer a statement of the amount owed.[29] The secured party can state the amount owed at any point from thirty-five days earlier or thirty-five days later.[30]

The second alternative is to send the secured party a statement of the amount the *debtor* believes is owing as of a specified date. The request must be signed (electronically or manually), must reasonably identify the transaction, and must ask the secured party to approve or correct the statement.[31] The secured party then has fourteen days to respond by sending the consumer an approval or correction of the amount stated.[32] The advantage of this procedure is that the secured party's reply will relate to a date chosen by the consumer.

The consumer is entitled to one free statement of either type per year. The cost of additional statements is capped at $25.[33]

A secured party that fails to comply with either of these requirements without reasonable cause is liable for the consumer's actual damages plus $500.[34]

---

20 15 U.S.C. § 1692g.

21 15 U.S.C. § 1692g(b). *See also* National Consumer Law Center, Fair Debt Collection § 5.7.3 (5th ed. 2004 and Supp.).

22 15 U.S.C. § 1692g(a)(4).

23 15 U.S.C. § 1692k.

24 U.C.C. § 9-616.

25 *Id.*

26 U.C.C. § 9-625(e). The $500 statutory damage award is available for violations of UCC § 9-616(b)(2) without a showing of a pattern or practice, but the awkward interplay between §§ 9-616(b) and 6-625(e)(5), (6) makes the applicability of this provision unclear.

27 U.C.C. §§ 9-625(b), (f). A few states alter or eliminate the $500 amount. *See* National Consumer Law Center, Repossessions and Foreclosures § 13.2.5 (5th ed. 2002 and Supp.).

28 U.C.C. § 9-210(a)(2).

29 U.C.C. §§ 9-210(b)(1), 9-102(a)(4) (definition of "accounting").

30 U.C.C. § 9-102(a)(4)(B).

31 U.C.C. § 9-210(a)(4).

32 U.C.C. § 9-210(b)(2).

33 U.C.C. § 9-210(f).

34 U.C.C. § 9-625(b), (f). A few states alter the $500 amount or eliminate it. *See* National Consumer Law Center, Repossessions and Foreclosures § 13.2.5 (5th ed. 2002 and Supp.).

16.1.2.8 Information About Charges on Monthly Statements for Credit Cards and Other Open-End Credit

For credit cards, home equity lines of credit, and other open-end credit, the Fair Credit Billing Act (FCBA) gives the consumer the right to dispute charges and request information about them.[35]

The FCBA allows a consumer to challenge

- unauthorized or unidentified charges or charges in the wrong amount;
- charges for merchandise or services that the consumer did not accept;
- charges for merchandise or services that were delivered late or in the wrong quantity or that were different from that agreed upon; and
- the card issuer's failure to apply a payment, send a statement, or properly compute the amount due.[36]

The consumer may also use the FCBA dispute procedure to request clarification, including documentary evidence, regarding an extension of credit shown on a periodic statement.[37] The FCBA does not apply to disputes over quality, however.[38]

The consumer must notify the card issuer in writing within sixty days of receipt of the disputed statement, identifying the name and account.[39] The notice should be sent to the special address designated by the card issuer.[40] The card issuer then must acknowledge receipt and either credit the amount or conduct an investigation within the rest of that billing cycle and the next two billing cycles. If the creditor resolves the dispute against the consumer, it must provide a written explanation.[41] If the consumer requests, it must also provide documentary evidence of the debt.[42]

TILA remedies for FCBA violations are forfeiture of the disputed amount up to $50, statutory damages up to $1000, actual damages, and attorney fees.[43]

35 15 U.S.C. § 1666. FCBA rights are discussed in detail in National Consumer Law Center, Truth in Lending § 5.8 (5th ed. 2003 and Supp.). The Truth in Lending Act also gives consumers the right to assert against the card issuer any defenses and claims, other than tort claims, that arise out of the transaction in which the credit card was used. 15 U.S.C. § 1666i. This right, which has some restrictions, is separate from the FCBA right to dispute a charge. *See* National Consumer Law Center, Truth in Lending § 5.9.5 (5th ed. 2003 and Supp.)

36 15 U.S.C. § 1666(b); 12 C.F.R. § 226.13(a). *See also* Official Staff Interpretation, § 226.13(a)(3)-1.

37 12 C.F.R. § 226.13(a)(6).

38 Official Staff Interpretation, § 226.13(a)(3)-1.

39 15 U.S.C. § 1666(a); 12 C.F.R. § 226.13(b)(1).

40 12 C.F.R. § 226.13(b)(1).

41 12 C.F.R. § 226.13(f)(1).

42 15 U.S.C. § 1666(a)(3)(B)(2); 12 C.F.R. § 226.13(f)(2).

43 15 U.S.C. §§ 1640, 1666(e).

16.1.2.9 Information About Payments Made Through Debit Cards and Other Electronic Fund Transfers

The Electronic Fund Transfers Act (EFTA)[44] has an error correction procedure somewhat similar to the Fair Credit Billing Act procedures discussed in the previous subsection. The EFTA applies to debit card transactions, direct deposits, automatic bill payment plans, and other forms of electronic transfers directly out of a consumer's bank account.[45] The consumer must give notice within sixty days of receipt of a bank statement that displays the error, identifying the consumer and the bank account and indicating the nature of the error.[46] The consumer can also request information to determine whether an error exists.[47]

If the bank does not credit the consumer's account immediately to correct the error, it must investigate the error and send notice of its results to the consumer.[48] If the bank denies the consumer's claim, it must provide a written explanation and offer the consumer the opportunity to see and request copies of the documents upon which the bank relied.[49]

For certain forms of non-compliance with these requirements, the bank is liable for treble damages[50] and, in any event, is liable for actual damages plus statutory damages not less than $100 nor more than $1000, plus attorney fees.[51]

16.2 Items to Seek in Formal Discovery

16.2.1 Original Files and Documents

Once the case is filed, it is important to begin formal discovery promptly. One experienced automobile fraud attorney recommends starting discovery with a document request that includes a demand for the entire dealer file, and then following up with a deposition of the salesperson, with instructions that the salesperson is to bring the original dealer file to the deposition. The consumer's attorney's staff

44 15 U.S.C. § 1693; 12 C.F.R. § 205.

45 15 U.S.C. § 1693a(6) (definition of "electronic fund transfer"). Even paper checks can be governed by these procedures when the payee does not deposit the check but uses it as a source document to initiate an electronic transfer out of the consumer's account.

46 15 U.S.C. § 1693f(a); 12 C.F.R. § 205.11(b).

47 12 C.F.R. § 210.11(a)(vii).

48 12 C.F.R. § 205.11(c), (d).

49 12 C.F.R. § 205.11(d)(1). *See also* Official Staff Interpretation, § 205.11)d)(1)-1 (documents must be converted to "understandable form").

50 15 U.S.C. § 1693f(e).

51 15 U.S.C. § 1693m(a).

then copies the original file as one of the first items of business during the deposition. It is surprising how often the original file includes documents that were not included in the copy produced in response to the document request.

Getting the originals and all copies of documents from the defendant can also uncover important information. There may be handwritten notes on the back of a document, for example. Motor vehicle dealers often keep multiple copies of repair orders, some of which have handwritten notes the mechanic wrote.

16.2.2 Pattern Evidence

Another important area to explore through formal discovery is similar-acts cases involving other consumers. This powerful evidence is relevant for many purposes, for example, to win punitive damages or to show intent, knowledge, plan, or absence of mistake.[52] Many courts have allowed consumers to discover information about other consumer's transactions with the same defendant.[53]

The consumer should be prepared for obdurate resistance to the release of information about other transactions and customers, however. If the court is reluctant to order this discovery, narrowing the request to a certain type of transaction or a shorter time period may help. Or the consumer could request documents for a random sample rather than all transactions. The selection of transactions should be supervised, however, to make sure that the sample is truly random.

Sometimes another way to get information about other transactions is to issue a subpoena to a state agency to which the defendant makes periodic reports. For example, in some states, vehicle dealers may have to identify buyers in reports that they file with the state motor vehicle department about sales or temporary tags. Issuing a subpoena to the state agency to produce this information casts the burden on the dealer to seek and justify a protective order and removes the argument that production of the documents puts too much of a burden on the dealer.

The defendant's training materials, manuals, and directives may also provide evidence of a pattern or practice of fraud. Even if they do not show fraud directly, they may show that the defendant's business practices were set up in a way that enabled fraud to flourish.

16.2.3 Net Worth Discovery

If punitive damages are sought, the consumer's attorney should also seek information about the defendant's income and assets. In many states the defendant's financial condition is a relevant factor in a punitive damages award. In some jurisdictions however, the plaintiff must make a prima facie showing of entitlement to punitive damages before being allowed to discover net worth information.[54]

16.3 Making the Most of Available Discovery Techniques[55]

Some discovery techniques are better than others for obtaining certain types of information. Interrogatories and

---

52 *See* § 21.2.2, *infra.*

53 Marks v. Global Mortgage Group Inc., 218 F.R.D. 492 (S.D. W. Va. 2003) (Gramm-Leach-Bliley Act does not prevent disclosure of identifying information about other customers in response to discovery); *Ex parte* Nat'l W. Life Ins. Co., 899 So. 2d 218 (Ala. 2004) (Gramm-Leach-Bliley Act does not prevent plaintiff from obtaining information about other insurance customers through formal discovery, but court should issue confidentiality order); *Ex parte* Nat'l Sec. Ins. Co., 773 So. 2d 461 (Ala. 2000); *Ex parte* First Nat'l Bank of Pulaski, 730 So. 2d 1160 (Ala. 1999) (declining to overturn trial court's order requiring discovery of names and addresses of all Alabama residents who borrowed money from bank through a particular agent over two-year period); *Ex parte* Union Sec. Life Ins. Co., 723 So. 2d 34 (Ala. 1998) (declining to overturn trial court's order requiring production of all credit life insurance applications from Alabama residents over five-year period); Colonial Life & Accident Ins. Co. v. Super. Court, 31 Cal. 3d 785, 647 P.2d 86, 183 Cal. Rptr. 810 (1982) (information about other claimants discoverable when Unfair Insurance Practices statute requires plaintiff to show that insurer's unfair claims settlement practices were a general business practice); Flores v. Super. Ct., 2002 WL 1613845 (Cal. Ct. App. July 19, 2002) (unpublished, citation limited) (identities of other customers discoverable, subject to appropriate orders to protect privacy and trade secrets); Fla. First Fin. Group v. De Castro, 815 So. 2d 789 (Fla. Dist. Ct. App. 2002) (ordering debt collector to produce records of correspondence and telephone calls to other debtors does not violate privacy protections of state and federal debt collection laws); Grange Mut. Ins. Co. v. Trude, 151 S.W.3d 803 (Ky. 2004) (discovery of other bad faith claims brought against defendant insurer is relevant to plaintiff's bad faith claim; plaintiff may also discover job-related information in personnel files of defendant's employees); Pleskach v. Chrysler Corp., Clearinghouse No. 53,518 (N.C. Super. Ct. Oct. 20, 1999) (imposing fine of $2000 per day, increasing to $5000 per day after eighth day, for manufacturer's failure to produce information about other buybacks), *later order at* Clearinghouse No. 53,518 (N.C. Super. Ct. Feb. 20, 2001) (entering default judgment against manufacturer for continued failure to produce documents, ordering documents held by clerk of court unsealed, and ordering manufacturer to produce vehicle identification numbers and names and addresses of owners and buyers of lemon buybacks over five-year period); Martino v. Barnett, 595 S.E.2d 65 (W. Va. 2004) (neither state insurance law nor Gramm-Leach-Bliley Act precludes party from obtaining information about other customers through discovery). *See also* Schmitt v. Lalancette, 830 A.2d 16 (Vt. 2003) (trial court abused discretion in ordering plaintiff not to contact other customers of defendant identified through investigation and was unjustified in denying discovery of identities of other customers, in UDAP and breach of contract suit).

54 *See* Wal-Mart Stores, Inc. v. Alexander, 868 S.W.2d 322, 332 n. 7 (Tex. 1993) (citing statutes and decisions from other states).

55 This section is based on a presentation made by Attorney

requests for production of documents are effective ways to obtain documents and identify witnesses. These discovery methods are also a good way to press defendants for evidence—such as the identities of other buyers—relating to a pattern of misconduct. Contention interrogatories, in which the defendant is asked to identify the facts supporting a particular contention, are also useful.

Interrogatories and document requests are also the basic tools for identifying the opponent's expert witnesses and obtaining financial statements. Financial statements that the defendant has provided when seeking to borrow money from financial institutions are the most useful, since the defendant probably will not have concealed assets when preparing these statements.

If the jurisdiction limits the number of interrogatories that may be asked, requesting documents may be another way to get the same information. There also may be no limit on the number of requests for admission, which can sometimes be used in place of interrogatories when the facts are straightforward. Requests for admission are also useful to nail down information obtained through other discovery methods. For example, they can be used to establish the authenticity of documents the defendant has produced so that the documents can be introduced more easily. Or, when facts have been discovered from one defendant, requests for admissions can be used to bind other defendants to them.

When seeking narrative responses, depositions are much more useful than interrogatories. Depositions under Rule 30(b)(6) of the Federal Rules of Civil Procedure, requiring a corporation to designate a representative to testify about a certain topic, are particularly helpful. Depositions under Rule 30(b)(6) or comparable state rules can define and limit the defendants' positions on important issues.

Scheduling of depositions should be planned carefully. It is important to schedule the deposition of the defendant so that there is time to follow up with additional discovery to deal with any defenses or issues that the deposition reveals.

16.4 Cadillac Discovery on a Buick Budget

Discovery costs can sometimes be reduced by conducting telephone depositions. Telephone depositions are particularly appropriate for short depositions of disinterested third-party witnesses, such as custodians of documents located in other states. Telephone deposition costs can be further reduced by working out an agreement that the witness will appear without the need for a subpoena or will accept a subpoena sent by fax. Any such agreement should be carefully documented.

Bernard Brown, a Missouri attorney with a specialty in automobile fraud, at NCLC's annual Consumer Rights Conference in 2001.

Another way to reduce costs is to try a request for admission first instead of conducting a deposition when the evidence sought is highly objective and routine, such as the foundation for admissibility of a third party's documents. Requests for admission are also a useful way to simplify the trial, and sometimes they produce concessions on important facts.

Deposition costs can be reduced by refraining from ordering unnecessary transcripts. Usually the court reporter's attendance fee is relatively modest, but the transcript is expensive. If a deposition is conducted purely for discovery, a transcript may be unnecessary. Even for depositions that will be used at trial, it may be possible to delay ordering transcripts until settlement efforts have been exhausted. Always be careful, though, to leave enough time for the deposition to be transcribed and presented to the witness for signature if it is to be used at trial.

Videotaping depositions is another cost-cutting strategy. Ordinary home video equipment may be sufficient. Some attorneys, though, favor investing in top-quality business video equipment, partly because it looks more impressive. In many jurisdictions, court rules require a disinterested person to swear in the witness and operate the tape. The opposing attorney may stipulate that the consumer's attorney, or an employee in the consumer's attorney's office, can perform this function. If not, the consumer's attorney can borrow an employee from another attorney's office. Audiotaping of depositions, allowed under the same rules, is also inexpensive. While audiotaping does not produce the visual record, and so may have less impact at trial, the equipment is less expensive and some witnesses may be more relaxed when being audiotaped than when being videotaped. Note that the federal rules require the officer taking the deposition to record certain statements at the beginning of each audiotape or videotape.[56]

The notice of a video deposition should state that the opposing party has the option of bringing a stenographer. The Federal Rules of Civil Procedure afford any party the right, upon notice, to record the deposition by another method in addition to the method specified by the party taking the deposition.[57] Even in a jurisdiction that does not make this a matter of right, it is a good idea to state in the deposition notice that the opposing attorney may arrange to bring a court reporter. If the opposing party brings a court reporter, the consumer saves having to pay the attendance fee but can still order a transcript if necessary.

By the same token, under the federal rules the consumer can arrange for an additional method of recording a deposition scheduled by the opposing party. For example, the consumer might want to make an audio or video recording of the testimony. Then the consumer will have a verbatim record of the testimony without having to pay for a transcript.

56 Fed. R. Civ. P. 30(b)(4).

57 Fed. R. Civ. P. 30(b)(3).

Video depositions can be vivid at trial, especially if the witness had not been advised to dress up or avoid arrogance, etc. Using them for impeachment can be cumbersome, but the key is to locate the most important answers in advance so that the tape can be shown without delay if the witness gives a different answer on the stand.

16.5 The Defendant's Deposition of the Consumer Plaintiff[58]

The defendant's deposition of the consumer is a critical point in the case. The defendant's attorney will be assessing how the trier of fact will respond to the consumer. If the consumer comes across poorly, it will strengthen the defendant's intransigence and give the defendant ammunition for cross-examining the consumer at trial. If the consumer comes across as sympathetic, the defendant may decide to settle the case.

Attorneys who represent elderly consumers have developed practice tips that may also be useful for non-elderly clients. Insist that the deposition be convenient and short. One possibility is holding the deposition at the client's home or at a friend's or relative's home.

Start early in the morning and make sure the deposition lasts only a few hours, entirely in the morning. Even if the client appears to be holding up well, do not continue the deposition into the afternoon. Many older clients wake up early in the morning and become markedly more tired by early mid-day. Once fatigue sets in, there is a greater danger of confusion, crankiness, pleasing the examiner, and the like.

Insist on adjourning early after a few hours, as originally arranged with opposing counsel. Prepare the client for the question, "You are doing great, don't you think you can go on for a bit more so we don't have to come back?" Effective answers provided by clients include "No. I'll take a rest now" and "No, I'm getting upset and worn out thinking about how they treated me. But don't get me wrong—I'll be back. I'm determined to get this case to a jury!"

Anticipate the client's physical problems. Make sure the client knows where the bathroom is and how to call a break. Do not forget that this is important for many older clients. If the client is a bit deaf, warn the opposing counsel in advance outside the client's presence and also see if the sound system can be adjusted. Tell the client how important it is not to pretend to hear something. If they miss some words, have them speak up and ask that the statement be repeated in a louder voice.

It helps to go over the case with the client the morning of the day before the deposition to refresh the client's memory of the story told the first time the client was interviewed. Then go over a few points quickly on the morning before the deposition. Make sure to review all the client's damages with the client so that none of them are forgotten at the deposition.

Clients must be reminded that their job is not to please the examiner. If the client wants to please anyone, it should be the client's own attorney. They should disagree with the questioner whenever appropriate. Also, they should disagree with assumptions made by the examiner. It is also important to build up the client's confidence so that he or she can withstand questioning from an attorney. Some attorneys use a funny hat or other visual cue when playing the role of cross-examiner during deposition preparation. This technique relaxes the client and helps break the ice.

In a fraud case, remind the client to remember what they knew at the time of the fraud and to relate this during the questioning. What they know now can be very different from what they knew then. Also warn the client not to be too chatty.

Older clients often feel quite guilty that they were deceived and view it as an indication of their lack of independence. Probe into why and how they were induced to trust the merchant and explain that "I trusted him" is a fine answer, if true.

It helps to keep the client reassured and relaxed. One way of doing that is to make sure the client's attorney also appears confident and relaxed. Any heated argument with the other side's attorney should be out of the hearing of the consumer. Keep objections to a minimum and step in only when the examining attorney appears to be browbeating or manipulating the consumer. But if the questions are ambiguous, confusing, or falsely premised, make a speaking objection explaining the ambiguity, confusion, or false premise. If the examiner is deliberately trying to confuse the consumer, instruct the consumer not to answer. Furthermore, do not let the examiner question the consumer's competence or criticize the consumer.

Be attuned to questions the client can not understand, and insist that they be rephrased. If the victim becomes tired, confused, emotional, or beaten down, demand a break.

Sometimes defense attorneys will ask a "contention question" at the plaintiff's deposition, asking the plaintiff to describe all facts that establish a contention in the complaint. At least one court has held that these questions are improper at deposition.[59] A lay plaintiff presumably knows at least some of the facts but can hardly be expected to know their legal consequences or sort through the facts and apply them on the spot to the legal theories. If the examiner is asking the consumer about the law or damages, object and say that it is an improper question, that the client gives his or her lawyer the facts, and the attorney takes those facts and uses legal training to draft the complaint, but the client should not be asked about the legal analysis involved in the case. This

58 This section is based on material supplied by Aurora Dawn Harris, a California attorney who practices consumer law.

59 Rifkind v. Super. Court, 22 Cal. App. 4th 1255, 27 Cal. Rptr. 2d 822 (1994).

same rationale may be a basis for objecting to questions asking the plaintiff what his or her damages are or what her or she wants out of the case, a question that plaintiffs often answer at deposition without adequate care. Plaintiff's attorney fee and cost agreements are generally not discoverable as they are not sufficiently relevant.[60]

Another strategy to prepare for questions about damages is to help the plaintiff make a written itemization of damages in advance of the deposition. The plaintiff can then pull out the list and refer to it in response to questions about damages. Before allowing the plaintiff to answer the question, the plaintiff's attorney may want to put an objection on the record that the plaintiff is not an attorney and does not necessarily know the law of damages. With respect to emotional distress damages or punitive damages, it is usually best for the plaintiff not to name a specific figure but instead to refer to "whatever the jury feels is appropriate" or some similar phrase.

The client should be prepared for the question, "Have you discussed your testimony with anyone?" Everyone knows that clients discuss their testimony with their attorneys before depositions, and the client should not feel a need to cover up this fact. An objection based on attorney-client privilege should be interposed to prevent any questioning about the substance of these discussions.

The consumer should be cautioned to bring nothing to the deposition that the opposing attorney should not see. For example, many consumers have a letter from their own lawyer in a purse or packet. The opposing attorney is likely to ask to see any documents the consumer has brought to the deposition.

Some consumer attorneys refuse to allow the consumers to disclose their social security numbers during depositions on a various grounds. The social security number is most commonly used to locate consumers but that is not necessary when the consumer is a plaintiff. The social security number will not lead to discoverable evidence. The social security number is private and confidential information that would be made publicly available, compromising there ability to avoid identity theft. If it is to be provided, it should only be provided in way that ensures its confidentiality.

60 *See* Sanderson v. Winner, 507 F.2d 477 (10th Cir. 1974) (fee agreement not discoverable as irrelevant, may or may not be confidential); Stahler v. Jamesway Corp., 85 F.R.D. 85, 86 (E.D. Pa. 1979) (fee agreement not discoverable as not relevant); Amherst Leasing Corp. v. Emhart Corp., 65 F.R.D. 121, 126 (D. Conn. 1974) (motion to compel deposition granted but inquiry about motive for bringing class action and fee arrangements excluded); Bogosian v. Gulf Oil Corp., 337 F. Supp. 1228 (D.C. Pa. 1971) (plaintiff deponent properly counseled not to answer questions about his fee agreement or net worth, as unlikely to lead to relevant evidence).

16.6 Videotaping the Deposition of the Consumer

Consumer attorneys should carefully consider a video recording of any deposition of the consumer plaintiff, particularly if the consumer is elderly or unsophisticated. Federal Rule of Civil Procedure 30(b)(2) states that the deposition may be recorded by audio and visual means, and the party taking the deposition shall bear the cost of the recording. Rule 30(b)(3) states that, with prior notice, any party may designate another method to record the deponent's testimony in addition to that specified by the person taking the deposition. The additional recording will be at that party's expense, unless the court orders otherwise. State rules, of course, may vary.

In other words, at least under the federal rules, the consumer's attorney can suggest that the defendant use a videotape to record the deposition (perhaps encouraging agreement by offering to pay part of the cost). If the defendant refuses, the consumer's attorney, with notice, can still arrange for videotaping at the consumer's expense. The consumer can even ask the court to order that the deposition be videotaped, either at the defendant's expense or split between the parties.

The videotaped deposition may become necessary to show at the trial if the client becomes incapacitated or dies before the trial. Moreover, particularly if the consumer is elderly or vulnerable, videotaping the deposition can have a profound effect on the other side's attorney. The attorney may become less aggressive and badgering and may even become flustered because the attorney knows that any aggressiveness by the attorney and its impact on the client becomes quite visible to the viewer. If shown at trial, the jury will be less skeptical of the client's testimony because it is a cross-examination. It also highlights the ordeal of litigation for the consumer, particularly for the elderly consumer.

On the other hand, the client may be disconcerted or distracted by the presence of the video camera. Knowing that the deposition is being filmed may make the client overly concerned not to appear confused or stupid and may lead the client to focus on appearance rather than content. The client may find it humiliating to be tape-recorded while being cross-examined, which may sap the client's resolve to continue with the case.

If the deposition is videotaped, make sure the camera is focused on the client at all times. Do not let the camera operator film the other parties at the deposition instead of the client. Some attorneys do, however, bring a second video camera to the deposition to film the opposing attorney's questioning. An attorney who is being filmed is less likely to be abusive toward the deponent.

16.7 Dealing with Missing Documents

Sometimes discovery reveals that documents are missing. For example, a dealer or manufacturer may claim to have purged records about a vehicle. If the consumer's attorney follows up with specific interrogatories about where, why, and by whom each document was destroyed, sometimes the defendant finds the documents.[61] If not, these questions can produce information that will be useful upon cross-examination.

If evidence or witnesses within the control of the defendant have disappeared, it may be appropriate for the judge to instruct the jury that they can draw adverse inferences from this fact. The court might even be willing to instruct the jury that there is a rebuttable presumption of wrongdoing or causation by the party responsible for the loss of the documents.[62]

---

61 Sample questions can include:

1. Please describe each document in connection with the ______________ contract that you have destroyed (including, but not limited to, altered, thrown out, discarded, lost, misplaced, given away, purged, and deleted from computerized records).

2. Please identify each person who authorized the destruction (including, but not limited to, the act of altering, throwing out, discarding, losing, misplacing, giving away, purging, or deleting from computerized records) of any document in connection with the ______________ contract.

3. Please identify each person who destroyed (including, but not limited to, threw out, discarded, lost, misplaced, gave away, purged, or deleted from computerized records) any document in connection with the ______________ contract.

The advocate should also request copies of the defendant's written policies for maintenance of records and purging of records, along with the date the policy was promulgated and the identity of the person who promulgated it.

62 *See* Sweet v. Sisters of Providence, 895 P.2d 484 (Alaska 1995) (rebuttable presumption of negligence and causation is appropriate in medical malpractice suit when hospital lost medical records); Manorcare Health Servs., Inc. v. Osmose Wood Preserving, Inc., 336 N.J. Super. 218, 764 A.2d 475 (Super. Ct. App. Div. 2001) (excluding all evidence obtained during or after repairs that destroyed evidence); National Consumer Law Center, Consumer Warranty Law § 10.1.2.5 (2d ed. 2001 and Supp.) (discussion of spoliation of evidence).

Chapter 17 Expert Witnesses

17.1 Selecting an Expert Witness

17.1.1 Is an Expert Witness Necessary?

An expert witness is by no means necessary in every consumer case. In many cases, no specialized expertise is necessary to enable the jury to understand the fraud or the violation. On the other hand, for warranty cases, an expert is often helpful, if not essential, to prove the existence of a defect and to quantify the resulting diminution in the value of the product. In auto fraud cases, it is usually important to have an expert establish that the odometer was in fact rolled back or that the car had in fact suffered wreck or flood damage and that this history would have been obvious to an experienced car dealer. Other cases may benefit from expert testimony about the nature of an industry, the vulnerability of the consumer, the readability of a document, the conclusions to be drawn from statistics, or a host of other issues.

If expert testimony is desirable, locating an appropriate expert should be one of the first tasks undertaken. If the expert's opinion will be central to the suit, it is best to locate the expert and obtain the opinion before suit is filed. Also, if the expert's opinion relates to the condition of a mobile home, car, or other product, the inspection should be done at the earliest possible moment because the condition of the product may change due to continued use, accidents, normal deterioration over time, or repairs and maintenance.[1]

When evaluating the need for expert witnesses in cases involving defects in automobiles or other products, remember that expert opinion may be necessary both on the existence of a defect and on the resulting diminution in the value of the product. Two experts may be necessary to cover this ground.[2] Sometimes diminution in value can be established without an expert, however, through requests for admission, testimony by the buyer, and cross-examination of the seller.[3]

17.1.2 Locating an Expert Witness

If the attorney expects to handle a number of cases in an area of law, it is helpful to develop a working relationship with one or more experts in that field. The expert need not be famous in the field or highly experienced. In car cases, the expert can be a local mechanic with a few years' training and experience. To be qualified as an expert, the mechanic only needs to have experience beyond the layperson's.[4] Whether the mechanic has two years experience or twenty years of experience is relevant to the weight rather than admissibility of the testimony. An expert who is new to inspection work may find it helpful to be put in touch with a more experienced inspector. An independent technician may have more credibility with the jury than a professional forensic expert. Selecting an expert who enjoys the respect of the industry can promote settlement and reduce objections to admissibility of the expert's opinions.

The expert need not have an advanced degree. In many cases, individuals have been qualified as experts based on on-the-job experience.[5] The attorney should, however, make

1 *See, e.g.*, Bogosian v. Mercedes-Benz of N. Am., Inc., 104 F.3d 472 (1st Cir. 1996) (expert's testimony excluded because, *inter alia*, there was no evidence that car, which had been tested by several other experts and then sold to a third party, was in same condition when he examined it as it was at time of accident).

2 *See, e.g.*, Finch v. Ford Motor Co., 2004 WL 2066917 (N.D. Ill. Aug. 27, 2004) (limiting one expert's testimony to existence of defects and the other's to valuation).

3 *See* National Consumer Law Center, Consumer Warranty Law § 10.5 (2d ed. 2001 and Supp.) (tips on proving diminution in value).

4 King v. Taylor Chrysler Plymouth, 184 Mich. App. 204, 457 N.W.2d 42 (1990) (licensed automobile mechanic qualified as expert); Schmidt v. J.C. Robinson Seed Co., 220 Neb. 344, 370 N.W.2d 103 (1985) (farmers were experts on whether corn could be detasseled). *But see* Fitzgerald v. Caterpillar Tractor Co., 683 S.W.2d 162 (Tex. Ct. App. 1985) (forklift driver with fifteen years experience and with driver's training was not a design mechanic nor an engineer and was not qualified to testify on forklift's design). *But cf.* Teerling v. Fleetwood Motor Homes of Ind., Inc., 2001 U.S. Dist. LEXIS 7481 (N.D. Ill. May 31, 2001) (barring expert's opinion because he had experience only with cars, not motor homes).

5 *See, e.g.*, Woodson v. McGeorge Camping Ctr., Inc., 1992 U.S. App. LEXIS 22747 (4th Cir. Sept. 15, 1992) (mechanical engineer with Bachelor of Science degree and experience with trailer design, hitches, and sway control could give opinion about whether hitch was defective); Finch v. Ford Motor Co., 2004 WL 2066917 (N.D. Ill. Aug. 27, 2004) (expert who had inspected vehicles for manufacturer's consumer appeals board

sure that the expert tests out all hypotheses thoroughly and is able to justify his or her techniques and conclusions in detail. An expert whose conclusions support the consumer but whose testimony is excluded on a *Daubert* motion[6] does not help the consumer.

The expert should be instructed to give his or her honest opinions. If the evidence does not support the consumer, it is best to learn this early in the case.

One way to locate an expert is to refer to catalogs, found in many law libraries and public libraries, which list forensic consultants by category. There are listings on the Internet also. Richard Goodman's *Automobile Design Liability* § 11.2 (3d ed. 1992 and Supp.) lists automobile experts by area of expertise and geographic location. The American Trial Lawyers Association and some private companies may also be able to help locate experts. Another source of information is reports of jury verdicts—which often identify the experts involved in the case—in publications and on the Internet.[7]

17.1.3 *Affording Expert Witnesses in Legal Services or Pro Bono Cases*

When it is not feasible to pay experts, the following potential sources of free assistance should be explored:

- High school and technical school teachers and graduate students or professors in the relevant field. If an instructor is unavailable or unwilling, he or she might be able to provide a referral to former students who have gone into business on their own.
- Experts advertising their services in the local legal newspaper, who may be willing to do a case pro bono
- Volunteer or salaried experts who provide technical advice to automobile arbitration panels in almost every large and medium-sized city
- Consumer arbitrators employed by the state attorney general or another state or local consumer agency. They may have developed expertise in a consumer-related field
- Local professional organizations, whose members may be willing to help
- Public officials such as police officers or consumer fraud investigators who have investigated the particular case or similar cases

and run own inspection business could testify concerning defects; expert who had assessed vehicle values for lenders could testify about vehicle value); S. Energy Homes, Inc. v. Washington, 774 So. 2d 505, 40 U.C.C. Rep. 2d 986 (Ala. 2000) (general contractor who built foundations for homes could testify about whether lot on which mobile home was situated was adequate; a second individual who had on-the-job experience in the mobile home business was allowed to testify as an expert about measurements of the home); Forest River, Inc. v. Posten, 847 So. 2d 957 (Ala. Civ. App. 2002) (RV salesperson testified as to actual value of RV); Schreidel v. Am. Honda Motor Co., 34 Cal. App. 4th 1242, 40 Cal. Rptr. 2d 576 (1995) (nineteen years of experience in auto repairs and mechanics qualified expert to testify); Hyler v. Garner, 548 N.W.2d 864 (Iowa 1996) (affirming admission of expert testimony of motor home's defects by journeyman mechanic, welder, machinist, and motor vehicle repairman who had taught welding and mechanics, supervised manufacture of trucks, consulted in cases involving vehicles and other machines, and disassembled an entire motor home); Sibley v. Bauers, 1999 Mich. App. LEXIS 1267 (Mich. Ct. App. July 16, 1999) (witness who had owned used-car business for seventeen years, had worked for agency that performed financing-related appraisals, and had experience in auto repair and refinishing was qualified to testify on value of used vehicle); King v. Taylor Chrysler Plymouth, 184 Mich. App. 204, 457 N.W.2d 42 (1990) (licensed automobile mechanic qualified as expert).

6 *See* § 17.2, *infra*.

7 A few experts are described in Appendix D, *infra*.

17.1.4 *Arranging for an Expert Inspection*

An expert who will be inspecting goods will need access to those goods. If the goods have found their way into the hands of an uncooperative third party, it may be necessary to use the state's procedure for subpoenaing documents and objects from a non-party.

If an expert inspection will destroy or change the goods, it is essential to notify all opposing parties of the inspection. Otherwise the consumer may face spoliation-of-evidence problems.[8]

The expert should preserve his or her field notes. If the jurisdiction requires a written report, the attorney should resist the temptation to help the expert write it, because that opens up the expert to cross-examination. If the jurisdiction does not require a report, the attorney should at least debrief the expert carefully and make detailed notes of his or her conclusions. The attorney should not press the expert to take a position with which the expert is uncomfortable, as this approach has the potential to backfire during cross-examination.

17.1.5 *Inspection by the Opposing Party*

In cases involving goods or other physical evidence, the seller will usually seek the opportunity to inspect the items. Section 2-515 of the Uniform Commercial Code provides that "either party on reasonable notification to the other and for the purpose of ascertaining the facts and preserving evidence has the right to inspect, test and sample the goods," including goods in the possession or control of the other party. Discovery rules generally allow parties a similar opportunity to have goods or other physical evidence produced for inspection and testing.

8 *See* § 23.3.6, *infra*; National Consumer Law Center, Consumer Warranty Law § 10.1.2.5 (2d ed. 2001 and Supp.).

The consumer's attorney should take precautions against alteration of the evidence by the seller during an inspection. At a minimum, the consumer's attorney or the consumer's expert should be present throughout the inspection. They should take notes about each test the seller's experts perform, what they inspect, any comments they make, and any written materials they consult. Discovery rulings support restrictions along these lines.[9]

One experienced lemon law attorney requires defense inspections of vehicles to follow these guidelines:[10]

- The defense must comply with the consumer's discovery requests before the inspection occurs.
- The defense inspection must be scheduled after the consumer's expert inspection.
- The consumer's attorney must be present during the entire inspection and must be allowed to videotape it.[11]
- The consumer must be allowed to attend.
- The consumer's attorney must be given a business card or other identification for every person participating in the inspection.
- The defense must provide a copy of any evidence generated by the inspection, such as photographs or diagnostic printouts, at the time of the inspection.
- The vehicle must never stay overnight.
- The inspection must take place at the selling or repairing dealership, and the consumer's attorney must be allowed to examine the originals of the dealer's sales and repair files at the same time.
- The defense must provide the consumer's attorney a written expert report within thirty days of completing the inspection.

The attorney also recommends recording the time when the inspection starts, each time the vehicle is moved, when the inspection ends, and the vehicle's odometer reading at start and finish. If the defendant refuses to allow videotaping and the court concurs, the plaintiff should take still photographs and audiotape the inspection, dictating a running description of the activities, with time marks throughout the dictation.

If the consumer takes the opportunity to attend the defense inspection, the attorney should caution him or her not to speak to anyone other than the attorney. If the consumer arrives early, he or she should stay in the car and wait for the attorney to arrive without speaking to anyone at the dealership or allowing any sort of preliminary inspection. The consumer may wish to take videos or photographs during the inspection and should be encouraged to bring a small notepad to make notes. If the inspectors take a test drive, the consumer should go along only if he or she can resist the temptation to talk to the inspectors, but the consumer should point out (preferably through the attorney) if the malfunction becomes apparent during the test drive.

Having a meticulous record of the seller's inspection can pay off during cross-examination. For example, the seller's inspector may not have duplicated the conditions under which the malfunction occurs, such as shimmying that occurs only over a certain speed. Then the expert's conclusion about whether the defect exists will lack foundation. Or the seller's inspector may have omitted certain tests that would have revealed the defect or may have failed to examine the parts that would be affected by the defect. A videotape can also demonstrate whether the problem appeared when the defense expert test drove the vehicle.

If a seller requests a pre-litigation inspection of a vehicle to verify the existence of the defects, the same guidelines as for an inspection during litigation should be used. Some consumer attorneys also require the seller to pay the fees for the buyer's expert to attend the inspection. In the alternative, some attorneys allow the inspection only if the seller stipulates that it will be the only inspection allowed during the course of any future litigation. In determining how to respond to a request for a pre-litigation inspection, the consumer's attorney should take into account whether the court is likely to admit evidence of any lack of cooperation if the case goes to trial.

17.2 Admissibility of Expert Testimony Under *Daubert*[12]

17.2.1 The Daubert *Ruling*

In *Daubert v. Merrell Dow Pharmaceuticals, Inc.*, the U.S. Supreme Court interpreted the Federal Rules of Evidence to require federal courts, before admitting expert testimony, to make "a preliminary assessment of whether

9 *See* Canter v. Am. Cyanimid Co., 5 A.D.2d 513, 173 N.Y.S.2d 623 (ordering that party who produces item for testing be allowed to observe tests), *as modified by* 6 A.D.2d 847, 174 N.Y.S.2d 983 (1958); State *ex rel.* Remington Arms Co. v. Powers, 552 P.2d 1150, 1153 (Okla. 1976) (as general rule, plaintiff or representative should be permitted to observe opponent's testing of item produced by plaintiff); Miller v. Goodyear Tire & Rubber Co., 40 Pa. D. & C.3d 430 (C.P. 1985) (defendant has right to test physical evidence but plaintiffs need not surrender custody and control; plaintiffs may send representative to monitor testing but must avoid overhearing conversations); Rea v. Schmocker, 5 Pa. D. & C.3d 434 (C.P. 1978) (ordering that plaintiffs' representative be allowed to attend defendant's testing to retain control of item during testing).

10 This discussion is based on guidelines used by Ronald L. Burdge, an attorney in Dayton, Ohio, who specializes in consumer law.

11 Be sure to bring plenty of film and batteries.

12 This subsection is based on a paper presented at the 2000 Consumer Rights Conference by Cary L. Flitter, a private attorney in Pennsylvania who concentrates in consumer law, and Stuart T. Rossman, Director of Litigation at the National Consumer Law Center.

the reasoning or methodology underlying the testimony is scientifically valid and of whether that reasoning or methodology properly can be applied to the facts in issue."[13] Six years later, in *Kumho Tire v. Carmichael*,[14] the Court held that this gatekeeping obligation applies to *all* expert testimony. This obligation is now codified by the Federal Rules of Evidence.[15]

The *Daubert* rule has spawned an enormous number of decisions, as a *Daubert* motion to exclude the opponent's expert witnesses' testimony has quickly become a routine part of pre-trial practice. This subsection merely sketches out the general outlines of the *Daubert* requirements.[16]

Prior to *Daubert*, expert testimony was admissible if the scientific theories were generally accepted in the field.[17] In one sense, *Daubert* liberalizes admission of expert testimony because it allows testimony based on new theories that have not yet been widely accepted. On the other hand, the *Daubert* test has placed federal courts in the role of gatekeepers, often requiring an exacting defense of the expert's methodology before the testimony can go to the jury. This defense can be required even when the expert is relying on widely accepted techniques. The test also goes beyond the former rule in that it requires scrutiny not only of testimony based on hard science, but also of testimony from experts such as accountants, economists, appraisers, social scientists, experts in survey technique, psychologists, human factor experts, and statisticians.[18] Even such routinely accepted expert witnesses as auto mechanics, mobile home repair technicians, carpenters, and plumbers will have to be prepared to meet the *Daubert* test. While the concerns that prompted the *Daubert* rule are of less significance in a bench trial, the *Daubert* standards must nevertheless be met.[19]

A court's decision whether to admit or exclude expert testimony as part of its gatekeeping function is subject to review pursuant to an abuse-of-discretion standard.[20] If the trial court's admission of expert testimony over a *Daubert* objection is reversed, however, the proponent of the testimony may not get another opportunity to prove the case. In *Weisgram v. Marley Co.*,[21] the Court of Appeals, upon holding that the trial court should have excluded the testimony of the plaintiff's expert on *Daubert* grounds, determined that the admissible evidence was insufficient to support a verdict for the plaintiff and ordered judgment entered for the defendant. The Supreme Court affirmed, rejecting the argument that the plaintiff should have been granted a new trial.

Many state courts have also adopted *Daubert*, but a substantial number continue to follow the prior rule or their own standards.[22] Because state courts are free to fashion their own criteria for admission of expert testimony, the practitioner should research the forum state's recent rulings before presenting expert testimony.

In addition to the *Daubert* tests, the federal rule requires that the expert's testimony "assist the trier of fact to understand the evidence or to determine a fact in issue."[23] Some states such as Ohio explicitly require that the expert's testimony relate to matters beyond the knowledge or experience of laypersons or dispel a misperception common among laypersons.[24]

17.2.2 The Daubert *Factors*

The objective of *Daubert* gatekeeping is "to ensure the reliability and relevancy of expert testimony."[25] The court must ensure that an expert, whether basing testimony upon professional studies or personal experience, employs the same level of intellectual rigor in the courtroom that characterizes the practice of an expert in the relevant field.[26] The expert's self-proclaimed accuracy is insufficient: "nothing in either *Daubert* or the Federal Rules of Evidence requires

13 509 U.S. 579, 113 S. Ct. 2786, 2796, 125 L. Ed. 2d 469 (1993).

14 526 U.S. 137, 119 S. Ct. 1167, 143 L. Ed. 2d 238 (1999).

15 Fed. R. Evid. 702.

16 National Consumer Law Center, Consumer Warranty Law § 10.1.7 (2d ed. 2001and Supp.), discusses *Daubert* in more detail. Helpful *Daubert* materials and case summaries can also be found at www.daubertontheweb.com.

17 Frye v. United States, 293 F. 1013 (D.C. Cir. 1923).

18 Summaries of *Daubert* cases, organized by type of expert, can be found at www.daubertontheweb.com.

19 Seaboard Lumber Co. v. United States, 308 F.3d 1283 (Fed. Cir. 2003).

20 Gen. Elec. v. Joiner, 522 U.S. 136, 138, 139, 118 S. Ct. 512, 139 L. Ed. 2d 508 (1997). This holding was reiterated in *Kumho Tire v. Carmichael*, 526 U.S. 137, 152, 119 S. Ct. 1167, 143 L. Ed. 2d 238 (1999).

21 528 U.S. 440, 120 S. Ct. 1011, 145 L. Ed. 2d 958 (2000). *See also* Nelson v. Tenn. Gas Pipeline Co., 243 F.3d 244 (6th Cir. 2001) (there is no right to an opportunity to cure the exclusion of expert testimony). *But cf.* Wilhite v. Rockwell Int'l Corp., 83 S.W.3d 516 (Ky. 2002) (when other evidence was sufficient to go to jury, court remands for new trial).

22 State decisions adopting and rejecting *Daubert* are cited in National Consumer Law Center, Consumer Warranty Law § 10.7.5.1 (2d ed. 2001 and Supp.). A state-by-state list of rulings may also be found in Manuel L. Real, *Daubert*—A Judge's View—A Reprise, American Law Institute—American Bar Association Continuing Legal Education, ALI-ABA Course of Study (Feb. 18–20, 2004) (available on Westlaw, Journals & Law Reviews database, SJ035 ALI-ABA 411). The website, www.daubertontheweb.com, includes *Daubert* decisions from selected states.

23 Fed. R. Evid. 702.

24 Ohio R. Evid. 702(A). *See* Pearn v. DaimlerChrysler Corp., 148 Ohio App. 3d 228, 772 N.E.2d 712 (2002) (expert's testimony concerning diminished value of vehicle was admissible, but testimony about dealer practices may not have been beyond knowledge or experience of laypersons). *See also* Pa. R. Evid. 702 (expert may testify concerning scientific, technical, or other specialized knowledge beyond that possessed by a layperson).

25 Kumho Tire v. Carmichael, 526 U.S. 137, 152, 119 S. Ct. 1167, 143 L. Ed. 2d 238 (1999).

26 *Id.*

a district court to admit opinion evidence that is connected to existing data only by the *ipse dixit* of the expert."[27]

Under Rule 702 of the Federal Rules of Evidence, a witness qualified as an expert by knowledge, skill, experience, training, or education may present expert testimony if "(1) the testimony is based upon sufficient facts or data; (2) the testimony is the product of reliable principles and methods; and (3) the witness has applied the principles and methods reliably to the facts of the case." This final requirement means that there must be a "fit" between the expert testimony and the disputed issues of the case. The expert need not accept the plaintiff's version of events exactly, however, if other eyewitness testimony supports the expert's analysis.[28]

The *Daubert* opinion lists five non-exclusive factors to guide a district court in its assessment of the admissibility of expert testimony:

- whether the theory or technique has been tested;
- whether the technique has been subjected to peer review and publication;
- the known or potential error rate of the technique employed;
- the maintenance of standards controlling the technique's operation; and
- whether the theory or technique is "generally accepted" in the scientific (or relevant) community.[29]

The Advisory Committee Note to Rule 702 lists the following additional factors as relevant:

- whether the expert developed his or her opinion expressly for the purpose of testifying or whether it grew naturally and directly out of independent research;
- whether the expert has unjustifiably extrapolated from an accepted premise to an unfounded conclusion;
- whether the expert has adequately accounted for obvious alternative explanations;
- whether the expert is being as careful as he or she would be in regular professional work outside paid litigation consulting;
- whether the field of expertise claimed by the expert is known to reach reliable results for the type of opinion the expert would give.[30]

Many courts rely on the Federal Judicial Center's *Reference Manual on Scientific Evidence*[31] in evaluating scientific evidence.[32]

These lists of factors should not obscure the fact that the district court's gatekeeper role is a flexible one. The factors are simply useful measures, not mandatory hurdles that a party must overcome in order to have expert testimony admitted. For example, *Daubert* recognizes that some propositions are too particular, too new, or of too limited interest to have been published in a peer-reviewed journal.[33] A party seeking to admit or exclude expert testimony must do more than enumerate the factors listed in *Daubert* and tally the number that are or are not met by a particular expert's testimony.

17.2.3 Application of the **Daubert** *Factors*

Courts have applied the *Daubert* factors to exclude expert testimony when the expert's opinion was based on insufficient or unreliable data;[34] was based on a methodology that

27 *Id.* at 157 (quoting Gen. Elec. v. Joiner, 522 U.S. 136, 146, 118 S. Ct. 512, 139 L. Ed. 2d 508 (1997)). *Ipse dixit* is "[s]omething asserted but not proved." Black's Law Dictionary 833 (7th Ed. 1999).

28 Lauzon v. Senco Prods., Inc., 270 F.3d 681 (8th Cir. 2001).

29 Daubert v. Merrell Dow Pharms., Inc., 509 U.S. 579, 594, 113 S. Ct. 2786, 2796, 125 L. Ed. 2d 469 (1993).

30 Advisory Committee on Evidence Rules Note to amended Fed. R. Evid. 702 at 43, 44.

31 Fed. Judicial Ctr., Reference Manual on Scientific Evidence (2d ed. 2000).

32 *See, e.g.*, Soldo v. Sandoz Pharms. Corp., 244 F. Supp. 2d 434 (W.D. Pa. 2003); Smith v. Wyeth-Ayerst Labs. Co., 278 F. Supp. 2d 684 (W.D.N.C. 2003).

33 Daubert v. Merrell Dow Pharms., Inc., 509 U.S. 579, 593, 113 S. Ct. 2786, 125 L. Ed. 2d 469 (1993). *Accord* Lauzon v. Senco Products, Inc., 270 F.3d 681 (8th Cir. 2001). *See also* Miller v. Burlington N. Santa Fe Ry. Co., 2001 U.S. Dist. LEXIS 16650 (N.D. Tex. Oct. 16, 2001) (magistrate's ruling) (math is not a proper subject of peer review); Coleman v. Dydula, 139 F. Supp. 2d 388 (W.D.N.Y. 2001) (admitting evidence based on generally accepted methods for calculating future lost wages even though expert did not cite scholarly treatises in support). *But cf.* Nelson v. Tenn. Gas Pipeline Co., 243 F.3d 244 (6th Cir. 2001) (citing lack of peer review as reason for excluding testimony despite plaintiff's claim that expert's novel opinions were at forefront of his field).

34 *See, e.g.*, Munoz v. Orr, 200 F.3d 291 (5th Cir. 2000) (calculation errors one of reasons for excluding testimony); Irvine v. Murad Skin Research Labs., 194 F.3d 313 (1st Cir. 1999); Dunn v. Sandoz Pharms. Corp., 275 F. Supp. 2d 672 (M.D.N.C. 2003) (small study size); *In re* Propulsid Prods. Liab. Litig., 261 F. Supp. 2d 603 (E.D. La. 2003); Soldo v. Sandoz Pharms. Corp., 244 F. Supp. 2d 434, 539–541 (W.D. Pa. 2003) (anecdotal case reports and adverse event reports are insufficient basis for conclusions about causation); Cayuga Indian Nation v. Pataki, 83 F. Supp. 2d 318 (N.D.N.Y 2000) (data errors one of reasons for excluding testimony); Telecomm Technical Servs. v. Siemens Rolm Commc'ns, Inc., 1999 U.S. Dist. LEXIS 21415 (N.D. Ga. Aug. 24, 1999) (use of too many estimates made underlying data unreliable). *See also* Metro. St. Louis Equal Hous. Opportunity Council v. Gordon A. Gundaker Real Estate Co., 130 F. Supp. 2d 1074 (E.D. Mo. 2001) (expert's failure to review accuracy of underlying survey data one factor in excluding his testimony); *In re* Ford Motor Co. Ignition Switch Prods. Liab. Litig., 194 F.R.D. 484 (D.N.J. 2000) (unreliability of data).

was untested, unsupported, or misapplied;[35] did not spell out the analysis in a step-by-step way so that others could review it for error;[36] was overly subjective;[37] strayed into areas beyond the witness's expertise;[38] or made selective use of evidence.[39] Nonetheless, courts are not to apply *Daubert* in a way that usurps the jury's role.[40] Nor are they to evaluate the expert's conclusions, as long as the expert's methodology is reliable and relevant to the case.[41] The fact that experts in other fields might also be able to form opinions about a question and would base those opinions on other factors does not disqualify an expert from testifying based on the factors that are relevant to his or her expertise.[42]

Expert witnesses need not have academic credentials but can base their testimony on skill or experience-based observation.[43] In such cases, some of the *Daubert* factors, such as error rate or acceptance in the field,[44] may be relevant, but many of the factors will not be.[45] Such an expert "must explain how that experience leads to the conclusion reached, why that experience is a sufficient basis for the opinion, and how that experience is reliably applied to the facts."[46]

17.2.4 Discovery of the Expert's Opinion

Under Federal Rule of Civil Procedure 26(a)(2), a party is required to disclose to all other parties involved in the action the identity of any person who may be used at trial to present evidence under Rules 702, 703, or 705 of the Federal Rules of Evidence. For a witness retained to provide expert testimony in the case, the disclosure must be accompanied by a written report prepared and signed by the expert. The report must contain a complete statement of all opinions to be expressed and the basis and reasons therefor; the data or information considered by the expert in forming the opinions; any exhibits to be used as a summary of or support for the opinions; the qualifications of the expert; the compensation to be paid for the study and testimony; and a listing of any other cases in which the expert has testified at trial or by deposition within the preceding four years.[47]

Although deposition of experts is, strictly speaking, discretionary, the prevailing practice is to allow a party to depose the opponent's testifying experts.[48] It may be appropriate to combine the discovery deposition of the expert for trial with a pre-*Daubert* deposition to develop facts to challenge the admissibility of the expert's testimony.

When seeking to challenge an opponent's expert on *Daubert* grounds, the advocate should look to build a record of gaps in the expert's qualifications, foundation methodology, or reasoning. The subjects might include

- a precise explanation of each step in the expert's reasoning, methodology, or application of principles supporting each conclusion;
- the factual bases and assumptions used by the expert;
- the sources of the factual bases or assumptions;
- other fact sources that were available but not used (especially when the expert relies solely on facts from his or her client);
- whether there is any standard, principle or reasoning that allows the expert to rely on his or her client for

---

35 Dunn v. Sandoz Pharms. Corp., 275 F. Supp. 2d 672 (M.D.N.C. 2003); Meister v. Med. Eng'g Corp., 267 F.3d 1123 (D.C. Cir. 2001) (affirming exclusion of medical opinion that was based on case reports rather than epidemiological studies); Metro. St. Louis Equal Hous. Opportunity Council v. Gordon A. Gundaker Real Estate Co., 130 F. Supp. 2d 1074 (E.D. Mo. 2001) (survey's reliability was undercut by variations in forms and protocols); Rockwell Int'l Corp. v. Wilhite, 83 S.W.3d 516 (Ky. 2002). *But cf.* Smith v. Wyeth-Ayerst Labs. Co., 278 F. Supp. 2d 684 (W.D.N.C. 2003) (case reports and an epidemiological study were sufficient basis for opinion).

36 Ebenhoech v. Koppers Indus., Inc., 239 F. Supp. 2d 455 (D.N.J. 2002) (report cited sources but failed to apply them to the analysis; also did not suggest modifications, alternate designs, or alternate warnings); Rogers v. Horseshoe Entm't, 766 So. 2d 595 (La. Ct. App. 2000).

37 *In re* Rezulin Prods. Liab. Litig., 309 F. Supp. 2d 531 (S.D.N.Y. 2004) (excluding testimony about ethical standards and defendants' motivation as not fact-based and too subjective); Cayuga Indian Nation v. Pataki, 83 F. Supp. 2d 318 (N.D.N.Y. 2000).

38 *In re* Rezulin Prods. Liab. Litig., 309 F. Supp. 2d 531, 548, 549 (S.D.N.Y. 2004) (witnesses who lacked expertise in Food & Drug Administration regulations could not testify about manufacturer's compliance); Schaaf v. Caterpillar, Inc., 286 F. Supp. 2d 1070 (D.N.D. 2003) (excluding portion of testimony); McGuire v. Davidson Mfg. Corp., 238 F. Supp. 2d 1096 (N.D. Iowa 2003) (excluding a portion of testimony); Gray v. Briggs, 45 F. Supp. 2d 316 (S.D.N.Y. 1999).

39 Concord Boat Corp. v. Brunswick Corp., 207 F.3d 1039 (8th Cir. 2000).

40 Deputy v. Lehman Bros., Inc., 345 F.3d 494 (7th Cir. 2003) (testimony should be excluded only on grounds of principles and methodology, not credibility); Maiz v. Virani, 253 F.3d 641 (11th Cir. 2001).

41 Union Bank v. Deutsche Fin. Servs. Co., 2000 U.S. Dist. LEXIS 1481 (S.D.N.Y. Feb. 14, 2000); Cayuga Indian Nation v. Pataki, 83 F. Supp. 2d 318 (N.D.N.Y 2000).

42 Smith v. BMW N. Am., Inc., 308 F.3d 913 (8th Cir. 2002).

43 Kumho Tire v. Carmichael, 526 U.S. 137, 151, 119 S. Ct. 1167, 143 L. Ed. 2d 238 (1999); Advisory Committee on Evidence Rules Note to amended Fed. R. Evid. 702 at 49 ("[i]n certain fields, experience is the predominant, if not sole, basis for a great deal of reliable expert testimony").

44 Kumho Tire v. Carmichael, 526 U.S. 137, 151, 119 S. Ct. 1167, 143 L. Ed. 2d 238 (1999).

45 First Tenn. Bank v. Barreto, 268 F.3d 319 (6th Cir. 2001) (expertise based on experience within an industry does not easily lend itself to scholarly review or scientific evaluation).

46 Advisory Committee on Evidence Rules Note to amended Fed. R. Evid. 702 at 49.

47 The practitioner should also check the district's local rules regarding disclosure obligations.

48 *In re* Paoli R.R. Yard PCB Litig., 35 F.3d 717, 739 (3d Cir. 1994) (it is important that each side have an opportunity to depose the other's experts).

important assumptions (for example, an AICPA rule or similar industry guide);
- whether the method or reasoning consists of a testable hypothesis;
- if so, whether it has been tested, and the results;
- what the test was, whether it can be reproduced, and whether there are other test protocols that have been used or described in the professional literature to test this hypothesis;
- whether the expert knows if authoritative tests or periodicals are published in the expert's field;
- what publications are used in the expert's education, practice or teaching;
- whether publications are peer-reviewed;
- what publications support the expert's work in the case;
- whether the expert's work in this case is subject to peer review;
- what professional standards apply to the expert's field;
- how, if at all, standards apply to the expert's work;
- how the expert explains any departure from any standards;
- whether the expert's method, reasoning, and application of principles are generally accepted and why;
- all sources—publications, standards, others—to which one could look in order to test the expert's work in this case;
- the relationship of the expert's technique to methods that have been established to be reliable;
- whether the expert has the qualifications necessary to meet professional standards in the field and apply the proposed methodology;
- whether and how the expert has used the proposed methodology in non-litigation contexts;
- whether the testimony is based directly on legitimate, pre-existing research unrelated to the litigation;
- objective sources for each step in the methodology; and
- objective sources for each factual assumption.[49]

The consumer's attorney should also go over this list of issues with the consumer's expert witnesses when reviewing their reports and preparing them for deposition and testimony.

17.2.5 *Timing of the Inquiry into Admissibility*

In *Daubert*,[50] the Supreme Court held that, when faced with the proffer of expert testimony, the trial judge "must determine at the outset, pursuant to Rule 104(a)," whether the expert meets the criteria to testify, but neither the Supreme Court's decisions nor the Rules of Evidence offer any other guidance on timing.[51] A *Daubert* challenge may be made at several different points: (1) in discovery, (2) at summary judgment, (3) by a stand-alone "*Daubert* motion" as part of a motion in limine, (4) at the pre-trial conference, or even (5) at trial (although challenges this late are disfavored).[52]

The decision on when and how to file the *Daubert* motion is as much art as science. One key factor is the trial judge's practice or reputation for strict enforcement of the Rule 26 disclosure deadlines. Attorneys should be prepared for *Daubert* challenges that are filed *after* the point at which the report could be amended, missing data obtained, or a new expert retained.[53] However, it may be an abuse of discretion not to permit a party to submit supplements to an expert's report in response to assertions by opposing experts that there are gaps in the expert's reasoning.[54] It is wise to ask for a pre-trial scheduling order that requires that *Daubert* motions be filed before the end of discovery, so that there is an opportunity to correct any problems with the admissibility of the expert's testimony.

17.3 Cross-Examining the Opponent's Expert Witness

17.3.1 *General Rules*

The first rule for cross-examining the opponent's expert is to know the expert. Review the expert's resume, written work, and testimony on prior occasions. Find out as much as possible about the expert and his or her testimony through interrogatories, pre-trial disclosures, and depositions. Use a Google search to locate, verify, and spot overstatements regarding the expert's publications, professional association memberships, honors, and affiliations.

The consumer's attorney should also become familiar with the expert's field by reviewing relevant treatises. The

49 Adapted from Robert M. Whitney, *A Practicing Lawyer's Guide to the Application of* Daubert *and* Kumho, 23 Am. J. Trial Advoc. 241 (1999).

50 509 U.S. at 592.

51 Advisory Committee on Evidence Rules Note to amended Fed. R. Evid. 702 at 51 ("The amendment makes no attempt to set forth procedural requirements for exercising the trial court's gatekeeping function over expert testimony").

52 *See* Elcock v. K-Mart Corp., 233 F.3d 734 (3d Cir. 2000) (ruling on admissibility of the expert testimony under *Daubert* based upon trial testimony when no pretrial *Daubert* hearing afforded); United States v. Alatorre, 222 F.3d 1098 (9th Cir. 2000) (trial court may resolve *Daubert* objections after *voir dire* of expert at trial). *See also* Macsenti v. Becker, 237 F.3d 1223 (10th Cir. 2001) (*Daubert* objection at trial must be made contemporaneously with the testimony); Alfred v. Caterpillar, Inc., 262 F.3d 1083 (10th Cir. 2001) (except in rare circumstances, *Daubert* challenge should not be made after proponent has rested).

53 *See, e.g.*, Nelson v. Tenn. Gas Pipeline Co., 243 F.3d 244 (6th Cir. 2001) (fairness does not require that plaintiff whose expert testimony has been excluded by pretrial motion be given second chance to marshal expert opinions).

54 Miller v. Pfizer, Inc., 356 F.3d 1326, 1332 (10th Cir. 2004).

consumer's expert witness can also help introduce the attorney to the field and point out weaknesses in the opposing expert's methods and reasoning.

The attorney should have all the records that relate to the expert's testimony organized for speedy reference during trial. Listen carefully to the expert's testimony, paying particular attention to what the expert reviewed and the facts used in any hypothetical question. Note especially what the expert does not say: what is left out can be as important as what is said.

Sometimes it is best not to cross-examine. The opponent's expert may not have hurt the consumer's case. There may be no effective points to make on cross-examination. Or the consumer's experts may have been clearly more persuasive.

The cross-examiner should control the expert's testimony through leading questions. Open-ended questions allow the expert to display his or her knowledge to the jury. It is usually more effective to break down big questions into several smaller steps. Cross-examination is most effective when it starts and ends with strong points and is kept simple. Overly technical questions will confuse the jury. The cross-examiner should follow up on non-responsive answers and should be prepared to rephrase questions when an objection is sustained as to form.

Advance preparation and organization are essential but, at the same time, the cross-examiner should not be so tied to written questions or an outline as to be unable to follow up on answers that need further probing.

17.3.2 Bringing Out Testimony That Supports the Consumer

Sometimes cross-examination of the opponent's expert witness can be used to support the consumer's own case. Supportive testimony by the opponent's expert is particularly helpful to point to in closing argument. Any supportive cross-examination should be done before any cross-examination that seeks to discredit other portions of the expert's testimony.

Techniques to bring out supportive testimony from the opponent's expert witness include

- bringing out the opposing expert's agreement with facts that the consumer wants to establish, to eliminate any dispute about those facts;
- repeating any testimony on direct examination that was favorable to the consumer;
- using treatises and other authoritative references to elicit the expert's support of generally accepted principles in the expert's field that help the consumer;
- obtaining concessions and admissions; and
- setting up questions that the consumer's expert will cover if that expert will testify later.

Sometimes it is helpful to use testimony of a prior witness when questioning the opposing expert. For example, the opposing expert may agree with selected statements made by the consumer's expert.

17.3.3 Discrediting the Opposing Expert on Cross-Examination

When seeking to discredit the opposing expert on cross-examination, the cross-examiner should avoid reviewing and repeating areas of harmful testimony already covered on direct examination. Arguing with the expert in front of the jury is also rarely effective.

Effective techniques for discrediting the opposing expert through cross-examination include

- pinpointing any weaknesses in the expert's education, training, and experience;
- demonstrating that the expert's true area of expertise is other than the specific one involved in the case;
- showing bias or interest on the part of the expert;
- showing that the opposing attorney or party supplied the information on which the expert's opinion is based;
- showing that the expert has previously testified for the same attorney, or normally testifies for the same position and the same side;
- bringing out alternative explanations for the expert's opinion;
- producing prior inconsistent statements;
- establishing a few significant defects in the data the expert relied on;
- exposing the expert's assumptions; and
- impeaching the expert through learned treatises in the field.

Chapter 18

"Keep Your Hands Up!"—Trade Secrets, Protective Orders, and the Smoking Gun

By Ian Lyngklip[1]

18.1 Importance of Defendant's Records in Consumer Litigation

If you think protective orders are esoteric, ethereal creations of the judiciary and academia, think again. As a consumer advocate, there are important public policy concerns you need to know about as well as practical realities you need to consider.

Every time a court refuses to compel discovery of "pattern evidence," rejects your request to inspect a predatory lender's procedures, or orders that records remain "confidential" or "sealed" during the litigation, the court is *effectively* granting a protective order. In short, every order that denies an opportunity to conduct discovery *is* a protective order. These orders are neither esoteric nor ethereal. Rather, protective orders barring discovery may put a "smoking gun" beyond the reach of the plaintiff. Likewise, protective orders that seal court records preclude other plaintiffs from using this same "smoking gun" evidence and prevent the public from protecting itself from further harm.[2]

Properly used, protective orders shield parties from abusive discovery and keep them from running amok in discovery practice. However, most often in consumer litigation, these orders stand as first line of defense of a bad actor who hopes to create a safe harbor for widespread wrongdoing. To an inexperienced attorney, the mere assertion that discovery materials are "confidential" can pollute the litigation with unnecessary motion practice and impenetrable procedure. Protective orders are the things that most often stand between the plaintiff and the "smoking gun" evidence of willful misconduct. If you stipulate to an unwarranted protective order, you agree to limit your ability to obtain and use the very information that you will need to effectively present your case.

If the information you are seeking is worth the battle for the defendant, it is doubly so for the plaintiff. In the end the protective order battle is one worth fighting. It affects both the settlement value of your case and the ability to present evidence at trial.

By refusing to agree to overly broad orders, you will be able to present a better case, put more pressure on the defendant to settle, show the court during discovery that the defendant's conduct is egregious and unworthy of judicial protection, inform the public of widespread wrongdoing, and ultimately save yourself the cost of fighting for admission of the documents down the road. On the other hand, by agreeing, you may keep the public from knowing of the wrongdoing, agree to the inadmissibility of evidence, cost your client money, and place yourself in a poor position for settlement and trial. This article addresses the proper limits on their use and some strategies to get past the defendant's unwarranted demands.

With this in mind, consumer advocates should be aware of the limits, uses, and procedure governing these orders.

18.2 How the Problem Arises

Battles over protective orders arise following a plaintiff's request for discovery of the defendant's documents. If the result of those requests would amount to public disclosure of evidence of the corporate wrongdoer's pattern of willful misconduct, the fear of further civil or criminal action will drive the defendant to refuse to produce unless a protective order is entered. The proposed orders may limit the use and disclosure of the documents, seal the court's record, or require that any proceedings involving these documents be kept secret. All the while, the Federal Rules of Civil Procedure do not permit a defendant to use proof of its own wrongdoing or the possibility of further litigation as the justification for sealing the court's record from public scrutiny. As such, the rules—if properly construed—will rarely allow for many of the confidentiality dictates of the corpo-

---

1 Ian Lyngklip is in private practice in Southfield, Michigan, near Detroit. He is a frequent speaker at continuing legal education conferences sponsored by NCLC, NACA, and other bar groups. He was presented NACA's Outstanding Advocate Award in 2003.

2 *See also* § 19.5.2, *infra*.

rate wrongdoers. Simply put, protective orders cannot be issued for the sole purpose of hiding a "smoking gun."[3]

With this in mind, most practitioners approach the problem as follows: Upon filing of the lawsuit, plaintiff's counsel will forward discovery requests that—if carefully drafted—should result in the production of the "smoking gun" evidence of wrongdoing and a general practice of malfeasance. In response, the defendant will fail to respond to the discovery. After several weeks of patient waiting, plaintiff's counsel will call to follow up and be told that that answers are in the mail. Upon inspection, plaintiff's counsel learns that *no* documents of any importance or relevance have been produced and that the defendant has asserted that all damning documents are "confidential" or "trade secrets" and will only be produced under a protective order. If only for the purpose of heading off a discovery motion, plaintiff will stipulate to a protective order requiring the documents be held as confidential, not used outside the litigation, and only be submitted to the court if the plaintiff files a motion under seal requesting to be able to use them. This tactic is simply wrong as well as unnecessary.

18.3 Rights Affected: Think Before You Stipulate

Before you agree to a protective order, recognize that these orders severely affect not only your client's rights but your rights and those of the public at large. Most often, protective orders will either deny the moving party access to discovery or prevent disclosure of the evidence obtained. If the discovery you are seeking is "pattern" evidence of widespread misconduct, then such a protective order will ensure that the evidence of misconduct will never see the light of day. Consequently, the effect of a protective order may be to ensure that the defendant will continue its wrongful practices, unimpeded by the possibility that its conduct will be remedied through the justice system. By the same token, if the court orders that all materials be sealed permanently, then you effectively limit your own first amendment right to publicly speak about the defendant's misconduct as well as the public's right to supervise the proceedings.[4]

So, for example, when the defendant *instructs* you that you will need to consent to an iron-clad protective order before you can see all the other certificates of title that it has forged, think twice about whether you wish to forfeit you client's right to put forward evidence obtained through discovery, your right to free speech, and the opportunity of the press to write about the misconduct and the court's handling of your case. At the same time, you limit the right of other plaintiffs who have been harmed to use the evidence developed by your clients.[5]

If these important constitutional considerations are not enough, consider the cost of these orders to you and your client down the road. Most often, the protective orders proffered by defendants will require that any materials disclosed through discovery must remain confidential and cannot be used in the litigation absent a court order. By agreeing to this, you have guaranteed that your trial preparation time will be consumed with motion practice over the relevancy of the "confidential" documents you have received, because you have effectively stipulated that the documents are presumptively irrelevant or cannot be admitted without a further order of the court. While defendants routinely require protective orders before producing any discovery, there is simply no basis for this procedure in the rules. Stipulating to an overly broad protective order may expedite getting the documents you need in the short run but, in the long run, they are costly.

18.4 What Is the Court's Authority?

Demands for protective orders often dissolve into unprincipled arguments over what one party does or does not feel like disclosing. The proper limits of the court's authority lie in Rule 26 of the Federal Rules of Civil Procedure and provide an answer to the defendant's demand for an overreaching protective order. Given the express limitations on the court's authority, you need not stipulate to a protective order that exceeds the scope of Rule 26 or improperly limits anyone's constitutional rights.

While Rule 26 provides limits on the court's authority, additional constraints arise from the Constitution. In order to understand the court's authority and its limits, advocates must recognize the inherent tension between discovery rules designed to facilitate trial preparation and the need to have open proceedings as required by the Constitution and common law. On the one hand, meritorious lawsuits should not be used as the justification for unwarranted prying into the private affairs of the litigants—a fact of which we are acutely aware when our own client's credit reports and tax returns are subpoenaed or made part of the public record.[6] On the other hand, when the courts uncover widespread

3 *See* Teresa M. Hendricks & Joseph W. Moch, *Protective Orders: The Industry's Silencer on the Smoking Gun*, 73 Mich. B. J. 424 (May 1994).

4 United States v. Nixon, 418 U.S. 683, 710, 41 L. Ed. 2d 1039, 94 S. Ct. 3090 (1974) (privileges contravene the fundamental principle that the "public . . . has a right to every man's evidence").

5 *In re* Grand Jury Subpoena, 836 F.2d 1468 (4th Cir. 1988). Protective orders should not be used to conceal wrongful conduct. In addition, a protective order can not serve as more than a stopgap measure to seal discovery materials. Incriminating information will normally be disclosed at trial even if the information is effectively suppressed prior to that time.

6 *See* US v. Amodeo, 71 F.3d 1044, 1051 (2d Cir. 1995) (recognizing that personal financial information is presumptively private). *See, e.g.*, Gattegno v. Price Waterhouse Coopers, L.L.P., 205 F.R.D. 70 (D. Conn. 2001). *Accord In re* Boson Herald, Inc., 321 F.3d 174 (1st Cir. 2003).

wrongdoing, the public's right to access the court's findings becomes a constitutional matter.

That is to say, the courts serve as a branch of the government, which like all others is open to public scrutiny. As such, the public and press alike have a right to review the activities of the courts to ensure their integrity and proper functioning.[7] Evidence elicited from the proceedings belongs to the public at large and may be used in other proceedings. Thus, the courts recognize the public's right of access. At the same time, the courts have been willing to carve out exclusions from this general rule for activities that do involve the disposition of the merits of cases and controversies under Article III of the Constitution.

In order to reconcile this tension, the courts have been willing to recognize that discovery is generally a matter of public record, but not all discovered information will become evidence. While discovery is a part of the Government's legitimate function, and is presumptively subject to open access,[8] any limitations flow from the court's authority under Rule 26 to control and limit discovery using the court's *sound discretion*.[9] Under Rule 26, the courts enjoy discretion to limit requests for, and the use of, discovery materials that the parties have not yet put before the court for the purpose of determining the merits of the case or approving settlements.[10] Simply put, the parties may request that the court exercise its discretion to limit public access to the discovery phase of litigation when justice so requires. However, once the court begins the review of evidence in the exercise of its Article III powers, that evidence and the proceedings are presumptively public matters, absent some compelling justification.[11]

Once discovery material is set before the court for the purpose of resolving the case or controversy, the public's right to know becomes paramount. This right to know is expressed through the litigant's right to speak publicly about the proceedings, the press's right to access and write about the proceedings, the public's right to supervise the judicial activities of its lifetime tenured judges,[12] the need of the public to understand the operation of the courts,[13] and right of litigants to a public trial. As such, any limitations on the sealing of the court's records from public view becomes subject to constitutional scrutiny, which requires a far higher justification than simply limiting the litigant's ability to publicize discovery documents that would not ultimately be admitted into evidence at the trial.[14]

18.5 Requirements for Issuance of a Protective Order

18.5.1 General

While Rule 26 provides a generously broad set of justifications for the issuance of a protective order, the Rule's requirements must be met.

18.5.2 Specific and Timely Objection

As with all other discovery matters, the responding party must respond to the discovery in a timely fashion and object to the disclosure in a timely fashion. The failure to raise timely objections to the discovery before it is due waives the objections. At the same time, any such objections must be specific and identify a clear basis for the objections. Generalized, boilerplate objections do not satisfy the discovery rules.[15]

18.5.3 Timely Motion

Rule 26's procedures for obtaining a protective order are not self-executing. A defendant cannot simply assert that the

7 Siedle v. Putnam Inv., Inc., 147 F.3d 7, 10 (1st Cir. 1998); *In re* Providence Journal Co., Inc., 293 F.3d 1 (1st Cir. 2002).

8 *See* United States v. Amodeo, 71 F.3d 1044 (2d Cir. 1995); Video Software Dealers Assoc. v. Orion Pictures Corp., 21 F.3d 24, 26 (2d Cir. 1994); *In re* Knoxville News Sentinel Co., 723 470 (6th Cir. 1983); Grove Fresh Distributors, Inc. v. Evefresh Juice Co., 24 F.3d 893 (7th Cir. 1994); FTC v. Standard Fin. Mgmt. Corp., 830 F.2d 404, 408-409 (1st Cir. 1987); *In re* Cont'l Ill. Secs. Litig., 732 F.2d 1302 (7th Cir. 1984); US v. Myers (*In re* Nat'l Broadcasting Co.), 635 F.2d 945 (2d Cir. 1980); Brown and Williamson Tobacco Corp. v. FTC, 710 F.2d 1165 (6th Cir. 1983); Am. Tel. & Tel. C. v. Grady, 594 F.2d 594 (7th Cir. 1978).

9 Harris v. Amoco Prod. Co., 768 F.2d 669 (5th Cir. 1985). Courts interpreting F.R.C.P. 26(c) have afforded trial courts much discretion with regard to the granting and fashioning of protective orders. "If the party from whom discovery is sought shows 'good cause,' the presumption of free use dissipates, and the district court can exercise its sound discretion to restrict what materials are obtainable, how they can be obtained, and what use can be made of them once obtained."

10 "While District Courts have the discretion to issue protective orders, that discretion is limited by the careful dictates of Fed. R. Civ. P. 26 and 'is circumscribed by a long-established legal tradition' that values public access to court proceedings. Brown & Williamson Tobacco Corp. v. FTC, 710 F.2d 1165, 1177 (6th Cir. 1983), *cert. denied*, 465 U.S. 1100, 80 L. Ed. 2d 127, 104 S. Ct. 1595 (1984)." P&G v. Bankers Trust Co., 78 F.3d 219, 227 (6th Cir. 1996).

11 *See* Press Enter. Co v. Super. Court, 464 U.S. 501, 509–510, 104 S. Ct. 819, 78 L. Ed. 2d 629 (1984).

12 United States v. Amodeo, 71 F.3d 1044, 1048 (2d Cir. 1995).

13 Leucadia, Inc. V. Applied Extrusion Techs., Inc., 998 F.2d 157, 161 (3d Cir. 1993).

14 United States v. Amodeo, 71 F.3d 1044 (2d Cir. 1995) a 1048 (comparing the discovery process by which no stone is left unturned to the litigation process through which the irrelevant evidence is discarded).

15 Cipollone v. Liggett Group, 785 F.2d 1108, 1121 (3d Cir. 1986); Burns v. Imagine Films Entm't, 164 F.R.D. 589, 592593 (W.D.N.Y. 1996); Chubb Integrated Sys. v. Nat'l Bank of Wash., 103 F.R.D. 52, 58 (D.C. 1984).

material sought is not discoverable, thereby seeking to withhold discovery based on an objection without also moving for the protective order. Even if such objections are accompanied by the offer to provide the documents once a protective order is entered, this does not constitute compliance with the rule. A party may not simply agree to make documents available at a later date under the proviso of restrictions which—in its unilateral judgment—it regards as being reasonable compliance with discovery.[16]

The fundamental principle of Rule 26 routinely ignored by defendants is that the rule requires the withholding party to either provide the discovery or move the court to issue a protective order. Consequently, a party who refuses to provide discovery based on the assertion of the need for a protective order has engaged in self-help and usurped the court's authority. It is improper to refuse to provide the required discovery without having received, or at least applied for, a protective order. If a party fails to timely move for a protective order, the order should be denied.[17] The proper time for such a motion is before the discovery is due rather than after.[18]

18.5.4 Good Cause

The party seeking the protective order must show good cause for the issuance and maintenance of the order.[19] As with all discovery, generalized blanket objections are not sufficient reason to withhold discovery.[20] Rather, the moving party must articulate "specific facts" showing "clearly defined and serious injury" resulting from the discovery sought; conclusory allegations of harm are not sufficient.[21] However, a party seeking to resist discovery may assert any of the reasons listed in Rule 26(c) as a basis for resisting disclosures. Most often, in the context of consumer litigation, the defendant will assert that the documents constitute a trade secret.[22]

Information that allows a business to gain a competitive advantage through exclusive use is a trade secret.[23] While courts may protect against the dissemination of these secrets if obtained through discovery, there is no *absolute privilege* for trade secrets or similar confidential information.[24] Rather, trade secrets must be disclosed if they fall within the general scope of discovery unless the court issues its protective order. Therefore, a party may not unilaterally designate the information as a trade secret—agreeing to make

16 Wagner v. Dryvit Sys., 208 F.R.D. 606, 611 (D. Neb. 2001). (citing Laker Airways Ltd. v. Pan Am. World Airways, 103 F.R.D. 42, 45–6 (D.C.D.C. 1984)).

17 Brittian v. Stroh Brewing Co., 136 F.R.D. 408, 412 (D.N.C. 1991); Nestle Foods Corp. v. Aetna Cas. and Sur. Co., 129 F.R.D. 483, 487 (D.N.J. 1990).

18 United States v. Panhandle E. Corp., 118 F.R.D. 346 (D. Del. 1988).

19 Phillips v. GM, 307 F.3d 1206 (9th Cir. 2002); Baxter Int'l, Inc. v. Abbot Labs., 297 F.3d 544, 548 (7th Cir. 2002); Chi. Tribune Co., v. Bridgestone/Firestone, Inc., 263 F.3d 1304, 1313 (11th Cir. 2001); San Jose Mercury News, Inc. v. United States Dist. Ct., 187 F.3d 1096, 1102 (9th Cir. 1999); Miscellaneous Docket Matter No. 1 v. Miscellaneous Docket, 197 F.3d 922, 926 (8th Cir. 1999); *In re* Wilson, 149 F.3d 249, 252 (4th Cir. 1998); P&G v. Bankers Trust Co., 78 F.3d 219, 227 (6th Cir. 1996); Glenmede Trust Co. v. Thompson, 56 F.3d 476 (3d. Cir. 1995); *In re* "Agent Orange" Prod. Liab. Litig., 821 F.2d 139, 145 (2d Cir. 1987); *In re* Standard Metals Corp., 817 F.2d 625, 628 (10th Cir. 1987); Farnsworth v. Procter & Gamble, Co., 758 F.2d 1545, 1547 (11th Cir. 1985); Harris v. Amoco Prod. Co., 768 F.2d 669 (5th Cir. 1985); Gen. Dynamics Corp. v. Selb Mfg. Co., 481 F.2d. 1204, 1212 (8th Cir. 1973).

20 *See* Pulsecard, Inc., v. Discover Card Servs., 168 F.R.D. 295, 303 (Kan. 1996). *See* St. Paul Reinsurance Co., Ltd. v. Commercial Fin. Corp., 198 F.R.D. 508 (N.D. IA 2000).

21 Avirgan v. Hull, 118 F.R.D. 252, 254 (D.D.C. 1987). *See, e.g.*, Zapata v. IBP, Inc., 160 F.R.D. 625, 627 (D. Kan. 1995) ("the initial inquiry is whether the moving party has shown that disclosure of the information will result in a 'clearly defined and very serious injury.' "); Deford v. Schmid Prods. Co., 120 F.R.D. 648, 653 (D. Md. 1987) (movant must show that disclosure would cause significant harm to its competitive and financial position, supported by affidavits and concrete examples; conclusory allegations of potential harm are insufficient.); Waelde V. Merck, Sharp, & Dohme, 94 F.R.D. 27, 28 (E.D. Mich. 1981) (movant must make a particularized showing and demonstrate specific examples of competitive harm in which good cause is predicated on claims of confidential trade secrets). *See* Koster v. Chase Manhattan Bank, 93 F.R.D. 471, 480 (S.D.N.Y. 1982). The moving party must also make "a particular and specific demonstration of fact, as distinguished from stereotyped and conclusory statements." Gulf Oil Co. v. Bernard, 452 U.S. 89, 102 n.16, 68 L. Ed. 2d 693, 101 S. Ct. 2193 (1981).

22 Under Fed. R. Civ. P. 26(c)(7), the party opposing discovery has the initial burden to demonstrate that the information requested is a "trade secret or other confidential research, development, or commercial information," and also that its disclosure would be harmful to the party's interest in the property. Sentry Ins. v. Shivers, 164 F.R.D. 255, 256 (D. Kan. 1996). In determining whether good cause exists to issue a protective order that prohibits the dissemination of documents or other materials obtained in discovery, "the initial inquiry is whether the moving party has shown that disclosure of the information will result in a 'clearly defined and very serious injury.' " Zapata v. IBP, Inc., 160 F.R.D. 625, 627 (D. Kan. 1995) (quoting Koster v. Chase Manhattan Bank, 93 F.R.D. 471, 480 (S.D. N.Y. 1982)). The moving party must also make "a particular and specific demonstration of fact, as distinguished from stereotyped and conclusory statements." Gulf Oil Co. v. Bernard, 452 U.S. 89, 102 n.16, 68 L. Ed. 2d 693, 101 S. Ct. 2193 (1981). The burden then shifts to the party seeking discovery to show that the information is relevant to the subject matter of the lawsuit and is necessary to prepare the case for trial. *In re* Remington Arms Co., Inc., 952 F.2d 1029, 1032 (8th Cir. 1991).

23 Whether a specific disclosure would constitute a trade secret is matter of state law. While there are some distinctions between the definition between states, most case law looks to the Uniform Trade Secrets Act for the applicable definition of a trade secret.

24 Fed. Open Market Comm. of Fed. Reserve Sys. v. Merrill, 443 U.S. 340, 362, 61 L. Ed. 2d 587, 99 S. Ct. 2800 (1979); Centurion Indus., Inc. v. Warren Steurer & Assocs., 665 F.2d 323, 325 (10th Cir. 1981).

documents available but placing restrictions on that offer—and be in compliance with discovery.[25]

To the contrary, the party seeking to withhold discovery of trade secrets must first establish that the information is, indeed, a trade secret or other confidential research, development, or commercial information. Additionally, the party must also demonstrate that disclosure of this information might be harmful. Only after the defendant establishes both trade secret and harm does the burden shift to the party seeking discovery to establish that disclosure is relevant and necessary to the action. If the information is necessary to the litigation, the court must then fashion its order by balancing the need for discovery against the possibility of harm.

18.6 Recommendations

In dealing with protective orders, plaintiff's counsel should heed the following caveats rather than simply signing away the right to litigate the case.

First, the protective order should follow the process of careful negotiation and not simply be an acquiescence to the desires of the defendant. Review the limitations carefully and make sure the defendant's order complies with the law governing the protective orders. If the defendant could not properly obtain the relief by an adversarial motion, there is no need to stipulate to that relief.

Second, never agree to the confidentiality of documents you have not seen. The protective order should have a procedure for designation and objection to the confidentiality of the documents. The agreement should require that the defendant retains the burden of moving to maintain confidentially in the event of disagreement over the designation. Do not agree to shift the burden to the plaintiff. While you can agree to hold these documents as confidential during the objection procedure, the defendant must have a deadline for moving to keep the documents protected, and the failure to move waives confidentiality.

Third, do not agree to seal the court's record at trial. Courts may only seal the record in the most extreme of cases and, in so doing, the public is denied its right to know of wrongdoing and to supervise the courts. Moreover, during the discovery phase of the trial—long before the parties know how the case will be presented at trial—it is exceedingly unlikely that the court could know whether the documents will need to be sealed from public view. Rather, the protective order should require the defendant to move to seal the record upon notice that a confidential document will be used in a dispositive phase of the case.

Fourth, if the defendant refuses to agree to discovery without an unreasonable protective order, bring the issue to the court promptly. The passage of time favors the defendant, so you must act diligently to get the documents and do not waste excessive amounts of time negotiating fruitlessly. Simply narrow the issues of disagreement for presentation to the judge, and only bring those issues in disagreement to the court. The major points for negotiation are whether the trial record is to remain sealed, whether plaintiff can challenge an improper designation of confidentiality, and who will ultimately bear the burden of showing whether or not the documents are confidential.

18.7 Conclusion

The issuance of protective orders affects the rights of the parties, their attorneys, and the public at large. Therefore, before an advocate agrees to the issuance of a protective order, the attorney should be certain that the protective order is justified by the disclosures and does not go beyond the bounds of what is proper. Advocates should never agree to allow the court to lend its imprimatur to orders that exceed the court's authority. While corporate wrongdoers may seek to have all of the "smoking gun" documents designated as secrets, many of these documents fail to meet the requirements of Rule 26(c). For the sake of the client, the public, and your freedom of speech, the expediency of obtaining the documents should never be allowed to outweigh the requirements of the rule. After all, a spurious claim of trade secrets most often cloaks the smoking gun, and a concealed weapon can be the most dangerous kind.

---

25 Wagner v. Dryvit Sys., 208 F.R.D. 606, 612. (citing Laker Airways Ltd. v. Pan Am. World Airways, 103 F.R.D. 42, 45–6 (D.D.C. 1984)).

Chapter 19 Settling Consumer Cases

By Carolyn Carter[1]

19.1 Negotiation[2]

19.1.1 Pre-Suit Preparation for Settlement

Preparation for settlement should start with the initial client contact and continue throughout the case. The client's expectations should be probed at the initial contact. Both overly high and overly low expectations create problems. The client's non-pecuniary goals should be explored and clearly understood.

If the case will be litigated, the client must be prepared to spend time, attend depositions and hearings, and live with uncertainty. The client should understand the negotiation and settlement process, the likely duration of the process, and the implications of such issues as confidentiality clauses, *cy pres* awards, and defendants' use of low attorney-fee offers to drive a wedge between attorney and client.

The attorney should have settlement potential in mind when framing the complaint. Not only parties but also claims should be chosen that will make settlement possible. For example, the primary defendant may have insurance coverage for negligent but not intentional acts. If so, the attorney should make sure to assert any claims of negligence that are available.

Investigating, documenting, and analyzing the facts before suit enables the consumer's attorney to start the case in a strong position. Obtaining an expert opinion before filing suit is equally critical in certain cases. Assessing the likeability of the client is also important. The defendant will have a number of occasions to observe the consumer over the course of the litigation and, in formulating a settlement position, will consider how a jury will respond to the consumer.

19.1.2 Framing the Initial Demand

The first settlement approach to the defendants is crucial for setting the tone of the negotiations. One of the first steps that the defense attorney will take is to present an analysis of the case and its likely value to any insurer for the defendants. The consumer's demand should be high but realistic and—most critically—the attorney and client should be prepared to follow through. An initial demand that is low or equivocal signals to the defendant that the case is not serious. By the same token, an inflated, unsupported demand from which the consumer's attorney quickly retreats signals not only that the case is weak but also that the consumer is not prepared to litigate it. It can be very difficult to correct an early misimpression about the seriousness of the case.

19.1.3 Constructive Engagement with Defense Counsel

Trial preparation should continue while settlement is negotiated. Pressing forward unabated with trial preparation unless and until a settlement is final tells the defendants that the case is serious and that the consumer is prepared to try it.

The consumer's attorney should strive for constructive engagement with defendants' counsel. Easing the defendants' and opposing attorneys' ego issues can be important in settling a case. The way a settlement is packaged may make it easier for a defendant to accept. For example, paying actual damages, other reimbursements, and attorney fees is much more palatable to defendants than paying punitive damages or emotional distress damages.

1 Carolyn Carter is Deputy Director of Advocacy at NCLC. She was formerly co-director of Legal Services, Inc., in Gettysburg, Pennsylvania, and director of the Law Reform Office of the Cleveland Legal Aid Society. She is the editor of *Pennsylvania Consumer Law* and the first edition of *Ohio Consumer Law*; co-author of *Automobile Fraud* (2003), *Consumer Warranty Law* (2d ed. 2001), *Unfair and Deceptive Acts and Practices* (6th ed. 2004), *Repossessions and Foreclosures* (5th ed. 2002 and Supp.); and contributing author to *Fair Debt Collection* (5th ed. 2004 and Supp.), *Truth in Lending* (5th ed. 2003 and Supp.), and *The Cost of Credit: Regulation, Preemption, and Industry Abuses* (3d ed. 2005). She is the 1992 recipient of the Vern Countryman Consumer Award and is currently a member of the Federal Reserve Board's Consumer Advisory Council.

2 This and the next subsection are based in large part on a presentation by Bernard Brown, an attorney in Kansas City who handles consumer cases.

It may take time and considerable litigation pressure before the defendant and the opposing attorney are prepared to recognize the strength of the plaintiff's case and reach the conclusion that settlement is better than trial. Giving a concession near the end of a negotiation, after a strong and determined course of pre-trial preparation and negotiation, may enable the opponent to save face and accept a settlement. It is prudent not to rush settlements and to be prepared at all times to take the case through trial if necessary but also to leave the door open for settlement discussions.

Consumer cases that seek significant damages are usually an educational process for culpable defendants, and it takes some time for defendants and their counsel to become accustomed to the defendants' real exposure. This process is often complicated by the fact that defendants who are guilty of fraudulent practices are frequently rather belligerent people, with no shortage of nerve. Once an attorney has won a substantial judgment or two at trial for consumers, defendants may be more willing to settle cases on reasonable terms. A newer attorney's settlement negotiations may be enhanced by obtaining co-counsel who have obtained substantial judgments in similar cases.

Obtaining partial summary judgment on liability or on one or two counts puts enormous pressure on the defense and can hasten settlement. In addition, if no settlement is reached, the case can proceed to trial with some degree of victory assured. A partial summary judgment can also simplify trial of the case and avoids jury confusion.

Also explore the defendant's status with any state licensing board. Is the alleged violation grounds for the defendant to lose its license? Has that licensing board previously taken action against that defendant or have other complaints been filed about the dealer? If the consumer reports the action to the licensing board, that agency may apply additional pressure on the dealer to resolve the case fairly. Even the possibility that the action may be reported to the licensing board may induce the dealer to agree to a settlement along the lines that the board would have encouraged. State licensing or bonding issues may also give the defendant an incentive to settle so that no judgment is recorded in the public records.

When defense counsel wants to discuss settlement right before trial, some consumer attorneys follow a practice of having another attorney in the firm handle negotiations, giving that attorney the parameters for settlement and the goal number. This approach allows the lead lawyer to continue concentrating on trial preparation.

19.1.4 Settling with Financially Shaky Defendants

Some defendants in consumer cases—such as automobile dealers, real estate agents, and home improvement contractors—may be required by state law to be bonded. The requirements for collection under such a bond should be kept in mind during settlement if the dealer is at all shaky financially. Is a finding of fraud or a violation of a particular state law necessary in order to recover against the bond? Will such a finding be more likely to be recognized by the bonding company if it is entered by the court after evidence has been presented? If the defendant does not pay the settlement figure, will the plaintiff need to ask that the case be reopened so that these issues can be litigated, or can they be litigated in a separate proceeding against the bond?[3]

Another approach is to have the defendants' payment guaranteed by an irrevocable letter of credit from a bank.[4] Settlements should provide that the case is not dismissed and the court retains jurisdiction until all payments are made.

The implications if a financially shaky defendant files for bankruptcy after agreeing to a settlement should also be considered. There are some steps that may reduce the problems this filing will create. First, bankruptcy is less of a problem if the settlement binds not just corporations but also collectable individuals. Second, presenting evidence and obtaining findings by the trial court as to fraud by individual defendants will help establish the non-dischargeability of their debts in bankruptcy. Another approach is to obtain an agreement to a judgment of the full amount sought, with a proviso that the judgment may be satisfied by payment of the settlement amount. Then at least the plaintiff is not stuck with the reduced settlement amount in bankruptcy court.[5]

Another concern is that a bankruptcy trustee can recapture property that a debtor transferred to or for the benefit of a creditor on account of an antecedent debt while the debtor was insolvent. This recapture is allowed if the transfer took place within ninety days prior to the debtor's bankruptcy filing and enables the creditor to receive more than the creditor would otherwise receive.[6] If the consumer's attorney receives the settlement amount and forwards it to the consumer, and the defendant then files for bankruptcy within ninety days, the consumer—or the consumer's attorney—may be required to return the settlement money to the bankruptcy trustee. It may be best for the consumer's attorney to hold the money, with the client's consent, until the ninety-day period passes.

Another question is the effect on the settlement agreement itself if the defendant files for bankruptcy before paying. The Supreme Court has ruled that signing a settlement agreement and release does not convert an underlying non-dischargeable fraud claim into a dischargeable contract

3 *See* National Consumer Law Center, Automobile Fraud § 9.13.4 (2d ed. 2003 and Supp.) (discussion of collecting against a dealer's bond).

4 *See* Uniform Commercial Code Art. 5.

5 *See* National Consumer Law Center, Automobile Fraud § 9.11.2.6 (2d ed. 2003 and Supp.)

6 11 U.S.C. § 547.

claim.[7] Thus, a consumer who has signed a release but has not yet received payment can still challenge the dischargeability of the debt on the ground that the underlying debt was procured by fraud. The Supreme Court did not rule out the possibility, however, that collateral estoppel might prevent the consumer from re-litigating the question of fraud.[8] Careful drafting of the release may avoid collateral estoppel problems, but it is safer to condition any release upon receipt of payment.

19.1.5 The Mechanics of Settlement

Often settlements are reached in the courthouse, either at a pre-trial conference or before or during trial. To prevent defendants from adding terms not bargained for, such as confidentiality clauses when drafting the settlement documents, it is helpful to recite the agreed-upon terms on the record with a court reporter. After reciting the terms, the consumer's attorney should ask the opposing attorney, still on the record, whether the recitation is correct and includes everything. It is also a wise precaution to ask the judge to retain jurisdiction in case it is necessary to enforce the settlement. For settlements reached outside the courthouse, many consumer attorneys offer to do the initial draft of the settlement documents in order to minimize the opposing attorney's opportunity to include onerous, one-sided terms in the agreement. Settlement terms are discussed in § 19.5, *infra*.

19.1.6 Documenting Settlement Efforts

Making and documenting settlement proposals is important. Even if the case is not settled but goes to trial, the court may look on an attorney-fee petition more favorably if it is clear that the defendants passed up many opportunities to settle the case for a reasonable amount at an earlier point when the plaintiff's fees were lower. Oral settlement proposals should be memorialized with a letter. If a defendant rejects an early settlement proposal, it may be helpful to reiterate it in writing (explaining any changes such as increasing attorney fees) at several critical junctures leading up to trial.

19.2 Mediation

Courts often suggest or mandate mediation to resolve cases. Careful preparation for mediation is essential.

Mediation is likely to be fruitful only if the defendant is seriously engaged in trying to settle the case. For this reason, many attorneys insist on a serious settlement offer from the defendant before they will agree to mediation. If the parties are taking incompatible positions about the value of the case, it may be best to postpone mediation until the case has been developed further.

If it appears that mediation may be fruitful, it is important to make sure that the defendant sends someone to the mediation who has the authority to offer the settlement that the consumer wants. Selection of the mediator is also critical. The mediator should be someone that the opposing party trusts. Mediation may be a pleasant experience with a mediator who favors the consumer, but the chances of reaching an agreement are much greater if the defendant perceives the mediator as neutral and trustworthy.

The mediator is likely to ask the consumer directly what would be a satisfactory resolution of the case. The consumer should be carefully prepared for this type of question. Sometimes consumers are so eager to appear compliant and cooperative with the mediator that they understate their case. If the consumer intends to go to trial if the defendant does not come to terms, the consumer has to be prepared to say so in a convincing manner and stick with it. The consumer should also be warned not to respond to settlement suggestions conveyed by the mediator without first speaking privately to the attorney. The consumer should also be warned about fatigue and not to abandon his or her position because of exhaustion.

As with any settlement negotiation, it is best to start high. It is easy to drop to a lower figure but almost impossible to move higher. The consumer's initial proposal should, however, be serious and realistic. Ridiculous settlement proposals undermine the consumer's credibility. When making a high early demand, the consumer should be cautioned that the case is unlikely to settle for the high initial demand.

Mediation is often the first time the defendant's decision maker actually has contact with the plaintiff and gets the real story of what happened. The mediator's impression of the strength of the consumer's case is also important. For these reasons, the consumer should be prepared to present a convincing, well-organized case. Charts and tables may be helpful.

The consumer's position at mediation should be reasonable and well supported. Even if mediation does not resolve the case, it is important that the consumer be perceived by the trial judge as having participated fully and reasonably in settlement efforts.

19.3 Settlement of Cases with Multiple Defendants

When multiple defendants are sued, the general rule is that the amount received in settlement with one defendant may be deducted from any court or jury award against a

7 Archer v. Warner, 538 U.S. 314, 123 S. Ct. 1462, 155 L. Ed. 2d 454 (2003).

8 *Id.*, 123 S. Ct. at 1468.

non-settling defendant for the same injury.[9] The consumer's attorney should check the jurisdiction's law on this topic carefully. There may be ways to document the settlement that will minimize the effect on the non-settling defendants.

One strategy to minimize the effect on non-settling defendants is to stipulate in the settlement agreement that the money is for some specific element of damages that the remaining defendants are not liable for. Examples are the attorney fees to date arising from the independent efforts against the settling defendant,[10] separate damages caused by the settling defendant's independent misconduct,[11] statutory damages, and punitive damages. As punitive damages are based on individual culpability, a payment by one defendant does not reduce the other's liability for punitive damages.[12]

Another concern is the effect on the jury if the judge allows admission of evidence of the settlement. If the plaintiff has already recovered a substantial sum from another defendant, the jury may feel that the plaintiff's case no longer has to be taken seriously. If the plaintiff settled with other defendants for a nominal amount, it may devalue the case in the jury's eyes.

Many states follow a rule similar to Federal Rule of Evidence 408 that evidence of compromise or an offer to compromise is not admissible on liability issues. This rule does allow such evidence to be admitted for other purposes—such as proving bias of a witness, negating a contention of undue delay, or proving an effort to obstruct a criminal investigation or prosecution—but courts tend to be reluctant to find it relevant for these purposes.[13] Even if relevant, such evidence can be excluded under Rule 403 if its value is substantially outweighed by the danger of unfair prejudice, confusion, or similar concerns.[14] If an offset is required because of the settlement, the majority rule is that the jury should still not be informed of the settlement, but the court should handle the offset after the verdict.[15] A motion *in limine* to exclude this evidence is recommended. If there is any chance that the evidence will be allowed in, many attorneys recommend alerting the jury to it beforehand, either in *voir dire* or in the opening statement.

Even if the jury is never informed of the terms of the settlement, the "empty chair" effect can be a problem, especially if the party who is no longer in the case is the one the jury is likely to perceive as the most culpable. In developing a trial strategy, the plaintiff's attorney should focus on ways to address the jury's discomfort and should stress the role that the culpable acts of the remaining defendants played in the overall fraud and in causing the plaintiff's injuries.

19.4 Attorney Fees and Settlements

19.4.1 Settlement Offers That Do Not Provide Sufficient Attorney Fees

Defendants often seek to "divide and conquer" by offering a settlement that does not include attorney fees, or includes an inadequate proposal for fees, creating a conflict between the consumer and the consumer's attorney. While the U.S. Supreme Court rejected a claim that it was unethical for a defendant to propose a settlement of a civil rights case that required waiver of attorney fees,[16] at least one state holds such a settlement offer to be unethical in a UDAP case.[17]

Problems of settlement offers that do not provide sufficient attorney fees can be minimized by a retainer that unites the consumer's interest with the attorney's. For example, the retainer could provide that, if the case is settled with insufficient provision for fees, the fees are satisfied first out of settlement proceeds. Or it could simply state that the client is responsible to pay the attorney at the agreed rate regardless of whether the case is won or settled. Public interest

9 Haynes v. Manning, 917 F.2d 450 (10th Cir. 1990), *rev'g in part* 717 F. Supp. 730 (D. Kan. 1989); O'Brien v. B.L.C. Ins. Co., 768 S.W.2d 64 (Mo. 1989) (trial court was correct in eliminating jury's actual damage award when plaintiff had already received a great amount in settlement against another defendant). *See also* Zivitz v. Greenberg, 279 F.3d 536 (7th Cir. 2002) (Ill. law) (no set-off when the damages awarded against non-settling defendant were not for identical injury). *Compare* Lemke v. Sears, Roebuck & Co., 853 F.2d 253 (4th Cir. 1988) *with* First Sec. Fed. v. McQuilken, 480 S.E.2d 485 (Va. 1997).

10 Wash. Trust Co. v. Fatone, 256 A.2d 490 (R.I. 1969). *See also* Beerman v. Toro Mfg. Corp., 1 Haw. App. 111, 615 P.2d 749 (1980) (citing attorney fee for which only one defendant was liable as example of payment that would not count against other defendant's liability).

11 Plath v. Schonrock, 64 P.3d 984 (Mont. 2003) (no set-off when settling defendant's liability was based on separate and distinct claim).

12 Beerman v. Toro Mfg. Corp., 1 Haw. App. 111, 615 P.2d 749 (1980); Exxon Corp. v. Yarema, 516 A.2d 990 (Md. Ct. Spec. App. 1986) (settlement with other defendants before trial can satisfy compensatory damages but not punitive damages liability of non-settling defendants); Freeman v. Myers, 774 S.W.2d 892 (Mo. Ct. App. 1989); Sanchez v. Clayton, 117 N.M. 761, 877 P.2d 567 (N.M. 1994) (settlement with one defendant does not offset other's liability for punitive damages); McGee v. Bruce Hosp. Sys., 545 S.E.2d 286 (S.C. 2001) (punitive damages awarded against one tortfeasor are not double recovery with respect to judgment against another tortfeasor, because purpose is to punish a particular offender rather than compensate victim for injury).

13 Graber v. City of Ankeny, 616 N.W.2d 633 (Iowa 2000).

14 Votolato v. Merendi, 747 A.2d 455 (R.I. 2000).

15 Morea v. Cosco, Inc., 422 Mass. 601, 664 N.E.2d 822 (1996); Southeastern Med. Supply, Inc. v. Boyles, Moak & Brickell Ins., Inc., 822 So. 2d 323 (Miss. Ct. App. 2002); Votolato v. Merendi, 747 A.2d 455 (R.I. 2000). *Cf.* Dynasty Hous., Inc. v. McCollum, 832 So. 2d 73 (Ala. Civ. App. 2001); Buccaneer Homes v. Pelis, 43 S.W.3d 586 (Tex. App. 2001).

16 Evans v. Jeff D., 475 U.S. 717, 106 S. Ct. 1531, 89 L. Ed. 2d 747 (1986).

17 Coleman v. Fiore Bros., Inc., 552 A.2d 141 (N.J. 1989).

attorneys who are handling a case without any obligation on the part of the client to pay fees should also have a clear understanding with the client, incorporated in the retainer, about how fee issues will be handled in the event of a settlement. Retainer issues are discussed in more detail in § 7.6, *supra.*

If the settlement involves the payment of money, sometimes it is easier to deal with a lump-sum proposal rather than a certain amount for the consumer and a certain amount for fees. Some defense attorneys will comply with a request that settlement proposals be in a lump-sum form. Sometimes a settlement that makes the client whole but requires the attorney to petition the court for a fee award is acceptable.

Some consumer attorneys make a practice of periodically sending the defendant's attorney a summary of their time records, to show them what the defendant's potential fee liability is and to make it clear that it is increasing. The defendant is less able to complain to the judge about the plaintiff's fees if the defendant has been given information about them all along and had the opportunity to settle when they were low.

19.4.2 Preserving the Right to Fees When Settling a Case

The consumer's attorney should pay careful attention to the language and structure of any such agreement. In federal courts and some state courts, the consumer is considered to be a prevailing party if an enforceable judgment on the merits or a court-ordered consent decree is entered, but not if there is a "private settlement" that does not involve judicial oversight and approval.[18] The following ways of settling a case are likely to preserve fees:

- Negotiation of payment of fees in an acceptable amount as part of the settlement on the merits
- An agreed judgment for money or other relief, as long as it is clear that fees have not been waived. An agreed judgment is an "enforceable judgment on the merits" and a "material alteration of the legal relationship of the parties," criteria that the Supreme Court has articulated as establishing prevailing-party status.[19]
- An agreed order, or even possibly a stipulation, that states that the consumer is the prevailing party or is entitled to fees in an amount to be determined by the court (although courts have not yet ruled on the viability of this approach)

The following settlement methods are less likely to preserve the right to fees:

- A stipulation resolving the merits of the case, even if filed with the court, that is signed only by the parties and does not state that the plaintiff is the prevailing party
- An entry of dismissal, even if the case is dismissed pursuant to an agreement signed by the parties under which the defendant agrees to the relief the plaintiff sought, unless the dismissal order embodies the settlement agreement or retains jurisdiction to enforce it

Preserving the right to fees when settling a case is discussed in greater detail in National Consumer Law Center, *Consumer Warranty Law* § 2.7.6.5 (2d ed. 2001 and Supp.).

19.5 Settlement Terms

19.5.1 Prompt Payment

Some defendants delay many months after agreeing to settle a case before making the actual payment. Insist that the settlement agreement specify a payment date. In the alternative, the agreement can be worded so that the settlement itself is contingent upon the defendants making payment within a certain time. It can provide that the consumer will not sign the release until the payment actually clears.

Another approach is to add a penalty for late payment, for example: "Defendant agrees to pay $10,000 if paid within thirty days. If this amount is not paid within thirty days, a judgment will be entered in the amount of $15,000." A similar approach that avoids the appearance of a penalty is to have a discount if payment is made within a certain time, for example: "Defendant will pay Plaintiff $15,000; however, if Defendant pays $10,000 by __________, Plaintiff will give Defendant a full and complete release." If a judgment has been entered, the agreement can state that the consumer will refrain from execution so long as payments are made as scheduled and that the consumer will have the judgment marked satisfied upon timely payment of the agreed-upon amounts.

It can also be helpful to negotiate a clause that the settling defendant will pay any court costs and attorney fees necessary to collect the judgment. Specifying the hourly rate in the agreement will reduce the number of disputed issues if it becomes necessary to invoke the clause. Negotiating a personal guarantee of payment by the individual who owns the corporate defendant also encourages prompt payment by the corporation and provides some protection if the company files for bankruptcy.[20] A letter of credit from a bank guaranteeing payment may be even better. The case should not be dismissed until payment is received and, even then, it is wise to have the court retain jurisdiction to enforce the settlement or with leave to reinstate the case should payment not be received.

18 Buckhannon Bd. & Care Home, Inc. v. W. Va. Dep't of Health & Human Resources, 532 U.S. 598, 121 S. Ct. 1835, 149 L. Ed. 2d 855 (2001).

19 *Id.*, 121 S. Ct. at 1840.

20 *See also* § 19.1.4, *supra.*

Another step to reduce delays is to add a clause to the settlement agreement that collection can proceed immediately upon expiration of the time for payment and that the defendant waives any appeal period during which collection would normally be precluded.

19.5.2 Confidentiality Agreements

Settling defendants often request that the settlement prohibits the parties from disclosing the terms of the settlement to anyone. A second, less extreme, clause does not prohibit disclosure altogether but prohibits publicity. Such clauses raise a host of concerns.[21] They enable defendants to cover up massive wrongdoing and create procedural obstacles if judicial enforcement of the settlement becomes necessary. Confidentiality agreements leave the litigation unsettled because they invite the defendant to sue the plaintiff years later alleging disclosure of the settlement.

It is arguable that use of such a clause to attempt to bar a subpoenaed witness from testifying in a future case amounts to witness tampering[22] and spoliation of evidence. The Rules of Professional Conduct prohibit a lawyer from attempting to restrain a person from giving evidence.[23] Another concern is the ethical rule that prohibits an attorney from offering or agreeing to a restriction on the lawyer's right to practice as part of a settlement of a case.[24] A number of U.S. Courts of Appeals have ruled that a stipulation of settlement that contains a confidentiality clause can not be approved unless good cause is shown, because such clauses have an adverse impact on the public interest.[25]

One reason confidentiality agreements are attractive to defendants is that they impede the plaintiff's attorney's representation of other clients against the same defendants. Some consumer attorneys refuse to agree to any confidentiality agreement that binds them, although the client has freedom to agree that he or she will not disclose the settlement. Another possible step is to insist that any confidentiality clause that applies to the attorney must include language that the non-disclosure agreement is void and unenforceable to the extent that it restricts the attorney's right to practice law. The attorney can also seek to narrow the non-disclosure provision such that it prohibits only disclosure of the amount of settlement, not the fact of settlement, which is a matter of public record in any event. To avoid ethical problems, any confidentiality agreement should also make an exception for evidence that is subpoenaed in another case.

It is wise to discuss these issues with the client at the outset of the case, before litigation is commenced. Some attorneys include provisions in their retainer agreements that reflect the understanding that has been worked out with the client about confidentiality clauses. The client retains ultimate authority to reject or accept settlement proposals, however.

If the client later becomes interested in a settlement that includes a non-disclosure provision, the client should be cautioned about the scope of such provision and the consequences of violating it. Confidentiality agreements place a great and usually lifelong burden on the client, forcing the client to live under the threat of suit if he or she ever discloses the settlement or if the defendant ever believes he or she disclosed it.

19.5.3 Other Terms and Clauses

Any release should be mutual, with each party releasing the other from the same scope of claims. If only the consumer signs the release, the consumer is vulnerable to suit by the defendant.

If one of the defendants holds a note or installment contract signed by the consumer, the settlement agreement should require it to be returned to the consumer, marked paid or cancelled. Otherwise, there is a danger that it will be treated as a continuing obligation and assigned to another entity, and the consumer will be dunned for payment or even sued.

19.5.4 Court Costs and Financing Costs

Most settlement agreements deal with responsibility for court costs incurred to date, but, in some jurisdictions, the clerk's office may charge additional court costs for entering the settlement order. Or the clerk's office may prepare a final court cost bill months after the case has been closed. The settlement agreement should deal with unanticipated court cost bills. For example, it could provide that any court costs owed to the clerk over and above the deposit posted by the plaintiff at the beginning of the case will be paid by the defendant.

---

21 *See* Ch. 18, *supra*. Also, Trial Lawyers for Public Justice has been active in opposing confidentiality agreements, especially in the class action context. They can be contacted at 1717 Massachusetts Ave., N.W., Suite 800, Washington D.C. 20036; by telephone at (202) 797-8600; and on the Internet at www.tlpj.org.

22 18 U.S.C. § 1512.

23 Model Rule of Professional Conduct 3.4.

24 Model Rule of Professional Conduct 5.6(b); ABA Comm. on Ethics and Prof'l Responsibility, Formal Op. 00-417 (2000). *See Settlement Agreements Create Ethical Dilemma*, N.Y.L.J., Oct. 12, 2000 (discussing New York State Bar Association ethics opinion).

25 *See, e.g.*, Citizens First Nat'l Bank v. Cincinnati Ins. Co., 178 F.3d 943 (7th Cir. 1999) (judge must find good cause before approving settlement agreement containing confidentiality clause); Pansy v. Borough of Stroudsburg, 23 F.3d 772 (3d Cir. 1994) (discussing confidentiality agreements, especially in relation to settlement papers that are not filed with the court); City of Hartford v. Chase, 942 F.2d 130 (2d Cir. 1991) (trial court may approve confidentiality order only after very careful, particularized review).

If the settlement figure includes the amount necessary to pay off a debt to a bank or other financier, remember that it should cover the amount that will be due when the check arrives, not the amount due at the time the settlement agreement is reached. It should cover not only interest that accrues up to the time the check arrives but also the loan payment that the client will have to make while waiting for the check.

19.6 Settlements of Consumer Disputes Should Address Consumer's Credit Report

19.6.1 Importance of Resolving Credit Reporting Issues

An important element of a settlement is protection of the consumer's credit record. If the dispute involves an obligation that the consumer ever failed or refused to pay or paid late, the creditor will already have reported its unfavorable experience with the consumer to at least one and probably more consumer reporting agencies. Even if the consumer later wins the case or pays the creditor's claim in full, the default may mar the consumer's credit reports for seven years.

The solution is to make sure that any settlement on the debt deals with credit reporting issues. The settlement should contain a clear and unequivocal requirement that, as part of the resolution of differences, the creditor will undertake to remove unfavorable information from the consumer's credit reporting file.[26] Model language that may be adapted and then included in settlement agreements is included below.[27]

Any settlement agreement should provide that the defendant will immediately take all steps necessary to ensure that no credit report or credit reference that is or could be construed as unfavorable to the consumer is made to anyone—and, in particular, any consumer credit reporting agency—with regard to any debts or claims involving the consumer. The agreement should further require the defendant to make a request to each credit reporting agency to whom it furnishes information, asking that the agency delete all references to the alleged debts or claims. The defendant should be required to sign a letter on its letterhead, prepared by the consumer's attorney, stating that its claims against the consumer have been fully released and that any adverse reports should be deleted and deemed unreliable. The defendant should also agree that, if it is asked by a reporting agency to verify that a debt was in fact ever in default, it will refuse to do so. Then, when the consumer asks the reporting agency to verify its information, it will be unable to do so and must delete the adverse reference from the consumer's file.

Credit reporting agencies are not required to withdraw information upon the request of a creditor, even from the creditor who supplied the information initially.[28] However, the agency is held to a standard of accuracy which, if violated, may render the agency liable for civil damages. Thus, in practice, when the source of information in a credit file requests that the information be withdrawn, suggesting that the information is not entirely accurate or reliable, the consumer reporting agency is likely to comply. If the reporting agency does not delete the item, the consumer can dispute it. The Fair Credit Reporting Act then requires the reporting agency to obtain re-verification of the item from the creditor. If the terms of the settlement prevent the creditor from verifying the information, the agency will have to delete the information.[29]

19.6.2 Selecting the Correct Settlement Language

Two alternative settlement provisions are provided below.[30] The first requires the creditor to withdraw the entire report of the disputed debt. This withdrawal is sometimes referred to as a "hard delete." The credit record will then be altogether silent about the debt and will not even provide a basis for another creditor, interested in the creditworthiness of the consumer, to inquire further. This is often the simplest solution for the consumer and the safest.[31] One drawback is that sometimes, if the debt is deleted, the consumer's credit record will be too sparse.[32] Some advocates report that a "soft delete" such as "cloaking" or "suppression" is inadequate and seems to lead to later re-reporting of the information. These advocates favor a "hard delete." Others report that re-insertion of the deleted information is actually

26 A creditor may be able to access a consumer report to make sure information has in fact been deleted as promised. Wilting v. Progressive County Mut. Ins. Co., 227 F.3d 474 (5th Cir. 2000).

27 *See* National Consumer Law Center, Fair Credit Reporting Ch. 13 (5th ed. 2002 and Supp.).

28 *See* Watson v. Credit Bureau, Inc., 660 F. Supp. 48 (S.D. Miss. 1986).

29 *See* National Consumer Law Center, Fair Credit Reporting § 7.4.2 (5th ed. 2002 and Supp.).

30 These clauses are also included in Microsoft Word format on the companion CD-Rom to this volume.

31 Some practitioners have encountered creditors who assert that they are unable to withdraw the entire report. On the contrary, however, the deletion can be accomplished through the Associated Credit Bureau's Universal Data Process or through the ACB's Metro 2 Format. Information regarding these mechanisms can be obtained from ACB's website at www.acb-credit.com. The settlement agreement should provide that the creditor will give the consumer's attorney a copy of the form that the creditor submits to the agency.

32 *See* National Consumer Law Center, Fair Credit Reporting § 13.6.1 (5th ed. 2002 and Supp.).

easier after a "hard delete."[33] The key for the consumer is that the agreement must include an iron-clad prohibition against re-reporting the debt or transferring or selling it, and the consumer must monitor his or her credit report to make sure the information does not reappear.

The second alternative permits reporting of the debt but requires the creditor to take steps to avoid having unfavorable information about the debt included in any credit report. The consumer may benefit from this approach if the resulting consumer report contains only information that suggests good consumer experience with credit management. It may benefit the creditor because it permits the reporting of the debt and any information that is uncontested or undisputed. The report could also reflect a debt, a dispute, and a successful resolution of the dispute.

For the second alternative to be successful, the settlement provisions must carefully delineate what information cannot be furnished to credit reporting agencies. Even so, there is always the risk that even the limited information reported, though accurate in a narrow sense, will permit another creditor using the report to fill in the gaps incorrectly or to draw its own negative inferences. For example, if the defendant is allowed to report that there was a dispute, a creditor might suppose there was a default as well.

There is another risk inherent in the second alternative, which should be addressed in the settlement agreement. The mere reporting of the existence of a debt may lead a future report user to call the creditor listed in the consumer report. A credit manager receiving such a call will naturally be inclined to give only the creditor's version of the facts, tinged perhaps with latent anger. As a result, the settlement must deal explicitly with oral inquiries made to the creditor directly. However, this will be a difficult provision to police.

Creditors may balk at promising to correct credit information before they can verify that the consumer will live up to any obligations imposed by the settlement agreement, especially if the agreement requires the consumer to make payments. To meet this concern, the consumer can agree that unfavorable information will be withdrawn or withheld only so long as the consumer complies with the settlement agreement. If the consumer breaches any part of the settlement agreement, for example by missing a payment, then the creditor may make a full report to the consumer reporting agency without the limitations otherwise inherent in the agreement. Nevertheless, because of the possibilities that a consumer will miss a payment, the settlement might only allow the creditor to report the delinquency in the rescheduled payment plan.

Creditors that routinely report their experiences to reporting agencies by computer tape or transmission will generally simply correct their tapes.[34] Other creditors may notify the agency by letter. The consumer's attorney may wish to retain a hand in the drafting of the letter the creditor will submit to the credit reporting agency.[35] In an appropriate case, the consumer's attorney may want to specify the agency-specific codes that will be used in the creditor's report on the debt's status to the agency.[36] It is important, especially under the second alternative, that the tone of the letter reflect the true nature of the settlement and not seem to mask some mismanagement of the credit by the consumer. This has been resolved in the past by providing that the notice to the consumer reporting agency shall be in a letter using language agreed to at the time of settlement by both parties. Upon posting, a copy of the letter should be sent to the consumer.

A common problem is the "recapture" of information from the monthly or periodic computer tapes or transmissions from creditors that fail to adjust their internal records to reflect the corrections made to the tradeline. The result is that the inaccurate information will then resurface in the consumer's report. The FCRA was amended in 1996 to prevent this abuse.[37] However, the settlement agreement itself should provide for the creditor to correct its internal records, including those already stored, with the specific intent to prevent accidental re-reporting of the transactions involved. If the settlement is with a credit reporting agency, the agreement can provide for a periodic review of the consumer's file to ensure that the offending information has not been reinserted. Although the 1996 amendments provide that the agency is supposed to notify the consumer when

33 *See id.* § 7.5.

34 Some consumer attorneys have found that credit reporting agencies will refuse to delete derogatory information that is "technically accurate" when the creditor submits it manually. In such a case, having the creditor submit the updated information via automated tape may accomplish the change. Failing that, the consumer may dispute the information directly with the credit reporting agency. The agency must drop the information from the report unless the creditor verifies it. 15 U.S.C. § 1681i. *See* National Consumer Law Center, Fair Credit Reporting § 7.3 (5th ed. 2002 and Supp.). The agreement can require that the creditor not verify it, and the creditor should take steps to make sure that the information is not unwittingly verified. A reminder of the new obligations imposed on furnishers may help. 15 U.S.C. § 1681s-2. *See* National Consumer Law Center, Fair Credit Reporting Ch. 3 (5th ed. 2002 and Supp.).

35 In drafting a letter for the creditor to submit to a credit reporting agency, it may be prudent to identify the consumer by present and any recent address, social security number, and name(s). Many creditors use a "Universal Data Form" to correct consumer credit records. The form allows the option of deleting or updating account information and can be included in the letter if appropriate. Associated Credit Bureaus, Inc., a trade association of credit reporting agencies, makes such a form available to its members and includes it in a universal electronic reporting program, called Metro 2, which also may be used to submit changes to all the major agencies.

36 See sample credit reports in National Consumer Law Center, Fair Credit Reporting Appx. F (5th ed. 2002 and Supp.).

37 *See* National Consumer Law Center, Fair Credit Reporting § 7.5 (5th ed. 2002 and Supp.).

once-deleted information is reinserted,[38] the settlement agreement should provide for additional verification.

The settlement agreement should also provide that the creditor will not assign the debt. A collection agency or assignee creditor can cause the disputed information to reappear in the consumer's credit report, and they may claim that the settlement agreement does not bind them.

19.6.3 Alternative I: Deleting All Mention of the Debt

The following is proposed settlement language that would require the creditor to request deletion of all reference to a disputed debt in a consumer's credit reporting file—complete deletion is far preferable to amendment of the information:

> It is further agreed that [name of creditor] shall take all steps necessary to ensure that no credit report or credit reference that is unfavorable or that may be construed unfavorably to [name of consumer] shall be made by it or by any consumer reporting agency with regard to any debts or claims as between [creditor] and [consumer]. Without limiting the effect of the foregoing obligation, [creditor] shall also within 10 days hereof send notice [in writing or electronically or both] [in the form attached hereto as Appendix A], to each consumer reporting agency to which the creditor has reported any information about [consumer], deleting from their files all references to the [alleged] debt which is the subject of this settlement agreement. To that end, [creditor] shall submit a [Metro II form coded with "DA" (delete account)] [and/or] [a Universal Data Form with the "Delete Tradeline" option box checked] to each consumer reporting agency to which the creditor has reported any information about the consumer. Prior to any execution of any release of claims by [consumer], [creditor] shall submit to counsel for [consumer] proof that [creditor] has submitted these forms. In the event Plaintiffs discover, more than 45 days following [creditor's] submission of the [Metro II form] [Universal Data form] as described, that any consumer reporting agency still reports the alleged debt, [consumer] may notify [creditor] in writing, and [creditor] will within 10 business days re-submit a request for deletion of all reference to the debt.
>
> [Creditor] shall adjust its relevant internal records in a manner that will permanently reflect the agreed-upon status of the debt. [Creditor] agrees to take all steps necessary or appropriate to prevent the re-reporting of any information about the [alleged] debt. In the event any such information is re-reported to any consumer reporting agency, [creditor] agrees to take all steps necessary or appropriate to ensure that the re-reported information is deleted from the files of every consumer reporting agency to which the information was re-reported. [Creditor] further agrees that it will not assign the [alleged] debt to another creditor, a collection agency, or any other third party and that it will not alter the account number or otherwise re-label the account. The parties agree that time is of the essence of this contract.

19.6.4 Alterative II: Correcting the Status of an Account But Retaining Information About the Account

The following is proposed settlement language that would require the creditor to request correction of a disputed credit account but would leave the account listed in the consumer's credit reporting file: This option is recommended only when there is a significant benefit to the client of maintaining information about the account, for it is far more likely to raise post-settlement problems:

> It is further agreed that [creditor] shall take all steps necessary to ensure that no credit report or credit reference that is unfavorable or that may be construed unfavorably to [consumer] shall be made by it or by any consumer reporting agency with regard to any debts or claims as between [creditor] and [consumer]. Without limiting the foregoing obligation, the [creditor] shall, within 10 days hereof, send written or electronic notice of the current status of the debt which is the subject of this settlement agreement to each consumer reporting agency to which the creditor has reported any information about [consumer], such notice to be in a form [approved by counsel for consumer] [or, attached hereto as Appendix A], and shall cause the deletion of all information that is unfavorable or may be construed unfavorably to [name of consumer]. For this purpose, the parties agree that the current status of the debt is [describe]. [Creditor] shall submit a [Metro II form coded with [describe codes]] [and/or] [a Universal Data Form [describe marks to be made on Form]] to each credit reporting agency to which the creditor has reported any information about the consumer. Prior to any execution of any release of claims by [consumer], [creditor] shall submit to counsel for [consumer] proof that [creditor] has submitted these forms. In the event Plaintiffs discover, more than 45 days following [creditor's] submission of the [Metro II form] [Universal Data form] as described, that any consumer reporting agency still reports the [alleged] debt other than as described above, [consumer] may notify [creditor]

38 FCRA § 611(a)(5)(B), 15 U.S.C. § 1681i(a)(5)(B). *See also* National Consumer Law Center, Fair Credit Reporting § 7.5 (5th ed. 2002 and Supp.).

in writing, and [creditor] will within 10 business days re-submit a request for reporting of the [alleged] debt, as described above. Furthermore, should a consumer reporting agency ever notify [creditor] that [consumer] is disputing the [alleged] debt, [creditor] will re-report the [alleged] debt only as described above; in such an event, [creditor] will also submit to counsel for [consumer], within 45 days after receiving the notification of the dispute from the consumer reporting agency, clear and complete copies of the notification of the dispute and any and all forms (including electronic forms) by which it responds to such notification (with [creditor's] subscriber password code redacted if [creditor] chooses).

Creditor shall further refrain from reporting any information that is unfavorable or may be construed unfavorably to [consumer] about said debt, so long as [consumer] remains in compliance with [specify the paragraphs of the settlement that deal with future payments].

[Creditor] shall adjust its relevant internal records in a manner that will permanently reflect the agreed-upon status of the debt. [Creditor] agrees to take all steps necessary or appropriate to prevent the re-reporting of any information about the debt that is inconsistent with the current status of the debt or the payment history from the date of this settlement agreement. In the event any such information is re-reported to any consumer reporting agency, [creditor] agrees to take all steps necessary or appropriate to ensure that the re-reported information is deleted from the files of every consumer reporting agency to which the information was re-reported. [Creditor] further agrees that it will not assign the [alleged] debt to another creditor, a collection agency, or any other third party and that it will not alter the account number or otherwise re-label the account. The parties agree that time is of the essence of this contract.

If [creditor] receives inquiries about said debt from anyone not a party to this settlement agreement, [creditor] will report only the current status of the debt as described above and the payment history from the date of this settlement. [Creditor] shall not provide, directly or indirectly, any information regarding the status of the debt before the date of this settlement, including [delinquencies] [repossessions] [deficiencies] [judgments] [foreclosures] [collection efforts].

19.6.5 Obtaining Court Approval

Practice varies by jurisdiction and by status of a case as to whether courts must approve a settlement agreement. Nevertheless, it may be in the consumer's interest, when possible, to obtain a court approval of any settlement involving correction of a credit report. A reporting agency is not required to take any action requested by a creditor but only has an obligation to ensure maximum possible accuracy. Having the request for correction appear in a document approved by a court may prove more persuasive to a reporting agency.

19.6.6 Court Orders Should Cover Credit Reporting Issues

Consumer attorneys must consider a consumer's credit rating not only while drafting settlement agreements but also when the dispute will be resolved through a court order. If the consumer has prevailed or partially prevailed in an action, the consumer should seek a court order requiring the creditor to take action to clear up the consumer's credit record relating to the dispute. Otherwise, even if the debt is no longer listed as currently due, indications that the debt was once considered delinquent and once subject to a collection action may remain on the consumer's record.

Even if a consumer loses a case, the consumer should consider seeking a court order that will minimize the impact of the dispute on the consumer's credit record. For example, consider the situation in which a consumer disputed a debt in good faith and made payments into escrow for several years pending resolution of the case. The consumer might seek a court order that the creditor should attempt to correct any reference in the consumer's reporting file to the two-year delinquency if the consumer pays the judgment promptly.

Chapter 20 Consumer Litigation's Tax Consequences for Prevailing Clients[1]

20.1 Introduction

A recent United States Supreme Court case, *Commissioner of Internal Revenue v. Banks*,[2] has put the spotlight on questions of client federal income tax liability resulting from successful consumer litigation. While *Banks* deals solely with the tax consequences for the client of contingent fees paid to the client's attorney, this chapter will examine tax issues more broadly.

***An important caveat**: The National Consumer Law Center is not staffed by tax lawyers, tax laws often change, and each client's tax situation is different. This article seeks to place individual client tax issues in a coherent context, highlight problem areas, and suggest possible solutions. But the specifics of a particular client's tax return and tax planning must be based on a tax professional's analysis of the facts specific to that individual.*

20.2 Double Taxation of Attorney Fees

Banks holds that, to the extent that a settlement or trial award is taxable income, the full amount of the award must be included in the individual's gross income, even that portion paid to the individual's attorney as a contingent fee. The individual can take the attorney fee payment as a miscellaneous itemized deduction on Schedule A of Form 1040 to the extent that the deduction exceeds 2% of the individual's adjusted gross income. Under a standard tax calculation this deduction neutralizes much, but not all, of the tax impact of including the contingent fee in the individual's gross income.

For substantial awards, a further problem comes with application of the Alternative Minimum Tax (AMT).[3] The effect of the AMT is to treat the contingent-fee portion of the award as part of gross income but to disallow itemized deductions, including the deduction for the attorney payment. This effect can result in a dramatic increase in a client's tax liability. Furthermore, both the client and the attorney must pay tax on the same fee, resulting in a form of double taxation.

20.3 Contingent Fee Not Includable in Gross Income When Underlying Award Not Taxable

Banks will certainly have an impact on client tax obligations for certain contingency awards. But not all such awards will create additional tax liability and, in many other cases, the AMT consequences will not be dramatic.

The *Banks* AMT problem for contingency fees disappears when a settlement or court award is not treated as part of the taxpayer's gross income.[4] When an award is non-taxable, no portion of that award is added to the consumer's gross income, including the contingent-fee portion, so there is no AMT problem.

Common situations in which all or part of a settlement or court award is non-taxable are discussed in § 20.9, *infra*, and include cases in which actual damages merely return to the consumer amounts unfairly paid for a product, service, finance charge, or fee and cases in which the recovery includes personal injury damages.

A damage award may include taxable portions (for example, lost earnings or punitive damages) and non-taxable portions. In such cases, a percentage of the contingent fee is included in the taxpayer's gross income and taken as an itemized deduction, equaling the percentage of the full award included in gross income. Reducing the amount of the fee included in gross income reduces the possibility of AMT consequences.

20.4 Inclusion of Fees in Gross Income May Not Trigger the AMT

The fact that contingent attorney fees may expose the consumer to the AMT does not mean that a particular award

1 Adapted from articles in NCLC REPORTS *Deceptive Practices and Warranties Edition*.

2 125 S. Ct. 826 (Jan. 24, 2005).

3 The AMT is described later on this page.

4 The rule may be different though for statutory attorney fees, as discussed below.

will trigger a sizeable AMT or even any AMT liability at all. Instead, the exact consequences for the particular taxpayer depend on an individualized AMT calculation.

The AMT replaces miscellaneous itemized deductions, such as the attorney fee payment, state and local taxes, home equity interest, and personal exemptions, with an AMT exemption of $58,000 (this exemption applies to married couples filing jointly with gross incomes up to $150,000, at which point the exemption begins to phase out). The AMT calculation still allows deduction of home mortgage interest and charitable contributions. Gross income minus the AMT exemption and other allowable deductions is taxed at 26% up to $175,000 and 28% over that amount. The resulting AMT is compared with the taxpayer's standard tax liability, and the taxpayer pays whichever amount is higher.[5]

Application of this formula when contingent attorney fees are in the $5000 to $15,000 range may produce little or no additional tax.[6] Even for a multi-million dollar award, the AMT consequences of the contingent fee will be significant but not crippling. A good estimate is that application of the AMT to a $3 million award (with a $1 million attorney fee) might reduce the consumer's net recovery (after tax and after paying the attorney) from around $1.3 million to around $1.18 million.[7]

20.5 *Banks* Does Not Address Tax Consequences of Statutory Attorney Fees

Of greater significance for most consumer litigation is a related question: the tax treatment of a statutory attorney fee award. Statutory attorney fees raise similar tax issues as contingent fee awards. Must the fees be treated as part of the consumer's gross income, with an itemized deduction for their full amount when paid to the attorney, thus creating potential AMT issues? Or are statutory fee awards income only to the attorney and not included in the consumer's gross income?

When statutory attorney fees are in the $10,000 to $20,000 range, whether the fee is included in gross income (and then taken as an itemized deduction) will have minimal AMT implications for many consumers, in light of the $58,000 AMT exemption. But when statutory attorney fees are large and actual damages less so, this issue takes on special significance. Even when the underlying award is not taxable, a large statutory fee could result in an AMT obligation exceeding the actual damages award, resulting in a net negative award to the consumer!

Banks declined to address the issue of whether a statutory fee is included in the client's gross income but did opine on the subject in ways that indicate that the Court may find such fees not taxable to the consumer. The Supreme Court stated: "plaintiff usually has little control over the amount awarded." Furthermore, the Court wrote that, when statutory fees are greater than the damage award, "[t]reating the fee award as income to the plaintiff in such cases, it is argued, can lead to the perverse result that the plaintiff loses money by winning the suit. Furthermore, it is urged that treating statutory fee awards as income to plaintiffs would undermine the effectiveness of fee-shifting statutes in deputizing plaintiffs and their lawyers to act as private attorneys general."[8]

Statutory fees are meant to allow consumers to pursue litigation even when a corporation utilizes a scorched earth strategy. The strategy would succeed and fair settlements would be discouraged if large potential AMT obligations prevented the consumer's attorney from matching the hours spent by the corporation's lawyers.

Until the courts resolve the question of whether a statutory fee is income to the taxpayer, the safest course for the consumer is, prior to the litigation, to irrevocably assign over to the attorney any right to the attorney fee and any control over the attorney fee claim.[9] The United States Solicitor General, representing the IRS, gave qualified endorsement to this strategy in its *Banks* reply brief: "If such an assignment [of statutory attorney fees to the attorney] is viewed as a transfer of the entirety of the attorney's fee claim to the lawyer, such that the prevailing party retains no meaningful interest in or control over the claim, then it may be possible to view any recovery on that claim as income only of the lawyer."[10] A number of cases also state that the client does not own statutory attorney fees.[11]

5 AMT taxes paid in one tax year because of the attorney fees being treated as income can not be taken as a tax credit in future years because the fees are exclusion items. U.S. Dept. of Treasury, Lawsuits Awards and Settlements (Training 2123-009 (11-00)).

6 Take, for example, a married couple with moderate income and minimal itemized deductions who receive a taxable $20,000 court award, with $8000 of that amount paid to their attorney as a contingent fee. Because of the $58,000 AMT exemption, the loss of the $8000 deduction may not be a problem, and the AMT calculation may in fact indicate that the $8000 contingent fee creates no additional tax liability.

7 This figure assumes that the award would result in a standard tax bill of $700,000. The AMT calculation might produce a tax bill of approximately $820,000, meaning the consumer's tax liability would increase $120,000.

8 Comm'r v. Banks, 125 S. Ct. 826, 834 (2005).

9 See Appendix A, *infra*, for sample retainer forms.

10 Reply Brief of Petitioner, Comm'r v. Banks, 2004 WL 2190372 (U.S. Sept. 22, 2004).

11 *See, e.g.*, Citizens Legal Env't v. Premium Standard Farms, Inc., 397 F.3d 592 (8th Cir. 2005) (plaintiff not entitled to keep statutory attorney fees).

20.6 Settlement Characterization of Attorney Fees As Statutory or Contingent Can Affect Client Tax Liability

In many cases, a client retainer letter is flexible enough to allow payment of attorney fees either in a statutory amount or as a contingent fee. In that case, care should be taken in drafting any settlement agreement to properly characterize the nature of the consumer attorney's fee.

The AMT implications of a contingent fee will depend on whether and what portion of the full award is taxable. If the full award is not taxable, then a contingent fee will have no AMT consequences, and the consumer is best off structuring the settlement to include a contingent fee, not a statutory fee award. Similarly, if part of the award is taxable and part is non-taxable, it may be best to treat the award as a contingent fee if a tax calculation indicates that the AMT consequences are minimal.

On the other hand, if the attorney fee's AMT consequences are significant, it may be best to structure the award as a statutory fee, rather than a contingent fee, and then take the legal position that statutory fees are excludable from gross income. This issue is one that *Banks* did not decide. The statutory fee will be either totally included or totally excluded from the taxpayer's gross income, depending on the outcome of the legal issue.

20.7 Fees Are Never Taxable in "Civil Rights" Cases

The Internal Revenue Code states that, for judgments and settlements awarded after October 22, 2004, attorney fees and court costs paid by or on behalf of the taxpayer "in connection with any action involving a claim of unlawful discrimination" are not treated as part of the taxpayer's gross income.[12] This rule applies universally—to contingent-fee awards, statutory-fee awards, and attorney fees awarded from a class action common fund. Because the fees are not part of gross income, there are no AMT problems.

Significantly, the Internal Revenue Code does not require the consumer to prevail on the discrimination claim or that this claim be the "primary" claim, only that the action involve a claim of unlawful discrimination. "Unlawful discrimination" is a defined term in the Internal Revenue Code. It includes claims under 42 U.S.C. §§ 1981, 1983 or 1985, Fair Housing Act claims, Americans with Disabilities Act (ADA) claims, and "(18) Any provision of Federal, State, or local law, or common law claims permitted under Federal, State, or local law—(i) providing for the enforcement of civil rights."[13] This provision would seem to include Equal Credit Opportunity Act (ECOA) discrimination claims and claims under state credit discrimination statutes. Of course, the definition also includes 42 U.S.C. § 1983 due process claims that may be alleged in many repossession, foreclosure, and garnishment cases.

20.8 Applicability of Banks to Class Actions

Class attorney fees are awarded pursuant to a statute or a common fund theory. In either case, the issue is whether the fees are included in the gross income of only the class representatives, the class as a whole on a pro rata basis, or are excludable from gross income. As a practical matter, including them on a pro rata basis as income to the whole class will rarely have tax consequences, because the amounts involved will be so small as to create no additional AMT liability. This fact leaves the key question being whether the full amount of either statutory or common fund attorney fees are taxable to the class representatives, an issue not discussed in *Banks*. A May 6, 2005, IRS Private Letter Ruling states that attorney fees paid pursuant to a settlement agreement to class counsel are not included in the gross income of either the class representatives or the class members. In addition, the fees should not be reported by the class defendant to the IRS as gross income for either the class representatives or class members.[14] While indicative of the IRS's present position on this issue, the letter ruling states that, pursuant to 26 U.S.C. § 6110, the letter "may not be used or cited as precedent."

Strong arguments can be made that class representatives do not control the litigation the way they do in an individual case, a key factor in the *Banks* outcome. The class attorney has obligations to the whole class, any class member can oppose a settlement, and the court must approve any settlement and attorney fee award. Amendments to Federal Rule of Civil Procedure 23, effective in December 2003, further increased court supervision of the attorney award and selection of the attorney.

It is also hard to see how the class representative should report as income the full portion of the common fund going to attorney fees without also having to report as income the whole common fund. This approach, of course, would produce impossible tax liabilities for class representatives and would be inconsistent with the general judicial approach of not placing special financial burdens on class representatives. For example, a class representative does not have to agree to bear the total cost of a class action litigation, only

12 26 U.S.C. § 62(a)(19).

13 26 U.S.C. § 62(e).

14 Internal Revenue Service Private Letter Ruling 200518017, 2005 WL 1060971 (May 6, 2005).

a pro rata share of that litigation.[15] Thus the Ninth Circuit, while holding that attorney fees are income to the plaintiff taxpayers, even if the defendant pays the plaintiffs' counsel directly, still assessed each class member only a pro rata share of such fees.[16] The May 6, 2005, IRS Private Letter Ruling offers the better solution.

20.9 What Portion of a Consumer's Damage Recovery Is Taxable?

20.9.1 General

Whether a consumer's damage award is included in the consumer's gross income has two consequences. It determines whether the consumer must pay taxes on the portion of the award the consumer keeps, and it also determines whether there is a potential AMT liability based on a contingent attorney fee.

In general, a settlement or court award providing money to a consumer is considered taxable income, including the following:

- Punitive damages[17]
- Loss of wages or income
- Pre- and post-judgment interest[18]

But there also are a number of important types of recoveries in consumer litigation that are not taxable. In fact, these exceptions to the general rule may be more common in consumer litigation than are instances of the general rule. In addition, as discussed in § 20.11, *infra*, if the consumer wins cancellation of a debt rather than an affirmative award, there are a number of additional theories why the amount cancelled may not be income.

20.9.2 Damages in Personal Injury Cases Are Not Taxable

The Internal Revenue Code states that gross income does not include damages (other than punitive damages) in a suit or settlement on account of personal physical injuries or physical sickness.[19] Such cases must involve tort or tort-type rights.[20] State law decides whether a tort-type injury is involved.[21]

If an action has its origin in a physical injury or physical sickness, then all damages (other than punitive damages) that flow from the physical event are treated as damages received on account of personal physical injuries or physical sickness, whether or not the recipient of the damages is the injured party.[22] If the tortious act causes physical injuries, which in turn cause other damages such as lost wages or pain and suffering, then all of the damages are "on account of" physical injury.[23]

20.9.3 Treatment of "Pain and Suffering" Damages

"Pain and suffering" damages accompanying physical injury are non-taxable, but "emotional distress" damages standing alone are taxable.[24] Moreover, emotional distress symptoms, such as insomnia, headaches, and stomach disorders, will likely be treated as emotional and not physical.[25]

Nevertheless, even when no physical injury is present, emotional distress damages are not taxable, up to the amount paid for medical expenses attributable to treat emotional distress.[26] Because the Code refers to the amount "paid" as opposed to the amount paid by the consumer, amounts paid by insurers should count toward this amount. A judgment or settlement need not say that part of an emotional distress award is compensation for medical expenses for that portion to be non-taxable.

20.9.4 Damages Relating to Overpayment for Goods, Services, and Related Charges Are Not Taxable

Typical consumer cases focus on damages resulting from breach of warranty, deception, or breach of contract. The consumer paid an amount for goods or services or related charges and did not receive in full what the consumer should have received. Consider a consumer who pays for a $10,000

15 Weber v. Goodman, 9 F. Supp. 2d 163, 174 (E.D.N.Y. 1998) (New York Disciplinary Rule 5-103 requiring client to agree to bear cost of litigation in contingent-fee cases only requires client to agree to bear *pro rata* share).

16 Sinyard v. Comm'r, 268 F.3d 756 (9th Cir. 2001).

17 In some states, part of the punitive damages go to a state fund or other governmental recipient. One would expect that that portion of punitive damages would not be taxable to the consumer because the consumer has no control over its disposition.

18 Brabson v. United States, 73 F.3d 1040 (10th Cir. 1996).

19 26 U.S.C. § 104(a)(2). *See also* O'Gilvie v. United States, 519 U.S. 79, 117 S. Ct. 452, 136 L. Ed. 2d 454 (1996) (punitive damages are taxable).

20 Comm'r v. Schleier, 515 U.S. 323, 115 S. Ct. 2159, 132 L. Ed. 2d 294 (1995).

21 Brabson v. United States, 73 F.3d 1040, 1044 (10th Cir. 1996).

22 *See* H.R. Conf. Rep. No. 104-737, at 301 (1996), *reprinted in* 1996 U.S.C.C.A.N. 1474, 1589.

23 *See* Banaitis v. Comm'r, 340 F.3d 1074 (9th Cir. 2003).

24 26 U.S.C. § 104(a).

25 "It is intended that the term emotional distress includes symptoms (e.g., insomnia, headaches, stomach disorders) which may result from such distress." H.R. Conf. Rep. No. 104-737, at 301.2 n.56.

26 26 U.S.C. § 104(a).

car, but the seller delivers a rebuilt wreck worth only $6000 or fails to perform $4000 worth of promised repairs. If the consumer successfully recovers the $4000 overpayment, this recovery should be non-taxable. A recovery in a case in which a car dealer improperly marks up government fees or keeps finance charges as undisclosed kickbacks should also be non-taxable.

Such awards are non-taxable because they are a recovery of capital, not income. Examine the origin of the claim to determine what the damages were paid in lieu of. In many consumer cases, actual damages are unrelated to lost wages or income or emotional distress but instead just represent return of amounts improperly taken from the consumer.

20.9.5 Taxability of Multiple and Statutory Damages

In general, statutory and minimum damages are taxable, unless they can be viewed under state law as compensatory.[27] Sometimes state law treats them as compensatory, as a proxy for a compensatory award that is difficult to prove, when public policy requires the consumer to be fully compensated despite such proof problems. Also consider the situation in which the statute awards minimum or actual damages, whichever is greater. At least a portion of a minimum damages award should be non-taxable if the taxpayer can show the IRS that non-taxable actual damages existed but were not awarded because the minimum damages were greater.

Of course, it will be important to separate out actual damages from the rest of a multiple damages award. For example, when treble damages are awarded, only two-thirds of the award should be automatically considered taxable, with the other third being examined to determine the exact nature of the harm being compensated for to see if that portion of the award is non-taxable.

20.9.6 Distinguishing Non-Taxable Damages from Taxable Damages in Settlement Documents

When a settlement involves both taxable and non-taxable damages, it is important to distinguish what percentage of the settlement relates to which source of damages. The IRS will initially rely on how the settlement agreement allocates the recovery between taxable and non-taxable damages.[28] But this allocation is not controlling, and courts will look past this division to determine the amount that should be counted as to each type of damages.[29] What motivated the company to pay the settlement amount,[30] the allegations contained in the taxpayer's complaint, the evidence presented, and arguments made in any court proceeding are all factors in determining the proper allocation.[31] Other factors include jury awards or any court orders in other cases.[32] Letters from the defense denying liability for certain types of taxable damages should be preserved for possible later litigation with the IRS.

20.10 Recovering As Actual Damages Any Excess Tax Obligations Created by the Need to Litigate

In reaching the dollar amount of a settlement, the tax consequences of the settlement should be considered. The client may want to insist on a higher recovery to offset taxes on the award and any AMT implications of the attorney fee award. Otherwise, such taxes could prevent the client from being made whole.

Some consumers have even successfully sought supplements to court-ordered damages to reflect that the consumer will not be made whole because of the tax implications of the award. For example, in one case, the plaintiff presented evidence that receiving back wages in one tax year and the AMT implications of the attorney fee would prevent the individual from being made whole. The state appellate court agreed that adverse tax consequence are actual damages and should be awarded, based on the broad scope of actual damages under the state statute and the statute's legislative intent to deter misconduct and make victims whole.[33]

20.11 Advantages of Characterizing a Recovery As Loan Forgiveness

20.11.1 Introduction

Consumers frequently bring seller-related claims against the creditor, and the litigation reduces the consumer's debt.

27 Taxable punitive damages are not defined in either the Internal Revenue Code or the Treasury Regulations. They have been defined by the courts, however, as damages that are non-compensatory as determined pursuant to state law. *See* Bagley v. Comm'r, 105 T.C. 396 (1995), *aff'd*, 121 F.3d 393 (8th Cir. 1997).

28 *See* Bagley v. Comm'r, 105 T.C. 396 (1995), *aff'd*, 121 F.3d 393 (8th Cir. 1997).

29 Robinson v. Comm'r, 70 F.3d 34, 37 (5th Cir. 1995).

30 Knuckles v. Comm'r, 349 F.2d 610, 613 (10th Cir. 1965), *aff'g* T.C. Memo. 1964-33, 23 T.C.M. (CCH) 182 (1964).

31 Threlkeld v. Comm'r, 87 T.C. 1294, 1306 (1986), *aff'd*, 848 F.2d 81 (6th Cir. 1988).

32 Miller v. Comm'r, T.C. Memo. 1993-49, 65 T.C.M. (CCH) 1884 (1993), *supplemented by* T.C. Memo. 1993-588, 66 T.C.M. (CCH) 1568 (1993), *aff'd*, 60 F.3d 823 (4th Cir. 1995).

33 Blaney v. Int'l Ass'n of Machinists & Aerospace Workers, Dist. No. 160, 55 P.3d 1208 (Wash. Ct. App. 2002).

The settlement often can then be structured, not as an affirmative recovery to the consumer, but as forgiveness of debt, which may provide new grounds to claim the amount as non-taxable. These grounds—principally the consumer's insolvency or bankruptcy—will be discussed below.

20.11.2 Four Exceptions When Loan Forgiveness Not Treated As Client Income

Debt that is canceled, forgiven, or discharged is often called DOI (discharge of indebtedness) income and is generally treated as part of the taxpayer's gross income.[34] The taxpayer declaring this income should use IRS Form 982.[35] But there are four important exceptions to the rule that DOI is taxable income.

20.11.3 Bankruptcy

The Internal Revenue Code specifically excludes from gross income any DOI income resulting from a discharge made in a bankruptcy case.[36] The timing of the bankruptcy filing is crucial. The bankruptcy exception does not apply if a debt forgiveness agreement is reached before the bankruptcy is filed. If the debt is discharged after the bankruptcy is filed, the DOI is entirely excludable from gross income.[37]

20.11.4 Insolvency

The Code specifically excludes from gross income any debt cancellation made while the debtor was insolvent,[38] to the extent of the insolvency. Consider, for example, a taxpayer with assets valued at $18,000 and liabilities of $26,000. This taxpayer is insolvent by $8000. If $12,000 of the debt is forgiven, the debtor has $12,000 worth of DOI income. $8000 of the DOI income would be excludable but not the other $4000 (because the taxpayer is no longer insolvent once the first $8000 has been forgiven).

Insolvency is defined as excess of liabilities over the fair market value of assets, as determined immediately prior to the discharge.[39] It is uncertain whether exempt assets should be included in the asset value. A long-established rule provided that exempt assets did not count as part of the consumer's assets.[40] However, a 2001 Tax Court ruling held the contrary, relying on 1980 tax law changes. This ruling has not been reviewed by an appellate court, and commentators have criticized it.[41] Contingent liabilities are counted as liabilities if it is "more likely than not" that the taxpayer will be called upon to pay the obligation in the amount claimed.[42]

20.11.5 Disputed or Contingent Debts

In many consumer cases, the amount of a debt or even the existence of a debt is disputed. "Forgiveness" of such a debt does not give rise to income.[43] This doctrine usually applies to unliquidated, disputed debts, and some courts even require fraud or material misrepresentation.[44] A related doctrine involves a purchase price reduction, in which the price of personalty or realty bought on credit is lowered, resulting in a lowering of the indebtedness. Such debt forgiveness is not taxable.[45]

For example, consider a consumer claim against the creditor under the FTC Holder Rule that a seller's deception resulted in the consumer paying too much for a motor vehicle, causing an excessive amount financed and finance charge in the loan agreement. Reduction of such an indebtedness should fall under the purchase price reduction and disputed debt exceptions and not be taxable.

In addition, contingent liabilities that are canceled are not treated as discharge of indebtedness income.[46] For example,

---

34 26 U.S.C. § 61(a)(12). It is also called cancellation of debt income (COD income).

35 This form, "Reduction of Tax Attributes Due to Discharge of Indebtedness," appears in many respects to be directed only at corporate taxpayers. Nevertheless IRS personnel recommend that the form be used by individual consumers as well. It is clear, however, that most individual taxpayers do not have any tax attributes that can be reduced. Therefore, only Part I of the form will be relevant.

36 26 U.S.C. § 108(a)(1)(A).

37 26 U.S.C. § 108(d)(2). If the bankruptcy exclusion applies, the taxpayer, to be safe, should file Form 982 but not include any amount in gross income on his or her tax return. IRS special procedures personnel recommend that an explanatory statement be attached to the tax return explaining the basis for not including the amounts reported on the 1099-C form. This statement can be in the simple form of: "The 1099-C DOI income reported by XYZ Bank is based on a discharge of indebtedness in bankruptcy under Title 11 United States Code. Therefore it is not includable as gross income pursuant to 26 U.S.C. § 108(a)(1)(A)."

38 26 U.S.C. § 108(a)(1)(B). The taxpayer has the burden of proving that an exception applies. *See* Danenberg v. Comm'r, 73 T.C. 370 (1980). In order to qualify for the insolvency exclusion, the taxpayer must file Form 982 together with a description of the taxpayer's assets and liabilities as of the date of the debt cancellation.

39 26 U.S.C. § 108(d)(3).

40 *See* Marcus Estate v. Comm'r, 34 T.C.M. (CCH) 38 (1975); Cole v. Comm'r, 42 B.T.A. 1110 (1940).

41 *See, e.g.*, Note & Comment, *Measuring Assets and Liabilities Under the I.R.C. 108 Insolvency Exclusion*, 19 Bank. Dev. J. 429 (2003).

42 Merkel v. Comm'r, 109 T.C. 463, 483 (1997), *aff'd*, 192 F.3d 844 (9th Cir. 1999).

43 Zarin v. Comm'r, 916 F.2d 110 (3d Cir. 1990).

44 Preslar v. Comm'r, 167 F.3d 1323 (10th Cir. 1999).

45 *See* Zarin v. Comm'r, 916 F.2d 110 (3d Cir. 1990).

46 *See* Priv. Ltr. Rul. 96-42-041, 1996 PLR LEXIS 1411 (July 18, 1996).

if a car sale is contingent on financing and falls through, no taxable income is created by the cancellation of the indebtedness.

20.11.6 Forgiveness of Interest and Fees Is Not Taxable; TIL Rescission As an Important Example

In most consumer transactions, only principal amounts canceled are DOI income. Canceled interest and fees are generally not counted as income, because such amounts were never available as income to the debtor. It may be advantageous to draft a settlement agreement to specify that a portion of the loan forgiveness relates to canceled interest or fees, instead of to principal.

Truth in Lending rescission of a home mortgage is an important example of a non-taxable event involving forgiven interest and fees. The rescission does not forgive any principal but just erases any liability for interest and fees. Past payments made toward interest and fees are returned or applied to reduce the principal, and the consumer tenders the net amount financed.

20.11.7 The Amount Saved in Interest and Fees Is Not Income

What happens, though, when a consumer has already taken a deduction for the interest portion of past payments and that past interest payment is returned or re-characterized as a payment toward principal? According to one court, the amount previously taken as a deduction becomes income in the current year, under the "tax benefit" rule.[47]

Practice Tip[48]

Settlement agreements should include a provision that the creditor not report to the IRS the debt cancellation as income. Provide the creditor with a letter spelling out the reasons why the cancellation is not taxable—for example, the debt is contested, the settlement is a non-taxable purchase price reduction, or the debtor is insolvent. Inform the creditor that there is no IRS penalty for not reporting a debt as income "if it is shown that such failure is due to reasonable cause and not to willful neglect,"[49] which reasonable cause is provided by the letter to the creditor. The maximum penalty for failure to report income is $100 per return,[50] so the creditor has little at stake. By contrast, there is a great deal at stake for the consumer if a creditor incorrectly reports the forgiveness as income, as the consumer will have to obtain tax representation to properly complete the tax return.

20.12 Implications of Client's Receipt of Form 1099-C, Evidencing Debt Cancellation

20.12.1 The Form 1099-C Reporting Requirement

When a settlement reduces the consumer's loan obligation, creditors frequently report to IRS the amount as income to the consumer on IRS Form 1099-C. A lender must file this form with IRS to report all debts over $600 forgiven at less than full consideration pursuant to an agreement between the financial entity and the taxpayer.[51] Any information the creditor provides to IRS in Form 1099-C must also be furnished to the taxpayer in a written statement sent on or before January 31st of the year following the year in which the cancellation was made.[52]

20.12.2 Taxpayer Need Not Always Treat DOI Reported on 1099-C As Includable in Gross Income

The filing of a Form 1099-C does not necessarily reflect a taxable event under the Internal Revenue Code. The lender is likely to file Form 1099-C without regard to whether one of the several exclusions from gross income discussed above applies. In addition, some 1099-C forms are filed by creditors in error in situations in which filing is not required by the IRS at all. Of course, a settlement agreement involving debt forgiveness can cover this issue by addressing whether the creditor will submit a 1099-C form and in what amount.

When taxpayers receive a 1099-C, they or their tax professional must make an independent analysis, distinct from that performed by the creditor, about whether the discharge of indebtedness must be included as part of the taxpayer's gross income or whether one of the exclusions applies.

47 Schlifke v. Comm'r, 61 T.C.M. (CCH) 1697 (1991).

48 Thanks to Dianne Thompson of Land of Lincoln Legal Assistance Foundation for the practice tip.

49 26 U.S.C. § 6724(a).

50 26 U.S.C. § 6721.

51 *See* 26 C.F.R. §§ 1.6050P-1(a), 1.6050P-1T(b)(2)(B), 1.6050P-1(b)(2)(F).

52 *See* 26 C.F.R. § 1.6050P-1(f)(2).

20.12.3 Consequences of Creditor Filing an Improper 1099-C

A creditor is unlikely to be liable to the consumer simply for inaccurately reporting income on a 1099-C Form. However, if an improper motive can be shown, there may be an unfair and deceptive act or practice involved. In addition, some creditors have used the threat of filing a 1099-C Form as a collection device. Such conduct is illegal because the threat itself is a collection effort and therefore the debt has not actually been forgiven.[53]

Similarly, a creditor's submission of a 1099-C form indicates that the debt is forgiven. Unless the creditor first amends the form, this submission should stop any collection action and end the consumer's liability on the debt.[54] A creditor that aggressively sends out 1099-C forms may actually be helping the consumer as well as opening itself up for debt collection harassment liability if it continues to collect on the debt.

20.13 Ten Tax Planning Tips

These ten tips are explained in more detail throughout this issue. Practitioners should consult a tax professional before following one of these tips in a particular case.

53 *See* Sledge v. Sands, 182 F.R.D. 255 (N.D. Ill. 1998).

54 *In re* Crosby, 261 B.R. 470 (Bankr. D. Kan. 2001).

- Determine which has better tax consequences—structuring a settlement with a contingent or a statutory attorney fee award.
- Plead and prove physical injury whenever possible.
- Add a civil rights claim whenever possible.
- Document all medical costs relating to pain and suffering, including payments by insurance companies.
- Draft settlements and retain documents substantiating that a high percentage of a damage award is of a non-taxable nature.
- Compute the after tax value of a settlement or judgment and consider seeking additional damages to cover tax losses caused by the need to litigate.
- File bankruptcy before a debt is forgiven, not after.
- Settlements may be more advantageous if they forgive interest and fees instead of principal.
- That a 1099-C lists debt forgiveness as income does not always mean the taxpayer must declare the debt forgiveness as income.
- A creditor sending a 1099-C must stop all collection efforts against the client on the forgiven debt.

Chapter 21 Trial of Consumer Cases

By Carolyn Carter[1]

21.1 Jury Trial

21.1.1 Right to Jury Trial

Federal consumer protection statutes typically do not specify whether there is a right to trial by jury. As a result, the question is controlled by the Seventh Amendment, which guarantees a right to jury trial "in suits at common law" in which the amount in controversy exceeds $20. The Supreme Court has interpreted the constitutional right to jury trial to extend to any claim that involves rights and remedies of the type traditionally enforced in an action at law.[2] If a statutory claim is "at least analogous to" matters tried at common law, and the plaintiff seeks legal as opposed to equitable relief, then there is a right to jury trial.[3] Since plaintiffs under most federal consumer protection statutes seek money damages for statutory versions of traditional claims such as fraud, defamation, and breach of contract, they should have a Seventh Amendment right to jury trial. Accordingly, courts have held that the Seventh Amendment guarantees a right to jury trial in cases under the Fair Debt Collection Practices Act[4] and the Truth in Lending Act,[5] both of which are part of the Consumer Credit Protection Act (CCPA). While there is little or no case law, it is likely that courts will find a right to jury trial under other portions of the CCPA, too.

The Seventh Amendment does not apply to state law claims filed in state court.[6] Instead, whether jury trial is available depends on the state constitution and whether a state statute grants or denies jury trial. Jurisdictions split on whether jury trial is available for UDAP claims.[7] The Eighth Circuit holds that the Seventh Amendment governs state claims that are tried in federal court, so jury trial is available for UDAP money damage claims even when state law precludes jury trial in state court.[8]

21.1.2 Demanding a Jury Trial

In federal court, where cases pursuant to the federal Consumer Credit Protection Act are usually brought, a demand for trial by jury must be made "not later than 10 days after the service of the last pleading."[9] The better practice is to request a trial by jury in the consumer's complaint. The method of requesting a jury trial—for example, doing so in the caption—is often governed by local

1 Carolyn Carter is Deputy Director of Advocacy at NCLC. She was formerly co-director of Legal Services, Inc., in Gettysburg, Pennsylvania, and director of the Law Reform Office of the Cleveland Legal Aid Society. She is the editor of *Pennsylvania Consumer Law* and the first edition of *Ohio Consumer Law*; co-author of *Automobile Fraud* (2003), *Consumer Warranty Law* (2d ed. 2001), *Unfair and Deceptive Acts and Practices* (6th ed. 2004), *Repossessions and Foreclosures* (5th ed. 2002 and Supp.); and contributing author to *Fair Debt Collection* (5th ed. 2004 and Supp.), *Truth in Lending* (5th ed. 2003 and Supp.), and *The Cost of Credit: Regulation, Preemption, and Industry Abuses* (3d ed. 2005). She is the 1992 recipient of the Vern Countryman Consumer Award and is currently a member of the Federal Reserve Board's Consumer Advisory Council.

2 Curtis v. Loether, 415 U.S. 189, 94 S. Ct. 1005, 39 L. Ed. 2d 260 (1974) (jury trial required in Civil Rights Act case). *See also* Feltner v. Columbia Pictures TV, 523 U.S. 340, 118 S. Ct. 1279, 140 L. Ed. 2d 438 (1998) (Seventh Amendment provides right to jury trial in action for statutory damages under Copyright Act).

3 City of Monterey v. Del Monte Dunes, 526 U.S. 687, 708, 119 S. Ct. 1624, 143 L. Ed. 2d 882 (1999) (section 1983 suit for damages for regulatory taking); Chauffers, Teamsters & Helpers Local 391 v. Terry, 494 U.S. 558, 110 S. Ct. 1339, 108 L. Ed. 2d 519 (1990) (workers' suit under NLRA for wages lost due to union's failure to represent them properly); Tull v. United States, 481 U.S. 412, 107 S. Ct. 1831, 95 L. Ed. 2d 365 (1987) (Clean Water Act penalties).

4 Kobs v. Arrow Serv. Bureau, Inc., 134 F.3d 893 (7th Cir. 1998); Sibley v. Fulton DeKalb Collection Serv., 677 F.2d 830 (11th Cir. 1982).

5 Barber v. Kimbrell's, Inc., 577 F.2d 216 (4th Cir. 1998).

6 City of Monterey v. Del Monte Dunes, 526 U.S. 687, 719, 119 S. Ct. 1624, 143 L. Ed. 2d 882 (1999); Gasperini v. Ctr. for Humanities, 518 U.S. 415, 418, 116 S. Ct. 2211, 135 L. Ed. 2d 659 (1996).

7 National Consumer Law Center, Unfair and Deceptive Acts and Practices § 7.9.2.2 (6th ed. 2004).

8 Grabinski v. Blue Springs Ford Sales, 136 F.3d 565, 571 (8th Cir. 1998) (UDAP claim); Kampa v. White Consol. Indus., Inc., 115 F.3d 585 (8th Cir. 1997) (jury trial available in federal court notwithstanding provisions of Minnesota human rights act).

9 Fed. R. Civ. P. 38(b).

rules. Once a trial by jury has been demanded, it may be withdrawn only upon the consent of all parties.[10]

21.1.3 Preparing for Jury Trial

Many cases are best presented to a jury rather than a judge. Juries are more likely to empathize with a consumer or fraud victim.

It is important to keep the case simple and the themes clear for the jury. Technical or trivial claims should be avoided.

Many experienced practitioners prepare the jury instructions at the beginning of the case, before discovery is commenced. Then they use the instructions as a guide to what evidence will be needed to establish the elements of each cause of action and to refute all the defenses. Preparing jury instructions early in the case helps focus discovery and avoid unnecessary battles. Sample jury instructions, *voir dire* questions, and opening and closing arguments are found on the companion CD-Rom to this volume.[11]

Practicing at least opening and closing arguments before a mock jury is a valuable way to evaluate a case and shape its themes. Ideally, the mock jury will reflect the demographics of the jury pool, but one experienced consumer attorney recruits five random people off the street on a Saturday morning and pays them $20 each to listen to mock opening and closing arguments and to then give their candid comments over pizza at lunchtime. This technique, while less scientific, is simple and produces useful results. It can also be invaluable to have an office staff member observe the opening argument—and, if possible, the whole trial—and report periodically on the responses of the judge and jury.

After a case is over, whether successful or unsuccessful, it is valuable to ask the trial judge or the bailiff for suggestions about how to improve. Approaching jurors to discuss how they reacted to the case is also extremely helpful.[12] It can help the attorney build on success and avoid mistakes in the future.

21.1.4 Voir Dire

The procedure for selecting juries differs from state to state and between federal and state courts. In some courts, the attorneys conduct the *voir dire*; in other courts, the judge does the questioning, and may or may not accept suggested questions from the attorneys. Sample *voir dire* questions can be found on the companion CD-Rom to this volume and on National Consumer Law Center, *Consumer Law Pleadings* (Cumulative CD-Rom and Index Guide).

In a jurisdiction in which the attorneys conduct *voir dire*, the consumer's attorney should use the opportunity to begin selling the consumer's case to the jury. The attorney should convey interest in the jurors as individuals and show appreciation that they are there. Using open questions, the consumer's attorney should ferret out any juror bias toward the attorney, the consumer, the consumer's experts, or consumers in general. Is the client rich, poor, young, old, black, white, Spanish-speaking, highly educated, uneducated, a celebrity, gay, disabled, a welfare recipient, unemployed, cross-eyed, or blonde? Is the consumer's expert female? Would a juror be able to give the same weight to an American expert as to the Mercedes expert whose accent is German?

The attorney must decide if any personal prejudice may affect the outcome and must confront this issue without blame or shame at the outset. Trial lawyers themselves are not popular these days. Some citizens are so disgusted with the process that they can not be trusted to be a fair part of it. Consumers themselves—and plaintiffs' trial lawyers—may have been portrayed poorly in the media, particularly around election time when industry pours money into advertising campaigns against consumer causes. A *voir dire* question that may be helpful in weeding out jurors who are prejudiced against consumer protection lawsuits is: "How many of you think there are too many lawsuits against car dealers (or whatever type of seller or lender is involved in the case) for cheating people?"

Voir dire is also a good occasion to bring up potentially damaging evidence or themes that the defense is likely to raise. The consumer's attorney can characterize these issues in a way sympathetic to the plaintiff and ask whether any of the jurors agree with the defense position. Finally, it is important to find out attitudes toward authority. Some otherwise intelligent people think that, if a large corporation does something, it must be okay. These subtle sub-surface biases can create havoc in jury deliberation rooms.

The attorney should ascertain potential jurors' attitudes toward various categories of damages, including punitive damages or civil penalties. If the case seeks punitive damages, some attorneys make a point of describing what they are in *voir dire* and asking whether any jurors have any objection to, or a fixed opinion against, awarding punitive damages. One experienced automobile fraud attorney stresses to the jury in *voir dire*, opening, and closing that the consumer is seeking only appropriate punitive damages and that a runaway verdict is not justice. By making it clear that the consumer is not greedy, this approach builds credibility with the jury and also makes it less likely that the defense will succeed on a post-trial motion to overturn a punitive

10 Fed. R. Civ. P. 38(d).

11 *See also* § 21.5, *infra*.

12 Jurors in some states may not be approached in way that would embarrass them or dissuade them from future jury service. *See* Comm. for Lawyer Discipline v. Benton, 980 S.W.2d 425, 41 Tex. Sup. Ct. J. 1250 (1998). *See also* Haeberle v. Texas Int'l Airlines, 739 F.2d 1019 (5th Cir. 1984) (local rule limited post-trial communications with jurors, and leave to interview jurors was denied).

damages award. Another useful *voir dire* question is whether any jurors have a fixed opinion against a person seeking money damages in a court of law.

It is a judgment call whether to ask potential jurors about bad experiences with the defendant's industry. For example, in an automobile fraud case the attorney might ask if any juror has ever been cheated by a car dealer or has a family member who has. If *voir dire* is conducted in front of the whole panel, a "yes" answer may provoke feelings of solidarity among the jurors, especially if the defendant's attorney then has that juror removed. The plaintiff's attorney may be able to rehabilitate such a juror by asking whether the juror will be able to separate the prior bad experience from his or her ability to decide the case based solely on the evidence. On the other hand, if the judge readily excuses jurors for bias, a "yes" answer may disqualify sympathetic jurors. The consumer's attorney can balance the question about having been cheated by a car dealer by also asking whether there are any members of the jury panel whose experience with car dealers has been so good that they would be reluctant to accept testimony that was critical of a car dealer. An alternative way to explore these issues is to ask if there are any members of the panel who would not mind it if they purchased a rebuilt wreck and that fact had not been disclosed to them. This more hypothetical question also has the advantage of conveying to the jury that the normal response is to be upset by the sale of an undisclosed wreck.

21.2 Evidence

21.2.1 Use of Exhibits at Trial

Exhibits can make the case vivid and concrete for the trier of fact. Examples include

- photographs of damaged or defective parts of a vehicle or the parts themselves;
- blow-ups of critical documents; and
- charts tracing a car's title history.

Computerizing trial exhibits can be effective, especially if the case involves a large number of documents that the jury will have to scrutinize. Some companies such as court reporting services will computerize trial exhibits for attorneys. A law office with a scanner and a computer can also handle the work. Each document should be given an identifying number, and data fields should be set up for the date, description, and other relevant information about each document. In the courtroom, the attorney needs to have an assistant to pull up the relevant documents on the computer screen. There must be enough monitors, close enough to the jury, so that jurors can see the documents easily. With some presentation programs, relevant parts of a document can be blown up or highlighted during testimony or argument.

21.2.2 Evidence of Other Bad Acts

Evidence of the defendant's similar acts toward others is powerful evidence. Many people are reluctant to believe that a seller or lender deliberately misled or cheated someone, so they naturally incline to accept the "innocent error" defense. Proof that the defendant has acted the same way toward others explodes this defense. Proof of similar wrongdoing toward others is also an extremely important factor in winning punitive damages.

The general rule under Rule 404 of the Federal Rules of Evidence and analogous state rules is that a consumer can not introduce evidence of other bad acts to prove the defendant's character. In most cases, however, the consumer will be seeking to introduce this evidence to prove matters other than the defendant's character. Nonetheless, there are at least ten exceptions that make this evidence admissible in many, if not most, consumer cases:

1. *Other bad acts are admissible to show intent or motive.*[13] Intent is certainly relevant to any fraud or RICO claim. Some UDAP statutes require a showing of intent as a precondition for enhanced damages. A number of other consumer protection statutes make intent explicitly relevant. For example, the Fair Credit Reporting Act makes punitive damages available only for "willful" violations,[14] and the

13 Bird v. John Chezik Homerun, Inc., 152 F.3d 1014 (8th Cir. 1998); United States v. Mora, 81 F.3d 781 (8th Cir. 1996), *cert. denied*, 519 U.S. 950 (1996); United States v. Guyon, 27 F.3d 723 (1st Cir. 1994); United States v. Harvey, 959 F.2d 1371 (7th Cir. 1992); Kerr v. First Commodity Corp., 735 F.2d 281 (8th Cir. 1984); Austin v. Loftsgaarden, 675 F.2d 168 (8th Cir. 1982), *rev'd on other grounds*, 478 U.S. 647 (1986); Shoals Ford, Inc. v. McKinney (Ala. 1992); Lee v. Hodge, 180 Ariz. 97, 882 P.2d 408 (1994); Smith v. Walt Bennett Ford, Inc., 864 S.W.2d 817, 828 (Ark. 1993); Walter v. Hall, 940 P.2d 991 (Colo. Ct. App. 1996), *aff'd on other grounds*, 969 P.2d 224 (1998); Meyers v. Cornwell Quality Tools, Inc., 41 Conn. App. 19, 674 A.2d 444 (1996) (evidence of prior acts admissible to prove intent); Dix v. Am. Bankers Life Assurance Co., 429 Mich. 410, 415 N.W.2d 206 (1987); Cates v. Darland, 537 P.2d 336 (Okla. 1975); Rugemer v. Rhea, 153 Or. App. 400, 957 P.2d 184 (1997) (evidence that defendant told exactly the same lie on another occasion is admissible to show that he lied to plaintiff and that he acted in bad faith); Schmitt v. Lalancette, 830 A.2d 16 (Vt. 2003) (trial court abused discretion in ordering plaintiff not to contact other customers of defendant identified through investigation, and was unjustified in denying discovery of identities of other customers in UDAP and breach-of-contract suit). *See also* Brockman v. Regency Fin. Corp., 124 S.W.3d 43, 51 (Mo. App. 2004) (other acts admissible to show intent in malicious prosecution action).

14 15 U.S.C. § 1681n. *See* National Consumer Law Center, Fair Credit Reporting § 11.4.1.2 (5th ed. 2002 and Supp.).

Fair Debt Collection Practices Act lists intent as one of the factors for determining the amount of statutory damages.[15]

2. *Evidence of other bad acts may be admissible to show preparation or a plan on the part of the defendants.* Such evidence is particularly relevant in cases alleging a civil conspiracy.[16] It also may be an essential element of a claim against a principal who was not directly involved in the deception against the consumer but who may be liable for directing others in their fraudulent activity.

3. *Evidence of other acts is admissible to show the defendants' knowledge.* A principal's knowledge of the fraudulent activities of agents is relevant, for example, to establish the principal's liability for the fraud committed against a particular consumer[17] or to establish that the defendants had the specialized knowledge necessary to run the fraudulent scheme.[18] Some courts require proof of the defendant's knowledge as a condition of UDAP liability for non-disclosure.[19] Treble damages or attorney fees may also depend on proof that the violation was knowing.[20] *Scienter* is an element of a fraud claim.[21] Even a consent order can establish the defendant's knowledge.[22]

4. *Evidence of other bad acts is admissible to prove absence of mistake or accident.*[23] Thus it is highly relevant to rebut any claim that the defendant made an innocent error. Even settlement of prior claims can be admissible for this purpose.[24]

5. *That the defendant's conduct against the consumer was in conformity with the defendant's habit or routine practice is another basis to introduce evidence of other bad acts.*[25] In other words, if there is a dispute as to how the defendant handled a transaction, the way it normally handled transactions is relevant evidence.

6. *Evidence of other bad acts is admissible in support of punitive damages.* In *BMW v. Gore*, the United States Supreme Court noted: "Certainly, evidence that a defendant has repeatedly engaged in prohibited conduct while knowing or suspecting that it was unlawful would provide relevant support for an argument that strong medicine is required to cure the defendant's disrespect for the law. . . . [R]epeated misconduct is more reprehensible than an individual instance of malfeasance."[26] This evidence is relevant for the same reason in states where the judge has discretion about whether to award multiple UDAP damages, depending on factors such as reprehensibility.[27]

7. *Evidence of other bad acts is required for claims under state and federal RICO statutes because the elements of a RICO claim include showing of a pattern of racketeering activity.*[28] The consumer not only can, but must, introduce pattern evidence if such a claim is added as an additional count in a UDAP case.

8. *Evidence of prior bad acts is relevant when the state imposes a "public interest" requirement on UDAP suits, requiring the consumer to show that the defendant's misdeeds have been repeated or affect others.*[29]

9. *Certain prior convictions relate to a crime involving dishonesty or false statement and thus are admissible for impeachment under Federal Rule of Evidence 609(a)(2).*[30] It is helpful to have a certified copy of the court record of the conviction available for introduction. Evidence of other bad

---

15 15 U.S.C. § 1692k(b).

16 United States v. Gold Unlimited, Inc., 177 F.3d 472 (6th Cir. 1999) (prior acts admissible in pyramid scheme criminal case to show knowledge or plan); Duval v. Midwest Auto City, Inc., 425 F. Supp. 1381 (D. Neb. 1977), *aff'd*, 578 F.2d 721 (8th Cir. 1978); Shoals Ford, Inc. v. McKinney, 605 So. 2d 1197 (Ala. 1992).

17 *See, e.g.*, Parrish v. Luckie, 963 F.2d 201 (8th Cir. 1992); United States v. Hugh Chalmers Chevrolet-Toyota, Inc., 800 F.2d 737 (8th Cir. 1986).

18 *See* United States v. Massey, 48 F.3d 1560 (10th Cir. 1995), *cert. denied*, 515 U.S. 1167 (1995); Commonwealth v. Source One Assocs., 436 Mass. 118, 763 N.E.2d 42 (2002).

19 *See* National Consumer Law Center, Unfair and Deceptive Acts and Practices §§ 4.2.14.3.4, 4.2.4.2 (6th ed. 2004).

20 *See* National Consumer Law Center, Unfair and Deceptive Acts and Practices §§ 8.4.2.3.1, 8.8.2.1 (6th ed. 2004).

21 *See* National Consumer Law Center, Automobile Fraud § 7.4 (2d ed. 2003 and Supp.).

22 Kerr v. First Commodity Corp., 735 F.2d 281 (8th Cir. 1984).

23 United States v. Murphy, 935 F.2d 899 (7th Cir. 1991); United States v. Gomez, 927 F.2d 1530, 1534 (9th Cir. 1991); United States v. Greenwood, 796 F.2d 49, 53 (4th Cir. 1986); Orkin Exterminating Co. v. Jeter, 832 So. 2d 25 (Ala. 2001); Lee v. Hodge, 180 Ariz. 97, 882 P.2d 408 (1994); Brockman v. Regency Fin. Corp., 124 S.W.3d 43, 51 (Mo. App. 2004).

24 Bradbury v. Phillips Petroleum Co., 815 F.2d 1356 (10th Cir. 1987).

25 *See* Fed. R. Evid. 406. *See also* Mobil Exploration & Producing U.S., Inc. v. Cajun Constr. Servs., 45 F.3d 96 (5th Cir. 1995).

26 517 U.S. 559, 116 S. Ct. 1589, 134 L. Ed. 2d 809, 827 (1996) (citations omitted). *Accord* State Farm Mut. Auto. Ins. Co. v. Campbell, 538 U.S. 408, 123 S. Ct. 1513, 155 L. Ed. 2d 585 (2003); TXO Prod. Corp. v. Alliance Resources Corp., 509 U.S. 443, 113 S. Ct. 2711, 125 L. Ed. 2d 366 (1993) (evidence of defendant's wrongdoing in other parts of the country was a proper factor for punitive damages); Pacific Mut. Life Ins. Co. v. Haslip, 499 U.S. 1, 111 S. Ct. 1032, 113 L. Ed. 2d 1 (1991) (frequency of similar past conduct is a proper factor for punitive damages); Bird v. John Chezik Homerun, Inc., 152 F.3d 1014 (8th Cir. 1998) (evidence of prior sales of concealed wrecks admissible in support of punitive damage claim); *Ex parte* Nat'l Sec. Ins. Co., 773 So. 2d 461 (Ala. 2000) (plaintiff who seeks punitive damages may discover names and addresses of consumers who entered into similar transactions); MacTools, Inc. v. Griffin, 126 Idaho 193, 879 P.2d 1126 (1994); Burbach v. Investors Mgmt. Corp., 484 S.E.2d 119 (S.C. App. 1997) (approving jury instructions). *See* National Consumer Law Center, Automobile Fraud § 7.10.6 (2d ed. 2003 and Supp.).

27 *See* National Consumer Law Center, Unfair and Deceptive Acts and Practices § 8.4.2.3 (6th ed. 2004).

28 *See id.* §§ 9.2, 9.3.

29 Burbach v. Investors Mgmt. Corp., 484 S.E.2d 119 (S.C. App. 1997); Cotton v. Kronenberg, 111 Wash. App. 258, 44 P.3d 878 (2002). *See generally* National Consumer Law Center, Unfair and Deceptive Acts and Practices § 7.5.3 (6th ed. 2004).

30 *See* United States v. Harris, 512 F. Supp. 1174 (D. Conn. 1981).

acts can also be used to impeach a defendant who claims that the company always follows certain proper procedures or has a sterling record.[31]

10. Evidence of prior acts is admissible when they are necessary to complete the story of the main transaction or are inextricably intertwined with it.[32] For example, evidence of a dealer's prior sales of the same defective vehicle is admissible.[33]

If other acts are offered under Rule 404 of the Federal Rules of Evidence or a state analog, they must be similar to those involving the plaintiff. One court has suggested that, in determining whether evidence of acts toward others is admissible, courts should consider the length of time between the past incidents and the current incident; the factual similarity of the incidents; the similarity of the defendant's conduct, the advantage the defendants secured, and the harm to the victims in the past incidents and the current incident; and the number of prior incidents as compared to the number of prior opportunities to conduct the unfair conduct.[34] The trial court has discretion to exclude evidence of satisfied customers offered by the defendant, as such evidence merely shows that the fraud is succeeding.[35]

When deciding whether to admit evidence of other bad acts, in most jurisdictions the court will have the duty to weigh its probative value against any prejudicial effect that it may have.[36] Also, the court will not want to try twenty-five cases when it is possible to try just one, so the evidence should be presented in a way that will not overwhelm the main case.

If evidence of other bad acts is relevant to the case, it is also discoverable. Decisions allowing discovery of customer lists and other sources of information about similar transactions are discussed in § 16.2.2, *supra*. Use of evidence of a defendant's other bad acts is examined in more detail in § 9.8.1 of another National Consumer Law Center manual *Automobile Fraud*.

31 *See, e.g.*, S. Energy Homes, Inc. v. Washington, 774 So. 2d 505 (Ala. 2002); Colony Cadillac & Oldsmobile, Inc. v. Yerdon, 505 A.2d 98 (Me. 1986).

32 *See, e.g.*, United States v. Stitt, 250 F.3d 878, 888 (4th Cir. 2001).

33 Canada v. Hudson Chevrolet-Olds-Pontiac-GMC Truck, Inc., 2003 WL 1406601 (Ky. App. Mar. 21, 2003).

34 Burbach v. Investors Mgmt. Corp., 484 S.E.2d 119 (S.C. App. 1997).

35 United States v. Ciccone, 219 F.3d 1078 (9th Cir. 2000). *See also* FTC v. Five-Star Auto Club, Inc., 97 F. Supp. 2d 502 (S.D.N.Y. 2000) (existence of satisfied customers is no defense).

36 *See, e.g.*, Fed. R. Evid. 403.

21.3 Witnesses

21.3.1 Helping Fraud Victims Prepare for Testimony

Fraud victims often are naive and have low self-esteem—that is why they were easy prey. They are often helpful, cooperative people who like to please others and are easily manipulated, both in a sales situation and on cross-examination. The consumer lawyer's job is to help such victims present their stories to a judge or jury without collapsing on cross-examination.

In preparing fraud victims for deposition or trial testimony, it can be helpful to make a vivid, concrete dichotomy between the victim's lawyer and the defense lawyer. One attorney puts on a funny hat when playing the role of the defense attorney, believing that this helps victims visualize the role of the defense attorney and gives them a funny mental image of the questioner that will help them relax later.

The consumer's attorney needs to prepare the victim for questions about why the victim did not read the contract. The number of people who hide illiteracy is surprising. If the victim shows any signs of reading problems, ask the consumer and the consumer's family about how well the consumer can read.

Prepare the consumer for other likely questions, such as "Did you talk to anybody about your testimony today?" Make sure consumer witnesses know not to answer questions they do not understand, to ask that unintelligible questions be rephrased, to wait until the judge rules on an objection before answering a question, and to tell the truth courageously no matter how painful.

At trial, if the consumer becomes confused, emotional, or beaten down, use redirect examination to rehabilitate the client. Ask short, simple questions:

- "Does money matter to you?"
- "Are you short on money?"
- "Did anyone tell you that you were paying $10,000 for this car?"
- "Did you want to give the dealer any extra money?"
- "Did you have any extra money to give anyone?"

21.3.2 Order of Witnesses

In presenting a fraud case, remember that jurors remember best what they hear first and last. Starting the trial with an expert witness[37] who has examined the transaction and can explain the economic and personal dynamics of the fraud can help the trier of fact understand the transaction.

37 Chapter 17, *infra*, discusses the use of expert witnesses.

Then the trier of fact is more likely to view the victim's weaknesses and vulnerabilities in the context of the fraud. The attorney should weigh, however, whether this approach over-complicates the issues or implies that special expertise is necessary to understand them. Having the plaintiff testify first also gives the jury an understanding of what the case is about. Either the plaintiff or an expert will usually face vigorous cross-examination, however.

Another approach is to call the defendant or an employee of the defendant first, to nail down the defendant's story so that it can be attacked throughout the trial. This strategy is particularly effective if the jury gets an early impression that the defendant is lying or unscrupulous. If compelling photos are going to be introduced, another effective approach is to blow them up, start with a witness who can identify them, and then keep them on an easel to refer to during the trial. Most attorneys wait to present evidence about damages until the last part of the trial.

21.4 Countering Defense Arguments

In preparing a consumer case for trial, the attorney should develop evidence to counter the themes that the defense is likely to raise. One common defense theme is that the defendant has the right to sell its product, and legitimate selling involves promotion and praise. For example, is it wrong for a salesperson to tell a customer that a terribly ugly hat looks beautiful on the customer? To counter this argument, stress the reasons that the consumer believed the dealer's particular statements. The dealer may have stressed its trustworthiness in its advertisements. The salesperson may have taken specific steps to secure the consumer's trust and reliance. In addition, the misrepresentations may relate to specific, fundamental facts rather than matters of mere opinion or subjective taste, which people can be expected to discount.

A related defense argument is that a consumer who has entered into similar transactions before is, or should be, aware of the pressures and temptations that are part of the process. If the consumer's prior experiences were with honest businesses, however, the consumer's description of these experiences may backfire against the defendant by showing the contrast between the defendant's practices and those of legitimate businesses. Consumers may also be able to testify about specific practices that they never suspected.

Another common defense theme is that consumers have some obligation to act intelligently: to read the documents before signing and to ask for any promises in writing. To counter this argument, stress any vulnerabilities on the part of the consumer—age, language, education level, extreme need. Deceptive acts and practices (UDAP) case law makes it clear that vulnerable consumers are entitled to special protection.[38] The judge may be willing to give the jury an instruction along these lines. Also highlight any techniques the defendant used to discourage the consumer from reading the contract or from getting promises in writing. The documents that the consumer is supposed to have read may themselves be persuasive if they are technically worded and part of a large packet.

On a related note, juries may fault consumers for being foolish enough to trust the defendant at all and may want to blame the consumer for not having double-checked all the defendant's representations. Some members of the jury may think along these lines even if the defense does not raise this argument. It may be possible to persuade the judge to give the jury an instruction that a consumer does not have to deal as though dealing with a liar or a scoundrel, that the law protects the trustful who have been victimized by fraud, and that one who has defrauded another can not defend on the ground that his or her own word should not have been believed.[39] If the defense does raise this argument, it can be turned on its head as an admission of predatory practices. The consumer's attorney should be careful to develop the facts that will show the reasonableness of the consumer's actions.

General impatience with lawyers and lawsuits may also play into a defense theme that consumers—sometimes ones with bad credit histories—are swamping the courts with trivial suits as a means of bleeding money from businesses. As discussed in § 21.1.4, *supra*, a *voir dire* question such as "How many of you think there are too many lawsuits against car dealers (or the industry in question) for cheating people?" can address this concern. Stressing the seriousness and the criminal nature of the dealer's acts is important. If the consumer is seeking punitive damages, evidence of a pattern of similar acts by the same defendants may make the importance of the litigation clearer to the jury.

Another defense argument is that the only reason the case is in court is to justify fees for the consumer's attorney.

38 *See* National Consumer Law Center, Unfair and Deceptive Acts and Practices § 4.2.11 (6th ed. 2004).

39 See Schmidt v. Mulhauser, 212 Md. 585, 130 A.2d 572 (1957) (quoting from Bishop v. E. A. Strout Realty Agency, 182 F.2d 503 (4th Cir. 1950)) ("There is nothing in law or in reason that requires one to deal as though dealing with a liar or a scoundrel, or that denies the protection of the law to the trustful who have been victimized by fraud. The principle underlying the caveat emptor rule was more highly regarded in former times than it is today; but it was never any credit to the law to allow one who had defrauded another to defend on the ground that his own word should not have been believed."). The Supreme Court's statement in *Mourning v. Family Publications Serv.*, Inc., 411 U.S. 356, 377, 93 S. Ct. 1652, 1664, 36 L. Ed. 2d 318 (1973) is also apposite: "The Truth in Lending Act reflects a transition in congressional policy from a philosophy of let the buyer beware to one of let the seller disclose. By erecting a barrier between the seller and the prospective purchaser in the form of hard facts, Congress expressly sought 'to . . . avoid the uninformed use of credit.' "

Since the question of fees is reserved for the court under most fee-shifting statutes, evidence and arguments about fees should not be presented to the jury at all. A motion *in limine* to preclude this or other irrelevant lines of questioning may be appropriate. This issue is discussed in more detail in § 21.5.3, *infra*.

Placing the consumer's suit in the general context of consumer protection can be helpful: why these laws exist, why they do what they do, why the consumer's attorney believes in these laws, and why the jury should care about them also. The consumer's closing argument can stress that these laws mean that consumers do not have to take the type of treatment that they did in the past; now, when the company does not treat their customer right, the law gives the jury the power to make things right. Stressing the importance of personal responsibility and accountability on the part of the defendant may resonate even with the most conservative judges and juries.

As some consumer protection laws are fairly technical, attorneys representing consumers should give thought to educating the judge before the trial. If the same judge will be hearing pre-trial motions and conducting the trial, filing a partial summary judgment motion will familiarize the judge with the laws involved as well as establish liability and reduce the number of issues for trial.

21.5 Jury Instructions and Special Verdict Sheets

21.5.1 Timing Issues

Most courts require advance submission of proposed jury instructions and special verdict sheets as well as trial briefs. Check the local court rules to determine those requirements. The consumer's proposed jury instructions should address the issues that will be decided by the jury. Well-drafted jury instructions will not only enhance the likelihood of success but will also protect the record on those issues that may be raised upon appeal. Samples can be found on the companion CD-Rom to this manual and in National Consumer Law Center, *Consumer Law Pleadings* (Cumulative CD-Rom and Index Guide).

Many practitioners prepare draft jury instructions at the same time as they prepare the complaint. Then, as the case develops, they evaluate whether they have gathered the evidence to prove each point that the instructions cover.

21.5.2 Drafting

Jury interrogatories and special verdict sheets may be submitted to the jury pursuant to Rule 49 of the Federal Rules of Civil Procedure. The jury may be asked to determine what violations the defendant has committed and then specify the award of actual damages and statutory damages. Often local rules will elaborate upon this process.

Many practitioners believe that it is best to submit separate jury forms for each theory or even for each element of liability if the court allows. The separate forms cause the jury to focus in on its award, which can be helpful to the plaintiff. It also reduces uncertainty if the consumer has to select between two awards. On appeal, if judgment for the consumer is reversed on one claim, having separate jury forms may make it clear that other claims are unaffected by the error.[40] As a result, the award may stand or only part of the case will have to be retried. If separate jury forms are submitted for each cause of action, the judge should be asked to instruct the jury that they are not to concern themselves with the total amount the plaintiff should receive, that the judge will calculate the final recovery, and that it is entirely possible that the plaintiff's award will be based on only some of their answers rather than the total of all their answers.

21.5.3 Attorney Fee Awards Not for Jury to Determine

Jury instructions and verdict sheets should not, as a general rule, address attorney fees. The determination of attorney fees under the fee-shifting provision of the typical consumer protection statute is a matter for the judge, not the jury.[41] The jury should not even be told of the possibility of fees being awarded:

> In a case where the plaintiff is entitled to compensatory damages, informing the jury of the plaintiff's potential right to receive attorney fees might lead the jury to offset the fees by reducing the damage award. Even more troubling, however, is the case where actual damages are small or nonexistent. When damages are nominal, there is a risk that the jury may believe that the "harm" does not justify the payment of a large fee award. The jury may thus decide to find for the defendant rather than allow the plaintiff's attorney to recover fees.[42]

40 *See, e.g.*, S. Energy Homes v. Washington, 774 So. 2d 505, 40 U.C.C. Rep. 2d 986 (Ala. 2000). *See also* Brzezinski v. Feuerwerker, 2000 Ohio App. LEXIS 4145 (Ohio Ct. App. Sept. 14, 2000) (refusing to treble damages because court could not tell from jury's general verdict whether its damage award related to a UDAP violation).

41 Brooks v. Cook, 938 F.2d 1048, 1051 (9th Cir. 1991) (section 1983 case). *See generally* National Consumer Law Center, Automobile Fraud § 9.12.4 (2d ed. 2003 and Supp.); National Consumer Law Center, Unfair and Deceptive Acts and Practices § 8.8.12 (6th ed. 2004).

42 Fisher v. City of Memphis, 234 F.3d 312, 319 (6th Cir. 2000) (section 1983 case); Brooks v. Cook, 938 F.2d 1048, 1051 (9th Cir. 1991) (section 1983 case). *See also* Lee v. Robins Preston Beckett Taylor & Gugle Co., L.P.A., 1999 U.S. Dist. LEXIS

Presenting fee issues to a jury detracts attention from the consumer's case and feeds into these defense arguments. If there is any ambiguity in the fee-shifting statute about when evidence of fees is to be presented, the consumer's attorney should clear it up in advance with a motion to bifurcate the trial, with liability and damages presented to the jury and fees presented to the judge. Also consider a motion *in limine* to bar the defense from mentioning attorney fees. An order *in limine* is justified because fee issues are irrelevant to the consumer's case, any argument about the consumer's attorney's motives is pure speculation, and discussion of fees would create prejudice that a limiting instruction would not cure.

12969 (S.D. Ohio July 9, 1999) (granting motion *in limine* precluding defendant from mentioning the availability of attorney fees to the successful FDCPA plaintiff). *But cf.* Lanham v. Whitfield, 805 F.2d 970, 972 (11th Cir. 1986) (civil rights case) (no error in light of curative instruction to jury to disregard closing statement's reference to attorney fees).

Chapter 22 Consumer Law Remedies in Individual Suits

By Carolyn Carter[1]

22.1 Introduction

One of the great benefits of consumer protection statutes is their powerful remedies. Many consumer protection statutes offer statutory damages, multiple damages, and attorney fees—remedies rarely available for contract or common law claims. Some explicitly contemplate class actions, some authorize punitive damages and injunctions, and some authorize special forms of relief such as rescission or cancellation of contracts. By providing these remedies, consumer protection statutes encourage private enforcement of the laws and deter violations.

Common law tort claims can also achieve a significant impact on the consumer marketplace. While a common law tort claim will not carry statutory or multiple damages, a substantial punitive damage award can expose abusive practices and deter their repetition, while at the same time doing justice for the individual consumer.

The remedies to be sought in a case need to be analyzed from the outset and taken into account in case selection. The lawyer's and client's objectives must be aligned with each other for the case to work. If the case must be litigated as a class action to serve the attorney's requirements for an adequate award of attorney fees—or the office's need to obtain a broad injunction protecting the public from harm—and the client only cares about receiving individual relief, the case is not a good match and should not be pursued by that lawyer for that client.[2]

When selecting remedies, it is important to make sure that they will actually be effective. If the defendant has few resources but is likely to put most of them into litigation, the pursuit of injunctive or declaratory relief could be fruitful whereas a suit for damages would likely result in an uncollectible judgment. A case in which the defendant has substantial resources for litigating against a consumer's claim often requires the joining of a number of plaintiffs' firms to reach a counter-leveling of the resources necessary to prevent overwhelming pressure to make a premature settlement of the claim.

This chapter surveys the various types of remedies that are available in consumer cases.

22.2 Compensatory Damages

22.2.1 General Principles

22.2.1.1 Assessing and Developing All Damage Claims

A common and costly mistake is to pay scant attention to the nature and extent of the consumer's actual damages. The client should be interviewed about the full range of potential damages.

A 1989 debt collection abuse case illustrates the tendency to undervalue consumers' actual damages. The litigation was brought as a claim in a bankruptcy proceeding. The bankruptcy judge's nominal award of $100 actual damages was modified on *de novo* review by the district court with a ten-fold increase. Reviewing the record, the district court judge found:

> In assessing the effect of the [single] letter [deceptively threatening imminent foreclosure] on the plaintiff, I must look at her actions, as well as at her own evaluation of the letter's effect. While plaintiff's testimony is uncorroborated, neither is it contradicted by any testimony offered by defendant. Plaintiff [a recently widowed, elderly, disabled woman] says she lost both sleep and weight,

1 Carolyn Carter is Deputy Director of Advocacy at NCLC. She was formerly co-director of Legal Services, Inc., in Gettysburg, Pennsylvania, and director of the Law Reform Office of the Cleveland Legal Aid Society. She is the editor of *Pennsylvania Consumer Law* and the first edition of *Ohio Consumer Law*; co-author of *Automobile Fraud* (2003), *Consumer Warranty Law* (2d ed. 2001), *Unfair and Deceptive Acts and Practices* (6th ed. 2004), *Repossessions and Foreclosures* (5th ed. 2002 and Supp.); and contributing author to *Fair Debt Collection* (5th ed. 2004 and Supp.), *Truth in Lending* (5th ed. 2003 and Supp.), and *The Cost of Credit: Regulation, Preemption, and Industry Abuses* (3d ed. 2005). She is the 1992 recipient of the Vern Countryman Consumer Award and is currently a member of the Federal Reserve Board's Consumer Advisory Council.

2 Chapter 24, *infra*, discusses consumer class actions.

> factors admittedly hard to value. But in addition to that assertion, we are told that plaintiff did a number of things. She called defendant's office. She called an attorney. She borrowed money from a friend to pay Fleet. All of these were rational acts. She quit her job so as to cash-in her pension contributions. That was an irrational act. To have done that shows that she was upset. Defendant, in taking plaintiff's deposition, spent much time and many questions trying to show plaintiff's sophistication as a debtor. What all of that testimony adds up to is a picture of an old woman, with an annual income of $5,160.00 (doubtless less than the legal fees and expenses in this case), trying desperately to maintain her independence. That she should be driven to "eating her seed corn" (eliminating her job earnings and cashing her pension contributions) shows the degree of that desperation. Whatever else may have been affecting plaintiff's peace of mind, I have no doubt that this letter was an important factor. Assessing all of these factors, I am changing the actual damages from the nominal amount of $100.00 to $1,000.00, an amount more nearly reflecting the harm done.[3]

A sociologist's survey of judgment debtors estimated that nearly half of all low-income consumer judgment debtors surveyed suffered specific injuries, and about a quarter of all the judgment debtors consulted a physician about stress-related illnesses arising from their financial troubles.[4] This suggests that a case should always be assessed for actual damages resulting from that type of injury, whether the claim is based on a statute or tort. Such actual damages may lead to greater punitive damages in a tort case and greater statutory damages in a consumer protection act claim. In addition to emotional distress, other types of actual damages that often arise are out-of-pocket expenses and "relational" injuries such as injury to reputation, that is, damage which is to the debtor's relationships with family, employers, or the community.

Consumers often experience multiple illnesses and injuries as a result of marketplace wrongs. For example, the consumer may have suffered from a combination of nausea, sleeplessness, and loss of concentration after a fraud was perpetrated or after debt collection abuse. Each of those types of suffering gives rise to compensable damages.[5]

Low-income clients often receive government subsidies paying for many types of out-of-pocket losses and often forego obtaining relief from unsubsidized injuries or losses. As a result, their out-of-pocket losses are often slight or inconspicuous. Counsel should be alert for charges not covered by subsidies, for example, extra fees for medical treatment, over-the-counter medications such as aspirin or sleeping aids, child care expenses, toll calls, or transportation expenses. In a case in which a consumer complained about a finance company's unfair use of distant forums, the actual damage sufficient to state a cause of action under a state's consumer protection statute consisted of a telephone toll call of a few dollars made by the consumer to consult with a lawyer in the distant forum.[6]

22.2.1.2 Maximizing Damage Awards Benefits the Community As Well As Clients

Successful negotiation or trial of the damages issues in a consumer case has important repercussions beyond the individual case. It sets a standard for future settlements. It may deter future misconduct by businesses throughout the affected community. Large settlements or awards also increase the legal resources available to low-income consumers by increasing the financial incentive for more private lawyers to become involved in consumer cases.

A working knowledge of the law and practice of proving damages is crucial in both the negotiation and the trial stage of a consumer case. An attorney inexperienced in preparing for trial has little idea of where to start negotiating and when to settle, although the advice to not accept the adversary's first offer is generally sound. The inexperienced lawyer should analyze how a jury would react to the case before negotiating the settlement of the case.[7] Reviewing that analysis with an attorney experienced in such cases is a sound practice.

22.2.1.3 Interpreting the Remedy Provisions of Consumer Protection Statutes

Consumer protection statutes typically provide that a consumer injured by a violation of the statute may recover "actual damages," "restitution," or "damages." In interpreting these provisions, it is important to remember the purpose of consumer protection statutes to overcome the inadequacies of common law remedies.[8] Counsel must be vigilant in avoiding the imposition of common law restrictions on consumer protection statutes that were enacted to provide new, more effective remedies. Strong and flexible remedies are key to strong consumer protections.

The rule that a consumer protection statute is entitled to a liberal construction applies to its remedy provisions just as

3 Crossley v. Lieberman, 90 B.R. 682, 698 (E.D. Pa. 1988), *aff'd*, 868 F.2d 566 (3d Cir. 1989).

4 *See* David Caplovitz, *Consumers in Trouble* 280, 281 (1974); National Consumer Law Center, Fair Debt Collection § 2.1.2 (5th ed. 2004 and Supp.).

5 *See* § 22.2.3, *infra*.

6 *See* Schubach v. Household Fin. Corp., 376 N.E.2d 140 (Mass. 1976).

7 *See also* Ch. 19, *supra* (settling consumer cases).

8 *See, e.g.*, National Consumer Law Center, Unfair and Deceptive Acts and Practices §§ 3.1.2, 4.2.3.1 (6th ed. 2004).

it applies to its substantive prohibitions.[9] For example, UDAP statutes should be construed to authorize the broadest remedy possible.[10] Without a liberal construction of UDAP remedies, deception is more likely to recur, the public will be less protected, and fraudulent practices will continue unchecked while a multiplicity of damage suits develops.

Until recently, the common law rules of damages developed largely through litigation in commercial situations. This has sometimes resulted in the attempt to apply common law rules which, though legitimate in the commercial context, unjustly deny or diminish recoveries for real injuries in consumer cases. Although the law is changing, in a particular jurisdiction the law of consumer damages may be more restrictive than in other jurisdictions. Careful additional research of local damages law is required. When the law of damages under a particular consumer protection statute is not fully developed, or is limited by confused or aberrational decisions, attorneys should explore whether to plead other claims such as breach of warranty, fraud, or rescission.

22.2.1.4 Legal Labels for Damages May Have More Than One Meaning

The law of damages has developed special categories and labels for damages. Some of these labels have a special meaning in the context of a particular cause of action and so are easily confused or misapplied. For example, the terms "special damages" and "general damages" have specific meanings and a variety of substantive implications when used in libel and slander cases. In that context, general damages are those inferred by law from the defamatory act and valued by the trier of fact without the plaintiff having to prove the existence, extent, or value of the injury to reputation. In the same context, special damages are those caused by the defamation and supported by evidence as to the existence, extent, and value of the injury. Special damages may be necessary in order for a cause of action to exist for libel or slander in some circumstances.[11]

These same two terms, however, are used differently in other contexts, with "general damages" referring to damages ordinarily suffered in a particular type of cause of action and "special damages" referring to compensation for other types of legally recognized damages. Thus, the rules for and meaning of general and special damages will vary depending on the cause of action.

Although courts in consumer protection cases often distinguish between types of damages, there is not always a clear dividing line. Direct or general damages are those directly and immediately resulting from the unfair or deceptive act or practice and pertain directly to the goods or services involved in the transaction. For example, if a used-car dealer sells the consumer a defective automobile, direct damages are the decreased value of the automobile.

Proximate or consequential damages are damages other than direct damages that are forseeable as flowing from an unfair or deceptive act or practice. For example, in the case of a defective used car, consequential damages may include the costs of substitute transportation, repairs to the car, towing expenses, lost earnings due to the inability to drive to work, and the like.[12]

"Nominal damages" are a trivial sum awarded to vindicate a legal right when there was no harm done or when the plaintiff failed to prove substantial damages.[13] However, damage awards of less than several hundred dollars are sometimes referred to as nominal damages simply because of their comparatively low amount.

"Punitive damages" are damages awarded to punish or make an example of a defendant or to provide compensation for expenses or injuries for which the law has not provided a recovery (for example, attorney fees or mental anguish). They are sometimes called "exemplary damages."

"Actual damages" should generally be regarded as a developing term of art due to its widespread use in consumer protection statutes that create new rights and protections and its developing use in cases thus far.[14] The term should be broadly construed to remedy the injuries that the statute was designed to prevent.

Consumer protection statutes often permit recovery of damages, according to a formula, beyond those awarded as

9 *See* National Consumer Law Center, Unfair and Deceptive Acts and Practices § 8.1 (6th ed. 2004).

10 *See, e.g.*, *In re* Bryant, 111 B.R. 474 (E.D. Pa. 1990); *In re* Jungkurth, 74 B.R. 323, 336 (Bankr. E.D. Pa. 1987), *aff'd*, 87 B.R. 333 (E.D. Pa. 1988); Young v. Joyce, 351 A.2d 857 (Del. 1975); Delgado v. J. W. Courtesy Pontiac GMC-Truck, Inc., 693 So. 2d 602 (Fla. Dist. Ct. App. 1997) ("economic loss doctrine" does not limit UDAP damages); Gour v. Daray Motor Co., 373 So. 2d 571 (La. Ct. App. 1979); Heller v. Silverbranch Constr. Corp., 376 Mass. 621, 382 N.E.2d 1065 (1978); Neveroski v. Blair, 141 N.J. Super. 365, 358 A.2d 473 (App. Div. 1976); Roane-Barker v. Southeastern Hosp. Supply Corp., 99 N.C. App. 30, 392 S.E.2d 663 (1990); Smith v. Herco, Inc., 900 S.W.2d 852 (Tex. App. 1995); March v. Thiery, 729 S.W.2d 889 (Tex. App. 1987) (greatest amount provable under any acceptable theory); Johnson v. Willis, 596 S.W.2d 256 (Tex. App. 1980); Woo v. Great Southwestern Acceptance Corp., 565 S.W.2d 290 (Tex. App. 1978). *See also* Process Components, Inc. v. Balt. Aircoil Co., 89 N.C. App. 649, 366 S.E.2d 907 (1988), *aff'd*, 323 N.C. 620, 374 S.E.2d 116 (1988); Bernard v. Cent. Carolina Trade Sales, 68 N.C. App. 228, 314 S.E.2d 582 (1984).

11 *See* National Consumer Law Center, Fair Debt Collection § 10.5 (5th ed. 2004 and Supp.).

12 *See* National Consumer Law Center, Unfair and Deceptive Acts and Practices § 8.3.3.1 (6th ed. 2004).

13 *See* Dan B. Dobbs, 1 *The Law of Remedies* § 3.3(2) (2d ed. 1993).

14 *See* National Consumer Law Center, Unfair and Deceptive Acts and Practices § 8.3 (6th ed. 2004); National Consumer Law Center, Fair Debt Collection § 6.3 (5th ed. 2004 and Supp.); National Consumer Law Center, Truth in Lending § 8.5 (5th ed. 2003 and Supp.); National Consumer Law Center, Fair Credit Reporting § 11.2 (5th ed. 2002 and Supp.); National Consumer Law Center, Credit Discrimination § 11.7 (4th ed. 2005).

actual damages. These damages may be termed "statutory damages" to avoid implicating a set of inappropriate common law rules, as might occur if they were labeled "punitive," "liquidated," or "general" damages. Courts have noted that statutory damages serve a variety of functions that make existing labels for other types of damages and their corresponding constructions inappropriate.[15] Statutory damages probably represent the legislature's estimate of the amount or range of damages for which a consumer injured by a statutory violation would not otherwise be compensated because of the difficulty or expense of proving the damages.

22.2.2 *Methods to Calculate Direct Damages*

22.2.2.1 Liberal Interpretation for Consumer Cases

There are three basic methods, derived from contract, warranty, and fraud cases, for calculating direct damages. "Out-of-pocket" damages are calculated as the difference between what the consumer paid and received. A second method is "loss-of-bargain" damages, calculated as the difference between what the consumer expected to get and what the consumer actually got. The UCC adopts this method as the standard way to calculate damages for breach of warranty. A third measure of damages is "cost-of-repair," which is the cost to the consumer to alter the product or service so that the product or service matches what was promised.[16] These three alternatives are discussed in the following subsections.

The measure of damages under a consumer protection statute is of course limited by the language of the statute's remedial provisions, such as by language authorizing only "restitution" instead of "actual damages." But the mandate of liberal construction and the purposes of consumer protection statutes to correct imbalances in common law and commercial law should prompt courts to construe the statutory language expansively. While courts should borrow from the state's common law on damages, consumer protection damage awards should not be limited to contract damages.[17] Just as courts fashioned different rules of damages for different types of contract, equity, and tort actions, they should fashion new remedial rules of damages under consumer protection statutes, adopting the most favorable measure of damages for a given case and discarding outdated doctrines limiting damages.

15 *See* National Consumer Law Center, Truth in Lending § 8.6.1 (4th ed. 1999 and Supp.).

16 Formosa Plastics Corp. v. Presidio Engineers & Contractors, Inc., 960 S.W.2d 41 (Tex. 1998). For a Maryland case enunciating the same three rules, see *Hall v. Lovell Regency Homes Ltd.*, 121 Md. App. 1, 708 A.2d 344 (1998).

17 Poor v. Hill, 138 N.C. App. 19, 530 S.E.2d 838 (2000).

22.2.2.2 Loss-of-Bargain Damages

Normally, loss-of-bargain damages are more than out-of-pocket damages. For example, consider a seller's claim that a product priced at $100 is really worth $200. If the product is actually worth $50, loss-of-bargain damages are $150 and out-of-pocket damages are $50.

Unless the language in the statutory damage provision specifically limits damages to "restitution," courts will normally grant loss-of-bargain damages. Thus, in UDAP cases, courts have awarded as loss-of-bargain damages the difference between the value of the product as represented and as sold, an amount equaling the difference between the final sale price and the lower price originally agreed upon, the lost profit from a purchase that the defendant's UDAP violations prevented, or even the difference between the final sale price and the lower price originally advertised.[18]

Loss-of-bargain damages can be sizeable. A court has awarded as loss-of-bargain UDAP damages the difference between what an investment scheme was expected to be worth ($65,000) and what it was actually worth ($0).[19]

Loss-of-bargain damages are especially helpful in cases dealing with credit terms. For example, a creditor disclosed a stated interest rate that was lower than the actual rate because the amount financed was disbursed in two installments. The court calculated the consumer class's damages as the difference between the actual total of payments and the total correctly adjusted for the two disbursements of the amount financed, assuming the interest rate remained constant.[20] Similarly, when a buyer could not obtain financing at the rates promised by the seller, the buyer's damages were the difference between the interest payments as promised and the rates then available.[21] Although the eventual length of the financing period could not be precisely determined (the buyer might pre-pay or refinance the mortgage), this did not make damages too indeterminate to be reasonably calculable.[22] When a lessor promised a purchase option of $1.00 but then demanded the market value of the property, the measure of damages was calculated as the difference between the market value and the $1.00 price.[23]

Loss-of-bargain damages can also be helpful when the consumer does not want to repair a product and keep it.

18 *See* National Consumer Law Center, Unfair and Deceptive Acts and Practices § 8.3.2.2 (6th ed. 2004).

19 Nottingham v. Gen. Am. Commc'ns Corp., 811 F.2d 873 (5th Cir. 1987) (Texas law). *Accord* Anthony's Pier Four v. HBC Assocs., 411 Mass. 451, 583 N.E.2d 806 (1991) (damage award based on lost profits and fair market value of property if defendant had not breached contract). *But see* Schwanbeck v. Fed. Mogul Corp., 31 Mass. App. 390, 578 N.E.2d 789 (1991) (in commercial case, court declines to award lost profits), *aff'd on other grounds*, 592 N.E.2d 1289 (Mass. 1992).

20 Leibert v. Fin. Factors Ltd., 788 P.2d 833 (Haw. 1990).

21 Stephenson v. Capano Dev., Inc., 462 A.2d 1069 (Del. 1983).

22 *Id.*

23 A.V.I., Inc. v. Heathington, 842 S.W.2d 712 (Tex. App. 1992).

When failure to make repairs lowers the market value more than the cost of those repairs, the consumer can recover the larger diminished market value.[24]

22.2.2.3 Cost-to-Repair Damages

Often, the consumer's best option is to receive damages based on the cost to repair a purchased item. Such cost-to-repair damages are measured as the cost of making the repairs, not just the diminished value of the property left in an unrepaired state. Damages are the amount necessary to repair property to meet the seller's representations.[25] For example, damages for failure to complete a contract are the cost of properly fulfilling the contract.[26]

While cost of repair is a legitimate basis for awarding damages, courts may not award such damages when it will lead to economic waste. The courts will instead award loss-of-bargain or out-of-pocket damages. For example, when a $44,000 house was situated on a dangerous site, a court refused to award $83,000, which would be the cost to move the house to another site. Instead, it held that $44,000 was the proper damage award, since the consumer could purchase a similar house with that award.[27]

22.2.2.4 Out-of-Pocket Damages or Restitution

In some cases, restitution or out-of-pocket damages may be preferable to other forms of damage calculations. In granting restitution, courts may award both return of the purchase price plus the consumer's other out-of-pocket expenditures as damages.[28] Some courts may allow restitution only in the amount that the defendant has benefited from the unlawful act. For example, an earlier version of the Maine UDAP statute, which allowed a consumer to sue for "restitution" but not actual damages, was interpreted to require that the dealer benefit from the act that harmed the consumers.[29]

A UDAP provision requiring sellers to "restore money acquired in violation" of the act has been interpreted as allowing full restitution of all money paid for a franchise.[30] Even when a statute limited recovery to "actual damages," since there was a legislative intent to encourage private UDAP litigation, the court allowed a consumer to return a defective car and obtain a refund of the original purchase price, thereby depriving the seller of any profit.[31]

To obtain restitution of the purchase price of a product, the consumer may have to return the product or deduct its value (if any) from the restitution award. A number of decisions, however, hold that the seller is not entitled to an adjustment for the consumer's use of the product.[32] Traditional equitable defenses such as laches may be available to the defendant when the consumer seeks restitution.[33]

22.2.3 Emotional Distress

22.2.3.1 History and Availability in Tort Actions

An important form of actual damages is for mental or emotional distress. A number of states allow emotional distress damages to be awarded for intentional fraud.[34] This approach is consistent with the *Restatement of Torts*, which allows recovery of emotional distress damages for extreme and outrageous conduct that is intentional or reckless and that causes severe emotional distress.[35] These states would probably also allow such damages for fraud-like claims, such as violation of a state or federal odometer statute.

---

24 Brighton Homes, Inc. v. McAdams, 737 S.W.2d 340 (Tex. App. 1987).

25 *See* National Consumer Law Center, Unfair and Deceptive Acts and Practices § 8.3.2.3 (6th ed. 2004).

26 Pierce v. Drees, 607 N.E.2d 726 (Ind. Ct. App. 1993). *Accord* Cox v. Sears, Roebuck & Co., 138 N.J. 2, 647 A.2d 454 (1994).

27 Guest v. Phillips Petroleum Co., 981 F.2d 218 (5th Cir. 1993) (Texas law); Hall v. Lovell Regency Homes Ltd., 121 Md. App. 1, 708 A.2d 344 (1998).

28 Catucci v. Ouellette, 25 Conn. App. 56, 592 A.2d 962 (1991).

29 Kleinschmidt v. Morrow, 642 A.2d 161 (Me. 1994); Dudley v. Wyler, 647 A.2d 90 (Me. 1994).

30 United Postage Corp. v. Kammeyer, 581 S.W.2d 716 (Tex. App. 1979).

31 Gour v. Daray Motor Co., 373 So. 2d 571 (La. Ct. App. 1979). *See also* Aurigemma v. Arco Petroleum Prods. Co., 734 F. Supp. 1025 (D. Conn. 1990) ("actual damages" language in statute authorized restitution, but not appropriate when it would be extremely difficult to unravel a five-year business relationship between plaintiffs and defendants). *But see* Colonial Lincoln-Mercury Sales, Inc. v. Molina, 152 Ga. App. 379, 262 S.E.2d 820 (1979).

32 *See* National Consumer Law Center, Unfair and Deceptive Acts and Practices § 8.3.2.4.2 (6th ed. 2004).

33 Cortez v. Purolator Air Filtration Prods. Co., 23 Cal. 4th 163, 999 P.2d 706 (2000) (noting that such defenses "may not be asserted to wholly defeat a UCL claim since such claims arise out of unlawful conduct").

34 *See, e.g.*, Orkin Exterminating Co. v. Jeter, 832 So. 2d 25 (Ala. 2001) (fraud and breach of contract; concealment of extent of termite damage); Firstbank of Ark. v. Keeling, 312 Ark. 441, 850 S.W.2d 310 (1993) (affirming lower court's award of emotional distress damages); Trimble v. City County of Denver, 697 P.2d 716 (Colo. 1985) (mental suffering damages allowed for fraud); Kilduff v. Adams, Inc., 219 Conn. 314, 593 A.2d 478 (1991) (foreclosure fraud; emotional distress damages can be recovered if they are the natural and proximate result of fraud, even if there is no bodily injury or risk of harm from bodily impact); Osbourne v. Capital City Mortgage Corp., 667 A.2d 1321 (D.C. Ct. App. 1995) (foreclosure fraud; plaintiff may recover emotional damages that are the natural and proximate result of intentional misrepresentation); Crowley v. Global Realty, Inc., 474 A.2d 1056 (N.H. 1994) (plaintiff can seek enhanced compensatory damages based on mental suffering; state does not allow punitive damages). *See generally* National Consumer Law Center, Automobile Fraud § 9.10.3.2 (2d ed. 2003 and Supp.).

35 Restatement (Second) of Torts § 46(1) (1965).

Courts in the past were reluctant to permit compensation for mental anguish or distress unless the mental distress resulted from a physical injury or impact. This became known as the "impact rule." Considerable confusion resulted from the courts distinguishing between physical injuries caused by physical trauma and those caused by stress, such as heart attacks, fainting, vomiting, and headaches. Many jurisdictions have now abandoned these distinctions even for common law claims, and it is even less likely that they will be given effect for claims under consumer protection statutes.

22.2.3.2 Emotional Distress Damages for Breach of Warranty

Many cases recite a general rule that emotional distress damages are unavailable for breach of contract. However, some states make an exception to this general rule when the subject matter is "so closely associated with mental concern, or with the emotions of the party to whom the duty is owed that a breach . . . can reasonably be expected to result in mental anguish."[36] Several states have also ruled that emotional distress damages are available for at least some breaches of warranty.[37] The typical example is a contract to build or repair a consumer's home, including a mobile home, but the rationale could apply equally to a car because of the safety issues.

22.2.3.3 Emotional Distress Damages for Violations of Consumer Protection Statutes

In general, mental distress damages should be available under a consumer protection statute at least to the same extent that they are recoverable at common law.[38] A number of states allow emotional distress damages to be awarded in UDAP cases.[39] The argument in favor of emotional distress damages in UDAP cases has particular appeal since UDAP statutes are remedial statutes that should be liberally construed. In states that have not yet ruled on whether emotional distress damages are available, the consumer's attorney can point out that the law in this area is developing, with more states recognizing the right to seek such damages at least in some circumstances.[40]

Federal consumer protection statutes providing for "actual damages" generally permit recovery of mental anguish damages without the common law predicates of outrage, severe injury, or intentional wrongdoing.[41] For example, awards of actual damages for emotional distress pursuant to the Fair Debt Collection Practices Act[42] do not require proof of physical injury or outrageous conduct as may be required to demonstrate a state law claim for the intentional infliction of emotional distress: "Existing state laws would, in many cases, afford no relief at all to the victim of abusive debt collection practices. This is particularly true when state law requires proof of physical injury before a plaintiff can recover for the intentional infliction of emotional distress."[43]

22.2.3.4 Developing and Proving an Emotional Distress Damages Case

The consumer's attorney should be careful to reserve emotional distress claims for egregious cases and to develop corroborating evidence and witnesses. An impression that the victim is "whining" can undercut the victim's case. It is often better for a friend or relative to give most of the damage testimony to avoid attributing a whining image to the plaintiff.

Jurisdictions differ on whether expert medical testimony is required for proof of emotional distress damages.[44] If physical injury and physical symptoms are not required, a plaintiff may need to show that the distress substantially

---

36 Sexton v. St. Clair Fed. Savs. Bank, 653 So. 2d 959 (Ala. 1995).

37 *See, e.g.*, Lutz Farms v. Asgrow Seed Co., 948 F.2d 638 (10th Cir. 1991) (Colorado law) (damages for mental suffering recoverable for willful or wanton breach); Grant v. Cavalier Mfg. Inc., 229 F. Supp. 2d 1332 (M.D. Ala. 2002) (Alabama law allows emotional distress damages for breach of warranty claim involving purchase of new home, here a mobile home). *See generally* National Consumer Law Center, Automobile Fraud § 9.10.3.2 (2d ed. 2003 and Supp.); National Consumer Law Center, Consumer Warranty Law § 10.6.3.3 (2d ed. 2001 and Supp.).

38 Hart v. GMAC Mortgage Corp., 246 B.R. 709 (Bankr. D. Mass. 2000) (requiring proof of elements of intentional infliction of emotional distress in order to recover UDAP damages for emotional distress); Kish v. Van Note, 692 S.W.2d 463 (Tex. 1985); Brown v. Am. Transfer & Storage Co., 601 S.W.2d 931 (Tex. 1980); Mercedes-Benz of N. Am. v. Dickenson, 720 S.W.2d 844 (Tex. App. 1986).

39 *See* National Consumer Law Center, Unfair and Deceptive Acts and Practices § 8.3.3.9 (6th ed. 2004).

40 For discussions of the developing judicial view of emotional distress damages, see Robert L. Dunn, *Recovery of Damages for Fraud* §§ 4.7-4.10 (3d ed. 2004); A. Merritt, *Damages for Emotional Distress in Fraud Litigation: Dignitary Torts in a Commercial Society*, 42 Vand. L. Rev. 1 (1989); Michael G. Walsh, *Recovery for Mental Anguish or Emotional Distress, Absent Independent Physical Injury, Consequent Upon Breach of Contract or Warranty in Connection with Construction of Home or Other Building*, 7 A.L.R.4th 1178 (1981 and annual Supp.).

41 *See* § 22.3.3, *infra*.

42 15 U.S.C. § 1692k(a)(1).

43 Smith v. Law Office of Mitchell N. Kay, 124 B.R. 182, 189 n.6 (D. Del. 1991).

44 *Compare* Bi-Rite Petroleum v. Coastal Refining & Marketing, Inc., 282 F.3d 606 (8th Cir. 2002) (for negligent infliction of emotional distress, Missouri requires expert opinion to establish causation of medically diagnosable distress) *with* Laurents v. La. Mobile Homes, 689 So. 2d 536 (La. Ct. App. 1997) (expert testimony is not required to prove mental anguish claim in mobile home sale case).

disrupted daily routine.[45] The plaintiff's proof should show that emotional distress was reasonably foreseeable as a result of the defendant's actions.[46] The plaintiff should also take care to tie the emotional distress damages to specific wrongful acts of the defendants.[47]

Courts may be reluctant to allow emotional distress damages based solely on the plaintiff's testimony.[48] Whether or not the court requires it, testimony of friends, relatives, and co-workers about the visible changes in the plaintiff's life—restrictions in activities, unhappy demeanor—are of great help in proving emotional distress damages. Signs and symptoms of emotional distress to which the plaintiff may be able to testify, and that others may be able to corroborate, include

- aggravation of existing illness;
- anxiety;
- appetite loss;
- periods of being bedridden;
- chest pain;
- loss of concentration;
- loss of consortium;
- crying;
- dizziness;
- fear;
- headaches;
- humiliation or embarrassment;
- hypertension;
- hysteria;
- illness;
- irritability;
- effect on job performance;
- job loss;
- medical expenses;
- medication;
- muscle spasms;
- nausea;
- nightmares;
- loss of privacy;
- effect on relationships;
- effect on reputation;
- shortness of breath;
- stomach pain; and
- weight gain or loss.[49]

Decisions awarding damages for these and other symptoms may be found in National Consumer Law Center, *Fair Debt Collection* § 2.5.2.2.2 (5th ed. 2004 and Supp.).

22.2.3.5 Damages for Aggravation and Inconvenience

Some jurisdictions refuse to award damages for mere aggravation and inconvenience. An Illinois appellate court, however, has affirmed a UDAP damage award for aggravation and inconvenience resulting from misrepresentations in a car sale.[50] Likewise, a New York court awarded $500 for disappointment, humiliation, and annoyance suffered when the defendant sent a different singer to the plaintiff's wedding than the one she had contracted for.[51] Several Oklahoma appellate decisions[52] and a Fourth Circuit decision based on West Virginia law[53] hold that losses such as annoyance, loss of time, inconvenience, travel, and telephone expenses are compensable.

45 Gill v. Boyd Distribution Ctr., 64 S.W.3d 601 (Tex. App. 2001) (UDAP claim).

46 *See, e.g.*, St. Paul Fire & Marine Ins. Co. v. Clark, 566 S.E.2d 2 (Ga. App. 2002) (emotional distress damages available for intentional wrong, here fraud by insurance agent, if natural result of act is mental suffering; when insurance company notified consumers' healthcare providers that insurance was rescinded, emotional distress damages affirmed); Signorino v. Nat'l Super Markets, 782 S.W.2d 100 (Mo. Ct. App. 1989) (element of emotional distress damages claim is that defendant should have realized that conduct involved an unreasonable risk of causing the distress); Cleveland v. Dyn-a-mite Pest Control, 57 P.3d 119 (Okla. App. 2002) (emotional distress damages available without physical injury if emotional distress is natural and probable consequence of wrongful act; damages affirmed when consumers bought home with swarms of live termites and major termite damage).

47 *See* Cousin v. Trans Union Corp., 246 F.3d 359 (5th Cir. 2001) (reversing FCRA damage award case because emotional distress was caused by denial of credit, not by disclosure of credit report); Wellisch v. United Servs. Auto. Ass'n, 75 S.W.3d 53 (Tex. App. 2002) (consumers failed to show that distress resulted from bad faith claims settlement practices rather than accident that killed their daughter).

48 *See* Cousin v. Trans Union Corp., 246 F.3d 359 (5th Cir. 2001) (emotional distress award requires a degree of specificity that may include corroborating testimony or medical or psychological evidence). *See also* Carey v. Piphus, 435 U.S. 247, 98 S. Ct. 1042, 1052 n.20, 55 L. Ed. 2d 252 (1978) (emotional distress award must be supported by evidence of genuine injury, such as evidence of injured party's conduct and third-party observations).

49 This list is based on a checklist used by Richard Feferman, an experienced consumer attorney in New Mexico.

50 Roche v. Fireside Chrysler-Plymouth, 600 N.E.2d 1218 (Ill. App. Ct. 1992) (affirming award of $750 for aggravation and inconvenience).

51 Griffin-Amiel v. Frank Terris Orchestras, 178 Misc. 2d 71, 677 N.Y.S.2d 908 (City Ct. 1998).

52 Brashears v. Sight N Sound Appliance Centers, Inc., 981 P.2d 1270 (Okla. App. 1999); Fuller v. Sight N Sound Appliance Centers, Inc., 982 P.2d 528 (Okla. App. 1999). *But see* Hedrick v. Spear, 138 Or. App. 53, 907 P.2d 1123 (1995) (damages can not include work time lost to attend trial).

53 Mirandy v. Allstate Ins. Co., 151 F.3d 1029 (4th Cir. 1998) (table, text available at 1998 U.S. App. LEXIS 10915). *See also* National Consumer Law Center, Consumer Warranty Law § 10.6.3.3 (2d ed. 2001 and Supp.) (mental anguish damages on warranty claims).

22.2.4 Physical Injuries

Some consumer protection statutes specifically disallow damages for physical injuries. The Magnuson-Moss Warranty Act is one example,[54] and some state UDAP statutes also have a specific exclusion.[55] However, when the statute allows the consumer to recover damages, without restricting the injury that is compensable, then the consumer can recover for physical injuries as well as monetary loss.[56]

A number of states require, as a condition of a UDAP suit, that the consumer have suffered "an ascertainable loss of money or property."[57] Courts in several states have misinterpreted this language to restrict the type of damages for which a consumer can be compensated only to those involving loss of money or property, not physical injury.[58] A better interpretation, more consistent with the liberal construction due UDAP statutes, is that, once the threshold requirement of an ascertainable loss of money or property is met, the consumer's damages are measured and limited only by general damage law principles.

54 15 U.S.C. § 2311(b)(2).

55 *See, e.g.*, T.W.M. v. Am. Medical Sys., Inc., 886 F. Supp. 842 (N.D. Fla. 1995) (denying recovery for personal injury because of Florida UDAP statute's explicit bar); Tex. Bus. & Com. Code Ann. §§ 122.50(b), (h), 122.49(e) (recovery limited to economic damages and mental anguish in some UDAP suits; damages for bodily injury or death excluded in most cases). *See also* National Consumer Law Center, Unfair and Deceptive Acts and Practices § 9.2.5.3.1 (6th ed. 2004) (RICO).

56 Maurer v. Cerkvenik-Anderson Travel, Inc., 181 Ariz. 294, 890 P.2d 69 (App. 1994) (California UDAP statute allows recovery for death of tourist caused by travel agency's failure to disclose risks of trip); Duncavage v. Allen, 147 Ill. App. 3d 88, 497 N.E.2d 433 (1986) (death claim allowed to proceed); Maillet v. ATF-Davidson Co., 407 Mass. 185, 552 N.E.2d 95 (1990). *See also* Kociemba v. G.D. Searle & Co., 680 F. Supp. 1293 (D. Minn. 1988) (Minnesota UDAP statute applies to product liability litigation); National Consumer Law Center, Unfair and Deceptive Acts and Practices § 2.2.11 (6th ed. 2004).

57 *See* National Consumer Law Center, Unfair and Deceptive Acts and Practices § 7.5.2 (6th ed. 2004).

58 Association of Wash. Public Hosp. Dists. v. Philip Morris, 2001 U.S. App. LEXIS 2561 (9th Cir. 2001); Wenrich v. Robert E. Cole, P.C., 2000 U.S. Dist. LEXIS 18687 (E.D. Pa. Dec. 22, 2000) (emotional distress damages probably not available for Pennsylvania UDAP violation); Blowers v. Eli Lilly and Co., 100 F. Supp. 2d 1265 (D. Haw. 2000); Northwest Laborers-Employers Health & Security Trust Fund v. Philip Morris, Inc., 58 F. Supp. 2d 1211 (W.D. Wash. 1999) (expenses for medical treatment paid by union health and welfare trust fund due to tobacco-related illnesses not compensable); *In re* Bryant, 111 B.R. 474 (E.D. Pa. 1990); *In re* Clark, 96 B.R. 569 (E.D. Pa. 1989); Beerman v. Toro Mfg. Corp., 1 Haw. App. 111, 615 P.2d 749 (1980); Gross-Haentjens v. Leckenby, 38 Or. App. 313, 589 P.2d 1209 (1979); Kirksey v. Overton Pub, Inc., 804 S.W.2d 68 (Tenn. App. 1990); White River Estates v. Hiltbruner, 953 P.2d 796 (Wash. 1998); Wash. State Physicians Ins. Exch. v. Fisons Corp., 122 Wash. 2d 299, 858 P.2d 1054 (1993); Keyes v. Bollinger, 31 Wash. App. 286, 640 P.2d 1077 (1982); Hiner v. Bridgestone/Firestone, Inc., 959 P.2d 1158 (Wash. App. 1998) (disallowing UDAP claim when property damage arose from automobile accident that caused personal injury), *rev'd in part on other grounds*, 138 Wash. 2d 248, 978 P.2d 505 (1999).

22.2.5 Consequential Damages

22.2.5.1 General

Direct damages, discussed in the preceding subsections, are those that result directly and immediately from the unfair or deceptive act or practice and pertain directly to the goods or services involved in the transaction. Consumer litigants may also obtain proximate or consequential damages—all damages forseeably flowing from an unfair or deceptive act or practice. Such consequential damages are often far greater than direct damages.

For example, in a defective car case, a consumer may be awarded as damages not only the appropriate part of the purchase price, but also the costs of repairs, towing, alternate transportation, storage, and various other inconveniences.[59] These costs flow from the misrepresentation and are a foreseeable consequence of it.[60]

22.2.5.2 Financing Costs As Consequential Damages

An important example of consequential damages is the various financing costs that relate to the unfair or deceptive practice. When a consumer recovers the purchase price of a defective car as actual damages, interest payments attributed to the car loan are also recoverable.[61] Similarly, courts award as additional UDAP damages any interest or finance charges the consumer was forced to pay by reason of a deceptive sale.[62]

Even when pre-judgment interest is not allowed, a consumer can still recover the interest lost when the consumer

59 Gent v. Collinsville Volkswagen, 116 Ill. App. 3d 496, 451 N.E.2d 1385 (1983); State *ex rel.* Guste v. Gen. Motors Corp., 354 So. 2d 770 (La. Ct. App. 1978), *rev'd on other grounds*, 370 So. 2d 477 (La. 1978); Hyder-Inrgram Chevrolet Inc. v. Kutach, 612 S.W.2d 687 (Tex. App. 1981) ($875 for use of a rental car). *See also* Tri-West Constr. Co. v. Hernandez, 43 Or. App. 961, 607 P.2d 1375 (1979); Atlas Amalgamated Inc. v. Castillo, 601 S.W.2d 728 (Tex. App. 1980).

60 Caldwell v. Pop's Home Inc., 54 Or. App. 104, 634 P.2d 471 (1981).

61 Gent v. Collinsville Volkswagen, 116 Ill. App. 3d 496, 451 N.E.2d 1385 (1983). *But see* Fort Lauderdale Lincoln Mercury v. Corgnati, 715 So. 2d 311 (Fla. Dist. Ct. App. 1998) (aberrant decision holding that financing costs and other consequential damages can not be included in UDAP award).

62 Jersild v. Aker, 775 F. Supp. 1198 (E.D. Wis. 1991); Antle v. Reynolds, 15 S.W.3d 762 (Mo. App. 2000); Quate v. Caudle, 381 S.E.2d 842 (N.C. Ct. App. 1989); Smith v. Baldwin, 611 S.W.2d 611 (Tex. 1980); Investors, Inc. v. Hadley, 738 S.W.2d 737 (Tex. App. 1987); Lone Star Ford, Inc. v. McGlashan, 681 S.W.2d 720 (Tex. App. 1984); Chrysler Corp. v. Scheunemann, 618 S.W.2d 799 (Tex. App. 1981).

had to take money out of a savings account to perform repairs the seller failed to perform.[63] And consumers may recover increased financing costs caused when building of a home was delayed by their refusal to pay a deceptively inflated real estate commission.[64]

22.2.5.3 Damages Based on Consumer's Lost Time or Earnings

Often a consumer's damages are not evidenced by payment of extra expenses but by additional efforts required of the consumer, and this lost time is a possible source of damages.[65] A consumer was awarded $5000 for his own efforts in supervising construction work necessary because a builder failed to complete the work.[66] Another consumer was awarded $400 for having to conduct her own title search on a mobile home when this was necessary because of the seller's deception.[67]

New Mexico's highest court has indicated it may consider a consumer's "lost paid vacation time" in calculating actual damages. This would be time the consumer had to take off from work to prepare for and appear at depositions and trial. "Certainly, high among the factors motivating legislatures to enact laws such as we are considering today is the frustration experienced by consumers having to run around to straighten out unfair or deceptive trade practices."[68]

Lost future earnings caused by a consumer protection violation should also be awarded as damages. For example, in a personal injury action based on a UDAP theory, a court approved $92,500 for loss of future earning capacity (which was then trebled).[69] In a commercial UDAP case, a graphics business that had purchased a printing system that did not perform as represented recovered $96,586 in lost profits.[70] Damages for loss of job, income, work time, or leave from a job have been awarded in a number of debtor abuse cases, usually based on a tort claim.[71]

Care must be taken to plead and prove such damages. They will be denied if the court finds them too conjectural.

22.2.5.4 Lost Use of a Product or Service

If, because of a defendant's wrongdoing, the consumer is deprived of the use of a product, this loss should be compensated as consequential damages. For example, a consumer may have lost the use of a vehicle because it was defective or delivered late or repairs were slow or inadequate. Actual car rental costs can certainly be considered within the contemplation of the parties and thus are appropriate for consequential damages.[72] Courts may also award the reasonable rental value of a substitute vehicle, even when there is no evidence that the consumer had in fact rented a substitute vehicle.[73]

The consumer may be reimbursed for the cost of purchasing a substitute car—calculated as the down payment—and tax, title and license fees, plus the monthly car payments for the period involved.[74] This was found to be appropriate even when the defective but running car was parked in the

63 Quate v. Caudle, 381 S.E.2d 842 (N.C. Ct. App. 1989); Orkin Exterminating Co. v. Lesassier, 688 S.W.2d 651 (Tex. App. 1985). *See also* Jersild v. Aker, 775 F. Supp. 1198 (E.D. Wis. 1991).

64 York v. InTrust Bank, 265 Kan. 271, 962 P.2d 405 (1998).

65 *See* Bump v. Robbins, 24 Mass. App. 296, 509 N.E.2d 12 (1987) (consumer awarded damages for lost time).

66 Ybarra v. Saldona, 624 S.W.2d 948 (Tex. App. 1981). *See also* Vill. Mobile Homes, Inc. v. Porter, 716 S.W.2d 543 (Tex. App. 1986) (affirming award of $750 for ten hours lost wages because the consumer had to use his lunch time to repair a damaged car).

67 Vill. Mobile Homes, Inc. v. Porter, 716 S.W.2d 543 (Tex. App. 1986) (affirming award of $750 for ten hours lost wages because the consumer had to use his lunch time to repair a damaged car).

68 Hale v. Basin Motor Co., 110 N.M. 314, 795 P.2d 1006 (1990).

69 Keller Indus., Inc. v. Reeves, 656 S.W.2d 221 (Tex. App. 1983).

70 Innovative Office Sys. v. Johnson, 906 S.W.2d 940 (Tex. App. 1995), *vacated pursuant to settlement*, 911 S.W.2d 387 (Tex. App. 1995).

71 *See, e.g.*, Rannels v. S.E. Nichols, Inc., 591 F.2d 242 (3d Cir. 1979) (allegations of loss of respect, pain and embarrassment, handicap in returning to profession, and loss of consortium were sufficient to plead special damages and to withstand a motion to dismiss); Hill Grocery Co. v. Carroll, 223 Ala. 376, 136 So. 789 (1931) (awarding tort damages to plaintiff who was fired from new job because creditor [a former employer] threatened new employer with loss of creditor's business if it did not either coerce payment of disputed debt or fire plaintiff); Long v. Newby, 488 P.2d 719 (Alaska 1971) (upholding $7600 damages when creditor, who was on board of hospital where plaintiff worked, obtained board resolution that plaintiff be fired unless disputed debt paid); London Guarantee & Accident Co. v. Horn, 206 Ill. 493, 69 N.E. 526 (1903) (upholding $800 award for employee who lost job because his refusal to settle a claim with an insurer led insurer to threaten his employer with cancellation of entire insurance policy); Barnett v. Collection Serv. Co., 214 Iowa 1303, 242 N.W. 25 (1932) (threat to consumer's employment part of basis for jury verdict against collector); Margita v. Diamond Mortgage Corp., 159 Mich. App. 181, 406 N.W.2d 268 (1987) (loss of work, irritability at work alleged); Long v. Beneficial Fin. Co., 39 A.D.2d 11, 330 N.Y.S.2d 664 (1972) (cause of action stated when collector regularly contacted consumer at her job, phoned her landlord, etc., causing mental distress, heart attack, and loss of employment); Duty v. Gen. Fin. Co., 154 Tex. 16, 273 S.W.2d 64 (1954) (loss of work, credit rating, and employment alleged).

72 Centroplex Ford, Inc. v. Kirby, 736 S.W.2d 261 (Tex. App. 1987) (slow repairs); Bob Robertson, Inc. v. Webster, 679 S.W.2d 683 (Tex. App. 1984) (late delivery).

73 Burgess Constr. Co. v. Hancock, 514 P.2d 236 (Alaska 1973); Malinson v. Black, 83 Cal. App. 2d 375, 188 P.2d 788 (1948); Meakin v. Dreier, 209 So. 2d 252 (Fla. Dist. Ct. App. 1968); Chriss v. Manchester Ins. & Indemnity Co., 308 So. 2d 803 (La. Ct. App. 1975); Luna v. N. Star Dodge Sales, Inc., 653 S.W.2d 892 (Tex. 1983), *aff'd*, 667 S.W.2d 115 (Tex. 1984); Milt Ferguson Motor Co. v. Zeretzke, 827 S.W.2d 349 (Tex. App. 1991); Metro Ford Truck Sales, Inc. v. Davis, 709 S.W.2d 785 (Tex. App. 1986); Holmes v. Raffo, 60 Wash. 2d 421, 374 P.2d 536 (1962).

74 Town E. Ford Sales, Inc. v. Gray, 730 S.W.2d 796 (Tex. App. 1987).

consumer's own garage, when the consumer was rightfully concerned with the car's safety and the dealer would not take it back.[75] But a consumer should not obtain a double recovery for a replacement vehicle and for lost use. Lost use damages should be calculated only until a replacement vehicle is purchased, and, from then on, the consumer should just recover for the cost of the replacement vehicle.[76]

22.2.5.5 Attorney Fees

Often one of the greatest consequential costs to a consumer of a UDAP violation is the expense of hiring an attorney to untangle the problems caused by the deceptive practice. Most UDAP statutes authorize a prevailing consumer to recover the attorney fees required to obtain the UDAP judgment, so it will be unnecessary to recover these same costs as consequential damages. But some UDAP statutes do not do so.

Moreover, even in states that provide statutory attorney fees, the consumer may have legal expenses relating to the UDAP violation that are in addition to the costs of prosecuting the UDAP case. Furthermore, being able to treat legal expenses as actual damages may allow the consumer to treble those costs in some circumstances.

There are situations in which a court will award attorney fees as UDAP consequential damages. Attorney fees expended to collect money due from one party are recoverable as UDAP damages against the third party responsible for forcing the plaintiff to resort to a collection action.[77] Attorney fees required to be paid to defend an earlier lawsuit are recoverable as actual damages when an insurer's unconscionable conduct required the expenditure of those fees.[78] Attorney fees incurred defending a prior suit that was filed in an illegally distant forum may be recovered.[79]

22.2.5.6 Other Out-of-Pocket Losses

Other out-of-pocket losses might include

- medical or counseling expenses;
- telephone toll charges;
- telephone charges for an unlisted number;
- payments on an invalid claim;
- transportation expenses;
- payment of a debt barred by a statute of limitations;
- conversion of consumer's property; and
- the amount of a tax refund intercepted to pay a student loan that had been discharged in bankruptcy and accountant fees for filing for the return of the intercepted funds.[80]

22.2.5.7 Damages to Personal Relationships

The following are examples of relational injuries:

- injury to reputation;
- loss of privacy;
- loss of consortium;
- strain to marriage;
- strain with family; and
- humiliation.[81]

22.2.5.8 Injury to Credit Rating

Consumers may also be able to recover damages for injury to their credit rating resulting from the deceptive practice. For example, when a trucker purchased a defective truck, leading to lost income, repossession of the truck, and a bad credit rating, the trucker recovered $50,000 damages for loss of credit.[82]

A claim under the Fair Credit Reporting Act may also be appropriate when a creditor makes an inaccurate report to a credit reporting agency regarding a consumer debt. In general, to hold a creditor liable for furnishing inaccurate information, the consumer must first ask the credit reporting agency to reinvestigate the entry. If the creditor fails to cooperate in the reinvestigation, the consumer has an FCRA claim against the creditor.[83]

---

75 *Id.*

76 Jeep Eagle Sales Corp. v. Mack Massey Motors, Inc., 814 S.W.2d 167 (Tex. App. 1991).

77 Fraser Eng'g Co. v. Desmond, 26 Mass. App. Ct. 99, 524 N.E.2d 110 (1988).

78 Columbia Chiropractic Group, Inc. v. Trust Ins. Co., 430 Mass. 60, 712 N.E.2d 93 (1999) (UDAP damages can include fees for defense of lawsuit that was filed to collect unreasonable and unnecessary charges); Nationwide Mut. Ins. Co. v. Holmes, 842 S.W.2d 335 (Tex. App. 1992).

79 Venes v. Prof'l Serv. Bureau, Inc., 353 N.W.2d 671 (Minn. Ct. App. 1984) (damages of $3900 for attorney fees for violating FDCPA).

80 National Consumer Law Center, Unfair and Deceptive Acts and Practices § 2.5.2.2.3 (6th ed. 2004).

81 *See* National Consumer Law Center, Fair Debt Collection § 2.5.2.2.4 (5th ed. 2004 and Supp.).

82 Metro Ford Truck Sales, Inc. v. Davis, 709 S.W.2d 785 (Tex. App. 1986). *See also* Phillips v. David McDermott Chevrolet, Inc., 1992 Conn. Super. LEXIS 888 (Mar. 24, 1992) ($5000 for damage to credit rating); Connell Chevrolet Co. v. Leak, 967 S.W.2d 888, 892 (Tex. App. 1998); Smith v. Herco, Inc., 1995 Tex. App. LEXIS 965 (1995); City Nat'l Bank v. Wells, 384 S.E.2d 374 (W. Va. 1989) (damage to credit rating is consequential damages under UCC). *But cf.* Page & Wirtz Constr. Co. v. Solomon, 110 N.M. 206, 794 P.2d 349 (1990) (no award when no evidence of UDAP violation); National Consumer Law Center, Fair Debt Collection § 10.5 (5th ed. 2004 and Supp.).

83 15 U.S.C. § 1681s-2(b). *See* National Consumer Law Center, Fair Credit Reporting Ch. 3 (5th ed. 2002 and Supp.).

22.2.5.9 Pre-Judgment Interest

Whether a court will provide pre-judgment interest on a UDAP claim will normally depend on a state's general treatment of pre-judgment interest. One court has ruled that the authority in the UDAP statute to award such equitable relief as it deems proper was not, in itself, broad enough to allow an award of pre-judgment interest.[84] But when state law provides for such interest, a court certainly has the power to award pre-judgment interest on its UDAP damages award.[85] Whether pre-judgment interest should be trebled with other UDAP damages is discussed in National Consumer Law Center, *Unfair and Deceptive Acts and Practices* § 8.4.2.22.5 (6th ed. 2004).

22.2.6 Proving Actual Damages

22.2.6.1 General

Whatever theory a consumer uses in seeking damages—such as out-of-pocket, restitution, or actual damages—the consumer has the clear responsibility to prove the occurrence and extent of those damages and how they were caused by the illegal conduct. While proof of damages may not require mathematical precision, it must be based on more than mere speculation.[86]

When damage is to be based on the difference between what was paid for a defective car and what it was worth, the consumer must offer evidence of what the car was actually worth when purchased, not the consumer's opinion of how much the car is now worth.[87] While the owner of property is usually considered competent to testify as to its value, such testimony can be disregarded if it is mere speculation.[88] A plaintiff seeking consequential damages should also take care to introduce evidence that these damages were the foreseeable consequence of the violations or that other state standards for consequential damages are satisfied.[89]

Documentary evidence may be introduced to corroborate the existence and value of out-of-pocket losses. For example, a receipt for medication, a pay check showing the amount of the victim's wages, an employer's personnel file showing the employer's view of a change in work habits, or a collector's record of a third-party contact may be introduced once a proper foundation is provided.

22.2.6.2 Proving Physical Injury and Emotional Distress Damages

Lawyers must carefully distinguish evidence that tends to prove the existence, cause, and extent (seriousness and duration) of an injury from evidence of the value of the injury. Evidence of the latter type is often unnecessary. While evidence of the value of damages suffered must be introduced for damages such as property losses, out-of-pocket losses, or loss of wages, this evidence need not be introduced for damages such as personal injury, mental anguish, or injury to reputation. The trier of fact may attach dollar amounts to the latter types of injury without any proof of their value, on the basis of the arguments of counsel, the trier's own experience, and very general legal standards.[90]

Evidence of the existence, extent, cause, and value of personal injury, mental anguish, and reputational damages usually comes from the victim of the injury, corroborating witnesses, expert witnesses, and (less often) documentary evidence. The victim of the injury may (and usually must, to present a convincing case) submit testimony concerning the injury's existence, severity, and duration. Rather than give opinions, the victim should simply state the observable manifestations of the injury. The severity and duration of each symptom of each injury should be detailed in order to maximize the recovery. Friends, clergy, and family may serve as corroborating witnesses and testify as to the physical manifestations or spontaneous declarations that accompanied each injury they observed. Corroborating witnesses may be able to provide dramatic details of suffering.[91]

A physician who either treated the victim or later became familiar with the victim's medical history is usually necessary to present a convincing case if the consumer has received medical treatment. The treating physician can corroborate the existence and extent of the injury. Any informed physician can answer hypothetical questions corroborating evidence of the extent and cause of an injury and

---

84 Nielsen v. Wisniewski, 32 Conn. App. 133, 628 A.2d 25 (1993).

85 Concorde Limousines, Inc. v. Moloney Coachbuilders, Inc., 835 F.2d 541 (5th Cir. 1987) (Texas law); Mill Pond Assocs. v. E. & B. Giftware, Inc., 751 F. Supp. 299 (D. Mass. 1990); State v. Bob Chambers Ford, Inc., 522 A.2d 362 (Me. 1987); Quintero v. Jim Walter Homes, Inc., 709 S.W.2d 225 (Tex. App. 1986). *But see* Am. Baler Co. v. SRS Sys., Inc., 748 S.W.2d 243 (Tex. App. 1988).

86 *See* National Consumer Law Center, Unfair and Deceptive Acts and Practices § 8.3.5.1 (6th ed. 2004).

87 Fort Lauderdale Lincoln Mercury v. Corgnati, 715 So. 2d 311 (Fla. Dist. Ct. App. 1998) (vacating damage award because of failure to prove diminished value of car); Hall v. Lovell Regency Homes Ltd., 121 Md. App. 1, 708 A.2d 344 (1998) (UDAP claim dismissed when evidence of actual value related solely to present time, not time of sale); Town E. Ford Sales, Inc. v. Gray, 730 S.W.2d 796 (Tex. App. 1987).

88 Hall v. Lovell Regency Homes Ltd., 121 Md. App. 1, 708 A.2d 344 (1998). *See generally* National Consumer Law Center, Consumer Warranty Law § 10.5.5 (2d ed. 2001 and Supp.).

89 *See* § 22.2.5, *supra*.

90 *See* J. Stein, 1 Personal Injury Damages §§ 1.5, 1.6 (3d ed. 1997); Dan B. Dobbs, *The Law of Remedies* §§ 3.1, 8.1(4) (2d ed. 1993). *See also* jury instructions on the companion CD-Rom to this manual.

91 Fed. R. Evid. 803(3).

the reasonableness of medical expenses. The absence of a treating physician as a witness may reflect negatively on the case.

22.2.6.3 Causation

Issues of causation must be carefully considered in any attempt to prove damages in consumer protection cases. Legal issues involving the concepts of proximate cause, intervening causes, and legally remote damages may arise in such cases. For example, a consumer suffering from abusive debt collection tactics is often in a financially distressed position that is stressful in itself and may have resulted from another traumatic event, such as illness, marital problems, or loss of employment. Suffering caused by different traumatic events must be differentiated as much as possible by counsel. Consumers suffering from financial stress are often subject to collection contacts from a variety of creditors; if the stress related to these combined collection efforts can not be separated according to each collector's activities, consideration should be given to joining all of them as joint tortfeasors.[92]

Some clients will be particularly susceptible to stress-related injuries and may benefit from the rule that a tortfeasor must take the victim as he or she is and must compensate the victim for his or her full measure of suffering. A likely issue in a case involving such a client is whether the client's suffering was actually exacerbated or triggered by the statutory violation or by the condition that made him or her particularly susceptible in the first place.[93] To overcome these problems, it is highly desirable to show the proximity in time between a collection contact and any suffering and to establish the collection contact as a substantial factor in the suffering.

A number of courts follow the common law rule that consequential damages are recoverable only if they were a foreseeable consequence of the wrong.[94] The Uniform Commercial Code also limits consequential damages for breach of contract to those resulting from requirements of which the seller had reason to know.[95]

Under the Texas UDAP statute, a deceptive practice need only have been the "producing cause" of the damage.[96] A producing cause is a substantial factor that brings about the injury and without which the injury would not have occurred and, unlike proximate cause, does not require a showing of foreseeability.[97]

22.2.7 Contractual and Other Limitations on Damages

22.2.7.1 Contractual Limitations on Damages

The Uniform Commercial Code allows sellers to limit the remedies available for breach of warranty.[98] Even under the Uniform Commercial Code, though, such a clause has no effect if it is unconscionable or if it deprives the consumer of the substantial value of the bargain.[99]

Few contractual limitation of remedy clauses even purport to apply to claims other than breach of warranty. Even if they are worded to apply beyond breach-of-warranty claims, courts reject the application of such clauses to fraud and other tort claims.[100] Furthermore, a waiver in a form contract of rights under consumer protection laws should be contrary to public policy and therefore void.[101]

In other words, a contractual provision limiting the consumer's remedies may be effective in limiting a consumer's damages resulting from a contract or warranty claim. But an action under a consumer protection statute is not based on a contract or a warranty but rather on the seller's unfair or deceptive practices.[102]

If there is an "as-is" clause in a contract, it may preclude the consumer from claiming an implied warranty, but most courts agree that such a clause will not preclude UDAP or tort claims.[103]

22.2.7.2 Collateral Source Rule

A defendant may argue that its liability should be reduced by any insurance proceeds received by a consumer for the

92 *See* Indus. Fin. Serv. Co. v. Riley, 295 S.W.2d 498 (Tex. App. 1956) (fifteen loan companies joined).

93 W. Page Keeton, *Prosser & Keeton on the Law of Torts* § 47 at 327 (5th ed. 1984); Dan B. Dobbs, *The Law of Torts* §§ 188, 313 (2000).

94 *See, e.g.*, Dimarzo v. Am. Mut. Ins. Co., 389 Mass. 85, 449 N.E.2d 1189 (1983) (entitled to all losses foreseeable consequent to insurer failing to settle claim); Taylor v. Medenica, 479 S.E.2d 35 (S.C. 1996).

95 U.C.C. § 2-715(2)(a). *See* National Consumer Law Center, Consumer Warranty Law § 10.6.3 (2d ed. 2001 and Supp.).

96 Tex. Bus. & Com. Code § 122.50.

97 Alexander v. Turtur & Assocs., 146 S.W.3d 113, 117 (Tex. 2004); Doe v. Boys Clubs of Greater Dallas, Inc., 907 S.W.2d 472, 481 (Tex. 1995); Union Pump Co. v. Allbritton, 898 S.W.2d 773 (Tex. 1995) (product liability case) (contrasting proximate cause, which requires foreseeability, with producing cause, which does not).

98 U.C.C. § 2-719.

99 *Id. See* National Consumer Law Center, Consumer Warranty Law Ch. 9 (2d ed. 2001 and Supp.).

100 *See* National Consumer Law Center, Consumer Warranty Law § 9.4.4 (2d ed. 2001 and Supp.).

101 *Id. See also* National Consumer Law Center, Truth in Lending § 22.5.4 (5th ed. 2003 and Supp.); National Consumer Law Center, The Cost of Credit: Regulation, Preemption, and Industry Abuses § 10.6.4 (3d ed. 2005.)

102 Martin v. Lou Poliquin Enters., Inc., 696 S.W.2d 180 (Tex. App. 1985).

103 *See* National Consumer Law Center, Consumer Warranty Law § 5.15 (2d ed. 2001 and Supp.); National Consumer Law Center, Automobile Fraud § 22.8.2 (2d ed. 2003 and Supp.).

same injury. In states with a collateral source rule, insurance proceeds received by the consumer should not reduce the recovery under a UDAP or other consumer protection statute. The Texas Supreme Court has held that the collateral source rule applies to UDAP claims.[104]

22.2.7.3 Mitigation of Damages

Some courts may find that the consumer has a duty to mitigate damages in UDAP and other consumer protection cases.[105] Even then, the defendant has the burden of proving that the consumer has not used reasonable diligence to do so.[106] The defendant must also prove that the steps it claims the consumer should have taken would have been effective to remedy the damage.[107]

22.2.7.4 Economic Loss Rule

The "economic loss doctrine" denies recovery in tort for the decreased value of a product and other economic losses.[108] Many courts apply this doctrine to preclude recovery in negligence for the diminished value of a defective product. Most courts hold that the economic loss doctrine has no application to UDAP claims, even those that are founded upon contracts.[109] UDAP claims are statutory causes of action rather than tort claims, and the legislature's decision to grant expanded remedies to consumers should not be overridden based on common law restrictions that the legislature did not explicitly adopt.[110] The same rationale should apply to other statutory causes of action. In addition, many courts hold that the doctrine has no application to fraud claims, reasoning that the purpose of the rule—to limit parties to their contract remedies—is not promoted when fraud has undermined the consumer's ability to negotiate the terms and remedies of the contract.[111]

104 Brown v. Am. Transfer & Storage Co., 601 S.W.2d 931 (Tex. 1980). *See also* Global Petrotech, Inc. v. Engelhard Corp., 824 F. Supp. 103 (S.D. Tex. 1993) (reluctantly following *Brown*; insurance proceeds will not reduce UDAP award).

105 Cambridge Plating Co. v. NAPCO, Inc., 85 F.3d 752 (1st Cir. 1996); Gunn Infiniti, Inc. v. O'Byrne, 996 S.W.2d 854 (Tex. 1999); Pinson v. Red Arrow Freight Lines, Inc., 801 S.W.2d 14 (Tex. App. 1990) (common law mitigation duties apply to a UDAP claim).

106 Pierce v. Drees, 607 N.E.2d 726 (Ind. Ct. App. 1993); York v. InTrust Bank, 265 Kan. 271, 962 P.2d 405 (1998) (defendant's proof insufficient).

107 Pierce v. Drees, 607 N.E.2d 726 (Ind. Ct. App. 1993).

108 *See* National Consumer Law Center, Consumer Warranty Law § 12.2 (2d ed. 2001 and Supp.).

109 *See* National Consumer Law Center, Unfair and Deceptive Acts and Practices § 4.2.16.2 (6th ed. 2004).

110 Delgado v. J. W. Courtesy Pontiac GMC-Truck, Inc., 693 So. 2d 602 (Fla. Dist. Ct. App. 1997). *See* § 22.3.1.1, *supra*.

111 National Consumer Law Center, Consumer Warranty Law § 11.4.4b (2d ed. 2001 and Supp.).

22.2.7.5 Relationship of Actual Damages to Other Damages

A consumer is entitled to only one compensatory recovery for a single injury.[112] Thus, for example, a consumer may not recover duplicative actual damages for the same act that is both a breach of contract and a UDAP violation. However, the consumer may receive actual, punitive, and/or statutory damages for multiple causes of action for the same wrongful conduct.[113]

22.3 Statutory and Multiple Damages

22.3.1 Minimum Statutory Damages

A common feature of consumer protection statutes is to allow private litigants to recover a minimum statutory damage award, such as $1000, regardless of the existence or amount of actual damages. The purpose of statutory damages is remedial rather than punitive.[114] Statutory damages are intended to encourage private enforcement of the statute[115] and provide an economic incentive for businesses to comply with it.[116] They also represent a recognition that many types of damages that consumers suffer will be difficult or expensive to prove, so a minimum award should be provided in all cases.

Examples of statutes under which statutory damages are available include the following:

- The Truth in Lending Act: Double the finance charge, with a minimum of $100 and a maximum of $1000 ($200 and $2000 in transactions secured by real property or a dwelling) for certain specified violations of the statute's disclosure rules and for violation of its substantive protections (which primarily affect credit cards)[117]
- The Fair Debt Collection Practices Act: Up to $1000,

112 Waite Hill Servs., Inc. v. World Class Metal Works, Inc., 959 S.W.2d 182 (Tex. 1998); Bekins Moving & Storage Co. v. Williams, 947 S.W.2d 568 (Tex. App. 1997).

113 *See* §§ 22.3.3, 22.4.6, *infra*.

114 Maberry v. Said, 927 F. Supp. 1456 (D. Kan. 1996). *See* National Consumer Law Center, Unfair and Deceptive Acts and Practices § 8.4.1.1 (6th ed. 2004); National Consumer Law Center, Truth in Lending § 8.6.1 (5th ed. 2003 and Supp.).

115 *See, e.g.*, Edwards v. Your Credit, Inc., 148 F.3d 427 (5th Cir. 1998) (TIL statutory damages); Rodash v. AIB Mortgage Co., 16 F.3d 1142 (11th Cir. 1994) (TIL statutory damages); Ives v. W.T. Grant Co., 522 F.2d 749 (2d Cir. 1975) (TIL statutory damages); Geismar v. Abraham & Strauss, 109 Misc. 2d 495, 439 N.Y.S.2d 1005 (Dist. Ct. 1981) (UDAP statutory damages).

116 *In re* Marshall, 121 B.R. 814 (Bankr. C.D. Ill. 1990), *aff'd*, 132 B.R. 904 (C.D. Ill. 1991), *aff'd*, 970 F.2d 383 (7th Cir. 1992) (TIL statutory damages); *In re* Perkins, 106 B.R. 863, 864 (Bankr. E.D. Pa. 1989) (TIL statutory damages).

117 15 U.S.C. § 1640(a).

based on factors specified in the statute, for any violation[118]

- The Telephone Consumer Protection Act: $500 (subject to trebling in the case of a knowing or willful violation) for violation of the statute's telemarketing rules, such as junk faxes and repeat violations of do-not-call rules[119]
- The federal odometer statute: $1500[120]
- The Real Estate Settlement Procedures Act (RESPA): $1000 for certain violations if a pattern or practice is shown[121]
- The Electronic Fund Transfer Act: $100 to $1000, based on factors listed in the statute, for violations other than those involving error correction procedures[122]
- The Fair Credit Reporting Act: $100 to $1000 for willful violations ($1000 against a natural person who obtains a consumer credit report under false pretenses or knowingly without a permissible purpose)[123]
- The Bankruptcy Code's restrictions on petition preparers: $2000[124]
- Article 9 of the Uniform Commercial Code: The finance charge plus 10% of the principal or cash price for violation of requirements regarding repossession and disposition of consumer goods collateral;[125] and a $500 statutory damage award for violation of certain miscellaneous requirements, such as failing to respond to certain requests for information[126]
- About half the state UDAP statutes: Amounts ranging from $25 to $5000, with enhanced statutory damages in a few states if the victim is elderly or disabled[127]

Other consumer protection statutes, such as the Home Ownership and Equity Protection Act[128] and the Credit Repair Organizations Act,[129] establish a right to damages in the amount of the payments made by the consumer. These provisions function like a statutory damages award because they provide a fixed award regardless of the amount of actual damages.

Statutory minimum damages for consumer litigants must be distinguished from provisions that allow the state attorney general or other public enforcement authorities to seek civil penalties. UDAP statutes, for example, typically allow the attorney general to seek civil penalties ranging from $500 to $25,000 for initial UDAP violations. Private litigants can not seek such penalties but are limited to statutory minimum damages, if available, and other private remedies.[130] However, this distinction is complicated because the phrase "civil penalties" in a UDAP statute may refer to private, minimum statutory damages.[131]

Statutory minimum damages not only allow consumers more sizeable recoveries when actual damage is small but also avoid problems of proving damages when the cost of proof may be high. Many consumer protection statutes make it clear that minimum damages can be awarded even if it is not feasible for the consumer to prove actual damages.[132] UDAP statutes are often less clear, but many have been interpreted as allowing statutory damages regardless of whether any actual damage is established.[133] Even UDAP statutes that require a showing of "ascertainable loss" as a precondition of suit have often been interpreted to require only that the loss be capable of being discovered and that the loss actually be established.[134] Damage or ascertainable loss requirements also have been interpreted as being satisfied with only minimal consumer damages.[135] Thus, minimum damages are awarded even in states that require ascertainable loss when there are only slight damages, as long as

118 15 U.S.C. § 1692k(a)(2).

119 47 U.S.C. § 227(b)(3), (c)(5).

120 49 U.S.C. § 32710(a).

121 12 U.S.C. § 2605(f). *See* National Consumer Law Center, The Cost of Credit: Regulation, Preemption, and Industry Abuses § 12.2.1.10 (3d ed. 2005).

122 15 U.S.C. § 1693m(2).

123 15 U.S.C. § 1681n(a). *See* National Consumer Law Center, Fair Credit Reporting § 11.3 (5th ed. 2002 and Supp.).

124 11 U.S.C. § 110(i). *See* National Consumer Law Center, Unfair and Deceptive Acts and Practices § 5.12.2.3 (6th ed. 2004).

125 U.C.C. § 9-625(c)(2). *See* National Consumer Law Center, Repossessions § 13.2 (6th ed. 2005).

126 U.C.C. § 9-625(e), (f). *See* National Consumer Law Center, Repossessions § 13.2 (6th ed. 2005).

127 *See* National Consumer Law Center, Unfair and Deceptive Acts and Practices § 8.4 (6th ed. 2004).

128 15 U.S.C. § 1640(a)(4) (all finance charges and fees paid by the consumer).

129 15 U.S.C. § 1679g(a)(1)(B).

130 Peery v. Hansen, 120 Ariz. 266, 585 P.2d 574 (Ct. App. 1978); Gramatan Home Investors Corp. v. Starling, 470 A.2d 1157 (Vt. 1983); Stigall v. Courtesy Chevrolet-Pontiac, Inc., 15 Wash. App. 739, 551 P.2d 763 (1976).

131 *See* Bell v. Kent-Brown Chevrolet Co., 1 Kan. App. 2d 131, 561 P.2d 907 (1977).

132 *See, e.g.*, National Consumer Law Center, Truth in Lending § 8.6.1 (5th ed. 2003 and Supp.) (actual damages not a prerequisite for award of TIL statutory damages); National Consumer Law Center, Fair Debt Collection § 6.4.4 (5th ed. 2004 and Supp.) (actual damages not a prerequisite for award of FDCPA statutory damages).

133 Perez v. Anderson, 98 B.R. 189 (E.D. Pa. 1989) (awarding statutory damages despite no actual damages); Clayton v. McCary, 426 F. Supp. 248 (N.D. Ohio 1976); Swanston v. McConnell Air Force Base Fed. Credit Union, 8 Kan. App. 2d 538, 661 P.2d 826 (1983); Carter v. Lachance, 766 A.2d 717 (N.H. 2001) (statutory damages are required even without proof of actual damages); Jones v. Gen. Motors Corp., 953 P.2d 1104 (N.M. App. 1998) (statutory damages allowed even if no actual damage shown); Dantzig v. Sloe, 115 Ohio App. 3d 64, 684 N.E.2d 715 (1996); Gaylan v. Dave Towell Cadillac, 15 Ohio Misc. 2d 1, 473 N.E.2d 64 (Mun. Ct. 1984). *See also* Page & Wirtz Constr. Co. v. Solomon, 110 N.M. 206, 794 P.2d 349 (1990); Couto v. Gibson, Inc., 1992 Ohio App. LEXIS 756 (Feb. 26, 1992). *But see* Shurtliff v. Northwest Pools, Inc., 120 Idaho 263, 815 P.2d 461 (Ct. App. 1991) (no statutory damages when no actual damages).

134 *See* National Consumer Law Center, Unfair and Deceptive Acts and Practices (6th ed. 2004).

135 *Id.*

these damages are capable of being shown, whether or not they are proven.

22.3.2 *Multiple Awards of Statutory Damages*

While statutory damages are designed to encourage private enforcement of consumer protection laws, in many cases the amounts are so low as to undercut this goal. For this reason, it is important to determine whether a consumer can recover multiple statutory damage awards for multiple violations of the same or different statutes or recover statutory damages on top of actual damages.

Some consumer protection statutes have an explicit provision about whether the consumer can recover multiple statutory damages for multiple violations. The Truth in Lending Act, for example, limits the consumer to a single statutory damage award even for multiple violations of its disclosure requirements.[136] However, multiple awards of statutory damages may be possible when the creditor violates requirements other than disclosure requirements, such as the right to rescind or the substantive rules for credit cards.[137] Article 9 of the Uniform Commercial Code also specifically forbids more than one recovery per transaction of the statutory damages of the finance charge plus 10% of the cash price or principal.[138]

Other statutes explicitly allow multiple statutory damages awards. Some UDAP statutes, for example, have been interpreted to allow statutory damages on a per-violation basis.[139] Article 9 of the Uniform Commercial Code provides for a supplemental $500 award for certain miscellaneous violations that is explicitly available on a per-violation basis.[140]

Even if a consumer can not recover multiple statutory damage awards under a single statute, the court may allow the consumer to recover statutory damages under each of two statutes. Such an award achieves each statute's goal of deterring violations. Thus, courts have awarded

- Fair Debt Collection Practices Act statutory damages and UDAP statutory damages for similar collection agency misconduct;[141]
- statutory damages under Article 9 of the Uniform Commercial Code for a commercially unreasonable sale of repossessed collateral, under the Truth in Lending Act for inadequate disclosure of the security interest, and under the state small loan act for other improper disclosures in the credit agreement;[142] and
- statutory damages under both the Article 9 of the Uniform Commercial Code and the Connecticut retail installment sales act.[143]

22.3.3 *Statutory Damages Plus Actual Damages*

Another question is whether statutory damages are in lieu of or in addition to actual damages. Some federal consumer protection statutes, such as the Fair Debt Collection Practices Act[144] and the Truth in Lending Act,[145] explicitly make both actual and statutory damages available for the same violation. On the other hand, under the federal Fair Credit Reporting Act a consumer may recover either actual or statutory damages, but not both, for willful violations (but punitive damages may be awarded in addition to either actual or statutory damages).[146] The federal odometer statute allows statutory damages of $1500 or three times actual damages, whichever is greater.[147] Article 9 of the Uniform Commercial Code allows statutory damages of the finance charge plus 10% of the principal as an alternative to actual damages.[148] A second $500 statutory damages provision, available for violation of certain specified Article 9 duties, is in addition to actual damages.[149]

While a statutory provision allowing "actual damages or civil penalties" could be construed to authorize the award of only one or the other,[150] an Oregon court held that a consumer could obtain actual damages for one UDAP violation and statutory minimum damages for another separate UDAP violation.[151] A court has also awarded actual UDAP damages on one count and statutory damages under the Truth in Lending Act on another count.[152]

136 15 U.S.C. § 1640(g).

137 *See* National Consumer Law Center, Truth in Lending § 8.6.3.1.1 (5th ed. 2003 and Supp.).

138 U.C.C. § 9-628(e).

139 *See* National Consumer Law Center, Unfair and Deceptive Acts and Practices § 8.4.1.2 (6th ed. 2004).

140 U.C.C. § 9-625(e).

141 *In re* Belile, 209 B.R. 658 (Bankr. E.D. Pa. 1997).

142 Merchandise Nat'l Bank v. Scanlon, 86 Ill. App. 3d 719, 408 N.E.2d 248 (1980).

143 Jacobs v. Healey Ford-Subaru, Inc., 652 A.2d 496 (Conn. 1995).

144 15 U.S.C. § 1692k(a).

145 15 U.S.C. § 1640(a).

146 15 U.S.C. § 1681n(a). *See* National Consumer Law Center, Fair Credit Reporting Ch. 11 (5th ed. 2002 and Supp.).

147 49 U.S.C. § 32710(a).

148 U.C.C. § 9-625(c).

149 U.C.C. § 9-625(e), (f).

150 Bell v. Kent-Brown Chevrolet Co., 1 Kan. App. 2d 131, 561 P.2d 907 (1977).

151 Tri-West Constr. Co. v. Hernandez, 43 Or. App. 961, 607 P.2d 1375 (1979).

152 Douglas v. G.E.E.N. Corp., 415 So. 2d 130 (Fla. Dist. Ct. App. 1982). *See also* Simpson v. Smith, 34 Ohio Misc. 2d 7, 517 N.E.2d 276 (Mun. Ct. 1987) (statutory damages for each of two UDAP violations, treble damages for a third UDAP violation, plus actual damages for a fourth violation); Sherwood v. Bellevue Dodge, Inc., 35 Wash. App. 741, 669 P.2d 1258 (1983) ($1000 statutory damages on UDAP count plus $1000 tort damages for infliction of emotional distress).

22.3.4 Statutory Damages in Class Actions

Another question is whether each class member in a class action can recover statutory damages. Some consumer protection statutes, such as the Truth in Lending Act and the Fair Debt Collection Practices Act, explicitly authorize statutory damages in class actions and provide factors for the court to use in setting the statutory damages award.[153] On the other hand, some UDAP statutes explicitly bar statutory damages in class actions.[154] When a statute is silent, courts attempt to divine the legislative intent and rely on general principles of law to determine whether statutory damages can be awarded on a class-wide basis.

22.3.5 Multiple Damages

Many consumer protection statutes offer multiple damages to consumer litigants. Examples include the federal Racketeer Influenced and Corrupt Organizations Act (RICO),[155] the Real Estate Settlement Procedures Act,[156] the Telephone Consumer Protection Act,[157] the federal odometer statute,[158] and the Electronic Fund Transfer Act.[159] About half of all UDAP statutes authorize treble or other multiple damage awards, often conditioning the award on a showing of willfulness, knowledge, or some other special level of wrongdoing.[160]

Unlike minimum damages, multiple damages are awarded only if actual damages are proven.[161] When an individual consumer's actual damages are nominal, three times this amount will still be nominal. But when actual damages are substantial, the possibility of multiple damages should significantly affect settlement negotiations and a consumer litigant's willingness to press the action.

153 15 U.S.C. § 1640(a)(2)(B) (TILA); 15 U.S.C. § 1692k(a)(2)(B), (b)(2) (FDCPA).

154 *See* National Consumer Law Center, Unfair and Deceptive Acts and Practices §§ 8.4.1.3, 8.5.7 (6th ed. 2004).

155 18 U.S.C. § 1964(c).

156 12 U.S.C. §§ 2607(d), 2608(b) (available for violations of duty to provide "controlled business arrangement" notice, prohibition against kickbacks, fee splitting and unearned fees, and title insurance steering).

157 47 U.S.C. § 227(b)(3), (c)(5) (if violation was willful or knowing).

158 49 U.S.C. § 32710(a) ($1500 statutory damages or three times actual damages, whichever is greater).

159 15 U.S.C. § 1693f(e) (for certain violations of the correction of error procedures).

160 *See* National Consumer Law Center, Unfair and Deceptive Acts and Practices Appx. A (6th ed. 2004).

161 Faris v. Model's Guild, 297 So. 2d 536 (La. Ct. App. 1974); Schafer v. Conner, 805 S.W.2d 554 (Tex. App. 1991); Sign-O-Lite Signs, Inc. v. Delaurenti Florists, Inc., 825 P.2d 714 (Wash. Ct. App. 1992). The Telephone Consumer Protection Act, 47 U.S.C. § 227(b)(3), (c)(5), is an exception, allowing the $500 statutory damage award to be trebled if the defendant acted knowingly or willfully.

Multiple damages have a number of purposes. They are an incentive for private individuals to ferret out deception and bring legal actions, they provide a remedy for those injured, they deter future seller misconduct, and they increase the incentive for the parties to reach a settlement.[162] Multiple damages can also compensate consumers for injuries that the law of damages does not recognize and for damages that the consumer, with only limited resources, is unable to prove at trial. Thus UDAP statutes' treble damage provisions are not penal but remedial[163] and should be liberally construed. There is no merit to the claim that treble damages should only be available when actual damages are small.[164] Detailed analysis of multiple damages is provided in National Consumer Law Center, *Unfair and Deceptive Acts and Practices* (6th ed. 2004).[165]

22.4 Punitive Damages

22.4.1 The Importance of Punitive Damages

Aggressive and effective pursuit of punitive damages on behalf of defrauded consumers can have dramatic benefits for clients, their community, and the capacity of a law firm to represent other clients effectively. With a punitive damage award, the consumer receives full compensation for all injuries suffered. Similar fraud is deterred, and the law firm has the resources to pursue similar cases. The attorney's recovery of punitive damages in one case will give that firm credibility in the next case for which it seeks punitive damages, making a just outcome that much easier to achieve.

The potential of hundreds of thousands of dollars in punitive damages justifies extensive factual investigation and discovery, which is often necessary to represent the client effectively. In this way the attorney can determine the actual facts and whether the business's conduct is intentional and part of a pattern of abuse. Simply bringing the corporation's practices to the light of day may be enough to stop the practice.

162 *See, e.g.*, State *ex rel.* Easley v. Rich Food Servs., Inc., 535 S.E.2d 84 (N.C. App. 2000) (purpose of treble damages and fees is to enable private citizens to prosecute claims that might otherwise involve prohibitive expense); Marshall v. Miller, 302 N.C. 539, 276 S.E.2d 397 (1981); Jim Walter Homes, Inc. v. Valencia, 690 S.W.2d 239 (Tex. 1985); Pennington v. Singleton, 606 S.W.2d 682 (Tex. 1980); Wilder v. Aetna Life & Cas. Ins. Co., 140 Vt. 16, 433 A.2d 309 (1981).

163 Holley v. Coggin Pontiac, 43 N.C. App. 229, 259 S.E.2d 1 (1979). *But see* Jones v. Sportelli, 166 N.J. Super. 383, 399 A.2d 1047 (Law. Div. 1979).

164 Mosley & Mosley Builders v. Landin Ltd., 389 S.E.2d 576 (N.C. Ct. App. 1990).

165 National Consumer Law Center, Unfair and Deceptive Acts and Practices § 8.4.2 (6th ed. 2004).

22.4.2 Preparing to Handle Punitive Damages Cases

Not unreasonably, many attorneys feel they have neither the expertise to jump into a jury trial seeking large punitive damages nor the resources to invest in discovery and trial and the eventual appeals that such a case will require.

The answer for most attorneys is to team up with another firm that has the expertise and the resources and that is willing to go to the mat in the case. Fortunately, a growing number of attorneys handling consumer cases have the resources and expertise to win large punitive damage awards.

Attorneys with specialties outside consumer fraud can also make successful partners. The legal aid office or private attorney with the consumer client can provide the legal theories and the client, and the partner can provide the discovery resources and the trial experience. After one or two such partnerships, the attorney may be ready and have the resources to handle such a case solo.

22.4.3 Availability of Punitive Damages

22.4.3.1 Availability Under Common Law

The general rule, in effect in all but a few jurisdictions,[166] is that punitive damages are available for at least some types of tortious conduct.[167] In some jurisdictions, punitive damages are also available for particularly egregious breaches of contract.[168] The consumer may have to plead an independent tort count although some cases allow punitive damages even without a tort count, as long as tort-like conduct is proven.[169]

Common law standards concerning when punitive damages are awarded vary from state to state. Common criteria for awarding punitive damages are malice, willful or wanton conduct, ill will, or reckless indifference to the interests of others.[170] When maliciousness or willfulness is required, it is seldom established by a direct admission by the defendant; usually it must be inferred from the nature and circumstances of the misconduct.[171] Unless a consumer protection statute specifies other standards, courts are likely to use a state's common law fraud standards in determining whether punitive damages are appropriate.[172]

In at least some jurisdictions, punitive damages can be awarded in common law fraud actions even if actual damages are not proven.[173] Some courts follow this rule in UDAP cases as well.[174]

Punitive damages are usually awarded to punish the defendant, hold the defendant up as an example to others, and deter future misconduct. Many jurisdictions allow evidence of the defendant's financial worth and profits to be admitted to ensure that the punitive damage award is sufficient to deter future misconduct.

166 The following jurisdictions are exceptions to the general rule:

LOUISIANA: Gray v. State, through the Dep't of Highways, 202 So. 2d 24, 30 (La. 1967) (punitive damages not permitted under civil law system); Ricard v. State, 382 So. 2d 190, 193 (La. Ct. App. 1980) (punitive damages not allowed unless specifically provided for), *aff'd*, 390 So. 2d 882 (La. 1980).

MASSACHUSETTS: Flesner v. Technical Commc'ns Corp., 575 N.E.2d 1107, 1112 (Mass. 1991) (punitive damages not allowed unless expressly authorized by statute); Santana v. Registrar of Voters, 502 N.E.2d 132, 135 (Mass. 1986).

NEBRASKA: Distinctive Printing & Packaging Co. v. Cox, 443 N.W.2d 566 (Neb. 1989) (interpreting Neb. Const. art. VII, § 5, to bar punitive damages); Miller v. Kingsley, 230 N.W.2d 472 (Neb. 1975) (interpreting Nebraska Constitution to bar punitive damages).

NEW HAMPSHIRE: N.H. Rev. Stat. Ann. § 507:16 (no punitive damages may be awarded in any action unless otherwise authorized by statute).

WASHINGTON: Steele v. Johnson, 458 P.2d 889, 890 (Wash. 1969) (punitive damages not allowed unless expressly authorized by legislature).

167 *See* Jacob Stein, *Personal Injury Damages* Ch. 4 (3d ed. 1997 with annual supp.); Dan B. Dobbs, 1 *Law of Remedies* § 3.11 (2d ed. 1993); National Consumer Law Center, Fair Debt Collection § 6.5 (5th ed. 2004 and Supp.) (discussion of punitive damages under the FDCPA).

168 *See* National Consumer Law Center, Consumer Warranty Law § 10.7 (2d ed. 2001 and Supp.).

169 *Id.*

170 *See* National Consumer Law Center, Automobile Fraud § 22.10.3 (2d ed. 2003 and Supp.); National Consumer Law Center, Unfair and Deceptive Acts and Practices § 8.4.3.3 (6th ed. 2004).

171 Jacob Stein, *Personal Injury Damages* § 4.9 (3d ed. 1997 with annual Supp.).

172 Boulevard Assocs. v. Sovereign Hotels, Inc., 861 F. Supp. 1132 (D. Conn. 1994) (Connecticut's UDAP statute expands purpose of punitive damages to include deterrence as well as compensation), *rev'd on other grounds*, 72 F.3d 1029 (2d Cir. 1995); Ford Motor Co. v. Mayes, 575 S.W.2d 480 (Ky. Ct. App. 1978); Deck & Decker Personnel Consultants, Ltd. v. Thomas, 623 S.W.2d 90 (Mo. Ct. App. 1981); Crooks v. Payless Drug Stores, 592 P.2d 196 (Or. 1979); Teague Motor Co. v. Rowton, 84 Or. App. 72, 733 P.2d 93 (1987); Dailey v. Sundance Ranches, Inc., 59 Or. App. 142, 650 P.2d 994 (1982); Mabin v. Tualatin Dev., 48 Or. App. 271, 616 P.2d 1196 (1980). *But cf.* MacTools, Inc. v. Griffin, 126 Idaho 193, 879 P.2d 1126 (1994) (approving use of UDAP statute's "repeated or flagrant violations" standard, which is less strict than general standard).

173 *See, e.g.*, Nappe v. Anschelewitz, Barr, Ansell & Bonello, 97 N.J. 37, 477 A.2d 1224 (1984). *See generally* National Consumer Law Center, Automobile Fraud § 22.10.1 (2d ed. 2003 and Supp.).

174 *See, e.g.*, Tillquist v. Ford Motor Credit Co., 714 F. Supp. 607 (D. Conn. 1989); Conway v. Am. Excavating, Inc., 41 Conn. App. 437, 676 A.2d 881 (1996).

22.4.3.2 Availability for Statutory Claims

Ten UDAP statutes explicitly authorize punitive damages,[175] and a separate Minnesota statute authorizes punitive damages for UDAP and other claims.[176] Some additional UDAP statutes authorize punitive damages for elderly or disabled victims.[177] Some federal consumer protection statutes, such as the Equal Credit Opportunity Act,[178] the Credit Repair Organizations Act,[179] and the Fair Credit Reporting Act,[180] also expressly allow punitive damages.

Even without express language, a court may find punitive damages to be implicitly sanctioned in statutory causes of action, particularly when courts award punitive damages for common law fraud.[181]

22.4.3.3 Common Law Fraud or Tort Punitive Damages When UDAP or Other Consumer Protection Statute Does Not Allow Punitive Damages

If a consumer protection statute does not authorize punitive damages, in appropriate cases consumer attorneys should add a common law fraud count and seek punitive damages under the common law fraud claim. This strategy has often been used successfully in UDAP cases.

There is no merit to the argument that the availability of UDAP remedies preempts common law tort claims or remedies.[182] Similarly, consumers should not have to elect between UDAP and tort remedies. There is nothing inconsistent or duplicative in recovering actual damages and attorney fees under a UDAP claim and punitive damages under a tort claim.[183]

175 Cal. Civ. Code § 1780 (West); Conn. Gen. Stat. § 42-110g(a); D.C. Code § 28-3905; Ga. Code Ann. § 10-1-399; Ky. Rev. Stat. Ann. § 3622.220; Idaho Code Ann. § 48-608; Mo. Rev. Stat. § 4022.025; Or. Rev. Stat. § 646.638; R.I. Gen. Laws § 6-13.1-5.2; Vt. Stat. Ann. tit. 9, § 2461 (exemplary damages capped at treble the consideration that consumer provides the merchant).

176 Minn. Stat. § 549.20 ("upon clear and convincing evidence that the acts of the defendant show a willful indifference to the rights or safety of others"). *See also* Wexler v. Brothers Entertainment Group, Inc., 457 N.W.2d 218 (Minn. Ct. App. 1990); Yost v. Millhouse, 373 N.W.2d 826 (Minn. Ct. App. 1985).

177 *See, e.g.*, Nev. Rev. Stat. § 598.09722.

178 15 U.S.C. § 1691e(b) (1976).

179 15 U.S.C. § 1679g(a)(2).

180 15 U.S.C. § 1681n(a)(2) (willful violations).

181 *See* National Consumer Law Center, Unfair and Deceptive Acts and Practices § 8.4.3.1 (6th ed. 2004).

182 Wildstein v. Tru Motors, Inc., 227 N.J. Super. 331, 547 A.2d 340 (Law Div. 1988).

183 United Labs. v. Kuykendall, 335 N.C. 183, 437 S.E.2d 374 (1993). *See* National Consumer Law Center, Unfair and Deceptive Acts and Practices § 8.4.3.8 (6th ed. 2004).

22.4.4 Constitutional Limits on the Size of Punitive Damages Awards

22.4.4.1 Introduction

The Due Process Clause prohibits a state from imposing grossly excessive punitive damages on a tortfeasor.[184] The Supreme Court has identified three guideposts for determining whether a punitive damage award is grossly excessive:

- The degree of reprehensibility on the part of the defendant
- The disparity between the harm or potential harm suffered and the punitive damages awarded
- The difference between the punitive damages awarded and the criminal or civil penalties authorized or imposed in comparable cases[185]

These three factors are discussed in more detail in the next three subsections. A comprehensive discussion of the constitutionality of punitive damages awards can be found in National Consumer Law Center, *Automobile Fraud* § 22.10.6 (2d ed. 2003 and Supp.).

22.4.4.2 Reprehensibility

The reprehensibility of the defendant's conduct is the most important factor in determining the constitutionality of a punitive damage award.[186] Factors that courts should consider when weighing the reprehensibility of a defendant's conduct include

- whether the harm is physical as opposed to economic;
- whether the tortious conduct shows an indifference to or reckless disregard of the health or safety of others;
- whether the target of the conduct had financial vulnerability;
- whether the conduct involved repeated actions or was only an isolated incident; and
- whether the harm resulted from intentional malice, trickery, deceit, or mere accident.[187]

Some of these factors are likely to be pronounced in consumer cases. The harm will usually be economic rather

184 The constitutional standards for punitive damages are discussed in detail in National Consumer Law Center, Automobile Fraud § 22.10.6 (2d ed. 2003 and Supp.).

185 State Farm Mut. Auto. Ins. Co. v. Campbell, 538 U.S. 408, 123 S. Ct. 1513, 155 L. Ed. 2d 585 (2003); BMW of N. Am., Inc. v. Gore, 517 U.S. 559, 116 S. Ct. 1589, 134 L. Ed. 2d 809 (1996).

186 BMW of N. Am., Inc. v. Gore, 517 U.S. 559, 575, 116 S. Ct. 1589, 134 L. Ed. 2d 809 (1996).

187 State Farm Mut. Auto. Ins. Co. v. Campbell, 538 U.S. 408, 123 S. Ct. 1513, 1521, 155 L. Ed. 2d 585 (2003).

than physical, but the creditor's actions may involve some threat to the consumer's health or safety, particularly if debt collection harassment, sale of a defective car, loss of a home, loss of utility service, or faulty home repairs are involved. The targets of fraud in consumer cases typically are financially vulnerable, and fraudulent businesses often specifically seek out these vulnerable consumers. Showing repetition and malicious intent is also often possible. The Supreme Court has stated: "Infliction of economic injury, especially when done intentionally through affirmative acts of misconduct or when the target is financially vulnerable, can warrant a substantial penalty."[188]

22.4.4.3 Ratio to Compensatory Damages

The Supreme Court has stated that "few awards exceeding a single-digit ratio between punitive and compensatory damages, to a significant degree, will satisfy due process."[189] Nonetheless, the Supreme Court also held that a higher ratio may be consistent with due process if an egregious act causes only a small amount of economic harm.[190] Many courts have applied this principle, upholding punitive damages well in excess of a single-digit ratio to compensatory damages when the compensatory damage award was relatively small.[191]

In calculating the ratio, some courts have compared punitive damages not just to the plaintiff's actual damages award but also to the potential damages that the defendant's actions could have caused or to the future harm that could occur. One particularly clear-cut example involved a drunk driver who crashed into the plaintiff's vehicle, pushing her into the lane of oncoming traffic. The plaintiff luckily escaped serious injury and was awarded only $8801.40 in compensatory damages. The court noted that the plaintiff could have died as a result of the defendant's misconduct and upheld a $200,000 punitive damages award—a 22.7-to-1 ratio to the actual damages award.[192]

It appears that the potential harm to others in the state may also be considered in calculating the ratio. In *Parrott v. Carr Chevrolet, Inc.*,[193] for example, the Oregon Supreme Court considered not only the actual injury to the plaintiff but also the potential injury that the misconduct might have caused to past, present, and future customers. While the United States Supreme Court's most recent punitive damages decision refers twice to the ratio between the punitive damages and the harm *to the plaintiff*,[194] a later portion of the opinion seems to acknowledge that harm to others in the state, if proven, could have been considered in calculating the ratio.[195]

22.4.4.4 Penalties for Comparable Misconduct

The third factor in analyzing the constitutionality of a punitive damages award is the civil and criminal penalties for comparable misconduct. Criminal penalties are available in some states for certain consumer protection violations, either under a UDAP statute or a criminal theft or other statute.[196] In addition, state UDAP statutes typically allow the Attorney General to seek substantial civil penalties for UDAP violations, often on a per-violation basis.[197] In certain states, additional penalties are available if the elderly are targeted.[198] The FTC Act is another useful analogy. It allows a civil penalty up to $10,000 per rule violation, with each day of non-compliance being treated as a separate violation.[199] The state may also be able to impose the "civil death penalty"—revocation of the wrongdoer's business license—for violations of the UDAP or related consumer protection statutes.[200] All of these are appropriate sources for comparison to a punitive damage award.

---

188 BMW of N. Am., Inc. v. Gore, 517 U.S. 559, 576, 116 S. Ct. 1589, 134 L. Ed. 2d 809 (1996) (citations omitted).

189 State Farm Mut. Auto. Ins. Co. v. Campbell, 538 U.S. 408, 123 S. Ct. 1513, 1524, 155 L. Ed. 2d 585 (2003).

190 *Id.*

191 *See, e.g.*, Mathias v. Accor Econ. Lodging, Inc., 347 F.3d 672 (7th Cir. 2003) (upholding 322.2-to-1 ratio when compensatory damage award to motel guest bitten by bedbugs was $5000). *See* National Consumer Law Center, Automobile Fraud § 22.10.6.3.4 (2d ed. 2003 and Supp.).

192 Craig v. Holsey, 590 S.E.2d 742 (Ga. Ct. App. 2003). *See also* Willow Inn, Inc. v. Pub. Serv. Mut. Ins. Co., 399 F.3d 224, 234 (3d Cir. 2005) (potential harm from an unsuccessful attempt at fraud may be considered, but not shown here); *In re* Exxon Valdez, 296 F. Supp. 2d 1071, 1104, 1105 (D. Alaska 2004) (accommodating potential future harm by allowing higher ratio; upholding $4.5 billion punitive damages award on $513 million compensatory damages in environmental tort class action).

193 331 Or. 537, 17 P.3d 473, 489 (2001).

194 State Farm Mut. Auto. Ins. Co. v. Campbell, 538 U.S. 408, 123 S. Ct. 1513, 1520, 1524, 155 L. Ed. 2d 585 (2003).

195 *Id.*, 123 S. Ct. 1513, 1525 ("With respect to the Utah Supreme Court's second justification [that State Farm's policies affected numerous Utah consumers], the Campbells' inability to direct us to testimony demonstrating harm to the people of Utah (other than those directly involved in this case) indicates that the adverse effect on the State's general population was in fact minor."). *See also* BMW of N. Am., Inc. v. Gore, 517 U.S. 559, 582, 116 S. Ct. 1589, 134 L. Ed. 2d 809 (1996).

196 *See* Grabinski v. Blue Springs Ford Sales, Inc., 203 F.3d 1024 (8th Cir. 2000) (citing criminal penalties for UDAP violations as reason to uphold punitive damage award).

197 *See* National Consumer Law Center, Unfair and Deceptive Acts and Practices § 10.22.3.1, Appx. A (6th ed. 2004).

198 *See generally* National Consumer Law Center, Unfair and Deceptive Acts and Practices § 10.7.3.7 (6th ed. 2004).

199 15 U.S.C. § 45(m).

200 Grabinski v. Blue Springs Ford Sales, Inc., 203 F.3d 1024 (8th Cir. 2000) (state's authority to refuse to issue or renew motor vehicle dealer's license to anyone who has obtained money by fraud, deception, or misrepresentation "weigh[s] heavily in favor of an award of punitive damages").

22.4.4.5 Practical Tips

That substantial punitive damage awards can be upheld in consumer cases is illustrated by *Grabinski v. Blue Springs Ford*.[201] The defendants there had sold the consumer a vehicle with concealed wreck damage. The Eighth Circuit upheld punitive damage awards ranging from 5 to 99 times actual damages against the various defendants. The court stressed that the defendants' actions were egregious and showed a clear and disturbing disregard for the consumer's safety and economic interests. The court held that the significant civil and criminal sanctions, including civil penalties of $1000 per violation, criminal fines and imprisonment, and loss of the license to do business, demonstrated the state legislature's judgment about the appropriate level of penalties.

In another case, involving the sale of a used car with concealed wreck damage and a rolled-back odometer, the Oregon Supreme Court upheld a punitive damages award of $1,000,000 when compensatory damages were $11,496.[202] The court found this an "extraordinarily egregious" UDAP violation and noted that there was evidence that this was the dealer's standard business practice, which the dealer had no intention of changing. In holding that the defendant had notice that UDAP violations could lead to such high financial loss, the court noted that the UDAP statute allowed courts to impose substantial civil penalties (up to $25,000 per violation) plus loss of a business license.

When presenting a case for punitive damages, it is important to keep in mind the factors that the trial court and appellate courts will use to review the jury's award. Evidence that the defendant is a repeat offender is a key factor in showing reprehensibility and is also powerful proof of fraudulent intent.[203] The jury should be encouraged to identify and quantify all damages, as any punitive damage award will ultimately be compared to the compensatory damages awarded. If there are elements of actual damage that can not be included in the actual damage award under the jurisdiction's law, consider asking the jury to quantify them anyway so that they can be included in the ratio analysis. Jury instructions must be prepared with care to inform the jury of the relevant factors and to caution against punishing the defendant for out-of-state conduct that was lawful in the state where it was committed.[204]

201 203 F.3d 1024 (8th Cir. 2000).

202 Parrott v. Carr Chevrolet, 331 Or. 573, 17 P.3d 473 (2001).

203 *See* National Consumer Law Center, Automobile Fraud § 9.8.1 (2d ed. 2003 and Supp.) (admissibility of evidence of other bad acts).

204 *See id.* §§ 7.10.6.3.9, 7.10.6.3.11.

22.4.5 State Statutory Caps on Punitive Damage Awards

About half the states have statutes that cap punitive damage awards for at least some types of cases. These statutes are often more restrictive than the limitations on punitive damages imposed by the Supreme Court, in that they tend to set rigid mathematical formulas instead of simply listing factors.

Consumer advocates must become familiar with any state statutory cap on punitive damage awards that is in effect in the jurisdiction. These caps may apply to UDAP or fraud claims in some states but not in others. For example, some caps apply only to product liability cases, while others apply to all civil actions. A state-by-state summary of these statutes is provided in *Automobile Fraud* § 22.10.4 (2d ed. 2003 and Supp.).

22.4.6 Interrelation of Punitive Damages with Other Remedies

Punitive damages are awarded in addition to compensatory damages.[205] Some courts hold that statutory damages are not considered punitive but compensatory, such that courts may award both statutory and punitive damages.[206] Some courts also allow both treble damages and punitive damages, particularly when they relate to separate violations and separate compensatory awards.[207] But other courts hold that a consumer can not receive both UDAP treble damages and punitive damages under a tort theory.[208] Instead, these courts usually allow the consumer to seek both treble and

205 United Labs. v. Kuykendall, 335 N.C. 183, 437 S.E.2d 374 (1993).

206 Equitable Life Leasing Corp. v. Abbick, 243 Kan. 513, 757 P.2d 304 (1988); Riviera Motors, Inc. v. Higbee, 45 Or. App. 545, 609 P.2d 369 (1980).

207 Aponte v. Aungst, 82 B.R. 738 (Bankr. E.D. Pa. 1988) (treble UDAP damages and punitive damages under Bankruptcy Code); Rhue v. Dawson, 173 Ariz. 220, 841 P.2d 215 (Ct. App. 1992) (state RICO treble damages and tort punitive damages); Colonial Lincoln-Mercury Sales, Inc. v. Molina, 152 Ga. App. 379, 262 S.E.2d 820 (1979) (for intentional violations treble damages and mandatory and exemplary damages are permissible); Crawford v. Bill Swad Chevrolet, Inc., 2000 Ohio App. LEXIS 4221 (Sept. 19, 2000) (allowing both punitive damages for fraud plus treble damages for UDAP violations); Mid Am. Acceptance Co. v. Lightle, 63 Ohio App. 3d 590, 579 N.E.2d 721 (1989) (punitive damages for fraud are recoverable along with UDAP treble damages); Freeman v. A&M Mobile Home Sales, Inc., 293 S.C. 255, 359 S.E.2d 532 (Ct. App. 1987) (awarding UDAP treble damages and punitive damages under common law fraud count); Winkle Chevy-Olds-Pontiac v. Condon, 830 S.W.2d 740 (Tex. App. 1992) (both may be awarded when there are different acts and practices and separate findings of actual damages).

208 *See* Lexton-Ancira Real Estate Fund, 1972 v. Heller, 826 P.2d 819 (Colo. 1992); Edwards v. William H. Porter, Inc., 1991 Del. Super. LEXIS 315 (July 26, 1991); Cieri v. Leticia Query

punitive damages and, after the court has set the size of both awards, the consumer can elect which award to accept.[209] State procedures differ as to when this election must be made, however, so practitioners should check their own state's law.

A buyer may be able to rescind a purchase and also receive punitive damages.[210] Punitive damages and attorney fees can both be awarded even when the cost of litigation is one of the factors used to justify punitive damages.[211] A somewhat unique issue arises in Oregon because a state statute specifies that punitive damages awards first go to pay the consumers' attorneys and the remainder is split between the consumer and a special state fund.[212] Oregon's highest court has ruled that UDAP attorney fees should still be awarded on top of the punitive damages award and that the total recovery should not be limited just because the attorney can be paid out of the punitive damages award.[213]

Realty, Inc., 905 P.2d 29 (Haw. 1995) (consumer must elect between treble damages and attorney fees on a UDAP claim or punitive damages on a fraud claim); 49 Prospect Street Tenants Ass'n v. Sheva Gardens, Inc., 227 N.J. Super. 449, 547 A.2d 1134 (App. Div. 1988) (when same practice results in award under different counts for treble and punitive damages, both awards may stand, but exemplary portion of treble damages (i.e., double damages) must be deducted from punitive damages award); Hale v. Basin Motor Co., 110 N.M. 314, 795 P.2d 1006 (1990); Hardy v. Toler, 288 N.C. 303, 218 S.E.2d 342 (1975); Smith v. Strickland, 442 S.E.2d 207 (S.C. Ct. App. 1994); Concrete Spaces, Inc. v. Sender, 2 S.W.3d 901 (Tenn. 1999) (plaintiff must make election before amount of punitive damages is awarded); Birchfield v. Texarkana Mem'l Hosp., 747 S.W.2d 361, 367 (Tex. 1987) (not reversible error to fail to award both treble UDAP damages and punitive damages for negligence in absence of separate and distinct findings of actual damages).

209 Roberts v. Am. Warranty Corp., 514 A.2d 1132 (Del. Super. Ct. 1986); Eastern Star, Inc. v. Union Bldg. Materials, 712 P.2d 1148 (Haw. Ct. App. 1985); Hale v. Basin Motor Co., 110 N.M. 314, 795 P.2d 1006 (1990); McLelland v. United Wisconsin Life Ins. Co., 980 P.2d 86 (N.M. App. 1999); Volt Sys. Corp. v. Raytheon Corp., 547 N.Y.S.2d 280 (App. Div. 1989) (claims for punitive and treble damages under different laws may be pleaded, but plaintiff may have to make election of remedies later); Ellis v. N. Star Co., 388 S.E.2d 127 (N.C. 1990); Mapp v. Toyota World, Inc., 344 S.E.2d 297 (N.C. Ct. App. 1986).

210 Sherrod v. Holzshuh, 274 Or. 327, 546 P.2d 470 (1976); Consol. Tex. Fin. v. Shearer, 739 S.W.2d 477 (Tex. App. 1987). *See* National Consumer Law Center, Automobile Fraud § 7.10.2 (2d ed. 2003 and Supp.).

211 Equitable Life Leasing Corp. v. Abbick, 243 Kan. 513, 757 P.2d 304 (1988). *See also* United Laboratories v. Kuykendall, 335 N.C. 183, 437 S.E.2d 374 (1993) (UDAP attorney fees and tort punitive damages not inconsistent or duplicative).

212 Or. Rev. Stat. § 31.735.

213 Honeywell v. Sterling Furniture Co., 310 Or. 206, 797 P.2d 1019 (1990). *But see* Ekl v. Knecht, 585 N.E.2d 156 (Ill. App. Ct. 1991) (no abuse of discretion to deny attorney fee when punitive damage award was sufficient to pay fee).

22.5 Rescinding or Voiding Contracts

22.5.1 Introduction

Canceling a contract may be preferable to a consumer than damages or an injunction. Cancellation can result in return of the consumer's payments or dismissal of a collection action without proof of the consumer's actual damages. When the consumer's loss is primarily the amount paid, or when the consumer has paid little or nothing but the contract is highly disadvantageous, voiding or rescinding the contract may be the ideal remedy.

This section summarizes the right to rescind or void a contract under a number of statutory and common law grounds. All of these grounds for voiding or rescinding contracts are discussed in detail in other National Consumer Law Center manuals. In addition, NCLC's manual *The Cost of Credit: Regulation, Preemption, and Industry Abuses* outlines the remedies for usury, which in some states include voiding and rescinding the loan contract.[214]

22.5.2 Cooling-Off Period for Door-to-Door and Other Off-Premises Sales

If the consumer wants to cancel a contract, the attorney should always investigate when the negotiation and sale took place. The FTC requires door-to-door and other off-premises sellers to give consumers a three-day cancellation right,[215] and each state has a similar statute that applies to at least some home solicitation sales. Most courts hold that the cancellation period begins to run only when the seller properly notifies the buyer of the right. Thus, the buyer can exercise the right to cancel months or even years after the sale if the seller did not provide proper notice of the right to cancel.[216]

The FTC cooling-off period applies not just to door-to-door sales but to any sale away from the seller's principal place of business.[217] Consequently, sales in motels, at the consumer's place of work, or in booths set up in shopping center parking lots should be covered. The FTC rule and the state statutes are examined in detail in *Unfair and Deceptive Acts and Practices* § 5.8.2 (6th ed. 2004).

214 National Consumer Law Center, The Cost of Credit: Regulation, Preemption, and Industry Abuses § 10.8 (3d ed. 2005).

215 16 C.F.R. § 429.

216 *See* National Consumer Law Center, Unfair and Deceptive Acts and Practices § 5.8.2.6.3 (6th ed. 2004).

217 16 C.F.R. § 429.0(a).

22.5.3 *Statutory Right to Cancel Other Specific Types of Contracts*

Many states have laws that provide similar cancellation periods for specific types of sales other than door-to-door sales. State health-spa legislation is a common example of a statute that allows a consumer to back out of a long-term membership agreement.[218] Some states also have laws allowing cancellation of contracts with buyer's clubs, time shares, or membership campgrounds.[219]

The federal Credit Repair Organizations Act[220] provides a three-day right to cancel contracts, and in many states there are similar state laws.[221] The scope of these statutes is surprisingly broad, and coverage should be investigated whenever a seller, broker, or other middleman has offered to improve the consumer's credit rating or arrange credit for the consumer. These laws are analyzed in depth in National Consumer Law Center, *Fair Credit Reporting* Ch. 15 (5th ed. 2002 and Supp.).

22.5.4 *Truth in Lending Rescission for Home-Secured Loans*

The Truth in Lending Act provides a three-day right to rescind a credit transaction when the creditor takes a security interest in the consumer's residence and the credit is not used to purchase the home. If the creditor fails to give the consumer certain material disclosures at the time the transaction is consummated, or fails to inform the consumer properly of the right to rescind, the consumer can exercise the right for up to three years after cancellation of the transaction.

The procedures to rescind a contract specified by the Truth in Lending Act and regulations are different in important ways from those for common law rescission. First, the creditor is required to void the security interest and return the consumer's payments before the consumer has a duty to tender back the proceeds of the loan.[222] A number of courts have concluded that they have equitable authority to modify this sequence of steps, however.[223] In addition, the Truth in Lending Act and regulations are explicit that rescission voids the consumer's obligation to pay interest and fees.[224] This means that a consumer who rescinds a home-secured loan after several years of payments will be entitled to a substantial refund of interest and fees already paid. Another advantage of Truth in Lending rescission is that statutory damages and attorney fees can be recovered along with rescission.[225] This important consumer cancellation right is discussed in detail in Chapter 6 of another NCLC manual *Truth in Lending*.

22.5.5 *Right to Reject or Revoke Acceptance of Purchased Goods; Automobile Lemon Laws*

The Uniform Commercial Code provides consumers with the right to reject an offered good as non-conforming or to revoke acceptance of the good if a substantial defect is later discovered. These UCC rights apply to the sale of all goods and are analyzed in detail in another NCLC manual.[226]

The federal Magnuson-Moss Warranty Act also gives consumers a right, when the seller offers a "full" written warranty, to receive a new product or a refund if the seller is not able to repair the purchased item.[227] Full written warranties are relatively rare, however.

More important for consumers are new-car lemon laws that all states have enacted and that give the consumer a right to a replacement car or refund in the case of automobile defects that the dealer can not repair.[228] A few states have similar legislation providing the right to cancel used-car sales under specified circumstances.[229] New- and used-car lemon laws are discussed in detail in National Consumer Law Center, *Consumer Warranty Law* §§ 13.2, 14.6 (2d ed. 2001 and Supp.).

22.5.6 *Unconscionable Contracts*

UCC §§ 2-302 and 2A-108 allow courts to refuse to enforce unconscionable contracts or contract terms. State credit codes based on the Uniform Consumer Credit Code generally have a similar provision. A number of other states have statutes prohibiting unconscionable contract terms in certain types of transactions,[230] and unconscionability is

218 *See* National Consumer Law Center, Unfair and Deceptive Acts and Practices § 5.10.3 (6th ed. 2004).

219 National Consumer Law Center, Unfair and Deceptive Acts and Practices §§ 5.10.5, 5.10.6 (6th ed. 2004).

220 15 U.S.C. § 1679 *et seq.*

221 *See* National Consumer Law Center, Fair Credit Reporting § 15.3, Appx. B.3 (5th ed. 2002 and Supp.).

222 *See* National Consumer Law Center, Truth in Lending §§ 6.6.1, 6.6.4, 6.7 (5th ed. 2003 and Supp.).

223 *Id.* § 6.22.

224 *Id.* § 6.4.2.

225 15 U.S.C. § 1640(a).

226 National Consumer Law Center, Consumer Warranty Law Ch. 8 (2d ed. 2001 and Supp.).

227 15 U.S.C. § 2301. *See* National Consumer Law Center, Consumer Warranty Law Ch. 2 (2d ed. 2001 and Supp.).

228 15 U.S.C. § 2301. *See* National Consumer Law Center, Consumer Warranty Law Ch. 13, Appx. F (2d ed. 2001 and Supp.).

229 Haw. Rev. Stat. §§ 481J-1 to 7; Mass. Gen. Laws ch. 90, § 7N1/4; Minn. Stat. § 325F.662; N.J. Stat. Ann. § 56:8-67 to 80 (West); N.Y. Gen. Bus. Law § 198-b (McKinney); R.I. Gen. Laws § 31-5.4-2. *See* National Consumer Law Center, Consumer Warranty Law § 14.8 (2d ed. 2001 and Supp.).

230 *See, e.g.*, Ala. Code § 5-19-16; Alaska Stat. § 45.12.108 (leases); Cal. Civ. Code § 1670.5; Cal. Fin. Code § 22302 (consumer loans by finance lenders); D.C. Code § 28-3812 (consumer credit transactions or direct installment loans); Ind.

also a common law doctrine.[231] Generally a consumer is allowed to cancel an unconscionable contract, although this may not result in the return of monies already paid. Unconscionability is more fully analyzed in *Consumer Warranty Law* (2d ed. 2001 and Supp.).[232]

22.5.7 Rescission Under State UDAP Statutes

A few state UDAP statutes explicitly list rescission or voiding the transaction as a remedy.[233] The more typical UDAP statute does not explicitly state whether a court can void or rescind a transaction based on UDAP violations. Consumer litigants should begin by closely examining the remedy section of the UDAP statute to determine what remedies are specifically mentioned, such as "other equitable relief" or "other appropriate remedies."

Even if no statutory language suggests the availability of the rescission or voiding remedies, a number of courts have found such inherent authority, particularly in light of the legislative intent to have broad and effective private UDAP remedies.[234] For example, a New Jersey case offered three theories for finding an automobile repair contract unenforceable when the repair shop violated UDAP regulations requiring written authorization for repairs. First, the contract was void against public policy. Second, the contract was illegal, and an illegal contract can not be enforced. Third, since the regulations specified that written authorization was a condition precedent to forming the contract, the contract was never consummated and was thus unenforceable.[235]

The UDAP statutes that contain an explicit rescission remedy may establish special procedures for rescission actions. For example, the Ohio UDAP statute specifies that the consumer must rescind within a reasonable time of discovering the grounds for rescission and before any substantial change in the subject of the consumer transaction.[236]

A consumer who seeks to rescind a contract under a UDAP statute that does not specify rescission procedures should be careful to follow common law requirements such as notice and tender.[237] Courts may also apply UCC principles that relate to revocation of acceptance.[238] When a contract has been assigned to another entity, the best practice is to notify both the assignee and the original seller.[239] If the consumer has used the item, the seller may be entitled to a setoff for its rental value and any damage to it.[240]

22.5.8 Misrepresentation or Fraud

Fraud is probably the most common ground for canceling a contract.[241] The defrauded party is entitled to be restored to the position he or she was in before the contract was made.[242] In many jurisdictions, punitive damages are available in addition to cancellation of the contract.[243] Remedies for fraud are discussed in more detail in another NCLC manual.[244]

Code § 24-7-6-5 (rental purchase agreements); Kan. Stat. Ann. § 58-2544 (residential rental agreements); La. Rev. Stat. Ann. § 9:3551 (consumer credit transactions); Mont. Code Ann. § 70-24-404 (residential rental agreements); N.Y. Gen. Bus. Law § 396-r (sale of goods or services at unconscionably excessive price during period of abnormal disruption of market due to disaster, strike, etc.); N.C. Gen. Stat. § 25A-43 (consumer credit sales); Vt. Stat. Ann. tit. 9, § 2485 (agricultural finance leases); W. Va. Code § 46B-2-2 (rent-to-own).

231 *See generally* National Consumer Law Center, The Cost of Credit: Regulation, Preemption, and Industry Abuses § 12.7 (3d ed. 2005).

232 *See* National Consumer Law Center, Consumer Warranty Law § 11.2 (2d ed. 2001 and Supp.).

233 Rev. Stat. § 480-12; Idaho Code § 48-608(1) (allows consumer to treat contract as voidable if it is incident to UDAP violation); La. Rev. Stat. Ann. § 9:3551 (court may refuse to enforce an unconscionable agreement); Ohio Rev. Code Ann. § 1345.09 (allows election between rescission and damages); Tex. Bus. & Com. Code § 122.50(b)(3). *See* National Consumer Law Center, Unfair and Deceptive Acts and Practices § 8.22.2 (6th ed. 2004).

234 Buyers Club v. Hayes, 46 Ill. App. 3d 270, 361 N.E.2d 1383 (1977); Am. Buyers Club v. Honecker, 46 Ill. App. 3d 252, 361 N.E.2d 1370 (1977); Lorentz v. Deardan, 834 S.W.2d 316 (Tenn. Ct. App. 1992); Smith v. Scott Lewis Chevrolet, Inc., 843 S.W.2d 9 (Tenn. Ct. App. 1992); Allen v. Am. Land Research, 95 Wash. 2d 841, 631 P.2d 930 (1980); Moonlight v. Boyce, 125 Wis. 2d 298, 372 N.W.2d 479 (Ct. App. 1985). *See also In re* Fricker, 115 B.R. 809 (Bankr. E.D. Pa. 1990) (awarding remedy similar to rescission by disregarding all illegal and unconscionable charges, recalculating interest, and subtracting the borrower's payments). *But see* April v. Union Mortgage Co., 709 F. Supp. 809 (N.D. Ill. 1989); *In re* Soto, 221 B.R. 343 (Bankr. E.D. Pa. 1998); Little v. Paco Collection Servs., 156 Ga. App. 175, 274 S.E.2d 147 (1980).

235 Huffmaster v. Robinson, 221 N.J. Super. 315, 534 A.2d 435 (Law Div. 1986). *See also In re* Fleet, 95 B.R. 319 (E.D. Pa. 1989) (New Jersey law); National Consumer Law Center, Unfair and Deceptive Acts and Practices § 9.5 (6th ed. 2004).

236 Ohio Rev. Code Ann. § 1345.09.

237 *See, e.g.*, David McDavid Pontiac, Inc. v. Nix, 681 S.W.2d 831 (Tex. App. 1984).

238 Peterman v. Waite, 1980 Ohio App. LEXIS 13565 (June 25, 1980) (buyer's continued use of vehicle, and failure to tender possession of it to seller, were inconsistent with revocation).

239 Nations Credit v. Pheanis, 102 Ohio App. 3d 71, 656 N.E.2d 998 (1995).

240 Davis v. Wholesale Motors, Inc., 949 P.2d 1026 (Haw. App. 1997).

241 Dan B. Dobbs, *The Law of Remedies* §§ 9.1-9.3 (1993).

242 *Id.*

243 *See* National Consumer Law Center, Automobile Fraud § 7.10.2 (2d ed. 2003 and Supp.).

244 National Consumer Law Center, Automobile Fraud Ch. 7 (2d ed. 2003 and Supp.). *See also* National Consumer Law Center, Consumer Warranty Law Ch. 11 (2d ed. 2001 and Supp.).

Rescission may be available for a misrepresentation even when all the elements of common law fraud can not be established. Many jurisdictions allow rescission for innocent misrepresentations.[245]

In most jurisdictions, the party seeking avoidance and restitution on grounds of fraud or misrepresentation must offer to return whatever was received under the contract.[246] The consumer's offer may be conditioned upon the seller's return of consideration.[247] Upon discovering a fraudulent or material misrepresentation, the aggrieved party must act with reasonable promptness to avoid the contract or will be held to have ratified it.[248]

Though the general rule is that rescission will not be ordered when a party can not be returned to the status quo, that rule will not always be strictly enforced. When, for example, the party resisting rescission is a wrongdoer who is exploiting its change of position, courts may allow rescission despite the inability to place the parties where they were.[249]

22.5.9 Contract Law Grounds for Voiding Contracts

22.5.9.1 Incapacity

An otherwise valid contract may be voidable under the common law when one party does not have the capacity to make the contract because of minority, mental disability, or intoxication.[250] The other party must return whatever the incompetent party gave under the contract, and the incompetent party must usually restore to the other party what the incompetent party received under the contract.[251] In general, the right to cancel must be exercised promptly after the disability is removed.

245 *See* National Consumer Law Center, Unfair and Deceptive Acts and Practices § 9.5.9.1 (6th ed. 2004).

246 J. Calamari & J. Perillo, Contracts § 9-23 (5th ed. 2003).

247 *Id. See also* Karapetian v. Carolan, 83 Cal. App. 2d 344, 188 P.2d 809 (1948).

248 *Id. See, e.g.*, Merritt v. Craig, 130 Md. App. 350, 746 A.2d 923 (2000).

249 *See, e.g.*, Bland v. Freightliner, L.L.C., 206 F. Supp. 2d 1202, 1208, 1209 (M.D. Fla. 2002) (rescission may be ordered even though parties can not be returned to their status quo, if the balance of equities justifies it); Weed Wizard Acquisition Corp. v. A.A.B.B., Inc., 201 F. Supp. 2d 1252, 1259 (N.D. Ga. 2002); Sokolow, Dunaud, Mercadier & Carreras, L.L.P. v. Lacher, 747 N.Y.S.2d 441, 447 (N.Y. App. Div. 2002).

250 Dan B. Dobbs, *The Law of Remedies* § 13.4 (1993). *See* National Consumer Law Center, Unfair and Deceptive Acts and Practices § 9.5.7 (6th ed. 2004).

251 17A Am. Jur. 2d *Contracts* §§ 28, 580 (2004).

22.5.9.2 Illegality

An illegal contract is generally void and unenforceable.[252] One important example of a contract that is illegal when made is when a seller enters into a consumer contract without the proper licensing required by state law, particularly when the licensing statute was enacted for the protection of the public and not just to raise revenue.[253] Courts, however, may refuse relief based on illegality when the seller of goods or services has substantially complied with the licensing requirements, has caused no harm to the consumer, or poses no grave threat to the public.[254]

A contract can also be illegal if a consumer protection statute prohibits a contractual provision found in the contract. Thus a security agreement violating the FTC Credit Practices Rule is unlawful and unenforceable.[255] A contract that does not include language or terms required by state law, such as a three-day cooling-off period or a specific description of the work to be performed, may also be void.[256] The Wisconsin Supreme Court has held that a lease is unenforceable in its entirety if it includes a prohibited clause.[257] Merely severing the illegal clause and allowing the rest of the lease to be enforced would mean that a landlord would suffer no consequences for including the illegal clause yet would reap the benefits of its chilling effects.

22.5.9.3 Duress and Undue Influence

An essential element in the formation of a contract is the parties' exercise of free will.[258] If one party overpowers the will of another, the contract is not binding on the second party. Accordingly, a contract entered into as a result of duress or undue influence is voidable by the victim of the

252 Restatement (Second) of Contracts §§ 178, 179 (1981). *See* National Consumer Law Center, Unfair and Deceptive Acts and Practices § 9.5.8 (6th ed. 2004).

253 *See* National Consumer Law Center, The Cost of Credit: Regulation, Preemption, and Industry Abuses § 10.8.4 (3d ed. 2005.) (consumer remedies when creditor lacks required license).

254 J. Calamari & J. Perillo, Contracts § 22-3 (5th ed. 2003).

255 *In re* Raymond, 103 B.R. 846 (Bankr. W.D. Ky. 1989); Boyer v. ITT Fin. Servs. (*In re* Boyer), 63 B.R. 153 (Bankr. E.D. Mo. 1986).

256 Scott v. Mayflower Home Improvement Corp., 363 N.J. Super. 145, 831 A.2d 564 (Law Div. 2001) (home improvement contract void when salesperson unlicensed and contract did not state costs, finance charges, and specific description of work as required by state law). *See also* Donnelly v. Mustang Pools, Inc., 84 Misc. 2d 28, 374 N.Y.S.2d 967 (Sup. Ct. 1975). *But see* Wowaka & Sons, Inc. v. Pardell, 242 A.D.2d 1, 672 N.Y.S.2d 358 (1998) (failure of home improvement contract to contain all the information required by statute does not render it unenforceable).

257 Baierl v. McTaggart, 629 N.W.2d 277 (Wis. 2001).

258 *See* G. Calamari & J. Perillo, Contracts § 9-2 (5th ed. 2003). *See also* 17A Am. Jur. 2d *Contracts* §§ 218–221 (2004).

coercion.[259] To avoid the contract, the coerced party must elect to rescind and communicate that election to the other party.

22.5.9.4 Failure of Consideration

To be binding and enforceable, the parties' promises must generally be supported by consideration. If both parties do not give up something of legal value, the contract is unenforceable because no contract was ever really formed.[260]

In a surprising number of consumer contracts, only the consumer is really obligated to do anything of value. For example, a buyer may pay for a service contract that merely duplicates the consumer's existing rights. The consumer has paid for the contract, but the seller has given up nothing. Although a distinction exists between want of consideration and failure of consideration, both generally are an excuse for non-performance of a promise.[261]

As a general rule, courts will not substitute their opinions as to what is adequate consideration for the opinions of the parties. The issue is not whether both sides made a reasonable bargain but whether there was *any* consideration.[262] Nevertheless, an exception may be made when a gross inequality between the things exchanged suggests fraud, duress, unconscionability, or mistake.

22.5.9.5 Mistake

Rescission may also be available on grounds of mistake. The Uniform Commercial Code expressly preserves this common law contract doctrine unless it is displaced by some particular UCC provision.[263] As expressed by the *Restatement (Second) of Contracts* § 152, if both parties are mistaken at the time of contracting as to a basic assumption on which the contract was made, and the mistake has a material effect on the agreed exchange of performance, then the contract is voidable by the adversely affected party. The doctrine of mistake is discussed in more detail in National Consumer Law Center, *Automobile Fraud* § 8.3 (2d ed. 2003 and Supp.).

22.5.10 Relationship of Rescission to Other Remedies

Historically a claim for rescission was viewed as inconsistent with a suit for damages; a suit for damages affirms the contract while a claim for rescission disaffirms the contract. Nonetheless most states allow the plaintiff to plead both actions, in the alternative.[264] However, given the historical view, practitioners must tread carefully and make sure that the jurisdiction will not deem a suit for damages as an irrevocable affirmation of the contract that will block a request for rescission.

Though a plaintiff may usually plead both rescission and damages, the plaintiff may not recover both but must elect a remedy. Jurisdictions vary on when the plaintiff must make the election. Some allow the election at any time before the court enters a final judgment. In these jurisdictions, the plaintiff can choose from the verdicts returned by the jury.[265] Other jurisdictions require an election at an earlier stage.[266]

Some UDAP statutes specify the relationship of the UDAP rescission remedy to other UDAP remedies. The Ohio UDAP statute specifically allows consumers only an election between rescinding the contract and damages.[267] If the consumer rescinds, the consumer can also recover any amount already paid on the contract but can not treble that amount.[268] The consumer also can not recover statutory damages for the UDAP violations that led up to the transaction.[269] The election between rescission and a damage remedy must be made *prior* to going to trial.[270]

One Texas decision allows a consumer to rescind a transaction and still obtain UDAP damages to the extent that the rescission has not made the consumer whole,[271] but another disagrees.[272] A Pennsylvania court has ruled that both rescission and treble damages based on the purchase price are allowed, noting that the UDAP statute does not make an exception to the treble damages rule for cases in which rescission is granted.[273] A Hawaii appellate court has not only authorized damages in a case in which the trans-

259 Richard A. Lord, Williston on Contracts § 3.4 (4th ed. 1990).

260 *See* National Consumer Law Center, Unfair and Deceptive Acts and Practices § 9.5.14 (6th ed. 2004).

261 17A Am. Jur. 2d *Contracts* §§ 648–650 (2004).

262 Richrad A. Lord, Williston on Contracts § 22.3 (4th ed. 1990).

263 U.C.C. § 1-103.

264 National Consumer Law Center, Automobile Fraud § 22.11.3 (2d ed. 2003 and Supp.).

265 *See, e.g.*, Jones v. Childers, 18 F.3d 899 (11th Cir. 1994); Ace Chem. Corp. v. DSI Transports, Inc., 115 N.C. App. 237, 446 S.E.2d 100 (1994); Garrett v. Mazda Motors of Am., 844 S.W.2d 178 (Tenn. Ct. App. 1992).

266 *See, e.g.*, Merritt v. Craig, 746 A.2d 923 (Md. App. 2000) (consumer must elect before trial between rescission on common law grounds and damages on UDAP theories).

267 Ohio Rev. Code Ann. § 1345.09. *See also* Bramley's Water Conditioning v. Hagen, 27 Ohio App. 3d 300, 501 N.E.2d 38 (1985); Bierlein v. Alex's Cont'l Inn, 16 Ohio App. 3d 294, 475 N.E.2d 1273 (1984).

268 Mid Am. Acceptance Co. v. Lightle, 63 Ohio App. 3d 590, 579 N.E.2d 721 (1989). *See also* Credit Acceptance Corp. v. Banks, 1999 Ohio App. LEXIS 6058 (Dec. 16, 1999) (rescission award can include money judgment for return of buyer's payments).

269 Eckman v. Columbia Oldsmobile, Inc., 65 Ohio App. 3d 719, 585 N.E.2d 451 (1989).

270 Williams v. Banner Buick, Inc., 60 Ohio App. 3d 128, 574 N.E.2d 579 (1989).

271 LaChalet Int'l, Inc. v. Nowik, 787 S.W.2d 101 (Tex. App. 1990).

272 Kargar v. Sorrentino, 788 S.W.2d 189 (Tex. App. 1990).

273 Metz v. Quaker Highlands, Inc., 714 A.2d 447 (Pa. Super. 1998). *See also* Lorentz v. Deardan, 834 S.W.2d 316 (Tenn. Ct. App. 1992); § 22.4.6, *supra*.

action was rescinded but directed that any trebling of damages be calculated before setting off the seller's claim for rental value and damages to the item purchased.[274]

22.5.11 Negotiating Cancellation of a Debt in Settlement of a Damage Claim

In many instances, a consumer will have a damage claim against a creditor at the same time as the creditor has a claim of debt against the consumer. Canceling the underlying debt, if owed, can provide meaningful relief to the consumer, since the amount of the debt may well exceed the damages recoverable on the consumer claim. However, consumer's counsel must use some caution in exploring forgiveness of the debt in return for dismissal or reduction of the amount claimed in litigation of a consumer case. One district court stated that it would consider awarding attorney fees to the debt collector should the evidence demonstrate that the consumer filed suit "to gain leverage in the dispute over a debt plaintiffs legitimately owe."[275]

Since the consumer may be judgment proof or eligible for bankruptcy, this type of compensation may be appealing to the collector because cancellation costs the creditor little or nothing in those situations. However, a consumer who is filing bankruptcy, or who is judgment proof, may have little interest in trading real dollars as damages for forgiveness of the debt in settlement negotiations. Retirement of the debt as settlement of damage claims should be accepted only when it has real significance to the consumer. Another concern is that canceling the debt may be beyond the authority of a defendant who is a collection agency or attorney. In certain circumstances, forgiveness of a debt may also be considered by the IRS to be taxable income to the consumer, requiring the payment of taxes.[276]

22.6 Injunctions and Other Equitable Relief

22.6.1 Advantages of the Injunctive Remedy

Because of their broad scope and flexibility, UDAP statutes are an ideal vehicle for enjoining marketplace misconduct. One of the most effective remedies is for a private individual to seek a court-ordered injunction preventing a business from engaging in specified conduct in the future. A merchant may treat occasional damage awards, even if trebled or increased with punitive damages, as an acceptable cost of business, not deterring future misconduct. But a properly framed and monitored injunction can eliminate the seller's use of the challenged practice against all future customers. Some of the most virulent consumer frauds are perpetrated by businesses that are immune to suits for damages because they hide their assets or have no assets. There is a lot to be lost pursuing such businesses for damages when relief with some teeth may be obtained by an injunction.

Legitimate merchants will comply with court-ordered injunctions, and judges will deal harshly with those who challenge the court's authority by disobeying the injunction. A judge will be far more strict with a seller who violates the court's own order than with a company that just deceives consumers.

Consumer litigants can also seek temporary restraining orders or preliminary injunctions to halt illegal practices. A consumer who quickly goes to court seeking such preliminary relief will put the seller on the defensive, expedite the case, obtain early discovery, and gain other tactical advantages.

While an injunction can be an effective remedy, it need not be an onerous one. It does not penalize a business for its misconduct but solely orders it not to repeat the practice, putting the company on clear notice of specifically defined prohibited practices. In theory, judges should enjoin future conduct when they are unwilling to order a company to pay for past conduct that was not clearly deceptive.

In every state, the state attorney general or similar state official can seek to enjoin UDAP violations. However, these state officials have limited resources and their own priorities. Attorney general offices must also make priority decisions regarding when to follow up to determine if a seller is complying with an injunctive order. Private litigants not wishing to be bound by state attorney general priority decisions find it useful to act as "private attorneys general," bringing their own injunctive actions and monitoring seller's compliance with the court order themselves.

22.6.2 Does a UDAP Statute Authorize Private Injunctive Relief?

22.6.2.1 Statutes That Explicitly Authorize Private Injunctive Relief

Most UDAP statutes explicitly authorize private injunctive actions. Eleven UDAP statutes[277] modeled after the

274 Davis v. Wholesale Motors, Inc., 949 P.2d 1026 (Haw. App. 1997).

275 Lewis v. Hanks, 1991 U.S. Dist. LEXIS 21807 (E.D. Mo. Feb. 26, 1991).

276 *See* National Consumer Law Center, Consumer Bankruptcy Law and Practice § 14.5.5.6 (7th ed. 2004); National Consumer Law Center, Repossessions and Foreclosures § 21.7.3 (5th ed. 2002 and Supp.).

277 Del. Code tit. 6, § 2533; Ga. Code Ann. § 10-1-373; Haw. Rev. Stat. § 481:A-4; 815 Ill. Comp. Stat. § 510/3; Me. Rev. Stat. Ann. tit. 10, § 1213; Minn. Stat. Ann. § 325D.45; Neb. Rev.

Uniform Deceptive Trade Practices Act (UDTPA)[278] provide that a "person likely to be damaged by deceptive practices of another" may seek injunctive relief. A primary function of the UDTPA is to provide businesses with a means of enjoining deceptive and thus unfairly competitive practices of other businesses. In most states the UDTPA has also been found to provide injured consumers with an injunctive remedy.[279] Therefore, for violations of the specific prohibitions found in state UDAP statutes patterned after the UDTPA, a private injunctive remedy is available. In addition, in twenty-three jurisdictions, UDAP statutes not patterned after the UDTPA explicitly authorize a private injunctive remedy.[280]

In Delaware, Georgia, Hawaii, Illinois, Maine, Minnesota, Nebraska, Ohio, and Oklahoma, consumer litigants should not confuse the UDAP statute patterned after the UDTPA[281] with the state's other UDAP statute that provides a private damages remedy, with which they may be more familiar.[282] Aggressive consumer litigants will select the more advantageous statute for a particular case or will even bring claims under both statutes.

22.6.2.2 Implying an Injunctive Remedy in Other States

Private injunctions may also be available even when the UDAP statute does not explicitly authorize this relief. Some statutes are drafted so that private injunctions are clearly foreclosed, as when a statute indicates that a damage award is the exclusive individual remedy.[283] But often a UDAP statute will allow a court to grant private plaintiffs "other equitable relief" or "other relief the court deems appropriate." These phrases may be terms of art in a particular state with specific state precedent as to their meaning.

When it is unclear whether injunctive relief is authorized, or when the statute is completely silent on the issue, consumer litigants should rely on the legislative intent and liberal construction of UDAP statutes to argue for injunctive relief. Allowing injunctive relief promotes the purposes of UDAP statutes—to prevent deception from recurring[284] and to protect the public.[285] If private injunctive actions are allowed, consumers can serve as private attorneys general, bringing to the court's attention seller misconduct that the state attorney general does not have the resources to pursue.

22.6.3 Injunctive Relief Under Other Consumer Protection Statutes

Article 9 of the Uniform Commercial Code, which regulates repossession and sale of collateral, explicitly allows a consumer to seek injunctive relief.[286] The federal laws prohibiting invidious credit discrimination also provide explicitly for injunctive relief in private actions.[287] A wrongful denial[288] or termination of utility services may be remedied by injunctive relief.[289]

Other consumer protection statutes are silent about whether injunctive relief is available. Federal courts have inherent power to issue equitable relief, and, while Congress may limit that power with respect to a particular statute, the Supreme Court has made clear that such limits are not assumed: "Absent the clearest command from Congress, federal courts retain their equitable power to issue injunctions in suits over which they have jurisdiction."[290] This

Stat. § 87-303; N.M. Stat. § 57-12-10; Ohio Rev. Code Ann. § 4165.03; Okla. Stat. Ann. tit. 78, § 54; Or. Rev. Stat. § 646.638.

278 *See* National Consumer Law Center, Unfair and Deceptive Acts and Practices § 3.4.2.4 (6th ed. 2004).

279 *See* National Consumer Law Center, Unfair and Deceptive Acts and Practices § 8.6 (6th ed. 2004).

280 Ala. Code § 8-19-10; Cal. Civ. Code § 1780 (West); Cal. Bus. & Prof. Code §§ 17203, 17204 (West); Conn. Gen. Stat. § 42-110g(d); D.C. Code § 28-3905(k); Fla. Stat. Ann. § 501.211(1) (West); Ga. Code Ann. § 10-1-399; Haw. Rev. Stat. § 480-13; Idaho Code Ann. § 48-608; 815 Ill. Comp. Stat. 505/10a; Kan. Stat. Ann. § 50-634; Me. Rev. Stat. Ann. tit. 5, § 213; Mass. Gen. Laws Ann. ch. 93A, § 9 (West); Mich. Comp. Laws § 445.911; Mo. Rev. Stat. § 4022.025(2) (authorizing private injunctions in class actions); Neb. Rev. Stat. § 59-1609; N.H. Rev. Stat. Ann. § 358-A:10; N.Y. Gen. Bus. Law § 349; Ohio Rev. Code Ann. § 1345.09 (Baldwin); R.I. Gen. Laws § 6-13.1-5.2; Tenn. Code Ann. § 47-18-109; Tex. Bus. & Comm. Code Ann. tit. 2, § 122.50(b) (Vernon); Utah Code Ann. § 13-11-19; Wash. Rev. Code § 19.86.090.

281 Del. Code Ann. tit. 6, § 2531; Ga. Code Ann. § 10-1-370; Haw. Rev. Stat. § 481A; 815 Ill. Comp. Stat. 510/1 *et seq.*; Me. Rev. Stat. Ann. tit. 10, § 1211; Minn. Stat. Ann. § 325D.43; Neb. Rev. Stat. § 87-301; Ohio Rev. Code Ann. § 4165 (Baldwin); Okla. Stat. Ann. tit. 78, § 51 (West).

282 Del. Code Ann. tit. 6, § 2511; Ga. Code Ann. § 10-1-390; Haw. Rev. Stat. § 480-1; 815 Ill. Comp. Stat. 505/1 *et seq.*; Me. Rev. Stat. Ann. tit. 5, § 206; Minn. Stat. Ann. § 8.31; Neb. Rev. Stat. § 59-1601; Ohio Rev. Code Ann. § 1345.01 (Baldwin); Okla. Stat. Ann. tit. 15, § 751 (West). *See* Greenberg v. United Airlines, 206 Ill. App. 3d 40, 563 N.E.2d 1031 (1990) (comparison of the two statutes).

283 *See* Wyo. Stat. Ann. § 40-12-114.

284 State *ex rel.* Guste v. Crossroads Gallery, Inc., 357 So. 2d 1381 (La. Ct. App. 1978); Hockley v. Hargitt, 82 Wash. 2d 337, 510 P.2d 1123 (1973). *See generally* National Consumer Law Center, Unfair and Deceptive Acts and Practices § 8.1 (6th ed. 2004).

285 Weigel v. Ron Tonkin Chevrolet Co., 298 Or. 127, 690 P.2d 488 (1984); Fisher v. World-Wide Trophy Outfitter Ltd., 15 Wash. App. 742, 551 P.2d 1398 (1976).

286 U.C.C. § 9-625(a). *See* National Consumer Law Center, Repossessions § 13.2.2 (6th ed. 2005).

287 National Consumer Law Center, Credit Discrimination § 11.7.5 (4th ed. 2005).

288 *See* National Consumer Law Center, Access to Utility Service § 3.4.2 (3d ed. 2005).

289 *See* National Consumer Law Center, Access to Utility Service § 12.4.5 (3d ed. 2004).

290 Califano v. Yamasaki, 442 U.S. 682, 705 (1979). *See* National Consumer Law Center, Truth in Lending § 8.4 (5th ed. 2003 and Supp.).

precedent is highly persuasive authority for federal courts to grant injunctive relief under federal consumer protection statutes.

Notwithstanding the Supreme Court's broad directive, courts are split on whether injunctive relief is available under the Fair Credit Reporting Act, with some courts concluding that Congress' grant of authority to the FTC to seek injunctive relief implies that private litigants lack such authority.[291] In addition, several courts have held that the silence of Congress regarding private FDCPA injunctive relief is fatal to such an action.[292] While these decisions present a hurdle to obtaining private FDCPA injunctions, courts have continued to entertain FDCPA injunctive suits since these decisions were rendered. However, the better tactical approach may be to seek declaratory relief or injunctive relief pursuant to a state statute or common law.[293]

22.6.4 Preconditions for Private Injunctive Relief

22.6.4.1 Must the Plaintiff Be Injured?

Not every individual can seek an injunction against merchant misconduct. While some individuals or organizations may wish to act as private attorneys general to combat marketplace abuses, UDAP statutes often specifically limit those who can seek relief to those who have suffered actual monetary loss, have been aggrieved, or have been adversely affected by a violation. Care must be taken in reviewing the UDAP statute for such limiting language by scrutinizing not only the provision for injunctive relief but also other sections dealing with private remedies.

A notable exception, the District of Columbia Code, was amended in 2000 to allow any person to bring an injunctive action.[294] One of California's UDAP statutes was similar until it was amended in 2004.[295] The Massachusetts UDAP statute allows a plaintiff to obtain an injunction before suffering actual damages, as long as the defendant's unfair practices may have the effect of causing a future loss of money or property.[296] The Alaska UDAP statute provides that, with prior notice, any person who is a victim of a UDAP violation may bring an action for injunctive relief, whether or not that person suffered actual damages.[297]

22.6.4.2 Must the Plaintiff Benefit from the Injunction?

While federal issues of Article III case-or-controversy standing will not apply to state court actions, consumer litigants seeking a court injunction from which they will derive little or no individual benefit should carefully review any applicable state standing doctrines. It will also be important to review the language of the statute under which the consumer is proceeding.

A Florida appellate court has interpreted its statute as requiring that the consumer be aggrieved by the practice but not that the injunction would benefit the consumer.[298] Thus a person who has suffered damage due to a practice may pursue a claim for declaratory or injunctive relief, even if the effect of those remedies would be limited to protection of consumers who have not yet been harmed by the practice. The District of Columbia Code allows any person, organization, or group, whether acting in its own interests, on behalf of its members, or for the general public, to bring suit.[299]

More typical are statutes patterned after the UDTPA,[300] which include language allowing private injunctions when a litigant is "likely to be damaged." The test is thus prospective, not retrospective, so the plaintiff must benefit from the injunction.[301] Legislative drafters may have had in mind

291 *See* National Consumer Law Center, Fair Credit Reporting § 11.5 (5th ed. 2002 and Supp.).

292 *See, e.g.* Zsamba v. Cmty. Bank, 56 F. Supp. 2d 1207 (D. Kan. 1999) (FDCPA does not specifically provide for injunctions; minor who sought to enjoin the sale of a horse she owned securing a debt of her parents was not entitled to an injunction); Sibley v. Diversified Collection Servs., 1998 WL 355492 (N.D. Tex. 1998) (injunctive relief not available under FDCPA); Sokolski v. Trans Union Corp., 178 F.R.D. 393 (E.D.N.Y. 1998) (FDCPA contains no injunctive relief remedy); Ditty v. Check-Rite, Ltd., 973 F. Supp. 1320 (D. Utah 1997) (private injunctive relief not available under the FDCPA); Gammon v. GC Servs. Ltd. P'ship, 162 F.R.D. 313, 320 (N.D. Ill. 1995); Zanni v. Lippold, 119 F.R.D. 32, 34 (C.D. Ill. 1988); Strong v. Nat'l Mgmt. Co., 600 F. Supp. 46 (E.D. Ark. 1984); Duran v. Credit Bureau of Yuma, Inc., 93 F.R.D. 607, 608 (D. Ariz. 1982). *See generally* National Consumer Law Center, Fair Debt Collection § 6.9 (5th ed. 2004 and Supp.).

293 *See* Gammon v. GC Servs. Ltd. P'ship, 162 F.R.D. 313 (N.D. Ill. 1995) (declaratory relief was appropriate in FDCPA litigation; injunctive relief was not available to the private litigant under the FDCPA).

294 D.C. Code § 28-3905(k).

295 Cal. Bus. & Prof. Code § 17203. *See* Stop Youth Addiction, Inc. v. Lucky Stores, Inc., 17 Cal. 4th 553, 71 Cal. Rptr. 2d 731, 950 P.2d 1086 (1998).

296 Warner-Lambert Co. v. Execuquest Corp., 691 N.E.2d 545 (Mass. 1998).

297 Alaska Stat. § 45.50.535.

298 Davis v. Powertel, Inc., 776 So. 2d 971 (Fla. App. 2000). *See also* Coronado Prods., Inc. v. Stewart, 1988 WL 116371 (Tenn. App. Nov. 2, 1988) (granting injunction against future deception under UDAP statute allowing anyone affected by a violation to seek injunction).

299 D.C. Code § 28-3905(k).

300 *See* National Consumer Law Center, Unfair and Deceptive Acts and Practices § 3.4.2.4 (6th ed. 2004).

301 *See, e.g.*, Glazewski v. Coronet Ins. Co., 108 Ill. 2d 243, 483 N.E.2d 1263, 1267 (1985) (consumer can not bring UDTPA injunctive action when consumer will not be deceived by the practice in the future); Smith v. Prime Cable, 658 N.E.2d 1325 (Ill. App. 1995) (no right to injunction when consumer could not show likelihood of future damage); Popp v. Cash Station Inc.,

businesses suing to halt competitors' deceptive practices that were placing the plaintiff at a competitive disadvantage. For private individuals, the applicability of this standard may be a bar to injunctive relief because a litigant who knows about a deceptive practice is unlikely to be damaged by it in the future.

There are obvious exceptions. For example, when there is only one merchant of a certain type in the area or there is an ongoing contractual relationship with the seller, the plaintiff must continue to deal with that seller. Apartment rentals, mobile home parks, migrant farm camps, campground memberships, health spas, vocational schools, and debt collection are other areas in which a consumer's injury may be continuing and injunctive relief particularly appropriate.

Thus in one UDAP case the court ordered the landlord not to evict any tenants without the court's prior approval.[302] Similarly, a court ordered a developer to use abutting property as conservation areas as promised the consumers.[303] A preliminary injunction to freeze the seller's assets should also be permitted when such assets may be necessary to satisfy an eventual judgment.[304]

Even when the UDAP statute does not expressly require that the plaintiff be likely to benefit from an injunction, sellers may argue that courts should not grant an injunction that will not benefit any named party to the action. This, of course, creates an anomalous situation. If only a consumer likely to suffer future damages can seek an injunction, then only those unaware of a deceptive practice could challenge it. Thus, a Texas court has stated that an injunction could be granted when other consumers were being injured or when the seller intended to repeat its deceptive practice.[305]

Moreover, judicial economy and the public interest in stopping a deceptive practice before a multiplicity of individual damage suits are filed outweighs any argument that the relief does not benefit any of the parties to the action. Framing a lawsuit as a class action may ease this problem, and class injunctive actions pose fewer procedural problems than class damage actions.

Federal courts have held that, assuming injunctive relief is available, the named plaintiff in a class action must be subject to the same substantial, immediate threat of irreparable injury as the class seeking the injunction. In a Truth in Lending Act case, this threat of injury was held absent when the named plaintiff stated in a deposition that he did not intend to do business with the defendants in the future.[306] In FDCPA cases, the named plaintiff is unlikely to have a comparable degree of control over future relations with a collector, since the collector is chosen solely by the creditor and the same collection agency may be used by many different creditors. In addition, a collector's discontinuance of practices violating the FDCPA does not preclude the issuance of an injunction.[307]

22.6.4.3 Does an Adequate Remedy at Law Prevent Injunctive Relief?

Litigants who have been damaged by a practice and who seek to enjoin the seller's future use of that practice may have to respond to a defense that equitable relief is not appropriate because a damage remedy could make them whole. This common law doctrine is being eroded and should not apply at all when equity jurisdiction is specifically conferred by the statute in question.[308] Thus, a court has ruled that recovery of even treble damages does not preclude injunctive relief.[309] When the underlying transaction involves real property, an analogy to specific performance may help overcome any judicial reluctance to grant injunctive relief.[310]

22.6.5 Other Equitable Relief

Equitable relief other than injunctions may also be available. For example, many UDAP statutes allow the court to grant "other relief" or "other equitable relief" that it deems proper. Language along these lines should give the court authority to exercise the equitable power of reformation of a contract or to order specific performance.

The Connecticut Supreme Court has interpreted its UDAP statute's authorization of "such equitable relief as [the court] deems necessary or proper" in the broad spirit appropriate

---

613 N.E.2d 1150 (Ill. App. Ct. 1992) (consumer is unlikely to be confused in the future and therefore can not seek injunction under Illinois Deceptive Trade Practices Act).

302 Hernandez v. Stabach, 145 Cal. App. 3d 309, 193 Cal. Rptr. 350 (1983).

303 Brandt v. Olympic Constr., Inc., 16 Mass. App. 913, 449 N.E.2d 1231 (1983).

304 Finkelstein v. Southeast Bank, N.A., 490 So. 2d 976 (Fla. Dist. Ct. App. 1986).

305 David McDavid Pontiac, Inc. v. Nix, 681 S.W.2d 831 (Tex. App. 1984). *See also* Adkinson v. Harpeth Ford-Mercury, Inc., 1991 Tenn. App. LEXIS 114 (Feb. 15, 1991); Hockley v. Hargitt, 82 Wash. 2d 337, 510 P.2d 1123 (1973); Connelly v. Puget Sound Collections, Inc., 16 Wash. App. 62, 553 P.2d 1354 (1976).

306 Rivera v. Dick McFeely Pontiac, Inc., 75 F.R.D. 1 (N.D. Ill. 1977).

307 Chavez v. Northwest Collectors, Inc., 1999 U.S. Dist. LEXIS 14979 (N.D. Ill. 1985); Smith v. Mikell, Clearinghouse No. 34,362C, 17 Clearinghouse Rev. 585 (N.D. Ill. 1982); Wiginton v. Pac. Credit Corp., 2 Haw. App. 435, 634 P.2d 111 (1981). *But see* Grassley v. Debt Collectors, Inc., 1992 U.S. Dist. LEXIS 22782 (D. Or. Dec. 14, 1992) (denying injunctive relief because of absence of proof that collector poses an ongoing threat of continued unlawful debt collection practices).

308 *See* Greenfield Country Estates Tenants Ass'n v. Deep, 423 Mass. 81, 666 N.E.2d 988 (1996).

309 David McDavid Pontiac, Inc. v. Nix, 681 S.W.2d 831 (Tex. App. 1984).

310 *See* Greenfield Country Estates Tenants Ass'n v. Deep, 423 Mass. 81, 666 N.E.2d 988 (1996).

for a remedial statute.[311] It held that a trial court had authority to reopen a judgment that a seller deceptively obtained, notwithstanding a general state procedural law that set a four-month period for reopening judgments.

22.7 Declaratory Relief

Declaratory relief is available in consumer actions in federal court.[312] The basis for declaratory relief in federal suits is found at 28 U.S.C. §§ 2201 and 2202. It should be noted that the Fourth Circuit cited the failure to seek and obtain declaratory relief as a factor in affirming a district court's reduced award of attorney fees under the Fair Debt Collection Practices Act (FDCPA).[313]

Declaratory or injunctive remedies for class relief are desirable when the collector's violations are part of a pattern or practice affecting a large number of people. Class action requirements for declaratory or injunctive relief may be considerably less than those for damages. Notice to the class of the pendency of a declaratory or injunctive action is not ordinarily required. The problems encountered in proving and distributing damages among class members are not raised by class actions seeking declaratory or injunctive relief.[314]

22.8 Putting a Business Scam into Involuntary Bankruptcy

Bankruptcy may be a favorable forum to proceed against a business that is largely operating illegally and is not paying judgments and claims against it.[315] An involuntary petition may be filed under chapter 7 or chapter 11 by three or more creditors with liquidated, non-contingent, undisputed,[316] and unsecured claims aggregating at least $12,300.00.[317] If the petition is opposed, the bankruptcy court will hold a hearing and will enter an order for relief if the debtor is failing to pay its debts as they become due.[318]

An involuntary order for chapter 7 relief against the business can provide many benefits for consumers. It results, among other things, in the appointment of a trustee to take control of the debtor's assets.[319] Creditors can elect a trustee of their own choosing at the meeting of creditors.[320] Forcing an involuntary bankruptcy can trigger useful disclosure requirements as well as other asset discovery procedures.[321] It can also prevent a dishonest debtor from transferring away assets that might have been available to satisfy a judgment and from otherwise mismanaging the business. Similarly, an involuntary case can be used to recover assets that have already been fraudulently transferred.[322] Two other potentially useful powers in an involuntary bankruptcy are the trustee's power to avoid any preferential transfers the debtor has made within the previous ninety days (or within one year to insiders)[323] and the court's power to appoint new management for the debtor.[324]

One example of a case in which consumers as creditors used an involuntary bankruptcy strategy involves a rent-to-own company against whom consumers had obtained a judgment for usury.[325] Several other unreported cases have involved large mismanaged apartment complexes in which tenants had judgments requiring damage payments and sub-

311 Yeong Gil Kim v. Magnotta, 249 Conn. 94, 733 A.2d 809 (1999).

312 Ballard v. Equifax Check Servs., Inc., 186 F.R.D. 589 (E.D. Cal. 1999) (Fed. R. Civ. P. 23(b)(2) class certified when predominate relief was declaratory); Ballard v. Equifax Check Servs., 27 F. Supp. 2d 1201 (E.D. Cal. 1998) (Declaratory Judgment Act, 28 U.S.C. § 2201(a), permits court to enter declaratory judgment notwithstanding absence of corresponding injunctive relief); Young v. Meyer & Njus, P.A., 183 F.R.D. 231 (N.D. Ill. 1998) (denying motion by defendant to decertify class, because requirements for Rule 23(b)(2) class certification had been met); Gammon v. GC Servs. Ltd. P'ship, 162 F.R.D. 313 (N.D. Ill. 1995). *But cf.* Sibley v. Diversified Collection Servs., 1998 WL 355492 (N.D. Tex. 1998) (denying certification pursuant to Rule 23(b)(2) of a proposed FDCPA national class because declaratory relief did not predominate: the declaratory relief was for declaring defendant's act violative of the FDCPA, not for an injunctive-like purpose, and the lawsuit sought actual damages).

313 Carroll v. Wolpoff & Abramson, 53 F.3d 626 (4th Cir. 1995).

314 *See* National Consumer Law Center, Consumer Class Actions: A Practical Litigation Guide §§ 6.3.3, 6.6 (5th ed. 2002 and Supp.). *But cf.* Goldberg v. Winston & Morrone, 1997 WL 139526 (S.D.N.Y. 1997) (finding that the FDCPA suit primarily sought damages, not declaratory relief, the court denied certification of a Rule 23(b)(2) class).

315 11 U.S.C. § 303. For a more complete discussion of involuntary bankruptcy, see National Consumer Law Center, Consumer Bankruptcy Law and Practice §§ 17.2.2, 13.8 (7th ed. 2004).

316 On the question of whether the creditor's claims are subject to a bona fide dispute, the bankruptcy court should be willing to give the consumers' earlier judgment effect under the doctrine of collateral estoppel. *In re* DEF Invs., Inc., 186 B.R. 671 (Bankr. D. Minn. 1995).

317 11 U.S.C. § 303(b). The $12,300 amount is adjusted periodically for inflation, under 11 U.S.C. § 104. If the debtor has fewer than twelve qualifying creditors, one or more creditors with over $12,300 in qualifying claims may file the petition.

318 11 U.S.C. § 303(h)(1). *See also* 11 U.S.C. § 303(h)(2).

319 11 U.S.C. § 701.

320 11 U.S.C. § 702.

321 An order for relief in an involuntary case triggers the requirement that schedules and a statement of affairs be filed within fifteen days. Fed. R. Bankr. P. 1007(c). Debtor's examinations are also available under Fed. R. Bankr. P. 2004. An involuntary debtor will not necessarily be cooperative in filing schedules and appearing for questioning, however. See National Consumer Law Center, Consumer Bankruptcy Law and Practice § 17.5.8 (7th ed. 2004).

322 The trustee's powers to avoid transfers are discussed in National Consumer Law Center, Consumer Bankruptcy Law and Practice Ch. 14 (7th ed. 2004).

323 11 U.S.C. § 547. *See id.* § 10.4.2.6.4.

324 11 U.S.C. § 303(g).

325 *In re* DEF Invs., Inc., 186 B.R. 671 (Bankr. D. Minn. 1995).

stantial repairs. An involuntary bankruptcy case in the latter situation may force a change of ownership if the debtor has effectively abandoned the building. It may also create opportunities to commence discussions about the future of the building with secured creditors. An involuntary bankruptcy may also be used to bring related parties and their assets before the bankruptcy court when there has been a voluntary bankruptcy by only one of several related parties (partners, spouses, subsidiaries and affiliated corporations, joint owners of real estate, and so forth).

However, advocates should keep in mind that there are substantial risks to an involuntary bankruptcy strategy. The bankruptcy court may require petitioners to post a bond against the debtor's expenses and potential damages to the debtor's business.[326] The penalties for bringing an involuntary bankruptcy that is dismissed include the possibility of compensatory and punitive damages as well as attorney fees and costs.[327]

22.9 Consumers' Attorney Fees and Costs

22.9.1 Purpose of Fee-Shifting Provisions of Consumer Protection Statutes

Virtually all UDAP statutes and many other types of federal and state consumer protection statutes offer attorney fees and costs to successful consumer litigants. By requiring merchants and creditors who violate consumer protection statutes to pay the consumer's legal expenses, these statutes make it possible for attorneys to devote the resources necessary to prosecute a case successfully, even if the consumer's dollar losses are relatively minor. This not only removes a barrier to consumers seeking to remedy marketplace abuses but also deters businesses from engaging in unfair and deceptive practices.[328] By ensuring that plaintiffs with bona fide claims are able to find lawyers to represent them,[329] fee-shifting provisions implement the private attorney general approach taken by consumer protection statutes.[330] Courts should construe statutory attorney fee provisions in favor of consumers since such provisions promote these underlying legislative purposes.[331]

Other grounds for attorney fee awards include the common fund doctrine, which applies in class actions whether or not the basis for the claim provides for fee shifting.[332] In addition, a number of states provide by statute that, if a contract clause requires the consumer to pay fees if the seller or creditor wins a case, then the seller or creditor is liable for fees if the consumer wins.[333]

Attorney fees are discussed in more detail in other NCLC treatises.[334]

22.9.2 Calculating the Amount of an Attorney Fee Award

The most common method for calculating statutory attorney fees is the lodestar method. The court determines the number of hours reasonably expended on the case and multiplies it by a reasonable hourly rate based on the prevailing rate in the community for an attorney of that level of skill and experience. Either party then may attempt to show why that amount should be adjusted up or down. Common reasons for downward adjustments are limited overall success or excessive, duplicative, or inadequately documented hours.[335]

Most courts recognize that, if the purpose of fee-shifting statutes is to enable consumers to pursue relatively small claims, it will often be appropriate to award fees that exceed

---

326 11 U.S.C. § 303(e).

327 11 U.S.C. § 303(i).

328 Parker v. I&F Insulation Co., 89 Ohio St. 3d 261, 730 N.E.2d 972 (2000); Taylor v. Medenica, 331 S.C. 575, 503 S.E.2d 458 (1998).

329 Lettenmaier v. Lube Connection, Inc., 162 N.J. 134, 741 A.2d 591 (1999); Chattin v. Cape May Greene, Inc., 243 N.J. Super. 590, 581 A.2d 91 (1990), *aff'd per curiam*, 124 N.J. 943, 591 A.2d 943 (1991).

330 *See, e.g.*, Graziano v. Harrison, 950 F.2d 107, 113 (3d Cir. 1991) (FDCPA); DeJesus v. Banco Popular de Puerto Rico, 918 F.2d 232 (1st Cir. 1990) (TILA); Parker v. I&F Insulation Co., 89 Ohio St. 3d 261, 730 N.E.2d 972 (2000) (UDAP). *See also* National Consumer Law Center, Fair Debt Collection § 6.8.1 (5th ed. 2004 and Supp.); National Consumer Law Center, Truth in Lending § 8.9.1 (5th ed. 2003 and Supp.); National Consumer Law Center, Unfair and Deceptive Acts and Practices § 8.8.1 (6th ed. 2005).

331 Jordan v. Transnational Motors, Inc., 537 N.W.2d 471 (Mich. Ct. App. 1995); Tanner v. Tom Harrigan Chrysler Plymouth, 82 Ohio App. 3d 764, 613 N.E.2d 649 (1991) (attorney fee provision should be construed liberally).

332 *See* National Consumer Law Center, Consumer Class Actions: A Practical Litigation Guide (5th ed. 2002 and Supp.); § 7.6.5, *supra*.

333 Ark. Code Ann. § 16-22-308; Cal. Civ. Code § 1717; Conn. Gen. Stat. § 42-150bb; Fla. Stat. Ann. § 522.105(7); Haw. Rev. Stat. § 607-14; Mont. Code Ann. § 28-3-704; N.H. Rev. Stat. Ann. § 361:C-2; N.Y. Gen. Obligations Law § 5-327; Or. Rev. Stat. § 20.096; Utah Code Ann. § 78-27-56.5; Wash. Rev. Code § 4.84.330. *See also* Mo. Stat. Ann. § 408.092 (fees to enforce credit agreement).

334 *See* National Consumer Law Center, Truth in Lending § 8.9 (5th ed. 2003 and Supp.); National Consumer Law Center, Fair Credit Reporting § 11.6 (5th ed. 2002 and Supp.); National Consumer Law Center, Fair Debt Collection § 6.8 (5th ed. 2004 and Supp.); National Consumer Law Center, Credit Discrimination (4th ed. 2005); National Consumer Law Center, Unfair and Deceptive Acts and Practices § 8.8 (6th ed. 2005).

335 Hensley v. Eckerhart, 461 U.S. 424, 533 S. Ct. 1933, 76 L. Ed. 2d 40 (1983). *See* National Consumer Law Center, Truth in Lending § 8.9.4 (5th ed. 2003 and Supp.); National Consumer Law Center, Unfair and Deceptive Acts and Practices § 8.8.11 (6th ed. 2004).

the consumer's recovery.[336] However, the Fourth and Fifth Circuits have indicated that the consumer's attorney fee may be greatly reduced or denied when there is little success[337] or no award of FDCPA damages.[338]

Almost all courts award attorney fees under consumer protection statutes when the individual is represented on a no-fee basis by a pro bono or legal services attorney.[339]

22.9.3 Procedure for Seeking Fees

The first step in a successful fee application is keeping detailed accounting of time spent and work performed on the case. Some courts may accept reconstructed records, but contemporaneous time records are by far the preferred practice. Courts often disallow time if there are no contemporaneous time records or if the records are insufficiently detailed. The time records should identify the nature of the task, who performed it, and the claims and defendants to which each time entry relates.

The fee petition should include a detailed breakdown of all time spent on the case, plus justification for the hourly rate claimed. An affidavit from a local attorney regarding the prevailing rate in the community for an attorney of similar skill and experience is helpful. A sample fee petition with supporting documentation is found on the companion CD-Rom to this manual.

Courts differ as to whether a hearing on the fee application is required. The Federal Rules of Civil Procedure allow courts to adopt special local procedures for resolving fee issues without extensive evidentiary hearings.[340]

To avoid the defense strategy of settling a case with the consumer directly without providing for the consumer's attorney fees, the consumer's attorney needs to be sure that the retainer agreement with the client provides protections for the consumer's attorney fee. A sample retainer is included as an appendix to this volume and on the companion CD-Rom.

When a case is settled, the form in which the settlement is documented can affect whether fees can be awarded or not. In federal court and some state courts, the consumer is considered to be a prevailing party entitled to a fee award under a fee-shifting statute only if an enforceable judgment on the merits or a court-ordered consent decree is entered. A "private settlement" that does not involve judicial oversight and approval is insufficient.[341] Courts have held that stipulations, even if they are filed with the court, are mere "private settlements" if they are signed only by the parties.[342] Negotiating the fee award as part of the settlement avoids these issues.

336 *See* Zagorski v. Midwest Billing Servs., Inc., 128 F.3d 1164 (7th Cir. 1997) (it was an abuse of discretion to not award attorney fees when the collector had admitted liability for $100; fees sufficient to compensate the attorney for the time spent on the case must be awarded to encourage enforcement of the FDCPA); National Consumer Law Center, Truth in Lending § 8.9.4.1 (5th ed. 2003 and Supp.); National Consumer Law Center, Unfair and Deceptive Acts and Practices § 8.8.11.1 (6th ed. 2004).

337 Carroll v. Wolpoff & Abramson, 53 F.3d 626 (4th Cir. 1995).

338 Johnson v. Eaton, 80 F.3d 148 (5th Cir. 1996).

339 *See* Gallegos v. Stokes, 593 F.2d 372 (10th Cir. 1979); Manning v. Princeton Consumer Discount Co., 533 F.2d 102 (3d Cir. 1976); Rodriguez v. Taylor, 569 F.2d 1231, 1244 (3d Cir. 1977) (Civil Rights Act); Rios v. Enter. Ass'n Steamfitters (UAW) Local 638, 400 F. Supp. 993, 995 (S.D.N.Y. 1975), *aff'd*, 542 F.2d 579 (2d Cir. 1976) (Equal Employment Opportunity Act). *See also* National Consumer Law Center, Truth in Lending § 8.9.3.2 (5th ed. 2003 and Supp.).

340 Fed. R. Civ. P. 54(d)(2)(D).

341 Buckhannon Bd. & Care Home, Inc. v. W. Va. Dep't of Health & Human Resources, 532 U.S. 598, 121 S. Ct. 1835, 149 L. Ed. 2d 855 (2001).

342 *See* National Consumer Law Center, Consumer Warranty Law § 2.22.6.5 (2d ed. 2001 and Supp.).

Chapter 23 Common Defenses and Defense Tactics

By Carolyn Carter and Steve Gardner[1]

23.1 Introduction

> Nothing is more difficult than the art of maneuvre. What is difficult about maneuvre is to make the devious route the most direct and to turn misfortune to advantage.

Sun Tzu, The Art of War[2]

One of the banes of representing plaintiffs, particularly in consumer cases, is dealing with the variety of tactics defense counsel throw out in an effort to avoid trial on the merits. These tactics are in addition to the expected motions to dismiss and for summary judgment and often border on the unprofessional and unethical. Indeed, in some instances, they are fully groundless and deserving of sanctions.

The most important consideration in responding to defense tactics is to avoid, at all costs, letting the tactics overwhelm the merits. For every defense tactic discussed in this chapter, there are ways to respond and to neutralize that tactic.

Although defense tactics are limited only by the imagination and the vestigial professional courtesy of the bottom feeders among the defense bar, this chapter will focus on the most common:

- Thin capitalization
- Discovery abuse
- Settlement offers
- Arbitration
- Counterclaims
- SLAPP suits
- Bona fide error or ignorance as a defense
- Preclusion of a pending consumer class through a class action settlement in another case

23.2 The Fly-by-Night Merchant: Thin Capitalization

If your client tells a story of a business that is so outrageous that there is no way that it would escape legal liability, inquire about its assets. One strategy adopted by some unscrupulous merchants is to plan their business so that they can make a quick profit and completely spend it or invest the money out of the country before they can be subjected to a civil or criminal judgment. These merchants are not generally good targets for the civil litigant who may spend thousands of dollars pursuing litigation against them only to end up with an unenforceable judgment. There are some industries in which this type of operation has been more common in the past, for example, travel tour scams,[3] alu-

1 Stephen Gardner is Director of Litigation for the advocacy group, Center for Science in the Public Interest, based in Washington, D.C. He is also Of Counsel to the National Consumer Law Center. Previously, Steve was Assistant Dean of Clinical Education at Southern Methodist University School of Law (1994–1995); Visiting Assistant Professor of Law at Southern Methodist University School of Law (1992-1995); Assistant Attorney General in the Consumer Protection Division of the State of Texas (1984–1991); Assistant Attorney General in the Bureau of Consumer Frauds of the State of New York (1982–1984); Students Attorney at the University of Texas (1981–1982); and a staff attorney at the legal aid office in Austin, now part of Texas Rio Grande Legal Services (1976–1981). He is a frequent author and speaker on consumer advocacy issues.

Carolyn Carter is Deputy Director of Advocacy at NCLC. She was formerly co-director of Legal Services, Inc., in Gettysburg, Pennsylvania, and director of the Law Reform Office of the Cleveland Legal Aid Society. She is the editor of *Pennsylvania Consumer Law* and the first edition of *Ohio Consumer Law*; co-author of *Automobile Fraud* (2003), *Consumer Warranty Law* (2d ed. 2001), *Unfair and Deceptive Acts and Practices* (5th ed. 2001), *Repossessions and Foreclosures* (5th ed. 2002); and contributing author to *Fair Debt Collection* (5th ed. 2004), *Truth in Lending* (5th ed. 2003), and *The Cost of Credit* (2d ed. 2000). She is the 1992 recipient of the Vern Countryman Consumer Award and is currently a member of the Federal Reserve Board's Consumer Advisory Council.

Section 23.8 on SLAPP suits is based on the work of Paul Bland, a staff attorney, and Candace Hom, a law clerk, with Trial Lawyers for Public Justice, whose kind agreement to allow the inclusion of their work is much appreciated. Thanks to Dick Rubin who helped prepare § 23.4 on offers of judgment. Thanks also to Robert Hobbs and Mary Kingsley for their work on this Chapter.

2 Sun Tzu, The Art of War 102 (Samuel B. Griffith, trans., Oxford Univ. Press 1971). Because Oxford is in England, it permits the variant spelling of "maneuvre."

3 *See* National Consumer Law Center, Unfair and Deceptive Acts

minum siding and driveway paving scams,[4] investment Ponzi schemes,[5] vocational schools,[6] and debt poolers.[7] In such situations, the consumer may be better off pursuing a complaint with the consumer protection office of the state attorney general or with the district attorney.[8]

If a civil suit is pursued with such a merchant, an attachment of assets should be considered early in the litigation and injunctive relief may be the most effective. If a judgment is obtained and no assets can be located, it may be worthwhile to hire a collection firm specializing in hunting down hidden assets, including foreign investments. Another approach may be to seek an involuntary bankruptcy if the illegality and insolvency are very clear.[9]

Another approach is to investigate the possible liability of other defendants. Are the principals of the business collectable and can they be held individually liable? Can a claim be asserted pursuant to the FTC Holder Rule[10] against the entity that financed the transaction for the consumer? Did other entities—a franchisor, manufacturer, telemarketing firm, collector, repossession company, endorser, advertising agency—contribute to the fraud or deception?[11]

Many businesses have insurance and some are required by law to post a bond. If the consumer's claim can be framed so that it falls within the coverage of the insurance or bond, then collectability is less of a concern. However, when a business is closing down, there are often many claimants to the limited bond fund, and there is a danger that the bond will be exhausted before the particular consumer's claim can be paid.[12]

23.3 Discovery Abuse

23.3.1 General

Any plaintiff's lawyer is familiar with the approach taken by far too many defense counsel, who attempt to win through various discovery abuses. Because virtually every necessary document and fact in a consumer case resides with the defendant and not the plaintiff, it is essential to counter these abuses. Fortunately, for each abuse, there is at least one effective counter-maneuver.

23.3.2 Invalid Objections to Written Discovery

The most common abuse is raising invalid objections to written discovery and then refusing to answer. The traditional response is simply to move to compel[13] and seek attorney fees. However, although courts are likely to grant a motion to compel, many are loathe to grant fees in what they view as a good-faith dispute (often because the judge came from a defense firm). Thus, although the discovery is obtained, it costs time and money to do so.

An alternative response is to notice a corporate witness deposition and ask the same questions orally. Only then may it be necessary to move to compel the written responses if the deposition is less than complete.

23.3.3 Inappropriate Objections at Depositions

Nothing is less conducive to the free flow of brilliant deposition questioning than deliberate and invalid objections and interruptions by defense counsel. These can range from unnecessary objections to "speaking" objections, wherein counsel say what the witness should have said, to which the witness adds a "Me, too."

Do not tolerate any significant degree of this conduct, or defense counsel will control the deposition.

One approach is to object each time it occurs and threaten to terminate the deposition and obtain a court order to prevent future abuse. Although this can often produce the desired result in the end, terminating the deposition (especially if defense counsel dragged their heels in making the witness available) may be just what defense counsel want.

A better method is to object to the conduct but continue the deposition to completion, making sure to get the witness's answer to each question to which objection was raised. Then, adjourn the deposition without passing the witness and go to court to seek sanctions for improper conduct. At a minimum, if the defense counsel objections are indeed worthless, the court will award attorney fees to the plaintiff and will usually order the resumption of the deposition, to be paid by the defendant.

It is very important to know and understand both the civil procedure rules in your own jurisdiction and the way trial judges interpret them. Some state civil procedure laws are

and Practices § 5.4.13 (6th ed. 2004); National Consumer Law Center, Consumer Law Pleadings (Cumulative CD-Rom and Index Guide).

4 National Consumer Law Center, Unfair and Deceptive Acts and Practices § 5.6.1 (6th ed. 2004).

5 *See id.* § 5.13.1.2.

6 *See* National Consumer Law Center, Student Loan Law Ch. 9 (2d ed. 2002 and Supp.).

7 *See* National Consumer Law Center, Unfair and Deceptive Acts and Practices § 5.1.2.3 (6th ed. 2004).

8 *See* § 6.2.3, *infra*.

9 *See* § 22.8, *supra*.

10 16 C.F.R. § 433.

11 *See* National Consumer Law Center, Unfair and Deceptive Acts and Practices Ch. 6 (6th ed. 2004).

12 *See id.* § 6.10 (merchant bonding, insurance, and consumer recovery funds); National Consumer Law Center, Automobile Fraud § 9.13 (2d ed. 2003 and Supp.) (auto dealer bonds).

13 Motions to compel discovery are included on the companion CD-Rom to this manual and in National Consumer Law Center, Consumer Law Pleadings (Cumulative CD-Rom and Index Guide).

better than others in this regard. For example, Texas adopted new discovery rules in 1999 that provide that the *only* objections to questions are "Objection, leading" and "Objection, form." If not stated in this concise form, objections are waived. The objector may not explain the objection unless requested to do so. "Argumentative or suggestive objections or explanations waive objection and may be grounds for terminating the oral deposition or assessing costs or other sanctions."[14]

23.3.4 Delay in Producing Documents or Making Witnesses Available

After much delay in providing a complete response to written discovery, defense counsel may next delay the actual production of documents or delay in responding to dates for depositions.

As to written documents, there is always the simple motion to compel, which often results in production even before hearing. As a quicker alternative, consider simply sending a short and courteous letter that demands production by a certain date, within a week or so. If that does not result in production, then the only alternative is a motion to compel, but the judge is more likely to award fees when there was first a sincere attempt to avoid involving the court. Indeed, many jurisdictions require attempted resolution prior to filing the motion.

When defense counsel delays a deposition by failing to respond to an informal request for available dates on which counsel and the witness are available, simply notice the deposition. The best practice is usually to send a letter to defense counsel advising of the need for a deposition and asking for available dates within a week. After the week has passed, send out the deposition notice. The burden is now on defense counsel to go to court for protection. Few courts countenance delay in depositions, especially when the lawyer seeking the deposition first sought dates informally.

Of course, a corollary to this rule is that one should always be ready to change the noticed date if defense counsel makes a reasonable request for a short delay. No court is going to be sympathetic to a lawyer who insisted on seeking a court order to take a deposition that the defense counsel was willing to give only a few days later. In any event, the calendars of most courts will result in an even greater delay before the hearing can be held.

23.3.5 Late Discovery Supplementation

Most civil procedure rules require the supplementation of discovery responses. One relatively common defense trick is to give only minimal responses when first asked but then to supplement copiously shortly before trial and after the close of discovery. One effective means to prevent this tactic in advance is to take a deposition of a corporate representative as allowed by Fed. R. Civ. P. 30(b)(6) and analogous state rules. The deposition notice must identify the matters on which information is sought, and then the corporation is required to designate someone to testify as to matters known or reasonably available to it. A human being, no matter how well coached, is likely to try to tell at least some of the truth and to fill out the brevity of the written responses.

Another approach is to seek sanctions, including striking defenses, at the time of the late response supplementation. Although it is not likely that a court will grant all relief sought, it is probable that a court will at least revive discovery deadlines and possible that the court will force the defendant to pay the cost of the additional discovery.

23.3.6 Destruction of Documents

Very few defendants actually engage in destruction of documents that are sought in discovery, just as very few suborn perjury. Because it is rare, and subject to severe sanctions, it is unlikely that a plaintiff's counsel will ever catch a defendant in the act. However, there is one method of determining whether it is going on—if the practitioner is lucky enough to have laid hands on a document of the "smoking gun" variety. In written discovery, ask the defendant to produce all documents of the nature of the document you already have (but which the defendant does not know that you have). If the defendant fails to produce the document, then you have clear proof that something fishy is going on, which will serve both as grounds for sanctions and as a basis for persuading a court to order very broad discovery in order to lessen the possibility of it happening again.

A business may routinely purge its business records to reduce its storage expense, and sometimes the period for destruction may be quite short. Some business defendants have also tried to cover up their wrongdoing by destroying incriminating documentary evidence. A good tactic to counter such loss of important documentary evidence is to move soon after filing your complaint for a protective order forbidding the destruction of documents related to the consumer's claim.[15] It is also wise to pursue discovery of the defendant's records as quickly as allowed so that they may be reviewed before the defendant discovers which of its records consumer's counsel is unaware of. When the defendant has a duty to retain documents, the destruction of documents may lead to a presumption that the documents would be inculpatory.[16]

Another concern is electronic documents. The ephemeral nature of electronic materials and the variability of record

14 Tex. R. Civ. Pro. 199.5(f).

15 *See* National Consumer Law Center, Consumer Law Pleadings (Cumulative CD-Rom and Index Guide).

16 *See* Park v. City Of Chi., 297 F.3d 606 (7th Cir. 2002).

retention programs combine to create a need to ensure the preservation of electronic discovery. As a precautionary measure, and until the rules of procedure are changed to deal with electronic discovery, it is advisable—very soon after filing a lawsuit—to learn the scope of existing electronic documents by serving an interrogatory seeking a description of all electronic materials relating to the subject matter of the lawsuit or by making that matter a subject of the initial conference.

23.3.7 Preparing for Discovery Battles

The consumer's attorney must be prepared for discovery battles, especially when seeking evidence that will pinpoint the fraud or establish a pattern of misconduct. To be in a position to win discovery battles, attorneys should avoid overreaching in discovery. There may be some advantages to requesting a few items that are not absolutely essential and that can be abandoned as part of a compromise, but a discovery request that is generally excessive is likely to antagonize the court.

It is important to be able to document reasonable efforts to resolve a discovery dispute before taking it to the court. If a defendant fails to respond to discovery, for example, a series of courteous and reasonable yet firm letters is appropriate: first a reminder letter, then a second reminder letter setting a deadline, and finally a third letter describing the motion that will be filed if the response is not received by a certain date. The letters should offer to work out any particular problems that have been raised. In some circumstances, offering a carefully limited protective order on subjects such as confidential financial information removes a basis for the defendant to resist discovery. It is important to make sure that the court's initial impression is that the consumer's attorney is acting reasonably and has made every effort to resolve the dispute before bringing it to the court. It is also important to come into court with clean hands, having complied with the defendant's discovery requests in a timely manner and with all the requirements of the civil rules, local rules, case law, and local procedures.

Courts tend to be impatient with discovery disputes, so motions and briefs should be concise. If the judge has not yet had to read the complaint, the motion should include a few basics about the case that will win the judge's sympathy.

Before a discovery hearing, the consumer's attorney should prepare a very concise oral description of the issue and the need for relief that immediately communicates the gist of the issue to the court. The attorney should also have thought through what discovery is absolutely essential and what is desirable but can be sacrificed if necessary. If the discovery dispute relates to evidence of a pattern of misconduct, it is helpful to marshal all evidence that suggests that a pattern exists so the court does not think that the consumer's attorney is on a fishing expedition. The consumer's attorney should also be prepared to rebut the defendant's contention that producing the information would be too burdensome or to pin the defendant down as to the nature of the burden and tailor the request in a way that will reduce the burden.

23.4 Offers of Judgment

Pursuant to Rule 68 of the Federal Rules of Civil Procedure, at any time more than ten days before trial, the defendant may make "an offer to allow judgment to be taken against the defending party for the money or property or to the effect specified in the offer, with costs then accrued." Defendants frequently make offers of judgment in consumer cases. Such an offer of judgment may be accepted within ten days by written notice. Thereafter, "either party may then file the offer and notice of acceptance together with proof of service thereof and thereupon the clerk shall enter judgment."[17] If the offer of judgment was not accepted and the judgment eventually obtained is less favorable than the offer, the plaintiff must pay the defendant's post-offer costs. A number of states have rules similar to Rule 68.

Offers of judgment are often less than crystal clear. Since the consequences of accepting or rejecting a Rule 68 offer are significant and the ten-day time limit is extremely short, the consumer's attorney should pay immediate attention to any Rule 68 offer and begin evaluating it as soon as it is received.

If a federal fee-shifting statute defines attorney fees as part of costs, then the term "costs" includes fees for purposes of Rule 68.[18] However, the various statutes within the Federal Consumer Credit Protection Act state that the successful litigant may obtain costs "together with a reasonable attorney's fee."[19] Although this language means that costs do not include attorney fees, dealing with the practical consequences of this legal distinction can be hazardous:

17 Fed. R. Civ. P. 68.

18 Marek v. Chesny, 473 U.S. 1, 9, 105 S. Ct. 3012, 3016, 87 L. Ed. 2d 1 (1985). Even when a statute that allows a prevailing party to recover fees defines fees as part of costs, a plaintiff who recovers less than the Rule 68 offer will not be saddled with the defendant's post-offer attorney fees. The plaintiff is still the prevailing party, despite winning less than the Rule 68 offer. Le v. Univ. of Pa., 321 F.3d 403, 411 (3d Cir. 2003); Payne v. Milwaukee County, 288 F.3d 1021 (7th Cir. 2002); Crossman v. Marcoccio, 806 F.2d 329 (1st Cir. 1986). *But see* Catalina Yachts v. Pierce, 105 P.3d 125 (Alaska 2005) (shifting defendant's post-offer fees to consumer under Alaska version of Rule 68; persuasive dissent).

19 15 U.S.C. § 1692k(a)(3) (Fair Debt Collection Practices Act); 15 U.S.C. § 1640(a)(3) (Truth in Lending Act); 15 U.S.C. § 1691e(d) (Equal Credit Opportunity Act); and 15 U.S.C. §§ 1681n(a)(3), 1681*o* (Fair Credit Reporting Act); 15 U.S.C. § 1679g(a)(3) (Credit Repair Organizations Act); 15 U.S.C. § 1693m(a)(3) (Electronic Fund Transfer Act). *See also* 49 U.S.C. § 32710(b) (federal odometer statute). *But see* 15 U.S.C. § 2310(d)(2) (Magnuson-Moss Consumer Warranty Act) (including attorney fees as part of costs).

- The question arises whether a plaintiff who accepts an offer of judgment that is silent as to fees and that instead offers, for example, a sum certain plus costs or just a sum certain is entitled to apply for an additional amount for reasonable attorney fees. This plaintiff is clearly the prevailing party and therefore entitled to a fee award.[20] However, the defendant typically argues that it intended that an allowance for fees was included in the sum offered. Federal courts analyze this question under prevailing contract principles construing ambiguities against the drafter. Accordingly, if the court finds that such silence creates an ambiguity, the plaintiff is entitled to apply for an additional fee award.[21]
- Determining whether an offer's silence regarding fees is ambiguous is nevertheless itself an issue that has divided the federal courts. The Ninth Circuit follows the bright line rule that an offer of judgment that does not explicitly mention and account for fees is always ambiguous and thus allows the plaintiff to apply for a fee award.[22] Other circuits do not require such a degree of specificity and instead hold that an offer that evinces a sufficiently clear intent to be inclusive of fees, such as by stating that the sum offered satisfies "all claims"[23] or is a "total sum as to all counts" of the complaint,[24] precludes an additional fee award.
- Knowing whether fees are included in, or may be added to, the sum offered is essential not only in evaluating whether to accept it but also in determining at the conclusion of the case whether the judgment eventually obtained is less favorable than the offer and whether the plaintiff therefore must pay the defendant's post-offer costs. The key is to make an apples-to-apples comparison, making sure that both of the amounts to be compared include the fees incurred as of the date of the offer.[25] Thus, if the defendant made a lump-sum Rule 68 offer of $20,000 to cover both attorney fees and compensation to the plaintiff, and fees incurred at the time amounted to $6000, the final judgment for the plaintiff would have to exceed $14,000 to be a better result.
- If the consumer rejects a Rule 68 offer, goes to trial, and recovers less than the offer, the consumer is responsible for court costs incurred after the date of the offer but can still force the defendant to pay post-offer fees under statutes that do not define fees as costs.[26] Even if a Rule 68 offer does not cut off post-offer fees, the court is likely to reduce or even eliminate the fee for work after the plaintiff rejects any offer of settlement that it considers to have been reasonable.[27]
- An offer of full payment of the underlying claim and statutory attorney fees may affect the continuing jurisdiction of the court. Some courts have held that an offer of judgment that pays all monetary claims in full and allows the court to award reasonable attorney fees and costs moots the case, leaving the court with no actual case or controversy to resolve.[28] An offer is unlikely to moot a case, however, if the plaintiff is seeking damages beyond an ascertainable liquidated sum, such as claims for emotional distress.

As a practical matter, the consumer who receives an unclear or ambiguous offer of judgment should ask that it be clarified. Even if the defendant refuses to clarify the offer, the consumer's request for clarification shows that the offer was ambiguous and thus should be construed against the drafter. Seeking clarification precludes the defendant from claiming later that the offer was more generous than it appeared to be.

If the defendant's offer of judgment does not explicitly include attorney fees, the consumer's attorney outside the Ninth Circuit should raise this matter and confirm it in writing. For example, when the defendant makes an offer of judgment to resolve the matter of damages and costs but agrees to leave the determination of attorney fees to the court, this should be spelled out in the offer of judgment. If not, the consumer should do so in the acceptance of the offer of judgment. On the other hand, if the offer of judgment does not include attorney fees because the defendant offers none, the consumer's attorney should confirm this in writing as well to protect against a later claim that the offer was more favorable than the ultimate judgment. When the offer of

---

20 Utility Automation 2000 v. Choctawhatchee Elec. Coop., Inc., 298 F.3d 1238 (11th Cir. 2002).

21 *See* Hennessy v. Daniels Law Office, 270 F.3d 551 (8th Cir. 2001); Webb v. James, 147 F.3d 617 (7th Cir. 1998); Nusom v. Comh Woodburn, Inc., 122 F.3d 830 (9th Cir. 1997).

22 Nusom v. Comh Woodburn, Inc., 122 F.3d 830 (9th Cir. 1997).

23 McCain v. Detroit Auto Fin. Ctr., 378 F.3d 561 (6th Cir. 2004).

24 Norby v. Anchor Hocking Packaging Co., 199 F.3d 390 (7th Cir. 1999).

25 Bevard v. Farmers Ins. Exch., 127 F.3d 1147 (9th Cir. 1997); Grosvenor v. Brienen, 801 F.2d 944 (7th Cir. 1986).

26 *Id.* Knight v. Snap-On Tools Corp., 3 F.3d 1398 (10th Cir. 1993) (when state consumer protection statute treated costs and attorney fees separately, unaccepted offer of judgment greater than the ultimate recovery entitled the defendant to recovery of post-offer costs but did not cut off post-offer attorney fees to the prevailing plaintiff); Grassley v. Debt Collectors, Inc., 1993 U.S. Dist. LEXIS 21375 (D. Or. Apr. 12, 1993).

27 Lee v. Thomas & Thomas, 109 F.3d 302 (6th Cir. 1997). *But cf.* NAACP v. Town of E. Haven, 259 F.3d 113 (2d Cir. 2001) (fact that parties were close to settlement before suit insufficient basis to deny fees; informal negotiations not a basis to deny fees); Ortiz v. Regan, 980 F.2d 138 (2d Cir. 1992) ("A district court should not rely on informal negotiations and hindsight to determine whether further litigation was warranted and, accordingly, whether attorney's fees should be awarded.").

28 *See generally* Murphy v. Equifax Check Servs., 35 F. Supp. 2d 200 (D. Conn. 1999). *But see* McCauley v. Trans Union, L.L.C., 402 F.3d 340 (2d Cir. 2005) (defendant's "make-whole" offer of judgment for all damages plaintiff claimed did not moot case because offer required judgment to be filed under seal).

judgment includes an unspecified amount of attorney fees, the amount of fees or the method of calculations should be confirmed in writing. By avoiding the confusion as to precisely what the offer of judgment includes and does not include, the consumer may avoid the result of an unintended waiver of counsel fees.

Another practical consideration is the filing of the offer of judgment and acceptance thereof. Most defendants wish to avoid a public record of judgment recorded against them. Therefore, many defendants will make a higher offer than that extended by the offer of judgment when the consumer agrees that the offer and acceptance will not be filed. It may be beneficial to the consumer to negotiate a larger settlement in lieu of filing the offer of judgment and acceptance. On the other hand, if the defendant does not make a higher offer, the offer of judgment and acceptance should be recorded with the clerk of the court, thereby creating a permanent public record of judgment against the defendant. An offer of judgment conditioned on confidentiality is ineffective.[29]

Defendants often use an offer of judgment to try to moot out a class action by settling the named plaintiff's claim.[30] Most courts reject this tactic—at least if a timely motion to certify the class has been filed—as inconsistent with the class action device.[31]

23.5 Stonewalling, Lying, and Attacking the Plaintiff's Character

A lawyer representing an abused consumer should endeavor early in the case to determine whether the abuse was committed by a rotten apple in the defendant corporation or whether the entire corporation is rotten. In the latter situation, the lawyer may want to reconsider the strategy of the case because a rotten corporation may go out of business or file bankruptcy rather than pay a money judgment that is based on a theory of law under which it can not operate. In such a situation, an injunctive action might be far swifter in reaching the same result.[32]

The most frequent response to a consumer's complaint against a corporation is that the underlying facts did not happen and that the consumer is lying. For this reason, most successful consumer cases are built on more than the consumer's word. They may be built on language in the contract or in advertisements, the client's tape recordings of telephone conversations,[33] title documents, or some other physical evidence. A case based on oral wrongdoing may be bolstered by the testimony of a former employee about the company's business practices, the testimony of other victims or witnesses, or a related claim based on physical evidence.

Defendants will sometimes attempt to portray the consumer as engaging in fraud, theft, or dishonesty. They may assert that the consumer is a deadbeat or never intended to pay. In one case in which the consumer's checkbook had been stolen and her name forged on her checks by the thief, the collection agency would not acknowledge that the thief was solely responsible despite his conviction in criminal court. If the consumer is the class representative, prior unrelated convictions may be raised, for example. These tactics are usually less effective if anticipated and discussed with the client.

23.6 Arbitration

Many lenders and retailers now incorporate mandatory arbitration clauses in their consumer contracts in an attempt to avoid court actions. By moving the consumer's dispute to arbitration, the company seeks to avoid injunctions, punitive damages, class actions, discovery, publicity, and juries. Companies also know that the high costs involved in arbitrating a dispute usually make it impractical for the consumer to arbitrate the claim.

While arbitration clauses are generally enforceable, there are several possible attacks on an arbitration requirement. These challenges meet with mixed success in the courts, and it is important for the consumer's attorney to develop the facts carefully, use the proper analysis, and cite to recent case law. An essential resource for anyone challenging the enforceability of an arbitration agreement is National Consumer Law Center, *Consumer Arbitration Agreements* (4th ed. 2004), written largely by the experts at Trial Lawyers for Public Justice. *Consumer Arbitration Agreements* lays out the torrent of recent case law and examines the most effective approaches. The companion CD-Rom includes sample discovery, briefs, and other key information.

23.7 Counterclaims

23.7.1 General

A common knee-jerk response to a consumer's lawsuit is a counterclaim. In some cases, the counterclaim is substantive, such as a claim on the debt that forms the basis for the affirmative claims. However, most counterclaims in con-

29 McCauley v. Trans Union, L.L.C., 402 F.3d 340 (2d Cir. 2005).

30 *See* National Consumer Law Center, Consumer Class Actions: A Practical Litigation Guide § 6.3.1 (5th ed. 2002 and Supp.).

31 *See, e.g.*, Weiss v. Regal Collections Lancer Investments, Inc., 385 F.3d 337 (3d Cir. 2004). *See generally* National Consumer Law Center, Fair Debt Collection § 2.4.1.3.2 (5th ed. 2004 and Supp.).

32 *See* § 22.6, *supra*.

33 Tape recording conversations may be criminal in some states without the consent of all parties and unethical for lawyers in additional states. *See* § 7.11, *supra*.

sumer cases are of the procedural "bad faith" variety. This section will discuss both types.

23.7.2 Substantive Counterclaims

Any careful defense counsel will advise the defendant to file a counterclaim for any damages that the defendant may actually have in connection with its transactions with that consumer. If the suit is for unlawful repossession, the counterclaim will be for the unpaid balance of the defaulted note. If the suit is filed in state court for violations of the Fair Debt Collection Practices Act, the counterclaim will be pleaded for the underlying debt.

From a defense perspective, a substantive counterclaim gives rise to at least three advantages. First, there is a risk that a defendant who does not raise the claim in the instant lawsuit will be precluded from suing on it later. Second, it gives the defendant some leverage in negotiation. Third, it can serve to give the consumer pause about continuing the lawsuit and risking an affirmative judgment of damages and possibly attorney fees to the defendant.[34]

If the counterclaim has merit and if the procedural rules of the jurisdiction in fact make it compulsory, such that it is waived if not pleaded, there is nothing to do but to reassure your client and proceed with the affirmative case, preparing also for the defense of the counterclaim (which will usually be the converse of the prosecution of the consumer's affirmative claim). However, a state law counterclaim to a suit filed in federal court may not be compulsory, so it may be possible to move to dismiss it. A federal court has some discretion to decline jurisdiction over a counterclaim that is not compulsory.[35] Many consumer claims do not involve the same case or controversy as the likely counterclaim. For example, a claim under the Fair Debt Collection Practices Act does not involve the same issues as a counterclaim on the underlying debt. The consumer's debt, including the question of whether it is owed, is immaterial to any issue regarding compliance with the Act.[36] Many courts have applied the same reasoning to decline jurisdiction over collection counterclaims when a consumer files a Truth in Lending suit in federal court.[37] If a consumer is worried about the possibility of a collection counterclaim, filing suit in federal rather than state court may be advantageous because of the discretion of federal courts to exercise their supplemental jurisdiction.

Counterclaims are particularly debatable in class actions, since the defendant will claim that the need to defend a counterclaim against the named plaintiff or absent class members will make the case sufficiently unmanageable to defeat class certification. Briefly stated, counterclaims of this nature are generally permissive and not compulsory, and a court does not have jurisdiction over counterclaims against absent class members. A counterclaim or defense that is peculiar to the class representative does not defeat certification. It may affect the named plaintiff's net recovery at trial, but it should not affect the presentation of the class claims.[38] If a defendant wishes to pursue individual counterclaims against absent individual class members, it must also establish the court's personal jurisdiction over those individuals.[39] If, on the other hand, the defendant wishes to bring a counterclaim against a *class* of absent class members, it must plead and prove that its counterclaim meets all the requisites of Rule 23.[40] The federal statute authorizing supplemental jurisdiction in federal courts may or may not slightly alter this analysis.[41] For a more thorough discussion of this issue, see National Consumer Law Center, *Consumer Class Actions: A Practical Litigation Guide* § 6.9 (5th ed. 2002 and Supp.).

23.7.3 Procedural "Bad Faith" Counterclaims

The more frequent counterclaim is based on the defendant's conclusory assertion that the lawsuit is so baseless that the plaintiff should be sanctioned in some way, usually by an award of attorney fees to the defendant. Counterclaims of this nature are based on either express provisions of consumer protection statutes or Federal Rule of Civil Procedure 11 or its state equivalent. The first type of bad faith counterclaim is the most common.

Legislatures often graft onto consumer protection laws a provision that, if the consumer's claim is brought in bad faith or for the purpose of harassment, the consumer is liable for the defendant's attorney fees. These provisions exist, in various permutations, in both federal and state consumer protection statutes.[42]

34 A related counterclaim is a SLAPP suit, which is based not on the transaction but rather on the desire to retaliate, intimidate, and punish the consumer for speaking out. SLAPP suits are discussed in § 23.8, *infra*.

35 28 U.S.C. § 1367(a).

36 *See, e.g.*, Peterson v. United Accounts, Inc., 638 F.2d 1134 (8th Cir. 1981); Drennan v. Van Ru Credit Corp., 950 F. Supp. 858, 859 n.3 (N.D. Ill. 1996); Azar v. Hayter, 874 F. Supp. 1314, 1317 (N.D. Fla. 1994); Strange v. Wexler, 796 F. Supp. 1117, 1118 (N.D. Ill. 1992); Kolker v. Duke City Collection Agency, 750 F. Supp. 468, 471 (D.N.M. 1990). *See* National Consumer Law Center, Fair Debt Collection § 7.4 (5th ed. 2004 and Supp.).

37 *See* National Consumer Law Center, Truth in Lending § 7.6.3.2 (5th ed. 2003 and Supp.).

38 H. Newberg & A. Conte, Newberg on Class Actions § 3:16 at 372 (4th ed.).

39 *Id.* § 4:34 at 303 (4th ed.).

40 *Id.*

41 *See* Jones v. Ford Motor Credit Co., 358 F.3d 205 (2d Cir. 2004).

42 *See, e.g.*, Fair Debt Collection Practices Act, 15 U.S.C. § 1692k(a)(3); Fair Credit Reporting Act, 15 U.S.C. § 1681n(c); Texas Deceptive Trade Practices Act, Tex. Bus. & Com. Code § 17.50(c). *See* National Consumer Law Center, Unfair and Deceptive Acts and Practices § 8.8.10 (6th ed. 2004).

Prior to filing suit, a consumer lawyer should consider the potential for such a counterclaim and should make the consumer aware of the possibility. If the consumer is very risk averse, it may be possible to plead a cause of action under a statute that does not have a bad faith counterclaim provision. However, usually the risk is unavoidable and the question is how to deal with such a counterclaim when it is raised.

The primary thing to bear in mind is that the defendant is probably not sincere in its assertion that the consumer's claims are bought in bad faith or for harassment and is merely bringing the counterclaim at the urging of defense counsel. Although the defendant may be irritated that it has been sued, that irritation does not establish bad faith on the consumer's part. Under the Fair Debt Collection Practices Act, the defendant's claim should be raised as a motion after the defendant prevails on the merits and not as a counterclaim for attorney fees.[43]

Regrettably, aside from Federal Rule 11, there is no counterclaim to a bad faith counterclaim, so the defendant has no disincentive to raising it. Of course, a successful consumer in a fee-shifting case will be awarded all reasonable attorney fees—which should certainly include time spent responding to a counterclaim that is itself groundless. However, it is important not to let the counterclaim-tail wag the dog—every effort should be made to get rid of the counterclaim as soon as possible.

Because a "bad faith" allegation is generally raised in boilerplate at the outset of the lawsuit, it is essential for the plaintiff to seek immediately to discover the facts and documents in support of the counterclaim. As a rule, there will be no such support aside from defense counsel's assertion that the plaintiff's lawsuit is no good. If indeed there is no factual basis for the counterclaim, it is subject to an early motion to dismiss or motion for summary judgment.

When the counterclaim seeks attorney fees, another responsive strategy is to seek full discovery of the defense counsel's time records in order to be prepared to argue that the fees sought are not reasonable. Because defense counsel are reluctant to disclose their billing records to anyone, especially to shore up a counterclaim they know is itself groundless, the defendant may drop the counterclaim rather than respond to discovery of this nature.

The other type of "bad faith" claim is not actually a counterclaim but rather a motion for sanctions, usually attorney fees, under Federal Rule of Civil Procedure 11 or its state equivalent. Rule 11 provides that an attorney who files anything with the court is "certifying that[,] to the best of the person's knowledge, information, and belief, formed after an inquiry reasonable under the circumstances," the filing is not for harassment or delay, is warranted by existing law or a non-frivolous argument for the change of existing law, and either has evidentiary support or is likely to have support after an opportunity for discovery.

Generally speaking, federal courts interpret Rule 11 to sanction only the most egregious of pleadings. Thus, it is only rarely that Rule 11 will be applied to a complaint. In the unlikely event a defendant does bring a Rule 11 motion arising out of the complaint, the response should be the same as to a "bad faith" counterclaim.

A recent case illustrates a novel variation on this defense strategy that resulted in a suit by a debt collector for a consumer lawyer making a frivolous claim in a demand letter. The court affirmed the award of sanctions pursuant to 28 U.S.C. § 1927 against the consumer's counsel for demanding $3000 to release a frivolous Fair Debt Collection Practices claim and continuing to pursue that claim that he knew to be improper. In addition, the appellate court reversed and remanded the district court's failure to award additional sanctions against the consumer's attorney pursuant to 28 U.S.C. § 1927, holding that the district court abused its discretion in declining to award sanctions for pursuing an unfounded FDCPA counterclaim against the debt collector's attorneys.[44]

23.8 SLAPP Suits[45]

23.8.1 General

Perhaps the most pernicious and intimidating defense tactic is the SLAPP suit. The term "SLAPP" (Strategic Lawsuit Against Public Participation) was coined by two scholars at the University of Denver, law professor George Pring and sociologist Penelope Canan.[46] A SLAPP suit is (1) a civil complaint or counterclaim for monetary damages and/or an injunction (2) filed against non-governmental individuals or groups (3) asserting liability resulting from their communications to a government body or official or the electorate (4) about an issue of some public interest or concern.[47] This definition has been endorsed and accepted by courts.[48]

SLAPP plaintiffs routinely seek to extend and delay the course of SLAPP suits, and SLAPP plaintiffs "win" the

43 *See* National Consumer Law Center, Fair Debt Collection § 7.2 (5th ed. 2004 and Supp.).

44 Riddle & Assocs., P.C. v. Kelly, 414 F.3d 832 (7th Cir. 2005).

45 The portion of this chapter on SLAPP suits is based on the work of Paul Bland, a staff attorney, and Candace Hom, a law clerk, with Trial Lawyers for Public Justice, whose kind agreement to allow the inclusion of their work is much appreciated.

46 Canan and Pring's books and scholarly articles on the subject include *SLAPPS: Getting Sued for Speaking Out* (Temple U. Press 1996); *Strategic Lawsuits Against Political Participation*, 35 Soc. Probs. 506 (1988); and *Studying SLAPPs: Mixing Quantitative and Qualitative Approaches*, 22 Law & Soc'y Rev. 385 (1988).

47 George Pring, SLAPPs, 7 Pace Envtl. L. Rev. 3, 8 (1989).

48 *See, e.g.*, Field v. Kearns, 682 A.2d 148, 153 (Conn. Ct. App. 1996).

lawsuit as long as they can continue to maintain the suit and aggressively pursue discovery, even though they seldom go to trial and almost never actually prevail. "Even if meritless, these suits caused the 'victim' to incur expensive legal fees, lose valuable personal time, and suffer the anxiety and uncertainty of litigation."[49] One scholar has noted:

> [N]o intimidation suit has ever resulted in a judgment for the plaintiff. Nonetheless, these suits achieve their objective of silencing citizens opposed to commercial interests. . . . [E]ven if the defendant is absolutely convinced he will prevail, the price of victory in time, money, and aggravation is very high. He must submit to the litigation process against his will. Typically, he will experience a very unpleasant deposition session, as well as the inconvenience of delays and uncertainty that invariably accompany litigation.[50]

23.8.2 Court Responses to SLAPP Suits

A number of courts have recognized SLAPP suits and have acted accordingly. While each of the SLAPP plaintiffs vigorously denied the fact, keen-eyed courts have regularly been able to look past the formalities of ostensibly legitimate suits and identify SLAPP suits.[51]

Well before the acronym was coined, courts were troubled by litigation brought to suppress the exercise of First Amendment rights and responded by holding that First Amendment activities—that is, speech on matters of public concern, peaceable assembly, and petitioning the government—were privileged. In the *Noerr-Pennington* line of antitrust cases, the Supreme Court held that speech and actions intended to influence government action could not be an antitrust violation, even if the intent and the results were anti-competitive.[52] The rule allowed a narrow exception for "sham petitioning," intended not to induce government action but to directly injure the plaintiff.[53]

In cases involving SLAPP suits, courts continue to emphasize that the right to petition is a fundamental right. The court in *Associated Contract Loggers v. U.S. Forest Service*[54] stated:

> The right to petition is absolutely fundamental to the First Amendment. To hold . . . that people can not freely inform the government of their wishes would . . . be particularly unjustified. The Constitution itself even makes it more clear: Citizens have the right to petition the Government for a redress of grievances. It is beyond conception that this cherished right is so cabined that it is lost at the very moment the petition might possibly achieve success.

In addition to the privilege derived from the First Amendment, most states provide a statutory or common law privilege for litigation, sometimes including quasi-judicial proceedings, pre-litigation activities, or reports to law enforcement authorities.[55]

23.8.3 Legislative Responses to SLAPP Suits

As of mid-2005, at least twenty-four jurisdictions had enacted statutes intended to curb SLAPP suits.[56] These statutes vary widely in scope. For example, Florida's statute

49 Vittands v. Sudduth, 671 N.E.2d 527, 530 (Mass. App. Ct. App. 1996).

50 Joseph J. Brecher, *The Public Interest and Intimidation Suits*, 28 Santa Clara L. Rev. at 114, 115 (1988) (citations omitted). *See also* Comment, *SLAPPs*, 27 Cal. W.L. Rev. at 409, 410.

51 *See, e.g.*, Westfield Partners, Ltd. v. Hogan, 740 F. Supp. 523, 524 (N.D. Ill. 1990) ("The court perceives this, with a great deal of alarm, as part of a growing trend of what have come to be known as 'SLAPP suits.' "); Gordon v. Marrone, 573 N.Y.S.2d 105, 109, 110 (N.Y. Sup. Ct. 1991), *aff'd*, 616 N.Y.S.2d 98 (A.D. 1994) ("petitioner's stated interest in [the case] is markedly disingenuous"; "this proceeding was undertaken primarily[,] if not solely, to harass or maliciously injure the conservancy."); Entm't Partners Group, Inc. v. Davis, 603 N.Y.S.2d 439, 440 (N.Y. Sup. Ct. App. Div. 1993) ("[h]ere, the underlying retaliatory and harassing SLAPP action, intended to stifle legitimate activity by community groups and time barred. . . . was, as the IAS court found, brought in bad faith and was without any reasonable basis in law or fact").

52 United Mine Workers v. Pennington, 381 U.S. 657, 85 S. Ct. 1585, 14 L. Ed. 2d 626 (1965); E. Rail Presidents Conference v. Noerr Motor Freight, Inc., 365 U.S. 127, 81 S. Ct. 523, 5 L. Ed. 2d 464 (1961).

53 Motor Transport Co. v. Trucking Unlimited, 404 U.S. 508, 92 S. Ct. 609, 30 L. Ed. 2d 642 (1972).

54 84 F. Supp. 2d 1029, 1034 (D. Minn. 2000), *aff'd per curiam*, 10 Fed. Appx. 397 (8th Cir. 2001).

55 *See, e.g.*, Jackson v. BellSouth Commc'ns, 372 F.3d 1250 (11th Cir. 2004) (alleged misconduct during settlement negotiations protected by absolute privilege); Buckley v. DirecTV, 276 F. Supp. 2d 1271 (N.D. Ga. 2003) (pre-litigation demand letters, accusing consumers who had purchased de-scrambling device of theft, threatening legal action, and demanding sum of money in settlement were petitioning activity); Kashian v. Harriman, 120 Cal. Rptr. 2d 576 (Cal. App. 2002) (privilege protects lawyer's letter to Attorney General, questioning tax-exempt status of healthcare provider and requesting investigation); Rubin v. Green, 17 Cal. Rptr. 2d 828 (Cal. 1993) (lawyer met with residents and discussed objectives of lawsuit; landlord's UDAP and tortious interference claims barred by absolute privilege); Reichardt v. Flynn, 823 A.2d 566 (Md. 2003) (absolute privilege applies to "quasi-judicial" proceedings); Kirchstein v. Haynes, 788 P.2d 941 (Okla. 1990) (preliminary matters—here, assembling documents and speaking with prospective witnesses—are privileged if a judicial proceeding is "under serious consideration, in good faith"). *See also* National Consumer Law Center, Fair Debt Collection § 10.1.3 (5th ed. 2004 and Supp.).

56 Ark. Code §§ 16-63-501 to 16-63-508; Cal. Civ. Pro. Code § 425.16; Del. Code Ann. tit. 10, § 8136; Ga. Code Ann. § 9-11-11.1; Guam Code Ann. tit. 7, §§ 17101–17109; Haw. Rev. Stat. §§ 634F-1–634F-4; Ind. Code Ann. §§ 34-7-7-1

applies only to actions brought *by* government entities,[57] and Pennsylvania's applies only in environmental matters.[58] The Delaware, Nebraska, and New York statutes apply only to suits against those who have commented on, challenged, or opposed an application or grant of a government permit, license, zoning change, or the like.[59] Even these relatively narrow statutes may be useful to consumers who are sued for asking state agencies to revoke a fraudulent vendor's or creditor's business license.

The broadest statutes protect petitioning and free speech on matters of public concern. The public concern requirement may be a problem in a consumer-merchant dispute, but some statutes of this type have been construed to cover petitioning on any subject whatever.[60] Thus, for example, when consumers sued a contractor, an anti-SLAPP motion would lie to challenge the contractor's abuse of process counterclaim, even though the dispute was purely private.[61] However, when a contractor, involved in a dispute over price and quality of the work began picketing and leafleting at a consumer's financial consulting business, the anti-SLAPP statute would not bar the consumer's defamation action: the picketing and leafleting were not petitioning (because these actions were not seeking government action) and the dispute was not a matter of public concern.[62]

Anti-SLAPP statutes are designed to provide a screening mechanism, to terminate abusive litigation before time, expense and stress can mount up, and to provide compensation to the person wrongfully sued. Most statutes provide for a special motion to dismiss, filed at an early stage with an expedited hearing. The court may, in its discretion, allow limited discovery on the issues raised by the special motion. The motion is then decided on the pleadings and affidavits. Typically, this is a two-step procedure. The first issue is whether the conduct in question is protected by the statute. If it is, then the court will consider whether the action is a SLAPP suit.

The showing necessary to overcome a special motion to dismiss, and the burden of proof, vary widely. Advocates should look closely at the wording of their jurisdiction's statute and the cases interpreting it. The original plaintiff may be required to show a likelihood of success on the claim; that its claim is well grounded in facts and law; that the alleged petitioning was devoid of factual or legal support or was a sham; or that any false statements alleged were made with actual malice. A showing of actual injury may also be required. Denial of an anti-SLAPP motion is usually immediately appealable, at least if a grant of the motion would terminate the litigation.

All the statutes permit—and most of them require—the award of costs and reasonable attorney fees if the special motion is granted. Several provide a cause of action (or a counterclaim in the existing action) for compensatory or, when appropriate, punitive damages.

When anti-SLAPP statutes are broadly worded, they have proven to be a double-edged sword.[63] In any state where petitioning is defined to include lawsuits or reports to government authorities, the anti-SLAPP statute may be a serious problem for a consumer alleging the misuse of the civil or criminal justice system, for example, the use of bad check or larceny charges against the consumer to gain advantage in a commercial dispute.[64] The California legislature, finding that there had been "disturbing abuse" of the anti-SLAPP

---

through 34-7-7-10; La. Code Civ. Pro. Ann. § 971; Me. Rev. Stat. Ann. tit. 14, § 556; Md. Cts. & Jud. Proc. Code § 5-807; Mass. Gen. Laws Ch. 231, § 59H; Minn. Stat. Ann. §§ 554.01–554.05; Mo. Rev. Stat. § 537.528; Neb. Rev. Stat. §§ 25-21,241–25-21,246; Nev. Rev. Stat. §§ 41.635–41.670; N.M. Stat. § 38-2-9.1; N.Y. C.P.L.R. § 3211(g), N.Y. Civ. Rights Law §§ 70-a and 76-a; Or. Rev. Stat. §§ 31.150–31.155; R.I. Gen. Laws §§ 9-33-1 to 9-33-4; Tenn. Code Ann. §§ 4-21-1001 to 4-21-1004; Utah Code Ann. §§ 78-58-101 to 78-58-105; Wash. Rev. Code §§ 4.24.500–4.24.520.

57 Fla. Stat. Ann. Ch. § 768.295.

58 Pa. Cons. Stat. tit. 27, §§ 8301–8305.

59 Del. Code Ann. tit. 10, § 8136; Neb. Rev. Stat. § 25-21,242; N.Y. Civ. Rights Law § 76-a. *See also* Gill Farms v. Darrow, 682 N.Y.S.2d 306 (A.D. 1998) (anti-SLAPP motion would not lie in lawsuit by farmer against anti-pesticide activist; farmer neither held nor sought pesticide permits, and activist did not seek adverse action against licensed applicators employed by farmer).

60 Briggs v. Eden Council for Hope and Opportunity, 19 Cal. 4th 1106, 969 P.2d 564 (1999) (subdivisions of California anti-SLAPP statute concerning petitioning do not limit their coverage to matters of public concern; subdivisions concerning free speech require a showing of an issue of public concern); Office One, Inc. v. Lopez, 769 N.E.2d 749 (Mass. 2002) (subject of "petitioning activity" need not be one of public concern).

61 Adams v. Whitman, 822 N.E.2d 727 (Mass. App. Ct. 2005).

62 Alfred L. Fillipini, PhD & Assocs., Inc. v. Fuller, 2003 WL 22181762 (Cal. App. Sept. 23, 2003) (unpublished, citation limited). *But cf.* Thomas v. Quintero, 24 Cal. Rptr. 3d 619 (Cal. App. 2005) (evicted tenant's demonstrating and leafleting against large commercial landlord were matter of public concern).

63 Jarrow Formulas, Inc. v. LaMarche, 31 Cal. 4th 728 (2003) (anti-SLAPP motions will lie in all cases alleging malicious prosecution or abuse of process); Duracraft Corp. v. Holmes Prods. Corp., 691 N.E.2d 935 (Mass. 1998) ("[b]y protecting one party's exercise of its right of petition, unless it can be shown to be sham petitioning, the statute impinges on the adverse party's exercise of its right to petition, even when it is not engaged in sham petitioning. This conundrum is what has troubled judges and bedeviled the statute's application.").

64 *See, e.g.*, Buckley v. DirecTV, Inc., 276 F. Supp. 2d 1271 (N.D. Ga. 2003) (letters sent to all consumers who purchased device that might be used for signal theft, threatening prosecution and demanding substantial sum as settlement; pre-litigation demand letters are "petitioning activity" within the meaning of Georgia statute; consumers' complaint dismissed with prejudice because not verified as required by anti-SLAPP statute); Dang v. Ehredt, 977 P.2d 29 (Wash. 1999) (anti-SLAPP statute provided immunity to bank employees who caused arrest of customer; customer innocently presented her paycheck, computer indicated that employer's account was closed because of stolen checks; bank called 911; after arrest police contacted employer and learned that check was good).

statute, "contrary to the purpose and intent" of the law, amended the statute in 2003 to bar its application to certain consumer causes of action.[65]

Even without special SLAPP legislation, courts in every jurisdiction have the authority to impose sanctions for frivolous or harassing litigation. A SLAPP suit's combination of retaliatory purpose and lack of merit will weigh heavily in favor of these sanctions.[66]

23.8.4 Responding to a SLAPP Suit

As with any defense tactic, the first response should be to avoid overreacting, either by caving in or by responding in kind. Instead, as Sun Tzu teaches, learn to turn misfortune to advantage.[67]

One approach is to use the SLAPP nature of the suit as an attack on its merits. In *Street Beat Sportswear, Inc. v. Nat'l Mobilization Against Sweatshops*,[68] for example, a clothing manufacturer brought suit against garment factory workers and non-profit organizations for the latter's tortious interference with the manufacturer's business by publicizing a boycott campaign. The court found that this was a "retaliatory SLAPP suit" meant to stifle defendants' existing claims against the manufacturer for violations of labor laws. Thus, in a case involving citizens who have previously voiced concerns in opposition to plaintiffs' plans, *Street Beat* supports dismissal of "retaliatory SLAPP suits" designed to stifle defendants from vocalizing their concerns.

Another positive response is to encourage the court to make the SLAPPer pay dearly for having brought a meritless lawsuit. Federal courts have authority under Rule 11, as well as inherent power, to sanction conduct that is inappropriate and frivolous and can use this authority to sanction plaintiffs who bring SLAPP suits.[69] Many states have a rule similar to Rule 11. State anti-SLAPP laws also typically allow, or even mandate, an order requiring the SLAPP plaintiff to pay the defendant's attorney fees if the court grants a special motion to dismiss the case.[70] Some state statutes provide for compensatory, statutory, or punitive damages.

The Ninth Circuit Court of Appeals has held that state anti-SLAPP suit provisions apply to state counterclaims that are brought in federal court and do not conflict with the Federal Rules of Civil Procedure.[71] Another court, however, has held that state anti-SLAPP statutes can not be applied to *federal* claims asserted in federal court.[72]

In summary, although critics have questioned the severity of the SLAPP suit problem, a considerable number of law review articles and cases reflect the growing concern in state legislatures and the legal community regarding the pernicious abuse of the legal system to burden the constitutional rights of those who oppose a party's actions. While courts will probably be reluctant to sustain a counterclaim that is based on an allegation that the plaintiff suite is a SLAPP suit, they are most likely willing to award attorney fees to a defendant for the costs incurred in defending a baseless lawsuit. In addition to awarding attorney fees to defendants, it is possible that courts may sanction plaintiffs for bringing a frivolous claim. Overall, the case law surrounding SLAPP suits has broadened considerably, with courts more willing to recognize the retaliatory intent behind such suits and their detrimental effects on constitutional rights.

23.9 Bona Fide Errors and Ignorance

Many federal and state consumer protection statutes follow the approach of the federal Truth in Lending Act that provides for strict liability but allows a defense for bona fide, unintentional errors despite the maintenance of procedures to avoid the errors.[73] This defense is limited to inadvertent errors and is not generally extended to mistakes of law.[74] Each element of the defense must be established for

65 Cal. Civ. Proc. Code § 425.17.

66 *See, e.g.*, Gordon v. Marrone, 573 N.Y.S.2d 105 (N.Y. Sup. Ct. 1991), *aff'd*, 616 N.Y.S.2d 98 (A.D. 1992); Entm't Partners Group, Inc. v. Davis, 603 N.Y.S.2d 439 (N.Y. Sup. Ct. A.D. 1993). *See also* Barnes Found. v. Twp. of Lower Merion, 242 F.3d 151 (3d Cir. 2001) (finding that § 1983 action against neighbors who opposed museum expansion was—just barely—not frivolous for purposes of awarding attorney fees because law not clearly established at time, but warning that parties "bringing suits to stifle First Amendment activity . . . will do so at [their] own peril.").

67 Sun Tzu, The Art of War (Samuel B. Griffith, trans., Oxford Univ. Press 1971).

68 Street Beat Sportswear, Inc. v. Nat'l Mobilization Against Sweatshops, 698 N.Y.S.2d 820, 825 (1999).

69 *See* Associated Contract Loggers v. U.S. Forest Serv., 84 F. Supp. 2d 1029, 1038 (D. Minn. 2000) (ordering plaintiffs to show cause why they should not be sanctioned for frivolous SLAPP suit).

70 *See* Conroy v. Spitzer, 70 Cal. App. 4th 1446, 1455, 83 Cal. Rptr. 2d 443, 449 (1999) (awarding fees); McLarnon v. Jokish, 431 Mass. 343, 350, 727 N.E.2d 813 (1999) (award of fees is mandatory).

71 United States v. Lockheed Missiles & Space Co., 190 F.3d 963, 972 (9th Cir. 1999).

72 Globetrotter Software, Inc. v. Elan Computer Group, Inc., 63 F. Supp. 2d 1127, 1129 (N.D. Cal. 1999).

73 15 U.S.C. § 1640 (c). *See also* National Consumer Law Center, Truth in Lending § 7.4.3 (5th ed. 2003 and Supp.); National Consumer Law Center, Fair Debt Collection § 7.5 (5th ed. 2004 and Supp.); National Consumer Law Center, The Cost of Credit: Regulation, Preemption, and Industry Abuses § 10.5.5 (3d ed. 2005); National Consumer Law Center, Unfair and Deceptive Acts and Practices § 4.2.6 (6th ed. 2004).

74 *E.g.*, Pipiles v. Credit Bureau, Inc., 886 F.2d 22 (2d Cir. 1989); Hulshizer v. Global Credit Servs., Inc., 728 F.2d 1037 (8th Cir. 1984); Baker v. G.C. Servs. Corp., 677 F.2d 775 (9th Cir. 1982). *But cf.* Johnson v. Riddle, 305 F.3d 1107 (10th Cir. 2002) (found errors could include mistakes of law based on erroneous comparison of the parallel provisions of the FDCPA and TILA).

the defendant to prevail.[75] Since the Act explicitly provides for this narrow bona-fide-error defense, courts generally decline to recognize any other "good faith" or "technical violation" defense.[76]

When contemplating a case in which the violation may have been the result of an error and when this defense is available, consumer's counsel should consider sending a demand letter to give the defendant a chance to explain that the violation was a result of an error.

23.10 Preclusion of a Pending Consumer Claim Through a Class Settlement in Another Case

One of the most frustrating defense tactics for a consumer attorney who has invested thousands of dollars in a consumer case is to be told that the client's claim has been determined by settlement in another class action against defendant. When the attorney is unaware of the other action, it is not unusual for the other action to provide attorney fees only for the consumers' attorneys involved in the other action. To avoid such surprises, it is advisable to propound a continuing interrogatory to the defendant requesting details of all pending litigation against it and periodically remind defense counsel that the interrogatory must be updated if additional litigation is filed against the defendant. Defense counsel who pursue a secret settlement in contravention of the interrogatory may be subject to bar sanctions. Federal Rule of Civil Procedure 23(e) provides class members with a procedure to object to a class settlement, but meritorious objections are many times rejected by courts anxious to clear their dockets.[77] The non-profit organization Trial Lawyers for Public Justice has a class action abuse prevention project through which it objects to class action settlements that provide little benefit to class members.[78]

23.11 Removal of Case to Federal Court

Sometimes a defendant will attempt to frustrate the consumer's choice of forum by removing a case filed in state court to federal court. Removal is allowed only if the federal court would have had original jurisdiction over the case.[79] A complaint that pleads no federal claims does not become removable because the defendant raises defenses based on federal law.[80]

As a general rule, removal is improper when the plaintiff has chosen to plead solely state law claims, even though federal claims might also have been pleaded.[81] There are two exceptions. First, under the "artful pleading rule," a case is removable if a consumer's state law claim is really a federal claim that is "artfully pled" as a state law claim.[82] Second, while federal preemption of a state claim is merely a defense that is not enough to make the case removable,[83] in a few areas of law Congress has so completely preempted the area that any claim is removable.[84] The Supreme Court has applied this complete preemption theory only under ERISA, § 301 of the Labor-Management Relations Act, and the National Bank Act.[85]

The best way to prevent removal is to deal with it at the pleading stage. If there are major advantages to staying in state court, the advocate should consider deleting claims under statutes such as the Fair Debt Collection Practices Act and the Truth in Lending Act that include a federal jurisdictional grant. Federal courts also have jurisdiction over suits between citizens of different states when the amount in controversy exceeds $75,000. The advocate should consider whether it is necessary to include defendants who are citizens of other states and whether the prayer for relief can be limited to an amount less than $75,000.

Procedurally, there is a thirty-day deadline for filing a notice of removal.[86] The plaintiff then has thirty days to file a motion asking the federal court to remand the case back to state court.[87] If the federal court grants the motion to remand the case, it may award the plaintiff the costs and attorney fees incurred as a result of the removal.[88]

75 *See* National Consumer Law Center, Truth in Lending § 7.4.3 (5th ed. 2003 and Supp.); National Consumer Law Center, Fair Debt Collection § 7.5 (5th ed. 2004 and Supp.).

76 *See* National Consumer Law Center, Truth in Lending § 7.5.1 (5th ed. 2003 and Supp.).

77 *See* National Consumer Law Center, Consumer Class Actions: A Practical Litigation Guide § 12.8 (5th ed. 2002 and Supp.).

78 *See* www.tlpj.org.

79 28 U.S.C. § 1441.

80 Beneficial Nat'l Bank v. Anderson, 539 U.S. 1, 123 S. Ct. 2058, 2062, 156 L. Ed. 2d 1 (2003).

81 Franchise Tax Bd. of Cal. v. Construction Laborers Vacation Trust for S. Cal., 463 U.S. 1, 23, 103 S. Ct. 2841, 77 L. Ed. 2d 420 (1983).

82 Rivet v. Regions Bank, 522 U.S. 470, 475, 118 S. Ct. 921, 139 L. Ed. 2d 912 (1998).

83 Franchise Tax Bd. of Cal. v. Construction Laborers Vacation Trust for S. Cal., 463 U.S. 1, 103 S. Ct. 2841, 77 L. Ed. 2d 420 (1983).

84 Beneficial Nat'l Bank v. Anderson, 539 U.S. 1, 123 S. Ct. 2058, 156 L. Ed. 2d 1 (2003).

85 *Id.*, 123 S. Ct. at 2063.

86 28 U.S.C. § 1446.

87 28 U.S.C. § 1447.

88 *Id.*

Chapter 24 Consumer Class Actions

By Stephen Gardner[1]

24.1 Introduction

Consumer class actions—though daunting even to experienced consumer lawyers—can be an important component of a meaningful, successful, and enjoyable consumer law practice. The United States Supreme Court has long recognized that a consumer lawsuit involving relatively small amounts of money for individual consumers is the paradigm for the existence of the class action rule: "Class actions . . . may permit the plaintiffs to pool claims which would be uneconomical to litigate individually. [In such a case,] most of the plaintiffs would have no realistic day in court if a class action were not available."[2] The Court more recently expanded on this concept: "The policy at the very core of the class action mechanism is to overcome the problem that small recoveries do not provide the incentive for any individual to bring a solo action prosecuting his or her rights. A class action solves this problem by aggregating the relatively paltry potential recoveries into something worth someone's (usually an attorney's) labor."[3] The economics of consumer law practice argue against offering to represent a consumer who has been defrauded but whose damages are too small to warrant bringing an individual lawsuit, but it may be possible to help that consumer and many others if you bring the case as a class action. The tactics of defense counsel frequently require numerous hours of lawyer time from the consumer's lawyer. Unfortunately, and despite plentiful court authority to the contrary,[4] some trial judges are loathe to award attorney fees commensurate with the work actually performed if the client's recovery is relatively small—another incentive to bring a consumer claim as a class action.[5]

When the consumer has been the victim of practices that apply to scores of consumers similarly situated and the defendant has substantial assets, it is worth considering bringing a class action on behalf of the entire class of consumers. If you are inexperienced in class actions or the industry involved, it is essential to bring in experienced co-counsel. The purpose of this chapter is to offer practical solutions to problems that arise in consumer class action litigation. This chapter is not, however, a treatise on the law of class actions. Two excellent sources already exist for that purpose. The first is NCLC's own *Consumer Class Actions: A Practical Litigation Guide*, which provides detailed discussion of both the law and the mechanics of consumer class action practice. The most exhaustive source on class actions is H. Newberg & A. Conte, *Newberg on Class Actions* (4th ed. 2002), a multi-volume set that contains the most thorough compendium of class action law. Any consumer law-

1 Stephen Gardner is Director of Litigation for the advocacy group, Center for Science in the Public Interest, based in Washington, D.C. He is also Of Counsel to the National Consumer Law Center. Previously, Steve was Assistant Dean of Clinical Education at Southern Methodist University School of Law (1994–1995); Visiting Assistant Professor of Law at Southern Methodist University School of Law (1992-1995); Assistant Attorney General in the Consumer Protection Division of the State of Texas (1984–1991); Assistant Attorney General in the Bureau of Consumer Frauds of the State of New York (1982–1984); Students Attorney at the University of Texas (1981–1982); and a staff attorney at the legal aid office in Austin, now part of Texas Rio Grande Legal Services (1976–1981). He is a frequent author and speaker on consumer advocacy issues.

2 Phillips Petroleum Co. v. Shutts, 472 U.S. 797, 809 (1985).

3 Amchem Prods., Inc. v. Windsor, 521 U.S. 591, 117 S. Ct. 2231, 2246 (1997).

4 *See* National Consumer Law Center, Unfair and Deceptive Acts and Practices § 8.8.11.3.1 (6th ed. 2004); National Consumer Law Center, Truth in Lending § 8.9.4 (5th ed. 2003 and Supp.); National Consumer Law Center, Fair Debt Collection §§ 6.8.2.4.1, 6.8.2.4.4 (5th ed. 2004 and Supp.); National Consumer Law Center, Automobile Fraud § 9.12 (2d ed. 2003 and Supp.); National Consumer Law Center, Credit Discrimination § 11.7.6 (4th ed. 2005); National Consumer Law Center, Fair Credit Reporting § 11.6.2 (5th ed. 2002 and Supp.).

5 *Compare* Zagorski v. Midwest Billing Servs., Inc., 128 F.3d 1164 (7th Cir. 1997) (fees commensurate with attorney time required even when $100 Fair Debt Collection Practices Act damages awarded); McGuire v. Russell Miller, Inc., 1 F.3d 1306 (2d Cir. 1993) (attorney fees are mandatory feature of a federal Odometer Act claim); Graziano v. Harrison, 950 F.2d 107 (3d Cir. 1991) (fees may be denied in a successful Fair Debt Collection Practices Act suit only in extraordinary circumstances); Pipiles v. Credit Bureau, Inc., 886 F.2d 22 (2d Cir. 1989) (Fair Debt Collection Practices Act fees are mandatory when consumer is successful) *with* Carroll v. Wolpoff & Abramson, 53 F.3d 626 (4th Cir. 1995) (only $500 attorney fees award justified in extensively litigated Fair Debt Collection Practices Act claim that resulted in $50 damages).

yer embarking on a class action practice should have both of these resources available, preferably in the firm library or at least at ready access. Other excellent resources are available for free on the Internet, such as the Federal Judicial Center's *Manual for Complex Litigation*, Fourth (2002), downloadable at www.fjc.gov, and Fred Misko's virtual treatise, *Misko on Class Actions* (2002), downloadable at http://classactions.misko.com/ManagingLitigation.html.

24.2 Initial Considerations: Case Selection and Formulation, Experience, and Capital

24.2.1 General

At the outset, there are a number of decisions to make. Regardless of the merits of the individual consumer's case, careful selection of the case and intelligent formulation of the claims to be made are essential. Equally important is ensuring that one has the resources, experience, and practical ability to bring and maintain a class action and to find good co-counsel.

24.2.2 Consumer Adequacy

The decision to bring a case as a class action involves several levels in addition to the usual case evaluation steps. In fact, evaluation of a potential class action presupposes that the facts of the case and the applicable law are such that it would qualify for your representation on an individual basis (possibly aside from the minimal damages problem, as discussed above).

Next it is necessary to evaluate the potential client on a different basis than used in accepting an individual case. Because class certification turns (often in significant part) on the individual adequacy of the class representative plaintiff, it is essential to ensure that: (1) the consumer understands that her duties as a litigant go beyond those of an individual litigant; (2) the consumer is willing to undertake those responsibilities and to participate actively in the lawsuit as it develops; (3) the consumer understands that she may be awarded damages only to the same extent as the other class members; and (4) there is nothing about the consumer that would interfere with her serving as a class representative. Each of these criteria is important and may vary slightly when state class action procedures apply.

Many consumers seek out a lawyer in order to turn the problem over to the lawyer and not worry about the case as it develops. This is often appropriate in the case of an individual action, but it may prove fatal to a class action. In a class action, it is almost certain that the defendant will try to disqualify the class representative plaintiff by showing that he has no idea of the substance or procedural posture of the lawsuit.

Therefore, it is necessary to explain this to the consumer and to obtain his commitment to the case at the outset, together with his agreement to read and review pleadings in the case as they are received, and to make sure he understands them in a general way.

To ensure that the consumer is typical of the class members, it may be necessary for the consumer to forgo relief that would be tied to his particular facts. For example, if a consumer is being considered as a class representative in a Fair Debt Collection Practices Act class action that will seek classwide relief for an improper form collection letter, that consumer may have to agree not to bring a claim for damages arising out of a statement made to him by the debt collector in a telephone call that does not appear to be standard practice directed at the entire class. Although different damages for the class representative do not absolutely disqualify that person from acting as class representative, the fact issue presents a complication that skilled defense counsel will use. This determination is something that must be made on the individual facts of the case. If the consumer has damages that are significant and different from damages incurred by other class members, then that consumer is probably not a good class representative. On the other hand, if those damages are indeed significant, then serious consideration should be given to bringing an individual action for that person rather than asking him to be a class representative.

A final consideration is whether there is anything in the consumer's background that could disqualify her in the eyes of the trial judge as an adequate representative of the class. Examples include criminal convictions involving moral turpitude, arrests, debt problems, or a history of litigious behavior. While none of these examples is likely to affect the actual adequacy or ability of the consumer to represent the interests of the class, they are exactly the sort of points that defense counsel use (regrettably with some success) to denigrate the consumer and the class claims in the eyes of the trial judge. Since the decision to certify a class action generally rests within the sound discretion of the trial judge, it is best to avoid, or at least be prepared to address, potentially explosive, or simply embarrassing, aspects of the consumer's background.

24.2.3 Evaluation of Claims

The second essential aspect of the decision to bring a consumer class action is the choice of claims to be asserted in the causes of action. Here, the watchword is simplicity. Bring only the claims that can be made for each class member and that, preferably, do not turn on complicated facts or facts that will be difficult to prove. The most successful class actions tend to have a very simple series of facts, often facts that are not disputable. In the debt collection example above, a form collection letter that went to hundreds of class members is exactly the type of thing to look for. Class actions depend on patterns that can be shown to apply uniformly—preferably identically—across the class.

This is not to say that significant claims should be abandoned but rather to reflect the need to use discretion in the choice of claims to be brought so as not to unnecessarily complicate or delay the lawsuit.

Similarly, it is best to avoid seeking relief for one wrongful act under a variety of legal theories that depend on different levels of proof. For example, if it is possible to use a statutory UDAP claim that is not dependent on establishing scienter or reliance, that should be used to the exclusion of a common law fraud claim that will often require class-wide proof of both intent to deceive and the class member's individual reliance on the fraudulent representation because the defendant will argue that individual proof of intent and reliance is required, making the class action unmanageable.

Equally important to the nature of claims and causes of action is the determination of the type of relief to be sought. Depending on the source of the claim (statutory or common law), relief can include actual damages, multiple damages, punitive damages, statutory damages, restitution, disgorgement, *cy pres* distribution, declaratory relief, and injunctive relief.

A practical consideration that may argue in favor of seeking only equitable relief (including injunction and restitution) is that certification of an injunctive-only class pursuant to Federal Rule of Civil Procedure 23(b)(2) does not require class counsel to give notice to the class that is required by Federal Rule of Civil Procedure 23(c)(2) for a damages class. If the class numbers in the thousands, the cost of giving notice after certification will prove beyond the financial resources of some consumer lawyers. Thus, if relief can be obtained for the class through injunctive relief and equitable restitution, it may be best to simplify the process by deciding not to seek to certify a damages class.

Another decision to be made at the outset is the geographical scope of the class members. If a defendant has committed the same act nationwide, it is tempting to try to correct that behavior on behalf of all consumers in the country. However, unless relief can be obtained under a federal statute such as the Fair Debt Collection Practices Act or the Fair Credit Reporting Act, successful prosecution may depend on proving that the wrongful behavior violated each separate state law, whether brought as common law fraud, breach of contract, or a violation of the consumer protection laws. Many courts are reluctant to certify classes that require the separate consideration of the laws of each state and territory. As with other complicating issues, there are ways to address these concerns. For example, it is feasible to conduct a survey of each state's applicable law to demonstrate that the elements of the cause of action do not in substance vary from state to state. However, this too will present complicating circumstances that may make the case more complex and time-consuming than if the class is confined to one state and one state's laws. In fact, in some circumstances, this may even be preferable. For example, home mortgage cases often are far more preferable in some states with better laws. Similarly, some federal consumer protection laws limit the total dollar amount that may be awarded in one class action against one defendant but do not limit the number of separate suits that may be brought.[6]

Of course, the 2005 amendments to federal removal rules allow for much easier removal of class actions. 28 U.S.C. § 1447. This will continue to be a concern for litigators who want to stay in state court—and a new opportunity for others who prefer federal court—but an explanation of the intricacies of these amendments is beyond the scope of this chapter. For details, see National Consumer Law Center, *Consumer Class Actions: A Practical Litigation Guide* (5th ed. 2002 and Supp.).

24.2.4 Experience

Although class action issues indeed fill one multi-volume treatise, *Newberg on Class Actions*, it is very possible for a good lawyer to bring a class action who has never brought one before. However, it often makes a lot more sense to join with co-counsel experienced in class action litigation and the substance of the claim.[7] To certify a class action, the court must usually find that the class is represented by experienced counsel, often looking specifically at counsel's experience in complex litigation. Although it is not necessary to be grounded fully in class action jurisprudence before bringing one's first class action, it is absolutely essential to be thoroughly familiar with the substantive law that forms the bases of the causes of action asserted and how class actions operate. Each area of consumer law and segment of the retail marketplace has its nuances that can come particularly into play in a class action. There is neither reason nor justification for class counsel to cut her teeth on a new area of the law at the same time she is learning class action practice. Therefore, no matter how good a claim seems under an unfamiliar statute, do not embark on a journey of discovery and personal growth at the expense of the class.

24.2.5 Co-Counsel

There is a way to plow new ground legally and still bring a class action—get an old workhorse. That is, associate with counsel experienced in bringing class actions in the area of

6 *See* National Consumer Law Center, Fair Debt Collection § 6.6.2 (5th ed. 2004 and Supp.); National Consumer Law Center, Consumer Class Actions: A Practical Litigation Guide § 3.6 (5th ed. 2002 and Supp.).

7 A sample co-counseling agreement is included in Appendix A.3, *infra*, and on the companion CD-Rom to this volume.

law and industry involved in your case. Your lack of knowledge will then present no impediment to a successful class action.

In fact, because class actions are by their very nature potentially more complicated than individual actions, it is best to make it a practice to associate with experienced class action counsel in every class action. This is the usual practice of even the most experienced class action lawyer. This need is particularly acute for the solo practitioner, who can always benefit from another ear to bend in any case and the human and organizational resources available in an affiliated firm. In class actions, the choices to be made are usually multiple at each step of the process, and an experienced lawyer can be of the utmost assistance.

Association can take many forms. Preferably, it will be co-counseling with equal effort performed by both lawyers. The best way to learn about class action litigation is to work alongside someone who knows what she is doing. However, the association can be more or less limited. The class counsel's responsibilities can be only those actions in the case directly related to the class issues, and the inexperienced counsel can be responsible for the substantive legal work and the discovery. Or the initiating lawyer can serve as little more than local counsel on the case, with all substantive legal work and discovery conducted by the experienced class counsel. It is even possible to agree that the lawyer experienced in class action work is essentially just a consultant, whose input is sought on an as-needed basis, although this is the least preferable alternative.

Whatever the arrangement, it is important to have a clear, written co-counsel agreement[8] that clearly spells out the nature and extent of work to be performed by each lawyer and the relative portion of attorney fees to be shared by each. This agreement should be in writing to avoid misunderstandings. It is possibly discoverable (because the sharing of fees is arguably related to adequacy of counsel), so you should draft your agreement to meet all ethical standards of the jurisdictions involved. The important thing is to have this understanding at the outset, to avoid both frustration based on different ideas of the nature of the arrangement during the pendency of the lawsuit and disagreement of counsel at the fee application stage.

24.2.6 Capital

Another consideration at the outset, and one that is directly related to co-counseling, is an accurate projection of the potential costs of the lawsuit. If a class action involves utility overcharges in one location in the lawyer's home town, this concern is minimal. Discovery is not likely to involve travel or significant deposition costs, nor will notice to a class of a few hundred tenants be prohibitive.

However, if the class action is to be statewide and filed outside of the initiating lawyer's locale, travel costs, deposition and motion costs, and costs of giving notice can be substantial. For this reason alone, it may be necessary to associate with co-counsel who can commit to advancing most or all of these costs.

An alternative is to simplify the lawsuit, as discussed above. Limit the size of the class to one state. Seek only equitable relief. Reduce the causes of action to those that do not involve significant proof problems, thus eliminating the need for significant discovery expense.

24.2.7 Balancing the Precepts

The foregoing precepts represent a distillation of the experiences of a multitude of class action lawyers and the lessons learned from a variety of sometimes contradictory appellate decisions. They were formulated with the intent of advising a lawyer inexperienced in class actions on the manner in which to bring and prosecute a successful class action. Accordingly, they should not be taken as inviolable truths but as guidelines. For this reason, the importance of associating with experienced class counsel, if only informally, can not be stressed too much.

24.3 Attorney Fees

The issue of attorney fees is an important issue in class actions today, both because it serves as a rallying point for defendants, and sometimes the press, to criticize class actions and because the criticisms of excessive fees are in some instances well based.

It is also by far the most complicated issue. There is no one problem and no one cure. The prime focus of criticism is the size of the fees. In many instances, this problem is more apparent than real. For example, when the individual recovery is $50 per consumer, an attorney fee of $500,000 seems excessive at first glance. However, if the dollars actually recovered by the individual class members in such a case were to be $10 million, then the fees represent just 5% of the total recovery achieved for the class. This makes the fees reasonable in relation to the total actual recovery. The basis for class action fee awards is discussed in National Consumer Law Center, *Consumer Class Actions: A Practical Litigation Guide* §§ 7.6.5, 7.14 (5th ed. 2002 and Supp.).[9]

There are two additional matters that a class lawyer should consider with respect to fees. First, it is not appropriate to discuss fees with defense counsel, regardless of the method by which they are to be calculated and regardless

8 A sample agreement can be found in Appendix A.3, *infra*, and on the companion CD-Rom to this volume.

9 *See also* National Consumer Law Center, Consumer Class Actions: A Practical Litigation Guide Ch. 15 (5th ed. 2002 and Supp.).

also of whether the case is a common-fund or fee-shifting case, until final agreement is reached as to the relief to be given the class. The best procedure is to obtain the defendant's binding agreement to all class relief and then to submit the fees issue to the court for determination. However, it is acceptable to negotiate fees after all relief has been agreed for the class and then to submit the entire agreement to the court and the class for review and approval.

A second essential in the area of attorney fees is that the maximum amount of attorney fees to be sought must be disclosed to the class members at the time the notice of proposed settlement is sent to them, stated as a total dollar amount. While it is appropriate to disclose the amount of fees per class member, the members of the class have the right to know how much overall their attorneys may be paid in total. That is, in the example above, the class *must* be told that the lawyers will receive $500,000 but could *also* be told that this amounts to only $10 per class member.

24.4 Ethical Issues in Settlements

The issue of attorney fees is not the only ethical issue confronting consumer class action lawyers. As with the issue of fees, other problems usually arise at the settlement stage. A study of class actions by the Federal Judicial Center demonstrates that, at least in the four districts the study surveyed, the statistical probability that a class action would go to trial is approximately the same as the probability that an individual civil action would go to trial.[10]

In too many settled class actions, the class counsel, who filed the lawsuit claiming at the time that it was greatest since sliced bread, become extraordinarily pessimistic of the possibility of victory once their fees are sewn up. They file motions with the court supporting settlement that express doubts as to the factual or legal merits of the very lawsuits that they have brought.

This sudden crisis of faith that occurs subsequent to settlement with many class counsel tends to confirm the presumption held by many in the public that class action lawyers are merely in it for the money. "Once a settlement is agreed, the attorneys for the plaintiff stockholders link arms with their former adversaries to defend their joint handiwork . . . ."[11]

As distinguished from virtually any other type of civil action, class actions involve a triad of responsibility. First, class counsel have a duty to represent the class adequately and to obtain the best relief possible. Second, the defense lawyers have a duty to defend their client with zeal. Third—and this is where class actions fundamentally differ from an individual civil lawsuit—the trial court has an affirmative duty to scrutinize class actions, both at the time of certification and at the time of settlement to ensure that the case is appropriately brought as a class action and that any settlement is fair, adequate, and reasonable to the class as a whole.

Unfortunately, sometimes only one part of this triad—the defense lawyers—are doing their jobs. The failure of class counsel to fulfill their fiduciary duty to represent the interests of the absent class members might not be a problem were it not for the signal fact that the trial bench has in many instances failed its independent duty to scrutinize any settlement and to ensure that the settlement is in fact fair, adequate, and reasonable.

This failure by the trial bench is understandable. In these days of ever-expanding dockets, trial judges do whatever they can to administer their dockets effectively and to encourage settlements. This approach works well with individual cases, in which all parties affected by a settlement are present in the litigation. However, it fails miserably with respect to class actions, in which the trial judges have a duty to ensure, after rigorous analysis, that the interests of the hundreds, thousands, or even millions of absent class members are guaranteed.[12] Rather than meet this duty, trial courts fall back on the hoary precept that settlements are to be viewed with favor and bend over backwards to find ways to approve them. "In deciding whether to approve this settlement proposal, the court starts from the familiar axiom that a *bad settlement is almost always better* than a good trial."[13]

Appellate courts sometimes exacerbate this problem, primarily by accepting the pro-settlement bias that the trial courts express. As Judge Friendly said in a dissent, "All the dynamics conduce to judicial approval of such settlements."[14] In addition, adequate and appropriate appellate review is hampered by the existing rule of law that trial court approvals are to be disturbed only upon a finding of abuse of discretion. This rule effectively turns appellate courts into rubber stamps rather than what they should be—another layer of protection to ensure that the interests of the absent class members are protected.

One case involving gas tanks in General Motors trucks is quite instructive as to what can go wrong when class counsel and the trial court do not do their jobs when a class action is settled before certification. It is actually two cases: (1) the federal Multi-District Litigation (MDL) proceeding that was reversed by the Third Circuit, *In re General Motors Corp. Pick-up Truck Fuel Tank Products Liability Litigation*,[15] and (2) a parallel Texas state case that was reversed both by a

10 Thomas E. Willging, Laural L. Hooper, & Robert J. Niemic, *Empirical Study of Class Actions in Four Federal District Courts: Final Report to the Advisory Committee on Civil Rules* 68, Table 16 (Federal Judicial Center 1996) ("FJC Study").

11 Alleghany Corp. v. Kirby, 333 F.2d 327, 347 (2d Cir. 1964) (Friendly, J., dissenting).

12 *See* Gen. Tel. Co. of the Southwest v. Falcon, 457 U.S. 147, 161 (1982); Weinberger v. Kendrick, 698 F.2d 61, 73 (1st Cir. 1982).

13 *In re* Warner Commc'ns Secs. Litig., 618 F. Supp. 735 (S.D.N.Y. 1985) (emphasis added).

14 Alleghany Corp. v. Kirby, 333 F.2d 327, 347 (2d Cir. 1964).

15 55 F.3d 768 (3d Cir.), *cert. denied sub nom.* Gen. Motors Corp. v. French, 116 S. Ct. 88 (1995).

Texas Court of Appeals and the Texas Supreme Court, *General Motors Corp. v. Bloyed*.[16] The facts of both cases are identical, as were the rejected settlements. The settlements failed to address the underlying basis for the lawsuit—exploding side-saddle gas tanks on General Motors pick-up trucks that were alleged to have burned to death hundreds of people and badly burned thousands more. The lawsuits claimed that the trucks were flawed by a dangerous and latent design defect—the placement of the gas tanks outside the frame rail—that increases the likelihood that their fuel tanks will rupture in side-impact crashes, causing fuel-fed fires.

Both state and federal class actions sought, *inter alia*, a recall of all General Motors trucks, with restitution and refunds to all class members, and an order directing General Motors to pay for the retro-fitting of all General Motors pickups to correct the fuel tank defects.

However, in the settlement, class counsel abandoned the recall/retrofit remedy in favor of an approach that limited class members' recovery to discount coupons to buy new General Motors trucks. There was no provision requiring General Motors to recall or repair the trucks, or to reimburse owners who made the repairs themselves, nor was there any provision requiring General Motors to warn consumers about the hazards of the trucks, despite the demand for such relief in the original petition filed by class counsel. In other words, nothing in the settlement addressed the animating principle of the lawsuit: that these General Motors pickup trucks pose a serious—but remediable—safety hazard.

If anything, the settlement would have adversely affected safety while increasing General Motors' profits at the expense of the consumer. In exchange for a promise of a discount that was nothing more than the type of marketing device often used by General Motors and other manufacturers and that only a very small portion of the class could use, the settlement allowed General Motors to walk away from its obligations to its customers after having created, and then concealed, one of the most serious safety problems in the history of the automobile.

In re General Motors Corp. serves as a useful model for consideration of abuses of existing Rule 23, for a number of reasons: (1) it was a settlement class; (2) the sole relief to the class members was in the form of coupons; (3) the compensation for class counsel was not in any way based on money paid to the class; (4) the Third Circuit opinion served as a warm-up to its decision in *Georgine v. Amchem Products, Inc.*;[17] (5) the Texas Supreme Court used the *In re General Motors Corp.* case as a vehicle to establish significant reforms to class action practices in Texas state courts; and (6) it is an example of a small claims class action that could and should have been brought. Although in *In re General Motors Corp.* both state and federal trial courts abused their discretion and thus failed to do their jobs, the appellate courts corrected those abuses of discretion.

Since the first edition of this book, the willingness of courts to examine settlements has increased significantly. As bad settlements—in which the lawyers make money but class members are left out in the cold—decrease, this is a good thing. But the increased scrutiny is often motivated by a heightened antagonism to class actions in general—and that, of course, is a bad thing as it promotes small, wasteful injustices in the marketplace.

Another ethical consideration is the notice of settlement to the class members. The current methods of giving notice to absent class members of the settlement of a class action virtually ensures that the class members will not have adequate information to make an informed and knowing choice as to whether or not to accept the settlement. Settlement notices frequently omit significant and pertinent information and are worded in a way as to make it virtually impossible for the class member to understand any aspect of the settlement.

This issue was reviewed in the FJC Study.[18] The study found that settlement notices generally failed to provide (1) the net amount of the settlement; (2) the estimated size of the class; and (3) the dollar amount of attorney fees to be requested by settling class counsel.[19] In the Texas case, *In re General Motors Corp.*, class counsel failed to advise the class members of the dollar amount of attorney fees that they planned to seek. This failure alone caused the Texas Supreme Court to reject that settlement.[20]

These issues, and others, were considered by the National Association of Consumer Advocates, which adopted *Standards and Guidelines for Litigating and Settling Consumer Class Actions*, 176 F.R.D. 375 (1998).[21] The standards and guidelines were adopted by NACA after much consideration and debate, with input from a wide variety of experienced consumer lawyers and other interested parties. One of the purposes of *Standards and Guidelines* was to make available to courts a reasoned and principled approach to consumer class actions. When this edition was written, NACA was revising *Standards and Guidelines* to reflect the current realities and concerns of class action litigation and settlements.

16 916 S.W.2d 949 (Tex. 1996).

17 83 F.2d 610 (3d Cir. 1996), *aff'd sub nom.* Amchem Prods., Inc. v. Windsor, 521 U.S. 591, 117 S. Ct. 2231 (1997).

18 Thomas E. Willging, Laural L. Hooper, & Robert J. Niemic, *Empirical Study of Class Actions in Four Federal District Courts: Final Report to the Advisory Committee on Civil Rules* 68, Table 16 (Federal Judicial Center 1996) ("FJC Study").

19 *Id.* at 50, 51.

20 Gen. Motors Corp. v. Bloyed, 916 S.W.2d 949, 957 (Tex. 1996).

21 Available also in National Consumer Law Center, Consumer Class Actions: A Practical Litigation Guide Appx. B (5th ed. 2002 and Supp.).

24.5 Summary

Although a class action is a journey not to be embarked upon lightly, it can prove to be a very effective way to redress broad-scale consumer fraud in an effective fashion that permits litigation and vindication of consumer damages that are individually small but significant when combined with those of others similarly situated.

Bringing a class action is within the ability of any relatively experienced consumer lawyer, providing that she prepares adequately, retains co-counsel with complementary resources, and knows what is in store for her.

Chapter 25 Preparing Your First Appellate Argument

By Dmitry Feofanov, Bob Erwin, Pat Tulinski, Craig Jordan, Ellen Friedman, Carolyn Carter, Dan Wulz, Pat Tulinski, Blaine Elliott, Jim Shackelford, Jim McMillen, and Robert Hobbs

How do I prepare for my first appellate argument? I have been bringing consumer cases for years and this is my first appeal to reach argument. Should I rehash my brief? Do I assume the judges have read my brief? Will they grill me on the cases I cite? This case involves a forged car contract.

Dmitry Feofanov:[1] Do not rehash your brief; they probably have already made up their minds anyway.

So what's the best approach? Give them the facts and invite questions. Our appellate courts will have bench memos already reviewed. Be aware that often the person who gets the most hostile questions wins.

"Will they grill me on the cases I cite?" Someone might ask you how you distinguish them, if you do. But this is pretty much irrelevant. Sometimes they would ask you to concede a very obvious point, which you should promptly concede. (They are checking your credibility.)

DO NOT bring the client for the argument—you will be more constrained to concede points you really should in his/her presence. Be very honest about your weak points—the law clerks already gave them chapter and verse, anyway (been there, done that), and calmly explain why, despite the weaknesses, you should win anyway.

Bob Erwin:[2] I try to use oral argument on appeal to tell the Judges *why* they should rule in my favor. If you have briefed the appeal correctly, you have already shown the panel *how* to rule in your favor—that is, you have cited cases and statutes that support your position and permit them to come to a favorable conclusion for you. You can usually assume they have read the briefs and understand the "how."

Now your job is to persuade them why they should do so. It sounds like you will want to be focusing on who the "innocent" parties are before the court (maybe both, but who is more innocent) and who is in the best position to spot and stop the forgery and/or in a better position to take the brunt of its effects, etc. Address the implications for future conduct if they rule for you and why that's better than what will result from an opposite ruling.

If you get interrupted with questions (which you will), answer the question and then get right back to "why." I believe the only valuable time spent at an oral argument on "how" to reach a conclusion in my favor is in distinguishing cases that seem to support my opponent's position, especially when I haven't had a chance to do so in writing.

Pat Tulinski:[3] If you can look at your brief and the opposing brief, then imagine what the opinion will look like. That is what I argue—the Court's opinion. That way, you appear fair, honest, and balanced in your comments. Also, know who is on the panel and find cases they have authored that state principles you will talk about. If nothing else, you can always find a recent case that cites the standard of review. It is very impressive to say, "Well, Justice _____, as you stated in _____ v. _____ the standard of review is . . . ."

They will be impressed that you did your homework, and every appellate judge likes to be quoted. Just make sure the history on the case is good. You don't want to mention a case that they got reversed on or otherwise criticized on.

Craig Jordan:[4] Listen to Pat, she knows what she's talking about. By way of addition to what she and others have said, focus on the deciding issue and the reasons it should go your way. Start your argument with the phrase "this case all boils down to . . . ." You'll draw out the panel's objections to your position the fastest this way, which will give you more time to deal with them, and you won't get interrupted before you

1 After a career in music, Dmitry Feofanov got tired of being poor and graduated from the Chicago—Kent College of Law in 1994. After serving as a law clerk for the Iowa Supreme Court and Illinois Appellate Court, he did municipal law and, in 2002, established www.ChicagoLemonLaw.com. Surprisingly, though, it did not make him rich. E-mail: Feoanov@ChicagoLemanLaw.com.

2 Bob Erwin is in private practice in Baltimore, where he specializes in consumer law cases. He was previously a consumer law specialist in the Maryland Attorney General's office and with the Legal Aid Bureau of Baltimore.

3 Pat Tulinski was in private practice doing consumer cases at the time of this discussion.

4 Craig Jordan is a NACA member with a consumer law practice in Dallas, Texas, and has a broad range of consumer law experience.

make the point that is most important for you to make. If you start somewhere else, you may never get there.

Ellen Friedman:[5] I was the Litigation Director at Legal Aid, and I believe that the best preparation for oral argument is to find two or three of your smartest colleagues, give them copies of all briefs and do a mock oral argument, letting them interrupt you as will the appeals panel. Tell them to be hard on you and critique you when you are finished. After a grilling like that, the questions of the real judges will seem a piece of cake.

Karen Cordry:[6] I used to do oral arguments a lot for a federal agency (National Labor Relations Board) and I agree a moot court would be the most useful preparation. Your interested but not involved colleagues would be in the same position as the court—intelligent but not overly knowledgeable about the specifics of your case. That, way if there is something about the facts or the law that they don't get from your brief or that bother them, it's probably the same thing that will bother the court.

Even if you can't get that, do it yourself—work out your opponent's argument for him—and then figure out how to answer what he will raise. Know every single factual nuance of your case—the judges may pick up on some obscure fact that just bothers them, and you'll need to be able to answer it. And there are often hidden gems that didn't seem to surface before but are always nice to have around to throw into the mix.

As far as the argument goes, think of it as a conversation between you and the judges—stay loose. I always pictured myself as playing tennis—they were on one side lobbing questions at me and I was on my toes bouncing ready to lob them back. You can't play tennis if you're tense and flat-footed and you can't do oral arguments if you're tongue-tied. Sound confident and be confident; if you're hesitant about your case, why shouldn't they be?

It is good to try to boil your brief and your case down to a single clear sentence or two that encapsulates the facts that the jury or the court found—and the law that's applicable. You want to get that out as practically the first thing out of your mouth after you say, "may it please the court, my name is . . . ." Something like, "I am appearing on behalf of Joe Smith to ask that you affirm the decision of the court below that the defendants can not obtain title to my client's property based on a forged deed of conveyance. This is an issue of first impression in this district but the court below properly concluded that the forgery made the transaction void *ab initio*. On appeal, the defendants [do not/can not] dispute the court's factual findings; they only argue that the forgery does not invalidate the transfer because . . . . The court below properly rejected that argument because . . . ."

Ideally, you would like to get the meat of your case before the court in the first minute of your case—think Al Gore and opening statements. Granted, he didn't answer the question, but most courts usually give you a minute or so before they start peppering you, so with luck you should be able to get out a coherent statement of your position before you get interrupted, as long as you boil it down to its bare essence.

And, if you can't get out your opening statement, you know you're in trouble. Contrary to someone else's comment, I usually figured if I got hostile questions, I was the one in trouble. I was in front of the Sixth Circuit one time and I knew I was sunk when I tried to give that one- or two-sentence synopsis of my case four times and never once was allowed to finish the sentence.

So, best of luck. And have fun—I (usually) did.

Carolyn Carter:[7] To add to Karen's comments, I recommend having a two-sentence opener written out word for word and memorized, in case words fail you, plus one sentence to close with when the light goes on or you otherwise get the hint that it's time to sit down. For what's in the middle, I recommend bringing an outline with you so that you have a logical progression to follow if you aren't peppered by questions.

Some people find an oral argument three-ring binder helpful, with the open and closing sentences and the outline under one tab, then tabs for certain questions you anticipate, and other tabs for special things like a copy of the trial court's opinion, the contract, the complaint, or some really critical statement from the transcript.

Dan Wulz:[8] My first appellate oral argument was as an associate with two years' experience, and I had two cases scheduled to argue in the 10th Circuit back to back. As such, I was terrified. So I had the time to find a book on appellate advocacy and read the chapters on oral argument. Try that if you have the time. If not, at least find an article (for example, trial lawyer's magazine) written by an appellate judge on the ten mistakes lawyers make at oral argument (or, conversely, the ten things you should do).

In my opinion, you should never rehash your brief. This depends to a certain extent on whether the court is hot (has read the briefs and a bench memo prepared by staff) or cold (knows nothing). You need to find this out. Today, I believe most courts are hot.

In most of my arguments, I've not been able to argue what I prepared. Most of the time was taken up with questions, usually involving facts. But I've seen other cases in which that did not occur.

Generally, you introduce yourself, state the issue succinctly, state how the case got there (for example, on appeal

5 Ellen Friedman is a NACA member with a practice in Louisville, Kentucky, with experience in car and fair debt cases.

6 Karen Cordry is the consumer law coordinator at the National Association of Attorneys General in Washington, D.C.

7 Carolyn Carter is Deputy Director of Advocacy at the National Consumer Law Center and a former staff person with legal aid in Gettysburg, Pennsylvania, and Cleveland, Ohio.

8 Dan Wulz is a senior attorney with Clark County Legal Services in Las Vegas, Nevada.

from summary judgment; appeal after jury verdict), give a brief factual statement, and argument, in that order. As in a lower court, you explain the matter like you are explaining it to someone with a high school education who does not know anything about the case. You don't memorize things from your brief and you try not to sound like a lawyer. In other words, you make it interesting. It helps to practice the argument in front of someone without any legal training (a spouse, a high-school-aged child) for feedback on whether you're being clear. You want to be blunt, clear, and concise.

I've never had an appellate judge quiz me on the facts or holding of a case I cited. They are all human beings and presumably want to be fair. You've got to hit them in the gut with what was unfair about what happened and the result (if you're the appellant).

If I lost below, I never trash the lower court judge. They probably know him/her and may respect them.

One thing I've read is that you need to come up with something—today's "sound bite"—that sticks in their head about the case and your argument. This is because usually they don't meet to deliberate until a week or two after argument, and it helps if you've said something that makes one of them say, "Oh yeah, this was the case about . . . ."

Try not to use all your time. They love that. If you're the appellant, save time at the beginning for rebuttal. Know the rules on time keeping (for example, light system or whether you have to ask for a five- or four- or three-minute warning). Try to watch an argument a few days or hours before yours.

Pat Tulinski:[9] I have one more suggestion to add to the wealth of good responses you have already received. If you are asked a question and are not sure of the answer or are weak on it, request leave to file a "letter brief" on the issue (standard time is within ten days, but let them set the time, as they might leave it open). Usually it will be granted, and it also provides you an opportunity to add in something you may have forgotten (but be careful not to abuse it). Make sure your letter brief is brief—don't go more than a page or two, or else you run the risk that the judges will think you have abused the process. This is a valuable escape valve, so don't get thrown if you don't know a specific answer.

Blaine Elliott:[10] Some views from a person who was in your shoes. Astoundingly enough, it was the little things that took me most by surprise in my first oral argument. "I have to be introduced to the Court?" That was my reaction at my introduction to one of the unwritten but "well known" rules of the Missouri Court of Appeals—Western District. I also had the pleasure of drawing a panel headed by the judge who authored the opinion I was arguing to have overturned. I was relieved to arrive at the court and see that there were two cases on the docket in front of mine (at least I would get to watch a few pitches before having to bat in the big leagues). The relief turned to disbelief as the Court announced that the two cases on the docket had been disposed of, bringing me to the number one spot arguing on behalf of the appellant (so much for getting to watch). I began by introducing myself and offering a short synopsis of the case just to give them the overall flavor, not heavy on the facts, just my view as to what the case was about. No sooner did the words leave my mouth than I was directed by the lead judge to answer a series of pointed, and rather well-chosen, questions.

Was the judge getting his jollies from this? In my opinion, no. He was looking to the strengths and weaknesses of my argument. When asked by the judge, what about ADB v. XYZ (his case which had doomed my clients from the word go), I looked him right in the eye and told him it was bad law (it's not often that you get a chance to tell a judge this to his face, even less often that you will get a favorable result after doing so).

Did the Court have its mind made up before the argument? Can't say. They definitely had it made up by the time the arguments were over (my opponent, the man who gave me a glowing introduction to the Court, was grilled mercilessly for the evil deeds of the dealer he represented). After all was said and done, I can honestly say that my oral argument was the best day of lawyering I have had to date.

My recommendations: just know your case forward and backward. Being knowledgeable about the case made it easier for me to relax. This shouldn't be hard, after all—this is your case. Who would know it better? By the time I got to the appeals court I had worked on the case for approximately sixty hours prior to the grant of summary judgment and another fifty to sixty in preparing the appeal. I knew the case, my strengths and weaknesses as well as my opponent's, better than I knew my family. I was still nervous, of course, but that fades quickly if you are comfortable in the case and your position.

Jim Shackelford:[11] In addition to what everyone else has told you, I'll put in my two cents worth. Assuming the judges have read the briefs, oral arguments are a chance for the judges to clarify key legal or factual issues. While many may have already decided the issue, an effective oral presentation can persuade those undecided and sometimes even get a judge to change his or her mind. I just attended a CLE at which an appellate judge said she had written a draft opinion for a unanimous court based on the briefs but changed her mind after the argument. The dissenter offered to let the other judges use her draft majority opinion, so she wound up actually writing both the majority and dissenting opinions.

Here a few specific suggestions:

1. Not only should you not read from your brief but you should not try to memorize most of your argument. It will be less wooden and you'll do better if interrupted by questions.

9 Pat Tulinski was practicing consumer law in Houston, Texas, at the time of this discussion.

10 Blaine Elliott is in practice in Belton, Missouri, where he specializes in consumer law, particularly car cases.

11 Jim Shackelford is an assistant attorney general in Kentucky.

(Personally, I like a lot of questions because it shows they are thinking about it.) That doesn't mean you should not practice your argument—just don't get hung up on specific phraseology unless it is important. I like to memorize my opening comments (usually the issue) and a closing sentence or two.

2. Be passionate without being emotional or argumentative.

3. Listen to the questions just like you listen to testimony. Sometimes they indicate the judges have a different take on the issues than the way either party has briefed the issue. However, if a judge asks a question that misses the major issue or is irrelevant, answer directly (even if it is "I don't know") and then get back to the main points. If you get in trouble, grab any lifelines thrown to you by a judge. Every once in a while a judge will throw you one by asking something like, "What public policy would be supported by declaring the deed void *ab initio*?" That's a hint. Take it.

4. On a fifteen- to twenty-minute argument, I usually reserve only two minutes for rebuttal. Many times you won't have anything to rebut since the issues have been discussed during your argument. This does give you time, however, to quickly rebut anything new that may have come up.

Jim McMillen:[12] Prepare, Prepare, Prepare. Do not read to the court. If you can find out who is on your panel and read what they have written. Be prepared to argue, but don't be disappointed if they just ask questions. If you don't know the answer to a question, don't guess, be straight forward. When that red light comes on, STOP. You will get a yellow warning.

Robert Hobbs:[13] You should also consider whether it makes sense to bring in a lawyer who specializes in appellate cases or who has a good appellate track record. Your client may be better served and the case put on even stronger footing. For example, Dick Rubin, Rand Bragg, and Joanne Faulkner are lawyers with proven appellate track records in Fair Debt Collection Practices cases to consider.

If the case is in the U.S. Supreme Court, the litigators at Public Citizen should be brought into the case to get it on its strongest footing in that highly specialized forum. This is a major focus of their work.

12 Jim McMillen practices in Houston, Texas, and is a frequent speaker at national conferences on bankruptcy and consumer law.

13 Robert Hobbs is the Deputy Director of the National Consumer Law Center.

Chapter 26 Historical Development of Consumer Law: Usury Laws[1]

26.1 Introduction

Usury laws may be one of the earliest examples of consumer protection laws and are instructive about the cyclical nature of some consumer protection efforts over time. They are also instructive on the point that the roots of many consumer laws are ancient moral principles and that consumer laws are fundamental legal protections and not revolutionary at all. Because of the breadth of poverty in the 1930s, there are many court opinions from that era that are more sympathetic of the plight of low-income households than opinions written in better economic times.

26.2 Early Attitudes Toward Interest

The history of usury regulation[2] is in large part a history of the tension between the conviction that the lending of money at interest is predatory and immoral and the fact that such money lending is necessary for the formation of capital and the flow of commerce. The tension between these views continues to the present day, albeit in a somewhat altered scope. The question today is not whether the charging of interest per se is moral or proper, but rather what limits, if any, should be placed on the interest charged.

The lending of money or commodities such as grain in return for interest has been documented as early as 3000 B.C.[3] and no doubt pre-dates that. From its inception, the practice seems to have caused controversy in many societies. In part, the charging of interest was condemned on moral and religious grounds; it was considered ungodly and uncharitable for one man to profit from the need of another. Yet there were also many concrete grounds for opposing money-lending. In hard times, a borrower could lose all his property and be sold into slavery to pay his debts. The evils caused by usury were very real, and money lending was at times banned outright. For example, under the laws of the Old Testament, one Jew was forbidden to lend at interest to another.[4]

---

1 This chapter is based on materials from National Consumer Law Center, The Cost of Credit: Regulation, Preemption, and Industry Abuses (3d ed. 2005), and its predecessors.

2 The historical discussion contained in this section is admittedly cursory. It is designed to be an overview of credit regulation rather than a detailed analysis. Those interested in more detail should consult the following sources: Bodfish, History of Building and Loan Associations in the U.S. (1931); Cobb, Federal Regulation of Depository Institutions: Enforcement Powers and Procedures (1984); The Consumer Finance Industry: Its Costs and Regulation (Chapman & Shea, eds., 1967); Curran, Trends in Consumer Credit Legislation (1966); Homer, A History of Interest Rates (1963); Hubachek, Annotations on Small Loan Laws (1938); Kawaja, Regulation of the Consumer Finance Industry: A Case Study of Rate Ceilings and Loan Size Limits in New York State (1971); Murray, History of Usury (1866); Saulnier, Industrial Banking Companies and Their Banking Practices (1940); Sherman, Modern Story of Mutual Savings Banks (1934); Welfling, Mutual Savings Banks (1968); 1 Credit Union Law Service Ch. 1 (Matthew Bender 1987); Note, *Interest Rates and the Law: A History of Usury*, 1981 Ariz. St. L.J. 61; Curran, *Legislative Controls As a Response to Consumer-Credit Problems*, 8 B.C. Ind. & Com. L. Rev. 409 (1966–67); Lynn Drysdale & Kathleen Keest, *The Two-Tiered Consumer Financial Services Marketplace: The Fringe Banking System and Its Challenge to Current Thinking About the Socio-Economic Role of Usury Laws in Today's Society*, 51 S.C. L. Rev. 445 (Spring 2000); David J. Gerber, *Prometheus Born: The High Middle Ages and the Relationship Between Law and Economic Conduct*, 38 St. Louis L.J. 673 (1994); Edward L. Glaeser & Jose Scheinkman, *Neither a Borrower Nor a Lender Be: An Economic Analysis of Interest Restrictions and Usury Laws*, 41 J. Law & Econ. 1 (1998); Jordan & Warren, *A Proposed Uniform Code for Consumer Credit*, 8 B.C. Ind. & Com. L. Rev. 441 (1966–67); Littlefield, *Parties and Transactions Covered by Consumer-Credit Legislation*, 8 B.C. Ind. & Com. L. Rev. 463 (1966–67); Redfield, *Savings Banks and Savings and Loan Associations: The Past and the Future*, 16 Bus. Law 170 (1960); *Combating the Shark*, 8 Law & Contemp. Prob. 1-205 (Winter 1941) (series of articles on usury, small loan laws, and loan sharking); Roster, *Modern Role of Thrifts*, 18 Loyola L.A. L. Rev. 1099 (1985); Vincent D. Rougeau, *Rediscovering Usury: An Argument for Legal Controls on Credit Card Interest Rates*, 67 U. Colo. L. Rev. 1 (1996).

3 The records are Sumerian. *See* Homer, A History of Interest Rates 25 (1963). The discussion of ancient commercial practices is taken primarily from this source.

4 *See* Exodus 22:25, Leviticus 25:35–37, Deuteronomy 23:19–20. *See also* Commonwealth v. Donoghue, 63 S.W.2d 3 (Ky. App. 1933) (quoting 4th century Christian theologian's views of usury and referring to Old Testament prohibitions). Similar concerns face Muslims based on the teachings of the Koran. *See* N. Bennett & N. Foster, *Alternative Financing: Issues and Opportunities for Lenders and Interest-Averse Communities*,

The complete abolition of money-lending at interest is not, however, a realistic solution to the problems that lending can cause or exacerbate. First, if one person has money or some commodity that another needs, it will be difficult to thwart the combined self-interest of the former and desire of the latter. Loan contracts are, after all, consensual agreements, even if not always even-handed ones. Second, loans bearing interest do not invariably spell doom for the borrower. They can and do benefit both parties in most cases, especially in commercial transactions in which they assist capital formation and commerce. Not surprisingly, early commercial societies were tolerant of money-lending, although they frequently imposed limits on the interest rates that would be permitted. Conversely, even in societies that prohibited loans with interest, means were found to overcome the prohibitions. Thus, even while the Old Testament condemned usurers and forbade one Jew from collecting interest from another, it allowed the collection of interest from foreigners.[5]

Medieval Europe, under the powerful influence of the Catholic Church, followed a similar path. The church repeatedly condemned the assessment of "usury" (that is, interest),[6] but Jews were permitted to operate pawnshops. As trade gradually increased through the centuries, Christian merchants developed various schemes to avoid the prohibitions, such as assignment of rents, "investments," and the use of bills of exchange. In England, it was not until 1545 that Parliament legalized charging interest in the modern sense,[7] and even this statute was repealed during the reign of Queen Mary, only to be reenacted in 1570 under Queen Elizabeth. From this date, interest ceilings in England were set at various rates below 10% until the ceilings were entirely removed in 1854.

Community Dividend 6 (Minneapolis Fed. Reserve Bank, Issue 1 2002).

5 *See* Deuteronomy 23:19–20.

6 In medieval terms the word "usury," derived from the Latin "usera," equated with what we would call "interest" today. The prohibition of usury was essentially a prohibition of charging for the use of money. However, common law distinguished reimbursement for a loss associated with a loan from charges for the use of money and permitted the former while forbidding the latter. This legal compensation for loss was known as "interesse" from the Latin "intereo" meaning "to be lost." Thus legal charges associated with a loan appear to have evolved to the modern notion of "interest," while illegal charges eventually came to be called "usury." *See* Homer, A History of Interest Rates 73–74 (1963).

7 37 Hen. 8, C. 9 (1545). The statute was entitled "An Act Against Usury," doublespeak apparently having preceded George Orwell by several centuries. *See also* Commonwealth v. Donoghue, 63 S.W.2d 3 (Ky. App. 1933) (discussing the development of English usury law).

26.3 General Usury Statutes in the United States

English usury statutes, particularly the Statute of Anne, were adopted by the American colonies prior to independence. Variations on these statutes remain in effect to this day in many states and are commonly referred to as "general" usury laws because they purport to set a ceiling for all loans of money or forbearance of debt in a jurisdiction, not just for particular types of lenders or credit transactions. With very few exceptions, general usury laws were the only statutes regulating credit costs in the United States prior to the twentieth century.

The influence of the general usury laws on modern credit regulation is difficult to over-emphasize. Their importance stems not so much from the language of the statutes or even from the particular interest ceilings they set, because these features are easily altered through legislation. Rather, the influence of general usury statutes lies in their heredity; when these statutes were borrowed from English law, they brought with them the interpretation placed upon them by the English courts. This gloss of case law was adopted by American courts and represents an important source of authority in the interpretation of modern usury statutes. It is, at least in effect, a common law of usury that, in the absence of express statutory treatment, governs issues such as the elements of proof of a usury case or the definition of interest.

Many of the inconsistencies and irrationalities that exist in current credit laws can be traced to English case law and, through it, to even earlier origins in common law or canon law. For example, the English courts ruled that a sale of goods on credit did not constitute a loan or forbearance and was thus exempt from the interest limitations of usury statutes.[8] This rule, known as the time-price doctrine, was adopted by American courts[9] and, despite much criticism, is still recognized in some states today.[10] In general, the time-price doctrine is the source of the separate regulation of loans and credit sales in virtually all states.

Another example of the ancient roots of modern usury law principles is the distinction between interest on a loan and "penalties," such as late fees, which can be assessed on overdue accounts, usually without usury limitations. (In many modern consumer statutes, however, late fees are separately regulated.) This distinction, which has been codified in most states, appears to have come to American law, through English case law, from a canon law rule that one could not exact gain from a loan (that is, charge any interest) but could be compensated for loss incurred through a loan,

8 *See* Beete v. Bidgood, 7 B. & C. 453, 108 Eng. Rep. 792 (K.B. 1827).

9 *See* Hogg v. Ruffner, 66 U.S. (1 Black) 115 (1861).

10 *See* National Consumer Law Center, The Cost of Credit: Regulation, Preemption, and Industry Abuses §§ 2.2.3.2, 2.3.2.2 (3d ed. 2005).

including the loss suffered when the loan was not promptly repaid.[11] This convenient doctrine appears to have been used in the Middle Ages to evade the church's prohibition against interest,[12] just as it is used today to evade laws that limit the amount of interest that a lender may charge.[13]

26.4 Special Usury Laws

26.4.1 General

Although some states have repealed the general usury laws, the structure of credit statutes in most states today is a general usury ceiling riddled with statutory exceptions for particular creditors or transactions. These statutory exceptions are known as "special" usury laws because of their individually limited scopes. However, special usury laws have proliferated to such an extent that to view them as exceptions to a general usury ceiling is misleading. Today, the average credit transaction is governed, if at all, by a special usury statute. In order to understand the evolution of special usury laws, it is necessary to consider the United States credit market of the nineteenth century when only general usury laws were on the books.

26.4.2 Laws Governing Loans

Consumer credit as we know it today did not exist, for practical purposes, prior to the twentieth century.[14] Pawnbrokering, of course, had been around for millennia, and personal loans secured by real estate were not unknown. Yet the vast majority of credit transactions were commercial. The total amount of credit available in the nineteenth century United States was limited, and most of it was directed toward industrial development when the profits available were higher and the risks lower than for individual loans. Furthermore, demand for individual credit was lower than it is today. Not only was individual borrowing socially frowned upon, but the economy was not oriented toward the production of consumer durable goods. In the days before automobiles, televisions, refrigerators, and other modern appliances, there was less for an individual to buy on credit.

This is not to say that individual Americans had no need to borrow for personal expenses prior to the twentieth century or that there was no demand for goods; rather, the official credit system simply did not extend to the average wage-earner. Given interest ceilings under general usury statutes in the neighborhood of 6%, and the proportionately higher administrative expense in small personal loans than in large commercial loans, banks could make more money lending to businesses. Thus individuals in need of personal loans had to resort to loan sharks or "salary lenders." The typical arrangement seems to have been a loan for $5 on a Monday, repayable on Friday (pay day) for $6. Ignoring compounding, this is an annual interest rate of 1040%.[15]

The problem of loan-sharking was pervasive in the nineteenth century,[16] leading to increased recognition of both the financial plight of wage earners and their need for a legitimate source of credit. Early attempts to reform were small-scale, informal, and uncoordinated but seemed to follow one of three basic strategies. First, cooperative societies were formed, generally following models pioneered in Europe in which individuals pooled their money for their mutual benefit. The earliest of these societies took the form of mutual savings banks, organized under existing banking laws but catering to and owned by small depositors. As the name implies, however, mutual savings banks were primarily concerned with encouraging thrift rather than providing credit. Building and loan associations, on the other hand, were cooperative organizations established primarily to provide mortgage money to members. Both of these institutions, which were the precursors of modern savings banks and savings and loan associations respectively, had become widespread by the turn of the century.[17] A later model of the cooperative society, which did not emerge in the United States until the first decade of the twentieth century, was the credit union. Like its predecessors, credit unions emphasized the pooling of resources but further required the existence of some common bond among the members, typically a common employer.[18]

---

11 The common law rule in turn seems to derive from Roman Law. *See* Homer, A History of Interest Rates 73–74 (1963).

12 J.B.C. Murray, History of Usury (J.B. Lippincott & Co. 1866).

13 For a discussion of delinquency charges under modern usury law, see National Consumer Law Center, The Cost of Credit: Regulation, Preemption, and Industry Abuses § 7.2.4 (3d ed. 2005).

14 *See generally* Note, *Interest Rates and the Law: A History of Usury*, 1981 Ariz. St. L.J. 61; Curran, *Legislative Controls As a Response to Consumer Credit Problems*, 8 B.C. Ind. & Com. L. Rev. 409 (1966–67).

15 See *Commonwealth v. Donoghue*, 63 S.W.2d 3 (Ky. App. 1933) and National Consumer Law Center, The Cost of Credit: Regulation, Preemption, and Industry Abuses § 2.5 (3d ed. 2005) for a discussion of modern incarnations of this type of credit. For a fuller discussion of the historical antecedents of today's fringe lenders, see also Lynn Drysdale & Kathleen Keest, *The Two-Tiered Consumer Financial Services Marketplace: The Fringe Banking System and Its Challenge to Current Thinking About the Socio-Economic Role of Usury Laws in Today's Society*, 51 S.C. L. Rev. 445 (Spring 2000).

16 *See generally Combating the Loan Shark*, 8 Law & Contemp. Probs. 1-205 (Winter 1941) (issue devoted to articles on usury, small loan laws, and loan sharking).

17 *See generally* Bodfish, History of Building and Loan Associations in the U.S. (1931); Cobb, Federal Regulation of Depository Institutions: Enforcement Powers and Procedures (1984); Sherman, Modern Story of Mutual Savings Banks (1934); Welfling, Mutual Savings Banks (1968); Redfield, *Savings Banks and Savings and Loan Associations: The Past and the Future*, 16 Bus. Law 170 (1960).

18 For a brief description of the evolution of credit unions, see 1

A second response to the loan shark problem was more strictly philanthropic.[19] Organizations supported by donated funds made small loans at no charge except administrative expenses. Some employers apparently followed the same route. However, the money available through such organizations does not appear to have been sufficient to have made much of a dent in the demand for small loans.

The third and, chronologically, last strategy aimed at combating loan-sharking was to attract credit, which had previously been extended only to businesses, to the consumer credit market by making consumer lending a profitable prospect. While the philanthropic organizations and, at least in their early stages, the cooperative credit organizations posed no challenge to the existing general usury laws, the essence of this third strategy created exceptions to the general usury law for small, unsecured loans, thereby making them attractive, profitable investments for legitimate creditors. The concept of making small loans available by increasing their yield is most clearly manifested in the small loan laws and the industrial bank laws, both of which were first adopted in the early twentieth century.[20]

The small loan laws, pioneered by the Russell Sage Foundation[21] and the research that it supported, took a direct approach to attracting capital to the consumer market. The Uniform Small Loan Law, the first draft of which was issued in 1916, created a licensed class of small-loan lenders authorized to charge rates significantly in excess of the general usury ceilings. In return, these lenders accepted regulation, the risk involved in personal lending, and the higher administrative expense of small loans. For example, the fourth draft of the uniform law[22] allowed the charging of 3 1/2% *monthly* on loans of $300 or less. This rate was much higher than the general usury ceiling but was nevertheless vastly lower than the rates charged by loan sharks.[23]

Industrial banks, first organized under regular state banking laws early in the twentieth century, took a less direct approach to increasing the yields on consumer credit.[24] These institutions accepted individual deposits and made loans secured by those deposits. Arthur Morris devised a plan that treated loans as repayable in a single lump sum at the end of the agreed term and computed interest accordingly. However, the Morris Plan required the borrower to make regular "deposits" in the bank that were calculated to equal the total amount of principal and interest due at the end of the term. Essentially, the Morris Plan allowed industrial banks to increase yields by charging interest on sums the borrower had already repaid (that is, by ignoring the declining principal balance on the loan). Although this device was really an evasion of existing general usury laws rather than a clear-cut legal exception to them, many states adopted statutory exceptions to general usury laws to validate the practice, and industrial banks came to serve a market of consumers seeking loans in excess of the $300 limits set for small-loan licensees.[25]

Carving out statutory exceptions to the general usury laws proved an effective means of expanding the amount of available consumer credit. Not surprisingly, it also proved to be a trend that, once started, was difficult to limit. Although credit laws developed differently in each state, statutory usury exceptions were soon made not only for small-loan lenders but also for industrial banks, as discussed above, credit unions, mortgage lenders such as savings banks and building and loan associations, and eventually banks[26] making "installment loans" to finance consumer purchases.

26.4.3 Laws Governing Sales

It should be emphasized that the statutes discussed in the previous subsection were adopted as exceptions to the general usury statutes that, as interpreted by the courts, regulated only loans or forbearances of debt and not sales of goods on credit. Since the effective interest rate (technically, the "time-price differential") that a seller could impose in a credit sale was not limited by the general usury laws, there was no need to loosen the regulatory reins through special legislation as there was with loans. Consequently, consumer credit sales were largely unregulated by state legislatures until after the Second World War and were governed instead by regular contract law.

When the attention of state legislatures finally did turn to credit sales transactions, the motivation was reversed from that for previous special usury laws; the idea was to tighten controls rather than to loosen them.[27] The retail installment sales acts (RISAs) and motor vehicle retail installment sales

---

Credit Union Law Service Ch. 1 (Matthew Bender 1987).

19 *See* Kawaja, Regulation of the Consumer Finance Industry: A Case Study of Rate Ceilings and Loan Size Limits in New York State 23 (1971).

20 The idea of increasing yield was applied to other creditors as well. For example, the early credit union statutes, modeled after a 1909 Massachusetts law, permitted credit unions to charge interest at rates above most general usury law limits.

21 *See generally* Curran, Trends in Consumer Credit Legislation (1966); Hubachek, *The Development of Regulatory Small Loan Laws*, 8 Law & Contemp. Probs. 108 (1941).

22 *Reprinted in* Hubachek, Annotations on Small Loan Laws (1938).

23 *See* National Consumer Law Center, The Cost of Credit: Regulation, Preemption, and Industry Abuses § 2.3.3.2 (3d ed. 2005).

24 *See generally* Curran, Trends in Consumer Credit Legislation 52 *et seq.* (1966); Saulnier, Industrial Banking Companies and Their Banking Practices (1940).

25 *See* National Consumer Law Center, The Cost of Credit § 2.3.3.4 (3d ed. 2005).

26 Although installment loan laws seem primarily to address banks making consumer loans, their precise scope varies significantly from state to state. *See* Curran, Trends in Consumer Credit Legislation 65 *et seq.* (1966).

27 A more cynical view may be taken, however. At the time that many RISAs were being adopted in the 1950s and 1960s, there was a clear trend in the courts toward the abolition of the time-price usury exception. The ultimate result of such a trend would have been the application of the low general usury

acts (MVRISAs) adopted after the war frequently imposed limits on finance charges where none had previously existed, and they universally emphasized consumer protections such as disclosure of credit terms and limitations on creditor remedies.[28] There is, of course, a sense in which the special lending laws were also protective; they allowed regulated lenders to charge high rates, thus sparing small borrowers from the even greater ravages of the loan sharks. Moreover, RISAs and special lending statutes address many of the same subjects, which is not surprising, since a credit sale is merely a secured loan in different legal clothing. For these reasons, this manual treats RISAs and MVRISAs as a subclass of special usury law. Yet, remember that the law has historically treated credit sales and loans distinctly and that these historical distinctions still occasionally crop up in modern consumer credit cases.[29]

ceilings to credit sales. RISAs and their relatively high ceilings can be seen as an attempt to preclude this result.

28 See, for example, *Zachman v. Whirlpool Acceptance Corp.*, 841 P.2d 27 (Wash. 1992) for a discussion of the purpose and origins of RISAs. *See generally* Curran, Trends in Consumer Credit Legislation *et seq.* (1966).

29 *See* National Consumer Law Center, The Cost of Credit §§ 9.2.3.3 (3d ed. 2005).

26.5 Will the Pendulum Swing?

Since the 1980s the pendulum of usury regulation has swung toward deregulation. Federal bank regulators have increasingly carved out federal preemption of state law that would limit bank charges and rates. Most consumer credit has sought to fit within this federal deregulation. One of the consequences is that banks are becoming one of the primary sources of high-rate lending that consumers have to be warned about. The backlash to this increase in predatory lending has been slower to materialize than one would expect.

Chapter 27

The Use of Testers and Investigators in Civil Litigation

By Professor David Hricik[1]

27.1 Introduction

27.1.1 Background

> Counsel: Telling the truth in civil litigation is, of course, a very attractive proposition. But, I would like to visit with your Honor further examining that proposition, because while that might be nice in a perfect world, it is not the way the system operates in litigation in this country.
>
> The Court: Sad comment, counsel.[2]

Only a few courts and bar associations have addressed the precise issue of whether it is ethical for a lawyer to hire a third party to contact an actual or potential party under deceitful circumstances to obtain evidence. The authorities that have addressed the issue have split. Furthermore, identically worded rules implicated by the use of investigators are being interpreted differently by the various jurisdictions. With this split, and with a lack of case law on the issue in most jurisdictions, lawyers who rely on undercover investigations do so at some peril.

This section begins with choice of law. Since those rules and the principles underlying them are directly implicated by the cases addressing undercover investigators, the section then discusses the split in the case law concerning whether lawyers may engage in *ex parte* contacts with persons who are or were employed by party opponents and, is so, when they may do so. If the applicable rule permits a lawyer to contact a low-level employee, for example, then having an investigator, instead of the lawyer, make that contact cannot be unethical. Finally, this section turns to the question of the use of undercover investigators to contact opposing parties, before or during litigation, and examines how the courts have split over the propriety of using lies to uncover wrongdoing. In civil cases, lawyers have long used undercover investigators who are hired to misrepresent their identity, purpose, or both in order to gather evidence.

The use of undercover investigators in trademark actions is apparently fairly longstanding. *See generally* John J. Steele, *Ethics Issues in Trademark, Copyright, and Unfair Competition Practice,* SF87 ALI-ABA 461 (March 22, 2001). In trademark actions, undercover investigators can be used in various ways. Mr. Steele posits two examples:

> Client, upset about a cybersquatter, hires a non-attorney investigator to make discrete inquiries with the URL owner, without revealing the client's identity, about the sale of the site. The owner does not respond. Client hires you to initiate legal proceedings, which you do. Opposing counsel makes an appearance. The next day, the owner contacts the investigator and indicates a willingness to sell. Client wants you to counsel investigator on how to handle the negotiations . . . .
>
> After winning a trademark . . . injunction, you test the defendant's compliance by hiring an investigator to approach the defendant and purchase items that were banned by the injunction. In doing so, the investigator lies about her identity and purpose.[3]

1 Professor David Hricik teaches at Mercer University School of Law in Macon, Georgia. E-mail: David@Hricik.com.

2 Monsanto Co. v. Aetna Cas. & Sur. Co., 593 A.2d 1013 (Del. Super. Ct. 1990) ("I embrace the proposition that in civil litigation in this jurisdiction one who is in search of the truth must tell the truth."), *modified*, 1990 WL 200471 (Del. Super. Ct. Dec. 4, 1990).

3 Steele, SF 87 ALI-ABA at 470 (citations omitted).*See generally* David B. Isbell & Lucantonio N. Salvi, *Ethical Responsibility of Lawyers for Deception by Undercover Investigators and Discrimination Testers: An Analysis of the Provisions Prohibiting Misrepresentation Under the Model Rules of Professional Conduct*, 8 Geo. J. Legal Eth. 791, 797–802 (1995) (discussing case law addressing housing and employment discrimination testers); Julian J. Moore, *Home Sweet Home: Examining the (Mis)Application of the Anti-Contact Rule to Housing Discrimination Testers*, 25 J. Legal Prof. 75, 78–79 (2001) (same, in housing context).

27.1.2 Overview of the Ethical Issues

In order to understand the ethical issues underlying undercover investigations, some background is necessary. Put in context, a contact by an undercover investigator may be an *ex parte* contact with a represented person. If so, Model Rule 4.2 prohibits the contact. Even if the person is not represented within the scope of Rule 4.2, Rule 4.3 requires certain disclosures be made by lawyers engaging in *ex parte* contacts; since the lawyer may not hire a person to do indirectly what he cannot do directly, Rule 4.3 would seem to apply.

Thus, the first section will accomplish two goals: First, it analyzes the law governing *ex parte* contacts and, second, it provides the groundwork for understanding the ethical issues that arise when a lawyer uses undercover investigators.

27.1.3 The Impact of Choice of Law Makes Even the Clearest Rule Vague

In litigation in which a lawyer considers contacting a former employee who resides in another state, or in which the suit is pending in a state other than the lawyer's or employee's state, which state's ethical rules govern the propriety of any contact? Is the lawyer obligated to follow his or her state's rules even if the forum's rules are more lenient? Can the lawyer do something which is unethical in his or her home state if it is ethical in the other state?

The choice-of-law issue is important because some states absolutely prohibit *ex parte* contacts with present or former employees, while others permit it almost unconditionally and still others have rules along the spectrum. Which rule applies if the employee is in California, the lawyer in Minnesota, and the suit in Oklahoma? What is the "national standard"—to be applied by federal courts in those "national standard" circuits—if the national authorities openly disagree about what approach should be used?

The federal district court in *McCallum v. CSX Transp. Inc.* faced this precise issue in the context of an *ex parte* contact with employees of a party opponent, disregarded all notions of choice of law based upon a state disciplinary rule, and instead reasoned as follows:

> This court has adopted a code of conduct in its local rules. Local Rule 505 utilizes the Code of Professional Responsibility promulgated by the Supreme Court of North Carolina. Notwithstanding, this Court must look to federal law in order to interpret and apply those rules. That is, even when a federal court utilizes state ethics rules, it cannot abdicate to the state's view of what constitutes professional conduct, even in diversity cases. Therefore, while this Court has adopted the North Carolina Professional Code as its code of conduct, it still must look to federal law for interpretation of those canons and in so doing may consult federal case law and other widely accepted national codes of conduct, such as the ABA Model Rules. In addition, the Court may presume the attorney to be familiar with and bound by the ethical rules of the courts in which the attorney is admitted to practice.[4]

The court rejected the plea, from the attorney whose conduct was at issue, to follow only the North Carolina rules:

> This Court may apply its ethical code of conduct to out-of-state attorneys who practice before this Court and can sanction conduct which takes place in other states. By choosing to litigate in this Court, counsel submit to this Court's federal law interpretation of ethical canons wherever the conduct takes place. Plaintiffs' counsel has not shown that the interpretation set out today is in direct contradiction of any duty imposed by the state where he was admitted to practice or where the conduct occurred. *Even if those states permitted the conduct at issue, that does not give an attorney permission to operate in contravention of the ethical duties as determined by this Court. If there is a disparity between ethical obligations of different states, counsel's only choice is to follow the more expansive duty or seek guidance from this Court.*[5]

Likewise, a Maryland Federal district court analyzed for the first time the propriety of *ex parte* contacts with former employees of a party opponent. Noting that the Maryland Rules of Professional Conduct were merely "the point of departure" for its analysis, the court analyzed authorities applying the Model Code, the Model Rules, and the Restatement of the Law Governing Lawyers.[6] The court held that *ex parte* contacts with former employees could be improper *even though Maryland's bar opinions had held precisely the opposite*.[7] Although recognizing that the law regarding *ex parte* contacts was "blurry" and that the question was one of first impression, the court disqualified the lawyers for violating its newly-minted rule, stating:

> The issue is not whether counsel incorrectly interpreted unsettled law, but whether [counsel] displayed an inappropriate disregard for the unsettled nature of that law. . . . [As] appellee stated in *Cagguila v. Wyeth Lab, Inc.*, 127 F.R.D. 653 (E.D. Pa. 1989)], "in such an uncertain area of ethical

4 McCallum v. CSX Transp. Inc., 149 F.R.D. 108 (M.D.N.C. May 4, 1993 (citations omitted).

5 *Id.* at 112 (emphasis added).

6 Camden v. State of Md., 910 F. Supp. 1118 (D. Md. Jan. 24, 1996).

7 *See id.* at 1119.

> conduct, we believe that a prudent attorney would have given notice to opposing counsel of the intent to take such a statement."[8]

Camden v. State of Md., 910 F. Supp. 1124 (D. Md. Jan. 24, 1996) (quoting Cagguila v. Wyeth Lab, Inc., 127 F.R.D. 653 (E.D. Pa. 1989), *as quoted in* University Patents, Inc. v. Kligman, 737 F. Supp. 325, 329 (E.D. Pa. 1990)).

27.2 *Ex Parte* Contacts with Current Employees of an Opposing Party

27.2.1 Model Code

ABA Model Code DR7-104(a) provides that a lawyer shall not

> [c]ommunicate or cause another to communicate on the subject of the representation with a party the lawyer knows to be represented by another lawyer in that matter unless the practitioner has the prior consent of the other practitioner representing such other party or is authorized by law to do so.

Courts have split on the scope of the prohibition in DR7-104(a) as applied to corporate party current employees, disagreeing on which employees should be considered to be "represented" by a lawyer representing the corporation.[9] Courts had reasoned that:

1. only *ex parte* communications with those in the "control group"—were prohibited;
2. only *ex parte* communications with "upper level" personnel—broader than the "control group"—were prohibited;
3. only *ex parte* communications with any agent with authority to bind the corporation were prohibited; *or*
4. all *ex parte* communications were prohibited.[10]

27.2.2 Model Rule 4.2

Model Rule 4.2 provides: "In representing a client, a lawyer shall not communicate about the subject of the representation with a party the lawyer knows to be represented by another lawyer in the matter, unless the lawyer has the consent of the other lawyer or is authorized by law to do so."[11]

In the case of organizations, the comment to Rule 4.2 explains that the rule prohibits contacts "with [1] persons having a managerial responsibility on behalf of the organization, and [2] with any other person [a] whose act or omission in connection with that matter may be imputed to the organization for purposes of civil liability or [b] whose statements may constitute an admission on the part of the organization."[12]

The comment has been subject to wide-ranging interpretations, particularly the comment with respect to the "admissions" prong.[13]

To exhaustively survey the interpretations would take a law review article. A recent case catalogs the potential categories of current employees who may be subject to Rule 4.2 and, in this particular jurisdiction, *all* of them are protected:

1. current officials of the corporation or organization who have managerial responsibility;
2. other current corporate or organizational employees whose act or omission in connection with the matter may be imputed to the corporation or organization for purposes of civil or criminal liability;
3. those who are responsible for implementing the advice of the corporation's or organization's lawyers;
4. any members of the corporation or organization whose own interests are directly at stake in a representation; and
5. an agent or servant of the corporation or organization whose statements concerns a matter within the scope of the agency or employment, which statement was made during the existence of the relationship and which is offered against the corporation or organization as an admission.[14]

---

8 Camden v. State of Md., 910 F. Supp. at 1124, quoting *University Patents, Inc. v. Kligman*, 737 F. Supp. 325, 329 (E.D. Pa. 1990) (quoting *Cagguila v. Wyeth Lab, Inc.*, 127 F. R. D. 653 (E.D. Pa. 1989)).

9 *See* Brown v. St. Joseph County, 148 F.R.D. 246, 249–51 (N.D. Ind. 1993).

10 *See id.* at 253–54 (collecting cases).

11 *See generally id.* at 254–55. The "ethics 2000" version of Model Rule 4.2 provides: "In representing a client, a lawyer shall not communicate about the subject of the representation with a person the lawyer knows to be represented by another lawyer in the matter, unless the lawyer has the consent of the other lawyer or is authorized to do so by law or a court order." The comments explains: "In the case of a represented organization, this Rule prohibits communications with a constituent of the organization who supervises, directs or regularly consults with the organization's lawyer concerning the matter or has authority to obligate the organization with respect to the matter or whose act or omission in connection with the matter may be imputed to the organization for purposes of civil or criminal liability. Consent of the organization's lawyer is not required for communication with a former constituent."

12 Model Rule 4.2, Comment 7.

13 *See, e.g.,* Camden v. State of Md., 910 F. Supp. 1115 (D Md. 1996) (collecting cases that take varying approaches).

14 Paulson v. Plainfield Trucking, Inc., 210 F.R.D. 654, 657–58 (D. Minn. 2002) (citing and collecting cases).

Because the rule has been subject to disparate interpretations, careful analysis should be given to whether a particular current employee comes within the scope of the prohibition. Indeed, as next shown, the rules themselves are not always identical to the Model Rule, thus making predictability that much more difficult.

27.2.3 The Federal Court "National Standard" of Ex Parte *Contacts with Current Employees*

Under the "national standard" approach to determining the rules of ethics governing attorney conduct in federal court litigation, consideration must be given to the approach of the Model Code, the Model Rules, and any applicable state rules. Thus an attorney seeking to contact a present employee of a party opponent must carefully evaluate the propriety of the contact under each of these three approaches and weigh the relative merits of each. If the contact is improper under one or more approaches, extreme care should be given before engaging in any *ex parte* contact.

27.3 *Ex Parte* Contacts with Former Employees of an Opposing Party

27.3.1 Model Code

Courts interpreting DR7-104(a) also had applied different interpretations to prohibitions against contacting former employees, including the following:

1. all *ex parte* communications were prohibited;
2. only *ex parte* communications with former employees whose acts or omissions could be attributed to the corporation were prohibited;
3. only *ex parte* communications with former managerial or "upper level" employees were prohibited; or
4. no *ex parte* communications with former employees were prohibited.[15]

27.3.2 Model Rule 4.2

By the late 1980s, most states adopted versions of ABA Model Rule 4.2.[16] Courts had, however, split as to whether the rule applied to *ex parte* contacts with *former* employees and, if so, how the rule applied. The source of the split was the comment to Model Rule 4.2, quoted in § 27.2.2, *supra*. Focusing on the comment, courts had inconsistently interpreted the state rules—some courts concluding that they did not apply to former employees, one holding that its state rule barred all communication, and others concluding that its rule permitted *ex parte* communication under certain circumstances.[17]

Very few courts have adopted a virtually absolute ban on *ex parte* contacts with all but the lowest-level former employees.[18] Although other courts have rejected the total ban, including the judge who authored the *PSE & G* opinion,[19] the total ban still has some support:

> The *PSE&G* decision is appealing in several respects. First, it provides a bright-line test for members of the Bar seeking to comply with ethical rules. Second, it advances one of the policy goals underlying the ethical rule: to protect parties and witnesses from overreaching by attorneys. Third, it arguably aids in the development of clear factual records in the sense that it fosters use of depositions. While depositions are admittedly a more expensive discovery technique than informal, *ex parte* interviews, they protect "the rights of all parties without unduly favoring or prejudicing" either, and they are "far more reliable and ethically sound" than informal discovery tools.[20]

In 1991, the ABA specifically stated that Model Rule 4.2 did not apply to former employees under *any* circumstances.[21] Since that time, *almost* every decision has reasoned that the state counterparts to Rule 4.2 do not apply to former employees.[22]

---

15 *See* Hanntz v. Shiley, 766 F. Supp. 258, 271 (D.N.J. 1991).

16 *See, e.g.*, Univ. Patents, Inc. v. Kligman, 737 F. Supp. 325 (E.D. Pa. 1990).

17 *See* Valassis v. Samelson, 143 F.R.D. 118 (E.D. Mich. 1992) (collecting cases).

18 Public Serv. Elec. & Gas Co. v. Associated Elec. & Gas Ins. Serv., Ltd., 745 F. Supp. 1037 (D.N.J. 1990).

19 *See* Andrews v. Goodyear Tire & Rubber Co., Inc., 2000 WL 175098 (D.N.J. 2000).

20 Shearson Lehman Bros., Inc. v. Wasatch Bank, 139 F.R.D. 412, 416 (D. Utah 1991) (quoting *PSE&G*).

21 ABA Formal Op. 91-359 (1991).

22 *See* Smith v. Kansas City So. Ry. Co., 87 S.W.3d 266 (Mo. App. 2002); Shearson Lehman Bros., Inc. v. Wasatch Bank, 139 F.R.D. 417–18 (D. Utah 1991); Brown v. St. Joseph County, 148 F.R.D. 253–54 (N.D. Ind. Apr. 12, 1993). *See also* Ohio Comm'n on Grievances and Discipline Op. 96-1 (Feb. 2, 1996) (no bar to *ex parte* contacts with former employees). The vast majority of courts have concluded that the rule does not apply, at all, to former employees. *See, e.g.*, Johnson v. Ohio Dept. Of Youth Serv., 231 F. Supp. 2d 690 (N.D. Ohio 2002) ("*Ex parte* contact with a former employee is not, however, prohibited."); *In re* Grievance Proceeding, 2002 WL 31106389 (D. Conn. July 19, 2002) (prohibition of Rule 4.2 does not apply to former employees); Wallace v. Valentino's of Lincoln, 2002 WL 31323811 (D. Neb. Oct. 17, 2002) ("former employees of a corporate party may be interviewed by adverse counsel without the permission of the corporate counsel if the former employees are not individually represented in the same matter"); Humco, Inc. v. Noble, 31 S.W.3d 916 (Ky. 2000) ("A former employee with no present relationship with the organizational party is not a 'party' under the rule . . . ."); Hanntz v. Shiley, Inc., 766 F. Supp. 258, 267 (D.N.J. 1991) (the policies of Rule 4.2 "do not

However, the earlier authority remains "good law" in many states, and some contrary decisions came after the 1991 ABA opinion.[23] This means that a charge of unethical conduct could be based upon cases decided before the 1991 ABA opinion, and it could be difficult to get a court to reject prior state law decisions on the strength of the ABA's 1991 opinion.[24]

In addition, some state rules may in fact be broader than, even though worded the same as, Model Rule 4.2. Even as of 2002, the precise scope of Rule 4.2 as it applies to former employees is an open question in some jurisdictions.[25]

27.3.3 The Federal Court "National Standard" of Ex Parte *Contacts with Former Employees*

Under the "national standards" approach to determining the rules of ethics governing attorney conduct in federal court litigation, consideration must be given to the approach of the Model Code, the Model Rules, and the relevant state's rules. Once again, an attorney seeking to contact a former employee of a party opponent must carefully evaluate the propriety of the contact under each of these three approaches and weigh the relative merits of each. If the contact is improper under one or more approaches, extreme care should be given before engaging in any *ex parte* contact: as shown below, improper *ex parte* contacts may result in severe sanctions, including disqualification, thus obviating any savings achieved by avoiding the costs associated with formal discovery.

A recent opinion from South Carolina illustrates the difficulty of predicting what a rule is, even when only a single state's rules might apply, and thus understates the difficulty in federal court litigation (as well as in states where there are as yet no clear judicial interpretations of the state version of rule 4.2):

> The Committee admonishes the Bar to be careful when contemplating contact with former employees. "The attorney who seeks [prior] court approval does not risk an ethical violation, but one who does not acts at his or her own peril." *In re Aircrash Disaster,* 909 F. Supp. 1116 (N. D. Ill. 1995). Such an interview is "a veritable minefield in which . . . short and tentative steps are the most appropriate." *Driggs Reorg. Corp. v. Driggs*, 217 B.R. 67 (D. Md. 1988). Because the American Bar Association Standing Committee on Ethics and Professional Responsibility or the South Carolina Ethics Advisory Committee provides a particular analysis and interpretation of Rule of Professional Conduct 4.2, does not mean that a particular court in or outside the State of South Carolina will draw the same conclusions. Of particular note is that federal law governs the conduct of attorneys in federal courts. *In re Snyder*, 472 U.S. 634, 645 n.6 (1985).
>
> In the State of New Jersey, for example, three separate Federal District Court judges came up with three separate tests for allowing *ex parte* contacts with former employees. *See Public Service Electric & Gas Co. v. Associated Electric & Gas Insurance Services Ltd.*, 745 F. Supp 1037 (D.N.J. 1990); *Curley v. Cumberland Farms, Inc.*, 134 F.R.D. 77 (D.N.J. 1991); and *In re The Prudential Insurance Co. of America Sales Practices Litigation*, 911 F. Supp. 148 (D.N.J. 1995). To add confusion, the judge in the *PSE & G* case reversed his position recently in *Andrews v. Goodyear Tire & Rubber Co., Inc.*, 2000 WL 175098 (D.N.J. 2000). The Southern District of New York engaged in an excellent analysis of the issue, reaching the conclusion that interviews with former employees were allowed in *Polycast Technology Corp. v. Uniroyal, Inc.*, 129 F.R.D. 621 (S.D.N.Y. 1990). Likewise, courts in Illinois, Michigan, and Connecticut have allowed contact with former employees. *Orlowski v. Dominick's Finer Foods, Inc.*, 937 F. Supp. 723 (N.D. Ill. 1996); *Valassis v. Samuelson*, 143 F.R.D. 118 (E.D. Mich. 1992); and *Dubois v. Gradco Systems, Inc.*, 136 F.R.D. 341 (D. Conn. 1991). In Virginia, *ex parte* contacts with former employees have been precluded where the former employee's statements may impute liability to the former employer. *Armsey v. Medshares Management Services, Inc.,* 184 F.R.D. 569 (W.D. Va. 1998).
>
> In Florida, some courts draw the line not on the nature of the prior employment, but rather on the former employee's knowledge. Contact may be had with any ex-employee, but no confidential information may be elicited. *Rent Club Inc. v. TransAmerica Rental Finance Corp.*, 811 F. Supp. 651 (M.D. Fla. 1992). In another case, however, a Florida court decided that ex-employees can be freely interviewed *ex parte*, but only subject to a series of guidelines that range from counsel identifying him or herself as adverse to the former

---

justify a wholesale restriction on discovery of factual information, damaging or not"); DuBois v. Gradco Sys., *Inc.*, 136 F.R.D. 341, 345 (D. Conn. 1991).

23 *See, e.g.*, Schwartz v. Hood, 2002 WL 974678 (D. Mass. May 8, 2002) ("I will not distinguish between former and current employees since their statements and wrongful acts could be equally imputed to the defendant for purposes of liability."); Camden v. State of Md., 910 F. Supp. 1120–22 (D. Md. Jan. 24, 1996); Rent Club, Inc. v. Transamerica Fin. Corp., 811 F. Supp. 651, 657–58 (M.D. Fla. 1992).

24 *See* Concerned Parents of Jordan Park v. Hous. Auth. of City of St. Petersburg, 1996 WL 450263, at *1–2 (attempting to reconcile Florida's conflicting cases and Opinion 91-359).

25 *E.g.*, Patriarca v. Ctr. for Living & Working, Inc., 778 N.E.2d 877 (Mass. Sup. Jud. Ct. 2002) ("The question of the general applicability of rule 4.2 to former employees is one we need not address because, on the facts presented, the former employees in question would not have been protected, even while employed, from *ex parte* contact by rule 4.2.").

employer to counsel delivering all of his or her work product to the other side, listing the employees contacted and all interview notes. *Lang v. Reedy Creek Improvement District*, 888 F. Supp. 1143 (M.D. Fla. 1995).

Without being mindful of the views of various courts and jurisdictions on this subject, attorneys may find their evidence excluded and themselves disqualified from further representation. *See Zachair Ltd. v. Driggs,* 965 F. Supp. 741 (D. Md. 1997). It is the interpretation of this Committee, however, that Rule 4.2 does not, at present, preclude *ex parte* communications with former employees. Any other interpretation "should be made by a duly promulgated amendment to the rule itself, rather than by the gloss of case law." *Davidson Supply Co., Inc. v. P.P.E., Inc.*, 986 F. Supp. 956, 958 (D. Md. 1997) (disagreeing with the *Zachair* opinion and relying upon the interpretation of Rule 4.2 given by the Maryland State Bar Association).

COMMITTEE NOTE: This issue engendered much discussion among the committee members. Some members were of the opinion that a lawyer could not properly communicate *ex parte* with a former employee who was a member of the former employer's control group. Others believed that it was improper for a lawyer to communicate with a former employee whose act or omission may be imputed to the organization for purposes of civil or criminal liability.

S.C. B. Ethics Advisory Comm. Op. 01-01 (2001).

27.4 Even When *Ex Parte* Contact Is Proper, Model Rule 4.3 Establishes Ethical Duty of Disclosure

27.4.1 General Duties to Unrepresented Persons

Even when allowed by the applicable rules, an attorney contacting a present or former employee may not portray himself or herself as a disinterested, neutral party.[26] In addition, the lawyer must be careful not to obtain any privileged or work product information and *may* also need to ensure that he or she does not learn any trade secrets.[27] In short, "certain precautions need to be observed,"[28] namely the following:

> [P]rior to the interview, the attorney or investigator must (1) fully disclose their representative capacity to the employee, (2) state the reason for seeking the interview as it concerns the attorney's client and the employer, (3) inform the individual of his or her right to refuse to be interviewed, (4) inform the person that he or she has the right to have their own counsel present, and finally, (5) may not under any circumstances seek to obtain attorney-client or work product information from the employee.[29]

"Some courts have required a set script to be read to and signed by the employee."[30]

27.4.2 The Ethical Duty Not to Solicit Privileged Information

Numerous courts have emphasized the attorney's ethical obligation to avoid inducing disclosure of privileged information.[31]

The rationale underlying the prohibition against a lawyer inducing disclosure of privileged information is clear:

> [T]he decision to waive the privilege belongs to the client, but if *ex parte* interviews are permitted, it would be left to the employee to determine what information is subject to disclosure and what remains privileged. Those employees are not only unskilled in making such determinations, any error could, in addition, expose them to liability

26 ABA Formal Op. 91-359 (1991); Brown v. St. Joseph County, 148 F.R.D. 254–55 (N.D. Ind. Apr. 12, 1993); Action Air Freight, Inc. v. Pilot Air Freight Corp., 769 F. Supp. 899, 903 (E.D. Pa. 1991).

27 *See In re* Home Shopping Network, Inc., Secs. Litig., Fed. Sec. L. Rep. 94, 95 (M.D. Fla. 1989).

28 McCallum v. CSX Transp. Inc., 149 F.R.D. 112 (M.D.N.C. May 4, 1993).

29 *Id.* (collecting cases). *See* Sanfill of Ga., Inc. v. Roberts, 502 S.E.2d 345 (Ga. App. 1998); S.C.B. Ethics Advisory Comm. Op. 01-01 (2001); Ga. S. Ct. formal Advisory Op. 94-3 (Sept. 9, 1994) (concluding it would be "deceitful" to use false premises to obtain information from an employee, and so lawyer must make full disclosure before conducting interview).

30 McCallum v. CSX Transp. Inc., 149 F.R.D. 112 (M.D.N.C. May 4, 1993) (citing cases); Monsanto Co. v. Aetna Cas. & Sur. Co., 593 A.2d 1013, 1014 (Del. Super. Ct. 1990) (creating form for interviewers to use), *modified*, 1990 WL 200471 (Del. Super. Ct. Dec. 4, 1990).

31 *See, e.g.*, Camden v. State of Md., 910 F. Supp. 1120 (D. Md. Jan. 24, 1996); Fu Inv. Co., Ltd., v. Comm'r, 104 T.C. No. 20, ¶ 50,563 (CCH) (Tax Ct., Apr. 3, 1995) ("during the course of such an interview [the attorney] must limit her questions to factual matters and refrain from eliciting or inducing statements or disclosures by a former employee that involved privileged communications"); Lange v. Reedy Creek Improvement District, 888 F. Supp. 1143, 1148–49 (N.D. Fla. 1995) ("plaintiff's counsel shall advise the former employee to avoid disclosure of privileged materials. In the course of the interview, plaintiff's counsel shall not attempt to solicit privileged information and shall terminate the conversation should it appear that the interviewee may reveal privileged matters").

arising from an improper disclosure. As one court explained:

> This court places no restrictions on *ex parte* communications with former employees . . . to the extent that no attorney-client confidences are involved in such communications. Thus, an attorney communicating with the former employees . . . may not inquire into privileged attorney-client communications because "[a]ny privilege existing between the former employee and the organization's counsel belongs to the organization, and can only be waived by the organization."[32]

27.4.3 *Sanctions and Other Restrictions Can Result from Improper* Ex Parte *Contacts*

Courts look carefully at *ex parte* contacts, sometimes requiring disclosure of interview notes[33] or imposing sanctions.[34] Other courts have excluded or limited the use of evidence obtained by the *ex parte* contact.[35] While often sought, disqualification is infrequently granted, at least when privileged information has not been obtained.[36]

27.5 Do Model Rules 4.2 or 4.3 Apply to Undercover Investigative Proceedings?

27.5.1 *General*

In many cases, the evidence gathered by undercover investigations has been used without challenge.[37] It also appears fairly settled that government lawyers, in conducting criminal investigations, may use undercover investigations.[38] However, it is an open question in most jurisdictions as to whether the same holds true in civil litigation.[39]

At least three rules are implicated when a lawyer directs that a non-lawyer provide false information to third parties: (1) whether the conduct constitutes an impermissible *ex parte* contact with a "represented party" under Model Rule 4.2; (2) whether any statements made must comply with Model Rule 4.3, governing unrepresented parties; and (3) whether a dissembling investigator violates either Model Rule 4.1 or 8.4, which prohibit deceitful conduct. This section now turns to those issues.

Are there circumstances under which an investigator can engage in activities that fall within Rule 4.2? If not, do the duties under Rule 4.3 apply such that the investigator must disclose his or her purpose, thus defeating the entire purpose of undercover investigations? The answers to these questions depend upon interpretations of those rules as well as the timing of the investigation and its scope and structure.

It is clear, at the outset, that a lawyer cannot simply use an investigator to do what the lawyer cannot do in terms of soliciting privileged information or obtaining admissions.[40] A lawyer cannot hire an investigator to call up a person covered under Rule 4.2 and obtain information. Nor, if the person is not covered under Rule 4.2, may an attorney hire an investigator to engage in contact that violates rule 4.3. [41]

---

32 Cram v. Lamson & Sessions Co., Carlon Div., 148 F.R.D. 266 (S.D. Iowa Apr. 13, 1993) (quoting Sequa Corp. v. Lititech, Inc., 807 F. Supp. 653, 668 (D. Colo. 1992).

33 *See, e.g., In re* Infant Formula Antitrust Litig., 1992 WL 503465 (N.D. Fla. 1992).

34 *See, e.g.*, Camden v. State of Md., 910 F. Supp. 1124 (D. Md. Jan. 24, 1996) (disqualifying lawyers); Rent Club, Inc. v. Transamerica Rental Fin. Corp., 811 F. Supp. 651 (M.D. Fla. 1992) (disqualifying lawyers).

35 *E.g.*, Camden v. State of Md., 910 F. Supp. 1123 (D. Md. Jan. 24, 1996) (suppressing use of evidence); McCallum v. CSX Transp. Inc., 149 F.R.D. 113 (M.D.N.C. May 4, 1993); Brown v. St. Joseph County, 148 F.R.D. 255 (N.D. Ind. Apr. 12, 1993); Shearson Lehman Bros., Inc. v. Wasatch Bank, 139 F.R.D. 48 (D. Utah 1991).

36 *See* Allstate Ins. Co. v. Bowne, 817 So. 2d 994,999 (Fla. App. 2002).

37 *See generally* David B. Isbell & Lucantonio N. Salvi, *Ethical Responsibility of Lawyers for Deception by Undercover Investigators and Discrimination Testers: An Analysis of the Provisions Prohibiting Misrepresentation Under the Model Rules of Professional Conduct*, 8 Geo. J. Legal Eth. 797–802 (1995) (discussing numerous cases where evidence gathered in undercover investigations was admitted without questioning whether the practice in some way implicated legal ethical issues). *See also* Sanfill of Ga. Inc. v. Roberts, 502 S.E.2d 343, 344 (Ct. App. Ga. 1998) (investigator called defendant to find location of former employee).

38 *See* Utah State Bar Ethics Advisory Comm. Op. No. 02-05 (Mar. 18, 2002) (noting that both the ABA and other states had found undercover investigatory practices ethical when conducted by government lawyers to gather evidence); United States v. Parker, 165 F. Supp. 2d 431, 476 (W.D.N.Y. 2001) (holding that the rule prohibiting deceit "does not apply to prosecuting attorneys who provide supervision and advice to undercover investigations.").

39 *See* Utah State Bar Ethics Advisory Comm. Op. No. 02-05 (Mar. 18, 2002) ("We do not address in this opinion and specifically reserve the issue of whether the analysis and result of this opinion apply to a private lawyer's investigative conduct that involves dishonesty, fraud, misrepresentation or deceit."); Am. Bar Ass'n Comm. on Ethics and Prof'l Responsibility Formal Op. 01-422 (2001) ("The Committee does not address in this opinion the application of the Model Rules to deceitful, but lawful conduct by lawyers, either directly or through supervision of the activities of agents and investigators, which often accompanies nonconsensual recording of conversations in investigations of . . . discriminatory practices, and trademark infringement. We . . . leave for another day the . . . question of when investigative practices involving misrepresentations of identity and purpose nonetheless may be ethical.").

40 *See, e.g.*, Upjohn Co. Aetna Cas. & Sur. Co. 768 F. Supp. 1186 (W.D. Mich. 1991); *In re* Envtl. Ins. Declaratory Judgment Actions, 600 A.2d 165 (N.J. Super. Ct. 1991).

41 Model Rule 5.3 (responsibilities of lawyer for activities of

When the lawyer is not engaged in conduct simply designed to do indirectly what he cannot do directly—for example, incite an employee to reveal privileged information—the issue becomes more complex and the disagreement between among the courts more pronounced.

27.5.2 *Whether Undercover Investigations Are Within Rule 4.2*

The timing of the investigation may be critical to whether contact with an opposing party, or an employee thereof, violates Rule 4.2. If the investigation occurs before the investigating attorney knows that the other side is represented by counsel, then Rule 4.2 may not apply.[42] While the courts agree that, once litigation is filed, the opposing party is obviously "represented by counsel" and the question arises of whether individual employees of that party are "represented" in terms of rule 4.2 arises, they disagree on when a lawyer "knows" that a party that has not yet been sued is nonetheless "represented by counsel" under Rule 4.2.[43]

The leading commentators believe that the onset of litigation prevents the use of any evidence gathered from persons who are covered by Rule 4.2:

> [T]here is little room for doubt that in some circumstances a lawyer's use of discrimination testers to communicate with a party known to be represented by counsel with respect to the matter being investigated—that is, the particular discriminatory practices being investigated—would present a vicarious violation of Rule 4.2. *As a practical matter, this may mean that lawyers may make use of testers only in investigating whether a particular enterprise is engaging in discriminatory practices, and in preparing litigation challenging such practices, but not in gathering further evidence once the litigation has been commenced or announced, and the target of litigation has made known that it is represented by counsel in the matter.*[44]

The courts are split. One court has held that rule 4.2 is violated by a contact by an undercover investigator after litigation had begun. In *Midwest Motor Sports, Inc. v. Arctic Cat Sales, Inc.*,[45] the plaintiff had hired undercover investigators to pose as ordinary consumers and attempt to purchase snowmobiles that the defendants were not authorized to sell. In deciding that Rule 4.2 had been violated, the court held that the contacts with the defendant's owner, made for the purpose of obtaining admissions, violated Rule 4.2's prohibition against contacts with "represented persons."

Even if Rule 4.2 technically violated through use of undercover investigations to obtain admissions from "represented" employees, several courts have found no violation. They concluded that, for policy reasons not expressed in the rule, contacts that are not designed to solicit privileged information—even if they do solicit admissions—do not violate the rule. Most recently, in *Hill v. Shell Oil Co.*,[46] a putative class action was brought against Shell alleging that Shell required African-American customers to pre-pay more often than white customers. To prove their case, the class hired individuals to purchase gas, and videotaped the purchases to see if there was disparate treatment. Though noting that the gas station's employees in question were obviously not "high level" corporate employees, the court held that they were within the scope of Rule 4.2, since Rule 4.2 covers "employees whose acts or omissions in the matter can be imputed to the organization . . . and employees whose admissions would be binding on the organization."[47] The *Shell* court then held that the employees were "represented" by counsel within the context of Rule 4.2.

Following the ruling, the *Shell* court turned to the question of whether the contact was appropriate. The plaintiffs contended that the contacts consisted "of normal customer business transactions outside the scope of the rule's prohibition."[48] The court held that the contacts were proper:

> [W]e think there is a discernable continuum in the cases from clearly impermissible to clearly permissible conduct. Lawyers (and investigators) cannot trick protected employees into doing things or saying things they otherwise would not say or do. They cannot normally interview protected employees or ask them to fill out questionnaires. They probably can employ persons to play the role of customers seeking services on the same basis as the general public. They can videotape protected employees going about their activities in

supervised non-lawyers). The Ethics 2000 version of the comments to Model Rule 4.2 provide:

> Communications authorized by law may also include investigative activities of lawyers representing governmental entities, directly or through investigative agents, prior to the commencement of criminal or civil enforcement proceedings.[] This implies that a communication is not authorized by law[] when the lawyer conducting the activity is not representing a government entity.

42 *See generally* Weider Sports Equip. Co. v. Fitness First, Inc., 912 F. Supp. 502 (D. Utah 1996).

43 *See id.*

44 David B. Isbell & Lucantonio N. Salvi, *Ethical Responsibility of Lawyers for Deception by Undercover Investigators and Discrimination Testers: An Analysis of the Provisions Prohibiting Misrepresentation Under the Model Rules of Professional Conduct*, 8 Geo. J. Legal Eth. 823 (1995) (emphasis added; footnotes omitted).

45 Midwest Motor Sports, Inc. v. Arctic Cat Sales, Inc., 144 F. Supp. 2d 1147 (D.S.D. 2001), *aff'd*, 2003 WL 22382960 (8th Cir. Oct. 20, 2003).

46 Hill v. Shell Oil Co., 209 F. Supp. 2d 876 (N.D. Ill. 2002).

47 *Id.* at 878.

48 *Id.* at 879.

> what those employees believe is the normal course.[49]

Another court, in a trademark case, reached the same conclusion as the *Shell* court—Rule 4.2 is violated by contact even with low-level employees—but, like the *Shell* court, held that the fact that the rule was "technically" violated did not warrant exclusion of evidence. In *Gidatex, S.r.L. v. Campaniello Imports, Ltd.*,[50] the defendants filed a motion *in limine* to exclude evidence obtained by the plaintiff's undercover investigators from defendants' sales clerks which showed that the defendant had not complied with the plaintiff's cease-and-desist letter. The evidence showed that the investigators had misrepresented their purpose and identities in determining whether trademark violations were not ongoing.

The *Gidetex* court held that Rule 4.2 was "technically" violated—since the sales clerks' statements were being offered as "admissions"—and that the clerks were "represented by counsel" even though suit had not been filed because of the "permanent adversarial status of the parties."[51] However, the court then states:

> Although Bailey's conduct technically satisfies the three-part test generally used to determine whether counsel has violated the disciplinary rules, I conclude that he did not violate the rules because his actions simply do not represent the type of conduct prohibited by the rules. The use of private investigators, posing as consumers and speaking to nominal parties who are not involved in any aspect of the litigation, does not constitute an end-run around the attorney/client privilege. Gidatex's investigators did not interview the sales clerks or trick them into making statements they otherwise would not have made. Rather, the investigators merely recorded the normal business routine in the Campaniello showroom and warehouse.[52]

The court emphasized that its "analysis of the technical requirements of the disciplinary rules only underscores [the] earlier conclusion that these rules do not apply in the context of this case."[53]

Finally, a similar decision was reached in *Apple Corps. Ltd. v. Int'l Collectors Soc'y.*[54] In *Apple Corps. Ltd.*, the plaintiff filed a motion for civil contempt, alleging that the defendants had violated a prior order enjoining the defendants from selling certain stamps bearing the likeness of The Beatles except in a manner approved by the court. After the order had been entered, the plaintiff's attorney had her secretary order some of the stamps in a manner that had not been approved by the court. Specifically, she had several people call the defendants using false names and giving false reasons for why they wanted to order the stamps. The defendant then sold the stamps in a manner that was not approved by the court.

In addition to opposing the motion, the defendants sought sanctions, arguing that the plaintiffs had acted unethically in using undercover investigators to procure the stamps.[55] Under New Jersey's rule, however, only members of the "litigation control group" are covered by New Jersey's rule 4.2.[56] As a result, the contacts did not violate Rule 4.2.

In dicta, however, the court also reasoned that Rule 4.2 could not be violated by that sort of typical undercover investigation:

> There is no evidence that any of Plaintiffs' investigators asked the sales representatives any questions about instructions given or received with regard to Beatles/Lennon stamps. Plaintiffs' investigators did not ask the sales representatives about Defendants' practices or their own practices or policies with regard to Beatles/Lennon stamps. The sales representatives' communication with Plaintiffs' counsel and investigators were limited to recommending which stamps to purchase and accepting an order for Sell-Off Stamps. The investigators did not ask any substantive questions other than whether they could order the Sell-Off Stamps. The only misrepresentations made were as to the callers' purpose in calling and their identities. They posed as normal consumers. The investigator did not make any misrepresentation that he or she was a Beatles/Lennon Club member. In most instances, Plaintiffs' investigators told the sales representative that he or she was not a Beatles/Lennon Club member. Furthermore, Defendants charged all of Plaintiffs' investigators' the higher, non-member price for the Sell-Off Stamps.
>
> RPC 4.2 cannot apply where lawyers and/or their investigators, seeking to learn about current corporate misconduct, act as members of the general public to engage in ordinary business transactions with low-level employees of a represented corporation. To apply the rule to the investigation

49 *Id.* at 880 (holding taping was appropriate because the conversations were minimal—consisting of asking whether the pump permitted prepayment—and beyond the audio range of the cameras).

50 Gidatex, S.r.L. v. Campaniello Imps., Ltd., 82 F. Supp. 2d 119 (S.D.N.Y. 1999).

51 *Id.* at 124–25.

52 *Id.* at 125–26.

53 *Id.* at 126, n.3.

54 Apple Corps. Ltd. v. Int'l Collectors Soc'y, 15 F. Supp. 2d 456 (D.N.J. 1998).

55 The district court struggled mightily with the issue of choice of law, since the lawyers who engaged in the conduct were licensed in New York, but the court was in New Jersey, which did not have a rule specifying which rules applied. *Id.* at 472–73. The court ultimately held that New Jersey's rules applied.

56 Apple Corps. Ltd. v. Int'l Collectors Soc'y, 15 F. Supp. 2d 474 (D.N.J. 1998).

> which took place here would serve merely to immunize corporations from liability for unlawful activity, while not effectuating any of the purposes behind the rule. Accordingly, Ms. Weber's and Plaintiffs' investigators' communications with Defendants' sales representatives did not violate RPC 4.2.[57]

The net impact of these decisions could be disconcerting, since the decisions rely upon policies that may or may not be adopted by other courts or by the disciplinary agency responsible for licensing the lawyer involved. However, even assuming Rule 4.2 is not violated, the lawyer must still be concerned with whether Rule 4.3 is implicated.

27.5.3 Whether Undercover Investigations Are Within Rule 4.3

The structure of the investigation may bear on whether Rule 4.3 applies. Some argue that the typical undercover investigation is not of the kind covered under these rules. An investigation that is not designed to obtain information but instead intended to record conduct is different. Based in part on this, the leading commentators argue that Rule 4.3 does not apply:

> Like Rule 4.2, this Rule is clearly limited to circumstances where the lawyer is acting as a lawyer—in this case, "dealing on behalf of a client." Moreover, the prohibitions embodied in the Rule—on stating or implying to the unrepresented person addressed that the lawyer is disinterested, and on allowing such a person to persist in misunderstanding the lawyer's role—clearly have application only to a lawyer who is acting as a lawyer. Like Rule 4.2, Rule 4.3 is intended to prevent a lawyer from taking advantage of a third party. While Rule 4.2 turns upon the actual conduct of the lawyer, however, Rule 4.3 turns upon the presumed expectations of the third party in dealing with a lawyer. Thus, both of the prohibitions in Rule 4.3 rest on the premise that a person acting in the capacity of a lawyer engenders expectations as to probity and candor that the ethical rules require a lawyer to honor. A lawyer acting as a lawyer but disguising his identity as such in dealing with an unrepresented person can also violate Rule 4.3 because, although he is acting as a lawyer, he has allowed that person to misunderstand that fact.
>
> Since Rule 4.3 rests upon assumed expectations of persons dealing directly with lawyers, it should have no vicarious applicability to lawyers supervising the activities of undercover investigators and testers, for the latter by definition do not represent themselves as acting on behalf of a lawyer and so cannot engender expectations of the sort that Rule 4.3 is intended to protect. No unrepresented person is realistically likely to apply his or her expectations of lawyers to an investigator or tester. Rule 4.3 could apply, however, to the activities of an investigator who represented himself as acting on behalf of a lawyer.[58]

Several courts have accepted this conclusion. One court suggested in *dicta* that Rule 4.3 did not apply:

> Rule 4.3, Utah Rule of Professional Conduct treats contact with unrepresented persons. Icon, by this argument, assumes Thompson was not represented, either in an individual capacity, which he was not, or as a corporate representative which has not been established. The invocation of Rule 4.3 accepts Thompson's status as that of a non-represented person. Under Rule 4.3 the lawyer, in dealing with such a person, is not to imply that the lawyer is not disinterested. However, Rule 4.3 may apply only to lawyers not investigators since the expectations are those of the unrepresented person dealing with a lawyer. It has been suggested the rule "should have no vicarious liability to lawyers supervising the activities of undercover investigators and testers, for the latter by definition do not represent themselves as acting on behalf of a lawyer so they cannot engender expectations of the sort that Rule 4.3 is to protect." No unrepresented person is realistically likely to apply his or her expectations of lawyers to an investigator or tester. Rule 4.3 could apply, however, to the activities of an investigator who represented himself as acting on behalf of a lawyer. Icon has not shown a basis for invocation of Rule 4.3 under this analysis.[59]

In the trademark context, the court in *Apple Corps. Ltd. v. Int'l Collectors Soc'y*,[60] stated:

> The attorney disciplinary rules also restrict an attorney's communications with an unrepresented party. New Jersey RPC 4.3 specifically provides protection for unrepresented employees. RPC 4.3 states that:
>
> > In dealing on behalf of a client with a person who is not represented by counsel, a lawyer shall not state or imply that the lawyer is disinterested. When the lawyer knows or reason-

57 *Id.* at 474–75 (citations omitted).

58 David B. Isbell & Lucantonio N. Salvi, *Ethical Responsibility of Lawyers for Deception by Undercover Investigators and Discrimination Testers: An Analysis of the Provisions Prohibiting Misrepresentation Under the Model Rules of Professional Conduct*, 8 Geo. J. Legal Eth. 825 (1995) (footnotes omitted).

59 Weider Sports Equip. Co. v. Fitness First, Inc., 912 F. Supp. 502, 511–12 (D. Utah 1996) (citations omitted) (quoting the Isbell and Salvi article, *supra* note 58).

60 Apple Corps. Ltd. v. Int'l Collectors Soc'y, 15 F. Supp. 2d 456, 476 (D.N.J. 1998).

> ably should know that the unrepresented person misunderstands the lawyer's role in the matter, the lawyer shall make reasonable efforts to correct the misunderstanding . . . .
>
> It is clear from the language of RPC 4.3 that it is limited to circumstances where an attorney is acting in his capacity as a lawyer—"dealing on behalf of a client." Therefore, its prohibitions on allowing the unrepresented person to misunderstand that the lawyer is disinterested only apply to a lawyer who is acting as a lawyer. Like RPC 4.2, RPC 4.3 was intended to prevent a lawyer who fails to disclose his role in a matter from taking advantage of an unrepresented third party.
>
> Plaintiffs' counsel and investigators in testing compliance were not acting in the capacity of lawyers. Therefore, the prohibitions of RPC 4.3 do not apply here. RPC 4.3 does not apply to straightforward transactions undertaken solely to determine in accordance with Rule 11 of the Federal Rules of Civil Procedure, the existence of a well-founded claim—in this case a claim of contempt.[61]

At least one court has held, however, that Rule 4.3 and the admonitions required apply to undercover investigations. The federal court for the District of South Dakota reasoned:

> When an attorney or an investigator or other agent for the attorney attempts to conduct an *ex parte* interview with a current employee of an adversary organization or corporation, Rule 4.3 . . . controls.
>
> * * *
>
> The attorney or investigator shall: (1) fully disclose his or her representative capacity to the employee, (2) state the reason for seeking the interview as it concerns the attorney's client and the employer, and (3) inform the individual of his or her right to refuse to be interviewed. The attorney or investigator shall not, under any circumstances, seek to obtain attorney-client or work product information from the employee.[62]

Even if Rule 4.3 does not apply, the investigating attorney encounters some additional complications. The *Apple* court's statement that the investigation must, *before it is begun*, comply with Rule 11 obviously creates some additional issues: ostensibly, a lawyer may not use undercover investigators to determine whether a claim exists; he may use it only to confirm an otherwise well-founded claim. This creates, as one court observed, a "troubled" relationship between Rule 4.2 and the requirement in Rule 11 that lawyers conduct adequate pre-suit investigations:

> If read literally, and implying the broadest possible interpretation for the term admission, a construction could arise from the argument that any communication that could fit under Rule 801(d)(2)(D) F.R.E [defining "admissions"] would be prohibited, therefore, virtually any communication with an organization employee would be prevented without the organization's counsel being present or contacted if the organization is a party. This could prevent any pretrial inquiry that would gather evidence from an employee of an organization. In most instances, this would block acquisition of important evidence about corporate practices, for example, civil right violations, age discrimination, improper corporate or labor practices, improper commercial practices, and frauds. This application of Rule 4.2 would preclude, prior to litigation, the gathering of the necessary factual information to determine if a valid claim for relief could be maintained and in its most exaggerated context leave[s] a party without a factual basis to assert an avenue of redress. The troubling features of this application of Rule 4.2 are observed in *In re Air Crash Disaster Near Roselawn, Indiana,* 909 F. Supp. 1116 (D.N.D. Ill.1995). The purpose of preserving attorney/client integrity is not involved where there is no protected interest under the attorney/client relationship standard of *Upjohn.* The concern for the coercion of an employee who may make a statement and to protect against exploitation can be dealt with in the context of the conduct of counsel and the trustworthiness of the statement. The rule does not protect against organizational counsel's own misconduct in interviewing organizational employees. Further, Rule 4.2 creates an "ethical minefield" for counsel, therefore, the court finds the suggested conclusion in *In re Air Crash Disaster, supra,* not to be fully acceptable.[63]

Even if rule 4.3 does not require the investigator to reveal his or her true identity and admonish the interview subjects to obtain their own lawyers, Rules 4.1 and Rule 8.4 may be implicated, since a lawyer who hires an investigator to conduct a deceitful investigation may be indirectly misrepresenting material facts or engaging in dishonest conduct. If so, those rules are violated.

27.5.4 Model Rules 4.1 and 8.4: Is Dishonesty for Good Purposes Ethical?

27.5.4.1 General

It is clear that honesty is incompatible with the use of testers and undercover investigators. The question is: is the use of testers, as a result, incompatible with the ethics rules?

61 Citations are omitted.

62 Midwest Motor Sports, Inc. v. Arctic Cat Sales, Inc., 144 F. Supp. 2d 1157 (D.S.D. 2001) (citation omitted).

63 Weider Sports Equip. Co. v. Fitness First, Inc., 912 F. Supp. at 508–09 (citations and footnotes omitted).

Model Rule 4.1 requires that, "in the course of representing a client," a lawyer does not knowingly "make a false statement of material fact . . . to a third person" or "fail to disclose a material fact to a third person when disclosure is necessary to avoid assisting in a criminal or fraudulent act by a client . . . ." Model Rule 8.4(c) prohibits engaging "in conduct involving dishonesty, fraud, deceit or misrepresentation."

In the abstract, acting "ethically" would certainly include acting "honestly." Many would say that honesty is one of the core values of the legal profession. In that regard, disciplinary rules specifically require lawyers to be "truthful" in statements to others; require them to disclose material facts to avoid committing fraud; and prohibit them from engaging "in conduct involving dishonesty, fraud, deceit or misrepresentation."[64]

Yet, when lawyers are attempting to prove various wrongs, they often need to resort to tactics that clearly do not involve full disclosure of material facts and which clearly do involve deceit. For example, in employment or housing discrimination, it may be helpful for a lawyer to have minorities apply for jobs or seek to rent an apartment in order to obtain recordings or other evidence demonstrating that the would-be or actual defendant is violating the law. Likewise, in trademark disputes, it may be helpful to the trademark owner to purchase a product to demonstrate that "knock-offs" are being sold in violation of the trademark.[65]

These undercover investigations by their nature require that the actors be less than honest. These investigations also often include the use of surreptitious tape recording or video taping—an activity that can be illegal in some states and may be unethical in others. The minority applicant does not, in fact, want the job; the trademark owner, in fact, wishes the item were not available and has no need for it. In both circumstances, the goal of the contact is to gather evidence, not to rent an apartment or buy a product or service. They no doubt assist the victim of the wrongdoing by permitting evidence to be gathered that could not be obtained were total honesty required. Whether this form of inarguably dishonest and deceitful conduct violates the rules in the context of civil litigation is a question that has split the courts, bar associations, and commentators.

No one seems to dispute, for example, that a person who dissembles as to his or her purpose or identity in making a contact is, in fact, making a misrepresentation of material fact. The rules prohibit doing so.

That is where the disagreement begins.

On the one hand, perhaps a majority of authorities reason that the fact that the conduct violates the rules does not end the inquiry—the deeper issue should be whether the conduct furthers the goals of the profession and not whether, when viewed literally, the conduct violates the rule. Values—not literalism—matters most, some say, and the value of being free from discrimination or free from infringement of property rights exceeds the value furthered by enforcing a strict interpretation of the rules.

Others, however, say that because disciplinary rules are just that—quasi-criminal rules, the violation of which can result in forfeiture of the right to practice law—then a rule which does not mean what it says should be amended.[66] Furthermore, they point out that the use of deception imposes costs on innocent people as well as actual wrongdoers: a company that is not infringing a trademark or committing discrimination, but has its time and resources consumed by those who are not actually interested in buying its products or renting its homes, is harmed. One could imagine, also, lawyers using testers in order to create cases in which there had been no prior complaint of discrimination.

27.5.4.2 Authority Holding White Lies are Acceptable

Commentators have argued that the Model Rules can and should be interpreted as not prohibiting misrepresentations made by testers.[67] Both statutory-construction and policy arguments have been mustered to show that what is clearly a misrepresentation by an investigator is not a "misrepresentation" in terms of Rule 8.4(c).

The statutory-construction argument has been explained by the leading commentators, who take this position:

> That principle [of statutory construction] would require that Rule 8.4(c) apply only to misrepresentations that manifest a degree of wrongdoing on a par with dishonesty, fraud, and deceit. In other words, it should apply only to grave misconduct that would not only be generally reproved if committed by anyone, whether lawyer or non-

64 Rules 4.1; 8.4(c). In addition, by violating rule 8.4, the lawyer could violate Rule 4.4. *See* David B. Isbell & Lucantonio N. Salvi, *Ethical Responsibility of Lawyers for Deception by Undercover Investigators and Discrimination Testers: An Analysis of the Provisions Prohibiting Misrepresentation Under the Model Rules of Professional Conduct*, 8 Geo. J. Legal Eth. 826 (1995). In addition, an investigation that is illegal is clearly unethical.

65 Lawyers may not circumvent their ethical obligations by hiring a non-lawyer to do the work for them. Model Rule 5.3(c)(1) (providing that a lawyer is responsible for conduct by a non-lawyer that violates the rules if the lawyer "orders or, with the knowledge of the specific conduct, ratifies the conduct involved").

66 *See* Sean Keveney, *The Dishonesty Rule: A Proposal for Reform*, 81 Tex. L. Rev. 381, 398 (2002).

67 David B. Isbell & Lucantonio N. Salvi, *Ethical Responsibility of Lawyers for Deception by Undercover Investigators and Discrimination Testers: An Analysis of the Provisions Prohibiting Misrepresentation Under the Model Rules of Professional Conduct*, 8 Geo. J. Legal Eth. 791, 811–826 (1995).

> lawyer, but would be considered of such gravity as to raise questions as to a person's fitness to be a lawyer. Investigators and testers, however, do not engage in misrepresentations of the grave character implied by the other words in the phrase [dishonesty, fraud, deceit] but, on the contrary, do no more than conceal their identity or purpose to the extent necessary to gather evidence.[68]

One case adopted this statutory-construction argument.[69]

The policy argument has been used to justify several cases holding that investigators' misrepresentations are not "misrepresentations." In *Apple Corps. Ltd.,* for example, the court essentially reasoned that Rule 8.4(c) should not be construed to cover "misrepresentations," concluding that the rule simply did not apply to misrepresentations regarding identity or purpose:

> Undercover agents in criminal cases and discrimination testers in civil cases, acting under the direction of lawyers, customarily dissemble as to their identities or purposes to gather evidence of wrongdoing. This conduct has not been condemned on ethical grounds by courts, ethics committees or grievance committees. This limited use of deception, to learn about ongoing acts of wrongdoing, is also accepted outside the area of criminal or civil-rights law enforcement. The prevailing understanding in the legal profession is that a public or private lawyer's use of an undercover investigator to detect ongoing violations of the law is not ethically proscribed, especially where it would be difficult to discover the violations by other means.
>
> * * *
>
> Plaintiffs could only determine whether Defendants were complying with the Consent Order by calling [Defendants] directly and attempting to order [The Beatles] stamps. If Plaintiffs' investigators had disclosed their identity and the fact that they were calling on behalf of Plaintiffs, such an inquiry would have been useless to determine [Defendants'] day-to-day business practices in the ordinary course of business.[70]
>
> Similarly, the trademark case of *Gidatex, S.r.L. v. Campaniello Imports, Ltd.*,[71] recognized that statements by undercover investigators were "technical" violations of rules prohibiting misrepresentations but nonetheless stated:
>
> As for DR 1-102(A)(4)'s prohibition against attorney "misrepresentations," hiring investigators to pose as consumers is an accepted investigative technique, not a misrepresentation. The policy interests behind forbidding misrepresentations by attorneys are to protect parties from being tricked into making statements in the absence of their counsel and to protect clients from misrepresentations by their own attorneys. The presence of investigators posing as interior decorators did not cause the sales clerks to make any statements they otherwise would not have made. There is no evidence to indicate that the sales clerks were tricked or duped by the investigators' simple questions such as "is the quality the same?" or "so there is no place to get their furniture?"
>
> * * *
>
> These ethical rules should not govern situations where a party is legitimately investigating potential unfair business practices by use of an undercover posing as a member of the general public engaging in ordinary business transactions with the target. To prevent this use of investigators might permit targets to freely engage in unfair business practices which are harmful to both trademark owners and consumers in general. Furthermore, excluding evidence obtained by such investigators would not promote the purpose of the rule, namely preservation of the attorney/client privilege.
>
> In this case, Gidatex had a right to determine whether Campaniello had complied with Gidatex's "cease and desist" letter dated October 16, 1997. The evidence gathered by the investigators demonstrates that defendants' employees informed consumers that plaintiff's business no longer exists and that the other brands of furniture sold by Campaniello are "the same" as the Saporiti Italia brand. Neither of these statements are true. Courts have recognized the relevance of such evidence.[72]

27.5.4.3 Authorities Finding White Lies to Be Deceitful

The Oregon Supreme Court wrote the seminal case explaining that the rules literally do not permit white lies in *In re Gatti*,[73] The case presents multiple ironies. Several years before the relevant events, Gatti had previously complained to the Bar about the conduct of the DOJ in using undercover investigators to pose as injured workers for purposes of infiltrating chiropractors' and lawyers' offices in a sting involving fraudulent workers' compensation claims. The lawyer's complaint was rejected by the Bar, which advised him in writing that government lawyers "have more latitude

68 *Id.* at 817 (footnotes omitted).

69 Apple Corps. Ltd. v. Int'l Collectors Soc'y, 15 F. Supp. 2d 456 (D.N.J. 1998). *See also* Jane Shay Wald, *Trademark Searches and Investigations*, 668 PLI/Pat 9 (Nov. 2, 2001) (discussing cases).

70 Apple Corps. Ltd. v. Int'l Collectors Soc'y, 15 F. Supp. 2d 475 (D.N.J. 1998).

71 Gidatex, S.r.L. v. Campaniello Imps., Ltd., 82 F. Supp. 2d 119 (S.D.N.Y. 1999).

72 *Id.* at 122 (footnotes and citations omitted).

73 *In re* Gatti, 8 P.3d 966 (Or. 2000).

in carrying out the agency's regulatory powers in a surreptitious fashion than members of the Bar in the private sector."[74]

Later, the lawyer made some phone calls and introduced himself under false pretenses in order to gather information for possible litigation. A complaint was filed with the Bar against the lawyer, arguing that he violated disciplinary rules by making false statements in conducting this investigation. After rejecting the argument that the Bar was estopped from asserting that the lawyer's misrepresentations constituted an ethics violation because the Bar had advised him that government lawyers conducting such investigations did not violate the rules, the court concluded that the lawyer had committed willful violations of the rules since he had misrepresented his identity in conducting the investigation.[75]

The court then turned to whether the rule should be interpreted to allow for an exception for misrepresentations limited "only to identity or purpose and made solely for purposes of discovering information . . . ."[76] Noting that various civil rights and other organizations had filed amicus briefs supporting this view, the court reasoned that as a court it was powerless to create an exception:

> As members of the Bar ourselves—some of whom have prior experience as government lawyers and some of whom have prior experience in private practice—this court is aware that there are circumstances in which misrepresentations, often in the form of false statements of fact by those who investigate violations of the law, are useful means for uncovering unlawful and unfair practices, and that lawyers in both the public and private sectors have relied on such tactics. However, ORS 9.490(1) provides that the rules of professional conduct "shall be binding upon *all* members of the bar." (Emphasis added.) Faithful adherence to the wording of DR 1-102(A)(3), DR 7- 102(A)(5), ORS 9.527(4), and this court's case law does not permit recognition of an exception for *any* lawyer to engage in dishonesty, fraud, deceit, misrepresentation, or false statements. In our view, this court should not create an exception to the rules by judicial decree. Instead, any exception must await the full debate that is contemplated by the process for adopting and amending the Code of Professional Responsibility. *See* ORS 9.490(1) (describing process for formulating rules of professional conduct). Furthermore, this court is prohibited from inserting into ORS 9.527(4) an exception that the statute does not contain. ORS 174.010. That statute applies to a member of the Bar "whenever * * * [t]he member is guilty of willful deceit or misconduct in the legal profession[.]" We decline to adopt an exception to DR 1-102(A)(3) and DR 7-102(A)(5), and we are without authority to read into ORS 9.527(4) an exception that the statute does not contain. Those disciplinary rules and the statute apply to all members of the Bar, without exception.[77]

The Oregon court reached the same conclusions in *In re Ositis*,[78] a case in which the attorney had hired an investigator to misrepresent his identity by posing as a journalist in conducting some telephone interviews related to potential litigation. The court reiterated the reasoning in *Gatti* rejecting the argument that "an exception from the broad disciplinary rule prohibiting misrepresentation is necessary if lawyers are to succeed in discovering and rooting out wrongful conduct . . . ." [79] The court stated that "faithful adherence" to wording of the rule, as well as to its precedent, did not "permit recognition of an exception for *any* lawyer to engage in dishonesty, fraud, deceit, misrepresentation, or false statements."[80] Eventually, however, the Oregon legislature amended the rule to permit an exception for efforts "to obtain information on unlawful activity through the use of misrepresentations or other subterfuge."[81]

In addition to this authority, other authorities could be read to require disclosure by the investigator of the full facts. For example, the authorities discussed above regarding the propriety of *ex parte* contacts with *un*represented persons suggests that full disclosure is required. Georgia's bar association, for example, wrote that, while it was appropriate to engage in an *ex parte* contact with a former employee, since the former employee had the right to decide whether to give evidence against its former employer, "it would be unethical to use deceit and false pretenses to deny the former employee his or her right."[82]

27.6 Conclusion

Need the truth be told in civil litigation? On their face, the disciplinary rules say yes. As a result, at least two states, Virginia and Oregon, have attempted to eliminate the uncertainty and to provide a considered, binding view of which value trumps by addressing the issue in their disciplinary rules. Virginia provides in a comment that its rules are "not

74 *Id.* at 969.
75 *Id.* at 974.
76 *Id.*

77 *Id.* at 976 (citations and internal quotation marks omitted).
78 *In re* Ositis, 40 P.3d 500 (Or. 2002).
79 *Id.* at 502.
80 *Id. See also* Sequa Corp. v. Lititech, Inc., 807 F. Supp. 653 (D. Colo. 1992) (holding that a lawyer who believes that another lawyer has violated the rules must report it, not engage in his own investigation that relies upon dissembling and misrepresentation).
81 Or. D.R. 1-102(D). *See* Arthur Garwin, *Covert Work OK*, 1 No. 6 Am. Bar Ass'n. J. E-Report 9 (Feb. 15, 2002).
82 State Bar of Ga.—Formal Advisory Op. No. 94-3 (Sept. 1994).

intended to preclude traditionally permissible activity such as misrepresentation by a nonlawyer of one's role in a law enforcement investigation or a housing discrimination 'tester.' "[83] Likewise, Oregon after the *Gatti* decision amended its rule to allow lawyers to advise and supervise otherwise lawful conduct that is done in "an effort to obtain information on unlawful activity through the use of misrepresentations or other subterfuge."[84]

Without a binding rule or a statement from the particular court involved, lawyers are left to attempt to discern how a court will balance the competing values of honesty, on the one hand, with efficiently rooting out wrong-doing on the other. Care and thoughtfulness are obviously required.

83 Va. R. Prof. conduct 5.3, cmt.

84 Or. D.R. 1-102(D). *See* Arthur Garwin, *Covert Work OK*, 1 No. 6 Am. Bar Ass'n. J. E-Report 9 (Feb. 15, 2002).

Appendix A Client Retainer Forms and Co-Counseling Agreement

The retainer forms in Appendix A are provided for the purpose of demonstration. They must be adapted by a competent professional to meet actual needs and local law and ethical standards. The retainer form in Appendix A.1 was adapted from forms used by the National Consumer Law Center. The retainer form in Appendix A.2 was adapted from forms used by Steve Gardner in Texas. State ethical decisions must be consulted to adapt a retainer to local requirements. An analysis of some of the considerations involved in drafting a retainer agreement is contained in § 7.6, *supra*. Editable versions are available on the companion CD-Rom to this volume.

A.1 Retainer Agreement

I, [*client*], hereby retain [*attorney*] and [*co-counsel*] to represent me in connection with a potential legal action against [*defendant(s)*] for violations of [*describe claims*] and other federal and state laws. It is my understanding that [*attorney*] and [*co-counsel*] will provide such representation as co-counsel pursuant to a Co-Counseling Agreement, a copy of which is attached hereto.

LEGAL SERVICES

Unless this agreement is changed or canceled in writing by [*attorney*], [*co-counsel*] or myself as set forth below, [*attorney*] and [*co-counsel*] agree to bring the claims I may have against [*defendant(s)*] in an appropriate court, and to pursue those claims on my behalf competently and diligently. [*Attorney or co-counsel*] will serve as the lead counsel in the litigation and will be responsible for all communications with me, including, but not limited to, keeping me advised as to the progress of the case. In the event that I receive a negative decision on my claim, [*attorney*] and [*co-counsel*] will review again the legal claim to determine whether it will provide me with legal representation in an appeal of the decision. Similarly, if a separate legal action or the defense of a counterclaim becomes necessary as part of the litigation of my claim, [*attorney*] and [*co-counsel*] will have the right to determine whether to provide me with legal representation in any such separate case or defense of a counterclaim pursuant to a separate written agreement at a fee to be agreed upon at that time.

ATTORNEY FEES/COSTS

I understand that I will not be required to pay any attorney fees to [*attorney or co-counsel*] other than through a deduction for the payment of reasonable fees from a common fund created as part of the settlement of the class claims filed, or judgment entered, in the action as set forth below. I further understand that my case is one in which [*defendant(s)*] may be required to pay reasonable attorney fees to [*attorney*] and [*co-counsel*]. I authorize [*attorney*] and [*co-counsel*] to seek and collect reasonable attorney fees in addition to any relief they are seeking for me. I agree that [*attorney*] and [*co-counsel*] may keep any attorney fees that are obtained through court or agency order or settlement of the case pursuant to the provisions of the Co-Counseling Agreement.

I understand that [*attorney*] and [*co-counsel*] may have to pay certain costs in order to properly represent me in this case. These costs may include filing fees, fees for service of process and subpoenas, expert witness fees, stenographer fees, and other expenses related to litigation. Whenever possible, [*attorney*] and [*co-counsel*] will try to have [*defendant(s)*] pay for the costs. If [*attorney*] and [*co-counsel*] cannot obtain payment of costs from [*defendant(s)*], and I receive an award of money in this case, I agree to repay [*attorney*] and [*co-counsel*] for all costs for my case from the money I receive. I further understand that I may not impose a requirement to incur costs that the attorneys feel are not reasonable unless I am willing to advance and pay those costs myself.

I understand that, if my case is not successful and the court rules that the case is frivolous, unreasonable, or groundless, the court may order me to pay [*defendant(s)'*] litigation costs and/or attorney fees. In the event of such a court order, [*attorney*] and [*co-counsel*] agree to pay the entire amount of [*defendant(s)'*] fees and litigation costs awarded, **except that**: I agree that I, alone, will be responsible for the payment of such an award if (1) I misstate the facts to [*attorney*] or [*co-counsel*] and the court award is based upon facts found to be substantially and materially different than I have stated them; or (2) I refuse a settlement offer which [*attorney*] and [*co-counsel*] considers reasonable under the circumstances and/or given the objectives of the litigation.

I also understand that, other than litigation costs, I alone am responsible for paying any fines, penalties, or damages assessed against me personally.

SETTLEMENT

I understand that it may be possible to settle my case. [*Attorney*] and [*co-counsel*] will keep me informed of any settlement offers and consult with me about how to respond to any offers. No settlement will be made without my approval.

[*Attorney*], [*co-counsel*], and I will make best efforts to obtain a settlement that will adequately meet each of the following goals, with no single goal taking precedence over any other goal: (a) produce systemic reform of [*defendant(s)'*] policies or practices so other consumers will benefit from this litigation; (b) satisfy my individual goals; and (c) compensate [*attorney*] and [*co-counsel*] fairly for their reasonable attorney fees and litigation costs.

I understand that, as a public interest counsel, [*attorney*] and [*co-counsel*] face competing goals in seeking to maximize my personal recovery and in seeking reasonable attorney fees and costs. In order to satisfy both interests, I authorize [*attorney*] and [*co-counsel*] to negotiate a resolution of the class claims and my individual claims separate from any negotiation of attorney fees and litigation costs. In the event that [*attorney*] and [*co-counsel*] are unable to reach a settlement on the issues of attorney fees and costs, I understand that [*attorney*] and [*co-counsel*] may make an application to the Court for an award of attorney fees and costs as a prevailing party. I further understand that in making such application, [*attorney*] and [*co-counsel*] will calculate their fees using the "loadstar" method that reflects the number of hours worked multiplied by a reasonable hourly rate. I agree that [*attorney*] and [*co-counsel*] may be entitled to a multiplier, or enhancement, of the loadstar amount due to the novelty, complexity, and speculative nature of the claims brought in this matter.

I understand that [*defendant(s)*] may make a settlement offer that does not include a breakdown between my damages and attorney fees or litigation costs or otherwise requires me, as a condition of settlement, that I waive any claim for attorney fees or litigation costs. Regardless, [*attorney*] and [*co-counsel*] will convey to me any settlement offer made by [*defendant(s)*], even if it is conditioned on my waiving these fees and costs. I understand that [*attorney's*] and [*co-counsel's*] recommendation concerning the advisability of accepting or rejecting such a settlement proposal may reflect the fact that it is conditioned on my waiving attorney fees or litigation costs.

I understand that, if I agree to a lump sum monetary settlement of all my claims against [*defendant(s)*], including attorney fees, then the attorney fees to be paid to [*attorney*] and [*co-counsel*] will be ________ percent (__%) of the settlement—first deducting expenses and costs—or attorney fees calculated pursuant to the loadstar method, whichever is greater, from the lump sum. Costs and expenses incurred by [*attorney*] and [*co-counsel*] will be taken off the top before computing this amount. In the event that I agree to a monetary settlement which delineates the amount to be paid for my claims against [*defendant(s)*] and the amount to be paid for attorney fees, expenses, and costs, then I agree that [*attorney*] and [*co-counsel*] will be paid their legal fees, expenses and costs in accordance with the terms of the settlement agreement.

CLIENT RESPONSIBILITIES

I agree to make a full and honest disclosure to [*attorney*] and [*co-counsel*] of all facts relevant to my case, including new facts that may arise during the course of my case. I will keep [*attorney*] and [*co-counsel*] informed of my current address and telephone number.

As a client of [*attorney*] and [*co-counsel*], I understand that I have the responsibility (through ________ as my local counsel) to keep them informed of any significant changes in my circumstances, including any changes in my financial condition. I will promptly inform [*attorney*] and [*co-counsel*], through ________, if I should receive any settlement offers, documents, or other communications directly from [*defendant(s)*] or any third parties in regards to this matter. I understand that, as my counsel, [*attorney*] and [*co-counsel*] are to conduct all communication on my behalf with regard to this matter. I agree that I will not initiate any communication and that I will immediately terminate any communication I might receive from [*defendant(s)*] or third parties in regards to this matter.

I understand that I may have to appear in court or attend a deposition and will assist, and cooperate with [*attorney*] and [*co-counsel*], to the fullest extent possible in its representation of my interests in this matter.

I also understand that this case may be certified as a class action lawsuit and that, in making any decisions concerning this case, my attorneys and I must consider, in addition to my own interests, the interests of the class of people for whom I am a representative. In the event that I enter into a settlement of the class action with [*defendant(s)*] that is not recommended by my counsel, I recognize that [*attorney*] and [*co-counsel*] reserve the right to seek approval from the Court to withdraw as counsel if they believe that the terms of the proposed settlement do not adequately address the interests and claims of the putative or certified class.

[*For legal aid organizations*]: If at some time in the future my income or assets exceed [*attorney's*] eligibility guidelines, I understand that [*attorney*] may no longer be able to represent me and I may have to obtain other counsel. [*Attorney*] and/or [*co-counsel*] will assist me in obtaining other counsel and will continue to represent me until appropriate arrangements are made.

[*Attorney*] and [*co-counsel*] recommend that I seek tax advice on the possible tax consequences of this matter as there are some situations in which the attorney fee award may be considered my income for tax purposes and the minimum alternative tax may result in that income not being fully deductible.[1]

COUNSEL RESPONSIBILITIES

[*Attorney*] and [*co-counsel*] agree to handle my case competently and diligently, to exercise professional judgment free from any conflict of interest, to alert me of important developments in my case, and to respond promptly to my reasonable requests for information about my case.

TERMINATION

I understand that I am free at any time to discharge [*attorney*] or [*co-counsel*] from representing me by written letter. However, if I choose to discharge [*attorney*] or [*co-counsel*], the remaining counsel is under no obligation to find a replacement or to continue representation of me. In addition, if after discharging [*attorney*] and [*co-counsel*] I thereafter recover monetary relief through settlement or trial, I agree to pay [*attorney*] and [*co-counsel*] their normal hourly rates, up to the amount of recovery, for the services actually provided to me in the case prior to the time of discharge and for all litigation costs and expenses expended by [*attorney*] and/or [*co-counsel*] on my behalf.

I agree that [*attorney*] and [*co-counsel*] may, upon giving reasonable written notice, seek to terminate their involvement in my case if (a) the case becomes frivolous, unreasonable, or groundless in their view, or (b) the facts of my case are found to be materially and significantly different than I have stated them, or (c) the representation of me requires taking a position contrary to the public interest as determined by [*attorney*] and [*co-counsel*], or (d) I refuse a settlement offer which [*attorney*] and [*co-counsel*] consider reasonable under the circumstances and/or given the objectives of the litigation, or otherwise fail to cooperate. If [*attorney*] and/or [*co-counsel*] terminate their involvement in my case under any of these circumstances, I agree that they will retain

1 *See Commissioner of Internal Revenue v. Banks*, 125 S. Ct. 826 (Jan. 24, 2005).

their right to recover their costs and the market value of their legal services from me.

PUBLICITY

[*Attorney*] cases are of public interest, and [*attorney*] often seeks to further the rights of others by publicizing the cases it supports and the outcome of those cases. I understand that [*attorney*] and [*co-counsel*] may make recommendations to me concerning such publicity. Based on the public need to know the law and the facts of my case, I agree to reasonably cooperate with such efforts. Ultimately, however, I retain the right to decide whether [*attorney*] and [*co-counsel*] may publicize aspects of my case that are not already part of the public record.

MISCELLANEOUS

I recognize that no results have been guaranteed by [*attorney*] or [*co-counsel*] to me and that this Retainer Agreement is not based upon any such promises or anticipated results. I further acknowledge that I am exclusively responsible for any personal liability, including tax liability or potential liability, awarded against me by the Court for any claim or counterclaim or claimed by a tax official and that, by undertaking to represent me pursuant to this Retainer Agreement, [*attorney*] and [*co-counsel*] assume none of my personal liability.

_____________________ _____________________

[*client*] [*attorney*]

[Date]

____

____________, on behalf of [Co-Counsel]

[Date]

A.2 Sample Retainer Letter and Agreement

[*Client*]

Re: [*Client v. Defendant(s)*]

Dear [*Client*]:

I am writing to offer to investigate and, if appropriate, file suit on your behalf against [*defendant(s)*] with respect to [*summary of facts and description of claims*].

My normal hourly rate for a case of this nature is $350/hour, plus expenses. Expenses include expert witness fees, costs of travel, depositions, postage, copies, and long-distance calls. I offer to represent you on a reduced rate of $100/hour, with the remainder of my hourly rate contingent on success in this matter by settlement, judgment, or otherwise. Expenses are not contingent. I will bill you monthly for my fees (at the reduced $100/hour rate) and expenses incurred. Those amounts are due upon receipt.

I will keep track of all fees and expenses until this matter is concluded. If the matter is successfully litigated or settled, we will attempt to obtain an award of attorney fees and expenses, which will be applied (1) to any outstanding balance of attorney fees and expenses and then (2) to reimburse you for the attorney fees and expenses you have paid. If there is no separate award of attorney fees and expenses, the entire outstanding balance of attorney fees and expenses will be deducted from your gross recovery and the net proceeds will be paid to you.

If you reject a settlement offer against my advice and the matter is not successfully litigated or settled, you will be responsible for all fees calculated at my normal $350/hour rate and all expenses through conclusion of this matter. Aside from that unlikely instance, if the matter is not successfully litigated or settled, you have no liability for the remainder of my fees. You are, however, responsible for payment of all reduced-rate fees and all expenses through the conclusion of this matter.

If any aspect of this offer is unclear to you, or if it does not fully reflect our discussions, please call me. Otherwise, please sign below and return the original to me in the enclosed envelope. I enclose a copy for your files.

Sincerely,

[*Attorney*]

Accepted, on the __ of ______________, 200 __.

____

[*Client*]

A.3 Draft Co-Counseling Agreement

Re:

Dear ______________:

This letter is intended as a draft of the proposed co-counseling arrangement between ______________ and [*my firm*] relating to the representation of ______________, et al., ("________") and the putative class in their proposed legal action against ______________ and ______________ (collectively "______________") and/or any of their parent companies, subsidiaries, officers, directors and/or affiliates, relating to potentially illegal, fraudulent, and/or deceptive practices with respect to ________. I will be the attorney of record on behalf of [*my firm*]. ________ and [*my firm*] will share equally in the preparation and presentation of this case. Because of your direct, existing relationship with [*plaintiff representative*], we have agreed that you will serve as lead counsel in this litigation. While this shall mean that you will have the primary responsibility for carrying on the day-to-day activities of the litigation, it is expected that you will consult with us prior to taking any strategic actions and that you will regularly confer with us in the planning and direction of the case.

[*My firm*] will keep you advised at all times as to the status of the work performed by, or on behalf of, us. You will be responsible for advising [*plaintiff representative*] on the progress of the case. [*My firm*] will communicate with [*plaintiff representative*] only as requested by you or in response to direct inquiries received from him/her (in which case [*my firm*] will keep you informed of any such communications). Of course, [*my firm*] will preserve all client confidences.

Given the nature of the claims to be brought against [*defendant(s)*] in this matter and the availability of fee-shifting statutes, it is expected that we will attempt to obtain an order from the Court requiring [*defendant(s)*] to pay litigation expenses and attorney fees distributed on a *pro rata* basis calculated using hours worked times hourly rate as the relevant base. Similarly, if the case is settled, we will attempt to get the [*defendant(s)*] to pay such fees and expenses.

If the case is settled on behalf of a class and a common fund is created, we reserve the right to have our attorney fees and litigation expenses paid from said common fund. In recognition of the sharing of responsibility in representing the clients, while dividing the labor between us, you and [*my firm*] have agreed that, unless otherwise ordered by the Court, any lump sum amount provided for attorney fees as part of a court award or settlement will be divided between us [on the basis of __% for you and __% for [*my firm*]] *or* [on a pro rata basis, to be determined by our relative contributions to the litigation].

In the event that the amount of the attorney fees and expenses are disputed by [*defendant(s)*] or any other third party, we will each submit our respective fee applications to the Court. We will maintain contemporaneous time records and other documentation of our work so as to properly support a fee application. We will at all times endeavor to ensure that there is no duplication of the work performed. We will review each other's fee applications prior to filing with the Court and attempt to eliminate any duplicative entries.

[Initially, ________ will be responsible for litigation expenses] *or* [Initially, we will equally share in the litigation expenses necessary to prepare this case for trial up to a ceiling of $______ (i.e. $______ from [*my firm*] matched, dollar for dollar, against $ ______ from you)]. Each of us will maintain appropriate records of these costs and will periodically notify each other of the expenses incurred. No experts will be retained and no substantial costs will be incurred without the mutual agreement of [*my firm*] and you. Once the litigation expenses incurred to prepare this case for trial reach the designated ceiling, [*my firm*] and you will negotiate a supplemental agreement, in writing, concerning the allocation and payment of future costs and expenses.

[*My firm*] and you are committed to providing appropriate and fair notice to the class if a class is certified in the case. Determination of how such notice will be funded, however, will be made at a later time, when such a determination becomes necessary.

You will be primarily responsible for publicizing this case and the public interest issues it addresses. [*My firm*] will cooperate fully with all publicity and public education efforts and may publicize this case through its own publications and organizational memberships. Both parties must approve all press releases and press conferences in advance. In all written and oral communications with the press about the case, [*my firm*] will mention your involvement in the case and *vice versa*.

[*My firm*] reserves the right to terminate this agreement and to seek withdrawal of representation of [*plaintiff representative*] and the putative class if you do not honor the terms reached herein or for any just reason as permitted or required by the [*state*] Code of Professional Conduct or as permitted by rule of court. [*My firm*] will provide you with advance notice of our decision to seek withdrawal prior to any filing with the Court. [*My firm*] also retains the right to seek reimbursement of attorney fees or expenses from any court award or settlement for all work performed prior to the termination of the agreement or withdrawal. Of course, you shall also have the right to terminate this agreement in the event that [*my firm*] fails to honor its terms.

If it is subsequently decided by both [*my firm*] and you that additional counsel should be brought into the case to assist in the representation of [*plaintiff representative*] and the putative class, this agreement will be revised to reflect any new arrangements that are negotiated.

Finally, you understand that [*my firm*] will require [*plaintiff representative*] and any other named class representatives to sign a joint Retainer Agreement with [*my firm*] and you, in the form attached hereto, prior to proceeding with its representation of his/her interests in this action. You agree that you will be responsible for obtaining his/her signature on the document. In the event that [*plaintiff representative*] receives a negative decision on his/her claim, [*my firm*] will review again the legal claim to determine whether to provide legal representation in an appeal of the decision. Similarly, if a separate legal action becomes necessary as part of the litigation of [*plaintiff representative's*] claim, [*my firm*] will have the right to determine whether to provide him/her with legal representation in the ancillary case or cases.

If this letter accurately represents your understanding of our agreement, please sign a copy on the line provided and return it to me. We look forward to working with you on this case.

____

________________, Esq.

____

________________, Esq.

____

________________, Esq.

[Date]

Appendix B Intake and Investigation Practice Aids

In addition to the consumer dispute questionnaire and the postmaster request form in this appendix, the companion CD-Rom to this volume contains:

- Sample Client Intake Form—Car Purchase
- Sample Client Interview Sheet—Car Purchase
- Sample Client Interview Sheet—Home Improvements
- Sample Foreclosure Prevention Counseling Forms
- Debt Collection Abuse Case Preparation Checklists
- Bankruptcy Questionnaire

B.1 Consumer Dispute Questionnaire

Please give us some information about yourself and about your dispute. This will help us evaluate your case and decide what action to recommend to you.

Give as much detail as possible. If you need more room, attach extra pages.

1. CONTACT INFORMATION

Your name: ________________________________

Address: ________________________________

____

Telephones: Work ______________________

Home ______________________

Mobile ______________________

Email: ________________________________

Close relative or friend not living with you (to update your contact information, if needed):

Name: ________________________________

Relative's Address: ______________________

____

Relative's Telephone: ( ) __-____

YOUR COMPLAINT

Please describe your complaint. Give details such as dates, the names (and phone numbers and addresses if you have them) of other people or companies that are involved.

____

____

____

WHAT HAVE YOU DONE TO TRY TO RESOLVE YOUR DISPUTE? (For example, did you contact the company? Company's response?)

WHAT ARE YOUR DAMAGES? (Damages include things such as the cost of repairs or replacement, lost time, and anything else this dispute has cost you.)

HAS THE DISPUTE CAUSED YOU ANY EMOTIONAL HARM? (Emotional harm includes things such as aggravation, inconvenience, mental distress, discomfort, anxiety, loss of sleep, or depression. You may not have any emotional harm, but, if you feel that you do, please give details.)

WHAT DOCUMENTS DO YOU HAVE ABOUT THIS DISPUTE? (This could be a receipt, a sales agreement, a contract, or anything else in writing. List and describe them and attach a photocopy—*not the originals*—to this Questionnaire.)

____

____

____

____

____

WITNESSES—Who knows any facts about your dispute? (This could be a friend, a spouse, or even an employee of the company.)

Name: ____________________________

Address: ____________________________

____

Telephones: Work ____________________

Home ____________________

Mobile ____________________

Email: ____________________________

What this person knows:

____

____

____

____

Name: ____________________________

Address: ____________________________

____

Telephones: Work ____________________

Home ____________________

Mobile ____________________

Email: ____________________________

What this person knows:

____

____

____

____

MORE INFORMATION ABOUT YOU

Have you ever been involved in a lawsuit before?

Yes __ No __ If yes, give details:

____

____

Have you ever been convicted or pleaded guilty to a crime?

Yes __ No __ If yes, give details:

Have you consulted with any other attorney about this matter?

Yes __ No __

If yes, what are that attorney's name, address, and phone numbers?

Do you have any agreement of any kind with that attorney?

Yes __ No __ If yes, give details:

Is there anything else about your dispute that you have not already described?

B.2 Request to Postmaster for New Address or Boxholder Information Needed for Service of Legal Process

39 C.F.R. 265.6(d)(4)(ii) provides this form and its use to locate a person for the purpose of serving legal process.

Postmaster
U.S. Post Office

Date

____
City, State & Zip Code

REQUEST FOR CHANGE OF ADDRESS OR BOXHOLDER INFORMATION NEEDED FOR SERVICE OF LEGAL PROCESS

1) Please furnish the new address or the name and street address (if a boxholder) for the following:

Name:____

Address:____

Note: The name and last known address are required for change of address information. The name, if known, and post office box address are required for boxholder information. The following information is provided in accordance with 39 CFR 265.6(d)(4)(ii). There is no fee for providing boxholder information. The fee for providing change of address information is waived in accordance with 39 CFR 265.6(d)(1) corresponding Administrative Support Manual 352.44a.

2) Capacity of requester (e.g., process server, attorney, party representing himself):

____

3) Statute or regulation that empowers me to serve process (not required when requester is an attorney or a party acting *pro se* except a corporation acting *pro se* must cite statute): ______________________________

The names of all known parties to the litigation:

____

4) The docket or other identifying number if one has been issued:______________

5) The capacity in which this individual is to be served: ______________________
[Defendant] [Witness]

WARNING

The submission of false information to obtain and use change of address information or boxholder information for any purpose other than the service of legal process in connection with actual or prospective litigation or (2) to avoid payment of fee for change of address information could result in criminal penalties including a fine of up to $10,000. or imprisonment or to avoid payment of the fee for change of address information or not more than 5 years or both (Title 18 U.S.C. Section 1001).

I certify that the above information is true and the address is needed and will be used solely for service of legal process in connection with actual or prospective litigation.

____
Attorney   Address

____
Printed Name   City, State and Zip Code

FOR POST OFFICE USE ONLY

_____ No change of address on file.

_____ Not known at address given

_____ Moved and left no Forwarding Address

_____ No such address

New Address or Boxholder's

____
Name

____
Address

____
City, State & Zip Code

Appendix C Sample Pleadings, Discovery and Memorandum of Law

In addition to the sample complaint in this appendix, the companion CD-Rom to this volume contains:

- 16 complaints and answers;
- 15 interrogatories and document requests;
- 8 briefs regarding motion to dismiss and summary judgment and 4 other pre-trial documents;
- 17 trial documents including *voir dire*, opening and closing statements, testimony, jury instructions and verdict forms;
- 2 pleadings regarding attorney fees; and
- key Internet links.

Fair Debt Collection Practices Act Complaint Including Both Federal and State Causes of Action

UNITED STATES DISTRICT COURT
FOR THE [*name district*] DISTRICT OF [*name state*]

________________	)	
	)	Civil Action No. __
Plaintiff,	)	
	)	COMPLAINT AND
v.	)	DEMAND FOR JURY
	)	TRIAL
	)	
Defendant.	)	(Unlawful Debt Collection
________________	)	Practices)

COMPLAINT

I. INTRODUCTION

1. This is an action for damages brought by an individual consumer for Defendant's violations of the Fair Debt Collection Practices Act, 15 U.S.C. § 1692, *et seq.* (hereinafter "FDCPA") and the [*state*] Unlawful Debt Collection Practices Act, ______ § ______ *et seq.* (hereinafter, "state Act"), which prohibit debt collectors from engaging in abusive, deceptive, and unfair practices.

II. JURISDICTION AND VENUE

2. Jurisdiction of this Court arises under 15 U.S.C. § 1692k(d), 28 U.S.C. § 1337, and supplemental jurisdiction exists for the state law claims pursuant to 28 U.S.C. § 1367. Declaratory relief is available pursuant to 28 U.S.C. §§ 2201 and 2202. Venue in this District is proper in that the defendants transact business here and the conduct complained of occurred here.

III. PARTIES

3. Plaintiff, ____________, is a natural person residing in ____________ .

4. Defendant, ____________, is a ____________ corporation engaged in the business of collecting debts in this state with its principal place of business located at ____________. The principal purpose of Defendant ____________ is the collection of debts using the mail and telephone, and Defendant ____________ regularly attempts to collect debts alleged to be due another.

5. Defendant, John Doe, also known as ____________, is a natural person employed by Defendant ____________ as a collector at all times relevant to this complaint.

6. Defendants are "debt collectors" as defined by the FDCPA, 15 U.S.C. § 1692a(6).

IV. FACTUAL ALLEGATIONS

7. On or about ______, 19__, Defendant ____________, while employed as a collector by Defendant ____________, contacted ____________, Plaintiff's employer, and requested Plaintiff's employer to speak to Plaintiff regarding the importance of paying an alleged debt of $______ allegedly owed to ____________ for medical services. Plaintiff's employer informed Plaintiff of this contact the next day.

8. On or about ______, 19__, Plaintiff wrote requesting Defendants not to contact Plaintiff's employer or Plaintiff since the alleged debt was to be paid by Plaintiff's health insurance. A copy is attached as EXHIBIT A.

9. On or about ______, Defendants mailed a letter to Plaintiff which threatened legal action if payment was not received in 5 days and which is attached hereto as Plaintiff's EXHIBIT B and by this reference incorporated herein. No payment was made by Plaintiff and no suit was filed by Defendants against Plaintiff within 5 days of Plaintiff's receipt of EXHIBIT B.

10. As a result of the acts alleged above, Plaintiff suffered headaches, nausea, and embarrassment; lost weight; and incurred sick leave and expenses for medication and day care for dependents.

V. FIRST CLAIM FOR RELIEF

11. Plaintiff repeats and realleges and incorporates by reference paragraphs one through nine above.

12. Defendants violated the FDCPA. Defendants' violations include, but are not limited to, the following:

(a) The Defendants violated 15 U.S.C. § 1692c(b) by contacting a third party, the Plaintiff's employer, without the Plaintiff's prior consent.

(b) The Defendants violated 15 U.S.C. § 1692e(2)(A), (5) and (10) by misrepresenting the imminence of legal action by Defendants.

(c) The Defendants violated 15 U.S.C. § 1692c(c) by contacting the Plaintiff after the Plaintiff had requested the Defendants cease communication with the Plaintiff.

(d) The Defendants violated 15 U.S.C. § 1692g by making a threat of suit during the debt validation request period in a manner that overshadowed the notice of validation rights and would create confusion for a least sophisticated consumer about his rights.

(e) The Defendants violated 15 U.S.C. § 1692g(b) by failing to provide verification of the debt and continuing its debt collection efforts after the plaintiff had disputed the debt in writing within thirty days of receiving notice of the 15 U.S.C. § 1692g debt validation rights.

(f) [*Add other allegations of FDCPA violations*]

13. As a result of the above violations of the FDCPA, the Defendants are liable to the Plaintiff for declaratory judgment that defendants' conduct violated the FDCPA, and Plaintiff's actual damages, statutory damages, costs, and attorney fees.

VI. SECOND CLAIM FOR RELIEF

14. Plaintiff repeats and realleges and incorporates by reference the foregoing paragraphs.

15. Defendants violated the state Act. Defendants' violations of the state Act include, but are not limited to, the following:

(a) The Defendants violated __ § __ by contacting a third party, the Plaintiff's employer.

(b) The Defendants violated __ § __ by engaging in the business of collecting debts and by attempting to collect an alleged debt from Plaintiff without a valid license.

16. Defendants' acts as described above were done intentionally with the purpose of coercing Plaintiff to pay the alleged debt.

17. As a result of the above violations of the state Act, the Defendants are liable to the Plaintiff for injunctive and declaratory relief and for actual damages, statutory damages, and attorney fees and costs.

WHEREFORE, Plaintiff respectfully prays that judgment be entered against the Defendant for the following:

A. Declaratory judgment that defendants' conduct violated the FDCPA, and declaratory and injunctive relief for the defendants' violations of the state Act

B. Actual damages

C. Statutory damages pursuant to 15 U.S.C. § 1692k

D. Statutory damages pursuant to __ § __

E. Costs and reasonable attorney's fees pursuant to 15 U.S.C. § 1692k and __ § __

F. For such other and further relief as may be just and proper

Respectfully submitted,

Attorney for Plaintiff

[Address]

DEMAND FOR JURY TRIAL

Please take notice that Plaintiff demands trial by jury in this action.

Attorney for Plaintiff
[*name of client*]

Appendix D Consumer Lawyers' Brief Biographies

The initial practice of consumer law is usually characterized by a lawyer's focus on developing one type of legal claim involving a single type of retailer or financer. From there, practitioners often branch into other claims and sometimes into other types of retailers. *See* Chapters 3, 5, and 7, *supra*. Many consumer law practitioners have developed another specialty before moving into consumer law and may continue to take cases in both areas. This appendix is intended to give the reader a flavor of various mixes of specialties that are practiced by consumer lawyers. The descriptions of law practices in this appendix were initially submitted with pleadings that are included in the National Consumer Law Center, *Consumer Law Pleadings* (2005 Cumulative CD-Rom and Index Guide).

Irv Ackelsberg is a consumer specialist with Community Legal Services, Inc., (CLS) in Philadelphia (3638 N. Broad Street, Philadelphia, PA 19140; phone: 215-227-2400; fax: 215-227-2435; e-mail: Iackelsberg@clsphila.org), where he has practiced for twenty-nine years and now serves as a Managing Attorney. He has extensive experience in the areas of foreclosure defense, bankruptcy, real estate, student loans and consumer fraud. In recent years he has concentrated most of his work on the predatory lending practices of the subprime mortgage industry. He successfully litigated the first reported case decided under the Home Ownership and Equity Protection Act (HOEPA), *Newton v. United Companies Financial Corp.*, 24 F. Supp. 2d 444 (E.D. Pa. 1998), and is counsel in the case that successfully used chapter 13 of the Bankruptcy Code to avoid a mandatory arbitration clause, *In re* Mintze, 2003 WL 22701020 (E.D. Pa. 2003) (awaiting decision by the Third Circuit). He has testified before Congress and the Pennsylvania legislature on predatory lending and is leading a legislative effort in Pennsylvania to stop payday lending and to reduce home foreclosures.

Mr. Ackelsberg has authored a number of consumer practice articles and is a contributor to the Pennsylvania Consumer Law treatise. He is a frequent lecturer at training events for lawyers, Legal Services clients, and the larger community. NACA named him (and his CLS colleague, Alan White) its 2004 Consumer Attorney of the Year, and he was the 2001 recipient of the Philadelphia Bar Association's Andrew Hamilton Award for exemplary service in the public interest. Mr. Ackelsberg received his B.A. from Haverford College in 1972 and his J.D. from the Rutgers-Camden Law School in 1976.

Alan A. Alop is Deputy Director of the Legal Assistance Foundation of Metropolitan Chicago (111 West Jackson, Chicago, Illinois; phone: 312-347-8310; fax: 312-341-1041). Mr. Alop has over twenty-five years experience in litigating consumer cases, including consumer fraud, RICO, collection abuse, consumer credit matters, and defense of collection matters. He is the author of *Defending Hospital Collection Cases: A Practical Guide* and was lead attorney in *Rosario v. Livaditis*, 963 F.2d 1013 (7th Cir. 1992), a successful fraud class action against a vocational school.

Mr. Alop is a 1971 graduate of the University of Chicago Law School. He worked for six years with the Duval County Legal Aid Association in Jacksonville, Florida, from 1971 to 1977 as a staff attorney and later Director of Litigation. Since 1977, he has been employed as a supervisory attorney with the Legal Assistance Foundation of Chicago (LAFC), where he specializes in consumer fraud and consumer credit cases. In 1997, he was named Deputy Director of LAFC. In 1998, the National Consumer Law Center named Mr. Alop the Ninth Annual Vern Countryman Award winner. Mr. Alop has litigated over a hundred class action cases and lectured on consumer-law-related topics.

Paul Arons operates a law office with Sharon Grace (685 Spring Street, #104, Friday Harbor, Washington; phone: 360-378-6496; fax: 360-378-6498; e-mail: lopa@rockisland.com). He began his legal career representing plaintiffs in labor and employment law disputes. In the early 1990's, he began focusing his efforts on class actions under the FDCPA, suing debt collectors who collect on dishonored checks.

Alden L. Atkins is a private attorney with Vinson & Elkins L.L.P, 1455 Pennsylvania Avenue, N.W., Suite 700, Washington, D.C. 20004; phone: 202-639-6500; fax: 202-639-6604. Mr. Atkins has twenty years of experience litigating commercial and pro bono cases. He specializes in commercial and criminal litigation and arbitration, and his clients have included one of the high-profile entities involved in the Whitewater investigation. Among his other pro bono work, he prepared numerous briefs in *Martin v. Wilks*. Mr. Atkins is a member of the New York and District of Columbia bar associations.

Charles M. Baird has a private law practice in Atlanta, Georgia (235 Peachtree Street, Suite 400, Atlanta, Georgia 30303-1400; phone: 404-287-2383; fax: 404-627-6049; e-mail: charlesmbaird@att.net). He specializes in consumer representation (individual and class actions), primarily focused on predatory mortgage lending. Mr. Baird has over thirty years of experience in consumer law. Before entering private practice, he was with the Georgia Legal Services Program and Legal Services of Greater Miami, and he also worked one summer as a staff attorney at the National Consumer Law Center. Mr. Baird was counsel for the borrower in *Rodash v. AIB Mortgage Co.*, 16 F.3d 1142 (11th Cir. 1994), a Truth in Lending case that attracted some attention and provoked Congress to enact the "Rodash fix."

Charles H. Barr of Croen & Barr L.L.P. (250 East Wisconsin Avenue, Ste. 1550, Milwaukee, WI 53202; phone: 414-225-2080/414-226-2070), received his bachelor's degree from Cornell University in 1973 and his law degree from Harvard Law School in 1977. He has been engaged in the private practice of law since graduation from law school. He is a partner in the Milwaukee, Wisconsin, firm of Croen & Barr, L.L.P., which he and Frederick R. Croen founded in 1993. Croen & Barr is a three-attorney firm that concentrates its practice in the areas of business, real estate, consumer issues, and civil trials and appeals.

Mr. Barr is the former co-chair of the Milwaukee Bar Association's Bench/Bar Court of Appeals Committee, which initiated a comprehensive review of the rules governing Wisconsin appellate courts that eventually resulted in revision of those rules. He presently serves as Chair of the MBA's Messenger Committee, which publishes the MBA's legal newspaper. He also serves on the MBA's Courts, Bench/Bar Municipal Courts, and Bench/Bar Civil Committees. His other bar activities include those in the Eastern District of Wisconsin Bar Association (member, Board of Directors), the Wisconsin Municipal Judges Association, and the Litigation and Appellate Sections of the State Bar of Wisconsin. He is the Wisconsin Contributing Editor for *ABA Survey of State Class Action Law* and a contributing author for *Wisconsin Methods of Practice* (The West Group). He has served as a Moot Court Judge in Marquette Law School and in National High School Mock Trial Tournament regional competitions. He has taught continuing legal education courses on discovery, witness preparation, civil procedure, and written advocacy and has participated in numerous bar-sponsored volunteer activities to bring information about the legal system to the general public. He has authored several articles, published in the *MBA Messenger*, including: *Unpublished Opinions:* Stare Decisis *and the Nature of Judicial Power*; *Spotlight on the Wisconsin Court of Appeals: Can the Court of Appeals Overrule, Modify or Withdraw Language from Its Previously Published Decisions?*; and *Seventh Circuit Determinations of Wisconsin Law: Prediction or Prescription?*. In May 2000, Mr. Barr was appointed the Municipal Judge in Bayside, Wisconsin, and was elected to that position in 2001 and 2004.

Nancy Barron is a partner in the firm of Kemnitzer, Anderson, Barron & Ogilvie, L.L.P. (445 Bush Street, 6th Floor, San Francisco, CA 94108). The firm has represented consumers for twenty years in automotive affairs involving lemon law, dealer and finance fraud, deceptive practices, and products liability. She has served as a California-State-Bar-approved CLE provider for seminars on lemon law litigation and the Unfair Competition Law and is author of National Consumer Law Center's *Return to Sender: Getting a Refund or Replacement for Your Lemon Car* (2000) as well as numerous legal articles. She is Chairman *emeritas* of the National Association of Consumer Advocates (NACA) and a member of Consumer Attorneys of California, the San Francisco Bar Association, and the Fulbright Alumni Association.

Peter F. Barry is a licensed attorney admitted to practice in the State of Minnesota and the owner of The Barry Law Office, Ltd. (342 County Road D East St. Paul, MN 55117-1275; phone: 651-714-8800 ext. 135; e-mail: pbarry@lawpoint.com). His practice is dedicated exclusively to protecting consumers against illegal debt-collection activity. He was recently named by his peers as a Super Lawyer® for 2003 by *Minnesota Law & Politics Magazine*. In 1996, Barry graduated from William Mitchell College of Law in St. Paul, Minnesota, where he competed nationally on the school's trial advocacy team and won top honors for his appellate work. Barry did extensive clinical work with several organizations, including the Ramsey County Public Defenders Office, Legal Assistance to Minnesota Prisoners, and the St. Paul Tenants Union. He opened his law practice directly out of law school and has been enjoying his private plaintiff's practice ever since.

Barry volunteers annually with Habitat for Humanity and the Minnesota State Bar Association's High School Mock Trial Program as a judge. He also devotes volunteer time to various William Mitchell clinical programs and maintains an ongoing pro bono legal-services commitment in the area of consumer rights. In 2003, Barry was named an adjunct Professor of Law at William Mitchell College of Law, where he now teaches consumer rights law. In addition to being admitted to practice in Minnesota and Wisconsin state and federal courts, Barry was also recently admitted to the Northern District of Texas and the Eighth Circuit Court of Appeals. He was born in San Jose, California, in 1964 and lives in St. Paul, Minnesota.

Daniel L. Berger is a partner in the New York law firm of Bernstein Litowitz Berger & Grossmann, L.L.P (1285 Avenue of the Americas, New York, NY 10019; phone: 212-554-1400; fax: 212-554-1444; e-mail: dan@BLBGLAW.com). Mr. Berger served as an Assistant Attorney General of the State of New York, Civil Rights Division, and is principally responsible for his firm's discrimination and securities practice groups. Mr. Berger currently is a member of the faculty of the Practicing Law Institute and a member of the National Employment Lawyers' Association.

Marlowe J. Blake, P.A., attorney at law (520 W. Hallandale Beach Blvd., Hallandale, FL 33009; phone: 305-670-3379). Mr. Blake concentrates on Fair Credit Reporting Act violations and general civil litigation in state and federal courts. He is AV-rated by Martindale-Hubble and is admitted to the Florida, Eleventh Circuit Court of Appeals, and to the United States District Court (Southern and Middle Districts) bars.

F. Paul Bland, Jr., is a Staff Attorney for Trial Lawyers for Public Justice, where he handles precedent-setting complex civil litigation. He is a co-author of *Consumer Arbitration Agreements: Enforceability and Other Issues* (co-published by the National Consumer Law Center and TLPJ). He is a co-chair of the National Association of Consumer Advocates. He has argued or co-argued and won nearly twenty reported decisions from federal and state courts across the nation, including cases in the U.S. Courts of Appeal for the Fourth, Fifth, and Ninth Circuits and in the high courts of Florida (two cases), Maryland (four cases), and West Virginia. He was named San Francisco Trial Lawyer of the Year in 2002 and Maryland Trial Lawyer of the Year in 2001 for his role in two cases challenging abusive mandatory arbitration clauses. Prior to coming to TLPJ, he was a plaintiffs' class action and libel defense attorney in Baltimore. In the late 1980s, he was Chief Nominations Counsel to the U.S. Senate Judiciary Committee. He graduated from Harvard Law School in 1986 and from Georgetown University in 1983.

LaBarron N. Boone practices consumer law with the firm of Beasley, Allen, Crow, Methvin, Portis & Miles, P.C. (P.O. Box 4160, Montgomery, Alabama 36103-4160; phone: 334-269-2343; fax: 334-954-7555, email: labarron.boone@beasleyallen.com). His areas of practice include consumer fraud, insurance litigation, personal injury law, products liability law, and product liability. He is a graduate of the University of Alabama Law School (J.D., 1995) and Auburn University (B.I.E., 1990).

Mr. LaBarron concentrates his practice on product liability, consumer fraud, and personal injury. He is the recipient of the "Chairman's Award of Excellence" presented by MCDC Young Democrats on September 28, 2000. He is a lecturer for The Association of Trial Lawyers of America. He was president of Kappa Alpha Psi Fraternity. He was featured in the April 2001 edition of the Kappa Alpha Psi Journal discussing the law and how it relates to consumer issues. Mr. LaBarron was also featured in the December 1999 issue of Jet Magazine, which focused both on victories for consumers and on two cases he tried—*Merriweather v. Whirlpool* and *Aultman v. Terex Telelect*—that resulted in verdicts of $581 and $116 million, respectively. A cover story was done on Mr. LaBarron in the Urban Metro June 2000 issue entitled *Lawyer Makes Big Strides in Alabama's America's Community*. He was the 2000–2001 President of the Capital City Bar Association and also serves as president of the Alabama Lawyers Association.

Rand Bragg is a private attorney whose offices are at Horwitz, Horwitz & Associates (25 East Washington Street, Suite 900, Chicago, IL 60602; phone: 312-372-8822; fax: 312-372-1673; e-mail: rand@horwitzlaw.com). He specializes in consumers' rights class action litigation, particularly debt collection abuse pursuant to the Fair Debt Collection Practices Act. Previously, Mr. Bragg was a litigation coordinator with the UAW Legal Services Plans and practiced with Legal Services Corporation-funded programs in Pennsylvania and West Virginia. He graduated from West Virginia University College of Law in 1973 and has practiced law in West Virginia, Pennsylvania, Delaware, and Illinois as well as many federal courts. Since 1989, Mr. Bragg has co-authored National Consumer Law Center's *Fair Debt Collection* and annual supplements. Since 1995, he has written the chapter entitled "Fair Debt Collection Practices Act" for Ohio Consumer Law. Mr. Bragg has lectured and conducted trainings on the Fair Debt Collection Practices Act for various groups, including NCLC and NACA (1992–2005); Student Legal Services (2004); Montana Consumer Law Summit (2004); Practicing Law Institute (2000); Chicago Bar Association (1996, 1999, and 2001); Kansas City Metropolitan Bar Association (1996); Commercial Law League (1992); and UAW Legal Services Plans (1985–1992).

Brian Bromberg is in private practice at Brian L. Bromberg, P.C. (40 Exchange Place, Suite 2010, New York, NY 10005; phone: 212-248-7906; fax: 212-248-7908; e-mail: brian@brianbromberg.com) and has been a NACA member since 2001.

Paul A. Brooks is an attorney, working for the past nine years with Community Legal Services, Inc. (1424 Chestnut St., Fifth Floor, Philadelphia, PA 19102; phone: 215-981-3826; fax: 215-981-0434). He specializes in consumer and bankruptcy law. Mr. Brooks is a member of the Pennsylvania state and federal bars.

Bernard Brown has been in private practice in Kansas City since 1980 and is presently at the Brown Law Firm (3100 Broadway, Suite 223, Kansas City, MO 64111; phone: 816-960-4777; fax: 816-960-6777; e-mail: brlawofc@swbell.net). Between 1984 and 1996 his office was devoted entirely to representing victims of car fraud—such as fraudulent sales of rebuilt wrecks and cars with odometer rollbacks. More recently he also has worked on class actions relating to vehicle sales and financing and on home equity fraud cases. A sizable number of his cases have resulted in published court decisions of significance in these areas of the law.

Mr. Brown started doing public interest work when he was in college, beginning with volunteer work at the headquarters of Common Cause in Washington, D.C. He has worked regularly with National Consumer Law Center staff for many years and has contributed to or written many articles relating to consumer law. He is a founding member of the National Association of Consumer Advocates (NACA) and one of its two original co-chairs and he currently serves on the NACA board. He has worked closely on a number of issues with other leading consumer groups (Consumers Union, Consumer Federation of America, Public Citizen, U.S. PIRG, Center for Auto Safety, and Consumers for Auto Reliability and Safety) and has drafted legislation and testified for these groups before Congress and state legislatures. He is extensively involved in networking and in the idea-sharing efforts of consumer advocate attorneys across the country, and he regularly provides instruction for other attorneys, consumer advocates, and law enforcement personnel on various consumer law issues. He often is consulted by members of local and national media regarding car industry consumer issues. He also serves as an adjunct law school professor teaching consumer protection law.

Karen Brown is a staff attorney with Atlanta Legal Aid Society, Inc. Home Defense Program (340 West Ponce de Leon Avenue, Decatur, GA 30030; phone: 404-377-0701; fax: 404-377-2349). Her work includes representation of low-income and elderly homeowners in cases involving home improvement and predatory mortgage lending scams. Ms. Brown previously served as a staff attorney in Atlanta Legal Aid Society's Senior Citizens Law Project. She has been involved in a number of major litigation cases in the consumer area including pending lawsuits against Ford Consumer Finance Company regarding alleged violations of RESPA mortgage broker kickback provisions. Ms. Brown is a founding member and Vice Chair of the Consumer Law Center of the South and a participant in the Housing Action Team of Atlantans Building Leadership Through Empowerment.

Edward D. Buckley, III, is a founding partner in the law firm of Buckley and Klein, L.L.P. He was born in Atlanta, Georgia, and grew up in the Sandy Springs area. He is a 1978 graduate of the College of Charleston in Charleston, South Carolina, and a 1983 graduate of Emory University School of Law. He had worked his way through college and law school as a carpenter (building houses and hospitals) and a legal writing instructor. He is familiar with the trials and tribulations of working people and has built his law practice advocating their interests, specializing in civil rights and employment discrimination cases. He has represented people from virtually every walk of life, including truckers, secretaries, food industry workers, technicians, salespeople, teachers, professors, stockbrokers, CEOs, CFOs, dock-workers, and even other lawyers. Mr. Buckley is ranked as one of "America's Leading Business Lawyers" by Chambers and Partners and as a "Super Lawyer" by *Atlanta Magazine*. He is also listed in *Martindale-Hubbell's Bar Register of Preeminent Lawyers*.

Mr. Buckley is a trial lawyer. He has won six- and seven-figure verdicts in the federal court system in cases involving race discrimination, sex discrimination, sexual harassment and retaliation. He has also settled numerous cases on behalf of employees for six and seven-figure sums. He has obtained injunctive relief for employees who have been treated unfairly in the workplace. He has served as an advocate for employees in mediations and arbitrations. Mr. Buckley is past president of the Georgia affiliate of the National Employment Lawyers Association. He is president of the Atlanta Bar Association Labor and Employment Section. A popular speaker, Mr. Buckley recently chaired the seminars, "Trial of a Race Discrimination Case" and "Trial of a Sexual Harassment Case." He has been selected to participate in mock trials for the American Bar Association Labor and Employment Section and has spoken at national seminars for consumer groups and employment rights groups.

Mr. Buckley writes frequently and has authored numerous articles and papers on employment law and civil rights law as well as book chapters. He has an AV rating by Martindale-Hubbell and is admitted to practice in all state courts, appellate courts, and federal district courts in the State of Georgia and in the Eleventh Circuit Court of Appeals in the United States Supreme Court.

Mr. Buckley lives in Decatur, Georgia, with his wife, Patty, and his daughter, Hope. When not practicing law, he enjoys fishing, canoeing and other outdoor activities. Recently, working in conjunction with various charities, he has developed a passion for bringing potable water to people who otherwise would not have it in remote regions of the Caribbean.

Ronald L. Burdge is an attorney with the Burdge Law Office Co., L.P.A. (2299 Miamisburg Centerville Road, Dayton, OH 45459; phone: 937-432-9500; fax: 520-432-9503; e-mail: Ron@OhioLemonLaw.com; websites: www.OhioLemonLaw.com, www.RvLemonLaw.com, www.KentuckyLemonLaw.com, www.OhioConsumerLaw.com and others; co-counseling and coaching website: www.TheLawCoach.com). Ronald L. Burdge is in the private practice of law in Dayton, Ohio, and is known throughout Ohio as a leading consumer law attorney who has represented literally thousands of consumers in "lemon" car lawsuits over the last twenty years and who actively co-counsels and coaches other consumer law attorneys. He has authored articles and lectured on the Ohio Lemon Law, Assistive Device Lemon Laws, and Recreation Vehicle Lemon Laws. Although the majority of his court cases have involved defective motor vehicle litigation, he has also represented consumers in UDAP, product defect, odometer tampering, contract breach, fraud, and commercial litigation in both state and federal courts throughout Ohio, in Indiana and Kentucky. With extensive trial and appellate experience related to motor vehicles and dealership business practices, he has also successfully argued cases in various courts of appeals and the Ohio Supreme Court.

He was admitted to the Ohio Bar in 1978. His bar admissions include all Ohio state courts, several United States District Courts (Ohio and Indiana), Sixth Circuit Court of Appeals, and the United States Supreme Court. He is a member of numerous bar associations, has obtained several multi-million dollar verdicts, and has handled numerous ground-breaking consumer law and lemon law cases.

The Law Offices of **Sheldon V. Burman**, P.C. (110 East 59th Street, 23rd Floor, New York, NY 10022; phone: 212-935-1600; fax: 212-223-4911), with a concentration in the consumer class action field, has a national reputation, having been involved in landmark litigation in that area. Sheldon V. Burman is a graduate of New York University School of Law and has an extensive background as a lecturer and author of numerous articles on consumer class actions and consumer law. Reported cases in which the firm has been a lead counsel in consumer class actions include *Branch v. Crabtree*, 197 A.D.2d 557, 603 N.Y.S.2d 490 (2d Dept. 1994); *Weinberg v. Hertz Corp.*, 69 N.Y.2 979, 516 N.Y.S.2d 652 (1987), *aff'g*, 116 A.D.2d 1, 499 N.Y.S.2d 693 (1st Dept. 1986); *Weinberg v. Sprint*, 165 F.R.D. 431 (D.N.J. 1996); *Eisen v. Carlisle & Jacquelin*, 417 U.S. 156 (1974) (amicus curiae brief on behalf of N.Y.S. Trial Lawyers Association); *Karlin v. IVF America, Inc.*, 93 N.Y.2d 282, 690 N.Y.S.2d 495 (Ct. App. 1999); *Hayes v. County Bank*, 286 A.D.2d 371, 728 N.Y.S.2d 709 (A.D. 2d Dept. 2001), *aff'g*. 185 Misc.2d 414, 713 N.Y.S.2d 267 (Sup. Queens 2000); *Selby v Principal Mutual*, 197 F.R.D. 48 (S.D.N.Y. 2000); *Colbert v. Rank America, Inc.*, 273 A.D.2 209, 709 N.Y.S.2d (A.D.2 Dept, 2OOO). Mr. Burman's lectures include: "Current Class Action Litigation," Class Action Committee, N.Y.S. Bar Association, Jan. 1998; "Class Action Update," Consumer Affairs Committee, N.Y. County Lawyer's Association, Oct. 1996; "Legal Safari Through the Class Action Jungle," National Consumer Law Center Conference, Chicago, Illinois, Oct. 1993; "Arbitration and Class Actions," National Association of Consumer Agency Administrators, Chicago, Illinois, June 2000; and "Consumer Class Actions," Consumer Affairs Committee, Association of the Bar of the City of New York, February 2000. Mr. Burman has contributed a variety of publications: National Consumer Law Center, *Consumer Class Actions: A Practical Litigation Guide* (3d ed. 1995); *Class Actions on behalf of Bank Customers*, N.Y.S.B.A. Journal (Dec. 1987); *Newberg on Class Actions (2d ed.)*, New York Law Journal, p. 2 (June 6, 1986) (book review); *Class Actions in New York*; Class Actions, 23 Syracuse L. Rev. 53; and *A Terminal Case Gets Statutory Relief*, 4 Class Action Reports (May–June, 1975). He is a founding member of the National Association of Consumer Advocates; a former member of the editorial board of *Class Action Reports*; and a member of the Consumer Affairs Committees, Association of the Bar of the City of New York, and New York County Lawyers Association.

Linda J. Cahn is in private practice in New York City, where she is developing a consumer protection and healthcare litigation practice. She graduated *cum laude* from Princeton University in 1976 and graduated with honors from Hofstra Law School in 1979. She was admitted to the Bar of the state of New York in 1980 and thereafter to the Eastern and Southern Districts of New York. She clerked for a year in the Eastern District and practiced law with several firms in the interim.

Eric M. Carlson is an attorney in the Los Angeles office of the National Senior Citizens Law Center (3435 Wilshire Blvd., Suite 2860, Los Angeles, CA 90010; phone: 213-639-0930).

Mr. Carlson specializes in the law governing long-term care facilities, including nursing homes and assisted-living facilities. He counsels attorneys from across the country in issues relating to long-term care and also participates in litigation on residents' behalf. He was co-counsel in *Podolsky v. First Healthcare Corp.*, 50 Cal. App. 4th 632, 58 Cal. Rptr. 2d 89 (1996), which established that the guarantee agreements that had been used routinely by nursing facilities were illegal and unenforceable.

Mr. Carlson is the author of numerous publications and articles, including *Long Term Care Advocacy*, the leading legal treatise on long-term care issues. He is the principal author of NSCLC's *Nursing Home Law Letter*, a comprehensive bimonthly summary of developments in long-term care. He speaks regularly across the country on issues relating to long-term care. He has spoken at numerous national conferences and at several programs organized by state government agencies.

Mr. Carlson received his B.A. degree from the University of Minnesota in 1982 and his J.D. degree from the Boalt Hall School of Law at the University of California at Berkeley in 1988.

Steve R. Conley practices consumer law in Metairie, Louisiana (3350 Ridgelake Drive, Suite 200 Metairie, Louisiana 70002; phone: 504-734-9804; fax: 504-733-1744). He has been a member of the National Association of Consumer Advocates since 1998. Since 1992, he has had a solo practice concentrating on consumer protection litigation under a variety of federal and state laws, including the Fair Debt Collection Practices Act, Truth in Lending Act, Fair Credit Reporting Act, and Equal Credit Opportunity Act. He graduated from the Tulane University School of Law with a J.D. in 1991 and served on the Tulane Law Review. His publications include *Lejune v. Rayne Branch Hospital: Allowing Bystander Mental Anguish Claims in Louisiana*, 65 Tul. L. Rev. 918 (1991).

Eric L. Crandall is an attorney practicing at 275 South Third Street, Suite 101, Stillwater, Minnesota 55082; phone: 651-430-8187; fax: 651-439-1034; e-mail: ericleighton@mcleodusa.net. His practice is focused on representing consumers in the areas of unfair debt collection practices, privacy rights, mortgage fraud, and credit insurance abuse. Mr. Crandall is a member of the bars of, and licensed to practice in, Minnesota and Wisconsin. Mr. Crandall is a 1988 graduate of William Mitchell College of Law, Saint Paul, Minnesota.

Mark A. Chavez received his Juris Doctorate degree from Stanford Law School in 1979. During law school he served as a Judicial Extern for the Honorable Mathew O. Tobriner, then Senior Associate Justice of the California Supreme Court. Mr. Chavez was also a co-founder and the first Managing Editor of the Stanford Environmental Law Annual and a founding member of the Stanford Public Interest Law Foundation.

Mr. Chavez was selected through the Attorney General's Honors Program and joined the Civil Division of the United States Department of Justice in Washington, D.C., after graduating from law school. He spent three years representing the United States in labor, employment, housing, and national security cases filed in federal courts around the country. In 1983, Mr. Chavez entered private practice, working first at Pillsbury, Madison & Sutro and subsequently at Farrow, Bramson, Chavez & Baskin. In 1994, Mr. Chavez founded the law firm of Chavez & Gertler, L.L.P.

In the course of his career, Mr. Chavez has represented plaintiffs in a wide variety of class actions, private attorney general cases, and other complex civil litigation matters. His significant class action experience before the California Supreme Court includes arguing *Olszeweski v. ScrippsHealth*, 30 Cal. 4th 798 (2003) and *Linder v. Thrifty Oil*, 23 Cal. 4th 429 (2000) and acting as co-counsel for the plaintiff class in *Briseno v. Washington Mutual*, 24 Cal. 4th 906 (2001). He has served or is currently serving as lead or co-lead counsel in over eighty other class actions filed in federal and state courts in Arizona, California, Colorado, Florida, Idaho, Missouri, New Jersey, Ohio, Tennessee, and Washington. These class actions have produced some of the largest recoveries ever achieved in consumer cases. For example, see *Transouth Cases* (Judicial Council Coordination Proceeding No. 4237) ($76.6 million); *Moultrie v. Nissan Motor Acceptance Corp.* (San Francisco Superior Court No. 302601)

($68.5 million); *Clark, et al. v. Ford Motor Credit Company* (Alameda Superior Court No. 6745257) ($58.5 million).

Mr. Chavez regularly lectures on consumer and class action issues and has been widely recognized for his expertise in these areas. In recent years, he has given presentations at the annual convention of the American Bar Association, the National Consumer Rights Litigation Conference, the annual convention of the State Bar of California, the annual convention of the Consumer Attorneys of California, the California Bankers Association Conference, and the Banking Litigation Seminar of the Association of the Bar of the City of New York. For many years, he was the co-chair of the Practising Law Institute's Consumer Financial Services Litigation Program in New York and San Francisco, and he currently is a member of the Editorial Board of *Consumer Financial Services Law Reporter*.

Mr. Chavez was one of the eight founders of the National Association of Consumer Advocates and is its former co-chair. He serves on the boards of the National Consumer Law Center and the Stanford Public Interest Law Foundation. Mr. Chavez is AV-rated by Martindale-Hubbell.

Andrew Cogdell is a senior managing attorney with Legal Aid of North Carolina, Inc. (211 East Union Street, Morganton, NC 28655-3449; phone: 828-437-8280; fax: 828-437-9397). He specializes in federally subsidized housing and private landlord/tenant law. Mr. Cogdell briefed and argued *Stanley v. Moore* before the Supreme Court of North Carolina, 454 S.E.2d 225 (1995). He is a member of the North Carolina state bar and, while he still considers himself a novice at consumer law, has applied consumer law remedies to housing cases in a number of contexts.

Cathleen M. Combs is a named partner in the Chicago law firm of Edelman, Combs and Latturner, which practices in the area of consumer class actions. She formerly supervised the Northwest office of the Legal Assistance Foundation of Chicago, where she was lead or co-counsel in class actions in the areas of unemployment compensation, prison law, social security law, and consumer law. Decisions in which she has argued include:

—*Bessette v. Avco Financial Services*, 230 F. 3d 439 (1st Cir. 2000) (held that bankruptcy debtor induced to pay a discharged debt by means of an invalid reaffirmation agreement may sue to recover the payment)

—*Emery v. American General*, 71 F.3d 1343 (7th Cir. 1995) (practice of "loan flipping," in which consumers are solicited for new loans and are then refinanced with "short" credits for unearned finance charges and insurance premiums being given through use of the "Rule of 78s," found to state a claim for violation of mail fraud statute)

—*Miller v. McCalla Raymer*, 214 F. 3d 872 (7th Cir.) (held that demand letter by mortgage foreclosure attorneys which failed to inform the debtor the exact amount due under a mortgage in default violated the FDCPA).

Jean Constantine-Davis has been an attorney with the AARP and AARP Foundation (601 E Street NW, Washington, DC 20049; phone: 202-434-2158; fax: 202-434-6424) since 1985. She is currently working in the Foundation's litigation group on issues involving fraudulent and predatory mortgage lending practices targeted at elderly homeowners. Prior to joining the litigation group, Ms. Constantine-Davis worked for AARP's Legal Counsel for the Elderly representing low-income elderly residents of the District of Columbia who were threatened with eviction and foreclosure on their homes. In 1995, she was awarded the Jerrold Scoutt Prize for her work on behalf of the low-income and vulnerable elderly population of D.C. Ms. Constantine-Davis has been a consumer fellow of the American Bar Association's Consumer Financial Services Committee since 1995.

Frank N. Darras is a partner with the law firm of Shernoff Bidart & Darras, L.L.P. and heads the firm's Health and Disability Department. As one of the nation's top civil litigators specializing in bad faith insurance claims, Mr. Darras has made a career out of holding insurance companies accountable for their short-term, long-term, and individual disability policies.

Having evaluated over 6000 disability cases since the start of his career, Mr. Darras is widely recognized as one of the nation's foremost authorities on litigating disability claims. Mr. Darras also represents policyholders in bad-faith disputes concerning denials of cutting-edge medical procedures and skilled nursing care, restricted access to specialists, and pre-existing condition exclusions.

Mr. Darras is a frequent lecturer and media commentator on insurance bad faith, including disability coverage issues, bad faith, HMO liability, and ERISA preemption. Mr. Darras has been featured in *The Wall Street Journal*, *Medical Economics*, and *Lawyers Weekly USA* and is a regular contributor to Mealey Publications and Bottom Line Personal. Among his numerous articles, Mr. Darras has authored *Disabling the Disability Carrier: The Insurers' Top 10 Defenses and How to Defeat Them*, *Insureds' Health v. Insurers' Wealth: Bad Faith in the Healthcare Industry*, and *The Iceberg Is Melting: ERISA Preemption and How To Avoid It*. Mr. Darras has been a featured speaker for various conferences, including the Association of Trial Lawyers of America, the American Bar Association, the American Conference Institute, National Consumer Law Center, and Consumer Attorneys of California.

Mr. Darras has received from Martindale-Hubbell, an internationally recognized independent attorney rating organization, its highest rating ("AV"), which signifies that Mr. Darras is an attorney recognized for the highest levels of skill and integrity. Mr. Darras is also listed in The National Registry of Who's Who. Mr. Darras serves as President of the Board of Directors of the Western State University College of Law Foundation.

Mr. Darras received his J.D. from Western State University in 1986 and attended Emory University as an undergraduate. Before joining the firm in 1988, Mr. Darras trained with the Los Angeles County District Attorney's Office Trial Attorney Project. Mr. Darras is a member of the Los Angeles County, San Bernardino County, and American Bar Associations, the Association of Trial Lawyers of America, Trial Lawyers for Public Justice, Consumer Attorneys of California, and Consumer Attorneys Association of Los Angeles. He has sat on the American Trial Lawyers Executive Board on Insurance Litigation and is a faculty member at the National College of Advocacy of the Association of Trial Lawyers of America and currently co-chairs the Bad Faith Litigation Group of the Association. Frank N. Darras may be reached at Shernoff Bidart & Darras, 600 S. Indian Hill Blvd., Claremont, CA 91711; phone: 909-621-4935; e-mail: fdarras@shernoff.com.

Susan L. DeJarnatt began teaching legal research and writing at Temple in July 1996. Before entering teaching full time, she was a staff attorney from 1985 to 1996 at Community Legal Services, Inc. in Philadelphia, Pennsylvania, specializing in consumer protection and housing issues; and, from 1982 to 1984, she was an associate at the Philadelphia law firm of Litvin, Blumberg, Matusow and Young. Professor L. DeJarnatt also taught legal research and writing as an adjunct instructor at Rutgers-Camden School of Law from 1991 to 1995. She has served as faculty and co-author of course materials for numerous continuing legal education programs on consumer protection, housing, and bankruptcy issues sponsored by the Pennsylvania Bar Institute, the Eastern District of Pennsylvania Bankruptcy Conference, the Philadelphia Bar Education Center, and the Consumer-Housing Task Force of Pennsylvania Legal Services. Professor DeJarnatt received a B.A. from Oberlin College in 1974 and received a J.D. *magna cum laude* from Temple University School of Law in 1980. Following graduation from law school, she served for two years as law clerk to the Honorable Joseph S. Lord, III, Chief Judge of the Eastern District of Pennsylvania.

Dan Deneen of Deneen & Deneen (202 S. Eldorado Road, Bloomington, IL 61704; phone: 309-663-0555; fax: 309-663-0556) is an attorney in Bloomington, Illinois, concentrating in probate and estate planning, commercial law, and some consumer law. He has been involved in cases relating to automobile manufacturers, dealers, and other retailers. His published works include *Automobile Finance, Warranty, and Insurance Extras: What the Consumer Should Know and How an Attorney Can Attack the Deceptive Practices*, 6 Loyola Consumer Law Reporter 5 (1993); *900-Number Services: Abuses, Regulation and Relief*, 80 Ill. Bar J. 406 (1992); and Chapter 35 of *Causes of Action, Breaches of Fiduciary Duty* (Illinois Institute of Continuing Legal Education).

Thomas A. Dickerson is a Judge on the Westchester County Court, State of New York; Chairman of the Class Action Committee, New York State Bar Association, 1985–present; Member, Westchester County Bar Association; Member, Consumer Affairs Committee, 1986–1989, 1997–1999, 2000–2002; Association of the Bar of the City of New York; Member of the Editorial Boards of *Class Action Reports* and International Travel Law Journal.

Judge Dickerson has an M.B.A. from the Johnson Graduate School of Management, Cornell University, 1973, and a J.D. from Cornell Law School, 1973. He practiced law in New York City from 1975 through 1993, at which time he became Judge. During his years as a practicing attorney he specialized in litigation, consumer law, travel law, and class actions. He has written over two hundred legal articles, most frequently on class actions and travel law. Thomas A. Dickerson is the author of *Travel Law* (Law Journal Press 1981–2002) and *Class Actions: The Law of 50 States* (Law Journal Press 1988–2002). His webpages at http://members.aol.com/judgetad/index.html and http:www.classactionlitigation.com/articles_of_interest.htm provide additional information about his publications and decisions.

Tom Domonoske of the Law Offices of Dale Pittman (461 Lee Avenue, Harrisonburg, VA 22802; phone: 540-442-8616; fax: 540-442-7706) began practicing law in California in 1990 before moving to North Carolina, where he taught classes at the University of North Carolina Law School. He then practiced as a legal aid lawyer with the Virginia Legal Aid Society at its Farmville office from 1993 to 1996. From July 1996 through August 2000, he was a Senior Lecturing Fellow at Duke Law School. While at Duke, he maintained a small consumer law practice in Virginia through an Of Counsel relationship with the Law Office of Dale W. Pittman. He is now back in full-time practice of law in Virginia. His primary emphasis is on auto fraud and mobile home fraud issues, the reason being that both involve Certificates of Titles that require prescribed forms and both involve dealer-arranged financing. He has published articles about the titling laws and illegal lease termination provisions in NACA's *The Consumer Law Advocate* as well an article on processing fees in car sales in the Virginia Trial Lawyers Association's *The Journal*. Additionally, he has contributed to drafting new subsections of NCLC's manual, *Truth in Lending*. In the past four years, he has given over twenty consumer law trainings at various conferences around the country.

Michael D. Donovan, a founding member of the Philadelphia law firm of Donovan Searles, L.L.C., is admitted to practice before the Supreme Court of the United States; the United States Courts of Appeals for the Second, Third, Eighth, Ninth, and Tenth Circuits; the United States District Court for the Eastern District of Pennsylvania; the United States District Courts for the Southern and Eastern Districts of New York; as well as the state courts of Pennsylvania and New York and the courts of Washington, D.C. He is a graduate of Vermont Law School (J.D. *cum laude* 1984) and Syracuse University (A.B. 1981). He was the Head Notes Editor and a staff member of the Vermont Law Review from 1982 through 1984. While on the Law Review, he authored Note, *Zoning Variance Administration in Vermont*, 8 Vt. L. Rev. 370 (1984). Following graduation from law school, Mr. Donovan was an attorney with the Securities and Exchange Commission in Washington, D.C., where he prosecuted numerous securities cases and enforcement matters, including injunctive and disciplinary actions against public companies, broker/dealers, and accounting firms. Mr. Donovan has co-authored *Preserving Judicial Recourse for Consumers: How to Combat Overreaching Arbitration Clauses*, 10 Loyola Consumer L. Rev. 269 (1998); *The Overlooked Victims of the Thrift Crisis*, *Miami Rev.*, Feb. 13, 1990, and *Conspiracy of Silence: Why S&L Regulators Can't Always Be Trusted*, Legal Times, Feb. 5, 1990.

Mr. Donovan has served as co-lead counsel in the following securities class actions: *In re Sunterra Corp. Securities Litigation*, No. 6:00-cv-79-Orl-28B (M.D. Fla. 2000) (settled for $5,450,000); *In re: Worldport Communications, Inc. Securities Litigation*, No. 1-99-CV-1817-CC (N.D. Ga. 2001) (settled for $5,100,000); *Lines v. Marble Financial Corp.*, Nos. 90-23 and 90-100 (D. Vt. 1991) (settled for $2 million together with substantial changes to the company's loan loss reserve procedures); *Jones v. Amdura Corp.*, No. 90-F-167 (D. Colo. 1991) (action against directors settled for $4,962,500 and against company after bankruptcy for $1.2 million); *In re Columbia Shareholders Litigation* (Del. Ch. 1991) (merger case settled for $2 per share increase in amount paid to shareholders); *Rosen v. Fidelity Investments*, [1995–1996] Fed. Sec. L. Rep. ¶ 98,949 (E.D. Pa. Nov. 28, 1995) (opinion certifying class of mutual fund purchasers); *Selis v. KTI, Inc.*, No. 2:00 CV 1478 (JCL) (D.N.J. 2000) (settled for $3.8 million). In addition, Mr. Donovan has had a substantial role in the prosecution of the following cases, among others: *In re Trustcorp Securities Litigation*, No. 3:89-CV-7139 (N.D. Ohio 1990) (settled for $5,600,000); *Moskowitz v. Lopp*, 128 F.R.D. 624 (E.D. Pa. 1989) (opinion certifying class of stock and option purchasers in fraud on the market and insider trading case); *In re Hercules Corporation Securities Litigation*, No. 90-442 (D. Del. 1992) (settled for $17.25 million).

In the area of consumer justice, Mr. Donovan was one of three lead trial counsel in *Samuel-Bassett v. Kia Motors America, Inc.*, in which a Philadelphia jury rendered a $5,600,000 verdict on behalf of a Pennsylvania class of Kia Sephia purchasers/lessees alleging breach of express warranty and Magnuson-Moss violations arising from defective brakes on the Sephia cars. Mr. Donovan has also argued before the Supreme Court of the United States in *Smiley v. Citibank (South Dakota), N.A.*, No. 95-860, 116 S. Ct. 806 (argued Apr. 24, 1996); obtained favorable appellate rulings from the New Jersey Supreme Court in *Sherman v. Citibank (South Dakota), N.A.*, 668 A.2d 1036 (N.J. 1995) and *Hunter v. Greenwood Trust Co.*, 668 A.2d 1067 (N.J. 1995); and obtained favorable appellate rulings from the Pennsylvania Superior Court in *In re Citibank Credit Card Litigation*, 653 A.2d 39 (Pa. Super. 1995) and *Gadon v. Chase Manhattan Bank, N.A.*, 653 A.2d 43 (Pa. Super. 1995). Recently, Mr. Donovan obtained a landmark Truth in Lending Act decision from the Court of Appeals for the Third Circuit in *Rossman v. Fleet Bank* (R.I.), N.A., 280 F.3d 384 (3d Cir. 2002), in which it was held that a bank may not change a credit card promise of no annual fee. He also obtained landmark decisions from the Appellate Division of the New Jersey Superior Court and the New Jersey Supreme Court in *Lemelledo v. Beneficial Finance Co.*, 674 A.2d 582 (N.J. App. Div. 1996), *aff'd*, 150 N.J. 255, 696 A.2d 546 (N.J. 1997), concerning loan and insurance packing.

Mr. Donovan has appeared as a panel speaker at the Pennsylvania Bar Institute's Banking Law Update, the Practicing Law Institute's Financial Services Litigation Forum, the Consumer Credit Regulation Forum of the New Jersey Bar Association, and the National Consumer Rights Litigation Conference sponsored by the National Consumer Law Center. Mr. Donovan is a member of the American Bar Association (Litigation and Business Law Sections), the Pennsylvania Bar Association, the New York Bar Association, and the District of Columbia Bar Association. He is the Chair of the Consumer Law Subcommittee of the ABA Litigation Section's Class Actions and Derivative Suits Committee. He is also the former Vice Chair of the National Association of Consumer Advocates and an active member of Trial Lawyers for Public Justice.

Lynn Drysdale has been a staff attorney for seventy years with Jacksonville Area Legal Aid, Inc. (126 West Adams Street, Jacksonville, FL 32202; phone: 904-356-8371, 306; fax: 904-224-7050; e-mail: lynn.drysdale@jaxlegalaid.org). Her focus is in the area of consumer finance and bankruptcy with an emphasis on asset preservation and community economic development, fringe lenders, unfair and deceptive consumer practices, debt collection, and other consumer concerns raised by low-income individuals. She is involved in litigation, legislative advocacy, and community education. Ms. Drysdale is a 1985 graduate of the University of Florida College of Law. She is also a licensed mediator.

Daniel A. Edelman is a principal in Edelman, Combs, Latturner & Goodwin, L.L.C. (120 South LaSalle Street, 18th Floor, Chicago, IL 60603-3403); website: www.edcombs.com; e-mail: edcombs@aol.com). He is a 1976 graduate of the University of Chicago Law School. From 1976 to 1981, he was an associate at the Chicago office of Kirkland & Ellis was heavily involved in the defense of consumer class action litigation (such as the General Motors Engine Interchange cases). In 1981, he became an associate at Reuben & Proctor, a medium-sized firm formed by some former Kirkland & Ellis lawyers, and was made a partner there in 1982. Since the end of 1985, he has been in private practice in downtown Chicago. Virtually all of his practice involves litigation on behalf of consumers.

Mr. Edelman is the author or co-author of numerous publications on class actions and consumer protection law, including *Predatory Lending Litigation in Illinois* (2001); the second (1990) through fifth (2002) editions of National Consumer Law Center's *Consumer Class Action*; *Payday Loans: Big Interest Rates and Little Regulation*, 11 Loy. Consumer L. Rptr. 14 (1999); Chicago Bar Association's *Fair Debt Collection Practices Act Update 1999* (1999); *An Overview of the Fair Debt Collection Practices Act*, in Financial Services Litigation, Practicing Law Institute (1999); *Consumer Fraud and Insurance Claims*, in Bad Faith and Extracontractual Damage Claims in Insurance Litigation, Chicago Bar Ass'n 1992; Chapter 8 of Ohio Consumer Law's *Fair Debt Collection Practices Act* (1995 ed.); *Fair Debt Collection: The Need for Private Enforcement*, 7 Loy. Consumer L. Rptr. 89 (1995); *The Fair Debt Collection Practices Act: Recent Developments*, 8 Loy. Consumer L. Rptr. 303 (1996); *Residential Mortgage Litigation*, in Financial Services Litigation, Practicing Law Institute (1996); *Automobile Leasing: Problems and Solutions*, 7 Loy. Consumer L. Rptr. 14 (1994); *Current Trends in Residential Mortgage Litigation*, 12 Rev. of Banking & Financial Services 71 (1996); *Applicability of Illinois Consumer Fraud Act in Favor of Out-of-State Consumers*, 8 Loy. Consumer L. Rptr. 27 (1996); Chicago Bar Association's *Illinois Consumer Law* (1996).

Veronika Fabian is a law graduate of the University of Michigan Law School in 1993 and also holds a B.A. from Cornell University in 1990. She worked at DNA People's Legal Services, Inc., from 1994 to 2003 and was the Director of Consumer Law Project from 1996–2003. She was awarded the Sharon A. Fullmer Legal Aid Attorney of the Year Award in 2003. In March of 2003, she joined the firm of Choi & Fabian, P.L.C., where she continues to focus on a wide variety of consumer protection cases. She has extensive litigation experience in wrongful repossession, Indian law, Truth in Lending Act, consumer fraud, breach of warranty, Fair Credit Reporting Act, and the Fair Debt Collection Practices Act. Her efforts have resulted in the following published opinions: *Walker v. Gallegos*, 167 F. Supp. 2d 1105 (D. Ariz. 2001); *Wide Ruins Community School, Inc. v. Stago*, 281 F. Supp. 2d 1086 (D. Ariz. 2003); *Howell v. Midway Holdings, Inc.*, 362 F. Supp. 1158 (D. Ariz. 2005).

Joanne S. Faulkner is in solo private practice in New Haven Connecticut, that is restricted to consumer matters, preferably for persons who cannot afford to pay a lawyer. In October 2002, she received the prestigious Vern Countryman Award from the National Consumer Law Center "for excellence and dedication in the practice of consumer law on behalf of low-income consumers."

She is a past chair of the Consumer Law Section of the Connecticut Bar Association and edited its Newsletter for many years. She was a member of the Federal Reserve Board's Consumer Advisory Council and has served on advisory committees to the Connecticut Law Revision Commission. She was on the Board of Directors of the National Consumer Law Center (NCLC) and is a trustee thereof. Ms. Faulkner has lectured for the Connecticut Bar Association on consumer laws and has assisted NCLC in editing various manuals, including *Truth in Lending*, *Automobile Fraud*, *Credit Discrimination*, *Fair Credit Reporting Act*, *Fair Debt Collection*, and their respective supplements.

Her appellate successes include *Heintz v. Jenkins*, 514 U.S. 291 (1995) (FDCPA); *Connecticut v. Doehr*, 501 U.S. 1 (1991) (due process, prejudgment attachments); *Clomon v. Jackson*, 988 F.2d 1314 (2d Cir. 1993) (FDCPA violated by attorney who allows collection agency to use his name); *Bentley v. Great Lakes Collection Bureau, Inc.*, 6 F. 3d 60 (2d Cir. 1994) (FDCPA violated by threat of legal action when no action intended); *Nelson v. Chase Manhattan Mortgage Corp.*, 282 F.3d 1057 (9th Cir. 2002); *Jacobs v. Healey Ford-Subaru*, Inc., 231 Conn. 707 (1995) (statutory damages under both RISFA and UCC for repossession violations).

Ms. Faulkner has co-authored amicus briefs for NACA/NCLC in such appeals as *Bass v. Stolper, Koritzinsky, Brewster & Neider, S.C.*, 111 F.3d 1322 (7th Cir. 1997); *Charles v. Lundgren & Assoc.*, 119 F.3d 739 (9th Cir. 1997); *Newman v. Boehm, Pearlstein & Bright, Limited*, 119 F.3d 477 (7th Cir. 1997).

Richard N. Feferman of the Law Offices of Richard Feferman (300 Central Avenue, SW, # 2000E, Albuquerque, NM 87102; phone: 505-243-7773; fax: 505-243-6663) is a 1971 graduate of the University of Michigan Law School. Mr. Feferman spent thirteen years in Legal Services before entering private practice.

The firm handles a wide variety of individual and class action consumer cases throughout New Mexico, Arizona, and Colorado. Most of the firm's cases are federal suits against car dealers, debt collectors, and lenders. In 1999, the firm was nominated for "trial lawyers of the year" by the Trial Lawyers for Public Justice for obtaining a $669,000 jury verdict against a New Mexico car dealer for odometer fraud and tortious debt collection practices. Recent favorable published decisions include: *Yazzie v. Ray Vicker's Special Cars, Inc.*, 12 F. Supp. 2d 1230 (D.N.M. July 6, 1998) (pawn "storage fee" was undisclosed finance charge under TILA), *cert. granted*, 180 F.R.D. 411 (D.N.M. July 6, 1998); *Lee v. Gallup Auto Sales, Inc.*, 135 F.3d 1359 (10th Cir. 1998) (striking illegal regulation exempting older vehicles from federal odometer act); *Bitah v. Global Collection Services, Inc.*, et al., 968 F. Supp. 1997) (lawyer liability under FDCPA); *Halwood v. Cowboy Auto Sales, Inc.*, 124 N.M. 77, 946 P.2d 1088 (Ct. App. 1997) (upholding punitive damages for on-reservation tort by non-Indian).

Lohf Shaiman Jacobs Hyman & Feiger, 950 S. Cherry Street, Ste. 900, Denver, CO 80246. Ms. Feiger received her J.D. at the University of Southern California in 1971 and her M.S. in Law and Society from the University of Denver in 1974. She is one of the leading litigation attorneys in Colorado in the area of civil rights, including sex discrimination, sexual harassment, age and race discrimination, and employment law in general. In 1978, Ms. Feiger was the first attorney in the United States to try a Title VII sexual harassment case. She is also responsible for numerous landmark court decisions in the employment area, helping establish the enforceability of personnel policy handbooks in the seminal Colorado case of *Continental Airlines, Inc. v. Keenan*, and for developing public policy wrongful discharge law in Colorado. Ms. Feiger is listed in *Best Lawyers in America* and has received the top rating available in the Martindale-Hubbell Law Directory as rated by her peers. Ms. Feiger has tried many employment cases in the last two decades, obtaining numerous seven-figure verdicts and settlements. At her firm, Ms. Feiger spends considerable time developing the skills of the attorneys who work with her and has trained numerous plaintiffs' attorneys in Colorado. Ms. Feiger's professional affiliations in the past five years include Elected Fellow, ABA College of Labor and Employment Law, and Chairperson of Board of Directors of Colorado Plaintiff Employment Lawyers Association. Ms. Feiger's publications in the last ten years include numerous articles and chapters on employment litigation.

Dmitry Feofanov, after a career in music, got tired of being poor and graduated from the Chicago-Kent College of Law in 1994. After serving as a law clerk for the Iowa Supreme Court and Illinois Appellate Court, he did municipal law and, in 2002, established the website www.ChicagoLemonLaw.com. Surprisingly, though, it did not make him rich. He may be reached at Feofanov@ChicagoLemonLaw.com.

Michael Ferry is executive director of Gateway Legal Services, Inc. (200 N. Broadway, Suite 950, St. Louis, Missouri 63108; phone: 314-534-0404; fax: 314-652-8308; e-mail: mferry@gatewaylegal.org). He is co-chair of the Consumer Involvement Task Force of the ABA's Uniform Commercial Code Committee, a Fellow of the American College of Consumer Financial Services Lawyers, Uniform Law Commissioner for the State of Missouri, adjunct professor at Washington University School of Law, and chair of the Consumer Law Committee of the Bar Association of Metropolitan St. Louis. He is a former member of the Consumer Advisory Council of the Board of Governors of the Federal Reserve System and a former Fellow of the ABA's Consumer Financial Services Committee and Uniform Commercial Code Committee. He has contributed to several NCLC publications, including *Repossessions and Foreclosures* (1999) and *Consumer Warranty Law* (2001), sits on NCLC's Board of Directors, and was the 1994 recipient of the Vern Countryman Consumer Law Award.

James B. Fishman is a partner in the law offices of Fishman & Neil, L.L.P. (305 Broadway, Suite 900, New York, NY 10007; phone: 212-897-5840; fax: 212-897-5841). Mr. Fishman's practice involves consumer credit, deceptive business practices cases, credit reporting matters, and illegal debt collection claims, as well as representing tenants in all types of landlord/tenant litigation. Mr. Fishman is a graduate of Bard College (1976) and New York Law School (1979). He is admitted to the Bar of the State of New York as well as the bars of the United States Supreme Court, the United States Court of Appeals for the Second and Fifth Circuits and the Southern and Eastern District of New York. He is a charter member of the National Association of Consumer Advocates. Mr. Fishman served as an Assistant Attorney General in the Bureau of Consumer Frauds and Protection of the New York State Department of Law and as a Senior Staff Attorney with the Civil Division of The Legal Aid Society. Mr. Fishman's publications include *New York General Practice*, Consumer Law Chapter (West Publishing Company 1992); lemon law pleadings from *Walker v. General Motors*, published by Bender's Forms, CPLR Art. 75 (1994 edition); *Applying Consumer Protection Laws in Landlord-Tenant Disputes*, New York State Bar Association Continuing Legal Education Committee (October 1994); *Purchase Of New and Used 'Lemons*,' Caveat Venditor (Julius Blumberg, Inc. 1994); New York *Needs a Private Right of Action for Debt Collection Abuse*, New York Law Journal, p. 1 (June 23, 1983).

Cary Flitter is a partner with Lundy, Flitter, Beldecos & Berger, P.C. (450 N. Narberth Avenue, Narberth, PA 19072; phone: 610-822-0782; fax: 610-667-0552), practicing in suburban Philadelphia and southern New Jersey. He handles both individual cases and class actions. Mr. Flitter has served on the adjunct faculty at Philadelphia University (Commercial Law) and currently serves on the adjunct faculty at Widener University School of Law (Consumer Law and Litigation). He is a contributing author to the treatise, *Pennsylvania Consumer Law*; a graduate of the National Institute for Trial Advocacy; and a member of NACA.

William J. Flanagan is an attorney with Flanagan, William-Duran & Flanagan (2307 Fargo Street, Los Angeles, CA 90039). Mr. Flanagan specializes in home equity fraud and consumer litigation. He is a member of the California and Florida bar associations.

Neil J. Fogarty is a senior attorney with Northeast New Jersey Legal Services (574 Summit Avenue, Jersey City, NJ 07306-2797; phone: 201-792-6363), practicing bankruptcy and consumer law since 1977. He is admitted to practice in New Jersey and New York. He was a member of the Federal Reserve Board's Consumer Advisory Council from 1986 to 1988 and was the president of the Consumers League of New Jersey for eighteen years. He was a member of the New Jersey Supreme Court Committee on Special Civil Part for five years and a lecturer for five years at the Institute for Continuing Legal Education on consumer credit regulation. He has contributed to the National Consumer Law Center's publications: *Consumer Law in a Box*; forms for *Consumer Bankruptcy Law and Practice*; *Repossessions and Foreclosures*; and *Truth in Lending*. He has practiced before the Third Circuit Court of Appeal as well as the New Jersey Supreme Court. He represented the debtor in *Pulley v Legreide, Director, N.J. Motor Vehicle Commission*, 295 B.R. 28 (Bankr. D.N.J. 2003), *aff'd* 303 B.R. 81 (Dist. Ct, D.N.J. 2003), a case holding that New Jersey insurance surcharges are dischargeable in bankruptcy chapter 7, with the result that thousands of debtors will now be able to get their driver's license restored through bankruptcy.

Mary Catherine Fons is a sole practitioner operating the Fons Law Office in Stoughton, Wisconsin. Her practice is limited to representing consumers with claims including debt collection harassment, fraud, deceptive sales practices, wrongful repossession, credit reporting errors, tenant rights, and other cases involving state and federal consumer protection laws. Ms. Fons is a frequent presenter on consumer protection topics at state and national conferences and seminars. She has taught consumer law at Marquette University Law School in Milwaukee, Wisconsin. Ms. Fons serves on the Consumer Protection Committee and Public Interest Law Board of the State Bar of Wisconsin and on the Advisory Board to the University of Wisconsin Law School Consumer Law Litigation Clinic. She has also served on advisory committees advising on revisions to the Wisconsin Consumer Act and the Revised Uniform Arbitration Act and served in a similar capacity for the Wisconsin Department of Financial Institutions.

James A. Francis is a member of Francis & Mailman, P.C. (Land Title Building, 19th Floor, 100 South Broad Street, Philadelphia, PA 19110; phone: 215-735-8600; fax: 215-940-8000); e-mail: jfrancis@consumerlawfirm.com), a law firm located in center city Philadelphia that concentrates in consumer litigation. The firm was founded in early 1998 with the goal of providing zealous advocacy to consumers subjected to unfair business, industry and trade practices. The firm represents consumers in individual actions, as well as through class action lawsuits, in the areas of unlawful credit reporting and debt collection practices, unfair trade practices, truth-in-lending, and other consumer matters. The firm's attorneys have significant litigation experience both in federal and state trial courts throughout Pennsylvania.

James A. Francis is admitted to practice before the United States Court of Appeals for the Third Circuit, the United States District Court for the Eastern District of Pennsylvania, the United States District Court for the District of New Jersey, as well as the state courts of Pennsylvania and New Jersey. He is a 1992 graduate of Muhlenberg College (B.A., *cum laude*) and a 1995 graduate of the Temple University Beasley School of Law. While at Temple Law School, he won the 1995 Wapner, Newman & Wigrizer, P.C., award for excellence in civil trial advocacy and was awarded outstanding oral advocacy. Additionally, he served as President of the Student Bar Association from 1994–1995. Following law school, Mr. Francis worked with Kolsby, Gordon, Robin, Shore & Rothweiler in Philadelphia, where his practice was concentrated in the area of catastrophic injury litigation and medical malpractice. Since the formation of Francis & Mailman, P.C., in 1998, he has focused his practice in consumer litigation, with particular concentration on fair credit reporting, fair debt collection practices, and consumer class actions. He has tried and successfully litigated cases on behalf of many consumers throughout Pennsylvania. He has been certified to serve as class counsel by state and federal courts in both contested and settlement class actions. These cases include *Petrolito v. Arrow Financial Services, L.L.C.*, __ F.R.D. __, 2004 WL 515761 (D. Conn. 2004); *Orloff v. Syndicated Office Systems, Inc.*, 2004 WL 870691 (E.D. Pa 2004); *Bonett v. Education Debt Services, Inc.*, 2003 WL 21658267 (E.D. Pa. 2003).

In 2004, Mr. Francis was voted and named one of Pennsylvania's Top 100 Super Lawyers in a recent study by Law and Politics published by *Philadelphia Magazine* and *Pennsylvania Super Lawyers 2004*. Mr. Francis has lectured before judges, lawyers, and professional associations on the topics of consumer rights litigation. In June 2002 and May of 2004, he was a speaker at the National Associates of Consumer Advocates Fair Credit Reporting Act Conferences. He has appeared on the NBC Philadelphia affiliate News 10's Consumer Alert and ABC Channel 6's Action News programs to discuss credit reporting issues. Mr. Francis regularly serves as a certified arbitration panelist chair with the Court of Common Pleas of Philadelphia County-Trial Division Program. He is a member of the Pennsylvania Trial Lawyers Association, Philadelphia Trial Lawyers Association, Philadelphia Bar Association, and National Association of Consumer Advocates.

Eric L. Frank is an attorney with the law firm of DiDonato & Winterhalter, P.C., in Philadelphia, Pennsylvania, where he concentrates on personal and commercial bankruptcy and consumer protection law. Previously, he was a partner with Miller, Frank & Miller and was a supervising attorney at Community Legal Services, Inc., both in Philadelphia. Mr. Frank is a member of the federal Judicial Conference Advisory Committee on Bankruptcy Rules, on which he has served since his appointment by Chief Justice Rehnquist in 1998. He is the Contributing Author to Chapter 523 of the treatise, *Collier on Bankruptcy* (15th ed.). Mr. Frank is a member the National Association of Consumer Bankruptcy Attorneys. He is also a member of the Eastern District of Pennsylvania Bankruptcy Conference, for which he has served as Chair of the Steering Committee, co-chair of its Education Committee, and a member of the Local Bankruptcy Rules Advisory Committee. Mr. Frank is a past cresident and current member of the Board of Directors of the Consumer Bankruptcy Assistance Project in Philadelphia, which provides pro bono representation in bankruptcy cases to low-income persons. He lectures and writes regularly for continuing legal education organizations on bankruptcy and consumer-protection-related topics. He served as a law clerk to the late Justice Samuel J. Roberts of the Pennsylvania Supreme Court and to U.S. Bankruptcy

Judge Bruce Fox. He received his J.D. from the University of Pennsylvania Law School in 1976 and his B.A. from S.U.N.Y. at Binghamton in 1973.

Jamie S. Franklin is a 1997 graduate of the University of Chicago Law School and a 1992 graduate of Duke University. She is an associate at the Chicago law firm of Meites, Mulder, Burger & Mollica, where her practice is focused on employment and consumer class actions. Formerly she was an associate at the Chicago consumer law firm of Edelman, Combs, Latturner & Goodwin and an intern in consumer law at the Legal Assistance Foundation of Metropolitan Chicago.

Charli Fulton is a senior assistant attorney general in the West Virginia Attorney General's Consumer Protection Division (P.O. Box 1789, Charleston, WV 26326-1789; phone: 304-558-8986). In addition to her interest in automobile sales and financing practices, Ms. Fulton has litigated in the areas of sweepstakes and title pawning. A favorable appellate ruling in a title pawning case in which she was involved, *State ex rel. McGraw v. Pawn America*, 205 W. Va. 431, 518 S.E.2d 859 (1998), has precluded this industry from doing business in West Virginia. The West Virginia Court of Appeals' ruling in *State ex rel. McGraw v. Imperial Marketing*, 203 W. Va. 203, 506 S.E.2d 799 (1998), another case in which she was counsel, affirmed a permanent injunction that was granted as a summary judgment. The Supreme Court held that the question of whether sweepstakes solicitations violated the West Virginia Prizes and Gifts Act and the West Virginia Consumer Credit and Protection Act depended on the language of the solicitations and did not require the presentation of extrinsic evidence. (In response to the Court's ruling that the state could only obtain a single $5000 civil penalty for repeated and willful violations, the West Virginia legislature amended the Act to provide for a civil penalty of up to $5000 for each violation.) The Consumer Protection Division has also been active in the areas of payday loans, spurious open-end credit offers, loan packing, and student loan scams.

Stephen Gardner is Director of Litigation for the advocacy group, Center for Science in the Public Interest, based in Washington, D.C. He is also Of Counsel to the National Consumer Law Center. Previously, Steve was Assistant Dean of Clinical Education at Southern Methodist University School of Law (1994–1995); Visiting Assistant Professor of Law at Southern Methodist University School of Law (1992-1995); Assistant Attorney General in the Consumer Protection Division of the State of Texas (1984–1991); Assistant Attorney General in the Bureau of Consumer Frauds of the State of New York (1982–1984); Students Attorney at the University of Texas (1981–1982); and a staff attorney at the legal aid office in Austin, now part of Texas Rio Grande Legal Services (1976–1981). He is a frequent author and speaker on consumer advocacy issues.

Wyman O. Gilmore, Jr. is licensed to practice in Tennessee and Alabama (Gilmore Law Office, 116 Court Street P.O. Box 729 Grove Hill, Alabama; phone: 251-275-3115; fax: 251-275-3847; e-mail: wogilmore@mygalaxyexpress.com). Mr. Gilmore's practice primarily involves personal injury, consumer fraud, and class actions. Mr. Gilmore has been practicing law since 1983. He has served as Special Deputy Attorney General for the State of Alabama and has served on the executive committee of the Alabama Trial Lawyer's Association.

Mitchell D. Gliner is a 1984 graduate of New York Law School. He is admitted to practice in Nevada, Connecticut and New York. Mr. Gliner is a former Marine Captain. His Marine Corps service included both that of military prosecutor and Company Commander. Upon leaving the Marine Corps, Mr. Gliner successfully defended a black youth charged with the murder of a skinhead. This racially charged trial received substantial publicity.

Since 1994, Mr. Gliner has confined his practice to consumer litigation involving credit reporting disputes and debt collection abuse. His most notable case, *Nelson v. Chase Manhattan Mortgage Corp.*, 282 F.3d 1057 (9th Cir. 2002), was the first decision by a Federal Court of Appeals that empowered individuals to personally sue companies which furnish inaccurate information to credit reporting agencies.

Mr. Gliner's other significant decisions involving the establishment and advancement of consumer rights are *Romine v. Diversified Collection Services, Inc.*, 155 F.3d 1142 (9th Cir. 1998); *Myers v. Bennett Law Offices*, 238 F.3d 1068 (9th Cir. 2001); *Kuhn v. Account Control Technology, Inc.*, 865 F. Supp. 1443 (D. Nev. 1994); *Edwards v. National Business Factors, Inc.*, 897 F. Supp. 455 (D. Nev. 1995); *Edwards v. National Business Factors, Inc.*, 897 F. Supp. 458 (D. Nev. 1995); *Pittman v. J. J. MacIntyre Co. of Nevada, Inc.*, 969 F. Supp. 609 (D. Nev. 1997); *Perez v. Telecheck Services, Inc.*, 208 F. Supp. 2d 1153 (D. Nev. 2002); *Uhlig v. Berge Ford Inc.*, 257 F. Supp. 2d 1228 (D. Ariz. 2003); and Taylor v. Bryant, Inc., 275 F. Supp. 2d 1305 (D. Nev. 2003).

Mr. Gliner has lectured locally and nationally on both the Fair Debt Collection Practices Act and the Fair Credit Reporting Act.

Phil Goldsmith has practiced consumer law in Portland, Oregon, for over twenty-five years, representing plaintiffs in class actions and individuals with financial institution problems including predatory lending cases, at the Law Office of Phil Goldsmith (222 SW Columbia Street, Suite 1600, Portland, OR 97201; phone: 503-224-2301; fax: 503-222-7288; e-mail: phil@lopglaw.com). Since 1987, he has been the principal in a one- or two-lawyer firm. He is a 1978 graduate of the Yale Law School. He served as co-lead counsel in *Vasquez-Lopez v. Beneficial Oregon, Inc.*, a predatory lending case that resulted in a jury verdict in January, 2004, which included $500,000 in punitive damages. The punitives have subsequently been reduced on post-trial motions and the case is currently on appeal. Other recent significant cases include *Bruce v. EarthLink*, a class action for degraded Internet service that resulted in a $2,000,000 settlement; *Hutson v. US Bank, National Association*, a wage and hour class action which settled on terms favorable to the plaintiff class; and *Rosted v. First USA Bank*, a nationwide class action challenging a credit card bait-and-switch scheme that settled with non-monetary class relief valued by the court as being in excess of $86 million. He was a panelist at the 2004 NCLC predatory lending mini-conference session on trying predatory lending cases. He previously has spoken at NCLC and NACA conferences on credit card litigation and attorney fees in class actions. He is currently a member of NACA's Class Action Guidelines Revision Committee.

Samuel D. Gollis is a solo practitioner. His office is at 3939C San Pedro Drive N.E., Suite 5, Albuquerque, NM 87110; phone: 505-883-4696; fax: 505-884-4331. Mr. Gollis was previously an associate with Williams, Janov & Cooney in Albuquerque. Prior to that, he worked on the Navajo and Hopi Indian Reservations as a staff attorney for DNA-People's Legal Services, Inc.

Tara L. Goodwin of Edelman, Combs, Latturner & Goodwin, L.L.C. (120 S. LaSalle, 18th Floor, Chicago, IL 60603-3403), has a J.D. with High Honors from IIT Chicago-Kent College of Law and a B.A. from the University of Chicago. She is currently a member of Edelman, Combs, Latturner & Goodwin, L.L.C., in Chicago, Illinois, where she has practiced for fourteen years. She specializes in consumer class actions.

Robert S. Green of Green Welling, L.L.P. (595 Market St., Ste. 2750, San Francisco, CA 94104), has extensive experience representing consumers in telecommunication, telemarketing, credit card, and insurance cases. Mr. Green was co-lead counsel in the Providian Credit Card cases, which settled in December 2000 for $105 million. Mr. Green and his firm have also brought claims against Direct Merchants Bank, First National Bank of Marin, First Union, and the American Fair Credit Association (AFCA), among others. The firm obtained substantial settlements in actions against Capital One, General Electric Capital Consumer Card Co., First USA Bank, and Advanta Bank. Mr. Green obtained a Ninth Circuit opinion expanding the rights of credit card holders under TILA in *Demando v. Morris (Capital One)*, 206 F.3d 1300 (9th Cir. 2000). Mr. Green also serves on the Editorial Board of Consumer Financial Services Law Report and is a member of the NCLC Partners' Council. Mr. Green's firm also maintains a substantial practice in the area of antitrust law, securities litigation, and shareholder derivative cases.

Mark E. Griffin has been a partner since 1988 at Griffin & McCandish (111 SW Naito Parkway, Portland, OR 97204-3500; phone: 503-224-2348; fax: 503-224-3634). His firm emphasizes complex civil litigation in personal injury and products liability; franchise, consumer, and investment fraud; employment discrimination and wage claims; professional malpractice with an emphasis on legal malpractice; and class actions. He is a 1976 graduate of the Northwestern School of Law, Lewis & Clark College. He served as co-lead counsel in *Vasquez-Lopez v. Beneficial Oregon, Inc.*, a predatory lending case which resulted in a jury verdict in January 2004 that included $500,000 in punitive damages. The punitives have subsequently been reduced on post-trial motions and the case is currently on appeal. He has previously received other substantial punitive damage awards, including those in *Gleaves v. MacTools*, a franchise fraud case with a $2.4 million verdict including $2.2 million in punitive damages; *McNicholas v. Maring, Capital Resource Finance Corp.*, a breach of fiduciary suit by a minority shareholder that resulted in a substantial verdict for compensatory and punitive damages; and *Hobbs v. Care Ambulance*, a sexual discrimination case with a jury verdict of over $200,000 for lost wages and punitive damages. He is a member of the Oregon Trial Lawyers Association, the Association of Trial Lawyers of America, and Trial Lawyers for Public Justice. He has published articles on federal criminal procedure, state civil procedure, and privacy rights and is a frequent lecturer at Continuing Legal Education seminars.

Leah Guggenheimer is an associate in the New York law firm of Bernstein Litowitz Berger & Grossmann, L.L.P. (1285 Avenue of the Americas, New York, NY 10019; phone: 212-554-1400; fax: 212-554-1444; e-mail: leah@BLBGLAW.com). Ms. Guggenheimer is a member of the National Employment Lawyers Association and the Women's Bar Association. She also serves on the Women's Rights Committee of the New York County Lawyers Association. Ms. Guggenheimer served as law clerk to Hon. Stephen Eilperin, D.C. Superior Court.

W. Howard Gunn is a private attorney in Aberdeen, Mississippi, whose practice includes consumer litigation. He can be reached at W. Howard Gunn & Associates, 310 South Hickory Street, P.O. Box 157, Aberdeen, MS 39730; phone: 662-369-8533; fax: 662-369-9844.

Daniel L. Haller has worked as an attorney for more than thirty years with Neighborhood Legal Services (928 Penn Ave., Pittsburgh, PA 15222). He has concentrated on landlord and tenant, consumer, and bankruptcy law for over twenty years. He is a member of the Bankruptcy Bar and a former member of the Bankruptcy Judge Merit Selection Committee for the Western District of Pennsylvania. He is the former author of the mortgage foreclosure chapter in *Pennsylvania Consumer Law* and co-author of "Debtor's Power to Avoid" in *Consumer Bankruptcy* (Penn. Bar Inst). He is a member of the Allegheny County Bar Association.

Penny Hays is a partner with Alabama Injury Lawyers, P.C. Ms. Hays received her B.A. from Samford University and her J.D. from Cumberland School of Law in 1994. Since joining the firm in 1995, Ms. Hays has been representing individuals in their claims for workers' compensation, wrongful termination, and social security disability. For the past five years, her practice has focused on representing consumers in their claims under the FCRA, FDCPA, and Alabama state law claims. Alabama Injury Lawyers, P.C., is a small firm located at 401 Office Park Drive, Birmingham, AL 35223; phone: 205-870-9848; fax: 205-871-8882.

Daniel F. Hedges is director of Mountain State Justice (922 Quarrier St., Ste. 525, Charleston, WV 25301; phone: 304-344-3144; fax: 304-344-3145) and is also in private practice at 8 Hale Street, Charleston, WV 25301; phone: 304-346-0361; fax: (304) 346-1054. He has been a consumer law specialist in West Virginia since 1969 and was presented the Vern Countryman Award in 2003 for outstanding consumer advocacy.

Andrew R. Henderson is a partner in the Los Angeles law firm of Hall & Henderson, L.L.P. (10951 W. Pico Boulevard, 3rd Floor, Los Angeles, CA 90064; phone: 310-441-8300; fax: 310-474-7083). He graduated with honors in 1990 from the University of North Carolina School of Law, where he was a member of the North Carolina Law Review. From 1990 to

1994, he was an associate at O'Melveny & Myers in Los Angeles. Before law school, he was active in both real estate development and parkland preservation on the southern coast of North Carolina. He also received a Master of Business Taxation degree from the University of Southern California in 1981.

Mr. Henderson left corporate practice in 1994 to practice public interest litigation with his current partner, Carlyle W. Hall, Jr., one of the original founders of Center for Law in the Public Interest. Mr. Henderson has a broad-based litigation practice with emphasis on land-use environmental issues and consumer rights. Specifically concerning the latter, he co-counseled throughout the successful trial of the then-record-setting *Wenger v. Trans Union Corporation* case in 1996. He has since litigated two other impact cases against credit reporting agencies. Most recently he argued the case, *Andrews v. TRW Inc.*, before the Ninth Circuit Court of Appeals, resulting in ground-breaking appellate precedent concerning both the applicability of the discovery rule to the Fair Credit Reporting Act and the obligations of credit reporting agencies to protect the privacy of consumers' credit histories in light of the epidemic of identity theft. He has also been active in *pro bono publico* matters and was the principal draftsperson of the City of Los Angeles' 1995 Ordinance for the Protection of Medical Facilities. He also recently served the City of Los Angeles as an appointed commissioner, helping to revise the City's seventy-four-year-old charter.

Evan Hendricks has served since 1981 as Editor/Publisher of the *Privacy Times*, a biweekly newsletter in Washington that reports on privacy and freedom of information law. He has served as an expert witness in several cases involving the Fair Credit Reporting Act. He may be contacted at evan@privacytimes.com, Privacy Times, PO Box 302, Cabin John MD 20818; phone: 301-229 7002; fax: 301-229 8011. Mr. Hendricks is author of the books, *Credit Scores & Credit Reports* (2004) (2nd ed. 2005), *Your Right To Privacy* (So. Ill. Univ. Press 1990), and *Former Secrets*, a 1982 compilation of 500 examples of significant disclosures to the public under the FOIA. From 1977–80, he was Editor of Access Reports and a newsletter on FOIA/Privacy. A graduate of Columbia University, Hendricks regularly lectures on information policy issues in the United States, Canada, and Europe. Some of his recent lectures and expert presentations have taken place Harvard University's Kennedy School of Government, Brookings Institution, the 16th Annual Conference on Data Protection in the Hague, the Netherlands, and Reed College Lecture Series on Privacy and Censorship.

Mr. Hendricks has been qualified by federal and state courts as an expert in Fair Credit Reporting Act and identity theft cases. He has been interviewed on various FOIA and privacy issues by the *Oprah Winfrey Show*, *Geraldo*, *ABC Nightline* and *World News Tonight*, *NBC Nightly News*, *CBS Evening News*, *CNN News Watch*, *The Washington Post*, *New York Times*, *Wall Street Journal*, and radio talk shows on KABC (Ray Briem, LA); KFI (Tom Likus-LA); WLS (both Tom Johnson and Bob Wade); Scams Across America (Business Radio Network, Richard Cooper); WOR (New York); and KFYI (Phoenix). He has done contract research for the Office of the Canadian Privacy Commissioner and the Australian Human Rights & Equal Opportunity Commission, in response to these organizations' need for a survey of American experiences in the course of formulating their national policies. In 1991, Hendricks became Chairman of the U.S. Privacy Council, a new organization and the first dedicated to the protection of privacy and improving our nation's law and policy. Hendricks is a native of Portland, Oregon.

Edward A. Icove is a principal in the firm of Smith and Condeni, L.L.P. (Ohio Savings Plaza, Suite 900, 1801 East 9th Street, Cleveland, OH 44114; phone: 216-771-1760; fax: 216-771-3387; e-mail: Edward@smith-condeni.com). Mr. Icove was a VISTA attorney and legal services attorney with the Cincinnati Legal Aid Society and Southeastern Ohio Legal Services. He is a board member (and former Vice-President) of the Cleveland Legal Aid Society. He has handled numerous individual and class consumer cases in both state and federal courts, for example, *Barney v. Holzer Clinic, Inc.*, 110 F.3d 1207 (6th Cir. 1997) (ECOA); *Smith v. Transworld Systems, Inc.*, 952 F.2d 1025 (6th Cir. 1992) (FDCPA, adopting the "least sophisticated" consumer standard in the Sixth Circuit); *Pyles v. Johnson*, 143 Ohio App. 3d 720 (4th Dist. 2001) (CSPA, RISA, and fraud); *Edwards v. McCormick*, 136 F. Supp.

2d 795 (S.D. Ohio 2001) (FDCPA and CSPA); *Shorts v. Palmer*, 155 F.R.D. 172 (S.D. Ohio 1994) (FDCPA); *Lewis v. Marlin*, Clearinghouse No. 53021 (S.D. Ohio 1999) (FDCPA). A Cleveland collection attorney once complained that Mr. Icove was a "champion of the poor."

Raymond G. Ingalsbe received a B.A. from the University of Cincinnati in 1973 and his J.D. from the University of Miami in 1976. Mr. Ingalsbe has been a board-certified civil trial lawyer since 1985. He is a member of the Academy of Florida Trial Lawyers and has been involved in attempting to draft changes to Florida's Deceptive and Unfair Trade Practices Act as a member of the Consumer Protection Committee of the Florida Bar. Mr. Ingalsbe was the chairman of the Palm Beach County Bar Association Consumer Law Committee for four years. He is an occasional lecturer on sales fraud and deceptive and unfair trade practices, has received two pro bono awards from the Palm Beach County Bar Association for his work in consumer law, and has received an award for his work on the Journal of the Academy of Florida Trial Lawyers. Mr. Ingalsbe is a charter member of the National Association of Consumer Advocates. His office is at 4400 PGA Boulevard, Ste. 800, Palm Beach Garden, FL 33410; phone: 561-775-3505; fax: 561-624-3533; e-mail: rgingalsbe@aol.com. His practice is limited to consumer claims which, by default, typically involve motor vehicle dealers and motor vehicle lenders.

David B. Irvin is a Senior Assistant Attorney General and Chief of the Antitrust and Consumer Litigation Section of the Office of the Virginia Attorney General (900 East Main Street, Richmond, VA 23219; phone: 804-786-2116; fax: 804-786-0122). He specializes in consumer protection law and has been lead counsel in cases alleging advance fee loan fraud, usury (payday and title pawn loans), charitable solicitation fraud, credit repair fraud, and deceptive advertising. Mr. Irvin is a member of the Virginia state and federal bar associations.

Danita Ivory is an associate in the law firm of Edelman, Combs and Latturner. She is a 2000 graduate of DePaul College of Law. She has been working at Edelman, Combs, & Latturner since. The cases she has litigated include:

—*Chandler v. American General Finance Company*, 329 Ill. App. 3d 729, 768 N.E.2d 60 (1st Dist. 2002) (held that compliance with the Truth in Lending Act did not preclude liability under the Illinois Consumer Fraud Act and the Illinois Consumer Installment Loan Act when the fraud alleged occurred outside of the loan documents).

—*Mallen v. MyInjuryClaim.Com Corporation*, 2002 WL 598400 (1st Dist. 2002) (held that Illinois recognizes a private right of action for the unauthorized practice of law).

—*Phillips v. Associates Home Equity Services, Inc.*, 179 F. Supp. 2d 840 (N.D. Ill. 2001) (denying a motion to compel arbitration when the plaintiff would have to pay prohibitively high costs to arbitrate her claims).

Edward Josephson is the Director of Litigation, South Brooklyn Legal Services, Inc. (105, Court St., Brooklyn, NY; phone: 718-237-5500; fax: 718-855-0733). His main areas of practice are landlord/tenant and federally assisted housing law. Mr. Josephson is a member of the New York bar.

De Vonna Joy is a solo practitioner with the law firm Consumer Justice Law Center. Ms. Joy limits her practice to consumer protection, litigating for consumers under state and federal laws. This practice consists of redressing rights arising from consumer fraud in various areas. Some of these areas include identity theft, automobile fraud, time-share sales violations and other sales scams, illegal debt collection practices, credit report violations, and other consumer disputes.

Ms. Joy opened her law firm as a solo practitioner in 1999. She is the moderator for the Legal Action of Wisconsin Badgerlaw Consumer Group Section. She received her J.D. in 1987 from Marquette Law School and is a 2003 graduate of Gerry Spence's Trial Lawyers College. She is the 2002 recipient of the Association for Women Lawyers Pro Bono Award as well as the 2001 recipient of the Volunteer Lawyers Project Outstanding Pro Bono Attorney Award from the Waukesha County Bar Association and Legal Action of Wisconsin Volunteer Lawyers Project. She has presented on consumer issues to consumer and legal services groups.

Suzanne Keys is a private attorney with Byrd, Gibbs & Martin (P.O. Box 19, Jackson, MS 39205; phone: 601-354-1210; fax: 601-354-1250). Ms. Keys is an active member of the Mississippi bar and an inactive member of the Wisconsin bar.

Gary Klein is a partner at the law firm Roddy Klein & Ryan, Attorneys at Law, in Boston, Massachusetts (727 Atlantic Avenue, 2nd Floor, Boston, Massachusetts 02111; phone: 617-357-5500 x. 15; fax: 617-357-5030; e-mail: klein@roddykleinryan.com. Until January 2001, he was an attorney at the National Consumer Law Center in Boston.

Mr. Klein is a nationally recognized expert on consumer law and consumer education. His specialties include unfair business practice cases, consumer protections for predatory lending, and bankruptcy. Mr. Klein has been co-counsel in many recent successful class action cases including several national settlements involving predatory mortgage lenders. Mr. Klein has served as an expert witness in court cases and in Congress, has authored numerous books and articles on bankruptcy and consumer law, and has been counsel in hundreds of bankruptcy cases, class actions, and individual lawsuits. He is a former director of the American Bankruptcy Institute and a current director of the Coalition for Consumer Bankruptcy Debtor Education. He is a graduate of Yale University and Rutgers Law School.

Henry Korman is currently associate general counsel at The Community Builders, Inc., a non-profit developer of affordable housing. He worked as a legal services advocate from 1977 until 2001, as a paralegal and staff attorney at Western Massachusetts Legal Services, a housing specialist at the Massachusetts Law Reform Institute, and as Chief Counsel and office manager at Cambridge and Somerville Legal Services. The pleadings submitted in this volume were developed with the support and assistance of the National Consumer Law Center. He may be reached at The Community Builders, Inc., 95 Berkeley Street, Suite 500, Boston, MA 02116; phone: 617-695-9595 fax: 617-695-9483; e-mail: henryk@tcbinc.org.

Robert Lax is a partner in the firm of Robert I. Lax & Associates) (535 5th Avenue, Floor 21, New York, NY 10176; phone: 212-818-9150; fax: 212-682-9040), a firm that practices exclusively in the area of complex commercial litigation, placing particular emphasis on representing plaintiffs in class action and derivative suits in the state and federal courts. In a relatively short period of time, Robert I. Lax & Associates has become well known for its academic approach to the practice of law as well as its dedicated sense of client advocacy.

Robert I. Lax & Associates is actively involved in cases representing clients in actions involving issues of securities fraud and corporate governance, consumer finance, advertising fraud, and royalty and intellectual property disputes. The ability and expertise of Robert I. Lax & Associates in handling these matters has been recognized by both the judiciary as well as members of the bar, with the result that Robert I. Lax & Associates has been appointed class counsel and invited to serve on the litigation committees of several of the nation's most prominent class action litigations.

David A. Leen is a principal in the firm of David Leen & Associates, P.L.L.C. (520 E. Denny Way, Seattle, WA 98122; phone: 206-325-6022; fax: 206-325-1424). He specializes in real estate litigation and consumer class actions. He is a member of the Washington bar and of the Seventh, Eighth, and Ninth Circuit Courts.

Seth R. Lesser is a partner in the Locks Law Firm (with offices in New York, New Jersey, and Pennsylvania). Mr. Lesser specializes in consumer fraud class actions as well as mass tort cases. He is a 1988 *magna cum laude* graduate of Harvard Law School and has written and spoken extensively on matters related to consumer law, class actions, and privacy law. He has also served on numerous committees of the American Bar Association and the New York City Bar Association and is a member of a number of consumer organizations.

Michael Lewis formerly practiced law with his wife and law partner, Pauline S. Lewis, in Clarksdale, Mississippi. Mr. Lewis has been a member of the Mississippi Bar since 1977. His firm specializes in personal injury with an emphasis on medical malpractice, product liability, insurance, and consumer issues. Mr. Lewis authored the "medicaid tobacco recovery theory," which casts the state as victim and entitles it to recover damages caused by tobacco-related illnesses. Mr. and Mrs. Lewis represented the State of Mississippi in *Moore v. Phillip Morris, et al.*, and recovered a settlement of $4 billion on behalf of the state of Mississippi. Mr. Lewis is admitted to practice in all state and federal courts in Mississippi as well as the U.S. District Court of Tennessee (Western Division), the U.S. District Court of Texas (Southern Division), and the U.S. Supreme Court. The identity theft case in Chapter 1 of NCLC's *Consumer Law Pleadings*, Number Five, is one of several in which Mr. Lewis was involved.

Mark Leymaster, who designed and presented the exhibits in NCLC's *Consumer Law Pleadings*, Number 9, § 1.2 (Cumulative CD-Rom and Index Guide), consults on expert legal systems, electronic document assembly, and consumer finance and also develops custom computer software as the Managing Partner at Renaissance Software in Silver Spring, Maryland, phone: 301-495-4877. He was previously an administrative law judge, insurance regulator, and rate-maker with the Commonwealth of Massachusetts. As Assistant Attorney General for the Commonwealth of Massachusetts, he did adversary administrative litigation and other public protection law enforcement. Mark specialized in consumer credit mathematics, Truth in Lending, repossessions, and payment system law when he worked at the National Consumer Law Center in Boston. He is the author of National Consumer Law Center's *Consumer Usury and Credit Overcharges* (1982). He also contributed an analysis on APR mathematics for National Consumer Law Center's manual, *Truth in Lending* (1986), and wrote articles on electronic banking and the poor before the electronic benefit transfers were mandated. Mark created NCLC's Annual Percentage Rate Calculator software, the latest version of which is included with each *Truth in Lending* manual.

Dani K. Liblang, of the Birmingham, Michigan, law firm of Liblang & Associates, P.C. (260 East Brown Street, Suite 320, Birmingham, MI 48009; phone: 248-540-9270, 248-433-1989), has successfully handled thousands of consumer warranty claims. She is the author of the Breach of Warranty chapter in ICLE's *Michigan Causes of Action Formbook*. She has spoken on warranty litigation at the Consumer Rights Litigation Conference, at ATLA's annual convention, and in numerous ICLE courses. She is the Chair of the Consumer Law Council for the State Bar of Michigan (2004–2005). She is a member of the National Association of Consumer Advocates and a past Vice President of the Michigan Trial Lawyers Association—Oakland Chapter. Ms. Liblang graduated *cum laude* from the University of Detroit Mercy School of Law in 1982 and is certified as a civil trial attorney by the National Board of Trial Advocacy. In addition to warranty law, Ms. Liblang specializes in personal injury, no-fault insurance, and employment law.

Charles Lorant, the founding partner of Alabama Injury Lawyers, P.C., has been representing plaintiffs and consumers in Alabama for over twenty years. Charlie received his B.A. from the University of North Carolina Chapel Hill and his J.D. from the University of Alabama School of Law. While Charlie continues to represent injured individuals in their claims for personal injuries, fraud, and discrimination for the past five years, his practice has become focused on representing consumers in their claims under the FCRA, FDCPA, and Alabama state law claims. While their firm is small, the lawyers have done battle with numerous giants across the country, including Equifax, Experian, Trans Union, First USA, Wachovia, Bank of America, American Express, Direct Merchants/Metris, Capital One, National Financial Systems, Risk Management Alternatives, Arrow, NCO, and countless others. Alabama Injury Lawyers, P.C., is a small firm located at 401 Office Park Drive, Birmingham, AL 35223; phone: 205-870-9848; fax: 205-871-8882; e-mail: charlie@lorantlaw.com.

Michael P. Malakoff has been a member since 1971 of Malakoff Doyle & Finberg, P.C. (or its predecessors), where he specializes in class action litigation. He is a founding member of the National Association of Consumer Advocates (NACA) and served on its Board. He was Chairman of the NACA Issues Committee from 1994 to 2002.

Over the last thirty years, he has participated in over 200 class actions, beginning as a former Regional Smith Fellow working at Neighborhood Legal Services Association (NLSA) in Pittsburgh in 1970–1971. He and members of his law firm have continued to work on class actions with NLSA attorneys, Community Justice Project, and National Consumer Law

Center (NCLC) attorneys. He has also worked with multiple other non-profit organizations, including Public Citizens (Washington, D.C.) and Trial Lawyers for Public Justice (Washington, D.C.) as well as with private law firms. An example of a class action in which he has recently participated with Community Justice attorneys is the protracted tax lien litigation in *Pollice v. National Tax Funding, L.P.*, 59 F. Supp. 2d 474 (W.D. Pa. 1999), which was affirmed in part at 225 F.3d 379 (3d Cir.).

Throughout his years of legal practice, he has also participated in a number of NLSA and NCLC seminars and legal workshops. His post-1998 activities include contributing author to NCLC's manual, *Consumer Class Actions* (4th ed. 1999). His consumer law pleadings have been featured in a number of NCLC's *Consumer Law Pleadings* treatises, including No. 1 (1994), No. 4 (1998), No. 5 (1999), No. 6 (2000) and No. 7 (2001), CPL8 Chapter 21; and CLP9 Chapter 11. He also authored *Commentary on the Class Action Fairness Act*, Class Action Reports, Vol. 26, No. 2 (March–April 2005).

Mr. Malakoff assisted in drafting the NACA's class action guidelines entitled *Standards and Guidelines for Litigation and Settling Consumer Class Actions,* published in 176 F.R.D. 375-404 (Oct. 8, 1997) (NACA Guidelines). He has served as a consultant and was honored when selected by the United States Court of Appeals for the Third Circuit as one of five private attorneys, along with five District Judges, to participate in the Court Awarded Attorneys Fees Report by the Third Circuit Task Force, the report for which was republished at 108 F.R.D. 237 (October 8, 1985) (Reporter, Arthur R. Miller).

He has been on the editorial board of *Class Action Reports* since 1985 and has been a consumer advisor for Consumer Financial Services since 1998. He can be reached at 412-281-8400; fax: 412-281-3262; or e-mail: malakoff@mdfpc.com.

Marsha M. Mansfield is a partner with Lawton & Cates, S.C. (10 East Doty Street, Ste. 400, P.O. Box 2965, Madison, WI 53701; phone: 608-282-6200; fax: 608-282-6252), a law firm that specializes in complex litigation matters. Ms. Mansfield has participated in multi-plaintiff consumer litigation in Wisconsin, including successful prosecution of a consumer action against a manufacturer of prefabricated housing, *Leverance*, et al. *v. Tri State Homes, Inc.* She has also managed lemon law cases against Ford and General Motors and is currently working on several projects with the Consumer Law Litigation Clinic at the University of Wisconsin Law School. Other members of the firm serve on the Board of the Center for Public Representation, a non-profit organization that provides legal assistance and referrals in areas including consumer advocacy.

James A. Mayhew is the managing attorney with St. Ambrose Legal Service (321 East 25th Street, Baltimore, MD, 21218; phone: 410-366-8550; fax: 410-235-7180). He specializes in consumer protection law. Mr. Mayhew was formerly a staff attorney with the Legal Aid Bureau in Baltimore, where he specialized in public benefits and housing law. He is a member of the Maryland state bar association and is admitted to practice in the U.S. District Court for Maryland and the U.S. Fourth Circuit Court of Appeals.

Cyrus Mehri is a founding partner of the law firm Mehri & Skalet, P.L.L.C.

Mr. Mehri served as Class Counsel in the two largest race discrimination class actions in history: *Roberts v. Texaco Inc.*, which settled in 1997 for $176 million, and *Ingram v. The Coca-Cola Company*, which settled in 2001 for $192.5 million. Both settlements include historic programmatic relief, featuring independent Task Forces with sweeping powers to reform key human resources practices such as pay, promotions, and evaluations.

Trial Lawyers for Public Justice named Mr. Mehri a finalist for "Trial Lawyer of the Year" in 1997 and 2001 for his work on the Texaco and Coca Cola matters respectively.

On April 6, 2004, Mr. Mehri, along with Martha Burk and the National Council of Women's Organizations, announced a project called "Women on Wall Street." The project focuses on gender discrimination in financial institutions. The project emerged in the wake of corporate CEOs participation in the male-only Augusta National Golf Club.

On September 30, 2002, Mr. Mehri and Johnnie L. Cochran, Jr. released the report, *Black Coaches in the National Football League: Superior Performance, Inferior Opportunities*. The report became the catalyst for the NFL's creation of a Workplace Diversity Committee and the adoption of a comprehensive diversity program. The NFL now has a record number of African American head coaches. Mr. Mehri serves as counsel for the Fritz Pollard Alliance, an affinity group for minority coaches, front office, and scouting personnel in the NFL.

In July 2001, Mr. Mehri's law firm and Johnnie L. Cochran, Jr., commissioned and released a report evaluating the appellate success rates of employment discrimination litigants in federal courts. The report, entitled "Double Standard on Appeal," received national press coverage for shedding light on the judiciary's basis against employment-discrimination plaintiffs.

The business press has long followed Mr. Mehri's work. The *New York Times* stated: "Mr. Mehri's vision for corporate America involves sweeping change, not the piece meal kind." *Corporate Counsel* magazine described Mr. Mehri as "the one who pushed racial discrimination suits to the top of Corporate America's agenda." *Fast Company* says "He is something of a one-man army in the battle against business as usual . . . [H]is impact—both in terms of penalties and remedies—is undeniable." In 2001, he was named by *Regardie's Power* magazine as one of "Washington's Ten Most Feared Lawyers" and, in 2003, by *Workforce* magazine as "Corporate America's Scariest Opponent."

Mr. Mehri co-authored a series of articles on securities enforcement and corporate governance including *Labor & Corporate Governance* articles entitled *Stock Option Equity: Building Democracy While Building Wealth* (November 2002) and *The Latest Retreat by the SEC* (February 2003). Mr. Mehri and Steven Berk also co-authored an article in *The Journal of Investment Compliance* (Winter 2002/2003) entitled *Slipping Back to Business as Usual, Six Months After the Passage of Sarbanes-Oxley*.

He is also the co-author (with Andrea Giampetro-Meyer & Michael B. Runnels) of the article *One Nation, Indivisible: The Use of Diversity Report Cards to Promote Transparency, Accountability, and Workplace Fairness*, Fordham Journal of Corporate and Financial Law, 9, 99–152.

Mr. Mehri currently represents institutional investors concerned about securities fraud and corporate governance. Mr. Mehri has a long history of representing defrauded investors, pensioners, and consumers, as well as small businesses subjected to price-fixing, in other class actions. For example, in 1993, *Florin v. NationsBank* restored $16 million to a pension plan that was bilked by company insiders at Simmons Mattress Company. In 1991, *In re Bolar Pharmaceutical Co.* returned over $25 million to defrauded shareholders. Currently, Mr. Mehri serves as co-lead counsel in numerous consumer class actions.

Mr. Mehri graduated from Cornell Law School in 1988, where he served as Articles Editor for the Cornell International Law Journal. After law school, he clerked for the Honorable John T. Nixon, U.S. District Judge for the Middle District of Tennessee. Mr. Mehri has received the Outstanding Youth Alumnus Award from Hartwick College and the Alumni Award from Wooster School in Danbury, Connecticut, "for becoming a beacon for good, positively affecting the lives of many."

Last year, the Pigskin Club of Washington, D.C., granted Mr. Mehri the prestigious "Award Of Excellence."

In March 2003, the Detroit City Council passed a testimonial resolution honoring Mr. Mehri and wishing him "continued success in changing the fabric of America."

Tom Methvin began his legal career in 1988 with Beasley, Allen representing people who have been victimized by consumer fraud. He pioneered many legal theories that are still in use today throughout the country. Some of these theories include lender liability causes of action known as "loan flipping," "insurance packing," and "yield spread premiums." He also became a national spokesman for the rights of consumers and for the law which applies to such rights. He was the lead attorney in a landmark case involving a door-to-door sales and finance scam that resulted in a settlement of $581 million dollars. As a result of this litigation, the finance company in question ceased to be involved in such activities in the state of Alabama.

Since 1998, Mr. Methvin has been the managing shareholder of Beaseley, Allen. As a result of his reorganization of the firm, each lawyer has been allowed to focus on certain types of cases and to be on the cutting edge in their fields of expertise. He has helped Beasley, Allen, to become a national powerhouse in representing victims of wrongdoing.

Mr. Methvin was recently named by the Montgomery Advertiser newspaper as one of the "Top 40 under 40." This is a list of the top 40 business people in Central Alabama under the age of 40.

Tom has authored numerous papers including, "The Law of Unfair Competition—A Plaintiffs Perspective," "Business Torts from a Plaintiffs Perspective," "Preparing Yourself to Take an Experts Deposition," "Consumer Fraud Class Action: A Plaintiff's Perspective," "Damages, Theories & Trial Strategies," "The Workup of a Debit Insurance Fraud Case," "Mortgage Fraud," "Winning and Collecting Big Verdicts Against Fringe Market Sellers," "The Workup of a Consumer Credit Fraud Case," "Alabama's Poverty Industry," "Fraud in Alabama," "Binding Arbitration and Its Effect on Consumer Finance Cases," "When Business Needs a Trial Lawyer," "Negotiations and Settlements of a Civil Action from a Plaintiffs Perspective," and "Alabama—The Arbitration State."

Mr. Methvin is on the Board of Alabama Trial Lawyers for Children and the Cystic Fibrosis Advisory Panel. He also serves on the Board of the Let God Arise Ministries. Mr. Methvin is married to the former Amy Agee of Birmingham and they have two sons. He attends church at Christ Community Church in Montgomery. He can be reached at Beasley, Allen, Crow, Methvin, Portis, & Miles, P.C., P.O. Box 4160, Montgomery, AL 36130; phone: 334-269-2343; fax: 334-954 7555.

Elizabeth Miller is a 1982 graduate of Brown University and a 1990 graduate of Yale Law School. Ms. Miller is the coordinator of the Bet Tzedek Legal Program of Jewish Family & Children's Service in Waltham, Massachusetts. She has practiced consumer law for more than ten years and has worked with the National Consumer Law Center on fair debt collection issues; with Grant & Roddy in Boston, primarily bringing class and individual actions for violations of the Truth in Lending Act, Fair Debt Collection Practices Act, Fair Credit Billing Act, Fair Credit Reporting Act, Consumer Leasing Act, and Massachusetts consumer protection law and for predatory "equity skimming" foreclosures, and as a staff attorney at Greater Boston Legal Services representing homeowners in the Roxbury and Dorchester neighborhoods of Boston faced with foreclosure. She may be contacted at andresliz@comcast.net.

Donna Siegel Moffa is a member of Rodriguez & Richards (3 Kings Highway East, Haddonfield, NJ 8033; phone: 856-795-9002; e-mail: donna@rr-law.com). She is admitted to practice before the United States Courts for the Districts of New Jersey and the District of Columbia as well as the Supreme Court of New Jersey and the District of Columbia Court of Appeals. She is a 1982 graduate (with honors) of Georgetown University Law Center. She received her undergraduate degree, also with honors, from Mount Holyoke College in Massachusetts in 1979.

Prior to entering private practice, Ms. Moffa was a staff attorney at both the Federal Energy Regulatory Commission (FERC), where she worked in the Divisions of Administrative Law and Hydroelectric Licensing—and the Federal Trade Commission (FTC). At the FTC, as a member of the Bureau of Consumer Protection, she litigated cases involving allegations of deceptive and unsubstantiated advertising against R.J. Reynolds and General Nutrition Company. In addition, both at FERC and the FTC, Ms. Moffa was involved with a wide range of administrative and regulatory issues, including labeling and marketing claims, compliance, FOIA and disclosure obligations, employment matters, and licensing. She has also participated in a number of rulemaking proceedings and contributed to the Final Report to the Federal Trade Commission on the Children's Advertising Rulemaking Proceeding.

In private practice, Ms. Moffa has continued to focus on consumer protection litigation and has substantial experience in consumer class actions. On behalf of individuals and classes, she has prosecuted claims in cases involving consumer financing, automobile sale practices, force-placed insurance, senior-citizen housing, deceptive labeling practices, and anti-competitive conduct arising under the state and federal laws. Prior to joining the firm, Ms. Moffa worked with Ms. Rodriguez as co-lead counsel in successfully challenging the practices of certain companies in the rent-to-own industry in New Jersey. As a result of that case, a significant monetary recovery was obtained for consumers, and changes were made in the contracts these companies use to provide more information to consumers.

Ms. Moffa is currently involved in class actions against lenders, dietary supplement manufacturers, car dealers, and drug manufacturers. Additionally, Ms. Moffa's practice continues to include representation of individuals and businesses in commercial, contractual, and tort litigation. She has successfully represented such clients in invasion of privacy actions, wage and hour proceedings, and contractual disputes. She has also addressed consumer protection and litigation issues in presentations to consumer groups, unions, and organizations as well as to professional associates. In addition, she has contributed to professional publications for consumer advocates.

Manuel H. Newburger is the Vice-President of Barron & Newburger, P.C., the President of Fair Debt Consultants, L.L.C., and an adjunct professor at the University of Texas School of Law. A graduate of Trinity University and the University of Texas School of Law, Mr. Newburger is admitted to practice law before the Texas Supreme Court, the United States Supreme Court, the United States Courts of Appeals for the Second, Fifth, and Seventh Circuits, all four United States District Courts for the State of Texas, and the United States District Courts for the Eastern District of Wisconsin, the Central District of California, and the Northern District of Indiana. He is board certified as a specialist in consumer and commercial law by the Texas Board of Legal Specialization.

Mr. Newburger consults nationally and internationally on fair debt compliance, consumer litigation issues, and collection agency licensing. He defends and serves as an expert witness in FDCPA cases across the United States, and he provides FDCPA compliance training and reviews to collection industry members. He represented the Commercial Law League of America as an amicus curiae in *Heintz v. Jenkins*, 514 U.S. 291, 115 S. Ct. 1489 (1995); *Koons Buick Pontiac GMC, Inc. v. Nigh*, __ U.S. __, 125 S. Ct. 460, 160 L. Ed. 2d 389 (2004); *White v. Goodman*, 200 F.3d 1016 (7th Cir. 2000); and *Riviere v. Banner Chevrolet, Inc.*, 184 F.3d 457 (5th Cir. 1999).

Mr. Newburger is the co-author, with B. Barron, of *Fair Debt Collection Practices: Federal and State Law and Regulation* (Sheshunoff & Pratt 2002).

Stephen Norman is a staff attorney with Vermont Legal Aid, Inc. (P.O. Box 1367, Burlington VT 05401; phone: 802-863-5620; fax: 802-863-7152). He has twenty-four years' experience in individual and class representation on housing, consumer, and public benefit issues, including antitrust, bankruptcy, and mobile home park law.

Stephen H. Olden is a senior attorney at the Legal Aid Society (215 East Ninth Street, #200, Cincinnati, OH 45202; e-mail: solden@lascinti.org). He has practiced in the consumer and housing fields for over twenty years. He currently heads the office's consumer/homeowner practice team, which includes a student loan and trade school project initiated in 1996. He has represented defrauded students in class action litigation as well as in proceedings with the U.S. Department of Education. He has also been a trainer at numerous consumer and student-loan discharge training events. Mr. Olden is a member of the Massachusetts, Ohio, and federal bars.

David J. Philipps is a partner in the firm of Gomolinski & Philipps, Ltd. (9760 S. Roberts Road, Suite One, Palos Hills, IL 60465; phone: 708-974-2900; fax: 708-974-2907); e-mail: davephilipps@aol.com). The firm concentrates its practice on consumer class actions, including those involving the Fair Debt Collection Practices Act, consumer fraud, and securities. He is a member of the state and federal bars of Illinois and is a founding member of the National Association of Consumer Advocates. He is a member of the Chicago Bar Association's Class Litigation Committee and has served as the committee's recent developments coordinator and legislative liaison from 1992–1998. He has spoken about the FDCPA and class action lawsuits at various seminars and to many bar groups.

James M. Pietz, Malakoff Doyle & Finberg, P.C. (Suite 200, The Frick Building, Pittsburgh, PA 15219; phone: 412-289-8400; fax: 412-281-3262). The firm specializes in class action litigation and consumer and insurance issues. The firm has served as class counsel in seven class actions, which to date have recovered over $10 million for consumers purchasing interests in campgrounds. Mr. Pietz has extensive experience in consumer class action litigation, particularly involving financial institutions' liability for campground fraud and life-insurer sales practices.

Dale Pittman maintains a consumer protection litigation practice based in Petersburg. He is a 1971 graduate of Hampden-Sydney College and a 1976 graduate of the University of Richmond Law School. As one of the first consumer protection attorneys in Virginia, his litigation of consumer protection cases has resulted in numerous published opinions furthering the rights of victims of consumer credit overreaching and abuse. Opinions from some of his Fair Debt Collections Practices Act cases appear at *Creighton v. Emporia Credit Service, Inc.*, 981 F. Supp. 411 (E.D. Va. 1997); *Withers v. Eveland*, 988 F. Supp. 942 (E.D. Va. 1997); *Morgan v. Credit Adjustment Board*, 999 F. Supp. 803 (E.D. Va. 1998); and *Talbott v. GC Services Limited Partnership*, 53 F. Supp. 2d 846 (W.D. Va. 1999). Courts in North Carolina and Virginia have certified class actions against collection agencies in cases in which Mr. Pittman represented classes of consumers, including *Woodard v. Online Information Servs.*, 191 F.R.D. 502 (E.D.N.C., Jan. 19, 2000) and *Talbott v. GC Services Limited Partnership*, 191 F.R.D. 99 (W.D. Va. 2000). Mr. Pittman has been asked to speak by the American Bar Association, Virginia CLE, the Virginia Trial Lawyers Association, the National Association of Consumer Advocates, the National Consumer Law Center, and others. He has contributed to several National Consumer Law Center publications. Mr. Pittman serves on the governing body of the Virginia Trial Lawyers Association, and he chairs the VTLA's Consumer Law Section. He is a past president of the Petersburg Bar Association.

Bren J. Pomponio is an attorney who, in 2000, joined Mountain State Justice, Inc. (922 Quarrier St., Suite 525, Charleston, WV 25301; phone: 304-344-5565; fax: 304-344-3145; e-mail: bren@msjlaw.org). Prior to that, he was a law clerk for West Virginia United States District Judges Charles H. Haden II and Joseph R. Goodwin.

Kieron F. Quinn is a member of the bars of Maryland, New York, the District of Columbia, a number of U.S. Circuits, and the Supreme Court. He is a graduate of Georgetown University and the George Washington University School of Law, where he was a Trustee Scholar who graduated first in his class, served on the Law Review, and was elected to the Order of the Coif. He thereafter served as a Trial Attorney in the United States Department of Justice. His practice concentrates in representing plaintiffs in class actions. He served as Damages and Discovery Chair for the Environmental Plaintiffs in both the class and non-class Exxon Valdez litigation in state court in Alaska and was lead class counsel in Denver, Colorado, for plaintiffs in *Escamilla v. Asarco, Inc.*, a toxic tort action in which the jury awarded the class in excess of $30 million. He was lead counsel in *Chisolm v. Charlie Falk's Auto Wholesalers & TranSouth Financial Services, Inc.*, a RICO and consumer protection action that was taken to the Fourth Circuit four times and that ultimately resulted in a recovery of approximately $15 million for the class and for which he was awarded the Public Justice Award by the Trial Lawyers for Public Justice. More recently, Mr. Quinn litigated a class action against Blue Cross/Blue Shield—in which a class of Maryland subscribers recovered $2.3 million as a consequence of being required to pay excess co-payments to health care providers—several successful class actions against automobile dealers arising from phoney charges, and several class actions against mortgage brokers who victimized low-income homeowners. Mr. Quinn teaches at the University of Maryland School of Law and has also lectured at a number of law schools. He has written several articles and delivered a number of papers at CLE symposia. He is an editor of *Class Actions Reports* and two other legal periodicals. Mr. Quinn has been selected for inclusion in the publication, *The Best Lawyers in America*, each year since it began publishing in 1982. He was selected by *Baltimore Magazine* in March 1995 as one of the best lawyers in Baltimore and was the co-recipient in 1993 of the TLPJ Trial Lawyer of the Year Award.

Kieron Quinn is located at Quinn, Gordon & Wolf Chtd. 40 West Chesapeake Ave. Suite 408, Baltimore, MD 21204; phone: 410-825-2300; fax: 410-825-0066; e-mail: kfquinn@quinnlaw.com.

Michael J. Quirk is a staff attorney with Trial Lawyers for Public Justice in Washington, D.C., where he engages in socially significant and precedent-setting complex civil litigation. His work focuses primarily on representing consumers, workers, and injury victims in fighting mandatory arbitration clauses and federal preemption defenses and on addressing class action-related issues. He was co-counsel in *Sprietsma v. Mercury Marine*, 537 U.S. 51 (2002), which held that a survivor's state law wrongful death claims against a boat manufacturer for failing to install a propeller guard are not preempted by the Federal Boat Safety Act or a federal agency's abstention from regulation. He was also co-counsel and wrote the successful trial brief for a class of California consumers in *Ting v. AT&T*, 182 F. Supp. 2d 902 (N.D. Cal. 2002), *aff'd in part and rev'd in part*, 319 F.3d 1126 (9th Cir. 2003), in which the courts struck down AT&T's mandatory arbitration clause based on provisions stripping consumers of damages remedies and class-wide relief, imposing excessive forum costs, and mandating sweeping secrecy requirements. He was lead appellate counsel for successful plaintiffs in *Sanderson Farms, Inc. v. Gatlin*, 848 So. 2d 828 (Miss. 2002) and *Boghos v. Lloyd's of London*, 109 Cal. App. 4th 1728, *rev. granted*, 1 Cal. Rptr. 3d 447 (Cal. 2003), both holding a company's mandatory arbitration clause unenforceable and allowing plaintiffs to litigate claims in court. He was also lead counsel for objecting class members in *Dotson v. Bell Atlantic-Maryland, Inc.*, 2003 WL 23508428 (Md. Cir. Ct. Nov. 13, 2003), where the court threw out a proposed consumer class action settlement that would have paid the class $155,000 in total relief and class counsel $13 million in attorney fees. He is co-author of the first four editions of *Consumer Arbitration Agreements: Enforceability and Other Topics* (National Consumer Law Center and The TLPJ Foundation), part of NCLC's Consumer Credit and Sales Legal Practice Series. Before becoming a staff attorney, he was an Equal Justice Works Fellow with TLPJ. He previously held a fellowship with the Public Citizen Litigation Group, also in Washington, D.C. He received his J.D. *cum laude* from the University of Michigan Law School in 1999.

David Ramp was a senior litigator practicing consumer law with Mid-Minnesota Legal Assistance in Minneapolis and then with the Attorney General's Office (445 Minnesota St.,1100, St. Paul, MN 55101; phone: 651-297-5907). He is currently in private practice in Minneapolis. Mr. Ramp is nationally recognized for his expertise on the rent-to-own industry, an expertise arising from his class action litigation against the largest firms in an industry that often overcharges low-income consumers and structures its contracts to avoid many consumer protection laws. In 1997, David received the National Consumer Law Center's Vern Countryman award honoring the accomplishments of public interest lawyers contributing significantly to the rights and welfare of low-income consumers. He has testified before Congress and been invited to draft new consumer protections. Recently, he also became a founding member of the Minnesota Consumer Attorneys Association, a growing group of private and public and legal services attorneys specializing in consumer law, modeled after the National Association of Consumer Attorneys. In addition, Mr. Ramp has been especially active in tenant screening litigation. He continues to work with foundation- and Dayton-Hudson-supported efforts to create alternative resources for populations drawn to rent-to-own outlets.

John Rao is a staff attorney at the National Consumer Law Center, Inc. Mr. Rao focuses on consumer credit and bankruptcy issues and directs the Center's case consulting services, providing technical assistance and litigation support to attorneys in consumer law cases. He also participates in the Center's litigation efforts. He has served as a panelist and instructor at numerous bankruptcy and consumer law trainings and conferences. Mr. Rao is a contributing author and editor of NCLC's *Consumer Bankruptcy Law and Practice*; co-author of

NCLC's *Repossessions and Foreclosures* and *Guide to Surviving Debt*; and contributing author to NCLC's *Student Loan Law*, *Stop Predatory Lending*, and NCLC REPORTS *Bankruptcy and Foreclosures Edition*. He is also a contributing author to *Collier on Bankruptcy* (Matthew-Bender) and the *Collier Bankruptcy Practice Guide*. He is a member of the board of directors for the National Association of Consumer Bankruptcy Attorneys and the American Bankruptcy Institute. He is a graduate of Boston University and received his J.D. from the University of California (Hastings).

Elizabeth Renuart is a staff attorney with the National Consumer Law Center. She is responsible for writing and supplementing two of the treatises in NCLC's Consumer Credit and Sales Legal Practice series—*Truth In Lending* and *The Cost of Credit: Regulation, Preemption, and Industry Abuses*—and is the author and editor of NCLC's bimonthly newsletter titled NCLC REPORTS *Consumer Credit and Usury Edition*. She provides direct service to attorneys representing low-income and elderly consumers, including analyzing mortgage loan documents. In addition, she has testified and commented orally and in writing on proposed Congressional and administrative agency action affecting low-income and elderly consumers, particularly in the area of mortgage lending. She has conducted conferences and seminars on mortgage lending and defenses to foreclosure. NCLC hosts an annual conference in which she participates as a facilitator and speaker.

Prior to coming to the National Consumer Law Center, from 1991–1996, she managed a small legal services program in Baltimore, Maryland, that specialized in representing homeowners in danger of losing their homes. In this capacity, she handled numerous cases involving mortgage loans, real estate issues, foreclosure, and bankruptcy. Prior to that position, she managed a legal services office in Frederick, Maryland, for twelve years and served as a staff attorney in a legal services office in Augusta, Georgia, for a year and a half. In those capacities, she represented low-income clients in a wide variety of cases. She has been practicing law for over twenty-five years.

Ms. Renuart is a member of the Maryland Bar and the federal bars of the United States Supreme Court, the Fourth Circuit Court of Appeals, the District of Maryland, and the Southern District of Georgia. She graduated from the Columbus School of Law, the Catholic University of America, Washington, D.C., in 1977. Since coming to the National Consumer Law Center, she has been retained as an expert in several cases pending in state and federal courts, all of which involve mortgage loans.

John Roddy is a partner in the Boston law firm of Roddy, Klein & Ryan (727 Atlantic Avenue, Boston MA 02111; phone: 617-357-5500; fax: 617-357-5030), and he specializes in consumer credit litigation and class actions. He is a 1980 honors graduate of Boston College Law School. From 1980–1985, he enforced state and federal consumer laws in the Consumer Protection Division of the Massachusetts' Attorney General's Office. These lawsuits remedied unfair and deceptive business practices that harmed hundreds and sometimes thousands of consumers. From 1986–1987, he was legislative counsel to the Attorney General in the office's Executive Bureau.

Mr. Roddy has written and lectured on the substantive and practical applications of the Massachusetts consumer protection act for Massachusetts Continuing Legal Education, Inc.; has co-authored (with Francis X. Bellotti, former Massachusetts Attorney General) part of an ABA Teleconference Seminar on consumer protection laws nationally; has written for and lectured in national seminars by the National Association of Housing and Redevelopment Officials on remedying predatory lending practices in the core city; and frequently writes and lectures on consumer law and class action litigation for diverse organizations, including the Practicing Law Institute, the National Consumer Law Center, the Review of Banking and Financial Services, MCLE, and the Florida Bar Association. For the past seven years he has co-chaired the Practicing Law Institute's *Annual Institute on Consumer Financial Services Litigation*, held in New York City and San Francisco. He is a board member of the Massachusetts Appleseed Foundation and a sponsor member of the National Association of Consumer Advocates.

Lisa J. Rodriguez is a member of the firm of Trujillo Rodriguez & Richards, L.L.C. (3 Kings Highway East, Haddonfield, NJ 08033; phone: 856-795-9002, 856-795-9887), which has offices in Philadelphia, Pennsylvania; Cherry Hill, New Jersey; and Mexico City, Mexico. The firm's practice is concentrated in the area of complex litigation, with an emphasis on antitrust, consumer, securities, international, and general business litigation as well as white-collar criminal defense and international transactions. The firm's consumer practice has focused on litigation involving force-placed insurance, insurance packing, rent-to-own transactions, and other financial services issues. Recently, the firm and its co-counsel made headlines by obtaining summary judgment on liability and damages on behalf of a certified class against Thorn Americas, which operates the Rent-A-Center chain. Thorn itself has estimated that the judgment will require it to pay $120 million. Also, the firm and its co-counsel obtained an important decision from the District of New Jersey sanctioning a bank for attempting to coerce a class representative to breach her duties to other class members.

Lisa J. Rodriguez, a member of the firm, is a 1983 graduate (with honors) of the George Washington University Law School. She served as a law clerk to the Honorable Mitchell H. Cohen, Senior Judge of the United States District Court for the District of New Jersey. Ms. Rodriguez has appeared as a panel speaker for the Practicing Law Institute on Securities Regulation and has also appeared as a lecturer for the Philadelphia Bar Education Center on consumer and class action issues. Ms. Rodriguez is co-lead counsel in a case being litigated in New Jersey state court involving the rent-to-own industry in which the court entered summary judgment on liability against three defendants. In addition, Ms. Rodriguez is lead or co-lead counsel in litigation involving force-placed insurance and credit insurance packing.

Ms. Rodriguez is admitted to practice before the United States Court of Appeals for the Third Circuit, the United States District Courts for the Eastern District of Pennsylvania, the District of New Jersey, and the Northern District of California. She is also admitted to the Supreme Court of Pennsylvania, the Supreme Court of New Jersey, and the United States Supreme Court.

Phillip C. Rogers is a private attorney at 40 Pearl Street, N.W., Suite 336, Grand Rapids, MI 49503; phone: 616-776-1176, Fax: 616-776-0037. His practice is focused on representing consumers in the areas of fraud in the sale and finance of automobiles, Truth in Lending, and the Fair Debt Collection Practices Act. Mr. Rogers is a member of the Michigan state and federal bars.

Stuart Rossman is an NCLC staff attorney directing the Center's litigation efforts. He is an experienced trial attorney who, after thirteen years of private practice, served as Chief of the Trial Division and Chief of the Business and Labor Protection Bureau (consisting of the Fair Labor and Business Practices Division, the Insurance Fraud Division, the Medicaid Fraud Control Unit, and the Unemployment Fraud Division) at the Massachusetts Attorney General's Office. He also founded and chaired the Attorney General's Abandoned Housing Task Force, a project created to assist municipalities and community groups in seeking solutions to abandoned properties. Mr. Rossman is the former chairman of the Volunteer Lawyers Project, the oldest and largest pro bono legal services program in Massachusetts, and continues to serve on its Board of Directors. He is a member of the adjunct faculties of the Northeastern University School of Law, where he has taught Civil Trial Advocacy since 1993, and the Suffolk University Law School, where he has taught a consumer law class. Mr. Rossman and NCLC's co-counsel in the case of *Coleman v. GMAC* (auto finance discrimination claims under the Equal Credit Opportunity Act) were recognized by the Trial Lawyers for Public Justice as 2004 Trial Lawyers of the Year Finalists and as recipients of the 2005 Thurgood Marshall Award from the Rainbow/PUSH Coalition. Mr. Rossman is a graduate of the University of Michigan and Harvard Law School.

Richard J. Rubin is a private attorney with an office at 1300 Canyon Road, Santa Fe, NM 87501; phone: 505-983-4418; fax: 505-983-2050; e-mail: DickRubin@cs.com, whose federal appellate practice is limited to representing consumers in both federal consumer credit protection—including credit reporting and debt collection abuse litigation—and to consulting for other consumer rights specialists around the country. He and his solo practice were the subject of a profile published in the January 1993 ABA Journal. Mr. Rubin has taught consumer law at the University of New Mexico School of Law, is a regular contributor to the Consumer Credit and Sales Legal Practice Series manuals published by NCLC, and presents continuing legal education and attorney-training programs nationally in the areas of consumer credit, warranty law, and debt collection abuse. The United States Court of Appeals for the Seventh Circuit has acknowledged Mr. Rubin as a "nationally known consumer-rights attorney" (*Bass v. Stolper, Koritzinsky, Brewster & Neider, S.C.*, 1997 U.S. App. LEXIS 41397, *5 (June 6, 1997). Mr. Rubin is the past chair of the National Association of Consumer Advocates (NACA) and in 2000 was the recipient of the Vern Countryman Award.

Margot Freeman Saunders (margot@nclcdc.org) was Managing Attorney of the Washington office of the National Consumer Law Center (www.consumerlaw.org) from 1991–2005. Currently "of counsel" to NCLC, her duties include representing the interests of low-income clients in Congress on electronic commerce issues, predatory mortgages, other financial credit issues as well as water and energy matters. She has testified on numerous occasions before several Congressional committees on the impact of various proposals on low-income households and recently completed terms as a member of the Federal Reserve Board's Consumer Advisory Council and the American Water Works Association Public Advisory Forum. She is co-author of a number of books, including the original and revised editions of NCLC's *Consumer Banking and Payments Law* (3d ed. 2005), the original and the revised editions of NCLC's *Access to Utility Service* (1996, 2001), NCLC's *Energy and the Poor: The Crisis Continues* (1995), *Tenants' Rights to Utility Service* (1994), and *The Manual on Water Affordability Programs* (AWWA, 1998), and numerous articles on consumer and utilities laws as they affect low-income people in the United States.

Prior to coming to D.C. in September 1991, Ms. Freeman Saunders was the consumer specialist for North Carolina Legal Services. In North Carolina, she represented low-income clients before the state legislature, the appellate courts, and various administrative agencies. She also regularly lobbied the North Carolina General Assembly on consumer issues. For several sessions of the Assembly, she was voted by legislators, the press, and other lobbyists to be among the top twenty most effective lobbyists.

In May 1991, she was the recipient of the Vern Countryman Award, a national award recognizing attorneys for outstanding advocacy on behalf of low income consumers.

She is a graduate of Brandeis University and the University of North Carolina School of Law.

David A. Searles, of Donovan Searles, L.L.C. (1845 Walnut Street, Suite 1100, Philadelphia, PA 19103; phone: 215-732-6067), is a founding member of the firm and is admitted to practice before the Supreme Court of the United States, the United States Court of Appeals for the Third Circuit, the United States District Court for the Eastern District of Pennsylvania, as well as the state courts of Pennsylvania. He is a 1975 graduate of the American University School of Law, Washington, D.C., where he served on law review. Following graduation from law school, Mr. Searles was an attorney for Community Legal Services of Philadelphia, where he specialized in consumer and bankruptcy law. In 1990, he successfully argued the first consumer reorganization bankruptcy case considered by the U.S. Supreme Court, *Pennsylvania v. Davenport*, 495 U.S. 552 (1990), and has served as lead counsel and has presented argument in numerous bankruptcy and consumer law cases before the United States Court of Appeals for the Third Circuit. From 1992 through 1997, Mr. Searles was associated with the Philadelphia law firm of Drinker Biddle & Reath, L.L.P., where his practice focused on Chapter 11 bankruptcy and creditor's rights.

Mr. Searles is the Managing Editor of the Survey of State Class Action Law (ABA Section on Litigation, 2005) and is a contributing author to *Pennsylvania Consumer Law* (2005). Along with Mr. Donovan, he co-authored *Preserving Judicial Recourse for Consumers: How to Combat Overreaching Arbitration Clauses*, 10 Loyola Consumer L. Rev. 269 (1998). He has taught advanced bankruptcy law at Rutgers University School of Law—Camden, business law at Widener University, and bankruptcy law at Pierce Junior College, Philadelphia. He is a past co-chairperson of the Education Committee of the Eastern District of Pennsylvania Bankruptcy Conference.

Thomas R. Seel is a senior attorney at the Legal Aid Society of Greater Cincinnati (10 Journal Square, Suite 300, Hamilton, Ohio 45011; phone: 513-241-9400; fax: 513-894-7669; e-mail: tseel@lascinti.org). He has fifteen years general legal services experience, including experience in the areas of consumer law and bankruptcy. Mr. Seel now specializes in rental housing and homeowner litigation. He is member of the Ohio, Kentucky, and federal bar.

Nina F. Simon has been an attorney with AARP and the AARP Foundation since 1985. Ms. Simon is currently working with the AARP Foundation's Litigation Group on issues involving fraudulent and predatory mortgage lending practices targeted at elderly and minority homeowners. Prior to joining the Litigation Group, Ms. Simon worked for AARP's Legal Counsel for the Elderly representing low-income elderly residents of the District of Columbia. In 1995, she was awarded the Jerrold Scoutt Prize for her work on behalf of the low-income and vulnerable elderly population of D.C. She has been a Consumer Fellow of the American Bar Association's Consumer Financial Services Committee since 1995 and currently serves as the Vice chair of the subcommittee on Consumer Litigation. She also served as a member of HUD's Negotiated Rulemaking Committee on the Mortgage Broker Rule and is a frequent speaker on TILA, RESPA and predatory mortgage lending. Ms. Simon was an active consumer representative in the Mortgage Reform Working Group and in HUD's deliberations on reform of Truth in Lending and RESPA. Ms. Simon graduated *magna cum laude*, Phi Beta Kappa, from Brandeis University in 1975. She received her law degree *cum laude* in 1978 from New York University Law School, where she was made a member of the Order of the Coif.

Kimberly M. Skaggs is the Executive Director of the Equal Justice Foundation (88 East Broad Street, Suite 1590, Columbus, OH 83215; phone: 614-221-9800), a non-profit organization that provides civil legal services in the form of class-action litigation to indigent, minority, or disabled individuals. Ms. Skaggs is a former Assistant Federal Public Defender and a former law clerk to the Honorable R. Guy Cole, Jr., United States Court of Appeals for the Sixth Circuit, and to the Honorable John D. Holschuh, United States District Court for the Southern District of Ohio. She is a past president of the Columbus Chapter of the Federal Bar Association and the 2003–2004 recipient of The Ohio State University Moritz College of Law Alumni Society Public Service Award. In addition to her administrative duties, Ms. Skaggs actively litigates consumer class action cases including, for example, *Matthews v. New Century Mortgage*, 185 F. Supp. 2d 874 (S.D. Ohio 2002) (predatory lending); *Mick v. Level Propane Gases, Inc.*, 168 F. Supp. 2d 804 (S.D. Ohio 2001) (grant of preliminary injunction in consumer class action); *Mick v. Level Propane Gases, Inc.*, 203 F.R.D. 324 (S.D. Ohio 2001) (certification of 23(b) (3) class in consumer class action); *Turner v. City of Chillicothe*, Case No. C2-00-980 (S.D. Ohio 2000) (class action utilities termination case).

Henry J. Sommer is Supervising Attorney at the pro bono Consumer Bankruptcy Assistance Project in Philadelphia. He has litigated many major cases involving bankruptcy, consumer law, civil rights, and other issues. Previously, he was the head of the Consumer Law Project at Community Legal Services in Philadelphia, where he worked for over twenty-one years. Mr. Sommer has also served as a Lecturer-in-Law at the University of Pennsylvania Law School. He received his A.B. degree from Harvard College, *magna cum laude*, and his J.D. degree from Harvard Law School, *cum laude*.

Mr. Sommer is Editor-in-Chief of *Collier on Bankruptcy* and the entire Collier line of bankruptcy publications. He is the author of *Collier Consumer Bankruptcy Practice Guide* (Matthew Bender 1997); *Consumer Bankruptcy Law and Practice* (6th Ed. 2000), published by the National Consumer Law Center; *Consumer Bankruptcy: The Complete Guide to Chapter 7 and Chapter 13 Personal Bankruptcy* (John Wiley & Sons 1994); and numerous articles on bankruptcy law. He is the co-author of *Collier Family Law and the Bankruptcy Code* (Matthew Bender 1991). He is also a contributing author to the Matthew Bender treatise, *Debtor-Creditor Law*.

Mr. Sommer is a former member of the Federal Judicial Conference Advisory Committee on Bankruptcy Rules (appointed by the Chief Justice of the Supreme Court) and a member of the National Bankruptcy Conference, for which he served as Reporter for the Bankruptcy Code Review Project's Working Group on Individual Debtors. He is a Fellow of the American College of Bankruptcy, a member of the American Law Institute, and a former member of the Federal Reserve Board Consumer Advisory Council. He is also President of the National Association of Consumer Bankruptcy Attorneys (NACBA), a former Chairman of the Eastern District of Pennsylvania Bankruptcy Conference, and Vice President of the Coalition for Consumer Bankruptcy Debtor Education.

He has been asked to testify many times before the House and Senate Judiciary Committees, as well as the National Bankruptcy Review Commission, on bankruptcy and consumer law issues. He has served on the faculty of numerous continuing legal education programs including those presented by the Federal Judicial Center, New York University Law School, the National Conference of Bankruptcy Judges, the Southeastern Bankruptcy Law Institute, the Executive Office of U.S. Trustees, the ABA Family Law Section, NACBA, ALI-ABA and the Pennsylvania Bar Institute. Mr. Sommer was the first recipient of the National Consumer Law Center's Vern Countryman Consumer Law Award.

Andrew Spark of the Florida Attorney General's Office (3507 E. Frontage Rd., Ste. 325, Tampa, FL, 33607; e-mail: Andrew_Spark@oag.state.fl.us) is a *cum laude* graduate of The Wharton School at the University of Pennsylvania and an honors graduate of the University of Florida College of Law. He practices in the Economic Crimes Unit, which primarily involves consumer racketeering litigation. He served as Vice Chair of the Consumer Protection Law Committee of The Florida Bar in 2001–2002. He is admitted to practice in Florida, New York, and New Jersey and has served as a lemon law arbitrator under the auspices of the Florida Attorney General.

Mark H. Steinbach is a partner in the Washington, D.C., law firm of O'Toole, Rothwell, Nassau & Steinbach (1350 Connecticut Avenue Suite 200, N.W. Washington, D.C. 20036; phone: 202-775-1550; fax: 202-775-0008). From 1974–1977, he served as a staff attorney with the Center for Auto Safety, a non-profit consumer advocacy group in Washington, D.C. Since then, he has been in private practice, beginning his concentration in consumer law in 1982. He has represented many individuals and consumer groups (such as the Disgruntled Diesel Owners' Group, the Audi Victims Network, and the Fiero Firefighters) and has been involved in class action litigation against auto dealers and manufacturers. He has been active for many years as a member of the Consumer Affairs Committee of the D.C. Bar. He serves on the Board of Directors of the Maryland Consumer Rights Coalition. In 2002, he joined the Board of Directors of the National Association of Consumer Advocates.

Robert Stempler is an attorney in private practice. Robert Stempler, Attorney at Law, Consumer and Tax Law Office of Robert Stempler, APLC, 3400 Inland Empire Blvd., Ste. 101, Ontario, CA 91764-5577; phone: 909-972-6841; fax: 909-433-2132.

Robert S. Stevens is an attorney with Charlottesville Albemale Legal Aid (617 W. Main street #3, Charlottesville, VA 22902). Mr. Stevens has a concentration in consumer protection and debtor relief. He is a member of the Virginia bar association.

Darnley D. Stewart is a partner in the New York law firm of Bernstein Litowitz Berger & Grossmann L.L.P. (1285 Avenue of the Americas, New York, NY 10019; phone: 212-554-1400; fax: 212-554-1444; e-mail: darnley@BLBGLAW.com). Ms. Stewart clerked on the Massachusetts Court of Appeals. Along with Daniel Berger, she is the partner principally responsible for her firm's employment discrimination and employee rights practice group. Ms. Stewart is a member of the Title VII Committee of the National Employment Lawyers Association and the individual Rights and Responsibilities Committee of the New York State Bar Association. In addition, she serves as Plaintiffs' Co-Chair of the Class Action Subcommittee of the ABA's Employment Rights and Responsibilities Committee.

The Sturdevant Law Firm (475 Sansome Street, Suite 1750, San Francisco, CA 94111; phone: 415-477-2410; fax: 415-477-2420) is a firm of five lawyers that specializes in complex and class litigation on behalf of consumers exposed to unlawful business practices, financial services fraud, misrepresentation and overcharging, employment discrimination, environmental damage, toxic torts, civil rights, vocational school fraud, and insurance packing, among others. Most of the firm's work takes place in the state and federal trial courts in the Bay Area.

James C. Sturdevant, the founder of the firm, has been engaged in the practice of law for more than twenty-five years. *Badie v. Bank of America* (1998) 69 Cal. App. 4th 779, 79 Cal. Rptr. 2d 273 (compulsory non-consensual ADR imposed on consumers via bill stuffer found to be invalid attempt to modify existing account agreement) and *Beasley v. Wells Fargo Bank, N.A.* (1991) 235 Cal. App. 3d 1383, 1 Cal. Rptr. 2d 446 (credit card late and over-limit charges constitute illegal and excessive penalties for breach of contract) are two examples of his litigation. Mr. Sturdevant serves on the boards of several trial lawyers' organizations and has received numerous awards for his work on behalf of consumers.

Patricia Sturdevant has focused her practice on consumer protection for more than two decades. She has advocated on behalf of consumers in both the public and private sectors, in two legal services programs in Southern California and in private practice in San Francisco and Washington, D.C. In those capacities, she has recovered more than $160 million in damage awards in class actions and private attorney general cases, directed the work of multidisciplinary teams engaging in media and outreach campaigns and distributing those awards, and been instrumental in the development of the law.

Ms. Sturdevant is a co-founder of the National Association of Consumer Advocates and was its first executive director and General Counsel. She is credited with pioneering the modern use of *cy pres* remedies and has been responsible for providing indirect benefits to class members through awards to consumer advocacy organizations in amounts in excess of $6 million.

She is the only person ever to have received both the Vern Countryman Award and the William F. Willier Award from the National Consumer Law Center and has been recognized by the State Bar of California, the California Trial Lawyers Association, and the Bar Association of San Francisco for her work protecting consumers. She was a past president of the San Francisco Women Lawyer's Alliance, 1988–89, and a board member from 1984 through 1990; a board member and officer of the San Francisco Trial Lawyers Association, 1989–1997; a board member of the San Francisco Neighborhood Legal Assistance Foundation, 1992–1997; and a board member of Consumer Action, 1995 to present.

David A. Szwak a native of Baton Rouge, was admitted to the Louisiana Bar in 1991. He is a partner with Bodenheimer, Jones, Szwak & Winchell, L.L.P. (401 Market Street, Suite 240, American Tower, Shreveport, Louisiana 71101; phone: 318-424-1400; fax: 318-424-1476, email: dszwak@bjswlaw.com; bjks1507@aol.com). He is a double LSU graduate, having earned his Bachelor of Science in Quantitative Business Analysis from LSU and his law degree from LSU Law Center. He is a consumer credit attorney and partner with Bodenheimer, Jones, Szwak & Winchell, in Shreveport. Mr. Szwak is admitted to practice in Louisiana; the federal courts of the Eastern, Western and Middle Districts of Louisiana; the Eastern and Western Districts of Arkansas; the Northern, Eastern and Southern Districts of Texas; the District of Arizona; the Eastern District of Michigan; the Fifth Circuit Court of Appeals; the Eighth Circuit Court of Appeals; the Ninth Circuit Court of Appeals; the Eleventh Circuit Court of Appeals; and the Supreme Court of the United States. He also frequently practices *pro hac vice* in most other federal and state jurisdictions.

He has authored many legal articles, frequently lectures, and regularly litigates consumer credit, privacy, defamation, and fraud cases. His writings include *Theft of Identity—A Credit Nightmare*, Texas Bar Journal (1993); *Theft of Identity, Call It Data Rape*, The Alaska Bar Rag (Alaska Bar Association, 1994); *Theft of Identity: Roadkill on the Information Highway*,

Trial Bar News (New Hampshire Bar Association 1994); *Theft of Identity: Data Rape*, The Colorado Lawyer (Colorado Bar Association 1995); and *Credit Cards in America*, The Bar Review (Shreveport Bar Association 1995).

Mr. Szwak also provides expert witness services in Fair Credit Reporting Act cases and related issues. His services include consultation, evaluation, assistance in drafting pleadings and discovery, depositions, expert reports and analysis, and testimony. A listing of his expert witness cases is available on his law firm website at www.bjswlaw.com.

Thomas Tarter is the Managing Director of the Andela Consulting Group, Inc. (ACG) (15250 Ventura Boulevard, Suite 610, Sherman Oaks, CA 91403; phone: 818-380-3102; fax: 818-501-5412; e-mail: ttarter@earthlink.net), a consulting firm whose services include the providing of research; financial, management and turn around consulting services; and board of directorships and expert testimony services on a variety of matters, including banking and lending standards and practices involving processing. He has served as a management consultant and business advisor and on the board of directors of public, financially troubled, and closely held corporations (large and small), including serving as a reorganization advisor to The Bank of Saipan and for SEC reporting corporations such as First Alliance Mortgage Company. Mr. Tarter was appointed to First Alliance's board of directors subsequent to its filing for bankruptcy protection. First Alliance was active in the subprime lending market. It was accused of predatory lending practices and unfair and deceptive sales tactics involving consumer loans.

Mr. Tarter's experience in the financial institutions industry spans more than thirty-five years. He started his career at Lloyds Bank California, where he was Vice President in the Corporate Finance and California Divisions, and continued it as Vice President and the Senior Credit Officer for Southern California at the Sanwa Bank of California; Founding Director, President, and Chief Executive Officer at Bank of Los Angeles; Director, President and Chief Executive Officer at Center Nation Bank; Executive Vice President, First Los Angeles Bank; a director at Western States Bankcard Association; and ACG. He was also a director of the Fort Ord Credit Union, advisor to Matadors Community Credit Union, and a founder and organizer of Hancock Saving Bank. Mr. Tarter has been appointed to the mediator panel for the Bankruptcy Mediation Program of the United States Bankruptcy Court for the Central District of California and was a member of the Board of the Los Angeles Bankruptcy Forum. He received a Master of Business Administration degree from Santa Clara University and a Bachelor of Science degree in business from the University of California at Los Angeles.

Steven Taterka is in private practice in Kingston Springs, Tennessee. His practice is primarily in consumer law focusing on automobile cases, including lemon law, odometer fraud, salvage fraud, financing (TILA), leasing (CLA), and sales practice (UDAP) issues. He also litigates title pawn and check-cashing (check loan) cases.

Michael Terry is a partner in the Nashville law firm of Terry & Gore (1200 16th Ave So., Music Row, Nashville, TN. 37212; phone: 615-321-2750; fax: 615-250-4915; e-mail: tglaw@comcast.net). Mr. Terry is a former Deputy Attorney General for the State of Tennessee. Mr. Terry has been involved in federal litigation for more than thirty years, handling cases at all levels, including the United States Supreme Court.

Alec Trueblood has a private practice in Los Angeles, California, emphasizing unfair credit reporting, unfair debt collection practices, auto dealer fraud, lemon law, and class actions. He is a graduate of the University of California, Berkeley, and the UCLA School of Law. He began his career in the litigation department at Morrison & Foerster and subsequently worked for Chavez & Gertler in Mill Valley, California, where he specialized in class actions and unfair business practices.

Susan M. Warren joined the Law Offices of Richard Feferman (300 Central Avenue, SW, # 2000E, Albuquerque, NM 87102; phone: 505-243-7773; fax: 505-243-6663) in 1996. She graduated from Harvard Law School in 1990 and practiced with DNA-People's Legal Services for six years before joining the Law Offices of Richard Feferman.

The firm handles a wide variety of individual and class action consumer cases throughout New Mexico, Arizona and Colorado. Most of the firm's cases are federal suits against car dealers, debt collectors and lenders. In 1999, for their $669,000 jury verdict against a New Mexico car dealer for odometer fraud and tortious debt collection practices, the firm was nominated for trial lawyers of the year by the Trial Lawyers for Public Justice. Recent favorable published decisions include *Yazzie v. Ray Vicker's Special Cars, Inc.*, 12 F. Supp. 2d 1230 (D.N.M. 1998) (pawn "storage fee" was undisclosed finance charge under TILA) and 180 F.R.D. 411 (granting class certification); *Lee v. Gallup Auto Sales, Inc.*, 135 F.3d 1359 (10th Cir. 1998) (striking illegal regulation exempting older vehicles from federal odometer act); *Bitah v. Global Collection Services, Inc.*, et al., 968 F. Supp. (1997) (lawyer liability under FDCPA); *Halwood v. Cowboy Auto Sales, Inc.*, 124 N.M. 77, 946 P.2d 1088 (Ct. App. 1997) (upholding punitive damages for on-reservation tort by non-Indian).

Clint Watkins is a graduate of Vanderbilt Law School. Mr. Watkins is licensed in Tennessee as an attorney and certified public accountant (inactive). Mr. Watkin's practice is primarily federal litigation. Law Office of Clint W. Watkins, 5214 Maryland Way, Suite 402, Brentwood, TN 37027; phone: 615-376-7000; fax: 615-376-2628; e-mail: clint@clintwatkins.com.

Mary Welford is a partner in the law firm of Witten, Woolmington, Campbell, Boepple, Welford & Sawyer, P.C. in Manchester Center, Vermont (phone: 802-362-4281). Her main areas of practice are civil litigation, including consumer protection and landlord/tenant, family, Social Security disability, and elder law. Prior to joining her firm, Ms. Welford had a solo practice in Manchester for six years and spent the previous seven years as a staff attorney with Vermont Legal Aid and the Vermont Senior Citizens Law Project. She is a member of the state and federal Vermont bars.

Alan M. White has been an attorney and supervising attorney at the North Philadelphia office of Community Legal Services, Inc., for the past twenty-two years. He has also been a fellow and consultant with the National Consumer Law Center in Boston and adjunct professor with Temple University Law School and Drake University School of Law. His practice includes representation of low-income consumers in mortgage foreclosures, bankruptcies, student loan disputes, real estate matters, and consumer fraud class actions. He has published a number of research papers and articles on consumer law issues and testified at hearings held by the Federal Reserve Board and the U.S. Department of Housing and Urban Development on predatory mortgage lending. He lectures frequently for the Pennsylvania Bar Institute and other continuing legal education programs on a range of bankruptcy and consumer law topics. He is the author of *Risk-Based Pricing: Present and Future Research*, Housing Policy Debate 15:503 (2004), and co-author with Professor Cathy Lesser Mansfield of *Literacy and Contract*, which appeared in the 2002:2 issue of Stanford Law and Policy Review. Mr. White received his Bachelor of Science degree from the Massachusetts Institute of Technology in 1979 and his J.D. from the New York University School of Law in 1983.

Peter S. Wright is a Clinical Professor with Franklin Pierce Law Center (Two White Street, Concord, NH 03301). Mr. Wright specializes in cases involving usurious or illegal lending practices, debt collection abuses, and illegal home foreclosure. He was formerly a staff attorney with New Hampshire Legal Assistance and with Bucks County Legal Aid Society in Pennsylvania. Mr. Wright is a member of the New Hampshire Bar Association, National Association of Consumer Bankruptcy Attorneys, and the National Association of Consumer Advocates.

Appendix E Abbreviations and Consumer Lawyer Alphabet Soup

AAA	American Arbitration Association
AARP	American Association of Retired Persons
ADA	Americans with Disability Act
ADR	alternative dispute resolution
AMTPA	Alternative Mortgage Transactions Parity Act
APR	annual percentage rate
ARM	adjustable rate mortgage
ATB	ability-to-benefit certification
BBB	Better Business Bureau
BEOG	Basic Educational Opportunity grant
CCPA	Consumer Credit Protection Act
CFA	Consumer Federation of America
chapter 7	bankruptcy liquidation
chapter 13	bankruptcy repayment plan
CID	civil investigation demand
CLA	Consumer Leasing Act
CRA	Community Reinvestment Act
CROA	Credit Repair Organizations Act
CU	Consumers Union
DIA	Depository Institutions Act
DIDA	Depository Institutions Deregulation and Monetary Control Act
DMV	Department of Motor Vehicles
DOE	Department of Education or Department of Energy
EBT	Electronic Benefits Transfer
ECOA	Equal Credit Opportunity Act
EFTA	Electronic Funds Transfer Act
EITC	earned income tax credit
ERISA	Employee Retirement Income Security Act
E-SIGN	Electronic Signatures in Global and National Commerce Act
FAA	Federal Arbitration Act
FACTA	Fair and Accurate Credit Transactions Act of 2003
Fannie Mae	Federal National Mortgage Association
FCBA	Fair Credit Billing Act
FCC	Federal Communications Commission
FCRA	Fair Credit Reporting Act
FDCPA	Fair Debt Collection Practices Act
FDIC	Federal Deposit Insurance Corporation
FERC	Federal Energy Regulatory Commission
FFEL	Federal Family Education Loan
FHA	Federal Housing Administration

FICO	Fair Isaac & Co.
FISL	Federally Insured Student Loan
FIRREA	Financial Institutions Reform, Recovery and Enforcement Act
FmHA	Farmers Home Administration
FRB	Federal Reserve Board
Freddie Mac	Federal Home Loan Mortgage Corporation
FSLIC	Federal Savings and Loan Insurance Corporation
FTC	Federal Trade Commission
GAP	guaranteed automobile protection
Ginnie Mae	Government National Mortgage Association
GLB	Gramm-Leach-Bliley Act
GSL	Guaranteed Student Loan
HEA	Higher Education Act
HEAL	Health Education Assistance Loan
HELC	home equity line of credit
HHS	Department of Health and Human Services
HIDC	holder in due course
HMDA	Home Mortgage Disclosure Act
HMO	health maintenance organization
HOEPA	Home Ownership and Equity Protection Act
HOLA	Home Owners Loan Act
ICRP	income-contingent repayment plan
ISRP	income-sensitive repayment plan
LIHEAP	Low Income Home Energy Assistance Program
MIB	medical information bureau
MUNIs	municipal utilities
MVRISA	Motor Vehicle Retail Installment Sales Act
NAAG	National Association of Attorneys General
NACA	National Association of Consumer Advocates
NACBA	National Association of Consumer Bankruptcy Attorneys
NACHA	National Automated Clearinghouse Association
NADA	National Automobile Dealers Association
NAF	National Arbitration Forum
NAIC	National Association of Insurance Commissioners
NCLC	National Consumer Law Center
NCUA	National Credit Union Administration
NHTSA	National Highway Traffic Safety Administration
NLADA	National Legal Aid and Defenders Association
NSLDS	National Student Loan Data System
OCC	Office of the Comptroller of the Currency
OTS	Office of Thrift Supervision
PLUS	parental student loan
PMI	private mortgage insurance
POS	point of sale
PSC	public service commission
PUC	Public Utilities Commission
RAL	refund anticipation loan
RAM	reverse annuity mortgage
REC	rural electric cooperative
Reg. Z	Federal Reserve Board Regulation Z: Truth in Lending

RESPA	Real Estate Settlement Procedures Act
RHS	Rural Housing Service
RICO	Racketeer Influenced and Corrupt Organizations Act
RISA	Retail Installment Sales Act
RISC	retail installment sales contract
RTO	rent to own
SEOG	Supplemental Educational Opportunity Grant
SLS	Supplemental Loan for Students
SSI	Supplemental Security Income
STRF	state tuition recovery fund
TANF	Temporary Assistance for Needy Families
TCPA	Telephone Consumer Protection Act (or Tennessee Consumer Protection Act)
TILA	Truth In Lending Act
TISA	Truth in Savings Act
TLPJ	Trial Lawyers for Public Justice
TRIP	Tax Refund Intercept Program
UCC	Uniform Commercial Code
UCCC	Uniform Consumer Credit Code
UCITA	Uniform Computer Information Transactions Act
UDTPA	Uniform Deceptive Trade Practices Act
UETA	Uniform Electronic Transactions Act
UDAP	unfair and deceptive acts and practices
UNIP	Unfair Insurance Trade Practices Act
VA	Veterans Administration
VIN	vehicle identification number
VSI	vendor's single interest insurance

Appendix F NACA Consumer Class Action Guidelines

This appendix contains the National Association of Consumer Advocates (NACA) consumer class action guidelines. The NACA began revising these guidelines in 2005.

National Association of Consumer Advocates, Standards and Guidelines for Litigating and Settling Consumer Class Actions, 176 F.R.D. 375[1]

TABLE OF CONTENTS

INTRODUCTION

Consumer class actions serve an important function in our judicial system and can be a major force for economic justice. They often provide the only effective means for challenging wrongful business conduct, stopping that conduct, and obtaining recovery of damages caused to the individual consumers in the class. Frequently, many consumers are harmed by the same wrongful practice, yet individual actions are usually impracticable because the individual recovery would be insufficient to justify the expense of bringing a separate lawsuit. Without class actions, wrongdoing businesses would be able to profit from their misconduct and retain their ill-gotten gains. Class actions by consumers aggregate their power, enable them to take on economically-powerful institutions, and make wrongful conduct less profitable.

In recent years, class actions—and particularly class actions which are resolved by settlement—have been subjected to considerable public criticism. At times, this criticism has been warranted. However, much of the criticism has been generated by self-appointed professional objectors and by self-interested entities who are motivated by a desire to immunize themselves from liability for wrongs rather than by any concern for the public interest. Certain types of businesses, such as financial institutions and insurers, commonly deal with large numbers of consumers in similar ways. Often, such businesses are essentially immune from individual suits for damages since the amounts at issue as to any particular consumer are small. These entities harbor an expectable dislike for the class action procedural device, since it provides an effective tool for consumer redress in such situations. While such entities are entitled to have their voices heard in any public debate, it appears

1 The National Association of Consumer Advocates (NACA) is a nonprofit association of attorneys and consumer advocates committed to representing customers' interests. Its members are private and public sector attorneys, legal services attorneys, law professors, and law students whose primary focus is the protection and representation of consumers. NACA's mission is to promote justice for all consumers by maintaining a forum for communication, networking, and information sharing among consumer advocates across the country and by serving as a voice for its members and consumers in the ongoing struggle to curb unfair and abusive business practices that adversely affect consumers. NACA can be contacted at 1730 Rhode Island Avenue, N.W., Suite 805, Washington, D.C. 20036, (202) 452-1989, fax number (202) 452-0099, www.naca.net, or at info@naca.net.

that a concerted effort has been initiated in recent years to undermine the legitimate uses for class actions by over-emphasizing the relatively infrequent occasions when abuses of the procedure occur.

In *Deposit Guaranty National Bank v. Roper*, 445 U.S. 326 (1980), the Supreme Court stated:

> A significant benefit to claimants who choose to litigate their individual claims in a class-action context is the prospect of reducing their costs of litigation, particularly attorney's fees, by allocating such costs among all members of the class who benefit from any recovery. Typically, the attorney's fees of a named plaintiff proceeding without reliance on Rule 23 could exceed the value of the individual judgment in favor of any one plaintiff. Here the damages claimed by the two named plaintiffs totaled $1,006.00. *Such plaintiffs would be unlikely to obtain legal redress at an acceptable cost, unless counsel were motivated by the fee-spreading incentive and proceeded on a contingent-fee basis.* This, of course, is a central concept of Rule 23.

Id., 445 U.S. 326, 338 n. 9 [emphasis added].

In a similar vein, the California Supreme Court recognized in its landmark decision in *Vasquez v. Superior Court*, 4 Cal. 3d 800, 808 (1971) that:

> Protection of unwary consumers from being duped by unscrupulous sellers is an exigency of the utmost priority in contemporary society . . . The alternatives of multiple litigation (joinder, intervention, consolidation, the test case) do not sufficiently protect the consumer's rights because these devices "presuppose a group of economically powerful parties who are obviously able and willing to take care of their own interests individually through individual suits or individual decisions about joinder or intervention." [Citation omitted.]

The California court further recognized that class actions generally have beneficial by-products, including a therapeutic effect on sellers who indulge in fraudulent practices, aid to legitimate business enterprises by curtailing illegitimate competition, and avoidance of multiple lawsuits involving identical claims.

Even when individual actions could be brought, it is only through class action status and class-wide discovery that the defendant's wrongful practice and its effect on large numbers of similarly-situated consumers may be carefully and accurately determined. Class action discovery thus can improve the strength and size of the eventual recovery for affected consumers.

Class actions also can be abused. Moreover, any abuse is sure to be the focus of much adverse comment in the media and to be used in an attempt to change the law to disfavor class suits and thereby insulate abusive business practices from effective review. Through this paper, the National Association of Consumer Advocates (NACA) is undertaking to provide guidelines to specify what practitioners should be doing under the current state of the law. In some instances, the law does not require compliance with the standards set forth here, in others it does, and in yet others there is a split of authority. Except where expressly stated, this paper does not argue for a change in the law. Instead, NACA seeks to educate practitioners about how to avoid conduct which is, or may appear to be, improper and about the most appropriate and effective way to fulfill the special obligations of class counsel to the class. Thus, the paper addresses how to curb abuses, while advocating keeping class actions as a vehicle for protecting consumers and holding economically powerful interests responsible for the harm they do.

NACA is comprised of consumer lawyers and advocates. The views of many NACA members were solicited and received before this paper was written, as well as after it was circulated in draft form. Often, different members expressed opposing viewpoints. This paper is intended to reflect the majority view in those instances where there was any significant difference of opinion among members.

This paper is directed toward use of class actions within the context of consumer cases. It is not intended to address class actions in other contexts, such as mass torts or employment discrimination cases, which often involve more substantial individual recoveries and a different mix of public policy and procedural considerations.

ISSUES ADDRESSED

1. The Propriety of Class Actions When Individual Recoveries Are Small

A. The Issue

Questions recently have been raised about whether some illegal business practices are inappropriate for class treatment because individual recoveries are too small to warrant individual actions and the attorney's fees which are recovered dwarf the individual damages. The Preliminary Draft of the Proposed Amendments to the Federal Rules of Practice and Procedure issued by the Advisory Committee on Rules of Practice and Procedure of the Judicial Conference of the United States suggests a new subparagraph (F) to Rule 23(b)(3) which would allow courts, in deciding whether to certify a class, to weigh the probable relief to individual class members against the costs and burdens of class litigation. The Summary for Bench and Bar, distributed by the Administrative Office of the U.S. Courts, contains the following comment about proposed subparagraph (F): "In 'small claims' class actions, it may justify refusal to certify a class even though subparagraphs (A) and (B) would push toward certification because individual class members are not practically able to pursue separate actions."

B. Viewpoints

The new proposed subparagraph F requires consideration of the relief to individual class members instead of the size of the total sum that the defendant will pay to the entire class. The genesis of this proposal appears to be the viewpoint that some recoveries to class members may be so trivial that they do not warrant redress. Noting that the traditional justification for litigation is individual remedial benefit and that most private wrongs go without redress, proponents of this rule change urge that "we should not establish a roving Rule 23 commission that authorizes class counsel to enforce the law against private wrongdoers." Request for Comment at 26.

Attorneys who litigate consumer class actions hold the contrary view and believe that the focus on individual compensation misses a central point of class actions: deterring misconduct by the defendants. The class action device is particularly appropriate in consumer cases where individual recoveries are small, but which, in the aggregate, involve substantial sums, often millions of dollars in damages. Class actions serve an important purpose beyond simply compensating the injured. Often, class counsel and class representatives act as private attorneys general vindicating cumulative wrongs and obtaining significant injunctive relief or institutional change, and requiring disgorgement of illegal profits. HERBERT NEWBERG & ALBA CONTE, NEWBERG ON CLASS ACTIONS §§ 5.49 & 5.51 (3d ed. 1992) [cited herein as "Newberg"]. To refuse to permit class actions on the grounds that individual recoveries are small, while ignoring the aggregate amounts involved, would encourage wrongful conduct and largely immunize entities engaged in schemes to steal millions in $10 increments.

An illustrative example is found in the consumer class actions challenging excessive late and overlimit charges on credit card accounts which were criticized on the grounds that class members "are eligible for only a few dollars apiece in compensation" while class counsel get "millions." Max Boot, WALL ST. J., Sept. 19, 1996. If Rule 23(b)(3)(F) were adopted, it could provide a basis for refusing to certify these classes because individual recoveries ranged from $3 to $50, which a court might deem to be trivial. Such a constricted view disregards the facts. For example, in the related Wells Fargo Bank and Crocker National Bank cases, total damages of almost $10 million were recovered, plus interest, and more than $6.5 million was distributed directly to the plaintiff classes. Each class member received the full amount which he or she was overcharged, plus interest, through credits to current customers' accounts and refunds to former customers. Moreover, $3.3 million was given to consumer organizations which provided indirect benefit to absent class members, and the Banks were required to pay all but $115,668 of the $2,130,118 awarded in attorney's fees for work in the trial court. The plaintiff classes were required to pay only 1.28% of the fund for fees.

These charges were imposed by the Banks in violation of California law. It would be unsound as a matter of policy to allow these large corporations to enrich themselves by $10 million through illegal conduct simply because each affected customer was overcharged by $50 or less.

The Supreme Court has long recognized that without Rule 23 claimants with small claims would be unable to obtain relief. *See Deposit Guaranty National Bank v. Roper,* 445 U.S. 326, 338 n. 9 (1980), quoted above. To the same effect is *Phillips Petroleum Co. v. Shutts,* 472 U.S. 797 (1985). "Class actions . . . may permit the plaintiffs to pool claims which would be uneconomical to litigate individually. For example, this lawsuit involves claims averaging about $100 per plaintiff; most of the plaintiffs would have no realistic day in court if a class action were not available." *Id.* at 809.

In addition, assuming that it is desirable for a court to weigh the potential "costs" of class action litigation against its potential "benefits," it would be a mistake to focus solely on monetary relief recoverable as damages or restitution. Rather, many consumer class actions provide an additional social benefit—deterrence. Recovery of a significant aggregate sum from the defendant will have a deterrent effect on resumption of the same or similar wrongful practices in the future, both by that defendant and by other similarly-situated entities. This deterrent effect is present regardless of the amount recovered by individual class members. Moreover, injunctive relief can specifically prohibit resumption of a wrongful activity.

The importance of the deterrence factor in consumer cases is evidenced by the frequency with which Congress and the state legislatures have included fee-shifting provisions in consumer protection statutes. By including fee-shifting provisions, Congress and the state legislatures seek to encourage enforcement of these consumer laws through a system of "private attorneys general," even where the amount of damages at stake would be too small to support litigation if the plaintiff had to absorb the cost of attorney's fees. *See, e.g., De Jesus v. Banco Popular de Puerto Rico,* 918 F.2d 232, 234 (1st Cir. 1990) (construing the Truth in Lending Act). This recognition of the importance of enforcing consumer protection laws, even in cases where the amount of damage to an individual consumer is small, is at least as applicable in the class action context as in the individual case context.

Indeed, the use of class actions to deter widespread consumer fraud is probably preferable to the only practical alternative: punitive damage awards. If small compensation class actions are discouraged, the alternative will be to seek large punitive damage awards on behalf of a few consumers who, while litigating relatively small individual claims, can prove willful, wide-spread misconduct by the defendant. While both alternatives result in the appropriate extraction of a large payment from the defendant, class actions result in the distribution of that payment to the victims of the practice, rather than providing a seeming windfall to the few consumers who prevailed in their individual punitive damage claims.

Finally, what may seem "small" to those of us fortunate enough to be lawyers and judges may be significant to those consumers whose annual incomes are at or below the poverty level. The sum of $50.00 represents two percent of the total annual poverty guideline allotment per family member under the United States Department of Health and Human Services 1995 poverty guidelines. For a low income consumer, that "trivial" $50.00 individual recovery has significant value, equivalent, as a percentage of income, to a $2,000 recovery by a single person earning $100,000 a year.

While class actions, like any procedures, sometimes may be abused, protections against abuse already exist. Courts may and do refuse to allow classes to be certified where the potential recovery to each consumer is nominal or where a distribution would consume such substantial time and expense that the class members are unlikely to receive any appreciable benefit. *See e.g., Buchet v. ITT Consumer Financial Corp.,* 845 F. Supp. 684 (D. Minn. 1994); *Blue Chip Stamps v. Superior Court,* 18 Cal. 3d 381, 386, 134 Cal. Rptr. 393, 556 P.2d 755 (1976); *City of San Jose v. Superior Court,* 12 Cal. 3d 447, 459, 15 Cal. Rptr. 797, 525 P.2d 701 (1974). Further protections are found in the requirements that courts must find any settlements to be fair and reasonable to the members of the class, F. R. CIV. P. 23(e), and that courts must approve amounts to be paid as attorney's fees.

C. NACA Guideline

The class action device is particularly appropriate in consumer cases where individual recoveries are small, but which, in the aggregate, involve millions of dollars in damages. This is precisely the type of case which encourages compliance with the law and results in substantial benefits to the litigants and the court. Denial of class certification in such instances would result in unjust advantage to the wrongdoer. Class actions should be deemed appropriate precisely because individual damages are too small to warrant redress absent a class suit, so long as significant aggregate pecuniary and/or nonpecuniary benefits to the class are sought. This is particularly true in cases with claims for which a legislative body has provided a fee-shifting remedy to encourage private enforcement actions.

2. Certificate Settlements

A. The Issues

There appears to be an increasing use of certificate settlements, offering relief to the class members in the form of certificates that are redeemable on future purchases from the defendant. Questions have been raised about the propriety of such settlements.

It is important to differentiate between certificate settlements, which are discussed herein, and other settlements that do not deliver dollars directly into the hands of the class members, which may well be appropriate. An example of the latter type of settlement is one in which credits are issued to class members' accounts with the defendant. When credits are made to existing accounts, the effect is similar to delivering cash, with increased efficiency.

By contrast, the General Motors ("GM") sidesaddle pickup truck case is a good example of the type of certificate settlement that should never have been proposed for court approval. That class action sought to resolve the worst vehicle-fire safety hazard in history: exploding side-saddle gas tanks on GM pickups that have killed 400 people and badly burned more than 2,000 more. The plaintiffs alleged that these trucks are flawed by a dangerous and latent design defect—the placement of the gas tanks outside the frame rail—that increases the likelihood that their fuel tanks will rupture in side-impact crashes, causing fuel-fed fires. The class action sought a recall of these GM trucks, with restitution and refunds to all class members, and an order directing GM to pay for the retrofitting of all GM pickups to correct the fuel tank defects.

However, in the settlement, class counsel abandoned the recall/retrofit remedy in favor of an approach that limited class members' recovery to discount coupons to buy new GM trucks. There was no provision requiring GM to recall or repair the trucks, or to reimburse owners who made the repairs themselves, nor was there any provision requiring GM to warn consumers about the hazards of the trucks, despite the demand for such relief in the complaint. In other words, nothing in the settlement addressed the animating principle of this lawsuit: that these GM pickup trucks pose a serious—but remediable—safety hazard.

The settlement was criticized and rejected by both federal and state courts. *In re: General Motors Corp. Pick-up Truck Fuel Tank Products Liability Litigation*, 55 F.3d 768 (3d Cir.), *cert. denied*, 116 S. Ct. 88 (1995); *Bloyed v. General Motors Corp.*, 881 S.W.2d 422, (Tex. App.—Texarkana 1994), *aff'd, General Motors Corp. v. Bloyed*, 916 S.W.2d 949 (Tex. 1996). One of the main points of criticism was the inadequacy of the certificates as the sole redress for the injured class members.

The GM case and others have served to demonstrate the problems inherent in non-cash settlements. It is important to note, however, that settlements that do not actually deliver dollars into the hands of the class may be entirely appropriate. For example, credits to existing accounts are usually adequate substitutes for mailing checks to each class member; indeed, crediting is more efficient than mailing and should serve as the basis for increasing the amount paid to each class member. Similarly, if the amounts available to each class member are so small as to make delivery by checks economically unviable or if the class members are impossible to determine with certainty, distribution of the class benefit through *cy pres* awards is advisable, as discussed in Issue 6 below. The comments here are directed solely to certificate settlements that only offer class members the opportunity to purchase a product or service from the defendant in the future at a claimed discount from the regular price to the consumer.

B. Viewpoints

The potential problems with non-cash settlement of class members' damages are many:

- There is no principled reason why delivery of cash settlements cannot be achieved, aside from the fact that the defendant prefers not to do so.
- For most of the class, redemption may not be an option, because they are unwilling or unable to make a future purchase. Thus the class members are not equally compensated—some get more, others get less. This situation is at its most aggravated when the certificate requires purchase of a new car or other "big ticket" item.
- Even where the coupon is for a small ticket item or is freely transferable, the defendant may be able to use its specialized knowledge of the industry to recover the cost of the coupon in the marketing of the relevant product.
- Policy considerations disfavor rewarding the wrongdoing defendant with new sales from the victims of its illegal practices.
- The actual value of certificates is uncertain, making valuation of attorney's fees impossible on a percentage basis, especially where discounted prices are common.
- Proponents of certificate settlements claim that use of certificates makes settlements easier because the defendant is more willing to settle for terms that will only mean a discount from the retail price of the product or because the cost to the defendant is in the future, requiring the immediate outlay of less money. Proponents stress that the particular facts involved in a proposed certificate settlement may justify it, pointing for example to *In re Sears Automotive Center Consumer Litigation*, (N.D. Cal. No. 92-2227 RHS). Here these proponents averred that the certificates involved could be redeemed for any merchandise sold at Sears stores (not merely the services and merchandise at issue in the litigation) and that 99.6% of the certificates issued were redeemed.

C. NACA Guidelines

Certificate settlements have many disadvantages and should be proposed by class counsel only in the rare case. For example, if (1) the primary goal of the litigation is injunctive and the defendant agrees to an injunction, or the certificates are good for the purchase of small ticket consumable items which class members are likely to purchase, or the certificates represent true discounts that would not otherwise be available, (2) the certificates are freely transferable, and (3) there is a market-maker to insure a secondary transfer market, a certificate settlement might be appropriate. A few basic positions are clear:

- Certificate-based settlements should never require identifiable class members to purchase major, large ticket items from the defendant as the sole significant relief to the class.
- Certificates should have some form of guaranteed cash value. For example, the certificates could have a lesser cash redemp-

tion value (either upon issuance or within a reasonable period of time) that still gives the class members a benefit that is significant in relation to the actual damages which would be provable at trial. As a less-preferable approach, the defendant could contract with a market maker that would promise to purchase all available certificates for a set price that is significant in relation to the likely recovery at trial.

- Certificate settlements should never be proposed to the court unless it is apparent that the defendant is providing greater true value (i.e., not just the face value of the certificates or their potential value) to class members than would be available from an all-cash settlement. There may be legitimate tax or financial-accounting reasons why a greater recovery for class members can be had from a non-cash settlement. However, class counsel should inquire about the defendant's reasons for preferring a non-cash settlement. The beginning assumption should always be that the defendant prefers a non-cash to a cash settlement because it believes the true value to be less. Since the defendant will usually be in a superior position to predict the ultimate redemption rate and benefit to the class, its preference for a non-cash settlement should be viewed with skepticism.
- A settlement involving certificates should require a minimum level of redemption by the class members within a reasonable period of time. In the event actual redemption does not meet this minimum level, the defendant should provide alternative relief in the form of a common fund. This requirement protects against the use of a meaningless certificate settlement that has little or no impact on a defendant, and little or no compensatory value to the plaintiff class.
- Class counsel and defendants should submit to the court and all counsel of record detailed information about redemption rates and coupon transfers during the entire life of the coupon. By doing so, a public record will be made of what works and what does not work in non-cash settlement cases.

3. Settlements When Other Class Actions Are on File

A. The Issue

Settlement of a class action when other similar cases are pending requires consideration of a series of specific questions. How should class counsel approach settlement when other class actions, whether putative or certified, have been filed? How can "reverse auctions" be avoided? How should counsel deal with differing geographic and/or substantive scope of multiple class actions?

B. Viewpoints

This issue was the most complex of all issues considered. There is general agreement that class counsel should be sensitive to the potential for wiping out claims asserted in other pending cases by settling a case, and should resist doing so. This problem is particularly apparent where the defendants suggest expanding a settlement class beyond the class definition contained in the complaint or in a prior order certifying a class, or expanding the claims settled, but offer no increased benefit to the additional class members or for settlement of the additional claims. There is also concern about the filing of nationwide class actions and agreeing to settlements which do not exclude from the class cases pending in certain states or locales. In either instance, the interests of the classes will not be well served by settlements which do not maximize benefits to class members.

One particular area of concern exists when the multiple cases are pending in both state and federal courts and thus cannot be consolidated under the federal multi-district litigation rules. 28 U.S.C. § 1407. Class counsel from California might be concerned about becoming involved in a related case pending in a rural area of Texas or Louisiana, where they are unfamiliar with the rules and traditions of practice. The Manual for Complex Litigation addresses this issue, and proposes several procedural steps to increase coordination. These steps include (1) joint conference calls among all judges (2) coordination of discovery, and (3) joint appointment of experts. MANUAL FOR COMPLEX LITIGATION, THIRD §§ 30.3, 31.14, & 31.3 (1995).

Another area of concern is the settlement of cases through a "reverse auction" by which defendants propose a cheap settlement and shop around among plaintiffs' counsel until they find a lawyer willing to settle on their terms. Although there is no empirical evidence that this problem exists, anecdotes abound, and the potential for collusion and abuse is obvious if a lawyer agrees to a bad deal in order to secure fees.

Commenters agreed that class counsel in overlapping actions should communicate with each other and work together to ensure that class members obtain the maximum settlement benefit. The personal interests of particular class counsel in receiving attorney's fees could discourage such cooperation at times. One member proposed that courts should be encouraged not to approve settlements in "copy cat" actions and to consolidate actions whenever possible. However, experience in the federal securities area suggests that use of a "first to file" rule (whether used to determine who will be lead counsel or which should be favored for settlement approval) often produces unsatisfactory results.

Cooperation among class counsel through a variety of means including sharing discovery, conducting joint discovery, using joint experts, coordinating document production, and coordinating scheduling of important motions, including motions for class certification, can expedite the handling of cases and minimize the cost to each counsel.

C. NACA Guidelines

Class counsel should attempt to learn of any pre-existing cases and to communicate with other plaintiffs' counsel in such cases prior to or promptly after filing an overlapping case. Counsel should cooperate with each other to the maximum extent feasible in the pre-trial stage by agreeing to conduct joint discovery, use joint experts, and coordinate document production; or at a minimum sharing discovery among counsel in similar cases; and, where possible, by allocating responsibility for researching and drafting important pleadings and coordinating scheduling of important motions, including motions on the pleadings, for summary judgment, and for class certification.

Counsel should be alert to the possibility that a defendant in multiple cases may seek to conduct a "reverse auction," in which it negotiates separately with various plaintiffs' counsel and attempts to strike a settlement most favorable to it. Bearing in mind the entitlement of class counsel to a fair fee given all the circumstances, the interests of the class must remain paramount.

Counsel (1) should be reluctant to agree to expand the class definition at the settlement stage, (2) should refrain from agreeing to unnecessarily-broad releases which wipe out claims asserted in other pending cases, and (3) should be cautious about settling anything beyond what is alleged in the complaint and mindful of preserving the opt-out rights of class members.

When a settlement has been reached, counsel should always

notify class counsel and the court in other cases involving the same defendant and the same or similar issues. Such notice should occur well before the fairness hearing, in sufficient time to permit those counsel the opportunity to appear.

After settlement, class counsel should also consider notifying persons and groups who have an interest in the proceedings that a tentative settlement has been reached and that a preliminary hearing will be scheduled to consider the fairness and adequacy of the settlement. For example, Trial Lawyers for Public Justice and Public Citizen would routinely be notified of class action settlements, the National Association of Attorneys General would receive notice of settlements involving motor vehicles which states purchase in large quantities, the American Association of Retired Persons would receive notice of settlements involving schemes that adversely affect the elderly such as telemarketing fraud and home equity scams, and NACA and the National Consumer Law Center would receive notice of settlements in consumer class actions such as challenges to deceptive home improvement financing schemes or overcharges by financial institutions. While such notification should not be an invariable rule, it should be the practice usually followed.

4. Additional Compensation to Named Plaintiffs

A. The Issue

Is it appropriate to provide additional sums to named plaintiffs, beyond what each class member receives, and, if so, when and in what amounts?

B. Viewpoints

Earlier cases reflect a view that it is a conflict of interest for named plaintiffs to receive anything more than their proportionate share of damages in amounts which are equal to those received by absent class members. The theory was that named plaintiffs, like class counsel, are fiduciaries to the class, so every dollar they receive is taken from class members.

Recently, some decisions have recognized that modest incentive awards to named plaintiffs, in the range of $2,000–3,000, are generally desirable in order to compensate people for their efforts in achieving the results obtained and thereby encourage them to serve as class plaintiffs. *GMAC Mortgage Corp. of Pa. v. Stapleton*, 603 N.E.2d 767, 776 (Ill. App. 1 Dist. 1992); *In re GNC Shareholder Litigation: All Actions*, 668 F. Supp. 450, 451 (W.D. Pa. 1987); *Troncelliti v. Minolta Corp.*, 666 F. Supp. 750, 752 (D.Md. 1987); *In re Jackson Lockdown/MCO Cases*, 107 F.R.D. 703, 709–710 (E.D. Mich. 1985).

Payments of even larger sums may be appropriate and necessary to compensate class representatives for the time they spend on the litigation. It is sometimes the case that named plaintiffs are subjected to embarrassment and harassment by defense counsel, and are required to submit to multiple days of depositions or to turn over their financial records for review. Named plaintiffs also may contribute to the litigation by reviewing records, reviewing and commenting on pleadings, responding to written discovery, giving assistance or advice to counsel and testifying at depositions and trial. It is appropriate that they receive additional payments to reimburse them for expenses they incur and time they spend in participating in the litigation. *See, e.g., Bryan v. Pittsburgh Plate Glass Co.*, 59 F.R.D. 616, 617 (W.D. Pa., 1973), *aff'd*, 494 F.2d 799 (3rd Cir. 1974), *cert. denied.*, 419 U.S. 900 (1974), *reh'g den.*, 420 U.S. 313 (1975) (approving special awards to those members of the plaintiff class who were most active in the prosecution of the case and who devoted substantial time and expense on behalf of the class); *Thornton v. East Texas Motor Freight*, 497 F.2d 416, 420 (6th Cir. 1974) (approving granting earlier seniority to those class members who had protested and helped to end discriminatory employment policy); *Harris v. Pernsley*, 654 F. Supp. 1042, 1052–1053 (E.D. Pa. 1987) (approving damage award to named plaintiff based on meritorious conduct); *Genden v. Merrill Lynch, Pierce, Fenner & Smith*, 700 F. Supp 208, 210 (S.D.N.Y. 1988) (approving award of $20,085 to one named plaintiff who, as an attorney, rendered consultative services to class counsel).

C. NACA Guideline

Awards to named plaintiffs are appropriate compensation for the time and expense they incur in serving as class representatives. The consumers who fight on behalf of an entire class should be reasonably compensated for their efforts when those efforts are successful. For anything more than modest sums in the range of $2,000–3,000, the amounts of such awards should be based on the amount of time and money expended in connection with prosecuting the case, or other special circumstances.

5. Class Member Releases

A. The Issues

When is it appropriate to release class claims without individual class member signatures? May the scope of releases exceed the scope of the claims certified by the Court?

B. Viewpoints

In agreeing to settle a class action, the defendant understandably wishes to obtain protection against later suits by class members for the same alleged wrongs that are being settled through the class actions. Ordinary principles of res judicata and collateral estoppel apply in the class action context to bar subsequent re-litigation of claims, so long as there was adequate representation of the class in the earlier case. *Matsushita Electric Industrial Co., Ltd. v. Epstein*, 516 U.S. 367, 116 S. Ct. 873, 134 L. Ed. 2d 6 (1996). Nevertheless, as in individual cases, defendants generally insist upon the inclusion of releases within a negotiated settlement document. In some cases, defendants may also seek individual releases from class members, either as part of the language contained in claim forms or as an endorsement on settlement distribution checks. There does not appear to be any benefit from releases which do not exceed the scope of the res judicata bar, but neither does there appear to be any harm.

Prior to *Matsushita*, there was some uncertainty whether class-wide releases which were broader than the scope of the pleadings and/or certified claims were binding upon individual class members in subsequent litigation. As a noted commentator states: "A class action settlement agreement cannot release the claims of absent class members. Only absent class members can release their own claims." Newberg § 12.17, at 12-52 (3d ed. 1992). However, Newberg subsequently notes that an alternative to individual releases is the inclusion of "a constructive release clause in the settlement agreement" to the effect that acceptance of settlement benefits releases whatever claims are described in the settlement agreement. *Id.* at 12-52–12-56.

The Supreme Court's recent decision in *Matsushita, supra*, clearly holds that res judicata bars re-litigation of non-certified claims (and even claims not contained in the pleadings) which are released on a class-wide basis, so long as there is adequate representation and an opportunity to opt out. Court approval of a proposed settlement should include a determination that plaintiffs and class counsel adequately represent the class on all of the settled issues, even if certification of some of the issues was previously denied.

It was the unanimous view of those who submitted comments that individual releases are unnecessary and unproductive if the scope of the class-wide release is limited to those claims certified by the court for class treatment. There was also consensus that class counsel should be cautious in discussing settlement of claims beyond the scope of a prior class certification order (or, if no order has yet been entered, beyond the scope of the pleadings). Several comments suggested that counsel should seek additional settlement compensation if settlement of such claims is agreed to.

The opportunity to opt out of a proposed settlement is particularly important if claims are being settled which have not been previously certified by the Court. It is common practice to offer class members only one opportunity to opt out of a class action. When there is a contested class certification motion, that opportunity usually comes immediately after certification. A subsequently-proposed settlement requires notice of the settlement terms and an opportunity to object, but usually not a second opportunity to opt out. If claims are being settled which were *not* described in the initial class notice, serious fairness issues are raised by the lack of a second opt-out opportunity.

In addition, there are very serious, and probably fatal, objections to any settlement that purports to release potential future claims of persons who have not suffered any damage at the time of settlement. Settlements of this nature are rare, or even unknown, in consumer cases. Therefore, this paper will not discuss in depth the many issues relating to these settlements. However, we note that even if it were possible to notify such future-damaged class members, it is impossible to provide any meaningful notice and opportunity to opt out, since they have not been injured and thus cannot assess what the proposed settlement means to them. The Supreme Court addressed future-damage issues this past Term in *Amchem Products, Inc. v. Windsor*, 521 U.S. __, 117 S. Ct. 2231, 138 L. Ed. 689 (1997). In that case, the Court found that including future-damaged persons in the class defeated the predominance requirement of Rule 23(b)(3) and also made it impossible for the named class members (who were not future-damaged) to represent the interests of the absent future-damaged class members, as required by Rule 23(b)(4). 117 S. Ct. at 2250–51, 138 L. Ed. at 713–714. In addition, the Court noted that there were significant problems of adequate notice to a class that included persons who were not then aware of their damages. 117 S. Ct. at 2252, 138 L. Ed. at 716.

C. NACA Guidelines

Class counsel should proceed cautiously in discussing settlement of claims other than those alleged in the pleadings and certified by the court. However, since the doctrines of res judicata and collateral estoppel will preclude subsequent litigation based on alternative legal theories arising out of the same set of facts, it is often reasonable to release any such alternative claims which could have been asserted, even if not contained in the pleadings or specifically certified. Except in unusual circumstances, counsel should not agree to any settlement which releases non-certified claims unless class members will be given a subsequent opportunity to exclude themselves from the settlement.

If a defendant seeks a release of claims arising from factual circumstances not alleged in the complaint, or as to which certification has been sought but not granted, class counsel should seek additional compensation to the class for such releases. If possible, negotiation of the certified claims should precede negotiations as to non-certified ones. Adequacy of representation as to non-certified claims should be addressed in the briefs supporting a proposed settlement.

A "general release" may be appropriate for the named class representatives. However, absent class members should not be required to release independent individual claims or claims as yet unknown in order to receive settlement benefits. Specifically, if the class settlement only provides injunctive benefits that do not result in restitution or other monetary payments to individual class members, the release should provide that individual damages claims are not being released.

6. *Cy Pres* Awards

A. The Issue

It is typically the case that not all class members can be located to receive their pro rata share of a damage award, and questions arise concerning what happens to the undistributed residue. They include: Are there circumstances under which the residue should revert to the defendant? Under what circumstances is a *cy pres* distribution of all or part of the settlement fund appropriate? What is class counsel's role in recommending recipients of such awards?

B. Viewpoints

Respondents unanimously agreed that *cy pres* remedies are appropriate to ensure that undistributed residues are used to provide indirect benefit to absent members of the plaintiff class or to further the purposes of the statutes which formed the basis for the underlying litigation. This view is supported by the case law. *Bebchick v. Public Utilities Commission* (D.C. Cir.) (en banc), *cert. denied,* 373 U.S. 913 (1963) approved use of the funds collected in an invalid fare increase for the benefit of those who paid it, that is, those who use that transit system. A fund was created in this non-class case to be used by the Commission to benefit transit users in any pending or future rate proceedings or to cover costs which might otherwise lead to an increase in fares, or aid in determining whether fares should be reduced.

Several other circuits have approved the use of *cy pres* remedies. An early antibiotic antitrust class action settlement included the creation of a trust fund from which indirect benefit could be conferred upon consumers as a whole, and the settlement was approved, with the details of the *cy pres* remedy left to be resolved at later hearings. *State of West Virginia v. Chas Pfizer Co.*, 314 F. Supp. 710, 728 (SDNY 1970), *aff'd*, 440 F.2d 1079, 1083 (2d Cir. 1971). The Seventh Circuit has adopted an approach requiring a case-by-case analysis of whether the use of a *cy pres* remedy is consistent with the policy reflected by the statute violated and whether the statute embodies policies of deterrence, disgorgement, or compensation. *Simer v. Rios,* 661 F.2d 655, 676 (7th Cir. 1981), *cert. denied*, 456 U.S. 917 (1982) (finding an award inappropriate because it would not serve the goals of deterrence or disgorgement on the particular facts of that case).

In *Nelson v. Greater Gadsden Housing Authority,* 802 F.2d 405, 409 (11th Cir. 1986), the court held that compensatory damages which were not claimed by class member public housing tenants were to be used by the housing authority to increase the energy efficiency of the apartment units or to improve the appliances supplied by defendant. In *Six Mexican Workers v. Arizona Citrus Growers,* 904 F.2d 1301, 1307 (9th Cir. 1990), the Ninth Circuit noted that the Eleventh Circuit's decision "expressly approved the use of fluid recovery to distribute unclaimed class action funds" and expressed its agreement, holding that the district court properly considered *cy pres* distribution of unclaimed funds, although it found the specific use which had been approved inappropriate. The court reversed and remanded to the trial court to determine what remedy would best effectuate the goals of the underlying statute and the interests of the absent class members. *Id.* at 1309.

Similarly, the Second Circuit in *In Re Agent Orange Product Liability Litigation,* 818 F.2d 179, 185 (2d Cir. 1987), concluded that a district court may set aside a portion of settlement proceeds for programs designed to assist the class in order to maximize the beneficial impact of the settlement fund on the needs of the class. The Court distinguished its earlier decision in *Eisen v. Carlisle & Jacquelin,* 479 F.2d 1005 (2d Cir. 1973) (*"Eisen III"), vacated and remanded on other grounds*, 417 U.S. 156 (1974) which reversed a trial court order allowing fluid recovery through a price reduction. The court explained that the fluid recovery at issue in *Eisen III* would have allowed plaintiffs to satisfy the manageability requirements of Rule 23 where they otherwise could not and would result in a greatly increased number of doubtful but astronomical class claims in the federal courts. That concern was not present in *Agent Orange*, which was maintainable as a class action regardless of the form of recovery available to the plaintiff class. *In Re Agent Orange Product Liability Litigation, supra*, at 185.

Other courts approving *cy pres* remedies also have distinguished *Eisen* on the basis that the fluid recovery sought in that case would have eliminated statutorily required individual proof of damages and circumvented class action manageability requirements. *Nelson v. Greater Gadsden Housing Authority, supra*, at 409; *Six Mexican Workers v. Arizona Citrus Growers, supra*, at 1307. Those issues are very different from the question of *cy pres* distribution of unclaimed funds, an issue which does not subject defendants to greater liability or alter their substantive rights. *Id.* In addition, Newberg criticizes the *Eisen III* rationale as defective and inconsistent with the historic purposes of class action remedies and concludes that "*cy pres* distributions have long been recognized as appropriate exercises of the court's general equitable powers under appropriate circumstances." Newberg, § 10.22 at 10-57.

State courts have also approved *cy pres* remedies in a number of unreported decisions in California and Georgia. *See, e.g., Vasquez v. Avco Financial Services of Southern California*, Los Angeles Superior Court Case No. NCC-11833B; *Beasley v. Wells Fargo Bank*, San Francisco Superior Court Case No. 861555, and a related case, *Kovitz v. Crocker National Bank,* San Francisco Superior Court Case No. 868914; *McClendon v. Security Pacific National Bank,* Alameda County Superior Court Case No. 613722-5; *Patterson v. ITT Consumer Financial Corporation*, San Francisco Superior Court Case No. 936818; *In Re: Domestic Air Transportation Antitrust Litigation*, No. 1-90 C 2485 MHOS & MAL No. 861 (consolidated Nov. 2, 1990); and *Starr v. Fleet Finance, Inc.*, et al. Cobb County Georgia Superior Court Civil Action No. 9210-2314-06.

The propriety of fluid recovery, including creation of a consumer trust fund, was recognized by the California Supreme Court in *State of California v. Levi Strauss,* 41 Cal. 3d 460 (1986). Following the general principles that wrongdoing must be deterred and that deterrence requires disgorgement of ill-gotten gains, the court approved *cy pres* distribution of the portion of a damage fund which could not be distributed to the consumers who had been overcharged.

The court concluded that such awards are appropriate where there is a nexus between the proposed use of the fund and the class on whose behalf the case was litigated, or where the proposed use furthers the purpose of the statutes which formed the basis for the underlying suit. In either instance, the use of the fund will provide indirect benefit to absent class members. The rationale for such awards is further explained in McCall, Sturdevant, Kaplan and Hillebrand, *Greater Representation for California Consumers—Fluid Recovery, Consumer Trust Funds, and Representative Actions,* 46 Hastings Law J. 798 (1995).

Thus, the case law supports creation of *cy pres* remedies in cases which are litigated to conclusion. Moreover, it is clearly permissible to settle with defendants and include a *cy pres* provision in the agreement, because a defendant may agree to a settlement which provides for fluid recovery notwithstanding the *Eisen* rule, *Beecher v. Able,* 575 F.2d 1010, 1016 n.3 (2d Cir. 1978).

There are two views on allowing residues to revert to defendants. One considers that an unacceptable alternative which would reward defendants for engaging in wrongful conduct, except where there are no ill-gotten gains to be disgorged. The other is that it is appropriate where there is no incentive for defendants to fail to distribute the damage award or to assist in locating absent class members because allowing the return of the residue may enable counsel to negotiate better relief to known class members and obtain an agreement as to injunctive relief.

There are also two divergent views on the propriety of *cy pres* awards of the entire damage fund with no distribution to the class. One view is that counsel's fiduciary duty to the members of the class requires that there must always be a direct distribution to class members, and only the undistributed residue used for a *cy pres* remedy. The other view is that where individual recoveries are unduly costly to distribute or too small to warrant the cashing of checks, *cy pres* awards of the entire damage fund is appropriate.

There is some authority for using a *cy pres* remedy for the entirety of a statutory damage award when the amount of damages to each class member is too small to warrant distribution. *Gammon v. GC Services Ltd. Partnership,* 162 F.R.D. 313 (N.D. Ill. 1995) was a suit under the Fair Debt Collection Practices Act involving a proposed class of four million people, each of whom would be entitled to 13 cents if plaintiffs prevailed. Class counsel, moving to certify the class under Rule 23(b)(2) of the Federal Rules of Civil Procedure, suggested *cy pres* distribution of the entire damage award. The defendant did not dispute the propriety of this remedy, which the court assumed would be suitable. Citing *Newberg*, the court noted that class actions are designed not only to compensate individuals who have been harmed, but also to deter violations of the law, especially when small individual claims are involved. It concluded: "Disgorgement of illegal gains from wrongdoers, together with . . . application of the recovery for the benefit of class members under *cy pres* doctrines, would fulfill the deterrence objectives of class actions." *Id.* at 321, quoting Newberg, § 4.36. (Note that in *Mace v. Van Ru Credit Corporation,* 109 F.3d 338, 345, (7th Cir. 1997), *Gammon* was limited to its own unique facts.)

There is agreement that it is the role of class counsel, who have been found to be adequate representatives of the class, to recommend *cy pres* recipients. NACA has adopted the guidelines set forth in the McCall, Sturdevant, Kaplan and Hillebrand article at pp. 850–851.

Since it is the role of the court to protect the interests of absent class members, the court should carefully review the competence and record of organizations that are proposed as recipients. We believe that serious consideration should be given to using the unclaimed portion of the award for a long-term grant to an existing organization with competence in the issues raised in the underlying litigation. This will ensure that projects are of sufficient duration to result in real and concrete benefit to absent class members.

C. NACA Guidelines

In proposing a *cy pres* remedy, class counsel should propose a disposition of the unclaimed portion of the award that will either (1) protect the interests of the persons injured by the illegal conduct and thus indirectly benefit absent class members or (2) promote the purposes of the statutory prohibitions sought to be enforced in the underlying litigation. Counsel should also insist that the recipients of the award be accountable to the court and should enter into memoranda of understanding to that effect with recipient organizations.

If counsel wishes to propose that a new organization receive the unclaimed funds, class counsel should be prepared to show the court how that organization has the ability and competence to work for the interests the underlying litigation sought to protect. This can be accomplished by providing information to the court about the current or proposed officers, directors, and staff of the organization. The work to be done by an existing or new organization should be set forth in a comprehensive proposal, together with time tables for accomplishing that work, which should indicate how the class will be indirectly benefited or the purposes of the underlying statutes will be furthered by these efforts.

To ensure full accountability, counsel should usually negotiate a formal agreement with the proposed recipients which binds the recipients to restrictions on the use of the funds, and requires them to comply with accounting, auditing, and reporting requirements. Such a negotiated agreement offers assurance to the court that the proposed recipient will use the funds strictly in accordance with the terms of the court's order. For long term projects, counsel can oversee performance by requiring quarterly meetings with recipient organizations, semi-annual plans for work to be undertaken, and periodic reports of past accomplishments. Counsel should be entitled to compensation for work necessary to monitor implementation of the *cy pres* remedy at standard rates, with no enhancement or multiplier.

Class counsel should agree that undistributed residues revert to defendants only in unusual circumstances. For example, reversion may be acceptable where there is no incentive for defendants to fail to perform their obligations in connection with distribution of the damage award and where there are no ill-gotten gains to be disgorged.

Class counsel should insist on direct distribution of damages to class members before recommending a *cy pres* remedy for the undistributed residue except in unusual circumstances. These include instances where individual recoveries are unduly costly to distribute because, for example, defendants have no computerized records which would enable them to generate a list of class members' names and addresses, or where individual damages are too small to warrant the issuance, processing, and cashing of checks.

Class counsel should recommend *cy pres* remedies which will provide indirect benefit to absent members of the class or which will further the purposes of the underlying litigation. They should also recommend mechanisms which will provide for monitoring by class counsel, and, ultimately, judicial oversight of the expenditure of the funds.

7. Attorneys Fee Considerations

A. The Issue

The issue of attorneys' fees is extremely important in class actions today, both because it serves as a rallying point for criticism of class actions and because the criticisms of excessive fees are in some instances well grounded. This is also a difficult and complicated issue since fee awards may be made on three different bases: statutory fee shifting, in which defendant pays the fee; common fund, in which the class members pay the fee from their recovery; and common benefit, in which the defendant pays the fee. There is no one problem and no one cure.

The prime focus of criticism is the size of the fees. In many instances, this problem is more apparent than real. For example, when the individual recovery is $50.00 per consumer, an attorneys' fee of $2 million seems excessive at first glance. However, if the dollars actually recovered by the individual class members in such a case were $15 million, then fees are less than 14% of the total recovery achieved for the class. This makes the fee reasonable with respect to the total actual recovery.

However, the cases that receive the most criticism are those where the class does not obtain cash recovery that is several times the fees received by the attorneys. The strongest criticism is directed at cases in which the actual cash received by the class is minimal, if any, and the only other benefits received by the individual members are certificates, of questionable value. The *GM Pickup Truck* cases, *In re: General Motors Corp. Pick-Up Truck Fuel Tank Products Liability Litigation*, 55 F.3d 768 (3d Cir.), *cert. denied*, 116 S. Ct. 88 (1995); *Bloyed v. General Motors Corp., supra*, and the *Bronco II* case, *In re: Ford Bronco II Products Liability* litigation, 1995 U.S. DIST. LEXIS 3507 (E.D. La. 1995) (rejecting settlement of a class action challenging dangerous vehicles that provided relief to the class in the form of a flashlight and safety video but no damages) are well known examples of this problem, but it had its roots in cases such as the airline antitrust settlement, which also provided certificates to consumers and millions of dollars in attorneys' fees to the class lawyers.

B. Viewpoints

There are a variety of proposed solutions, none of which would take care of the problem entirely. One viewpoint holds that class counsel should be paid only by hourly lodestar rates, enhanced by multipliers when appropriate, and that percentage calculation of fees is not appropriate. The leading lodestar calculation cases, which primarily consider time spent, hourly rates, the work done, and the results obtained, are: *Johnson v. Georgia Highway Express, Inc.*, 488 F.2d 714 (5th Cir. 1974); *City of Detroit v. Grinnell Corp.*, 495 F.2d 448 (2d Cir. 1975); *Lindy Bros. Builders, Inc. v. American Radiator & Standard Sanitary Corp.*, 487 F.2d 161 (3d Cir. 1973), on remand, 383 F. Supp. 999 (E.D. Pa. 1974), *rev'd on other grounds*, 540 F.2d 102 (3d Cir. 1976) (en banc). Because the availability of multipliers of the lodestar fee is uncertain, prohibiting percentage fees could make some class actions impossible to bring, if the resources needed to commit to the litigation were so sizable that the only way a law firm could economically justify taking on the case, and running the risk of recovering nothing, would be the potential of a large percentage recovery. In addition, some commentators have suggested that basing a fee on an hourly rate could lead some class counsel to perform unnecessary work ("churning").

The opposite end of the spectrum from this viewpoint holds that a percentage recovery in the 20–30% range is entirely appropriate and should be left to court approval. Percentage fees have been held appropriate in common fund cases: *Boeing Co. v. Van Gemert*, 444 U.S. 472, 478–79 (1980); *In re Activision Securities Litigation*, 723 F. Supp. 1373 (N.D. Cal. 1989); *Paul, Johnson, Alston & Hunt v. Graulty*, 886 F.2d 268 (9th Cir. 1989); and have been required in cases not involving a fee shifting statute in *Swedish Hospital Corp. v. Shalala*, 1 F.3d 1261 (D.C. Cir. 1993) and *Camden I Condominium Association v. Dunkle*, 946 F.2d 768 (11th Cir. 1991). However, some commenters urge that this approach could in class counsel being unduly compensated for insufficient time and effort.

Others feel that a blended approach is best—evaluating both percentage and lodestar fees, to determine a reasonable fee for the particular case. Under this approach judges would make a lodestar calculation based on the hours spent and hourly rates and compare that figure with the percentage awards made in similar cases. *See Strang v. JHM Mortgage Sec. Ltd. Partnership*, 890 F. Supp. 499, 502–03 (E.D. Va. 1995) (comparing the lodestar and percentage of common fund calculations to conclude that 25% rather than 30% of the fund was a reasonable fee).

Still others urge that different bases for fee awards raise different issues and require different solutions. A complicating factor is that it is not always clear whether a case is a common fund, a fee-shifting, or a common benefit case. If the entire case is based on statutes that provide for fee-shifting (and most consumer class actions are primarily based on fee-shifting statutes), some commenters felt that it would be inappropriate for class counsel to seek fees based on a percentage of the amount awarded the class. This view finds support in case law holding that the lodestar calculation is required in fee shifting cases: *City of Burlington v. Dague*, 505 U.S. 557, 562 (1992); *Blum v. Stenson*, 465 U.S. 886, 895 (1984). These commenters found it even more objectionable if class counsel sought to obtain percentage fees out of the amounts awarded the class, rather than insisting that the defendant pay the fees over and above all amounts given the class. These commenters felt that this problem was particularly acute in instances where fees are assessed against members of the class who did not actually receive any monetary benefit. This situation can arise when class members' recoveries are credited to their accounts with the defendant but not every class member receives a credit.

These alternative bases for awarding fees are not necessarily in conflict: fees could be recovered from the defendant under a fee shifting statute or other theory and paid into the common fund, with class counsel receiving a percentage of the total recovery. This approach finds support in *Skelton v. General Motors Corp.*, 860 F.2d 250 (7th Cir. 1988), which involved the settlement of statutory fee shifting claims. The court noted that a settlement merges all claims, including the client's statutory fee shifting claim, into one common fund that belongs to the class clients, and ordered fees to be calculated under common fund principles. This view is also consistent with case law noting that the amount which an opposing party can be required to pay as a "reasonable" fee may be substantially less than a reasonable fee owed by the client (or class of clients). *Venegas v. Mitchell*, 495 U.S. 82 (1990).

Whatever the method of calculating fees there is no question that any contingent fee award must take into account the difficulty, complexity, and the risk of the case, the relief obtained for the class, as well as the fact that some cases will result in no fee at all. Therefore, it is entirely appropriate in most class action cases to award fees that are in excess of a fee calculated solely on an hourly basis without any multiplier.

When a fee is to be calculated on a percentage basis, there is no fixed percentage that is appropriate to all cases. A fee of 10% on a class recovery of $100 million might be excessive depending on the circumstances. On the other hand, a 40% fee award would be insufficient in a case where the primary relief sought is injunctive and the payment to the class minimal, but where thousands of hours of attorneys' time was required and the extent of the injunctive relief justified it.

Some commenters argue that there is an inherent problem with negotiating fees with opposing counsel, even when counsel have first agreed on relief to the class. Since the Court has an independent duty to examine the fees, these commenters feel, prior agreement does little but create the appearance of collusion between class counsel and the defendant. Others contend that settlement often would be impossible to achieve unless the defendants understand the extent of their total exposure, and urge that it is preferable to obtain relief promptly for class members and that there is no reason not to reach agreement on fees so long as negotiation of fees follows the obtaining of an agreement to relief for the class on the merits.

C. NACA Guidelines

Reasonable attorneys fees must be awarded in consumer class actions because fees are the incentive for lawyers to engage in private enforcement of the law, but excessive and unreasonable amounts should not be sought or awarded. Because the issue of reasonable attorneys' fees is one that will be determined by the merits of the lawsuit and the nature of the settlement, there is no one possible remedy for the abuses that exist. However, a variety of partial solutions will be beneficial.

- ***Time to discuss fees***. Because the Supreme Court has recognized that in a fee-shifting case the defendant has an economic interest in resolving the fee issues in a settlement negotiation along with all other statutory claims [*see White v. New Hampshire*, 455 U.S. 445, 452 n.14 (1982)], class counsel should avoid any conflicts of interest that may increase the danger of an improper quid pro quo detrimental to the class. For example, if a defendant offers a $5 million lump sum settlement, with $4 million for the class and $1 million to counsel, it would be improper to accept this offer contingent upon $3 million being made available to the class and $2 million available to counsel. It *would be* appropriate, however, to state that the $4 million for the class is acceptable as long as counsel's compensation is increased. One alternative is to obtain the defendant's binding agreement to all class relief and then to submit the fees issue to the court for determination. In statutory fee-type cases, an acceptable alternative is to obtain the defendant's agreement on class relief contingent on successfully negotiating an agreement on fees. It is also acceptable to negotiate fees after all relief has been agreed on for the class, and then submit the entire agreement as a whole to both the court and the class for review and approval. In common fund cases, there is no need to discuss fees with the defendant since the class clients, not the defendant, pay the fee from the fund that was created by their counsel, subject to court approval.
- ***Percentage Benchmarks for most Common Fund Cases.*** For the vast majority of common fund cases, courts and counsel should examine the reasonableness of the fees requested by the percentage benchmarks that have been recognized in

similar cases. *See, e.g., Camden I Condominium Ass'n v. Dunkle*, 946 F.2d 768 (11th Cir. 1991); *Paul, Johnson, Alston & Hunt v. Graulty*, 886 F.2d 268, 272 (9th Cir. 1989); *Brown v. Phillips Petroleum Co.*, 838 F.2d 451, 454 (10th Cir.), *cert. denied*, 488 U.S. 822 (1988); *Swedish Hosp. Corp. v. Shalala*, 1 F.3d 1261, 1272 (D.C. Cir. 1994); *Bebchick v. Washington Metro Area Transit*, 805 F.2d 396, 406–407 (D.C. Cir. 1986); *see also In re General Motors Corp. Pick-up Truck Fuel Tank Prods. Liab. Litig.*, 55 F.3d 768, 820–21 (3d Cir.), *cert. denied*, 116 S. Ct. 88 (1995); *In re Continental Illinois Secs. Litig.*, 962 F.2d 566, 572 (7th Cir. 1992). In the absence of special circumstances, including either an unusually large monetary recovery or a relatively small monetary recovery coupled with very beneficial but difficult to value equitable relief, the courts have recognized percentage benchmarks ranging from 19 percent to 45 percent of the common fund. *See, e.g., In re Greenwich Pharmaceutical Sec. Litig.*, [1995] Fed. Sec. L. Rep (CCH) ¶ 98,774, p. 92,523 (E.D. Pa. Apr. 26, 1995); *In re SmithKline Beckman Corp. Secs. Litig.*, 751 F. Supp. 525, 533 (E.D. Pa. 1990); *In re Unysis Corp. Retiree Med. Benefits ERISA Litig.*, 886 F. Supp. 445, 467 (E.D. Pa. 1995); *Mashburn v. National Medical Healthcare, Inc.*, 684 F. Supp. 679, 692 (M.D. Ala. 1988); *In re Activision Secs. Litig.*, 723 F. Supp. 1373, 1374–78 (N.D. Cal. 1989). As one court has observed, "[w]hen the 'prevailing' method of compensating lawyers for 'similar services' is the contingent fee, then the contingent fee is the 'market rate'." *Kirchoff v. Flynn*, 786 F.2d 320, 324 (7th Cir. 1986).

In the few (often highly publicized) cases in which the monetary relief, however valued or estimated, exceeds $30 million, reasonable fees will nearly always, though not necessarily, represent smaller than the benchmark percentages. In such cases, courts have encouraged use of a lodestar analysis to cross-check the reasonableness of fees in such large cases. *See, e.g., General Motors*, 55 F.3d at 822; *In re Washington Public Power Supply Sys. Litig.*, 19 F.3d 1291, 1295, 1298 (9th Cir. 1994). Although such cross-checks in typical cases simply add another level of analysis, and may even undermine the purposes of the percentage-of-the-fund approach, in large cases the cross-checks are a useful tool in protecting the class from windfall fee awards. Similarly, when the common fund is relatively small or difficult to value precisely and the common benefit is undoubtedly valuable but difficult to quantify, the lodestar approach may properly supplant the percentage-of-the-fund benchmarks. Provided the class receives real value and is receiving benefits commensurate with the fees to be awarded to class counsel, it is not per se unreasonable for counsel to set aside a monetary fund from which attorneys fees will be paid even though the class may be receiving primarily equitable benefits. However, counsel should be aware that "the timing of fee negotiations" in such cases may be considered as a factor by the courts in the "review of the adequacy of the class' representation." *General Motors*, 55 F.3d at 803–804.

- ***Recovering fees from the class.*** In a common fund case where the underlying claims are based on fee-shifting statutes, it is generally best to negotiate an additional amount representing the right to fees from the defendant directly, in order to limit the fees paid by class counsel's clients and maximize the total recovery to the class. It may be appropriate in such a case to merge the statutory fee into the common fund (*see Skelton, supra*) and to also obtain a portion of the fees from the common fund. The same is true in common benefit cases. In instances where the only source of fees is the common fund, class counsel must insure that (1) no class member is assessed fees if that member did not receive a benefit and (2) the percentage of fees assessed against any class member is a reasonable percentage of that class member's recovery. Class counsel must refuse to discuss any proposal by a defendant to pay one amount itself or to pay nothing itself but agree to class counsel seeking a greater amount from a common fund. If the defendant can be persuaded to offer an additional sum for fees, that can be accepted as a credit toward a common fund award made by the court. In a statutory fee shifting case which is not converted to a common fund case, fees should be recovered solely from the defendant and be based on the lodestar.
- ***Non-cash settlements.*** In a case where relief to the class is not paid in cash (or by credit to an existing account), the attorneys' fees should be based solely on a lodestar rate, with a multiplier when appropriate under existing case law. Otherwise, it is impossible to determine the value of the actual relief received by the class (as opposed to the theoretical value of non-cash relief) on which to base a percentage amount. If an agreement is negotiated with the defendant as to an amount of fees which the defendant will not contest, class counsel should still submit sufficient documentation to the court to justify, on a lodestar basis, whatever amount of fees is being sought. Alternatively, a percentage fee might be recovered, but only after a delay, as described below.
- ***Percentage fee request if cash value of settlement cannot be determined at time of settlement approval.*** In some situations, the total cash value of a settlement may not be calculable at the time the settlement is finally approved. The two most common situations where this is true are (1) certificate settlements, where it is unknown how many of the certificates will ultimately be redeemed; and (2) "claims made" settlements, where it is unknown what proportion of the available funds will be claimed by class members or paid to a *cy pres* recipient. In such cases, it is inappropriate for class counsel to seek a percentage fee unless one of the following is true: (a) the settlement provides for a minimum settlement level which is guaranteed to be paid (either to class members or as a *cy pres* payment) and the fee sought is based upon a percentage of the minimum amount; (b) the settlement provides for an initial payment to class members (or as a *cy pres* payment) and the fee is sought based on a percentage of that initial payment; or (c) approval of payment of the fee to class counsel is not requested until such time as the court can accurately assess the actual value of the settlement (i.e. after the deadline for class member claims are after the certificates expire).
- ***Notice to the class of fees.*** Another essential, but not sufficient, component of reform is a requirement that the maximum amount of attorneys' fees to be sought must be disclosed to the class members at the time the notice of proposed settlement is sent to them, stated as a total dollar amount. In a common fund case where a percentage will be sought, that fact and the specific percentage to be requested should be stated in the notice. In statutory fee shifting cases, the lodestar, if agreed to by the parties, should be disclosed in the class notice. If there is no agreement, the amount class counsel

intend to request from the court should be disclosed. It is also a good idea to disclose the amount of fees per class member, but the members of the class have the right to know how much their attorneys are making in total. For example, the class must be told that the lawyers will receive $2 million, but could also be told that this amounts to $6.67 per class member. The average fee per class member need not be disclosed when recoveries vary substantially among class members, since that number would not be meaningful.

8. Improved Notice of Settlement

A. The Issues

One significant problem with class action settlements is that Rule 23 does not specify the content of notice to the class. Consequently, the notices given to the class, whether individually or by publication, are not uniform and often are in such fine print and sufficiently complicated and unclear that the class members do not understand the nature of the relief sought or obtained in their names. They therefore do not actually have the information necessary to make an informed decision as to whether to remain members of the class, to opt out, or to object to the settlement.

B. Viewpoints

Currently, there is no group advocating or opposing improved notice to the class. However, industry groups and the defense bar are readying attacks on class actions that could be fatal to the ability of individual consumers to use class actions to stop deceptive and illegal practices and to obtain relief after being victimized. Part of any consideration of changing class action practice should include finding a way to insure that the absent class members have the best tools possible to decide whether or not to support a class action settlement. Both the MANUAL FOR COMPLEX LITIGATION, THIRD and the foremost treatise on class actions recommend the content of notices of proposed settlements. The Manual suggests that notice include a description of the essential terms of the settlement, information about attorneys' fees, disclosure of any special benefits for class representatives, specification of the time and place of the hearing to consider approval of the settlement, and an explanation of the procedure for allocating and distributing the settlement. § 30.212 (1995). Newberg & Conte recommend that notice contain a description of the litigation, summary of the proposed settlement, requested allowance for attorneys' fees, procedure for filing proofs of claims, procedure for filing appearances and objections, and procedure for obtaining documents related to litigation and settlement. Newberg, *supra*, at § 8.32.

C. NACA Position

NACA supports a drive for simplified, plain-language, standardized disclosure of the salient aspects of a settlement. Disclosure should be required only of those points that are most important for consumers to know. This simplified form would be the first page of the class notice, whether by publication or individual mail. The details would continue to be placed in the body of the class notice.

The standard form of notice should include the following:

- A clear statement of how the consumer can tell whether he or she is a member of the class.
- The number of members of the plaintiff class.
- The total amount of relief to be granted the class, stated in dollars where the payment is in cash or credit to an account.
- The individual relief to be received by each member of the class, broken down into sub-classes if necessary. Where this cannot be determined in advance of the claims process, there should be a good faith estimate of the range of individual recoveries for class members.
- The total maximum fees, in dollars, to be sought by the class attorneys, and the method whereby they were calculated (hourly, hourly with a multiplier, percentage, or a combination), as well as the source from which payment will be sought.
- Proposed distribution of any unclaimed funds, including whether they will revert to defendants.
- Options available to class members including at least opting out and objecting.
- An address to write for further information regarding the settlement.

9. Approval of Settlement Classes

A. The Issue

The growing use of settlement classes, especially when coupled with the increasingly-frequent proposals of settlements where the class members do not receive either monetary or equitable relief, raises serious concerns that the interests of the absent class members have not been adequately represented. The holdings in *Amchem Products, Inc. v. Windsor*, 117 S. Ct. 2231 (1997) and *In re: General Motors Corp. Pick-up Truck Fuel Tank Products Liability Litigation*, 55 F.3d 768 (3d Cir.), *cert. denied*, 116 S. Ct. 88 (1995) should serve as a harbinger of increased judicial scrutiny of settlements of this nature.

B. Viewpoints

Most commenters agreed that the preferred approach is to seek and obtain class certification prior to any discussion of settlement. By seeking court involvement at an early stage, the class has the advantage of an adversary-based determination of such vital issues as adequacy of representation of the class, adequacy of class counsel, and the exact make-up of the class.

Settlements before certification create problems. Commenters differed in the best approach to take. One approach to post-settlement certification entails a two-step process. First, the issue of certification would be the subject of a plenary hearing, after notice to the class but without notice of settlement of the merits. After the trial court has determined that the case should be certified as a class following hearing, the notice of settlement and of class certification would not need to be addressed again, and the trial court would focus on the Rule 23(e) determination that the settlement is fair, adequate, and reasonable to the class as a whole, as the law requires.

Another approach to post-settlement certification, which is acceptable under the holdings of the Third Circuit, combines the two hearings into one, with notice to the class of both the certification and the fairness issues to be considered. The trial court would conduct a plenary hearing into both the certification of the class and the fairness issues, only reaching the fairness issues after determining the nature of the class to be certified pursuant to both subsections (a) and (b) of the Rule.

Under Rule 23(c)(1), the trial court has always had the power to make certification conditional, before decision on the merits. It would appear to be within the scope of the Rule to make certification conditional on finality of the settlement, providing no subsequent res judicata effect if the settlement itself is rejected. Certainly, this approach adheres much more closely to the Rule than certification after less than full consideration of all Rule 23 requirements. This approach meets the holdings of the Third Circuit and also provides the salient benefit of avoiding both the appearance and the actuality of either collusion or inadequate representation of the absent class members.

Some commenters felt that negotiating settlement prior to obtaining class certification is appropriate because it enables counsel to obtain prompt resolution of cases to the benefit of the class. Those commenters also felt that it was a waste of time for a court to conduct a hearing on class certification if the defendant had agreed to class settlement and that the chance to opt out provided sufficient protection to the class members.

The Supreme Court reviewed the Third Circuit's holding in *Georgine v. Amchem Products, Inc.*, 83 F.3d 610 (3d Cir. 1996), *aff'd sub nom. Amchem Products, Inc. v. Windsor*, 117 S. Ct. 2231, 138 L. Ed. 2d 689. The opinion held that the decision of the Court of Appeal bears modification because it did not indicate that settlement is relevant to a class certification. It further held that the court did properly consider the terms of the settlement in concluding that the class certification could not be upheld because common questions did not predominate and future claimants' interests were not adequately represented.

The rule to be derived from that opinion is that a court must find that the requirements of Rule 23, subdivisions (a) and (b) are satisfied in order to approve a class certification in the context of a settlement. The analysis need not take into account the manageability of the case if it were to be tried, since if the settlement is approved there will be no trial, but must include consideration of the subdivision (a) requirements of numerosity, commonality of questions of law or fact, typicality of the claims or defenses of the representative parties with those of the class, and adequacy of representation in that the representative parties will fairly and adequately protect the interests of the class. Additionally, the court held that certification of a class requires compliance with the provisions of subdivision (b) (1), (2), or (3). In a Rule 23(b)(3) case such as this, in order to certify a class a court must find that common questions of law or fact predominate, but a common interest in a fair compromise can not satisfy the predominance requirement. In language that will be useful to litigators handling consumer protection cases, the court distinguished mass tort cases from consumer class actions, noting: "Predominance is a test readily met in certain cases alleging consumer or securities fraud or violations of the anti-trust laws." 117 S. Ct. at 2250; 138 L. Ed. 2d at 713.

The Committee on Rules of Practice and Procedure of the Judicial Conference of the United States ("Rules Committee") has recently proposed for comment an entirely new Rule 23(b)(4) that specifically permits use of a class in a settlement that did not otherwise meet the requirements of Rule 23(b)(3). *See* Preliminary Draft of Proposed Amendments to the Federal Rules of Appellate, Civil, and Criminal Procedure published in August, 1996. This proposal does not provide any criteria for a court's determination whether such settlement certification is proper; it is based solely on the agreement of the parties. Among others voicing strong opposition to this proposal is a group of some 150 law professors. The objections of the law professors are threefold: (1) the proposal contains no limiting guidelines or principles, (2) it fails to address serious constitutional and statutory problems, and (3) it formalizes what has until now been an extremely controversial practice and invites collusion.

C. NACA Guidelines

The specific Rule 23(b)(4) proposed by the Rules Committee fails to provide guidance for district courts' exercise of discretion in approving a settlement class and therefore must be rejected as it is currently worded. It is unnecessary to amend Rule 23 at all to obtain the positive benefits of appropriate settlement classes.

The preferable method is to obtain class certification prior to entering into settlement negotiations. However, the dynamics of settlement often create situations where settlement is reached early in the proceedings, before class certification. In those cases, as part of the settlement, class determination may be made contingent on finality of the approval of the settlement, as is commonly done when a court certifies a class "for settlement purposes only." If the Rules Committee proposes a revised new rule, NACA should address it, and this position may change.

10. Interlocutory Appeal of Class Certification

A. The Issue

The Rules Committee also proposes new Rule 23(f), permitting interlocutory appeals of a district court order granting or denying class certification. The right to appeal is discretionary with the court of appeals. The proposed rule provides also that such an appeal does not stay the proceedings unless the district or appellate court orders.

B. Viewpoint

It is difficult to imagine a scenario where a defendant would not attempt to appeal an order granting class certification. It is also difficult to imagine a scenario where if appeal is permitted, either the district court or the court of appeals would not stay the proceedings.

On the other hand, the likelihood of a plaintiff appealing a denial and seeking a stay of proceedings is minimal. However, it is virtually certain that, if the plaintiff did appeal a denial of certification, the defendant would seek, and likely obtain, a stay pending the appeal. Therefore, the rule as written does little to advance a plaintiff's situation, but does provide significant dilatory opportunities for defendants.

The California state court approach is a variant on this theme. It is silent on the issue of stay, but permits immediate appellate review only of denial of certification, on the ground that a denial is a "death knell" because it effectively terminates the entire action as to the class. Granting class certification is not such an order, and is only harmful to the defendant if the plaintiff prevails at trial and on appeal, both on certification issues and on the merits, so is not immediately reviewable. *See Stephen v. Enterprise Rent-A-Car*, 235 Cal. App. 3d 806 (1991) and *Rosack v. Volvo of America Corp.*, 131 Cal. App. 3d 741 (1988).

C. NACA Position

The California state court approach is a balanced approach that preserves the rights of both plaintiffs and defendants. Immediate appeal should be allowed only if certification is denied.

SUMMARY AND CONCLUSION

Most class actions work the way Congress and the courts intended. They provide an efficient and appropriate way to obtain relief for many individuals harmed by illegal practices. In the consumer law area, class actions are particularly appropriate because many people can be harmed by the same illegal practice, and the damages are often both quantifiable and individually too small to warrant separate lawsuits.

Nonetheless, there are abuses by class counsel and the public perception is that some of those abuses are increasing. Rather than precipitously attacking the problem by restricting the availability of the class action device to consumers, the better practice is a combination of increased court scrutiny of class action settlements and heightened commitment on the part of class counsel to avoid even the appearance of abuse.

The NACA guidelines and positions set forth in this paper are intended to give both bar and bench a reference point for aggressive yet responsible class action advocacy.

Appendix G Free Legal Resources on the Internet

Most of these links are available on line at www.ConsumerLaw.org (click on "Links") as well as on the companion CD-Rom to this volume.

General Legal Web Sites

Resident Agent Information and Links	www.residentagentinfo.com
Management Information Exchange	www.m-i-e.org
The Tenants Union	www.tenantsunion.org
COUNSEL QUEST: Business and Consumer Law	http://home.earthlink.net/~parajuris/CounselQuest/z-bus.htm
Cornell University Legal Information Institute	www.law.cornell.edu
Findlaw	www.findlaw.com
Villanova Center for Information Law and Policy	www.law.villanova.edu
American Bar Association	www.abanet.org/home.html
Ethics Opinions	www.legalethics.com
Expert Witness Databases	www.expertpages.com/index.htm
The Internet Law Library	www.internetlawyer.com
U.S. Federal Judiciary (directory of U.S. court websites, many with opinions)	www.uscourts.gov
Class Actions	http://members.aol.com/class50/index.html
Tobacco Bulletin Board System	www.tobacco.org

General Consumer

General Consumer Information for public interest organizations, consumer advocacy and education groups, and the general public

National Association of Consumer Advocates	www.naca.net
National Association of Consumer Bankruptcy Attorneys	www.nacba.org
Consumer Federation of America	www.cfa.ort
Center for Responsible Lending	www.responsiblelending.org
Consumers Union	www.consumersunion.org
Consumer Reports	www.ConsumerReports.org
American Association of Retired Persons	www.aarp.org
Bank savings and credit interest rates	www.bankrate.com
Class action notices	www.notice.com
Class actions	www.web-access.net/~aclark/current.htm
Consumer Law Page	http://consumerlawpage.com
Consumer World	www.consumerworld.org
FTC Credit Information	www.ftc.gov/bcp/menu-credit.htm
National Consumer Law Center	www.ConsumerLaw.org
ConsumerNet	www.consumernet.org
U.S. Consumer Information Center Links	www.pueblo.gsa.gov/textver/t_links.htm
Tenant Net Home Page (Netscape)	http://tenant.net/main.html
U.S. Landlord-Tenant Law	www.law.cornell.edu/topics/landlord_tenant.html
Nolo Law Books, Consumer Section	www.nolo.com/briefs.html

U.S. Consumer Credit Law	www.law.cornell.edu/topics/consumer_credit.html
Uniform Commercial Code (UCC)	www.law.cornell.edu:80/ucc/ucc.table.html
Consumer Action	www.consumer-action.org
National Center on Poverty Law	www.povertylaw.org
Consumers for Auto Reliability and Safety	www.carconsumers.com
The Hospice Patients Alliance	www.hospicepatients.org
FAMSA	www.funerals.org
Elder Law Answers	www.elderlawanswers.com
The National Association of Consumer Agency Administrators	www.nacaa.net
Federal Information Resources for Consumers	www.consumer.gov

Consumer Complaint Websites

consumer complaint website	www.complaints.com
internet scam busters	www.scambusters.org
identity theft and telefraud complaint site	www.consumer.gov/sentinel

Legal Services Back-Up and Resource Centers

Non-profit organizations devoting all of its resources to advocating equal access to justice for all Americans

National Senior Citizens Law Center	www.nsclc.org
National Veteran Legal Services Program	www.nvlsp.org
Center on Budget and Policy Priorities	www.cbpp.org
The Center for Law and Social Policy	www.movingideas.org
National Legal Aid and Defender Association	www.Nlada.org
Palmetto Legal Services (South Carolina)	www.logicsouth.com/~legalpal
Western New York Legal Center	www.wnylc.net
Bazelon Center	www.bazelon.org/what.html
Native American Rights Fund (NARF)	www.narf.org
National Health Law Program	www.healthlaw.org
Practicing Law Institute	www.pli.edu
Pine Tree Legal Assistance: Links to Other Legal Services Organizations	www.ptla.org/links.htm
Trial Lawyers for Public Justice (TLPJ)	www.tlpj.org

Car Information

Good collection of resources regarding cars, car pricing and safety information, lemon law summaries

AutoSite	www.autosite.com
CarFax	www.carfax.com
Carwizard	www.carwizard.com
Kelly's Blue Book	www.kbb.com
National Highway Traffic Safety Administration	www.nhtsa.dot.gov/cars/problems
Auto Finance Law	www.faircreditlaw.com
Don't Get Taken Every Time	www.takeneverytime.com

Helpful Tools

General Financial and mortgage calculators

"What is a dollar worth?"	http://minneapolisfed.org (click on inflation calculator)
financial calculators	www.interest.com/hugh/calc
mortgage calculators	www.mortgage-net.com

Travel Law Materials on the Web

Travel law articles on the Web	http://members.aol.com/travellaw/index.html
Take Your Travel Agent on a Trip to the Courthouse	http://courts.state.ny.us/tandv/travelagent.html

The Cruise Passenger's Rights and Remedies	http://courts.state.ny.us/tandv/cruiserights.html
Flight Delays, Rights, Remedies, Damages & Class Actions	http://courts.state.ny.us/tandv/flightdelays.html
What Tort Lawyers Should Know About Travel Law	www.courts.state.ny.us/tandv/travellaw.htm
The Licensing and Regulation of Travel Sellers in the United States	www.courts.state.ny.us/tandv/Aqtaed1.htm
The Internet, the "Solicitation Plus" Doctrine and Jurisdiction over Foreign Travel Suppliers	http://courts.state.ny.us/tandv/TLJInternetArticle99.htm
Sponsoring Group Travel: A Discussion of Liability Issues-1999	http://courts.state.ny.us/tandv/sgt.html
Travel Abroad, Sue at Home	http://courts.state.ny.us/tandv/tasah.html
Instant Travel Agents	http://courts.state.ny.us/tandv/ita.html
Tour Operators and Air Carriers: Modern Theories of Liability	http://courts.state.ny.us/tandv/toac.html
How Safe Are Student Tours	http://courts.state.ny.us/tandv/studtour.html
Hotel Restaurant Liability for Lost Overcoats	http://courts.state.ny.us/tandv/overcoat.html
Sporting Event Tours: Liability for Defaults, Performance Failures and Physical Injuries	http://courts.state.ny.us/tandv/SportingEventArticleCourtWebPage.htm
Judge Dickerson's Consumer Law Decisions, Articles, Papers & Books	http://members.aol.com/judgetad/index.html

Retailer & Trade Groups

American Bankers Association	www.aba.com
American Financial Services Association	www.americanfinsvcs.com
Better Business Bureau	www.bbb.org
Commercial Law League	www.clla.org
ACA International (formerly known as American Collectors Association)	www.collector.com
American Recovery Association Inc.	www.repo.org
APR Systems	www.aprsystems.com/RegZ.htm#latest
National Association of Retail Collection Attorneys	www.narca.org
National Credit Information Systems	www.wdia.com
Netbanker	www.netbanker.com
U.S. Chamber of Commerce	www.uschamber.com

Government Web Sites

Department of Justice	www.usdoj.gov
Federal case law	www.findlaw.com/casecode
Federal law	www.law.cornell.edu/uscode
The Federal Judicial Center	www.fjc.gov
FedStats	www.fedstats.gov
Library of Congress	www.loc.gov
Medline	www.ncbi.nlm.nih.gov/PubMed
State laws	www.washlaw.edu
U.S. Congress (bills and status)	http://thomas.loc.gov
U.S. Federal Courts	www.uscourts.gov
U.S. Government Accounting Office (GAO)	www.gao.gov
U.S. House of Representatives	www.house.gov
U.S. Senate	www.senate.gov
Washington Post Federal Internet Guide	www.washingtonpost.com
The White House	www.whitehouse.gov

U.S. Government Agencies

Extensive links to all U.S. Government agencies

Department of Agriculture	www.usda.gov
Department of Commerce	www.doc.gov

Department of Defense	www.defenselink.mil
Department of Education	www.ed.gov/index.html
Department of Energy	www.doe.gov
Department of Health & Human Services	www.os.hhs.gov
Department of Housing & Urban Development	www.hud.gov
Department of the Interior	www.doi.gov/index.html
Department of Justice	www.usdoj.gov
Department of Labor	www.dol.gov
Department of State	www.state.gov
Department of Transportation	www.dot.gov
Department of the Treasury	www.ustreas.gov
Department of Veterans Affairs	www.va.gov
Environmental Protection Agency	www.epa.gov
Federal Reserve System	www.federalreserve.gov
Federal Bureau of Investigation	www.fbi.gov
Federal Trade Commission	www.ftc.gov
Securities and Exchange Commission	www.sec.gov
Small Business Administration	www.sbaonline.sba.gov
Social Security Administration	www.ssa.gov
United States Postal Service	www.usps.gov
Federal Communications Commission	www.fcc.gov

URLs for State and District of Columbia Courts

Alabama	www.judicial.state.al.us
Alaska	www.state.ak.us/courts
Arizona	www.supreme.state.az.us
California	www.courtinfo.ca.gov
Colorado	www.courts.state.co.us/ct-index.htm
Connecticut	www.jud.state.ct.us
Delaware	http://courts.state.de.us
District of Columbia	www.dcwatch.com/courts/default.htm
Florida	www.flcourts.org
Georgia	www.georgiacourts.org
Hawaii	www.courts.state.hi.us/index.jsp
Idaho	www2.state.id.us/judicial
Illinois	www.state.il.us/court
Indiana	www.in.gov/judiciary
Iowa	www.judicial.state.ia.us
Kansas	www.kscourts.org
Kentucky	www.kycourts.net
Louisiana	www.lasc.org
Maine	www.courts.state.me.us
Maryland	www.courts.state.md.us
Massachusetts	www.state.ma.us/courts
Michigan	www.courts.michigan.gov
Minnesota	www.courts.state.mn.us
Mississippi	www.mssc.state.ms.us
Missouri	www.osca.state.mo.us
Montana	www.mtd.uscourts.gov
Nebraska	http://court.nol.org
Nevada	http://nvcourtaoc.state.nv.us
New Hampshire	www.state.nh.us/courts
New Jersey	www.judiciary.state.nj.us
New Mexico	www.nmcourts.com

New York	www.courts.state.ny.us
North Carolina	www.nccourts.org
North Dakota	www.court.state.nd.us/Court/Courts.htm
Ohio	www.sconet.state.oh.us
Oklahoma	www.oscn.net
Oregon	www.ojd.state.or.us
Pennsylvania	www.courts.state.pa.us
Rhode Island	www.courts.state.ri.us
South Carolina	www.sciway.net/gov/state_court.html
South Dakota	www.sdjudicial.com
Tennessee	www.tennessee.gov
Texas	www.txs.uscourts.gov
Utah	http://courtlink.utcourts.gov
Vermont	www.vermontjudiciary.org
Virginia	www.courts.state.va.us
Washington	www.courts.wa.gov
West Virginia	www.state.wv.us/wvsca/wvsystem.htm
Wyoming	http://courts.state.wy.us
National Center for State Court's directory of state court websites	www.ncsconline.org/D_KIS/info_court_web_sites.html

Finding a Lawyer

Search for a lawyer nationwide

National Association of Consumer Advocates	www.naca.net
National Association of Consumer Bankruptcy Attorneys	www.nacba.org
Elder Law Answers	www.elderlawanswers.com
Massachusetts Legal Services Programs	www.neighborhoodlaw.org
Other Legal Services Programs	www.ptla.org/links.htm
Legal Services Program Locator	www.lsc.gov/fundprog.htm

Reference Sites

a search engine for reference sites	www.refdesk.com
BabelFish (translation services)	www.babelfish.com/en
Language Line (fee-based telephone translation services)	www.languageline.com
Wikipedia (free encyclopedia)	http://en.wikipedia.org
Merriam-Webster Dictionary and Thesaurus On-Line	www.m-w.com
Verizon Telephone reverse number lookup	www22.verizon.com/utilities/reverselookup/
Webpage archives	www.archive.org

Fee-Based Legal Research and Legal Forms Sites

Lexis Nexis	www.lexis.com
LoisLaw	www.loislaw.com
Pacer	www.pacer.psc.uscourts.gov/index.html
WestLaw	www.westlw.com
Lawdisks (bankruptcy forms)	www.lawdisks.com

Index

References are to sections

References are to sections

References are to sections

References are to sections

References are to sections

References are to sections

Quick Reference to the Consumer Credit and Sales Legal Practice Series

References are to sections in *all* manuals in NCLC's Consumer Credit and Sales Legal Practice Series. References followed by "S" appear only in a Supplement.

Readers should also consider another search option available at ***www.consumerlaw.org/keyword***. There, users can search all seventeen NCLC manuals for a case name, party name, statutory or regulatory citation, or *any* other word, phrase, or combination of terms. The search engine provides the title, page number and context of every occurrence of that word or phrase within each of the NCLC manuals. Further search instructions and tips are provided on the web site.

The Quick Reference to the Consumer Credit and Sales Legal Practice Series pinpoints where to find specific topics analyzed in the NCLC manuals. References are to individual manual or supplement sections. For more information on these volumes, see *What Your Library Should Contain* at the beginning of this volume, or go to www.consumerlaw.org.

This Quick Reference is a speedy means to locate key terms in the appropriate NCLC manual. More detailed indexes are found at the end of the individual NCLC volumes. Both the detailed contents pages and the detailed indexes for each manual are also available on NCLC's web site, www.consumerlaw.org.

NCLC *strongly recommends,* when searching for PLEADINGS on a particular subject, that users refer to the *Index Guide* accompanying *Consumer Law Pleadings on CD-Rom*, and *not* to this *Quick Reference*. Another option is to search for pleadings directly on the *Consumer Law Pleadings* CD-Rom or on the *Consumer Law in a Box* CD-Rom, using the finding tools that are provided on the CD-Roms themselves.

The finding tools found on *Consumer Law in a Box* are also an effective means to find statutes, regulations, agency interpretations, legislative history, and other primary source material found on NCLC's CD-Roms. Other search options are detailed at page vii, *supra*.

Abbreviations

AUS = Access to Utility Service (3d ed. 2004)
Auto = Automobile Fraud (2d ed. 2003 and 2005 Supp.)
Arbit = Consumer Arbitration Agreements (4th ed. 2004 and 2005 Supp.)
CBPL = Consumer Banking and Payments Law (3d ed. 2005)
Bankr = Consumer Bankruptcy Law and Practice (7th ed. 2004 and 2005 Supp.)
CCA = Consumer Class Actions: A Practical Litigation Guide (5th ed. 2002 and 2005 Supp.)
CLP = Consumer Law Pleadings, Numbers One Through Eleven (2005)
COC = The Cost of Credit (3d ed. 2005)
CD = Credit Discrimination (4th ed. 2005)
FCR = Fair Credit Reporting (5th ed. 2002 and 2005 Supp.)
FDC = Fair Debt Collection (5th ed. 2004 and 2005 Supp.)
Fore = Foreclosures (2005)
Repo = Repossessions (6th ed. 2005)
Stud = Student Loan Law (2d ed. 2002 and 2005 Supp.)
TIL = Truth in Lending (5th ed. 2003 and 2005 Supp.)
UDAP = Unfair and Deceptive Acts and Practices (6th ed. 2004 and 2005 Supp.)
Warr = Consumer Warranty Law (2d ed. 2001 and 2005 Supp.)

References are to sections in *all* manuals in NCLC's Consumer Credit and Sales Legal Practice Series

References are to sections in *all* manuals in NCLC's Consumer Credit and Sales Legal Practice Series

References are to sections in *all* manuals in NCLC's Consumer Credit and Sales Legal Practice Series

References are to sections in *all* manuals in NCLC's Consumer Credit and Sales Legal Practice Series

References are to sections in *all* manuals in NCLC's Consumer Credit and Sales Legal Practice Series

References are to sections in *all* manuals in NCLC's Consumer Credit and Sales Legal Practice Series

References are to sections in *all* manuals in NCLC's Consumer Credit and Sales Legal Practice Series

References are to sections in *all* manuals in NCLC's Consumer Credit and Sales Legal Practice Series

NOTES

NOTES

NOTES

NOTES

NOTES

NOTES

NOTES

NOTES

NOTES

About the Companion CD-Rom

CD-Rom Supersedes All Prior CD-Roms

This CD-Rom supersedes the CD-Rom accompanying *The Practice of Consumer Law* (1st ed. 2003). Discard the earlier CD-Rom. The 2005 CD-Rom contains everything found on the prior CD and much additional material.

What Is on the CD-Rom

For a detailed listing of the CD's contents, see the CD-Rom Contents section on page xxv of this book. Highlights include:

- Retainer and co-counseling letters;
- Practice aids including checklists, questionnaires, a bankruptcy handout, and common abbreviations encountered in consumer law;
- 2 notice letters;
- 19 complaints and answers;
- 18 interrogatories and document requests;
- 8 briefs regarding motion to dismiss and summary judgment, 3 rebuilt wreck depositions and a debt collector's deposition in an FDCPA case, and 4 other pre-trial documents;
- 17 trial documents including *voir dire*, opening and closing statements, testimony, jury instructions and verdict forms;
- 2 pleadings regarding attorney fees;
- NACA's Consumer Class Action Guidelines and draft revised guidelines; and
- Key Internet links.

How to Use the CD-Rom

The CD's pop-up menu quickly allows you to use the CD—just place the CD into its drive and click on the "Start NCLC CD" button that will pop up in the middle of the screen. You can also access the CD by clicking on a desktop icon that you can create using the pop-up menu.[1] For detailed installation instructions, see *One-Time Installation* below.

1 Alternatively, click on the D:\Start.pdf file on "My Computer" or open that file in Acrobat—always assuming "D:" is the CD-Rom drive on your computer.

All the CD-Rom's information is available in PDF (Acrobat) format, making the information:

- Highly readable (identical to the printed pages in the book);
- Easily navigated (with bookmarks, "buttons," and Internet-style forward and backward searches);
- Easy to locate with keyword searches and other quick-search techniques across the whole CD-Rom; and
- Easy to paste into a word processor.

While much of the material is also found on the CD-Rom in word processing format, we strongly recommend you use the material in PDF format—not only because it is easiest to use, contains the most features, and includes more material, but also because you can easily switch back to a word processing format when you prefer.

Acrobat Reader 5.0.5 and 7.0.5 come free of charge with the CD-Rom. **We strongly recommend that new Acrobat users read the Acrobat tutorial on the Home Page. It takes two minutes and will really pay off.**

How to Find Documents in Word Processing Format

Most pleadings and other practice aids are also available in Microsoft Word format to make them more easily adaptable for individual use. (Current versions of WordPerfect are able to convert the Word documents upon opening them.) The CD-Rom offers several ways to find those word processing documents. One option is simply to browse to the folder on the CD-Rom containing all the word processing files and open the desired document from your standard word processing program, such as Word or WordPerfect. All word processing documents are in the D:\WP_Files folder, if "D:" is the CD-Rom drive,[2] and are further organized by book title. Documents that appear in the book are named after the corresponding appendix; other documents have descriptive file names.

Another option is to navigate the CD in PDF format, and, when a particular document is on the screen, click on the corresponding bookmark for the "Word version of . . ."

2 The CD-Rom drive could be any letter following "D:" depending on your computer's configuration.

This will automatically run Word, WordPerfect for Windows, or *any other word processor* that is associated with the ".DOC" extension, and then open the word processing file that corresponds to the Acrobat document.[3]

Important Information Before Opening the CD-Rom Package

Before opening the CD-Rom package, please read this information. Opening the package constitutes acceptance of the following described terms. In addition, the *book* is not returnable once the seal to the *CD-Rom* has been broken.

The CD-Rom is copyrighted and all rights are reserved by the National Consumer Law Center, Inc. No copyright is claimed to the text of statutes, regulations, excerpts from court opinions, or any part of an original work prepared by a United States Government employee.

You may not commercially distribute the CD-Rom or otherwise reproduce, publish, distribute or use the disk in any manner that may infringe on any copyright or other proprietary right of the National Consumer Law Center. Nor may you otherwise transfer the CD-Rom or this agreement to any other party unless that party agrees to accept the terms and conditions of this agreement. You may use the CD-Rom on only one computer and by one user at a time.

The CD-Rom is warranted to be free of defects in materials and faulty workmanship under normal use for a period of ninety days after purchase. If a defect is discovered in the CD-Rom during this warranty period, a replacement disk can be obtained at no charge by sending the defective disk, postage prepaid, with information identifying the purchaser, to National Consumer Law Center, Publications Department, 77 Summer Street, 10th Floor, Boston, MA 02110. After the ninety-day period, a replacement will be available on the same terms, but will also require a $20 prepayment.

The National Consumer Law Center makes no other warranty or representation, either express or implied, with respect to this disk, its quality, performance, merchantability, or fitness for a particular purpose. In no event will the National Consumer Law Center be liable for direct, indirect, special, incidental, or consequential damages arising out of the use or inability to use the disk. The exclusion of implied warranties is not effective in some states, and thus this exclusion may not apply to you.

System Requirements

Use of this CD-Rom requires a Windows-based PC with a CD-Rom drive. (Macintosh users report success using NCLC CDs, but the CD has been tested only on Windows-based PCs.) The CD-Rom's features are optimized with Acrobat Reader 5 or later. Acrobat Reader versions 5.0.5 and 7.0.5 are included free on this CD-Rom, and either will work with this CD-Rom as long as it is compatible with your version of Windows. Acrobat Reader 5.0.5 is compatible with Windows 95/98/Me/NT/2000/XP, while Acrobat Reader 7.0.5 is compatible with Windows 98SE/Me/NT/2000/XP. If you already have Acrobat Reader 6.0, we *highly* recommend you download and install the 6.0.1 update from Adobe's web site at www.adobe.com because a bug in version 6.0 interferes with optimum use of this CD-Rom. See the *Acrobat 6 Problem* button on the home page for details. The Microsoft Word versions of pleadings and practice aids can be used with any reasonably current word processor (1995 or later).

One-Time Installation

When the CD-Rom is inserted in its drive, a menu will pop up automatically. (Please be patient if you have a slow CD-Rom drive; this will only take a few moments.) If you do not already have Acrobat Reader 5.0.5 or later, first click the "Install Acrobat Reader" button. Do not reboot, but then click on the "Make Shortcut Icon" button. (You need not make another shortcut icon if you already have done so for another NCLC CD.) Then reboot and follow the *How to Use the CD-Rom* instructions above.

[*Note*: If the pop-up menu fails to appear, go to "My Computer," right-click "D:" if that is the CD-Rom drive, and select "Open." Then double-click on "Read_Me.txt" for alternate installation and use instructions.]

3 For instructions on how to associate WordPerfect to the ".DOC" extension, go to the CD-Rom's home page and click on "How to Use/Help," then "Word Files."